FLORIDA RV CAMPING

MARILYN A. MOORE

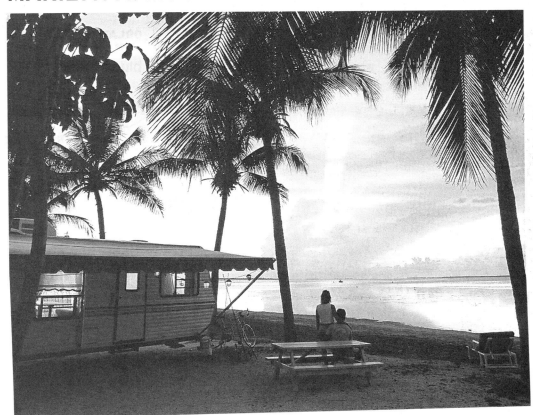

How to Use This Book

ABOUT THE CAMPGROUND PROFILES

The campgrounds are listed in a consistent, easy-to-read format to help you choose the ideal camping spot. If you already know the name of the specific campground you want to visit, or the name of the surrounding geological area or nearby feature (town, national or state park, forest, mountain, lake, river, etc.), look it up in the index and turn to the corresponding page. Here is a sample profile:

Campground name and number →

General location of the campground in relation to the nearest major town or landmark →

Map the campground can be found on and page number the map can be found on →

Icons noting activities and facilities at or nearby the campground

Rating of scenic beauty on a scale of 1–10 with 10 the highest rating

Symbol indicating that the campground is listed among the author's top picks

1 SOMEWHERE USA CAMPGROUND

Scenic rating: 10

south of Somewhere USA Lake

See map page 4   BEST (

Each campground in this book begins with a brief overview of its setting. The description typically covers ambience, information about the attractions, and activities popular at the campground.

Campsites, facilities: This section notes the number of campsites for tents and RVs and indicates whether hookups are available. Facilities such as restrooms, picnic areas, recreation areas, laundry, and dump stations will be addressed, as well as the availability of piped water, showers, playgrounds, stores, and other amenities. The campground's pet policy and wheelchair accessibility is also mentioned here.

Reservations, fees: This section notes whether reservations are accepted, and provides rates for tent sites and RV sites. If there are additional fees for parking or pets, or discounted weekly or seasonal rates, they will also be noted here.

Directions: This section provides mile-by-mile driving directions to the campground from the nearest major town or highway.

Contact: This section provides an address, phone number, and website, if available, for the campground.

ABOUT THE ICONS

The icons in this book are designed to provide at-a-glance information on activities, facilities, and services available on-site or within walking distance of each campground.

- 🚶 Hiking trails
- 🚲 Biking trails
- 🏊 Swimming
- 🎣 Fishing
- 🚤 Boating
- 🛶 Canoeing and/or kayaking
- ❄️ Winter sports

- ♨️ Hot Springs
- 🐕 Pets permitted
- 🛝 Playground
- ♿ Wheelchair accessible
- 🚐 RV sites
- ⛺ Tent sites

MAP SYMBOLS

Expressway	(80) Interstate Freeway	Airfield
Primary Road	(101) US Highway	Airport
Secondary Road	(29) State Highway	O City/Town
Unpaved Road	66 County Highway	▲ Mountain
Ferry	Lake	⬘ Park
National Border	Dry Lake	Pass
State Border	Seasonal Lake	⊙ State Capital

INTRODUCTION

COURTESY OF KOA

Author's Note

Welcome to Florida, the perfect place for an RV vacation. Whether you're coming to enjoy the beach, soak up the winter sun, or explore the Sunshine State's theme parks, forests, and nature spots, your RV is a first-class ticket to fun and adventure.

The RV lifestyle is the quintessential escape from the pressures of modern life. It's a way to spend quality time with your family or partner, make new friends, learn new skills, and rediscover the soul-restoring qualities of nature. You can use an RV park as your home base for anything that satisfies your psyche—from active sports like trail biking and canoeing, to more quiet pursuits like antiquing and bird-watching. You can spend as much time as your schedule and your budget allow. Perhaps, as so many people do, you'll spend your active retirement years on the road, either full-time or splitting the year between a more permanent abode and a long vacation in the sunny Florida winter months.

It's also a more cost-effective way to travel to Disney World or tour the state. Florida is a favored destination for RVers escaping the winter winds and seeking social and leisure lifestyles. Driving vacations are less hassle: no airport security, no delayed flights, no expensive restaurant bills, plus you get to bring your own pillow (and whatever other personal belongings you wouldn't bring on a plane). RV industry associations and RV manufacturers say that more and more people are discovering the joys of camping and the moving lifestyle.

In this age when your everyday life can follow you anywhere you go, when you have to monitor (and respond to) cell phones, personal digital accessories, and voice mail, it seems more important than ever to unplug now and then, to hit the road—and disconnect—at least for a little while. If that thought makes you nervous, know that you can always plug back in at the many RV parks that now offer wireless Internet service.

This book was written to help the RV traveler explore the Sunshine State and find the right park amid an enormous number of options, based on more than a decade's worth of research. After all, Florida is a big state. It's a hard day's drive from the state line to South Florida, and six hours traversing Florida from east to west. Even if you've decided where you're going, where will you stay on the way? What will you find when you get there?

Here are the answers to those questions—whether you're piloting a huge motor coach or a pop-top. Maybe you need a convenient stop on the highway as you travel. Perhaps you just want to hunker down for the winter in a deluxe resort with like-minded people. Possibly, you're only interested in finding a cheap place to stay while you visit tourist attractions.

Other details will help you make your choice, too. Are the mosquitoes worse by the lake? Shade may be nice, but maybe there are too many trees to put up your satellite dish. Is it hard to back a trailer into the spots at Campground A? Will you have to make reservations at Campground B? Are there showers with hot or cold water? Outhouses or restrooms? Is electricity available? Is it 50-amp service or 30-amp?

I hope to give you the insights you'll need to help you choose a campground where you and your companions will be happy.

Ready? Let's hit the road. Fire up the ignition on the Class A motor coach. Hitch up the Airstream or the Scamp (my favorite), or whatever trailer suits your appetites. Throw the cooler in the back of the car. This book will show you Florida in a way that no other RV guidebook does.

Best RV Parks and Campgrounds

Can't decide where to go this weekend? Check out these "bests" for the state in several categories:

◖ Best for Biking

Pine Log State Forest, Panama City, page 77

Kelly's RV Park, Tallahassee, page 103

Pine Creek Landing, Tallahassee, page 105

O'Leno State Park, Gainesville, page 130

Paynes Prairie Preserve State Park, Gainesville, page 132

Moonrise Resort, Orlando, page 232

Bay Aire RV Park, St. Petersburg, page 344

Alafia River State Park, Tampa, page 361

Markham Park, Gold Coast, page 477

Long Pine Key Campground, The Everglades, page 495

◖ Best for Equestrians

Coldwater Recreation Area, Pensacola, page 49

Navarre Beach Campground, Pensacola, page 59

Otter Springs RV Resort, Gainesville, page 135

Tillis Hill, Orlando, page 236

Wekiwa Springs State Park, Orlando, page 248

Lake Louisa State Park, Orlando, page 261

Clarcona Horseman's Park, Orlando, page 266

Lakeside Stables, Orlando, page 320

Wickham Park, Space Coast, page 333

Jay B. Starkey Wilderness Park, St. Petersburg, page 342

◖ Best for Families

Flamingo Lake RV Resort, Jacksonville, page 146

Sunshine Holiday Daytona RV Resort, Daytona, page 213

Disney's Fort Wilderness Campground, Orlando, page 284

Lake Magic RV Resort, Orlando, page 285

Kissimmee/Orlando KOA, Orlando, page 287

Fort Summit KOA Camping Resort, Orlando, page 291

River Ranch RV Resort, Orlando, page 312
Peace River Preserve, Orlando, page 316
Arcadia's Peace River Campground, Sarasota/Bradenton, page 380
Lion Country Safari KOA, Gold Coast, page 468

◖ Best for Fishing
Sunset King Lake Resort, Panama City, page 71
Leonard's Landing Lake Crescent Resort, St. Augustine, page 173
Chassahowitzka River Campground and Recreation Area, Ocala, page 191
Parramore's Fantastic Fish Camp and Family Resort, Ocala, page 203
Highbanks Marina and Camp Resort, Daytona, page 218
Pana Vista Lodge, Orlando, page 238
Camp Mack's River Resort, Orlando, page 310
Hide-A-Way RV Resort, Tampa, page 363
North Lake Estates RV Resort, Lake Okeechobee, page 405
The Marina RV Resort, Lake Okeechobee, page 413

◖ Best for Golf
Pacetti's Marina RV Park and Fishing Resort, St. Augustine, page 159
Grand Lake RV and Golf Resort, Ocala, page 181
Recreation Plantation RV Resort, Orlando, page 232
Lake Harris Resort, Orlando, page 242
Deer Creek RV Golf Resort, Orlando, page 291
Sanlan Ranch Campground, Orlando, page 298
Lily Lake Golf Resort, Orlando, page 308
River Ranch RV Resort, Orlando, page 312
Peace River Preserve, Orlando, page 316
Willow Lakes RV and Golf Resort, Space Coast, page 327
The Great Outdoors Resort, Space Coast, page 329
Hidden River Travel Resort, Tampa, page 360

◖ Best Natural Springs
Vortex Spring RV Park, Panama City, page 73
Ichetucknee Springs Campground, Gainesville, page 128
Ginnie Springs Resort, Gainesville, page 129
Manatee Springs State Park, Gainesville, page 135
Otter Springs RV Resort, Gainesville, page 135
Rainbow Springs State Park, Ocala, page 191

Salt Springs Recreation Area, Ocala, page 194

Kelly Park, Orlando, page 246

Wekiwa Springs State Park, Orlando, page 248

(Best Privately Owned Beachfront RV Parks

Playa del Rio RV Park, Pensacola, page 57

Emerald Beach RV Park, Pensacola, page 59

Navarre Beach Campground, Pensacola, page 59

Magnolia Beach Campground, Pensacola, page 60

Destin RV Beach Resort, Pensacola, page 64

Camping on the Gulf Holiday Travel Park, Pensacola, page 65

Flagler by the Sea, St. Augustine, page 168

Beverly Beach Camptown, St. Augustine, page 168

Gulf Beach Campground, Sarasota/Bradenton, page 382

Red Coconut RV Resort, Fort Myers/Naples, page 446

(Best Publicly Managed Beachfront Campgrounds

Mystic Springs Cove Airstream Park, Pensacola, page 49

Henderson Beach State Park, Pensacola, page 64

Grayton Beach State Park, Panama City, page 78

St. Andrews State Park, Panama City, page 82

T. H. Stone Memorial St. Joseph Peninsula State Park, Panama City, page 85

Huguenot Memorial Park, Jacksonville, page 148

Kathryn Abbey Hanna Park, Jacksonville, page 149

Anastasia State Park, St. Augustine, page 162

Gamble Rogers Memorial State Recreation Area, St. Augustine, page 169

Jetty Park Campground, Space Coast, page 330

Fort de Soto Park Campground, St. Petersburg, page 350

Long Key State Park, Florida Keys, page 503

Bahia Honda State Park, Florida Keys, page 505

(Most Luxurious

Roughing it? Not here. These parks can't be called campgrounds, really. They're more like resort hotels.

Destin RV Beach Resort, Pensacola, page 64

Grand Lake RV and Golf Resort, Ocala, page 181

◖ Most Unusual

Mystic Springs Cove Airstream Park, Pensacola, page 49, is for Airstream trailers only.

Falling Waters State Park, Panama City, page 73, has Florida's only waterfall.

Florida Caverns State Park, Panama City, page 74, has beautiful caves.

Torreya State Park, Tallahassee, page 91, has mountains. Well okay, steep hills.

Tresca Memorial Park/Advent Christian Village, Gainesville, page 125, is oriented to Bible study and a Christian lifestyle.

O'Leno State Park, Gainesville, page 130, has a river that goes underground and reappears three miles later.

Mike Roess Gold Head Branch State Park, St. Augustine, page 159, has a minicanyon.

Rock Crusher Canyon RV and Music Park, Ocala, page 190, has a big-time concert venue. Top-name artists like Willie Nelson and others perform here in an amphitheater.

Buttgenbach Mine Campground, Orlando, page 255, is nirvana for motorcylists, dirt bikers, and all-terrain cyclists.

Christmas Airstream Park, Orlando, page 267, welcomes both Airstreams and RVs made by other manufacturers.

Wallaby Ranch Flight Park, Orlando, page 290, is for hang gliders.

Manatee Hammock, Space Coast, page 330, is one of the closest campgrounds from which to watch space launches at Kennedy Space Center; several others also make that claim in the Space Coast chapter. The truth is you can see space launches take flight from campgrounds as far away as Kissimmee. It just depends on how good a view you want to get.

Pioneer Park of Hardee County, Lake Okeechobee, page 397, has a small wildlife refuge including bears and a cougar.

Lion Country Safari KOA, Gold Coast, page 468, is part of a wildlife park where lions roam.

Seven nudist campgrounds will give you the chance to get an all-over suntan: Riviera Naturist Resort, Pensacola, page 55; **Hidden River Resort,** Jacksonville, page 153; **Sunny Sands Nudist Resort,** Daytona, page 213; **Lake Como Club,** Orlando, page 275; **Sunnier Palms Nudist Campground,** Treasure Coast, page 428; **Sunsport Gardens,** Gold Coast, page 467; and **Seminole Health Club,** Gold Coast, page 477.

RV Travel Tips

FLORIDA TRENDS

Things move quickly in Florida, a state that always seems to be on the cutting edge of national trends. Consider the following:

- The Internet has changed the way people travel. New RVs now come equipped with desk areas for computers. Some of the most sophisticated campgrounds have installed wireless Internet networks or "instant-on" telephone service at each site. Others brag that they are "modem friendly" or place Web-accessible computers in their recreation halls so travelers can check their email and keep in touch with home. State parks, national parks, and public agencies that administer public lands post maps on their websites that you can download for general orientation and other details. On the negative side, countless gigabytes in commercial cyberspace are devoted to pseudo RV directories. Use these online directories at your own risk; they are often totally out of date. Once online, they make minimal effort to recheck the information on a regular basis.

- It's crucial to have up-to-date information at your fingertips. Many RV parks have closed in recent years, falling victim to the developer's bulldozer and being converted into housing subdivisions or shopping centers. Some older, private parks have simply filled to capacity, and many of their sites are now occupied by full-time RVers in retirement. Even newly built parks are filling up quickly, as they sell the Great American Dream of second-home ownership: a patch of land on which to park your rig that you can rent out to itinerant travelers when you've gone back home to Canada, the Northern states, or elsewhere. Other parks have been affected by hurricanes.

- Full-time camping has become a reality for many people. Early retirement, the aging of the Baby Boomers, or just plain old wanderlust have converted many a former working stiff into a roadmaster. The full-time RV lifestyle (estimated at about $1,500 a month in expenses) is more economical than ever.

- Middle-class parents, perhaps recalling the long drive-across-America trips they enjoyed as children, see camping as a budget-stretching way to take their own kids on Disney World vacations or to Florida beaches. The kids themselves, toughened by outdoors Scouting activities and the rage for "extreme sports," are happy to go, at least until they reach the age where they no longer go want to go anywhere with their parents.

- Our fast-paced modern lives have ignited a thirst for getting out of the city and into a more natural setting. The RV industry has noticed and is now producing both bigger, fancier RVs for affluent retirees and smaller, lighter, more efficient trailers and pop-tops for family campers.

- Older people are no longer "senior citizens." They're "active retirees searching for an active lifestyle." Many RV parks now have tennis courts, golf courses, exercise rooms, and full-time activities directors. Of course, the heated swimming pool and spa, shuffleboard courts, and stocked fishing ponds are still ubiquitous, as is the recreation hall with bingo, potluck suppers, and ice-cream socials. These parks have become the wintertime home address for both the affluent RVer and the penny-pinching retiree.

- Florida state parks previously banned pets, making these award-winning natural beauties inaccessible to many travelers. Now most parks allow you to bring dogs, provided they have proof of vaccination against rabies and behave on a leash. Tip: If you travel with a pet, you must carry proof of rabies vaccination. State parks also are now under a convenient, system-wide reservation system, relieving the uncertainty of being greeted with the equivalent of a "no vacancy" sign.

FLORIDA'S RV HISTORY

You're not alone, and here's a bit of historical perspective: Ever since the Model T was invented, Florida has been an RV mecca, drawing thousands of people seeking adventure and sunshine.

As early as 1916, the first "snowbirds" were packing up homemade house cars or trailers and heading south for the winter. Experts estimated that one-half of the 50,000 trailers on the road in the United States were hauled to Florida during one winter in the 1930s. Sunshine State hoteliers and boardinghouse owners howled that their business would drop. But the hotels remained crowded, and trailer parks began to spring up all over the state to accommodate RVs. It helped that the campers' money was as green as everyone else's.

These early campers formed their own version of the Good Sam Club, calling themselves the Tin Can Tourists of the World. Founded in a Tampa campground in 1919, the group grew to 30,000 members by 1938. Its goals were to provide members with "safe and clean camping areas, wholesome entertainment, and high moral values," according to Florida state archives. Their official emblem? A tin can soldered to the radiator cap of a member's car.

The origin of the tin can moniker isn't clear. It may have referred to campers' preference for canned foodstuffs. Or it could have been a reference to the Tin Lizzie, as Model T Fords were called.

The Tin Can Tourists gathered at parks around the state, usually in Tampa, Sarasota, Ocala, and Eustis. During the summer, they met at a campground in Michigan. Their favored Florida migration route: Dade City (Pasco County) at Thanksgiving and Arcadia (DeSoto County) for Christmas, where they celebrated with a community Christmas tree and a Santa Claus for the children, according to *The WPA Guide to Florida*, a book written during the Great Depression.

In 1931, the city of Sarasota opened a municipal trailer park that quickly became winter headquarters for the Tin Can Tourists. During its first season, 1,500 people in 600 trailers set up camp. Five years later, the population had grown to 7,460 people and nearly 3,000 cars, as noted in *So This Is Florida* (written by Frank Parker Stockbridge and John Holliday Perry; published in 1938).

The Sarasota Tourist Park was located on 30 acres wooded with Australian pines at a railroad crossing and Ringling Boulevard. The park even hosted the Tin Canners' annual convention, featuring a parade of new models and equipment — basically, a 1930s-style RV show.

Ocala and Arcadia also had municipal trailer parks in the 1930s, but the millionaire's city of Palm Beach allowed trailers to park for one hour only.

Conveniences at a park in Bartow in Polk County sound much the same as today's: water, electricity, hot and cold showers, laundry facilities, a recreation hall, shuffleboard courts, and horseshoe pits. The price? Stockbridge and Perry say that camping cost $1.30 by the week for two people, plus $0.25 for each additional person. Fees at other parks ranged from $1 to $5.

Camping in those days presented much the same spectacle as today. You would have seen dusty cars and trailers with license plates from all over the United States. Campers caught up with old acquaintances and made new friends. They played shuffleboard and cards, or they congregated in the recreation hall. They cooked in the open and hung laundry out to dry. And when dusk came, they lounged outdoors to watch the sun set.

So take a moment, as you embark on your journey, and think back to the Tin Can Campers. Americans have been enjoying the great outdoors of Florida in their own individual style for a long, long time.

- Some RV parks are getting more luxurious—and falling under corporate chains. A handful of RV parks are selling not just resort-style living or condominium lots, but "RV portes"—a luxury garage for the vehicle with attached housing. Several parks now offer "super" sites with spas, patio furniture, and barbecue grills. The jury is still out on this feature.

THINGS YOU SHOULD KNOW ABOUT RV TRAVEL IN FLORIDA

Here are some things learned in the course of researching this book and during many years of traveling in Florida:

When to Come

You can camp in Florida at any time—the weather's fine! On the other hand, it depends on who you are and what kind of experience you're looking for.

When are parks least crowded? For the purposes of most out-of-state visitors, Florida has two seasons. North Florida, particularly along the Gulf Coast in the Panhandle, sees its "high" season in the summer months when school is out. South and Central Florida campgrounds are busiest in the winter months, mainly mid-December–April.

Unless otherwise noted, most parks and campgrounds are open year-round. However, a few that are oriented to snowbird visitors, usually retirees, do close down in the long, hot Florida summer, generally May–October. Even if they don't close, that would be the "slow" season for this type of park.

Reservations

Most private campgrounds recommend that you make reservations, as noted in the listings. Often, they require a nonrefundable deposit ranging from $25 to $100 or more, depending on the length of your stay.

Overnighters, beware: Don't make reservations for an overnight stop unless you are ab-solutely certain you wish to stay in a particular place. If you're just traveling through, many private campgrounds will squeeze you in overnight even without a reservation. Just call ahead and tell them how big your rig is.

Using this method, you may not get the choicest spot, it's true. One private campground near Sarasota put me in a utility right-of-way under the telephone and electric poles. My view was of the back of some mobile homes, the perimeter fence, and the trash receptacle. But hey, I was there for only one night and just passing through on the way to someplace nicer.

For state parks, definitely make a reservation. Reservations are now handled by ReserveAmerica; call 800/326-3521. Previously, in most parks, only half the sites were available by reservation, and the rest were first-come, first-served. The old policy added to a lot of heartache and a kind of gambling mentality if you were planning a trip on a weekend when all the sites that could be reserved were full. For state parks, using the reservation system is almost mandatory now if you're sure you're going to be arriving at a particular park that night. In a pinch, call the park directly.

But making reservations at private campgrounds can have its pitfalls. Consider this tale: On a scorching-hot summer weekend a few years ago, I made reservations at a private campground in the Florida Keys. I drove south, chose a site as instructed by the office, unhitched the trailer, and plugged in the electric cord. Then I switched on the air-conditioning. Nothing. I jiggled the circuit breaker. Nope. I took the air conditioner apart trying to find a short circuit. Nada. Now the sweat was rolling down my hot little face. It was 90 degrees in the shade, and there really was no shade to speak of. After an hour of trying, it was clear there was to be no air-conditioning—and that I was not going to stay. I departed, but my $25 deposit was lost.

Snowbirds

Snowbirds are the exception to the rule on reservations. If you've come to Florida to stay for

RV ETIQUETTE

Miss Manners would have a field day if she ever deigned to visit some RV parks. Although most parks have published rules against noise, some managers are unable or unwilling to enforce them. Don't be inconsiderate of others. It boils down to respecting the rights of others:

- Keep radios turned down. Your taste in music may not appeal to everyone.
- If you have visitors, especially after dark, be attuned to other campers' rights to peace and quiet. Unnecessary noise is everyone's pet peeve. Observe quiet times and curfews.
- Children should be supervised at all times. It's safe practice against harm.
- Don't molest, tease, or feed wildlife. Never, ever give food to alligators; it's against the law in Florida. Furthermore, it makes them associate humans with food, and they can turn dangerous.
- Don't take shortcuts across occupied campsites. It's considered rude.
- Share the park. If tent campers are nearby, remember that they have no "walls." Noisy generators and air conditioners can be bothersome; most parks separate RVs from tent campers where possible.
- In the bathhouse, conserve hot water for others. Avoid taking long showers or leaving faucets running. If you see an open faucet, shut it off. Let the management know if supplies are running low, or if bathrooms are unclean. To avoid tracking dirt or mud into the bathhouse, wear flip-flops or sandals.
- Don't tie anything to trees or shrubs. Clotheslines are an eyesore, if sometimes necessary. Bring in towels and bathing suits when dry.
- Wash dishes in the appropriate place. Most parks frown on dish-washing in the bathhouses.
- Most publicly owned campgrounds, including state parks, prohibit alcohol, firearms, and BB guns.
- Put garbage in the correct bins; throw cans and plastic bottles into recycling containers. Don't leave household trash outside; it attracts animals and bugs.
- Check the rules before doing mechanical repairs, oil changes, and heavy auto maintenance.
- In the laundry, don't leave clothes in dryers or washers after the cycle ends. Fold clothes at your site or at the table provided in the laundry.
- Pets should be on a leash at all times. Don't tie pets to the RV and leave them behind. Barking dogs and aggressive behavior are explicitly prohibited at most places; they can be grounds for eviction.
- When you walk your pet, clean up after him/her. Use the dog walk area if one is provided.
- Park extra vehicles in the designated area. Store away toys and tools when not in use.
- Use the dump station when needed. Avoid spilling gray water on the ground.
- Where fires are permitted, use existing fire rings or grills. When leaving, put out the fire completely, pack out all trash from the fire ring, and scatter the ashes away from the site. Ground fires *can* be started by campfires that are not properly dismantled.
- Never litter. Scour your site for even the tiniest piece of trash and any other evidence of your stay.

winter or for several weeks, make a reservation early. Parks fill up fast during their big season. Many visitors return to the same park year after year, and this is the best way to guarantee you'll get the site you want.

If it's your first time in the area, you might scout for a park where you'd like to stay next winter. Try a few days at several places to get a feel for the crowd, the activities, and things to do in the area. Then make your reservation for the following year. Many parks accept reservations as early as the preceding spring, so you'll have to act quickly. Still, find out what the refund policy is before you send your check.

State Parks

Most of the best campgrounds in Florida are in state parks, where demand is high on weekends and holidays. Definitely make reservations, especially at the more popular places. You can go online and reserve a specific site.

Under the new system, state parks now accept reservations 11 months in advance of stay. (It used to be just 60 days in advance, which meant marking your calendar exactly 60 days before your planned visit, then calling first thing in the morning to reserve a spot.) Again, call ReserveAmerica at 800/326-3521. This company has a contract with the state park service to book your spot.

RV Restrictions

If you think the only rule limiting RVs is the length of your rig and the size of the available site, then think again. A few Florida RV parks don't allow pop-top campers, truck campers, vans, converted school buses, or RVs more than 20 years old. Some now restrict visitors to class A motor homes, or recreational vehicles more than 36 feet long. It seems unfair at first glance, but it's just basic free-market economics. Consider that the bread and butter of most private parks is the retired, long-staying RVer who has invested thousands of dollars in a rig and wants to mix with like-minded folks.

An alternative for people with small or unconventional trailers is to look beyond the private campgrounds. I'm particularly fond of Florida's award-winning state parks, which seek to maintain a setting as it looked when the first Europeans arrived in Florida the century after Columbus. But if you really want to get away from city lights, check out the little-known state forests and water management districts, as well as the primitive areas offered by the national forests and national parks to self-contained RVs. Some county parks are real gems, too.

Renting an RV

If you're not ready to take the plunge of investing in your own RV, renting is an option. In fact, a number of European visitors fly into Florida airports, rent a car or take a taxi to an RV rental company, and head for the open road.

A typical motor home, depending on length, sleeps 2–5 people. The advantage to a motor home is that you do not need a towing vehicle. You're less likely to find a travel trailer or pop-up camper for rent; though it's not impossible.

Rates are based on the availability of RVs at a particular location and vary by season. A typical winter rental of a motor home might cost $90–120 nightly. Add on $0.29 per mile traveled, taxes, and gasoline. Expect your mileage to be somewhere around 10 miles per gallon or less. Insurance is generally included in the rate, but it is wise to ask about coverage and be sure it is adequate since you will be responsible if the vehicle is damaged in any way.

Additional fees are charged for using the on-board generator or for towing a car behind the motor home. A refundable security deposit of $500 or so is also required.

You can bring your own gear, if practical, or rent it from the same company. Kitchen setup can be $85 per vehicle; sheets, pillows, blankets, and towels are $35 per person.

The rig must be returned to the place of origin. One-way rentals are unusual and require management approval.

RV RENTALS

Here are some companies that rent RVs:

Americas Best Cruising Motorhomes and RVs
13771 Northwest 19th Ave.
Miami, FL 33054
305/681-4811
www.americasbestrv.com

Camp USA RV Rentals
Fort Lauderdale: 954/971-8188
or 800/971-8840
Orlando: 407/944-0009
or 888/647-6665

Cruise America
Orlando office: 2915 North Orange
Blossom Trail
Kissimmee, FL 34744
407/931-1409
fax 407/931-1103
email: orlando@cruiseamerica.com
Headquarters office: 11 West Hampton Ave.
Mesa, AZ 85210

480/464-7300 or 800/327-7799
www.cruiseamerica.com
Has locations in Miami, Orlando, Pensacola, Tallahassee, Jacksonville, Gainesville, Tampa, Fort Lauderdale, Fort Myers, and other cities.

El Monte RV
562/483-4956 or 888/337-2214
www.elmonterv.com
Specializes in RV rentals across the United States. It has four locations in Florida, including one "fly-drive" site in Orlando.

Florida RV World
4260 U.S. 92 East
Plant City, FL 33566
813/754-6171 or 800/330-6171
fax 813/752-1046
www.floridarvworld.com
Rents motor homes 22-32 feet long, Class A motor homes over 33 feet long, travel trailers, and pop-up campers. Check with the company for rates.

Pets

Many Florida state parks now allow pets in their campgrounds. You must have proof of the pet's rabies vaccination and carry it with you. In addition, pets must be kept on a leash at all times and must be well behaved.

A few state parks, particularly those near beaches, may allow your pet in the campground but not on the beach.

Pets are allowed in most private parks, national forests, many county-run campgrounds, Florida Fish and Wildlife Conservation Commission campsites, many water management district sites, and U.S. Army Corps of Engineers sites.

Some places charge an extra fee of $2 or so per day per pet. Many RV parks restrict the size and weight of the pets they will allow (under 20 pounds, for example). Others prohibit specific breeds, such as pit bulls, rottweilers, or German shepherds; this has become more widespread because of insurance requirements.

Other times, the restrictions border on the downright ridiculous. One campground in the Panhandle told me pets are allowed, except for potbellied pigs. I guess you'll have to leave your potbellied pigs in the kennel at home.

Most parks have other requirements, such as walking your dog in a special area. It's fair to say that nearly all require you to clean up after your dog. They may even put all the pet owners in a special section. Of course, do not leave your pet unattended or tie him or her up to your RV while you hit the golf course or run down to the grocery store.

Which leads me to another point: Never leave your pet locked in your car. Even with the windows cracked, the temperature inside a car can quickly reach fatal levels in hot Florida.

Children

At many private RV parks, children are not welcome. The listings note when this is the case.

Some parks are willing to bend the rules if you look like a reasonable person and promise not to let your kids go unsupervised in the common areas, such as the swimming pool or restrooms. Others, even those that are strictly targeted to retirees, allow grandchildren to visit for, say, two weeks during the course of a year.

Then there are those parks that say they allow children but give you the third degree: "How big are the kids?" Some places frown on babies or small children, perhaps because they cry at night. Others are OK with little ones but dislike teenagers. Said one campground manager in Panama City: "Kids are OK, as long as they're not spring breakers."

Sometimes, it's clear that the rules are intended to keep out the working poor. There's a touch of elitism in a regulation that allows retirees to stay as long as they can pay, but wants no school-age children on the grounds for more than two weeks.

But like irresponsible pet owners who have made it difficult for everyone else, some lax parents have made it tough for other families. I was shocked when one campground owner near North Port cautioned me, "We allow kids, as long as you don't go off and leave them here alone for days." Huh? I certainly don't suggest such negligence unless you want the child and welfare investigators asking questions.

Age Restrictions

You've reached voting age, so you're an adult, right? Not necessarily. You may not be old enough. Not only do some campgrounds ban children, but there may be other complicated rules as well. Some require at least one camper to be over the age of 55; others say all visitors must be over 65. Yes, in Florida, a trailer park is not always a trailer park; it's a "retirement community" or an "adult resort."

Rates

The least-expensive parks are national and state forests, state parks, and county parks; a few are even free. State parks charge more for beachfront parks, less for inland ones.

Most private RV parks charge competitive rates, usually around $25–30 per night for two people. At deluxe resorts, charges can go as high as $70. In most places, cable TV service and sewer hookups are included in the base rate.

Then there are add-ons. Private parks usually charge a fee for each additional person, normally $2–5 each. Sometimes, discounts are given for children under 12. Extra people can cost as much as $8–15 in a handful of places.

Also, some private operators charge extra for use of air-conditioning, electric heaters, and washers or dryers (usually $2 daily). A few parks ask for $2 extra for cable TV.

More-desirable sites (closest to the beach, for example) go for a higher rate. And rates "in season" will be higher than those in slow times of the year. Finally, some campgrounds charge even more when there's a special festival or other crowd-drawing attraction, such as Biketoberfest in Daytona Beach.

On the other hand, national parks, county parks, and others offer discounted rates to folks over 65 or the disabled. You'll be required to provide proof of age or disability. (Under federal policy, disability is proven by showing proof of medically determined permanent disability, or eligibility for receiving benefits under federal law.)

Snowbirds who store their RVs on-site after the season ends can save money. After the sixth month, they do not pay the local tourist tax, which varies by location, but can be as high as 11 percent. In addition, most parks charge only nominal fees for storing a rig during the summer.

Just as an FYI: If you don't mind traffic noise, you can also camp for free in some Wal-Mart parking lots and those of a restaurant chain called Cracker Barrel. You'll need to ask the manager for permission to stay overnight. Some Moose lodges also allow RVs to hook up in their parking areas. Campground owners, naturally, don't like this trend, considering it competition. Frankly, I think Florida offers too many pretty places for me to consider staying in a parking lot.

Taxes

The rates in the listings are the base rates. They do not include sales tax. The reason for this is that each county charges a different rate, as much as a total of 11 percent in some cases.

Why so high? Florida has no state income tax. It derives its income from sales taxes. While most counties charge 6 or 7 percent sales tax when you purchase an item in a store, they tack on additional "bed" taxes for lodging. That way Florida residents unwittingly shift the tax burden to tourists and visitors. Some mighty strange things get funded with hospitality taxes—sports stadiums, local pet projects, and even advertising campaigns to get more tourists to come and pay bed taxes.

Using the Facilities

If you're not in a self-contained RV, you're going to have to face the communal restrooms and showers. Many parks brag that their facilities are sparkling clean. That may be, but some will give you pause. The drains don't drain, the hot water runs out, or you're forced to listen helplessly to endless palaver from your neighbors. Bring soap, shampoo, toothbrush and toothpaste, and other niceties in a separate bag; sometimes, a flashlight is needed for the walk. Don't forget a towel and a change of clothes. Most campgrounds perform a daily cleaning routine about 11 A.M., and that's it for the day. If you must take a shower at night, you'll likely find you have to wait your turn, and by then, things aren't so sparkling, or the water is tepid. Mornings are quieter, and you're more likely to have hot water. Get up early.

The Florida Effect

Things change here. From the time Henry Flagler's railroad came marching down the East Coast, change has been a constant in Florida. Hurricanes and wildfires roar through, eradicating buildings, washing out streets, and even eliminating big sections of forest.

Weather experts say we are now in a possibly 10-year period of highly active hurricane seasons. Certainly, the summers of 2004 and 2005 have borne this out. The 2005 summer set a record with 26 named storms. Some favorite parks were wiped out in these storms, or were so badly damaged that the owners simply gave up the operation. It happens even with state parks and national parks; for example, Fort Pickens Campground in the Gulf Island National Seashore near Gulf Breeze remains closed "indefinitely" as of May 2006 while basic roads are rebuilt. A $6 million beachfront state park near Pensacola was open just a short year before a storm caused $5 million in damage. Authorities are wrangling over whether the campground should be rebuilt at all, given its vulnerable location. In Fort Lauderdale, two top-notch nature parks are being used in 2006 and 2007 by the Federal Emergency Management Administration (FEMA) to house people displaced by Hurricane Wilma.

Another force, not spawned by Mother Nature but by the almighty dollar, is the increasing value of real estate. Mobile-home parks on the city/suburb edge get supplanted by subdivisions, sometimes in a matter of weeks. One example is the All-Star Resort in Perdido Key, near Pensacola. Just two years after it opened with brand-new, sparkling facilities, winning awards left and right, it was torn down, reportedly for a condominium. Well, it was right on the beach—the most valuable property there can be in Florida. More examples are in the Florida Keys, where some of the largest and longest-running campgrounds were sold to developers in the middle of the decade.

All this, and much more, can affect whether the information in this book is up-to-date. Although every effort has been made to be sure the data are current and accurate, you'll have to allow some wriggle room to account for the "Florida Effect."

Change can be a good thing—the state of Florida runs a remarkable, proactive land-acquisition program to preserve natural areas, and thousands and thousands of acres are added each year. Public access points and available facilities are subject to change, and new areas may be open after we go to press. If you have a specific need or concern, it's a good idea to call the responsible agency ahead of time. Websites for the larger state land resource management areas are listed (see *Resources*). Browse their websites often to see if new lands are open for hiking, camping, boating, or other activities. Often, you can download maps or recreation guides from these websites as information is updated through the coming months.

CLIMATE AND WEATHER PROTECTION

Camping in Florida rewards you with many surprises: Sunsets over the Gulf of Mexico, watching the golden orb drop into the horizon with a refreshing iced tea in your hand and a gentle sea breeze rustling your hair. Snorkeling in the Florida Keys just 20 steps from your beachfront tent. A herd of deer snooping around your campsite in the woods. Hiking in a shady pine forest, canoeing down the Peace River, casting a line into the surf, going to sleep on an island so secluded that you can only get there by boat. Mountain biking on lonely forest roads where you suddenly come across an abandoned homestead from the 1920s.

It can also be a shock—with sudden downpours that Floridians call "palmetto pounders"; gale-force winds that rock your trailer and blow down your tent; mosquitoes, gnats, no-see-ums, spiders, and roaches; or broiling-hot days with sticky humid nights.

Cold

When most people think of Florida, they envision warm weather and sunny skies. The truth is that Florida's climate is amazingly diverse—and subject to dramatic change. Even people who've lived in Florida a long time sometimes overlook this fact.

One spring break several years ago, I set out from Miami on a weeklong camping trip. In Miami, the temperature was near the 80s during the day and in the mid-70s at night, and I thought I'd packed all the personal gear I could possibly need—shorts, T-shirts, swimsuits, and sunglasses. By the time I reached Lake City in North Florida at the end of that first day, skies had turned cloudy and then stormy, as the leading edge of a cold front dipped south. Dinnertime in the campground was uncomfortable. Temperatures had dropped into the 60s and the wind had picked up.

It sounds ridiculous to think about wind-chill factors when there's no snow on the ground, but I had no long pants and no long-sleeved shirts, and I was cold! That arctic front never traveled south of Orlando, but tell that to my shivering kids as I bundled them up into the car and headed for the nearest store to buy jeans and sweatshirts.

Yes, Florida is hot in the summertime. But from October through May, the weather can vary significantly, depending on your location.

FLORIDA'S AVERAGE DAILY MAXIMUM TEMPERATURES

	Jan.	Mar.	May	July	Sept.	Nov.
Daytona Beach	68	75	84	90	87	76
Miami	75	79	85	89	88	80
Orlando	71	78	88	92	90	78
Pensacola	60	69	83	90	86	70
Tampa	70	77	87	90	89	78

Source: National Weather Service

North Florida—from the Panhandle east to Jacksonville—even has changing seasons. (See the temperature chart, earlier in this chapter.)

By the standards of most people who live outside Florida, though, winters are mild, offset by an occasional cold front that may bring freezing or near-freezing weather. And those fronts last for just a couple of days. Many visitors don't seem to mind them, and they don't let the weather interrupt their outdoors pursuits. It's common to see Canadians and Europeans accustomed to colder climes basking on the beach in 50-degree weather—giving truth to the old saying that you can tell who the tourists are because they have tans in winter.

Even without a weather report, you can often tell what's going to happen. A cold front usually sweeps south in a broad band. As the cold collides with the warm air, cloudy skies and swift winds are formed, sometimes accompanied by rain. As the front continues south, the skies often clear. You'll see crisp, sunny days and clear, starlit skies at night. Keep an ear on the radio weather reports throughout the year.

On any outing in winter, bring at least a long-sleeved shirt and a pair of long pants. A heavy jacket or windbreaker is also a good idea, even if you just leave it in the car. On one trip, when the mercury dipped into the 20s at night in O'Leno State Park near High Springs, I appreciated having saved my down jacket from long-ago mountaineering days out West.

Watch the weather reports and read the weather maps before you leave. If a cold front is a possibility, bring enough warm clothing to last for a couple of days. And don't forget to pack for everyone in your party, particularly children. When they get cold and miserable, it's hard for anyone to have a good time.

Heat

Yes, it's hot here. But as you can see from the temperature chart, it's often cooler in the hottest summer months than in many places, say, in the landlocked Midwest. Ocean breezes and frequent rains oblige with extra relief, and you can always jump into the nearest pool to cool off. If you're really desperate to get out of the heat, you can stop at a movie theater or a mall.

Still, it's nice to have air-conditioning during summer, both in your car and in your RV. For sitting outside, an inexpensive box fan stirs the air on hot nights and sometimes keeps bugs away.

Which brings me to a discussion on the dangers of heat. You need to be concerned about three things (listed here in order of seriousness): heat cramps, heat exhaustion, and heatstroke. The key to preventing all three is to drink plenty of liquids. Limit exercise in the hottest part of the day. Wear a hat. Look for shade. (After

---

THE DANGERS OF DEHYDRATION

Dehydration doesn't just mean that your body is in need of water. It also means that you're in danger of a rising body temperature, nausea, and – in hot weather – suffering from heat-related illness. The solution? Replace your body fluids by drinking lots of water – 8-10 cups per day – and up to one gallon if the weather is warm or if you're really active.

If you're feeling thirsty, you are mildly dehydrated. But if you're experiencing headaches and dry mouth – and your urine output is under two cups over 24 hours – chances are your case is serious. Replace electrolytes (salt, potassium, and bicarbonate) by drinking fruit juice or an energy drink such as Gatorade (which was invented at the University of Florida in Gainesville; their football team is known as the Gators).

Although physicians once recommended salt pills, they now believe that regular diets, including dehydrated foods that campers often consume, provide enough salts without supplements.

you've been in Florida awhile, you'll just instinctively cross the street to walk on the shady side.) Wear lightweight, light-colored clothing that reflects sunlight. Avoid getting sunburned, which makes you feel hotter and impedes the body's thermostat.

Heat cramps, usually painful spasms in the leg or abdominal muscles, are the first symptom that you're not handling your environment properly. It means that you're lacking salt, probably caused by losing more water (through sweat) than you're gaining. Stop exercising, get out of the sun, and drink salted water (one teaspoon of salt to a quart of water). Do NOT drink caffeine or alcohol because they make symptoms worse and are dehydrating. Massage the cramps gently.

Heat exhaustion comes on when your personal cooling system starts to shut down, usually after prolonged activity in hot, humid weather. Skin may become cold, pale, and clammy. You may become weak and may even vomit. Your body temperature will be normal or slightly lower. At these signs, lie down in the shade. Remove any restrictive clothing and raise your legs above your head to encourage blood flow. Drink salted water.

Heatstroke, also called sunstroke, is really dangerous. Usually, the skin is hot and dry. You will not sweat, and your internal body temperature may be 106 degrees or higher. Dizziness, vomiting, diarrhea, and confusion are also symptoms. If any of these symptoms occur, call 911 or go to a hospital without delay. If you are in the backcountry (or on the way to the hospital), remove your clothing. Lower your body temperature with cool water or sponges, fans, or air conditioners. Do NOT consume any liquids.

Rain

Be prepared for drenching downpours. Rain gear is essential year-round. Summer (May–October) is the rainy season, but thunderstorms and heavy rain are possible at all times of the year. Can you imagine 18 inches of rain in 24 hours in the middle of October? How about March? It happens.

Florida rains are rarely the gentle drizzling kind that last all day. They burst upon you with an intensity that may surprise people who have no experience with the subtropics. Driving is dangerous in these conditions, and flash flooding may occur. Fortunately, the skies often clear within a couple of hours. And since you're traveling in an RV, all you have to do is break out the cards or board games and wait for the storm to pass.

Sun

Many private campgrounds in Florida don't have tree canopies; or you may be assigned to a site as leafless as the desert. After you've spent all day swimming or hiking in the hot sun, you'll crave a chance to get into the shade. Fortunately, you can bring your own.

A sunroom or screen tent comes in handy to keep the broiling sun at bay. These 8- by 10-foot rooms go up just like a tent; some are big enough to slip over the campground picnic table. They cost about $200 at sporting goods or RV supply stores and as little as $20 at a big discount store. The kind with screens around them also keep out bugs.

Too much sunshine is a real health concern in Florida. Studies say that native Floridians with fair complexions and light-colored eyes run an extremely high risk of getting skin cancer. But no matter where you were born or what you look like, sunscreens are a must to prevent sunburn, which can cause problems later in life. In addition to skin cancer, excess exposure to sun can lead to cataracts, premature aging, and even damage to your immune system. Be especially careful with children, who will resist secondary applications of sunscreen after the first dip in the water. Plus, they often lose (or won't wear) hats.

You can buy sunscreens almost everywhere in Florida, from grocery stores to gas stations. Purchase the highest-rated sunscreen you can find; an SPF of 15 is considered the minimum recommended protection. On a prolonged outdoors trip, SPF 15 is not adequate for kids unless you want to be reapply it every hour or two.

Unfortunately, not even sunscreens may be enough to prevent melanoma, the most malignant and deadly form of skin cancer. Many dermatologists today recommend use of sunscreens in combination with two other caveats: Limit sun exposure, particularly between 11 A.M. and 1 P.M., and wear protective clothing, such as hats, long sleeves, and long pants.

Even on rare days when skies are overcast, you can still get a harmful sunburn. Ultraviolet rays are particularly dangerous when you're in a boat or at the beach; they reflect off the water or the sand, doubling their effects.

Most people are uncomfortable without sunglasses. If you forgot to bring a pair, cheap sunglasses ($5–10) are readily available in convenience stores, gas stations, and drugstores. But be forewarned: Unless the glasses promise 100 percent UV protection, they could do more harm than good, in some cases doubling the amount of UVA rays your eyes would experience without sunglasses. You can spring for a better pair from sunglasses kiosks in shopping malls. Don't forget to get a pair for the kids, and be prepared to replace them often.

You'll also want to invest in several tubes of lip protection balm. Some brands have sunscreens in their formulas. Soothe painful, sunscorched lips with Bag Balm or Vaseline. (Bag Balm can cure horrible swollen lip damage within hours.)

Boaters, canoeists, and kayakers should wear wide-brimmed hats, available at Army-Navy surplus stores or outdoors shops. Baseball caps are popular, but remember to use sunblock, particularly on your ears and neck. Bicyclists have the problem that they must wear helmets, but helmets don't provide sufficient sun protection. Slather on that sunscreen repeatedly, especially on the neck under the chin and areas you don't normally think will get burned. Look for a sunscreen that resists sweat, or you end up with the double whammy of irritated eyes from the sweat plus the sunscreen. Use a bandanna or sweatband under your bike helmet for a little control.

Hypothermia

Being exposed to wet, cold weather for an extended period can be fatal—even at 50 degrees. In fact, cases of hypothermia are a lot more common than you would expect in the Sunshine State. In part, that's because Florida's sunny reputation makes some campers blasé. A few years ago, rugged Army Rangers training in the Panhandle were severely stricken; some even died. They spent 10 wet hours in air that did not dip below 50 degrees.

So the first line of defense against hypothermia is the expectation that it could happen. Remember that being cold and wet at the same time can be deadly. Keep your clothes dry at all costs, and stay out of the wind. In short, remain warm and dry.

If you start to shiver, you could be on the way to hypothermia. Never ignore shivering. Get out of the wind and into dry clothes.

The second wave of symptoms may include uncontrollable shivering, slow or slurred speech, incoherence, uncoordinated movements, stumbling, exhaustion, and drowsiness.

If a person has entered this second stage of hypothermia, some exercise will help by burning calories and raising the internal body temperature. But remember, as those calories are burned, they must be replaced. A good choice is warm soup (not hot because blazing temperatures can shock a cold body and cause a heart attack). Another good choice is snacks with quick energy release such as candy or an energy bar.

Do not let anyone with such symptoms go to sleep! Get the person out of the wind and rain, take off all wet clothes (no need to be shy when you may be dying), and put on dry clothes. Administer warm drinks. Dry clothes and a warm sleeping bag are best until the victim recovers.

If the sufferer is only semiconscious, leave his or her clothes stripped off and get him or

DIAL-UP WEATHER REPORTS

If you don't have ready access to radio, TV, or the Internet, you can call the National Weather Service for recorded weather information, including local forecasts, tropical (hurricane) outlook, and marine conditions, among others:

- Jacksonville: 904/741-4370
- Key West: 305/295-1316
- Melbourne (Space Coast area): 321/255-2900
- Miami: 305/229-4550 (English and Spanish)
- Tallahassee: 850/422-1212
- Tampa Bay: 813/645-2506

her into a sleeping bag with another naked person. The best treatment then is skin-to-skin contact. In no case should the victim be left in wet clothing because it tends to wick heat away from the body.

Lightning and Severe Weather

Florida is home to some of the most extreme thunderstorms in the country, so you'll want to keep a close eye on the weather.

It is worthwhile to fork over a few bucks for a special NOAA Weather Radio. (NOAA is the National Oceanic and Atmospheric Administration, which runs the National Weather Service.) For as little as about $40, you get access to continuous-loop weather reports that are updated throughout the day. Weather on demand, in other words.

The radios are permanently tuned to the free NOAA service, and the only investment is the initial cost. Advisories are continuous, and bad-weather alerts are broadcast as soon as they are issued. The information is immediate, more complete, and thoroughly detailed, unlike the intermittent and brief weather reports on local radio stations. Weather radios are sold at Radio Shack, electronics and sporting goods stores, marine shops, and outdoors stores.

For up to $200, you can also get weather radios that, even when left in their inactive mode, will chirp to life and let you know when a weather alert has been issued in your area. These devices are particularly important if you're not watching TV regularly while you're on vacation.

A weather radio can provide good service even if you're camping in more urban conditions. Several years ago, a line of tornadoes rolled across Central Florida, flattening a campground near Kissimmee. Much was made of the fact that campers didn't have warning. There was talk of installing tornado warning sirens to alert folks that they should leave their RVs and take cover in a secure building on the grounds. The talk has come to little, so you are responsible for monitoring severe weather.

You're more likely to experience lightning than tornadoes. Lightning strikes more than 1,000 people a year in the United States, often in Florida. In fact, Florida is considered the lightning capital of the nation. Most victims are standing when they are hit. The electricity enters the head first, knocking them unconscious. Nerves and blood vessels speed the electricity through the body.

You may have some warning, or an inkling that something is up. People who are struck often see lightning or hear thunder in the distance and try to squeeze in one more round of golf or hook another fish. When you hear thunder, take precautions immediately. If you're

HURRICANE SHELTER TIPS

If a hurricane approaches and you are unable to drive out of the area or find lodging in a motel, you may be forced to go to a public shelter. These are usually located in schools, government buildings, or even stadiums. While you are probably not going to encounter conditions like those at the New Orleans Superdome during Hurricane Katrina in 2005, please note that most shelters do not allow pets, and that comforts are few. Here's what you should bring, according to the National Weather Service:

- First-aid kit
- Medicine
- Baby food and diapers
- Cards, games, books, etc.
- Toiletries
- Battery-powered radio (or television)
- Flashlight (one per person)

- Extra batteries
- Blankets or sleeping bags
- Identification
- Valuable papers and documents, such as insurance
- Cash

Source: National Weather Service

in a field or on open water, make for cover right away. Do not stand under a solitary tree or clump of trees. Nor should you stand near a fence or metallic objects. Ideally, you will find shelter in a building or car. If you're outdoors away from civilization, try to head for a forest. Do not stand under the tallest tree, but rather seek out the shortest. If you are caught in the middle of a field, lie down far away from objects that might attract lightning.

Hurricanes

First, the good news. You will have plenty of notice (usually several days) in advance of a hurricane if you pay attention to local news and weather reports. The bad news is that RVs and mobile homes are not safe for weathering a hurricane, and you may be required to evacuate to a safer area. Even if the storm's path is uncertain, tourists and RVers sometimes are ordered out of vulnerable places like the Florida Keys ahead of local residents.

The Atlantic hurricane season runs every year from June 1 through November 30. For statistical purposes, the coastal areas have the greatest risk, and storms tend to diminish in strength after they make landfall. Hurricanes are nature's way of blowing off steam, literally a way to release heat buildup into the upper atmosphere, and their pattern of formation varies in frequency. The mid-1990s saw the beginning of an accelerated cycle of hurricane activity that may last another 10 years or more.

Storms that reach wind speeds above 39 mph are designated in order of the alphabet, based on a predetermined list of names. So, for example, in 2005, the first storm of the season was named Arlene. The last would have been Wilma. But then the list ran out, and the record-breaking season pushed on. After Wilma, forecasters used letters of the Greek alphabet for the first time in history.

Weather experts monitor the Atlantic and Caribbean for "tropical depressions" or "tropical waves" that can grow in intensity to become tropical storms, and at 75 mph turn into hurricanes. As they grow in wind speed and destructive power, storms are rated from Category 1 through 5, with 5 being the most disastrous. For more information on hurricanes and weather, please see the National Weather Service National Hurricane Center website at www.nhc.noaa.gov. Another good website for storm information is www.wunderground.com/tropical.

If you are in Florida during a hurricane scare, you'll learn all this terminology quickly from radio and television. So let me fill you in on what will be happening on the ground and what you should be doing if your location is in the official "cone of uncertainty." First, plan your evacuation route and fill up your gasoline tank. Remember that everyone else will be getting out of Dodge at the same time, so highways will be crowded. Make sure you have cash, a battery-operated radio and flashlights, fresh drinking water, ice, and food. Those will be scarce after the storm passes.

One campground in Florida that has served as an official Red Cross shelter for many RVers is Spirit of the Suwannee Music Park in Live Oak, where it once hosted 8,000 storm refugees. Of course, RV parks all along the escape routes will be filled, too, so you may wind up staying in a motel or, in a worst-case scenario, a public shelter such as a school.

Hurricanes and severe weather usually knock out the electrical power for widespread areas. What does that mean for you? For one, gasoline stations need electricity to pump gas. You may face long lines at a gas station that has a generator to keep your journey going forward. For another thing, automatic bank teller machines, banks, and stores will have no power. That's why you should keep some cash handy. You won't be able to withdraw money or pay for anything with a credit card.

This all sounds very ominous, but don't worry. If you're alert, you can pretty much count on not being anywhere near a hurricane if and when it strikes. And if you leave early enough, you may beat the traffic.

BEASTS, BUGS, AND TOXIC PLANTS

I don't want to scare anyone. You're not likely to encounter many of these critters, but you ought to be aware that they are out there.

Alligators

Alligators are unlikely to hurt you, with a few important exceptions.

The myth of dangerous alligators is largely just that—a myth. Think about the reports you've heard of alligators attacking people. You hear, what, maybe one every few years? The very fact that such encounters make such big news is a clue to their rarity. In Florida, far more people are killed by lightning than by alligators.

One of my friends once waded through alligator-infested, chest-deep waters for long stretches on two consecutive days. It makes for a great story, but in fact he was largely unconcerned. The reason? He was in the middle of the Everglades, where gators have precious little contact with humans. And when Clyde Butcher, the famous photographic chronicler of Florida's outdoors, lowers his burly body into the waters to shoot his stunning black-and-white photos, he says he doesn't worry one bit about alligators snapping at his bare legs or any other part of him.

Which brings me to one big exception. With hundreds of people moving to Florida every day, more and more of the alligator's territory is being invaded. This is not usually a problem—at least from the human point of view—until people start feeding the beasts. A fed gator is a dangerous gator. It's as simple as that. Under normal circumstances, an alligator does not view an adult human as food. Once the marshmallows start flying, however, all bets are off.

So if you suspect an alligator has been fed—if he starts edging toward you, for instance, indicating he has lost his natural shyness—get the heck out of there, and by all means don't put your hand near his mouth.

Also, old, sick alligators may go after a person, particularly a child. Because of their size, children make a better target. Alligators six feet or longer present the greatest danger to kids. Those under four feet generally are not a problem. When you swim in freshwater in Florida, keep an eye out for large gators. Also, avoid swimming at dusk or at night, when they often are feeding. They might not recognize you as a human until it's too late.

Don't let your pets near any body of freshwater in Florida. Pets, also because of their size and posture, may be viewed as eligible fare for the dinner hour. A child splashing in the water with his dog can be a lethal mix.

Poisonous Toads

The nasty little South American import known as *bufo marinus* secretes a toxic substance and is chiefly a threat to pets. If you handle a greenish-gray toad with brown bumps that look like a bad case of warts, be sure to wash your hands thoroughly afterward. Don't let children or pets play with them. A dog that has had a bufo in its mouth may foam at the lips, cough, and gag. Try to get a hose or water bottle to wash out the dog's mouth.

Snakes

Most snakes in Florida are not poisonous. Like alligators, they are a largely overblown menace in the backcountry, especially when you consider how few people are killed by them. Still, I don't want to minimize their threat, because a snakebite is serious. At the very least, it will ruin your camping trip. As a rule, stay away from all snakes. Even a nonpoisonous snake can strike and break the skin.

Bear in mind that snakes, poisonous and nonpoisonous, are more scared of you than you are of them. Be careful where you plant your feet and hands when you are outdoors, and never, ever reach into a pile of wood. To gather firewood, use a downed branch to move individual pieces of wood to where you can see them and confirm they are not harboring a snake (or a scorpion or a spider, for that matter).

If bitten, forget the old wisdom of scratching an X on the spot and sucking out the venom. Doctors have found the sucking method to be ineffective, impractical, and messy, as well as potentially dangerous for the good Samaritan sucking the venom. The new wisdom: Stay calm and get medical help as soon as possible. Realize that most bites turn out to be dry bites, meaning no venom was injected.

If you're near your drive-up campsite when the bite occurs, simply get in the car and travel calmly to an emergency physician. If you're in the backcountry, walk out slowly; don't run because the venom may spread through your bloodstream more quickly. Better yet, sit down and get medical help to come to you. The U.S. Army advises its soldiers to lie quietly, move no more than necessary, and don't smoke, eat, or drink any fluids. Remove any jewelry from the bitten extremity because rings, bracelets, and the like may become a tourniquet if swelling occurs. If a limb was bitten, don't elevate it—keep the extremity level with the body. If you don't know what type of snake struck, then try to remember what the reptile looked like so you can describe it to a physician.

You may fashion a splint out of a tent stake or something similar in the meantime. Loosely tie it with a sock, T-shirt, or another piece of clothing. It should be tight enough to stop the flow of blood near the skin, the Army advises. But don't tie it tight enough that it becomes a tourniquet—or you'll risk losing the limb. If swelling is occurring quickly, place an inch-wide constricting band about two inches above the bite, suggests the Cooperative Extension Service of Mississippi State University. Remember: Make it loose enough that you can slip a finger underneath. Don't place a constricting band on a joint.

There are four types of poisonous snakes to worry about:

RATTLESNAKES

Florida is home to several species of rattlesnakes, including Eastern diamondbacks, which can grow up to eight feet long. Usually found in woodpiles and in the ubiquitous clusters of saw palmetto that dot Florida woodlands, they are an excellent reason to stay on hiking trails and watch your step around downed wood.

One time in the Big Cypress Swamp, a troop of about 25 Boy Scouts was hiking along a trail that was blocked by a fallen log. The guys and their scoutmasters all stepped over the log—until the 22nd or 23rd boy noticed a rattlesnake wedged under it. The laggards chose an alternate path.

WATER MOCCASINS

Also known as cottonmouths, these snakes are mottled brown and black pit vipers with cotton-white coloring on the inside of their mouths. If you're lucky, though, you'll never see the inside of one's mouth. That's a sign of warning! These snakes are usually found in or near the water. If you're swimming in freshwater, stay away from clumps of vegetation, particularly if enough of it is growing above the water's surface for a snake to hide. And watch where you are stepping when you're at the shoreline.

As a child, one of my friends was swimming in front of a dock on Lake Placid when his father commanded him to get out of the water immediately. Ignoring his father's objections, he swam around to where he could use the ladder at dockside—right next to a clump of vegetation where two big, fat cottonmouths were sunning themselves. He still remembers that cotton-white color.

CORAL SNAKES

These snakes have smaller injectors and inject less poison than the aforementioned pit vipers, but their venom packs more punch and rapidly affects the nervous system. Fortunately, they are not very aggressive. They're usually found under rocks or debris on the ground.

Coral snakes have black snouts and their bodies are ringed entirely with red, yellow or off-white, and black bands. Several nonpoisonous snakes, such as the scarlet king or the milk snake, look like coral snakes. Remember that coral snakes have black noses; the imitators have yellow or red noses. Although other nonpoisonous snakes have the same coloring, on the coral snake the red ring always touches the yellow ring. (Here's an old saying: "Red touch black, venom lack; red touch yellow, bad for fellow.")

COPPERHEADS

These snakes are pit vipers without rattles that live in dry upland areas in the Panhandle and grow up to four feet long. You can recognize them by their copper-colored head and the reddish hourglass on the body. Their venom is not as potent as rattlers'.

Raccoons

Of course raccoons look cute. Heck, the former Florida governor Lawton Chiles even compared himself with an old "he-coon" in a close-fought election campaign. But stay away from these masked marauders because some carry rabies.

And don't feed them. Some campers have been invaded on more than one picnic by raccoons rampaging across the table expecting a handout. It's tough to scare off the little buggers once they know people have food. Also take precautions against raccoons stealing food while you sleep. It's best to store food and water in your car or RV. If you're roughing it in the backcountry, you may want to keep food in the tent with you. Or, if you have a hard-sided cooler, store food and water inside and secure it with numerous loops of rope, tied tight. You need the rope because raccoons are clever enough to open some coolers. Use thick rope, not twine, so they can't chew their way through.

Bears

Although they once roamed most of the state, black bears in Florida now number fewer than 1,500 and are confined to scattered pockets. The biggest pockets are in the Big Cypress National Preserve and Osceola, Ocala, and Apalachicola National Forests, as well as the surrounding areas.

So rare are bears today that state biologists have to put electronic collars on the animals and drive 150 miles in a single day at times to find them. Females typically range 10 miles or so in a day, while the larger, 250- to 350-pound adult males will go farther.

These secretive, shy, little-seen mammals come out mostly at night and tend to be found around thick clumps of trees and underbrush. They consider the tender shoots of saw palmetto thickets a bear's answer to ice cream. You're extremely unlikely to encounter these officially designated "threatened" animals. The worst possibility is to unexpectedly come up against a mama bear and her cubs, usually in summer or fall.

If you're camping where bears are likely to be, place all food inside backpacks or nylon stuff sacks and hang the bags from a tree limb. Here's the process: Look for a sturdy tree limb that extends at least eight feet from the trunk of a tree. Throw a length of rope over the limb. Tie one end of the rope to a sack of food. Pull on the other end of the rope to haul the bag, pulley-style, into the air so the bag hangs 10 feet or higher above the ground. Then wrap the other end of the rope a few times around the tree trunk and tie it tightly.

Wild Hogs

Descended from domestic pigs that escaped from early settlers, wild hogs are a major nuisance. They root around in the ground, leaving big, plowlike ruts in their wake, destroying natural areas. They can be very dangerous when cornered. In many designated hunting areas, they are the only animal for which there is no bag limit. Spareribs all around, I say!

One of my researchers and his family were confronted with a wild hog in the campground at Myakka River State Park. The animal was rooting around, looking for food underneath the picnic table when they returned to camp. Feeling cornered (the picnic table was next to a wet marshy area), the hog grew agitated. Clearly, trouble was on the way. The family was lucky because they climbed onto the picnic table and the hog soon ran off.

If you see a wild hog, head the other way immediately and start looking for an escape route. Climb a tree, get into a car, or head inside a building. Merely backing away will usually defuse the situation. In any case, do not knowingly approach a hog. It will feel threatened and could charge.

Bees, Wasps, and Yellow Jackets

These insects can be a serious problem—even a fatal one for people who are susceptible. Obviously, you should never disturb their nests on purpose. Remember when you're walking in the woods that these insects strive to keep their nests dry. So don't poke your hand into a hollow log (good advice on numerous counts) or places where nests could be hidden.

In my experience, yellow jackets are the most aggressive of the three, followed by wasps, then bees. Unlike bees, which lose their stinger after one piercing, wasps and yellow jackets can return to sting you repeatedly.

If you are being attacked, run! If you are stung, watch for signs of allergic reaction: swelling, wooziness, shortness of breath, fainting, cramps, or shock. Should any of these symptoms seem to be occurring, head for the nearest emergency room.

As a stopgap measure, consider treating stings with a semiliquid mixture of water and baking soda. If you know you are allergic to such stings, be sure to bring along an antidote when you go camping.

Mosquitoes

Well, what would Florida be without mosquitoes? A lot more pleasant, that's what I say. But that's impossible and, besides, it wouldn't be the same mosaic of ecosystems. That's right—skeeters have their place in the ecological web.

Think of a camping trip without the soothing croaks of mosquito-eating frogs. What would the Florida outdoors be like without skeeter-munching dragonflies darting across hiking trails? And mosquito larvae are a major food for fish.

Mosquitoes are drawn by carbon dioxide—what we all exhale—so you can't very well avoid them altogether. Mosquitoes are worst in summer, of course, and are generally more of a problem in South Florida than North Florida. Most, but not all, mosquitoes prefer to bite at dusk. Some also swarm at night. All avoid direct sunlight, though, because it dries them out and kills them.

With rare exception, mosquitoes are merely pests. The exception is when they transmit disease. Although malaria has been wiped out (except in some third-world countries), you can contract encephalitis, which causes brain inflammation, through mosquito bites. More recently has been the spread of potentially fatal West Nile virus by mosquitoes. It's uncommon, yet it makes sense to avoid mosquito bites as much as possible.

In urban areas, so-called sentinel chickens are deliberately put out to be bitten by mosquitoes, then tested to see if the disease-carrying insects have done the deed. For years little evidence of disease transmission existed, but in recent years a few outbreaks have been reported.

What do we do to protect ourselves? We rub poison all over our bodies! Sad to say, but insecticides are the most effective way to keep skeeters away. I prefer formulations containing DEET—particularly when facing the 47 types of mosquitoes in Everglades National Park. Avon's Skin So Soft can be helpful, although it is not marketed as an insecticide and hence has not been tested as one. (Some people assume it's safer than DEET, but as far as I know, no one has checked.) The standard advice is to wear long sleeves and long pants, although I find this fairly uncomfortable in summer when mosquitoes are most numerous.

Make sure to cover any exposed skin with insecticide. In my experience, skeeters are particularly attracted to the ankles, arms, neck, and—while you sleep, if you're careless enough to let one into your tent or RV—face.

If possible, escape to your tent or RV at dusk. Another nicety is a dining fly enclosed by mosquito netting, although this is obviously impractical for backpackers and canoeists. Mosquitoes also tend to avoid smoke and heat, another great argument for having a campfire. Make a big, hot, smoky one, then sit back and enjoy.

Roaches

I hate roaches. But they are as much a part of the Florida landscape as the air. You'll find roaches in five-star hotels, luxury homes, and even cars. Folks here call them "palmetto bugs."

There's not much you can do about roaches if you're tent camping, except push them out of your way. In an RV, clean up Florida-style after every meal: Sweep the floor, wipe the counters, and get rid of crumbs. And please, don't spray the campsite with Raid. I was in a county park near Tampa having dinner at the picnic table when my neighbors decided to declare chemical war on bugs. Not very neighborly when the wind is blowing.

Ticks

Ticks are one of the more serious insect threats because they can spread Lyme disease. A vaccine is now available if you're really worried about Lyme disease or expect to be regularly exposed to ticks.

You'll tend to find ticks on your body if you've been in the deep woods, although they can appear in a standard commercial campground, too. You're most likely to encounter them if you're crashing through little-disturbed, low-lying brush during a hike. Stay on the trail to minimize this threat.

Get into the practice of surveying your skin any time you've been in the deep woods. If possible, have a camping mate look over your back, neck, and scalp. Don't forget to check under your clothes; ticks can be discovered in unmentionable areas! If you find a tick, it will look like a brown wart. What has happened is that the tick has been sucking on you all day, with its head burrowed in your flesh, and its body has become engorged with your blood.

Don't take the advice of some standard guides that prescribe covering the little bugger with gas, Vaseline, or some other toxic substance. The theory is that the tick will come out because it's short on oxygen. Another birdbrained idea is to burn the tick out by touching its back end with a cigarette. In my experience, these solutions don't work. Usually the tick dies and you're left with a dead tick partially burrowed into your flesh.

My remedy: Take a pair of tweezers and very carefully—as if you were a surgeon—burrow down around the tick's head, which is embedded in your flesh. Give a gentle pull, or two or three, until the tick comes out. You'll have to yank it out. The primary danger is crushing the tick's head or blood-engorged body. This can release its body fluids and the nasties they carry, so try hard not to let it happen. If you screw up and the tick's head remains embedded in you, go in again with the tweezers (after washing them in alcohol) and try to get it out. Check to see if the mouthparts broke off in the wound, and if so, seek medical attention. No matter what happens, wash the area thoroughly with alcohol. If the area becomes infected or a welt develops, then consult a doctor. You can buy a tick-removal kit at many camping stores.

More on Lyme disease: A few days or weeks after a bite, you may suffer flulike symptoms, headaches, a stiff neck, fever, aching muscles, and malaise. A rash usually develops at about the same time. The rash generally looks like an expanding red ring with a clear center (a kind of bull's-eye), but it can vary from a blotchy appearance to red throughout. See a doctor if you're suffering symptoms. A blood test will help determine if you have Lyme disease instead of just an allergic reaction to tick saliva. If you start taking antibiotics soon, the disease can be cured. If you don't get medical help, later possible complications can spell trouble: recurring acute arthritis (usually of the knees, hips, or ankles), heart palpitations, tingling in the extremities, and lethargy.

It should go without saying, but don't forget to check children and pets for ticks after spending any time in the woods.

Ants and Scorpions

The worst of the ants is the fire ant, imported from South America. In North and Central Florida, you'll see the big piles they call home. Just stay away from them. Red ants also inhabit South Florida, and although their piles are not as obvious, you can avoid them if you're careful.

If you get bitten, wash the affected area with soap and water or rubbing alcohol. Do not scratch open the white-headed blister that may form, because you risk an infection. If you are bitten numerous times, consult a doctor or go to an emergency room.

Scorpions are rare and are not a life-threatening problem in Florida. Ditto for centipedes. You're most likely to find them in woodpiles, but they've been known to turn up in people's tents. Check your shoes before putting them on in the morning; shoes are a favorite hiding place. If you are stung, it will hurt but won't kill you. Wash the wound, then see a doctor.

Chiggers

The term "chigger" is a common name used to describe the larval stage of parasitic mites. These minuscule insects can ruin an otherwise perfect camping trip. Much like a mite, they are impossible to see. But you'll know if you have them because they will start burrowing into your skin—usually your softest skin, often in private areas—and you will experience an incredible itching and small, red welts.

The best remedy for chiggers can be obtained from a doctor, although a good soap-and-water treatment may suffice. Another remedy is to seal the skin from contact with air: You can use home remedies such as nail polish, calamine lotion, Vaseline, cold cream, or baby oil. But you'll get more relief by using something that includes antihistamines, such as Caladryl, or hydrocortisone salves and creams, according to Iowa State University's Entomology Department. Or ask a pharmacist to suggest a local anesthetic or analgesic.

To avoid chiggers, stay away from Spanish moss. The gray-green moss commonly hangs in long intertwined curly strands from the branches of old oaks in Central and North Florida. It sways elegantly in the breeze until it falls in clumps onto the ground. So don't roll around on the forest floor. (Darn! That's my favorite part.)

Poison Ivy and Other Plant Pests

Poison ivy is the bane of adventuresome Florida campers. It can be such an innocent mistake to stumble into one of these itch machines. My main advice is to stay away from any plant with which you are not familiar, particularly because Florida's version doesn't look identical to the poison ivy Northern visitors know.

Locally, poison ivy comes in many forms— bush, ground cover, and vine. It has a special affinity for sabal palms. Remember: "Leaves of three, let it be." The leaves are a forest green, or perhaps a little lighter, and vaguely heart- or arrow-shaped. You can usually see beads of the poison, which often have hardened into little, black, wartlike eruptions on the leaves themselves. You may see white berries accompanying poison ivy—or you may not, depending on whether or not the plant is in bloom.

Keep your dog on the hiking trails. Otherwise, the next time you snuggle up to your four-legged buddy after his or her romp in the woods, you may find yourself scratching because the itchy sap has been transferred to you.

Many other plants in Florida are irritants at best, poisonous at worst. Among them are periwinkle, yellow allamanda, crape jasmine, oleander, crown of thorns, lantana, pencil tree, Brazilian pepper, and poinsettia. Even lime or mango trees can lead to problems; oil from the lime peel and mango skin and tree sap sometimes causes blistering and reddening.

RV LIVING TIPS

The RV lifestyle is pretty easy, especially in a big motor home or modern trailer equipped with ovens, microwaves, and showers.

Food

In an RV, your menu is pretty much whatever you wish. I like spaghetti, hamburgers, salads, and soups, just like at home. I like to grill outdoors as much as possible, too. Needless to say, don't store food outdoors.

Big grocery store chains in Florida are Publix

and Winn-Dixie. Most stores also sell wine and beer. You'll have to go to a liquor store or "package" store to find the hard stuff.

Grilling is easy, and Florida grocery stores offer fresh options beyond the obvious beef or chicken. You can grill shrimp, fish, vegetables, and even frozen foil-wrapped Italian garlic bread from the store. Side dishes can be the same as at home. Feel free to use frozen convenience foods if you wish; steamed vegetables and grains/rice are cooked just the way you do at home. My favorite approach on a trip is to keep one or two preserved, nonrefrigerated meals on hand for emergencies, and plan to shop every day for the "real" food, as the Europeans do. if the travel schedule allows. That way every day is fresh, except for planned meals away from stores.

Favorite camping meals:

Roast Steak à la Mari: This is an easy make-ahead, and it is 100 percent guaranteed to be a hit unless every one of your guests is vegetarian. Buy a flank steak, skirt steak, or other flat rectangular piece of tender beef. Put it in a plastic bag. Add a mix of 1/4 cup or so of olive oil, a few teaspoons of vinegar, a teaspoon of chopped garlic, a teaspoon of celery seed (this is a crucial ingredient for perfection, but you can go without as long as you keep the garlic or Worcestershire), ground pepper, and a tablespoon of Worcestershire sauce. Increase the liquids in order to make a nice marinade. Let it soak in a plastic bag or bowl for anywhere from 30 minutes to more than day. Cook the meat on a grill until nice and brown on both sides but rare on the inside.

Fast-cooking and healthful: Buy some boneless chicken breasts. Slice them in half widthwise, or pound them into thinner slices. Throw them into a hot frying pan or grill (carefully) for a few minutes. Serve with store-bought salad, steamed vegetables, rice, pasta, or potatoes.

Potatoes on the grill: I'm almost embarrassed to include this because it's such a camping classic. However, for all those non-Scouts out there, try this staple: Take an Idaho or other type of baking potato. If you're home, prick them with

PARK MODELS

Throughout this book, you'll find references to "park models" for sale or rent. What the heck is a park model?

A park model, sometimes called a "recreational park trailer," is an upscale resort cottage designed for part-time recreational use. Unlike mobile homes, they have wheels and can be moved by a big-haul truck to the owner's lot in an RV community.

With slide-outs and floor plans similar to a large travel trailer, they have 400 square feet of living space, fancy interior decorations, full-size appliances, and central air-conditioning. Less common in Florida are those styled to look like log cabins.

The average price is $30,409, though some can go as high as $60,000. That doesn't include the price of the lot. Some owners rent them out part-time, giving them a source of income. Since 1995, about 7,000 units have been shipped to Florida, according to an industry spokesman.

a fork and heat on high in a microwave for five minutes. Wrap in foil and pack. As you're building the fire, put the foil-wrapped potatoes in the base of the heat source. If you've microwaved the spuds, heat them on the grill or on top of the coals until they seem done. If not, wrap in foil and wait patiently for a long time.

Sausage: This is not something I like to eat everyday at home, but it is inexpensive and easy to grill or fry in the campground. Stores in Florida offer an amazing array of sausages, from the more familiar Italian or Southern styles, to ethnic concoctions such as Argentine, Chilean, Honduran, Mexican, and more. Whatever the skew, sausage is an appetite pleaser for the bigger eaters: grilled, fried, or boiled.

Spaghetti: I'm such a Boy Scout mom that my social life temporarily ended when my son outgrew the Scout troop. However, I will never forget my lessons as chief cook of the volunteer Scout spaghetti dinner fund-raisers. This is what I learned to carry over to RV cooking: You cook your pasta to completion at home, and store it in a plastic bag with a little water. To reheat, just boil water briefly and throw in the precooked pasta to heat. Do the same thing with your meat sauce or other "gravy."

Other meals: To save money, at least on some meals, don't neglect the light, easy-to-make stuff you can get right off the supermarket shelf. Consider ramen noodle soup; Lipton

Cup-a-Soup; instant oatmeal in single-serving pouches; macaroni and cheese; and the small cans of tuna, clams, and the like that go great on top of crackers. Fresh fruit and vegetables generally keep well, too. You can find even more interesting variations in stores today if you are open-minded.

No-cook indulgence: Buy delicious stone crabs (in season) from the grocery store. Be sure to request that they be "cracked." (If you don't have the fishmonger crack them, you'll have a messy and hard job on your hands, especially if you don't have a hammer or mallet handy.) Mustard-based sauce is a fabulous finishing touch, but you can make do with any creamy substance that has an acidic flavor like lime or vinegar.

Coffee? Many people view coffee as essential as a food group. You can bring an ordinary household coffeemaker from home, or use a coffee press. Now you can also buy premade coffee in glass flasks from name-brand coffee companies, whether ordinary, cappuccino, or espresso.

This being Florida, coffee styles are influenced by other cultures and a different menu of choices.

Hint: Way before coffee became the hip beverage of choice, Latin American and Caribbean immigrants to Florida brought their own jet fuel. That means you can ask for a Cuban-style *cortadito,* which is an espresso with foam on top and whipped by hand with sugar; or a "Cuban coffee" or *tiro,* which is an espresso "shot" served in a small cup with or without sugar; or "*colada,*" a larger serving usually "to go" that may have milk or sugar and is meant to share with other people (a colada is served to you in a small Styrofoam container and a bunch of small plastic containers like those used in hospitals for medications, so you distribute the caffeine to your friends).

Dishware

Although I once shared a camp with a guy who lugged along a miniature espresso maker, you don't really need a lot of kitchen accessories. Bring only what you'll use.

And what about the washing up? For some reason, RV manufacturers haven't made dishwashers standard issue in their rigs. That means you may be washing up outside. Susan Windrem of Miami Springs swears by a few drops of ammonia in a bucket or bowl. She even washes her hands in it before starting to cook or handle food. The little bit of ammonia presumably kills germs in the water and caked-on food. It's not a bad idea if you can stand the smell. Just don't use a lot, and bring some hand lotion for afterward.

Stoves

Even though my Scamp trailer had a built-in stove inside, I often preferred to cook outdoors on a hardy portable Coleman stove with propane. It just seems more like camping that way. A two-burner stove can handle the demands of a pasta dinner, or side dishes when you're cooking meat on a grill. Table-top grills, also powered by propane, are available for as little as $50. Trouble is, once you get all that heating equipment on the picnic table, will you have space to eat? It's all in the organization and planning.

Water

I don't worry about water quality much in most campgrounds because it's city water or well water. But if you're taking your RV to the back-

country or primitive spots in natural Florida, the water can be plain nasty. It's not dangerous, but it contains a lot of gunk, usually humus or some other by-product of rotting matter. So fill your tanks with all the water you will need.

Clothing

Shorts and sandals are pretty much the rule most of the year. And remember, it's not a fashion show. Even in an RV, you're likely to get more dirty than usual.

Most RV parks have laundry facilities and they frown on clotheslines as an eyesore. Unfortunately, that means your wet bathing suits or damp towels will have to be hidden from view or left to dry in the RV. Remember to bring or buy laundry detergent at a supermarket, and to stockpile quarters for using the washers and dryers.

When it's cold, layer your clothes. Usually a T-shirt, overshirt, and light jacket will be enough. But in North Florida and even the southern part of the state in winter, you'll sometimes want to give yourself four or more layers, including a decent jacket or even a winter coat. Don't forget a knit cap or other hat; much of your body heat is lost through your head.

In an RV, where you have closets, bringing extra clothes is not much of a space issue, especially if you use soft-sided luggage that can be stuffed into nooks and crannies. The important thing is to be prepared for any kind of weather, and be sure that you've considered everyone in your party. And don't count on a campfire to keep warm; most counties have outlawed ground fires because of the risk of starting a conflagration you didn't intend. In wintertime, forest areas are tinder-dry, and forest fires are a danger. (And don't light a fire on top of your picnic table, as I saw in one Florida Keys campground.)

Footwear

There's nothing wrong with bringing high-ankle hiking boots to an RV park or more nature-oriented campground. They'll keep your feet dry and warm, and you'll generally avoid

RV CAMPING CHECKLIST

Personal Items:
- Bathing suits
- Feminine hygiene products
- Hat with a broad brim to keep sun off your face, ears, and neck
- Hiking boots or sneakers
- Insect repellent
- Pants, long (airy weave in summer, thicker in winter)
- Personal prescription medicine
- Rain gear: jacket, poncho, rain pants
- Sandals or flip-flops for the bathhouse
- Shirt, long-sleeved (airy weave in summer, thicker in winter)
- Shorts
- Soap
- Sunglasses
- Sunscreen
- Toiletries
- Towels
- Water shoes

Gear:
- Barbecue utensils, such as a big fork, spatula, or tongs
- Blankets, comforter, or sleeping bag
- Broom
- Can opener
- Cookware, such as a frying pan, a set of pots
- Cutting board, mixing bowls, cooking utensils, and knives
- Dinnerware including glasses and cutlery
- Dish towels
- Dishwashing soap
- Entry rugs to keep dirt out of the RV
- First-aid kit
- Flashlight

twisted ankles on uneven terrain. If you have to trek to the restrooms in the middle of the night, they provide ease of mind as you walk through piles of leaves.

RV Maintenance

Always carry a well-equipped toolbox. A good idea is to include extra hose clamps in varying sizes, wire, tire-flat sealer, and other things that might come in handy in an on-road breakdown. Many mechanics advise that hoses should be replaced at the beginning of each summer, but Florida's heat is murder on car batteries, hoses,

and belts. Locals tend to think that five-year-guaranteed batteries last no more than three years in a Florida setting. (If you have to buy a new battery before the five years are up, the shop will prorate the cost.) Keep an eye on the engine temperature in hot weather and on hill climbs. If you're coming from northern climates, the heat may be a surprise for your engine parts.

An overheating engine is a major problem, especially when towing a trailer. I lost an engine in my towing vehicle when the car overheated suddenly, which "cracked the block," and cost

- Food
- Fuel
- Garbage bags, aluminum foil, and food-storage bags
- Hatchet
- Matches in waterproof container
- Mop
- Paper towels
- Screen-room tent or shade house
- Sheets and pillows
- Sponges and cleaning supplies
- Stove
- Toilet paper
- Weather-alert radio

Optional Items:
- Bag for dirty clothes
- Bicycles
- Board games, deck of cards
- Books, magazines
- Camera, with flash and extra batteries, film or memory card
- Canoe, kayak, or inflatable boat with paddles
- Cell phone or walkie-talkie
- Extra propane or stove fuel
- Firewood (buy at the store) or charcoal
- Fishing rod and tackle
- Folding chairs
- GPS (global positioning system) device
- Lantern
- Laptop computer with modem and network cables
- Laundry detergent
- Radio or stereo
- Tool kits for the car, RV, boat, bikes, and other needs
- TV satellite dish or wiring to connect to cable TV in the park

several thousand dollars to replace, plus a 50-mile tow from the Everglades into Miami.

Even the least-mechanical person should be sure that the towing vehicle or motor home is in good repair. That means checking the oil, fluids, and battery on a regular basis, as well as getting tune-ups as needed. Often overlooked before a trip is the spare tire; be sure it's inflated properly and carry a tire gauge. An auto-club membership and cell phone are also highly recommended.

PENSACOLA

COURTESY OF FLORIDA STATE PARKS

BEST RV PARKS AND CAMPGROUNDS

🌙 Equestrians
Coldwater Recreation Area, page 49
Navarre Beach Campground, page 59

🌙 Most Luxurious
Destin RV Beach Resort, page 64

🌙 Most Unusual
Mystic Springs Cove Airstream Park, page 49
Riviera Naturist Resort, page 55

🌙 Privately Owned
   Beachfront RV Parks
Playa del Rio RV Park, page 57
Emerald Beach RV Park, page 59
Navarre Beach Campground, page 59
Magnolia Beach Campground, page 60
Destin RV Beach Resort, page 64
Camping on the Gulf Holiday Travel Park, page 65

🌙 Publicly Managed
   Beachfront Campgrounds
Mystic Springs Cove Airstream Park, page 49
Henderson Beach State Park, page 64

If you think Florida is only tropical beaches, palm trees, and Caribbean style, then think again. Pensacola – which shares the same latitude as Cairo, Egypt, and Austin, Texas – is known as the "Western Gate to the Sunshine State." It's so far west and so far north of Miami, Orlando, and Tampa that you may forget this area in the so-called Panhandle is part of Florida. Culturally, it has more of the feel of Dixie, and you're more likely to hear Southern accents than not. That also means Southern hospitality is served up with a smile and a "yes, ma'am" and a "thank you, sir."

The Spanish explorer Tristan de Luna happened upon Pensacola long before the founding of St. Augustine, America's oldest city. In 1559, he was greeted by the now-extinct Panzacola tribe. Although the settlement was quickly abandoned, the territory was heartily and bloodily disputed, changing governments five times in the ensuing 400 years. During the Civil War, the city was occupied by both sides of combatants. A total of five flags have flown over Pensacola: Spain, France, England, the United States, and the Confederacy.

Today, Pensacola – also known as the "cradle of naval aviation" – is home to the Naval Air Station (where Navy, Marine, and Coast Guard personnel begin their flight training) and the National Museum of Naval Aviation, one of the world's largest museums dedicated to air and space technology. If you have an interest in military history, there's much to see: Fort Pickens, built in 1834, is the best known of four forts built in the area and a half-scale replica of the Vietnam veterans' memorial wall welcomes visitors and military reunions.

Pensacola makes much of its cultural diversity, with attractions such as historic Seville Square, where you'll find quaint restaurants, bars, and shops. The North Hill Preservation District is a residential area where the city's wealthy once lived in grand homes, and the Palafox Historic District embraces the commercial district and the industrial waterfront.

But don't think it's all about sightseeing. For the RV visitor, the area offers loads of nature camping, and in fact, some of the best "Old Florida" pine, oak, and scrub woods. Most of this area is heavily forested, with tall pines stretching from the northern state line down to some of Florida's prettiest beaches. The sand is blindingly white, thanks to years of wave action working its magic on crystals of quartz and silicon dioxide.

Several RV parks offer easy access to the beach and the Gulf of Mexico. Nearby Destin, "the world's luckiest fishing village," is a saltwater angler's delight. Each year, anglers catch more billfish in Destin than in all of the other gulf ports combined; they also hook king mackerel, cobia, and other game fish. Charter boats and guide services are widely available.

Farther north, you'll find natural camping in the woods, as well as canoeing and hiking in the Blackwater River State Forest and Blackwater River State Park. Don't miss this part of the area, even if you're focused on beachfront experiences.

If you're passing through on I-10, you'll cross a largely rural, undeveloped area. Many RV parks convenient to the highway are set in beautiful areas, making even an overnight stay a more pleasant experience.

Pensacola is on Central Standard Time. Unlike the rest of the state, the most popular times to visit are during the summer (basically April–Aug.). Crowds thin out in the cooler off-season, roughly August–March.

PENSACOLA

see Panama City page 70

© AVALON TRAVEL PUBLISHING,

1 LAKE STONE CAMPGROUND

Scenic rating: 4

in Century just south of the Alabama border

Large, grassy sites are set on a peninsula extending into an irregularly shaped artificial lake. The shimmering waters of Lake Stone (sometimes called Stone Lake) encircle this quiet, family-style campground favored by all ages, locals, and visitors from as far away as Canada. Some campsites slope down to the water, and guests can fish from their sites—when there is no drought, that is. A nearby boat ramp is part of the county-run park. The little campground was hard hit by the hurricanes of 2004–2005 and lost 500 trees. However, this is Florida, and foliage grows back more quickly than in other parts of the country. Activities include walking, fishing, playing cards and dominoes, and attending club meetings; the park also holds dances, potluck dinners, and concerts.

RV sites, facilities: All 77 sites have water, 20/30/50-amp electrical hookups, picnic tables, and fire rings. Some sites are waterfront, and 40-foot-long RVs and slide-outs can be accommodated. Restrooms, showers, a playground, two dump stations, and a boat ramp are provided. A camp store sells ice, snacks, and limited groceries. Most areas are wheelchair accessible. Groceries and restaurants are within three miles. Malls are 35 miles away, and the nearest hospital is 8 miles. Children are welcome. Leashed pets are permitted.

Reservations, fees: Reservations are not accepted. Sites are $10 per night for eight people. Credit cards are not accepted. Maximum stay is 30 days.

Directions: From U.S. 29 on the south end of Century, turn west on State Road 4 (across from the courthouse). Drive 1.5 miles to the park, on the left. The entrance is the second driveway.

Contact: Lake Stone Campground, 801 West State Road 4, Century, FL 32535, 850/256-5555.

2 MYSTIC SPRINGS COVE AIRSTREAM PARK

Scenic rating: 6

north of Molino just south of McDavid, off U.S.

BEST (

You'll need an Airstream to camp here. Reservations are a must on rally weekends 13 times a year, when the park fills up. This wooded, 10-acre park on the banks of the Escambia River is shaded by old oaks laden with Spanish moss. With the closing of Land Yacht Harbor near Melbourne in 2001, this is one of only two Airstream parks in Florida; the other one is near Christmas, Florida (see *Christmas Airstream Park* in the *Orlando* chapter).

RV sites, facilities: There are 56 sites with full hookups and 30-amp electrical service. Four are pull-through, 11 have 50-amp service. A recreation pavilion and communal kitchen are available. A convenience store is within one mile, and groceries are eight miles away in Century. Most areas are wheelchair accessible. Children are welcome. Leashed pets are permitted.

Reservations, fees: Reservations are required during rally weekends; the rest of the time, they are not necessary. Sites are $9–11 per night. Credit cards are not accepted.

Directions: From I-10, take Exit 10B onto U.S. 29 northbound. Drive about 23 miles north. Turn right on Mystic Springs Road and drive 0.7 mile.

Contact: Mystic Springs Cove Airstream Park, 591 Mystic Springs Road, McDavid, FL 32568, 850/256-3280, www.geocities. com/mystic-springs.

3 COLDWATER RECREATION AREA

Scenic rating: 9

in Blackwater River State Forest west of Munson

BEST (

Hankering for a trail ride amid oak, juniper, and soaring pine trees? This campground is restricted to horseback riders and to groups needing four or more campsites. Four horseback-riding trails diverge from Jernigan Bridge near the campground. There's also a swimming area and canoe launch at the bridge. This area is sometimes used for major bird dog field trials. As many as 132 horses can be accommodated in paddocks. Horses are not allowed in the creek.

RV sites, facilities: There are 69 sites with water, 30-amp electricity, picnic tables, and fire rings. Restrooms, showers, a dump station, two corrals, stables, and outside paddocks are on the property. Kennels for 124 dogs and a dining hall/pavilion accommodating 110 people are available for an extra charge. Children are welcome. Leashed pets are permitted. Proof of a current negative Coggins test is required for each horse.

Reservations, fees: Reservations are required. Sites are $13 per night for five people, or $7 for people 65 and over or who are disabled. Proof of age or 100 percent disability is required for the discount. Credit cards are not accepted. The maximum stay is 14 days.

Directions: From Milton, drive 15 miles north on State Road 191. At Hardy Road, turn west and drive 5.5 miles to the park.

Contact: Blackwater Forestry Center, 11650 Munson Highway, Milton, FL 32570, 850/957-6140, fax 850/957-6143.

❹ KRUL RECREATION AREA

Scenic rating: 9

in Blackwater River State Forest west of Bear Lake and east of Munson

A hiking trail begins at the campground and ends at Bear Lake. The Sweetwater Trail (leading to a wheelchair-accessible 2,900-foot boardwalk and a suspended bridge) is accessible by wheelchair for 0.5 mile. The campground also has a seven-acre swimming lake.

RV sites, facilities: There are 45 sites with water

and 30-amp electricity. Restrooms, showers, picnic tables, fire rings, and a dump station are available. Children are welcome. Pets are not permitted.

Reservations, fees: Reservations are not accepted. Sites are $13 per night for five people, or $7 for people 65 and over or who are 100 percent disabled. Proof of age or disability is required. Credit cards are not accepted. The maximum stay is 14 days.

Directions: From Munson, drive 0.75 mile east on State Road 4. The campground entrance is on the north side of the road.

Contact: Blackwater Forestry Center, 11650 Munson Highway, Milton, FL 32570, 850/957-6140, fax 850/957-6143.

❺ BEAR LAKE RECREATION AREA

Scenic rating: 9

in Blackwater River State Forest east of Munson

Located just east of the Krul Recreation Area (see previous campground), this spot is set on the shores of Bear Lake. Anglers can enjoy the 107-acre lake, but only boats with electric trolling motors are allowed. The fishing pier is wheelchair accessible. Mountain bikers can use a six-mile-long dirt trail. The Sweetwater hiking trail connects to the 4-mile Bear Lake Loop Trail, and then to the 21-mile Jackson Trail. The closest stores for supplies are in Munson, 2.5 miles west of the campground.

RV sites, facilities: There are 32 RV sites with water, and 20 have 30-amp electricity. Three sites are pull-through; RVs as long as 35 feet can be accommodated. Restrooms, showers, picnic tables, fire rings, a dump station, and a boat ramp are provided. Children are welcome. Leashed pets are permitted.

Reservations, fees: Reservations are not accepted. Sites are $12 per night for five people, or $7 for people 65 and over or who are 100 percent disabled. Proof of age or disability is required. Credit cards are not accepted. The maximum stay is 14 days.

Directions: From Munson, drive 2.5 miles east on State Road 4. The campground entrance is on the north side of the road.

Contact: Blackwater Forestry Center, 11650 Munson Highway, Milton, FL 32570, 850/957-6140, fax 850/957-6143.

6 HURRICANE LAKE RECREATION AREA

Scenic rating: 9

in Blackwater River State Forest north of Baker

Campsites overlook Hurricane Lake, a 318-acre impoundment that is popular for fishing. Half the sites are on the north side; the others are on the south. Boats with ele ctric trolling motors are permitted on the lake, but you may not use outboard motors. A canoe launch with access to the Blackwater River and a six-mile hiking trail are near the campground. Blackwater River State Forest is known for its longleaf pine/wire grass ecosystem, which once covered 60 million acres in the Southeast. Don't be alarmed if you see scorched areas: State foresters use fire to control hardwoods and to promote the flowering of wire grass. Fire also helps protect the habitat of the endangered red-cockaded woodpecker. Look for bogs of carnivorous pitcher plants. Throughout the forest, you'll find unpaved roads good for mountain biking. Horse trails are threaded through the western portion of the forest.

RV sites, facilities: There are two campgrounds here: one on the north side and one on the south. The north side has 13 RV sites with water and 30-amp electricity, plus 5 sites with water only. RVs longer than 35 feet cannot be accommodated; none of the sites is pull-through. Restrooms, showers, picnic tables, fire rings, a dump station, and a boat ramp are on-site. The south campground has 18 primitive sites with restrooms only. Children are welcome. Leashed pets are permitted.

Reservations, fees: Reservations are not accepted. Sites are $13 per night for five people, or $7 for people 65 and over or who are 100 percent disabled. Proof of age or disability is required. Credit cards are not accepted. The maximum stay is 14 days.

Directions: From Baker, drive six miles west on State Road 4. Turn north on Beaver Creek Road and proceed about 8.5 miles. At Bullard Church Road, turn east and follow the signs to the campground.

Contact: Blackwater Forestry Center, 11650 Munson Highway, Milton, FL 32570, 850/957-6143.

7 KARICK LAKE

Scenic rating: 9

in the far eastern part of Blackwater River State Forest north of Baker

Take a refreshing dip or cast your line for fish in 65-acre Karick Lake. Boats with electric trolling motors are allowed. The fishing pier is wheelchair accessible. One major attraction is the campground's location at the eastern terminus of the 21-mile-long Jackson Trail, which meanders through the state forest, crossing the Blackwater River at Peaden Bridge. The campground, set in a hardwood forest, is actually two in one; half of the sites sit on one side of the lake and half on the other.

RV sites, facilities: There are 30 sites with water and 30-amp electricity, 15 in the northern section and 15 in the southern section. Restrooms, showers, picnic tables, fire rings, a dump station, and a boat ramp are provided. Children are welcome. Leashed pets are permitted.

Reservations, fees: Reservations are not accepted. Sites are $13 per night for five people, or $7 for people 65 and over or who are 100 percent disabled. Proof of age or disability is required. Credit cards are not accepted. The maximum stay is 14 days.

Directions: From Baker, drive eight miles north

on County Road 189 to the campground entrance on the east side of the road.
Contact: Blackwater Forestry Center, 11650 Munson Highway, Milton, FL 32570, 850/957-6140, fax 850/957-6143.

☑ LAKESIDE AT BARTH

Scenic rating: 4

Frequented mostly by locals and families, this place offers country camping near the city. The area north of the paper mill town of Cantonment is off the well-worn tourist track, and you'll discover rolling hills of pine forests, tiny communities that are little more than crossroads, and people who say, "yes, ma'am" and "no, sir" in the Southern way. Nestled on 80 wooded acres, the campground has grassy sites with some shade. About 20 percent of the park is occupied year-round. The swimming lake is 0.5 acre in size; the fishing lakes are 5 and 8 acres. Favorite catches are bream, bass, and catfish. A large Winn-Dixie grocery store is 11 miles away near I-10, though a local grocery 3 miles away is recommended for "the best meat around."

RV sites, facilities: All 28 full-hookup sites have 30-amp electrical service. Sites are narrow and long, but large enough at 60 feet deep to accommodate big rigs and slide-outs. Restrooms, showers, a playground, a covered pavilion, two man-made fishing lakes, and one swimming lake are available. Children are welcome. Leashed pets are permitted.

Reservations, fees: Reservations are not necessary. Sites are $15 per night for two people, plus $3 for each additional person. Credit cards are not accepted.

Directions: From I-10 at Pensacola, take Exit 10B heading north on U.S. 29 and drive 16 miles. After you cross State Road 97, continue two miles to Barth Road. Turn east (right) and drive one mile to the campground.

Contact: Lakeside at Barth, 855 Barth Road, Molino, FL 32577, 850/587-2322.

☑ ADVENTURES UNLIMITED OUTDOOR CENTER

Scenic rating: 9

Billing itself as a getaway from city life, this privately run resort/canoe concessionaire overlooks the confluence of Wolfe Creek and Coldwater Creek at Tomahawk Landing. It's a sprawling, 88-acre, canoeing-oriented complex with large cabins for groups, a small inn, small cottages, "camping cabins," and group activities for family reunions, birthday parties, and youth retreats. Canoeing and tubing package trips and hayrides are available, as are challenge rope courses for team building. On the property you'll find an old dam and millpond, a historic cemetery, and two riverside beaches. Adventures Unlimited also arranges one- to three-day-long canoe trips. Canoes equipped with camping equipment are available (with reservations).

RV sites, facilities: There are 8 shady, grassy RV sites with water and 30-amp electricity and 10 primitive sites for pop-ups or small, self-contained units. The maximum length of RV is 38 feet, though slide-outs can be accommodated. Restrooms, showers, picnic tables, and fire rings are provided. A game field, a volleyball court, a limited store, a small playground, rental cabins, canoes, and inner tubes (for tubing on the river) are available. A camp store sells ice, camping supplies, a few groceries, snacks, souvenirs, fishing tackle, and bait. The four-room Schoolhouse Inn was once a school that served a tiny community nearby. The store and office are wheelchair accessible. Groceries, restaurants, and hospitals are 15 miles away. Families and groups are welcome. Pets are not permitted.

Reservations, fees: Reservations are recom-

mended. Sites are $20 per night for four people, plus $3 for each additional person. Credit cards are accepted. Long-term rates are available from November through February only; the high season here is the warmer time of the year.

Directions: From Milton, drive 12 miles north on State Road 87. Turn east at the Adventures Unlimited sign. Drive four miles to the campground, which is just south of the confluence of Coldwater Creek and Wolfe Creek.

Contact: Adventures Unlimited Outdoor Center, 8974 Tomahawk Landing Road, Milton, FL 32570, 850/623-6197 or 800/BE-YOUNG (800/239-6864), fax 850/626-3124, www.adventuresunlimited.com.

10 BLACKWATER RIVER STATE PARK

Scenic rating: 10

in Blackwater River State Forest

With just 30 sites, this campground fills up fast in the busy summer months, but it's worth the effort. The 590-acre state park is located on the south side of Blackwater River State Forest, the largest state forest in Florida at more than 200,000 acres. The tea-colored river, a popular stream for canoeing and kayaking, flows through the park. Don't expect rough water; the river is quite shallow in places and the bottom is sandy. It's one of the few rivers in the country with spectacular white-sand beaches. Canoe, kayak, and inner-tube concessions are located nearby. The closest is Blackwater Canoe Rental at 10274 Pond Road in Milton, located on the state park access road (850/623-0235 or 800/967-6789, www.blackwatercanoe.com). Prices range $19–22. The big sandbars on each bend in the river are strikingly white in contrast to the darkness of the water; stop now and then to swim or soak up some rays on the broad ivory banks. In the summer, you may glimpse a Mississippi kite, a graceful, hawklike bird with gray underparts and a pale head, winging

overhead. At other times, look for river otters, deer, turkey, and bobcats as you drift lazily downstream.

RV sites, facilities: There are 30 sites with water, 30-amp electricity, picnic tables, and fire rings. Sites vary in size, as they do in most state parks, where natural geographic contours are followed in the design of the park. Rigs up to 35 feet can be accommodated, as well as slide-outs. Canoe, tube, and kayak rentals, restrooms, showers, souvenirs, guided walks, and nature programs are available. The bathhouse and office are wheelchair accessible. Children are welcome. Pets are allowed with proof of vaccination.

Reservations, fees: Reservations are recommended; contact ReserveAmerica at 800/336-3521 or reserveamerica.com. Sites are $14 per night for eight people. Credit cards are accepted. The maximum stay is 14 days.

Directions: From I-10 at Milton, use Exit 31 on State Road 87 northbound. Travel 0.5 mile, then turn east on U.S. 90. Drive five more miles to Harold and turn north on the state park access road. The campground is three miles away.

Contact: Blackwater River State Park, 7720 Deaton Bridge Road, Holt, FL 32564, 850/983-5363, fax 850/983-5364, www.floridastateparks.org.

11 EAGLE'S LANDING RV PARK

Scenic rating: 7

near Holt east of Milton

The owners describe this all-ages, sunny park with huge lots as the perfect overnight stop. It's certainly close to the interstate, at 0.5 mile off the road, and convenient to shopping and outdoor recreation throughout the area. Clean, quiet, and well maintained, this 10-acre park has 60 large, grassy sites, 24 of which are available for seasonal stays. A few sites are occupied by year-round residents.

RV sites, facilities: There are 60 pull-through sites with full hookups, electricity, and picnic tables. Sites are a whopping 85 feet long and 35 feet wide, and some have 50-amp service. The biggest RVs on the market can be accommodated here, including multiple slide-outs. There's a wireless Internet network accessible in many parts of the park. Satellite dishes are no problem. Restrooms, showers, laundry facilities, a recreation room, a dog-walk area, and telephone service are available. Planned activities are held during the winter months by repeat visitors who value the peace and quiet here. Children are welcome. Leashed pets are permitted.

Reservations, fees: Reservations are recommended. Sites are $19 per night for two people, plus $2 per extra person over age four. Credit cards are not accepted. Long-term rates are available.

Directions: From I-10, take Exit 45 and go north 0.25 mile to the park entrance on the left.

Contact: Eagle's Landing RV Park, 4504 Log Lake Road, Holt, FL 32564, 850/537-9657, fax 850/537-9625, www.campingandcampgrounds.com/eagle.htm.

12 CEDAR LAKES RV PARK AND CAMPGROUND

Scenic rating: 5

near Milton

Opened in 2000, this park sits on 16 acres and features two 3-acre, spring-fed lakes surrounded by woods. It's an all-ages park, but older campers are preferred. Lots are shady, and the sunsets are beautiful. Campers can fish in the lakes for free, and they won't need fishing licenses. The park is continually being improved and enlarged. The management boasts the drinking water tastes great.

RV sites, facilities: There are 18 RV sites for overnighters, with 7 to 14 available for seasonal visitors. Both 30-amp and 50-amp sites are available. Almost all sites are pull-through,

with no length restrictions; the sites have full hookups. Restrooms, showers, laundry facilities, a dump station, and telephone service are available. Also on the premises are lakes, a small clubhouse (for potluck dinners, card games, and the like), and a dog-walk area. Children are allowed. Leashed pets are permitted.

Reservations, fees: Reservations are recommended. Sites are $16.50 per night for two people, plus $3 per extra person. Children under 10 are free. Credit cards are not accepted. Long-term rates are available.

Directions: If eastbound from I-10, take Exit 28 south to County Road 184 (Hickory Hammock Road) 0.75 mile away. Turn east and drive one mile to Coachman Road. Then go south to the park entrance on the left. If westbound, take I-10 Exit 31, and drive two miles south to County Road 184. Turn right on Coachman Road and proceed two miles. The park will be on the left.

Contact: Cedar Lakes RV Park and Campground, 4312 Coachman Road, Milton, FL 32583, 850/626-9291, www.cedarlakesrvpark.com.

13 MILTON/GULF PINES KOA

Scenic rating: 7

off I-10 near Milton

This convenient, easy-on, easy-off RV park offers respite to travelers passing through and to visitors seeking to explore the Panhandle area from a base with fancier amenities than are available at most spots near here. The wooded park has a store, a playground, miniature golf, a pool, and a recreation room. It was renovated after the storms of 2004 and 2005.

RV sites, facilities: There are 96 pull-through RV sites with full hookups, 50-amp electrical service, picnic tables, patios, cable TV, and optional phone service. Restrooms, showers, a dump station, laundry facilities, a pool, a clubhouse, miniature golf, a playground, volleyball, basketball courts, computers with Internet access, a store, rental cabins, and a dog-walk area are available. All areas are wheelchair accessible. Children are welcome. Leashed pets are permitted.

Reservations, fees: Reservations are recommended. Sites are $33–43 per night for two people, plus $3 per extra person. Continental breakfast is included. Credit cards are accepted. Long-term (up to six months) or seasonal stays are available.

Directions: From I-10, take Exit 31 at State Road 87 and drive north 300 feet to the campground.

Contact: Milton/Gulf Pines KOA, 8700 Gulf Pines Drive, Milton, FL 32583, 850/623-0808 or 877/684-2307, www.miltonkoa.com.

14 CEDAR PINES CAMPGROUND

Scenic rating: 7

north of Milton

Lots of oak trees provide shade at this pretty countryside campground near Blackwater River State Forest and Whiting Field Naval Air Station. Groceries and other supplies can be obtained within three miles. From here, you're just 31 miles from Brewton, Alabama, if you want to add another state to your "been there" list. Closer to home is the big town in this area, Milton, which once went by the names Scratch Ankle and Hard Scrabble.

RV sites, facilities: There are 40 RV sites with full hookups, 30/50-amp electrical service, and cable TV. Thirty-four sites are pull-through, and all can accommodate the largest RVs on the market and slide-outs. An Internet wireless network is available at sites and in the clubhouse. Many sites have patios or picnic tables. Restrooms, showers, laundry facilities, a clubhouse, a pool, a communal grill and fire pit, horseshoes, a screened pavilion, miniature golf, and a dump station are available. The restrooms, clubhouse, and library are wheelchair accessible. Children are welcome. Leashed pets are permitted.

Reservations, fees: Reservations are recommended. Sites are $23–25 per night for two people, plus $2 for each additional person. Credit cards are not accepted. Long-term stays are allowed.

Directions: From U.S. 90 in Milton (Exit 28 off I-10), drive four miles north on State Road 87. The park is on the east side of the road.

Contact: Cedar Pines Campground, 6436 Robie Road, Milton, FL 32570, 850/623-8869, fax 850/623-1520, www.cedarpines.com.

15 RIVIERA NATURIST RESORT

Scenic rating: 5

northwest of Pace and Milton

BEST (

Set on 16 shady, wooded acres, this family-oriented resort offers a haven for those who like to camp in the buff. Nudity is required—weather permitting. Guests are clothed when practical (in cold weather); nude when possible (other times). Identification is required because management doesn't want to encourage curiosity seekers. Cameras are not allowed without permission.

RV sites, facilities: This nudist campground has 29 grassy RV spaces, 10 with full hookups and electricity available for vacationers. A dial-up Internet connection is available in the clubhouse. The resort has picnic tables, restrooms, showers, a swimming pool and whirlpool tub, a volleyball field, horseshoes, *pétanque* (a French game similar to cricket), and a 0.5-mile nature trail. An area is set aside for sun-tanning. Children are welcome with parents. Leashed pets are permitted.

Reservations, fees: Reservations are recommended. Sites are $22–28 per night. Credit cards are accepted. The maximum stay is one month during the summer and three to five months during the winter.

Directions: From I-10 at Pensacola, take Exit 17. Turn east on U.S. 90. Drive 6.5 miles to County Road 197A/Woodbine Road. Turn

north on Woodbine Road and go two miles, then turn east on Guernsey Road. The park is 0.4 mile away, on the north side of the road.
Contact: Riviera Naturist Resort, 5000 Guernsey Road, Pace, FL 32571, 850/994-3665, fax 850/994-1906, www.riviera-resort.com.

16 TALL OAKS CAMPGROUND

Scenic rating: 2

on the west side of Pensacola

Set on five acres, this campground caters to overnight travelers, as well as long-term visitors. A shopping center 0.25 mile away offers citified essentials—groceries, a hair salon, and a restaurant, for instance. Within a five-minute drive are golf courses, a hospital, and the Five Flags Speedway. The urban location is convenient to Pensacola attractions such as historic Seville Square, where you'll find quaint restaurants, bars, and shops, and the National Museum of Naval Aviation (call 850/932-2229 for more information). The museum, one of the world's largest dedicated to air and space technology, displays the first airplane to cross the Atlantic and all manner of military aircraft. It also salutes the famous Blue Angels, the U.S. Navy's precision flight demonstration team based in Pensacola. Visitors here include tourists and families, although half the park is occupied year-round by locals.
RV sites, facilities: There are 65 grassy RV spaces with full hookups, most with 30-amp electrical service. Fifteen have 50-amp electricity. Picnic tables are provided at about half the sites. The biggest RVs and slide-outs can be accommodated. You'll have no trouble setting up your satellite dish here. Amenities include wheelchair-accessible restrooms, showers, laundry facilities, vending machines, a pay phone, and a dump station. Groceries and restaurants are within 0.5 mile, and malls and hospitals are 4 miles away. Children are welcome. Leashed pets are permitted.

Reservations, fees: Reservations are not necessary. Sites are $20 per night for two people, plus $5 per extra person. Credit cards are accepted. Long-term rates are available.
Directions: From I-10 eastbound, take Exit 5 onto Alternate U.S. 90/Nine Mile Road. Drive one mile east, then turn south on Pine Forest Road and continue to the park on your right. From I-10 westbound, take Exit 7 onto State Road 297/Pine Forest Road. Drive north for 0.5 mile to the entrance.
Contact: Tall Oaks Campground, 9301 Pine Forest Road, Pensacola, FL 32534, 850/479-3212

17 MAYFAIR MOTEL AND RV PARK

Scenic rating: 2

in west Pensacola

Shopping and restaurants are on hand, and you can swim in the motel's pool (next door). The park's urban location is convenient to Pensacola's historical attractions and the National Museum of Naval Aviation (for description, see previous campground); the beach is within a 15-minute drive.
RV sites, facilities: There are 24 RV sites with full hookups and 30-amp electricity; however, just a few are available for overnighters. Management says that big RVs can be accommodated. Restrooms, showers, a dump station, and laundry facilities are provided. Children are welcome. Leashed pets are permitted.
Reservations, fees: Reservations are recommended. Sites are $25 per night. Credit cards are accepted. Long-term rates are available.
Directions: From I-10, exit on State Road 297/Pine Forest Road and drive 3.5 miles south to U.S. 90/Mobile Highway. Turn east on U.S. 90 and look for the campground/motel complex.
Contact: Mayfair Motel and RV Park, 4540 Mobile Highway, Pensacola, FL 32506, 850/455-8561, fax 850/455-0090.

18 BIG LAGOON STATE PARK

Scenic rating: 10

on Perdido Key southwest of Pensacola

The campground at this 698-acre state park is located along a series of sandy ridges. Bird-watchers will be delighted here because the wind-whipped sand-pine scrub, gnarled slash pines, and swampy salt marshes harbor loons, grebes, cormorants, great blue herons, and many other species seen daily. During the fall, this is one of the last resting places for birds migrating south across the Gulf of Mexico. You may also see gray foxes, raccoons, skunks, and opossums. Hikers can improve their chances of spotting these animals by walking the 1-mile boardwalk; there's also the 3.5-mile "Girl Scout Cookie" hiking trail looping through the park. Two swimming areas are on Big Lagoon, near the Intracoastal Waterway. Boating, canoeing, windsurfing, and fishing opportunities are abundant because the park is encircled almost completely by water. If you're hankering for seaside fun on the Gulf of Mexico, registered campers are permitted to use the white-sand beach at Perdido Key State Park, located five miles west, at no additional charge. Special events are held here throughout the year, including a bluegrass festival in May, concerts on holiday weekends, and Christmas and Halloween celebrations. You can even rent the amphitheater for weddings.

RV sites, facilities: The state park campground has 49 sites with piped water and electricity. Twenty-five sites have 50-amp electrical service; the rest have 30-amp. None are drive-through. RVs up to 40 feet long and slide-outs can be accommodated; sites vary in size. Picnic tables, grills, restrooms, showers, a playground, and a dump station are provided. The park also has a boat ramp, three nature trails, an amphitheater, and two swimming areas. Campsites 8 and 9 are wheelchair accessible, as are the restrooms, boardwalks, and some picnic pavilions. Beach wheelchairs are available upon request. Chil-

dren are welcome. Pets are allowed in the campground with proof of vaccination.

Reservations, fees: Reservations are recommended; contact ReserveAmerica at 800/336-3521 or reserveamerica.com. From March 1 through August 31, sites are $16 per night for up to eight people. Credit cards are accepted. The maximum stay is 14 days.

Directions: From Pensacola, drive 12 miles west on State Road 292 to Perdido Key. Turn east on State Road 292A/Gulf Beach Highway and drive 0.5 mile to the park entrance.

Contact: Big Lagoon State Park, 12301 Gulf Beach Highway, Pensacola, FL 32507, 850/492-1595, fax 850/492-4380, www.floridastate-parks.org.

19 PLAYA DEL RIO RV PARK

Scenic rating: 10

on Perdido Key

BEST (

This resort-style park's location on Perdido Key and the white-sand Gulf of Mexico beaches can't be beat no matter where you wind up parking your rig. Fronting on the Ole River with a view of Ono Island, this park offers boat dockage for campground guests' boats—and even a free paddleboat and kayak for their use. Bird-watching and various boating tours are available, and the beach is across the street via a short path. Fish off the dock or try your hand at catching crabs from the dock. The hurricanes of 2005 wiped out the landscaping, leaving visible surrounding high-rise resorts. Repairs to the park have been completed, including a new dock and freshly planted shrubbery.

RV sites, facilities: There are 30 RV sites for rigs up to 45 feet. Some sites have concrete pads; all have full hookups, 30/50-amp electrical outlets, cable TV, and phone availability. Restrooms, showers, a dump station, laundry facilities, a fishing dock, a community room, barbecue grills, and a picnic area are on-site. The restrooms, laundry, community room, and boat docks are wheelchair accessible. Children are welcome. Leashed pets are permitted.

Reservations, fees: Reservations are recommended. Sites are $29–59 (highest rates are from March 1 through September 15) per night for two people, plus $2 per extra person. Credit cards are accepted. Long-term stays are allowed.

Directions: From I-10 westbound, take Exit 7 south onto Route 297 (Pine Forest Road) for 1.5 miles. At Blue Angel Parkway, turn right and head south 5.5 miles on Sorrento Road (Highway 292), which changes its name to Perdido Key Drive after the Intracoastal Bridge. The resort is 5.7 miles on the right. From I-10 eastbound, take Alabama State Road 59 south through the Alabama towns of Foley and Gulf Shores. At Alabama State Road 182, turn left and continue east. The road changes names to Florida Highway 292, then to Perdido Key Drive.

Contact: Playa del Rio RV Park, 16990 Perdido Key Drive, Perdido Key, FL 32507, 850/492-0904 or 888/200-0904, fax 850/492-4471, www.playadelrio.com.

20 PENSACOLA/ PERDIDO BAY KOA

🏊 ⛵ 🚐 🐕 🚐 ⛺

Scenic rating: 6

west of Perdido Key

Despite its name, this campground is actually in Alabama across Perdido Bay from Florida. It's less than a mile from the Florida state line and might be an option if the other parks are full. The owners call it "snowbird heaven."

RV sites, facilities: There are 50 full-hookup sites with 30-amp and 50-amp electrical service available for overnighters and seasonal visitors. Restrooms, showers, a dump station, laundry facilities, and telephone service are available. On the premises are a heated pool (open March 14–October 1), a boat dock, a

clubhouse, shuffleboard courts, a dog-walk area, and boat access to Perdido Bay and the Gulf of Mexico. Children are welcome. Leashed pets are permitted.

Reservations, fees: Reservations are recommended. Sites are $28 per night for two people, plus $3 per extra person and $2.75 for cable TV. Credit cards are accepted. Long-term rates are available.

Directions: From Perdido Key, drive west on U.S. 98 and cross the bridge to Alabama. Turn left (south) on State Route 99 to the park.

Contact: Pensacola/Perdido Bay KOA, 33951 Spinnaker Drive, Lillian, AL 36549, 251/961-1717, www.koa.com/where/FL/01102.htm.

21 FORT PICKENS CAMPGROUND

Scenic rating: 10

within Gulf Islands National Seashore on the western end of Santa Rosa Island

This once-gorgeous campground will be closed until at least fall of 2006, if not longer. Hurricanes in 2005 destroyed the road to the park. The campground will require repairs after the road is rebuilt to new storm-proof construction standards. Call the park or check the website for updates.

RV sites, facilities: This National Park Service campground offered 168 sites with water and electricity.

Reservations, fees: Once open, reservations will be accepted through the National Park Service reservations system; call 800/365-2267 or see www.reservations.nps.gov.

Directions: At the dead end of U.S. 98 in Pensacola Beach, drive west on Fort Pickens Road/State Road 399 for eight miles to the park entrance.

Contact: Gulf Islands National Seashore Park Headquarters, 1801 Gulf Breeze Parkway, Gulf Breeze, FL 32561, 850/934-2600, 850/934-2621, or 800/365-2267 (reservations).

22 PELICAN PALMS RV PARK

Scenic rating: 5

southeast of Milton

A good base for exploring the canoeing, cycling, hiking, and fishing opportunities nearby, this park is three miles from a PGA golf course and other courses. It's also a convenient overnight stop from the interstate. Sites are level and grassy. About 20 percent of the park is occupied year-round.

RV sites, facilities: Thirty-six sites are available; 23 are pull-through and all have full hookups. Six sites have 50-amp service, 29 have 30-amp, and 10 have picnic tables. Restrooms, showers, a dump station, laundry facilities, a recreation room (but no planned activities), and a pool are on-site. A wireless Internet network, a small store, and a book exchange were added in 2005. A camp store sells ice, camping supplies, snacks, souvenirs, and propane. Children are welcome. Leashed pets are permitted.

Reservations, fees: Reservations are not usually necessary. Sites are $23 per night for two people, plus $2 per extra person, and $2 for 50-amp service. Credit cards are accepted. Stay as long as you like; long-term rates are available.

Directions: From I-10, take Exit 26 and drive south on County Road 191 for 0.1 mile. The park is on the east side of the road.

Contact: Pelican Palms RV Park, 3700 Garcon Point Road, Milton, FL 32583, 850/623-0576, www.pelicanpalmsrvpark.com.

23 EMERALD BEACH RV PARK

Scenic rating: 10

on U.S. 98 between Fort Walton Beach and Pensacola

BEST (

This all-ages park slopes gently down to the water and a 300-foot sandy white beach. This area is marketed by local tourist councils as the "Emerald Coast," a reference to the emerald-green waters offshore. Although you won't find much shade here, especially after the 2004–2005 hurricanes, some lucky RVers can overlook the waters of Santa Rosa Sound. Post-storm building has energized the area, and the community is much busier than it was before. Everyone is parked close together, but campers in big rigs don't seem to mind; they are more interested in fishing, boating, swimming, and visiting the nearby Naval Aviation museum. The location of the park is central to Fort Walton Beach (14 miles east) and to Pensacola (18 miles west).

RV sites, facilities: There are 71 RV slots with full hookups and 30/50-amp electrical service; 36 are pull-through. Some sites are waterfront. Rigs up to 50 feet long and slide-outs can be accommodated. Sites range 26–27 feet wide to 45–60 feet deep. A wireless Internet connection, restrooms, showers, picnic tables, concrete patios, a dump station, a pool, rental cabins, a camp store with ice, snacks and limited groceries, and shuffleboard courts are available. Big grocery stores and restaurants are within 2 miles; malls and hospitals are within 15 miles. Most areas are wheelchair accessible. Streets are paved. Children are welcome. Leashed pets are permitted.

Reservations, fees: Reservations are recommended. Sites are $40 per night for two people, plus $3 per extra person. Credit cards are accepted. Long-term rates are available.

Directions: From Navarre, drive 1.5 miles east on U.S. 98. The park is on the south side of the road.

Contact: Emerald Beach RV Park, 8885 Navarre Parkway, Navarre, FL 32566, 850/939-3431, www.emeraldbeachrvpark.com.

24 NAVARRE BEACH CAMPGROUND

Scenic rating: 10

on U.S. 98 between Fort Walton Beach and Pensacola

BEST (

Palm trees give a tropical atmosphere to this manicured, resort-style family campground that boasts its own beach and a fishing pier on Santa Rosa Sound. Services are terrific: There's a computer room with PCs and high-speed access, and park employees will escort you to your site. The property is gated at all times. Children under 12 must be accompanied by an adult at all times, and all kids swimming in the pool must be supervised by a grown-up. Favorite thing to do: fish and go to the beach. This is an oasis against the backdrop of development sprawling along the U.S. 98 corridor with shopping centers, fast-food eateries, and other accoutrements of modern life rapidly moving in.

RV sites, facilities: All 137 sites have full hookups, 30-amp or 50-amp electrical service, concrete patios, picnic tables, and cable TV. Rigs up to 50 feet long and slide-outs can be accommodated. The most desirable sites are beachfront "ultra" sites with their own deck. There's a wireless Internet network in the office and clubhouse. Restrooms, showers, two laundry facilities, a dump station, a game room, a fishing pier, a pool, a hot tub, horseshoe pits, shuffleboard and basketball courts, a store, cabin rentals, and a playground are available. Campfires are permitted at a communal fire pit. A camp store sells ice, camping supplies, groceries, snacks, and souvenirs. During the winter, planned activities are available. All areas are wheelchair accessible. Children are welcome. Small pets are permitted at the discretion of the management; barking dogs, for example, are frowned upon, and campers are encouraged to report errant behavior to the office.

Reservations, fees: Reservations are recommended. Sites are $39–69 per night for two people, plus $3 for each additional person. Credit cards are accepted. Long-term rates are available.

Directions: From the Navarre Beach Bridge, drive one mile east on U.S. 98.

Contact: Navarre Beach Campground, 9201 Navarre Parkway, Navarre, FL 32566, 850/939-2188, fax 850/939-4712, www.nav beach.com.

25 MAGNOLIA BEACH CAMPGROUND

Scenic rating: 10

east of Navarre

BEST (

Swim on the park's sandy, 400-foot-long beach or cast a line for a seafood dinner from the long pier. Some sites overlook Santa Rosa Sound, which gets less boat traffic here than in other locations. From this five-acre park, you can combine your seaside delights with the wilderness. Just drive up State Road 87 toward Blackwater River State Park and the surrounding state forest for canoeing and other adventures.

RV sites, facilities: This campground has 50 RV sites with full hookups and 30-amp electricity. Restrooms, showers, laundry facilities, and a 600-foot-long fishing pier are provided. You can tie your boat up to the pier to load or unload passengers or gear, but the boat cannot be left there longer than that. The water around the pier is somewhat shallow, and jumping and diving are not permitted. Children are welcome, but those under 12 must be supervised at all times. Pets under 15 pounds are permitted on a leash; management can suggest several kennels nearby if your dog is larger.

Reservations, fees: Reservations are suggested. Sites are $27.50–35 per night for two people, plus $2 per extra person. Credit cards are not accepted. Long-term rates are available.

Directions: From Navarre, drive three miles east on U.S. 98. The park is on the south side.

Contact: Magnolia Beach Campground, 9807 Navarre Parkway, Navarre, FL 32566, 850/939-2717 or 877/375-4600, www.magnolia beach.com.

26 PLAYGROUND RV PARK

Scenic rating: 2

on the north side of Fort Walton Beach

Although located beside a busy highway with strip shopping centers and heavy commercial activity, this park is nearly always full. It's convenient to Eglin Air Force Base, and beaches are only four miles away. Most overnighters or vacationers are here for the beach or visiting relatives nearby.

RV sites, facilities: This mobile-home community and apartment complex has a total of 65 RV sites with full hookups, 30/50-amp electrical service, and cable TV. Nine pull-through sites are generally available for short-term visitors. Restrooms, showers, laundry facilities, and a dump station are available. Children are welcome. Small, leashed pets are permitted.

Reservations, fees: Reservations are accepted. Sites are $30 per night for two people, plus $2 for each additional person over the age of six. Credit cards are accepted. Long-term rates are available.

Directions: From the junction of U.S. 98 and State Road 189 in Fort Walton Beach, drive north on State Road 189 for four miles. The park is on the east (right) side of the road.

Contact: Playground RV Park, 777 Beal Parkway, Fort Walton Beach, FL 32547, 850/862-3513, email: playgroundrvpark@aol.com.

27 RIVER'S EDGE RV CAMPGROUND

Scenic rating: 9

south of Holt

Sprawling across 144 acres on the banks of the Yellow River, this campground is heavily wooded and peaceful, suitable as a destination park or as an overnight spot. Even the biggest rigs can be accommodated on the extra-large pull-through sites. The campground provides 24-hour security. While you're here, fish from the river's edge or on nearby Log Lake and hike the one-mile nature trail. A quaint bridge built in the 1920s once spanned the Yellow River; now it sits on the riverbank as a bit of a historical interest. Blackwater River State Forest is close by.

Supplies are available in Crestview, about 10 miles east of the park.

RV sites, facilities: Of the 110 RV sites, most have full hookups and 30-amp and 50-amp electrical service. Picnic tables, fire pits, restrooms, showers, laundry facilities, a dump station, a boat launch, a playground, a clubhouse, a pavilion, and a camp circle are on the grounds. Children are welcome. Leashed pets are permitted.

Reservations, fees: Reservations are recommended. Sites are $18–20 per night for two adults, plus $2 for each additional person. No credit cards are accepted. Long-term stays are okay.

Directions: From I-10 near Holt, take Exit 45 and drive south on State Road 189 for 1.5 miles to the park.

Contact: River's Edge RV Campground, 4001 Log Lake Road, Holt, FL 32564, 850/537-2267.

28 LAZY DAYS RV PARK

Scenic rating: 2

east of Niceville in Freeport

This roadside, 8.5-acre park usually attracts snowbirds in the winter and travelers passing through. In recent years, almost the entire park (98 percent) is occupied year-round, most recently by workers helping to repair hurricane damage or work on the many construction developments going up in the area. The beach is 10 miles away. Points of interest in the area include Eden State Gardens, Seaside, Grayton Beach, and Destin.

RV sites, facilities: There are 30 full-hookup RV sites with 30/50-amp electrical service, concrete patios, and optional cable TV and telephone service. RVs as long as 45 feet and slide-outs can be accommodated. An Internet connection is available in the office. Picnic tables, restrooms, showers, a dump station, laundry facilities, a game room where potluck dinners are held in the winter months, and horseshoe pits are available. Groceries and restaurants are within two miles. Children are welcome. Pets are allowed on a leash. Pop-top trailers are not allowed.

Reservations, fees: Reservations are recommended. Sites are $25 per night for two people, plus $2 for each additional person over age five. Credit cards are accepted. Long-term rates are available.

Directions: From I-10 at De Funiak Springs, take Exit 85 and head south on U.S. 331 for 17 miles. Or, from U.S. 98 west of Panama City, drive seven miles north on U.S. 331 to the park.

Contact: Lazy Days RV Park, 18655 U.S. 331 South, Freeport, FL 32439, 850/835-4606.

29 EGLIN AIR FORCE BASE

Scenic rating: 8

south of I-10 and between Pensacola and De Funiak Springs

One of the largest swaths of wilderness in Florida is controlled by the Department of Defense (DOD). Although most people don't think of the military as being in the wild-woods business, the DOD has been an admirable caretaker of the grounds in recent years. For instance, the military went so far as to take special steps to save endangered red-cockaded woodpeckers by planting trees and protecting the rare birds' homes from fire.

What you give up here in lack of amenities you get back in an astounding variety of natural settings for camping. They include sites on the Choctawhatchee and East Bays, which may be favored by saltwater anglers; six sites on ponds suitable for freshwater fishing; one on Metts Bluff overlooking the Yellow River; one at Gin Hole Landing, where boaters can launch onto the Yellow River; and others beside small creeks or bayous. Swimmers can take a plunge in the Gulf of Mexico, which is only a short drive away.

Wild animals you might spot include deer, coyote, wild turkey, wild hog, quail, rabbit, or, if you're exceptionally lucky, the secretive black bear. But remember also that hunting is allowed. The general gun season, when you'll want to be sure to wear orange-blaze vests and hats (or avoid the area altogether), varies from year to year but usually occurs on specific dates such as weekends between Thanksgiving and mid-January. Call ahead for the dates. Seasons for small-game and turkey hunters follow, but these present less of a threat to campers. Still, ask about hunting dates and bring along the orange-blaze outerwear. Also, if you come at these times, don't be surprised if you're sharing a campsite with hunters. Some areas of the base are closed to hunting, and others are designated for hunting only by bow and arrow. During certain periods, the base lands may be closed to the public for defense reasons; call 850/882-0007 for current status 24 hours a day.

RV sites, facilities: There's an improved campsite with water and electricity at Postal Point; however, only persons affiliated with the Department of Defense may stay here (call 850/882-3569 if you qualify). For the general public, primitive campsites for self-contained RVs are scattered across about 446,000 acres square miles. Children are welcome. Pets are also permitted, but they must be restrained and kept at least 50 yards outside your campsite. Supplies and restaurants are available in Niceville and Valparaiso, on the base's southern boundary.

Reservations, fees: Permits are required. They may be obtained in two ways: (1) At least three weeks before your stay, write to Eglin Air Force Base Natural Resources Branch, 107 Highway 85 North, Niceville, FL 32578. Include a photocopy of a valid driver's license for the main person in your camping party, as well as updated address information and phone number if different from that on the driver's license. Specify that you want a camping permit, which costs $5 for five consecutive days and is payable only by check or money order payable to DFAS-DE

DSSN 3801; or (2) Dropping by the office at the address above. It's open 7 A.M.–4:30 P.M. Monday–Thursday, 7 A.M.–6 P.M. Friday, and 7:30 A.M.–12:30 P.M. Saturday. The office is closed Sundays and holidays. The permit is valid for five consecutive nights for up to 10 people.

Directions: From I-10 near Crestview, take Exit 56 and head south on State Road 85 for about 15 miles to the base's Jackson Guard in Niceville.

Contact: Eglin Air Force Base, Natural Resources Division/Jackson Guard, 107 Highway 85 North, Niceville, FL 32578, 850/882-4164, www.eglin.af.mil/newcomers/leisure.htm.

30 FRED GANNON ROCKY BAYOU STATE PARK

Scenic rating: 9

near Niceville

This park on the edge of the Eglin Air Force Base territory has another military link: It was named after a colonel who helped develop the 357-acre parcel of land after the state acquired it from the U.S. Forest Service. Most visitors to the area focus on the beach, even though it's fairly narrow and not your typical post-card bathing beach. There are plenty of other water-oriented delights here in a forest setting of tall sand pines. Some trees are 300 years old. Swimmers, boaters, canoeists, and anglers can explore the treasures of Rocky Bayou, which opens into Choctawhatchee Bay; there's also a freshwater lake on the property. (You'll need the appropriate fishing license depending on whether you try your hand at fresh or saltwater fishing.) Ten campsites overlook the bayou. In 2005, several improvements were made to the park, including a new heated bathhouse, a bridge crossing Puddin Head Lake, and 50-amp electrical service at about one-fourth of the campsites. It'll take you about 25 minutes to explore each of the three

nature trails. If you choose only one, then pick the Sand Pine Trail, which leads along Puddin Head Lake and through the woods. Incidentally, the town of Niceville was once named Boggy, but folks didn't think that sounded too appealing.

RV sites, facilities: There are 42 campsites in this state park, offering water and electricity (31 are 30-amp, and 11 have 50-amp service), picnic tables, grills, and fire rings. Restrooms, showers, a dump station, a boat ramp, a pavilion, and a playground are available. RVs up to 45 feet long and slide-outs are permitted. Groceries and restaurants are within 0.5 mile. Two campsites, the bathhouse, office, store, and the boat ramp are wheelchair accessible. Streets are paved. Children are welcome. Pets with proof of rabies vaccination are allowed.

Reservations, fees: Reservations are recommended; contact ReserveAmerica at 800/336-3521 or reserveamerica.com. Sites are $12 per night for eight people. Credit cards are accepted. The maximum stay is 14 days.

Directions: From I-10 near Crestview, take Exit 56 and drive south on State Road 85 for 15 miles. Turn east onto State Road 20 in Niceville and drive nine miles to the park.

Contact: Fred Gannon Rocky Bayou State Park, 4281 Highway 20, Niceville, FL 32578, 850/833-9144, www.floridastate parks.org.

31 BAYVIEW RV RESORT

Scenic rating: 3

in Destin

Located across from Destin's main boat launch, this park offers boat storage for guests and is set in a quiet neighborhood. Long-term visitors are preferred, and usually only a few sites are available. You'll notice the park's lighthouse at the entrance.

RV sites, facilities: This tiny park has 12 RV sites with full hookups; call to see if any sites are available. Restrooms, showers, and laundry facilities are available. Children are welcome. Leashed pets are permitted.

Reservations, fees: Reservations are recommended. Sites are $25 per night for two people, plus $2 per extra person. Credit cards are accepted. Long-term rates are available.

Directions: From the U.S. 98 bridge in Destin, drive east 1.6 miles. Turn north on Beach Drive and continue 1.3 miles to the park on the left.

Contact: Bayview RV Resort, 749 Beach Drive, Destin, FL 32541, 850/837-5085, www.bayviewdestin.com.

32 DESTIN RV BEACH RESORT

Scenic rating: 10

east of Destin

BEST (

This beachside motor-coach resort, opened in 2001, offers luxury sites with private beach access, fancy landscaping and lighting, brick pavers instead of an asphalt road, and an intimate setting of just 36 sites. With this much investment, you can expect that upscale RVers are most welcome. Only Class A, B, and C motor homes, fifth wheels, and travel trailers are allowed; they must be at least 22 feet long and no more than 10 years old. Pop-ups, truck campers, and other hybrid travel trailers are prohibited.

RV sites, facilities: There are 36 full-hookup sites with 30/50-amp electrical service, concrete patios, professional landscaping, and cable TV. Lots are 30 feet wide by 60 feet deep, and they can accommodate RVs up to 45 feet long and slide-outs. Wireless Internet service is available for an additional charge. Restrooms, showers, laundry facilities, and telephone service are available. On the premises are a heated pool, two luxury rental units above the office building, brick-paved driveways, and a path to the beach. The bathhouse, office, and pool area are wheelchair accessible. Children are welcome. Leashed pets are permitted.

Reservations, fees: Reservations are recommended. Sites are $69–79 per night for a family of six (two adults and four children), plus $10 for each additional adult. Only six people are allowed per site. Long-term rates are available.

Directions: From U.S. 98 and MidBay Bridge Road (Highway 293), drive east on U.S. 98 about five miles. Turn right on Miramar Beach Drive to the park at the beach.

Contact: Destin RV Beach Resort, 362 Miramar Beach Drive, Destin, FL 32550, 850/837-3529, www.destinrvresort.com.

33 HENDERSON BEACH STATE PARK

Scenic rating: 10

in Destin

BEST (

Opened in March 2000, this is one of the newest campgrounds in Florida's award-winning state park system. Since opening, Henderson Beach State Park has doubled the size of its campground with the addition of another loop along the Gulf of Mexico. The park has 6,000 feet of white-sand shoreline (with a boardwalk from the campground to the beach) and 208 acres of sand pine, scrub oak, and other vegetation. Why is the sand so white? It's composed of quartz and silicon dioxide polished by countless years of wave action. You can scuba dive just one mile offshore, or swim in the gulf, or cast a line from the surf to while away the day. Restaurants and shopping are within one mile, and there's a Wal-Mart across the street. The campground has its own beach area separate from the day users' beach. On weekends, rangers hot interpretive programs, and the park is the site of festivals, such as a national surf-casting fishing event.

RV sites, facilities: Sixty sites have water, 30-amp electricity, picnic tables, and grills. Twenty-two sites are pull-through; 36 sites have 50-amp service. Big RVs and slide-outs are permitted. Restrooms, showers, and a dump station are available. Ice and souvenirs are for sale. Most areas are wheelchair accessible. Children are welcome. Leashed pets are permitted.

Reservations, fees: Reservations are recommended; contact ReserveAmerica at 800/336-3521 or reserveamerica.com. Sites are $23 for up to eight people. Credit cards are accepted. The maximum stay is 14 days.

Directions: From the intersection of US 98 and Midway Bridge Road in Destin, drive west on U.S. 98 one mile to the park entrance.

Contact: Henderson Beach State Park, 17000 Emerald Coast Parkway, Destin, FL 32541, 850/837-7550, fax 850/650-0290, www.floridastateparks.org.

34 CAMPING ON THE GULF HOLIDAY TRAVEL PARK

Scenic rating: 10

east of Destin

BEST (

If you've come to Florida to visit the beach, you'll love this family park, where you can book a site directly on the fabled white sands of the Gulf of Mexico. As the owners say, "You can't get much closer than this!" Beachfront spots, naturally, are the most dear, but shady, grassy sites and sites with concrete pads are convenient to the water and the oceanfront walkway. The campground "beach patrol" will help you park your rig, and the management offers "express check-in" for many reserved visitors.

RV sites, facilities: There are 221 RV sites with full hookups, 30/50-amp electrical service, cable TV, concrete patios, and picnic tables; some have telephone service. Twenty-one sites are pull-through. The average lot size of 30 feet wide by 70 feet deep accommodates RVs up to 45 feet long and slide-outs. Restrooms, showers, laundry facilities, a dump station, a heated pool, a gift shop, rental cabins, a 3,500-square-foot activity center with planned activities, a fishing guide, and a playground are provided. A wireless Internet connection is available in the clubhouse. The camp store sells ices, snacks, limited groceries, souvenirs, and propane. Groceries, restaurants, malls, and

hospitals are within two miles. All areas are wheelchair accessible. Children are welcome. Leashed pets are permitted, though not on the beachfront campsites.

Reservations, fees: Reservations are recommended. Sites are $45–107 per night for five people, plus $5 per extra person. Credit cards are accepted. Six-month stays are okay September–May.

Directions: From the U.S. 98 bridge in Destin, drive east for 10 miles to the park on the south side of the road.

Contact: Camping on the Gulf Holiday Travel Park, 10005 West Emerald Coast Parkway, Destin, FL 32541, 850/837-6334 or 877/226-7485 (reservations), fax 850/654-5048, www.campgulf.com.

35 TOPSAIL HILL STATE PRESERVE

Scenic rating: 10

in Santa Rosa Beach

If you own a large RV, this 140-acre private-campground-turned-state-preserve is where you'll want to be. One of the most deluxe RV parks in Florida, Topsail has resort-style amenities such as a heated swimming pool, fishing lakes, professional landscaping, over-sized lots, and immaculate grounds. Even the restrooms are heated and air-conditioned, according to season. The park is tucked into a pine forest near sandy beaches and upscale shopping centers. Free shuttle service is available to the beach.

Longtimers remember this park as Emerald Coast RV Resort, but the neighboring 1,639-acre state preserve—Topsail, home to one of the world's last remaining populations of the endangered Choctawhatchee beach mouse—took it over, and it is now part of the state park system. Tiny wildflowers bloom most months at the preserve, which features wispy savannas, cypress domes, coastal dune lakes, and, of course, the feature from which it derives its name, a 25-foot-high lakeside dune.

RV sites, facilities: All 156 RV sites have sewer hookups, 30/50-amp electricity, cable TV, and optional telephone service. Internet access is available. Picnic tables, grills, restrooms, showers, laundry facilities, a dump station, a heated pool, a recreation center, tennis courts, a lake, boat and canoe rentals, rental cabins, a driving range, horseshoe pits, and shuffleboard courts are on-site. The restrooms, office, and beach boardwalk are wheelchair accessible. Children and leashed pets are welcome.

Reservations, fees: Reservations are recom- mended; contact ReserveAmerica at 800/336- 3521 or reserveamerica.com. Sites are $38 per night. Credit cards are accepted. Long-term stays are okay.

Directions: From I-10 at De Funiak Springs, take Exit 85 and head south on U.S. 331 for 26 miles to U.S. 98. Turn west (right) and drive five miles to County Road 30A. Turn south (left) and drive 0.2 mile to the park entrance on your right.

Contact: Topsail Hill State Preserve, 7525 West Scenic Highway 30A, Santa Rosa Beach, FL 32459, 850/267-0299, fax 850/267-9014, www .floridastateparks.org.

PANAMA CITY

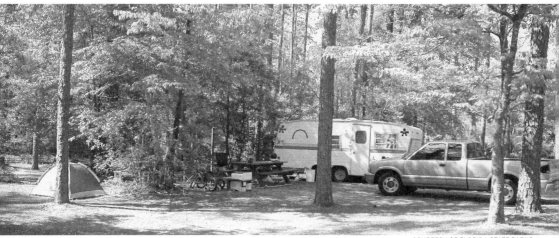

COURTESY OF FLORIDA STATE PARKS

BEST RV PARKS AND CAMPGROUNDS

(Biking
Pine Log State Forest, page 77

(Fishing
Sunset King Lake Resort, page 71

(Most Unusual
Falling Waters State Park, page 73
Florida Caverns State Park, page 74

(Natural Springs
Vortex Spring RV Park, page 73

**(Publicly Managed
Beachfront Campgrounds**
Grayton Beach State Park, page 78
St. Andrews State Park, page 82
T. H. Stone Memorial St. Joseph Peninsula
State Park, page 85

Panama City's beaches and surrounding coastline are legendary: Dazzling-white, sandy expanses offset by brilliant, emerald-green waters that will take your breath away as the sparkling water frames gorgeous picture-postcard vistas. A university professor who styles himself as "Dr. Beach" has officially designated some of these sugary sands as the best in the world. It doesn't stop here, though; saltwater anglers say the fishing is excellent as well.

The beachfront in Panama City is becoming populated with luxury condominiums and high-rises, although a few private RV parks remain. This family-oriented area beckons kids of all ages with amusement parks, water sports, reef and wreck diving, snorkeling, zoos, go-cart racing, and similar activities. Fortunately for the RV visitor, two state parks preserve a more nature-oriented beach experience: the award-winning T. H. Stone Memorial St. Joseph Peninsula State Park and St. Andrews State Park. Be sure to make reservations if you want to stay at these parks; they are hugely popular and for good reason.

Inland, you'll find vast acres of forest for a more woodsy feel, as well as natural springs, including one with associations to the fabled "fountain of youth." The explorer's quest is memorialized by Ponce de Leon Springs State Park, where two springs are surrounded by a wall built in 1926, when the waters were a "fountain of youth" tourist attraction. Although you can't camp here, consider making your base at Vortex Spring, on the outskirts of the city of Ponce de Leon, where scuba divers have a chance to explore the springs from the inside out.

RVers will enjoy side trips to De Funiak Springs, which hosts a spring-fed lake said to be one of the few perfectly round lakes in the world. In Marianna, visitors at the Florida Caverns State Park can tour the stalactites, stalagmites, columns, flowstones, and draperies that were formed tens of thousands of years ago; there's even a "wedding cake" formation in one chamber, where some couples have celebrated their nuptials.

This stretch of the Gulf Coast attracts thousands of visitors from the Florida Panhandle and surrounding Southern states such as Alabama, Mississippi, and Georgia. This is especially true during the summer months, a reverse of the traditional "winter season" busyness that befalls most of the state of Florida.

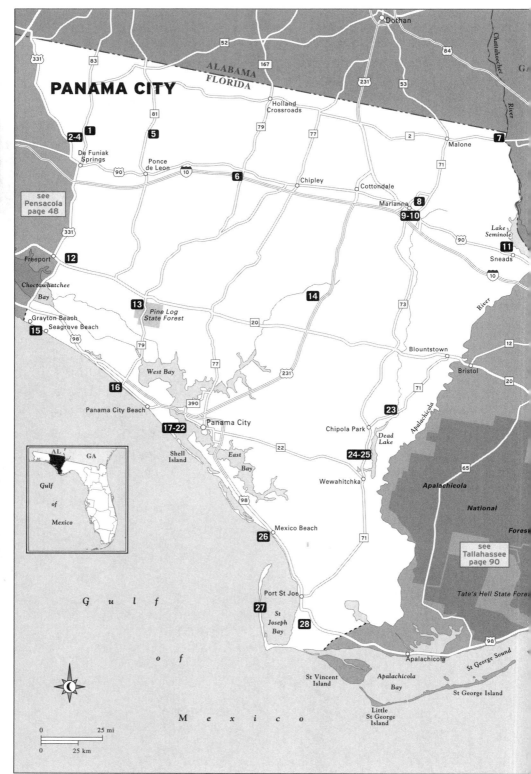

◼1 SUNSET KING LAKE RESORT

Scenic rating: 8

north of De Funiak Springs on Kings Lake

BEST (

Set on 580-acre Kings Lake, this park caters to anglers and campers who like lots of on-site amenities, such as miniature golf, croquet, basketball, volleyball, badminton, and much more. It's not so far from I-10 that it isn't a good stay-over option. Kids can play in the fenced playground, swim in the lake-view pool, or fish off the 75-foot lighted pier. The lake is stocked regularly with black bass, shellcracker, crappie, and bream; in 1987, it yielded a record-breaking bass weighing in at more than 17 pounds. Sites are sunny, with a few trees interspersed. A hired activities director organizes the fun stuff. Lots are for sale, as well. These people are really into technology: If you want to check the views online, the park has a dock-mounted and pool area Web cameras.

RV sites, facilities: This park has 100 large (40 foot by 90 foot) full-hookup RV sites with 50-amp electrical service and cable TV. Rigs up to 45 feet or more in length can be accommodated, as well as slide-outs. A wireless Internet connection is available in the clubhouse. Cable TV, picnic tables, grills, restrooms, showers, a dump station, a clubhouse, a pavilion, a pool, a boat ramp, boat docks, a playground, a game room, miniature golf, horseshoe pits, a store, and laundry facilities are on-site. A restaurant is open Wednesday–Sunday. The clubhouse and bathhouse are wheelchair accessible. Children and pets are welcome. Memberships are for sale, so you may see lots of repeat visitors.

Reservations, fees: Reservations are not necessary, but the peak season at the park is February–March and November–December. Sites are $27–45 per night for two people, plus $1 per extra person. Credit cards are accepted. Long-term rates are available.

Directions: If westbound: From I-10 west of De Funiak Springs, take Exit 70 and drive north on State Road 285 for 0.4 mile. Turn right onto U.S. 90 and drive 8.5 miles east. When you reach Kings Lake Road, turn north and follow the signs to the park. If eastbound: Take I-10 Exit 85 and turn right on Highway 331. Drive two miles to U.S. 90 and turn left. Continue five miles on U.S. 90 until you reach Kings Lake Road. Roads leading to the park are paved.

Contact: Sunset King Lake Resort, 366 Paradise Island Drive, De Funiak Springs, FL 32433, 850/892-7229 or 800/747-5454, fax 850/892-7998, www.sunsetking.com.

◼2 LONG LEAF RV PARK

Scenic rating: 3

near De Funiak Springs

Weary travelers on I-10 will find this park convenient, though it offers no pool or recreation room. It has long pull-through spaces on gravel roads just 3.5 miles south of the interstate. Overnighters are welcome. Shopping and restaurants are close by. Among your fellow campers will be European and American touring bicyclists coming for the open country and easy roads.

RV sites, facilities: There are 24 partially shaded RV sites, all with water and electricity. Nineteen sites have full hookups with 30- or 50-amp electricity. All have picnic tables. Restrooms, showers, laundry facilities, and telephone service are available. Most areas are wheelchair accessible, although the streets are gravel. On the premises is a dog-walk area. Children are welcome. Leashed pets are permitted.

Reservations, fees: Reservations are recommended. Sites are $20–22 per night for two people, plus $2 per extra person. Credit cards are not accepted. Long-term rates are available.

Directions: From I-10, take Exit 85 onto U.S. 331 and drive 3.5 miles south.

Contact: Long Leaf RV Park, 5687 U.S. 331 South, De Funiak Springs, FL 32435, 850/892-7261.

3 BASS HAVEN CAMPGROUND

Scenic rating: 5

north of De Funiak Springs on Juniper Lake

Rigs up to 40 feet long can be accommodated in this 1.5-acre park on Juniper Lake, which is famed for its bass fishing. Locals nurture the belief that the world-record largemouth bass will come from its waters. But there's more to do around here than fish: Take a 15-minute drive to Vortex Spring or explore the city of De Funiak Springs, which has dozens of spectacular Victorian homes that circle a spring-fed lake; it's said to be one of two perfectly round lakes in the world. Around the turn of the 20th century, this town was famous as the home of the Winter Chautauqua, a cultural and philosophical movement that brought lecturers and speech makers here to the still-standing Chautauqua Auditorium. Also nearby is the Chautauqua Winery (850/892-5887), the largest winery in Florida; tours are available. If you're feeling really energetic, take a drive north to the highest point in Florida—345 feet above sea level. It's just an imperceptible bump flagged with a sign and a granite marker, but you can say you bagged another peak. From De Funiak Springs, drive north on U.S. 331/State Road 285 about 20 miles until State Road 285 forks off to the northeast. Continue on State Road 285 about two miles; the marker is in a pine woods with a small picnic area.

RV sites, facilities: The campground has 19 RV sites, most with sewer hookups and 30-amp electrical service. Two pull-through sites have 50-amp, but no sewer. On the premises are picnic tables, restrooms, showers, a dump station, a boat ramp, boat docks, boat rentals, horseshoe pits, a volleyball field, a store, and laundry facilities. Groceries and restaurants are within five miles. The bathrooms and "sleeping room," a rental suite attached to the clubhouse, are wheelchair accessible. Children and pets are welcome.

Reservations, fees: Reservations are not necessary. Sites are $20 per night for a family of four,

plus $2 per extra person and $1 for cable TV. Credit cards are not accepted. The maximum stay is six months.

Directions: From I-10 at De Funiak Springs, take Exit 85 and drive north on U.S. 331 for two miles, then turn east onto U.S. 90 and go several blocks through town. At State Road 83, turn left and drive 2.5 miles north. At Juniper Lake Road, turn west (left) and follow the signs to the park.

Contact: Bass Haven Campground, 350 Bass Haven Drive, De Funiak Springs, FL 32433, 850/892-4043.

4 JUNIPER LAKE CAMPGROUND

Scenic rating: 5

north of De Funiak Springs on Juniper Lake

Juniper Lake is considered to be one of the area's finest fishing lakes for bass. In fact, those in the know are so confident that they believe a world-record largemouth bass will be pulled from here someday. Will you be the lucky angler? Stay a few days at one of the campsites right on the lakeshore of this 4.5-acre park and give it a try. The lake is 667 acres, and very "fishy."

RV sites, facilities: This park has 18 RV sites with full hookups and cable TV. Overnighters are welcome, and 50-amp service is available. On the premises are picnic tables, restrooms, showers, a picnic area, a clubhouse, covered boat slips with electricity, johnboats for rent ($30 per day), three docks, and laundry facilities. Children are welcome. Leashed pets are okay.

Reservations, fees: Reservations are suggested. Sites are $18 per night. Credit cards are not accepted. Long-term rates are available.

Directions: From I-10 at De Funiak Springs, take Exit 85 and drive north on U.S. 331 for two miles, then turn east onto U.S. 90 and go several blocks through town. At State Road 83, turn north and drive 2.5 miles. At Juniper Lake Road, turn west and follow the signs to the park.

Contact: Juniper Lake Campground, 363 Black

Bass Boulevard, De Funiak Springs, FL 32433, 850/892-3445, fax 850/892-9136, www.juni-perlakervcampground.com.

⑤ VORTEX SPRING RV PARK

🏊 🚤 〽️ 🐕 ♿ 🚐 ⛺

Scenic rating: 10

in Ponce de Leon

BEST (

For decades, Florida pitchmen have exploited the legend of Spanish explorer Juan Ponce de Leon, romanticizing his quest to find a fountain of youth in the flowery paradise he discovered on Easter Sunday in 1513 and named La Florida. Historians, however, portray him as a gold-hungry despot who arrived in the New World on Christopher Columbus' second voyage, then conquered the Carib Indians. He was hunting for hidden riches, not just a fountain, when he was mortally wounded by an Indian arrow at Charlotte Harbor in 1521. Nonetheless, his name has been attached ever since to Florida's myriad springs—natural wonders with supposedly curative powers that have drawn countless visitors and are now a resource for the state's thriving bottled water industry.

The family-run Vortex Spring camping resort, on the outskirts of the city of Ponce de Leon, capitalizes on another angle: scuba diving and underwater caving. The centerpiece of this 480-acre private campground is a spring and underwater cavern that spews 28 million gallons of water daily at a constant temperature of 68°F. The spring basin, crystal clear and 48 feet deep, is shared by catfish, freshwater eels, rare shadow bass, and a vegetarian piranha named Paco. The limestone cavern, restricted to cave-certified divers, meanders farther for 100 yards to a depth of 115 feet. Diving lessons are available. On the surface, the spring spills into Blue Creek, which is good for snorkeling, canoeing, or a paddleboat ride. The swimming area has a small waterslide, a nine-foot diving platform, a slide for small children, and an old-fashioned rope swing. The campsites are grassy and semishaded; wood for campfires is sold at the store, along with other supplies.

Near the campground is a 443-acre park named after you-know-who: Ponce de Leon Springs State Park, on State Road 181A, 0.5 mile south of U.S. 90. Two springs are surrounded by a wall built in 1926 when the waters were a "fountain of youth" attraction; they produce 14 million gallons daily that flow into the Choctawhatchee River. No camping is permitted, but there's a swimming beach with a bathhouse, a picnic area, and a couple of nature trails. Admission is $2 per car. For more information, call 850/836-4281.

RV sites, facilities: This park has 22 RV sites. Seven have full hookups and are pull-through; all have water and electricity. Additional boondock sites are primitive. Each developed site has a picnic table, a grill, and a fire ring. On the premises are restrooms, showers, scuba-diving facilities, a campground store, and a spring for swimming. Snorkel gear, paddleboat, canoe, kayak, and inner-tube rentals are available. A go-cart park is a mile from the campsites. Children are welcome. Pets are discouraged, but small leashed pets are permitted.

Reservations, fees: Reservations are recommended, particularly during holidays. Sites are $28 per night for two people, plus $6 for each additional person. Credit cards are accepted.

Directions: From I-10 east of De Funiak Springs, take Exit 96 to State Road 81 and drive five miles north to the park at right. Turn right at the sign and drive 0.5 mile to the campground.

Contact: Vortex Spring RV Park, 1517 Vortex Spring Lane, Ponce de Leon, FL 32455, 850/836-4979 or 800/342-0640, fax 850/836-4557, www.vortexspring.com.

⑥ FALLING WATERS STATE PARK

🥾 🏊 🐕 🛶 🚐 ⛺

Scenic rating: 10

near Chipley

BEST (

This 171-acre park is a fine overnight camping spot with a unique attraction: Florida's only waterfall. Sure, it's no Niagara, plunging just 67 feet into a cylindrical sinkhole where it vanishes into the limestone. The site, though, has a prehistoric feel, lush with ferns and ancient hardwoods. Slash pines shade the campground, and there's a trail leading to the swimming lake (swimming in the waterfall is not permitted). The trail continues past the site of an oil well drilled by wildcatters in 1919. It produced a dribble of crude and was capped three years later. Just above the falls, a whiskey still produced spirits for frontier railroad crews in the 1800s. The waterfall itself powered a gristmill for several years. Timbers from the old mill are on display.

RV sites, facilities: This state park has 24 campsites with water, 30-amp electricity, picnic tables, grills, and fire rings; 7 are pull-through sites. There are restrooms, showers, a dump station, a swimming lake, and a playground. Firewood is not provided, but you are welcome to bring your own. Children are welcome. Pets are permitted with up-to-date vaccination records. The picnic area is wheelchair accessible.

Reservations, fees: Reservations are recommended; contact ReserveAmerica at 800/336-3521 or reserveamerica.com. The fee is $15 for eight people. Credit cards are accepted.

Directions: From I-10 at Chipley, take Exit 120 onto State Road 77 and drive south for three miles to the park.

Contact: Falling Waters State Park, 1130 State Park Road, Chipley, FL 32428, 850/638-6130, fax 850/638-6273, www.floridastateparks.org.

⑦ NEAL'S LANDING

Scenic rating: 4

on the Chattahoochee River, near the Georgia border

Sites are shady and spaced far apart from each other in this campground, which was previously run by the U.S. Army Corps of Engineers. The Corps turned over maintenance responsibilities

to Jackson County government in late 2005, and the county is planning improvements here and at two other Corps facilities, Buenavista and Parramore's. However, it may be several years before everything is finalized, so call ahead. At this writing, visitors have access to a boat ramp on the Chattahoochee River but will find that it's typically very busy, attracting boaters and anglers from three states: Georgia is across the river to the east, and Alabama is just a hop, skip, and jump to the north. (Note that the bathroom facilities serve both the campground and the boat launch.)

RV sites, facilities: There are 11 sites, each with a picnic table, a grill, and a lantern hanger. There is no electricity or water hookups at the campsites. Restrooms, showers, a dump station, and a boat ramp are available. Children and leashed pets are welcome.

Reservations, fees: Reservations are not accepted. Sites are $5 per night for up to eight people. There's a self-pay station at the entrance. Credit cards are not accepted. Maximum stay is 14 days.

Directions: From the west side of Sneads at the junction of State Road 271 and U.S. 90, drive 22 miles north on State Road 271. At County Road 164, turn right (northeast) and drive 1.3 miles. At State Road 2, turn right (eastbound) and drive 0.9 mile. The campground is on the south side of the road, just before the bridge and the Georgia state line.

Contact: Jackson County Community Development Department, 4487 Lafayette Street, Marianna, FL 32446, 850/482-9637 or 850/718-0437.

⑧ FLORIDA CAVERNS STATE PARK

Scenic rating: 10

north of Marianna

BEST (

Caves in Florida? You bet. Be sure to take the 45-minute ranger-led tour to see the stalactites, stalagmites, columns, flowstones, and draperies that were formed tens of thousands of years ago. Although not as large as Kentucky's Mammoth Cave, the Florida Caverns are arguably just as interesting; there's even a "wedding cake" formation in one chamber, where some couples have celebrated their nuptials. The state park and the caverns were developed in the 1930s by the Civilian Conservation Corps, which built trails and passages and installed lighting to make the caverns accessible to the public. This is the only cave in Florida that the public can enter without a scientific research permit. However, you are not permitted to explore the caverns at whim. Tours are first-come, first-served; if your only reason for coming is to see the caves, then go directly there to buy your ticket ($2.50–5) because they sell out fast. The rest of the 1,300-acre park has much to offer: a swimming area at Blue Hole, a boat ramp on the Chipola River, canoe rentals, hiking and equestrian trails, and forests of American beech, southern magnolia, spruce pine, white oak, and some plants more typical of the Appalachian Mountains.

Another feature that makes this park special is that it was constructed by the Civilian Conservation Corps during the late 1930s. The CCC, formed by President Roosevelt to provide employment during the Depression, built several parks in Florida, using local rock to create charming buildings. At Florida Caverns, the Corps enlarged the caverns and installed lighting. In much earlier days, the caves were used by Native Americans and as a hiding place during the Civil War.

RV sites, facilities: There are 35 shady, gravel sites, all with water and 30-amp electricity, picnic tables, grills, and fire rings. Although the campground has plenty of trees, you'll also find spots suitable for raising a satellite dish. Rigs as long as 40 feet can be accommodated. Restrooms, showers, a dump station, a boat ramp, a playground, a museum, and a snack bar are provided. The bathhouse and visitors center are wheelchair accessible.

Children are welcome. Pets are permitted with proof of vaccination.

Reservations, fees: Reservations are recommended; contact ReserveAmerica at 800/336-3521 or reserveamerica.com. Sites are $17 per night for eight people. Credit cards are accepted. Maximum length of stay is 14 days.

Directions: From I-10 at Marianna, take Exit 142 and onto State Road 71 North for 5.8 miles. Turn right on State Road 166/Jefferson Street. That road becomes Caverns Road; keep going for 2.7 miles to the park entrance.

Contact: Florida Caverns State Park, 3345 Caverns Road, Marianna, FL 32446, 850/482-9598, www.floridastateparks.org.

9 ARROWHEAD CAMPSITES

Scenic rating: 5

in Marianna on U.S. 90

Arrowhead Campground borders on Mill Pond, a spring-fed, seven-mile-long lake where one angler caught a world-record shellcracker. It also overlooks the main drag into town, but situated as it is on a hill, the ambience is a bit more superior than sniffing highway exhaust. The campground has tall pines and elms and plenty of stuff for kids, including a swimming pool, a playground, and a game room. A whopping 180 sites are pull-through, which, located as they are on a slope, is a very good thing for drivers like me who remain back-up impaired. There's an RV dealership and service center on-site, a bit handy in this remote area. I have fond memories of this place, where I rendezvoused with my cousin and accoutrements. She came loaded with a vintage Winnebago and a little dog. The plan was to camp at the state park, but my cousin got stopped by the rangers at the then-pet-prohibited park. So I whiled away some hours here, and it was quite pleasant.

RV sites, facilities: There are 244 sites with full hookups, cable TV, and picnic tables. Restrooms, showers, laundry facilities, a dump station, a game room, a pool, a playground, a boat ramp, boat docks, canoe rentals, and five cabins are available. An RV supplies store is on-site. Children are welcome. Leashed pets are permitted.

Reservations, fees: Reservations are recommended. Sites are $16 per night for four people, plus $2 for each additional person. Major credit cards are accepted. Long-term stays are okay.

Directions: From I-10 at Marianna, take Exit 142 heading north on State Road 71 for 1.8 miles. At U.S. 90, turn left and drive 0.2 mile west. The park is on the right, on the lake.

Contact: Arrowhead Campsites, 4820 U.S. 90 East, Marianna, FL 32446, 850/482-5583 or 800/643-9166, fax 850/482-4713, www.arrowheadcamp.com.

10 DOVE REST RV PARK

Scenic rating: 4

south of Marianna

With many pull-through sites near the highway, this lushly wooded 26-acre campground offers easy on-and-off access for even the weariest interstate traveler. It's convenient to Florida Caverns State Park, restaurants, and shopping. The park is divided into two sections: one is sunny, and the other is shaded by some of the park's 300 trees. About one-third of the park is occupied by year-round residents or permanently placed units that are for rent. A Wal-Mart is 0.5 mile away.

RV sites, facilities: All 110 pull-through RV sites have full hookups, 30- and 50-amp electrical service, cable TV, and concrete pads. There's plenty of elbow room between sites, and the biggest rigs can be accommodated. Restrooms, showers, laundry facilities, a dump station, a basketball court, a recreation hall, and horseshoe pits are on-site. Restaurants are 0.5 mile away. Children are welcome. Leashed pets are permitted.

Reservations, fees: Reservations usually are not necessary. Sites are $25 per night for two people, plus $2 for each additional person. Credit cards are not accepted. Long-term rates are available.

Directions: From I-10 at Marianna, take Exit 142 and drive south on State Road 71 for 0.5 mile.

Contact: Dove Rest RV Park, 1973 Dove Rest Drive, Marianna, FL 32448, 850/482-5313.

11 THREE RIVERS STATE PARK

Scenic rating: 9

north of Sneads

Camping here is a lakeside affair in a forest of pines and hardwood trees, but most visitors come to fish, not explore the forest. Three Rivers State Park is so named because it is located at the junction of the Chattahoochee and Flint Rivers, which merge to form the Apalachicola River, and Lake Seminole. The 683-acre park fronts two miles of shoreline on Lake Seminole, which is a popular place for catching largemouth and smallmouth bass, catfish, and bluegill. Commonly seen around the lake are alligators and alligator snapping turtles; in the woods, you may encounter white-tailed deer. A shady, two-mile-long nature trail loop winds along the lakeshore. The fishing pier is 100 feet long, so don't worry if you don't have a boat or choose not to rent one from one of the nearby marinas.

RV sites, facilities: There are 30 sites with water, 30-amp electricity, picnic tables, grills, and fire rings. Firewood is available for sale in the park; however, you are not allowed to gather your own wood. Restrooms, showers, a dump station, a boat ramp, and a fishing pier are available. Children are welcome. Leashed pets with proof of rabies vaccination are accepted.

Reservations, fees: Reservations are recommended; contact ReserveAmerica at 800/336-3521 or reserveamerica.com. Fee is $12 per night for eight people. Credit cards are accepted. The maximum stay is 14 days.

Directions: From the west side of Sneads at the junction of State Road 271 and U.S. 90, drive two miles north on State Road 271. Turn north (right) at the sign for the state park.

Contact: Three Rivers State Park, Route 1, P.O. Box 15-A, Sneads, FL 32460, 850/482-9006, www.floridastateparks.org.

12 THE OUTPOST RV PARK

Scenic rating: 2

east of Freeport

Located on Black Creek near the Choctawhatchee Bay, this small rural store has 10 sites available for anglers, hunters, and overnighters. A boat ramp makes water access easy, and bait and tackle are available at the store.

RV sites, facilities: Ten RV sites with full hookups and 50-amp service are available. There are no restrooms or showers. A store, a boat ramp, a dock, and canoe rentals are available. Children are welcome. Small leashed pets are permitted.

Reservations, fees: Reservations are recommended. Sites are $18 per night for two people, plus $2 per extra person. Credit cards are not accepted. Long-term stays are permitted.

Directions: From the intersection of State Road 331 and County Road 3280 in Freeport, drive east five miles on County Road 3280. Look for the store on the right side of the road.

Contact: The Outpost RV Park, 4576 County Road 3280 East, Freeport, FL 32439, 850/835-2779, fax 850/835-2628.

13 PINE LOG STATE FOREST

Scenic rating: 10

south of Ebro

BEST (

Grassy, wooded sites form a half circle around a five-acre swimming lake fringed with slash pines and hardwoods. If the weather is clear,

you'll see spectacular sunsets over the water. Swimming is allowed (at your own risk) in the eastern lake only; signs warn of submerged objects. You can fish on all lakes and streams in the forest, but only carry-in boats and electric motors are permitted in the two lakes near the campground. A ranger's residence is within view, which makes for a secure feeling when there are few other campers about. Pine Log is the only developed campground in the 6,911-acre state forest, one of Florida's first. Acquired in the 1930s, it was clear-cut at that time, but replanting has created an enchanting place, thick with slash, longleaf, and sand pines, as well as oak, cypress, red maple, sweet gum, juniper, and magnolia trees. Horse trails and several miles of hiking trails, including an eight-mile section of the Florida National Scenic Trail, are nearby, and the forest roads are good for mountain bikes. Although the Florida trail is open only to foot traffic, the Crooked Creek Trail welcomes mountain bikers. It's a 9-mile, single-track, figure-eight loop (you can also do just 4.5 miles) opened by the division of forestry in conjunction with the Panama City Flyers Bicycle Club. The trail is closed during the first nine days of hunting season. Call ahead or see the kiosk at the parking area located on State Road 79 for the exact dates. At other times during the hunting season, cyclists should wear fluorescent orange and use extreme caution. This campground is a bit off the beaten path, so it gets use from locals as well as tourists from Florida, Alabama, and Georgia. However, as seems to be the rule rather than the exception in Florida, the area surrounding the park is beginning to come under development.

RV sites, facilities: Twenty campsites have 50-amp electricity, water, picnic tables, grills, and fire rings. They are grassy and level, with shady spots overlooking the water. Rigs as long as 40 feet can be accommodated. Restrooms, showers, a dump station, and two lakes are on-site. Children are welcome. Leashed pets are permitted.

Reservations, fees: Reservations are not taken.

Sites are $13 per night for five people. There's a self-pay station at the campground entrance. Credit cards are not accepted. The maximum stay is 14 days within one month.

Directions: From the intersection of U.S. 20 and State Road 79 in the town of Ebro, drive south on State Road 79 for 1.3 miles. Use the second state forest entrance, marked Environmental Road, and watch for signs indicating camping. Turn west on the dirt road and travel about 0.5 mile to the campground.

Contact: Florida Division of Forestry, 715 West 15th Street, Panama City, FL 32401, 850/872-4175, fax 850/872-4879, www.fl-dof.com/stateforests/pine_log.htm. Trail information is available from the Pine Log State Forest Field Office, 5583-A Longleaf Road, Ebro, FL 32437, 850/535-2888. For hunting and fishing information, contact the Florida Fish and Wildlife Conservation Commission, 3911 Highway 2321, Panama City, FL 32409, 850/265-3677 or 800/955-8771.

14 PINE LAKE RV PARK

Scenic rating: 5

north of Fountain

Under new ownership since 2005, this 45-acre, all-ages rural park caters to anglers and countryside-lovers with its two fishing lakes: the stocked 7-acre fishing pond on the property and nearby 150-acre Compass Lake. Feed the fish and the ducks, cast a line for dinner, or watch movies on the big-screen TV in the rec hall. Music is also popular. Some pickers live on-site, and country music jamborees are held frequently. Most sites are pull-through, and the staff is proud to offer easy, safe access for any-size RV. About 25 percent of the park is occupied year-round. Visitors come from the Northern states, as well as people working locally. Favorite things to do? Fish, relax, and join in the planned activities. Park models are for sale in an adjacent area under development.

RV sites, facilities: There are 100 RV sites with full hookups and picnic tables. One site has 100-amp electricity, 30 have 50-amp, and 39 have 30-amp. Sites average 30 foot wide by 60 feet deep. An Internet connection is available in the office. Planned activities include music making, potluck dinners, exercise classes, games, movies, and fishing tournaments. Restrooms, showers, laundry facilities, a dump station, and horseshoe pits are available. Groceries, restaurants, malls, and hospitals are 14 miles away. Families are welcome, and leashed pets are permitted.

Reservations, fees: Reservations are recommended but usually not necessary. Sites are $25–30 per night for two people, plus $2 for each additional person. Credit cards are accepted. Long-term rates are available.

Directions: From I-10 west of Marianna, take Exit 130 onto U.S. 231. Drive south for 15 miles. The park is just south of the intersection with State Road 167 on the east side of the road.

Contact: Pine Lake RV Park, 21036 U.S. 231, Fountain, FL 32438, 850/722-1401, fax 850/722-1403, www.pinelakerv.com.

15 GRAYTON BEACH STATE PARK

Scenic rating: 10

east of Destin

BEST (

Set on a stretch of coastline with spectacular beaches, this park is a notch above the rest. The beach here is on a peninsula ringed with marshes and the emerald waters of the Gulf of Mexico, and is protected by barrier dunes covered with sea oats. The sand is so white that it resembles snow. Use lots of sunscreen at the swimming beach because the white sand reflects ultraviolet rays and increases the chance of sunburn. Saltwater and ocean breezes have fashioned the trees into bonsailike shapes; you may see mature sand pines that resemble bushes. The intimate little campground is slipped into a pine scrub woods near a lake. Both freshwater and saltwater fishing are possible, and the boat ramp is in protected waters on Western Lake. Buy supplies before you arrive; there's not much around here except for Seaside, a planned resort community famed for its architecture. Just two miles east of the state park, Seaside's new Victorian-style buildings are often photographed for magazine advertisements or used as movie backdrops. They're a bit Disneyesque in their perfection.

RV sites, facilities: There are 37 gravel sites with water, 30-amp electricity, picnic tables, fire rings, and grills. Lots vary in size, and a few are waterfront. Some sites accommodate rigs up to 40 feet long and slide-outs. You can also use a satellite dish at some of the sunnier sites that are not blocked by trees. Restrooms, showers, a dump station, and a boat ramp are available. Canoes are for rent, as are cabins. There's also a boat ramp for small boats entering a lake. Rangers give nature talks in the summer months (remember, in the Panhandle, the tourist season is more summer-oriented than in southern parts of Florida). The bathhouse is wheelchair accessible. Groceries are five miles away, and restaurants are within one mile. Malls and hospitals are 20 and 10 miles away, respectively. Children are welcome. Pets are prohibited.

Reservations, fees: Reservations are recommended; contact ReserveAmerica at 800/336-3521 or reserveamerica.com. Sites are $19 per night for eight people. Credit cards are accepted. The maximum stay is 14 days.

Directions: From I-10 at De Funiak Springs, take Exit 85 and go south on U.S. 331 for 26 miles. At U.S. 98, turn left and drive two miles east to County Road 283. Turn south and drive three miles. At County Road 30-A, turn eastbound and go 0.5 mile to the park.

Contact: Grayton Beach State Park, 357 Main Park Road, Santa Rosa Beach, FL 32549, 850/231-4210, www.floridastateparks.org.

16 PEACH CREEK RV PARK

Scenic rating: 6

east of Destin

Set in a wooded area, the park is located on Peach Creek with access to the Choctawhatchee Bay and River and is only two miles from Eden State Park. Grayton Beach State Park is just five miles away.

RV sites, facilities: There are 14 full-hookup RV sites, with half available for overnighters. All have 50-amp service and picnic tables. Restrooms, showers, a dump station, laundry facilities, and telephone service are available. On the premises are a boat ramp, a campground store, propane sales, canoe and boat rentals, a dog-walk area, and a nature trail. Most areas are wheelchair accessible. Children are welcome. Leashed pets are permitted.

Reservations, fees: Reservations are recommended. Sites are $20 per night for two people. Credit cards are accepted. Long-term stays are okay.

Directions: From the intersection of U.S. 98 and Highway 331, drive east four miles. The campground is located one mile east of the intersection with County Road 395.

Contact: Peach Creek RV Park, 4401 Highway 98 East, Santa Rosa Beach, FL 32459, 850/231-1948.

17 PINEGLEN MOTORCOACH AND RV PARK

Scenic rating: 9

in Panama City Beach

Nicely secluded from the hurly-burly atmosphere of the beachfront, this modern but nature-blessed park boasts a covered gazebo for picnics along one of the three stocked fishing lakes. Tall pines shade the campground, which is close to the beaches, amusement parks, shopping, and restaurants. Families, take note: Children ages 11–17 are not welcome.

RV sites, facilities: This park offers 60 RV sites with full hookups or water and 30-amp electricity, picnic tables, grills, and cable TV. Sixteen sites are pull-through, and 30 have 50-amp service. Restrooms, showers, a dump station, laundry facilities, and telephone service are available. On the premises are a screened-in pool, a clubhouse, a dog-walk area, and three stocked fishing lakes. The bathhouses, laundry room, and pool area are wheelchair accessible. Children are welcome. Leashed pets are permitted.

Reservations, fees: Reservations are recommended. Sites are $29–39 per night for a family of two adults and four children up to age 10, plus $2 per extra adult. Children ages 11–17 are not permitted. Major credit cards are accepted. Long-term (up to six months) or seasonal stays are allowed.

Directions: From U.S. 98 at the intersection of State Road 79, drive east on U.S. 98 about four miles. The park is on the north side across from a large furniture store.

Contact: Pineglen Motorcoach and RV Park, 11930 Panama City Parkway, Panama City Beach, FL 32407, 850/230-8535, fax 850/230-2554, www.pineglenpark.com.

18 EMERALD COAST RV BEACH RESORT

Scenic rating: 10

west of Panama City Beach

Manicured to near perfection, this updated and modernized big-rig resort caters to families and snowbirds who want a beachside destination vacation near shopping and entertainment. Palms and pines cast shade over the paved roads and sites. The managers describe it as "upscale," and the park has won awards for its cleanliness and neatness. All campsites are lighted. Even the restrooms are heated or air-conditioned. About 10 percent of the lots are occupied by full-time residents. Management plans more improvements in the coming years, including premium "fire and water" sites on the lakefront, a pavilion, a basketball court, a spa, and a sauna. From May through September, the park provides free shuttle service to the beach.

RV sites, facilities: There are 138 full-hookup RV sites with 50-amp electrical service, concrete pads, picnic tables, and cable TV. All sites have wireless Internet access, though you can also go to the office to connect. Thirty-three sites are drive-through. Sites are paved and level, ranging in size from 20 by 39 feet to 20 by 111 feet. Big rigs and slide-outs are welcome. Sites 52–73 are closest to the pool, putting green, and clubhouse. Restrooms, showers, laundry facilities, and telephone service are available. On the premises are a heated pool, a turtle pond, a nature path, a clubhouse, horseshoe pits, shuffleboard courts, three dog-walk areas, a store (selling ice propane, snacks, souvenirs, and camping supplies), miniature golf, paddleboat rentals, and park model rentals. Movies, pancakes, cookouts, bingo, cards, arts and crafts, and local tours provide entertainment. Malls are within three miles. The clubhouse, office, store, pool area and paved streets are wheelchair accessible. Children are welcome. Leashed pets are permitted, but not German shepherds, Doberman pinschers, rottweilers, or pit bulls.

Reservations, fees: Reservations are recommended. Sites are $39–95 per night for two people, plus $3 per extra person and $2 for cable TV. The rate varies according to the season and whether the site is back-in or pull-through. Credit cards are accepted. Long-term rates are available.

Directions: From I-10, take Exit 17 southbound on State Road 79 about 35 miles to the junction with U.S. 98. At U.S. 98, go east 6.6 miles. Turn right on Allison Avenue (Exit A) and drive one block to the park. From Panama City at the bridge, head west on Alternate 98 for 1.5 miles and follow the directions above.

Contact: Emerald Coast RV Beach Resort, 1957 Allison Avenue, Panama City Beach FL

32407, 850/235-0924 or 800/232-2478, fax 850/235-9609, www.rvresort.com.

19 RACCOON RIVER CAMP RESORT

Scenic rating: 5

in Panama City Beach

Set centrally near the beach, this clean RV park backs onto a pretty lake. This is a not a mobile-home park; only 1 percent of the sites are occupied by year-round residents. It's favored by families and seasonal, repeat visitors from 48 states. From September through February, you'll find bingo, potlucks, cookouts, and horseshoe tournaments, but year-round entertainment can be had at a nearby water park, "goofy golf," the beach, and many festivals. Note: This area has seen a lot of condominium development in recent years.

RV sites, facilities: There are 135 full-hookup RV sites with 30-amp electricity and 5 sites with 50-amp. Forty-four sites are drive-through. All have picnic tables, cable TV, and concrete pads. Rigs up to 45 feet long and slide-outs can be accommodated. The grassy, level lots vary in size, with a mix of sunny and shady views. Restrooms, showers, laundry facilities, and telephone service are available. Internet access is available in the office. On the premises are two heated pools, a fenced-in playground, a clubhouse, a store, and a recreation hall. Ice, camping supplies, snacks, and souvenirs are available in the store; groceries and restaurants are within 0.5 mile. The bathhouse, clubhouse, office, store, and pool area are wheelchair accessible, and the streets are paved. Children are welcome. Leashed pets under 20 pounds are permitted.

Reservations, fees: Reservations are recommended. Sites are $35–45 per night for two people, plus $5 per extra person. Major credit cards are accepted. The maximum stay is six months. Long-term rates are available.

Directions: From Panama City Beach at the bridge over St. Andrews Bay, head west on U.S. 98A for about one mile. Turn right at County Road 392A/Hutchison Boulevard and continue west about 0.5 mile to the park on your left.

Contact: Raccoon River Camp Resort, 12209 Hutchison Boulevard, Panama City Beach, FL 32407, 850/234-0181, fax 850/234-1090.

20 CAMPER'S INN

Scenic rating: 4

in Panama City Beach

Set in the most commercial part of Panama City Beach, this park is across the street and about a block's walk from beaches and the Gulf of Mexico, although there's not much of a view. T-shirt and souvenir shops, amusement parks, bumper cars, a dog track, bars, and strip clubs are the milieu, as well as the condominium developments cropping up all around. But there's plenty to do without leaving the campground, from playing ball to swimming in the two pools. Small children and nonswimmers must be supervised in the pool areas. Camping supplies, gifts, toys, groceries, and rental bikes are available. About 10 percent of the park is occupied year-round, and there is an adjacent mobile-home section. It's a popular spot for families, seasonal visitors, anglers, and working people.

RV sites, facilities: Grassy and paved sites with concrete patios and picnic tables are available for 115 RVs in this 240-space mobile-home and RV park. All have 30/50-amp electrical service, full hookups, and wireless Internet access. Seventeen lots are pull-through. The sunny sites allow for satellite dish setup, and they vary in size from 30 to 50 feet wide and 40 to 80 feet long. Cable TV, restrooms, showers, picnic tables, laundry facilities, and a dump station are available. Also on-site are two pools, a recreation hall, a playground, a volleyball area, basketball and shuffleboard courts, several stores, cabins for rent, propane, a fishing guide, and a gasoline station. Planned activities include potluck dinners, karaoke, dances, cards, and bingo. Streets are paved, and the bathhouse, clubhouse, office, store, and pool area are wheelchair accessible. Groceries, restaurants, and shopping are within one mile. Children are welcome. Leashed pets are permitted.

Reservations, fees: Reservations are recommended. Sites are $18–50 per night for two people, plus $5 for each additional person over the age of 12 and $3 for cable TV. Credit cards are accepted. Long-term rates are available. The maximum length of stay is six months.

Directions: From the intersection of U.S. 98 and County Road 3033/Beckrich Road in Panama City Beach, drive south on County Road 3033. Turn east on County Road 392 and drive 0.7 mile. Continue for two miles on Thomas Drive to the park.

Contact: Camper's Inn, 8800 Thomas Drive, Panama City Beach, FL 32408, 850/234-5731 or 866/872-2267, http://pcbchcampersinn.com.

21 PANAMA CITY BEACH RV RESORT

Scenic rating: 9

in Panama City Beach

Located just outside St. Andrews State Park, this is a deluxe way to be near that park's marvelous beaches. The park caters to motor coaches, fifth wheels, and other big rigs. Three condo apartments are for rent above the park office. Only modern RVs at least 22 feet long and less than 10 years old are accepted; there is no space for pop-ups, hybrid travel trailers, truck campers, or converted horse trailers. The park is popular with families, seasonal visitors, and over-age-55 tourists from Florida, Georgia, Alabama, and Tennessee. What do they come for? The beach.

RV sites, facilities: There are 69 large, paved, full-hookup RV sites with professional landscaping to accommodate even the biggest vehicles. All sites have 30/50-amp electrical service, cable TV, and concrete patios. With lots ranging in size from 30 by 60 feet (back-in) to 30 by 80 feet (pull-through), there's plenty of room for slide-outs and rigs up to 45 feet long. Instead of concrete walkways, all driveways and paths are covered with pretty paver blocks. Palms, magnolias, wax myrtles, and oaks have been planted, and the lighting is designed to accent the greenery.

Restrooms, showers, laundry facilities, and telephone service are available. On the premises are a heated pool, an exercise room, a recreation hall, snacks, walking paths, beach access, and three luxury condo rental units. Lots are for sale. Groceries and restaurants are within two miles. All areas are wheelchair accessible. Children are welcome. Leashed pets are permitted.

Reservations, fees: Reservations are recommended. Sites are $50–70 per night for two people and four children under age 16. Each additional adult is charged $10. The maximum number of people per site is six. Prices are subject to change. Credit cards are accepted. Long-term rates are available.

Directions: From the intersection of U.S. 98 and County Road 3033/Beckrich Road in Panama City Beach, drive south on County Road 3033. Turn east on County Road 392 and drive 0.7 mile. Continue for 2.5 miles on Thomas Drive to the park.

Contact: Panama City Beach RV Resort, 4702 Thomas Drive, Panama City Beach, FL 32408, 866/637-3529, www.panamacityrvresort.com.

22 ST. ANDREWS STATE PARK

Scenic rating: 10

east of Panama City Beach

BEST (

Famed internationally for its clear waters and blinding white-sand beaches, this 1,260-acre state park gets hard use from tourists and locals, especially during the summer. Camping is split between the Pine Grove and Lagoon Campgrounds; both overlook Grand Lagoon, a narrow body of water separating the park from the rest of the barrier island. Some sites are directly on the water, and slash pines offer shade. The best swimming is on the gulf side of the park, where big rolling sand dunes separate the road from the beach. You can snorkel there or in a protected pool behind a rock jetty. Fishing is from the jetty, the beach, two piers, or by boat; among the fish caught here are dolphin, bluefish, flounder, Spanish mackerel, sea trout, redfish, and bonito.

Two short nature trails give hikers an opportunity to see alligators and birds in a salt marsh. Also in the park is a turpentine still that shows how early settlers derived the solvent from pine trees, a practice that became a major industry at the turn of the 20th century. World War II–era circular cannon platforms still stand in the park, which was used as a military reservation at the time. Across from the park is Shell Island, which is reachable by park shuttle in spring and summer or by boat year-round; it's a 700-acre oasis that remains almost untouched by development. Unfortunately, this park is so close to major tourist areas and the urban area that it can get crowded.

RV sites, facilities: There are 176 sites with water, electricity, picnic tables, and grills. Restrooms, showers, a dump station, two fishing piers, a boat ramp, a store, picnic areas, and swimming beaches are available. Children are welcome, but pets are not allowed.

Reservations, fees: Reservations are recommended; contact ReserveAmerica at 800/336-3521 or reserveamerica.com. From October 1 through February 28, sites are $10 per night for four people, plus $2 for electricity and $2 for a waterfront location. From March 1 through September 30, sites are $17 per night, plus the extra charges mentioned. Major credit cards are accepted. The maximum stay is 14 days.

Directions: From the intersection of U.S. 98 and County Road 3031/Thomas Drive in Panama City Beach, turn south on County Road 3031. Drive five miles to the dead end at the beach and turn left. The park entrance is just ahead.

Contact: St. Andrews State Park, 4415 Thomas Drive, Panama City, FL 32408, 850/233-5140.

23 SCOTTS FERRY GENERAL STORE AND CAMPGROUND

Scenic rating: 5

south of Blountstown

Nearly hidden under the highway bridge over the Chipola River, this canoeing-oriented campground is slipped into a hardwood forest sloping down to a little boat dock. It's a shady spot with an open-air pavilion, but you may hear road noise from the bridge. The campground rents canoes and has a boat launch; the affiliated store sells hunting and camping supplies, bait, and gasoline. For a fee, you can rent covered picnic tables, some of which are large enough to accommodate a group.

RV sites, facilities: The 25 campsites have water, 50-amp electric hookups, and picnic tables. Restrooms, showers, a boat ramp, a pavilion, rental cabins, and a store are on-site. The store sells bait and tackle, groceries, hardware, ice, and gasoline. Children are welcome. Leashed pets are permitted.

Reservations, fees: Reservations are not necessary. Sites are $18 per night. Credit cards are accepted. Long-term stays are okay.

Directions: From Blountstown, drive south on State Road 71 for 11 miles. The park is on the west (right) side of the road, just before you cross the bridge.

Contact: Scotts Ferry General Store and Campground, 6648 State Route 715, Blountstown, FL 32424, 850/674-2900.

24 PARKER FARM CAMPGROUND

Scenic rating: 1

on the northwest side of Wewahitchka

Little more than an open, grassy field in the countryside, this no-frills campground is located next to the North Florida Motor Speedway, which claims to be the fastest dirt track in the nation. It also adjoins a field for flying remote-control airplanes. An air show is held the second week of October. Restaurants and groceries are available within one mile. About one-third of the park is occupied by full-time residents. The park also draws hunters and anglers because of its proximity to the Chipola and Apalachicola Rivers.

RV sites, facilities: All 16 grassy, sunny sites have full hookups, 30-amp electrical service, and 2 of the sites have optional telephone service. Big rigs and slide-outs are welcome. A dump station can be used for a $2 fee. There are no showers or restrooms. Alcoholic beverages are prohibited. Children are welcome. Leashed pets are permitted, but they must be kept inside your rig. The owner says that all areas of the park are wheelchair accessible.

Reservations, fees: Reservations are not necessary except during special events. Sites are $14 per night. Credit cards are not accepted. Long-term stays are okay.

Directions: From the junction of State Roads 71 and 22 in Wewahitchka, drive west on State Road 22 for 0.3 mile. Turn north on County Road 22A and drive three miles to the park.

Contact: Parker Farm Campground, 440 Parker Farm Road, Wewahitchka, FL 32465, 850/639-5204.

25 DEAD LAKES PARK

Scenic rating: 9

north of Wewahitchka

This county park's eerie beauty and its name stem from the thousands of bleached tree trunks rooted in the lake water. The trees drowned when a sandbar formed in the Apalachicola River, blocking the mouth of the Chipola River and flooding 12,000 acres of swamp. Before this event, there were twin lakes that the Indians called "water eyes," or Wewahitchka, a name that was adopted by the nearby town. Two other ponds in the park were dug in 1936 and held a fish hatchery until 1951. Half a century ago, turpentine was tapped from the pines, and honey, harvested by bees from the hardwood tupelo trees, was barreled for medicinal purposes. Spanish moss that draped the trees was a commodity used for packing and furniture stuffing. Such commerce is history today, and the Dead Lakes area is primarily a recreational retreat surrounded by swamp and flat-wood forests. These vistas made the silver screen in Peter Fonda's 1997 movie, *Ulee's Gold,* a critically acclaimed drama in which Fonda played a beekeeper. The bees in this area really do produce a succulent honey called "Tupelo Gold." The park is popular with hikers, anglers, bird-watchers, and boaters.

The campsites are shaded by native longleaf pines and carpeted with wire grass. There's a hiking trail for viewing wildlife, and the boat ramp provides access to the Dead Lakes and the Chipola River. The tree trunks create an obstacle course for those in canoes and fishing boats. You can hook bass, bream, and carp in the old hatching ponds as well as in the lakes, where the drowned forest makes casting a real challenge.

RV sites, facilities: There are 22 sites for RVs up to 50 feet long, all of which have water and electricity. Each site has a picnic table, a grill, and a fire pit. Facilities include restrooms, showers, a dump station, and a boat ramp. Children are welcome. Pets are allowed with proof of vaccination.

Reservations, fees: Reservations are not necessary. Sites cost $10 per night for four people, plus $2 per extra person, $2 for electricity, and $2 for pets. The maximum length of stay is 14 days.

Directions: From Port St. Joe, take State Road 71 north for 24 miles to Wewahitchka. Drive one mile north of town and turn east on Gary Rowell Road. Continue 0.5 mile to the park. From Panama City, take State Road 22 east for 25 miles to State Road 71 and turn north. Go one mile to Gary Rowell Road, turn east, and proceed to the park.

Contact: For information about Dead Lakes Park, contact Paula Ramsey Pickett of the Gulf County Tourism Development Council at 850/229-7800, email: info@VisitGulf.com. The park is located at 510 Gary Rowell Road, Wewahitchka.

26 EL GOVERNOR RV CAMPGROUND

Scenic rating: 2

in Mexico Beach

Set in the center of Mexico Beach, a family-oriented community of vacation homes and waterfront motels on the Gulf of Mexico, this RV park has a small creek and a good location across the street from the water. Don't expect much shade, greenery, or water views, which are blocked by the motels. Charter boat services, fishing guides, and boat storage and dockage are available in town. There is a similar campground in the area: Rustic Sands Resort, on 15th Street north of U.S. 98.

RV sites, facilities: This campground has 59 RV sites (10 pull-through) with sewer hookups, 30-amp electrical service, and cable TV. Restrooms, showers, picnic tables, laundry facilities, and a dump station are on-site. Children and leashed pets are permitted.

Reservations, fees: Reservations are recommended. Sites are $31 per night for four people, plus $2 for each additional person. Credit cards are not accepted. Stays up to six months are allowed.

Directions: Drive through Mexico Beach on U.S. 98. The park is in the middle of town at the corner of 17th Street, across from the big El Governor Motel.

Contact: El Governor RV Campground, 1700 Highway 98, Mexico Beach, FL 32410, 850/648-5432.

27 T. H. STONE MEMORIAL ST. JOSEPH PENINSULA STATE PARK

Scenic rating: 10

near Port St. Joe

BEST (

Surrounded by water on three sides, this secluded, woodsy state park boasts one of the best beaches in Florida, with broad expanses of sugar-white sand, dunes studded with sea oats and struggling grasses, and trees twisted by the wind. Year after year, "Dr. Beach," a university professor who rates these things, has named this America's No. 1 beach. You can swim in either the Gulf of Mexico or St. Joseph Bay. The water is clear enough for snorkeling; be sure to use a dive flag. On the bay side, you may see bay scallops, octopus, and three types of crabs (hermit, fiddler, and horseshoe). Canoes are available for rent.

When you can tear yourself away from the water, try hiking on nine miles of heavily forested trails. Bike riders will find paved roads with little traffic inside and outside the park. Here's a tip: Buy groceries in Port St. Joe, 22 miles away, and bring wood along for a campfire; supplies in the community of vacation homes on the peninsula are limited. Sprawling over 2,516 acres, the park dominates the northern tip of the peninsula, which has seen little development since the Army used it for training during World War II. More than 200 species of birds have been seen here. In fall, campers may see hawks heading south or monarch butterflies flying to their winter home in Mexico. There's plenty of other wildlife; even a black bear has been spotted—look in the campground office for a photo of the creature.

RV sites, facilities: The state park has two campground loops: Gulf Breeze, which has larger sites for big rigs, and Shady Pines, which is wooded and more secluded. There are a total of 119 campsites with 30-amp electrical service and 15 with 50-amp. Two sites are drive-through. Rigs up to 38 feet and slide-outs can be accommodated. Each site has water, a picnic table, a grill, and a fire ring. On the premises are restrooms, showers, a dump station, a boat ramp and basin, docks, beaches, a playground, and rental cabins. All areas are wheelchair accessible. Children are welcome. Pets are not allowed except for guide dogs.

Reservations, fees: Reservations are recommended; contact ReserveAmerica at 800/336-3521 or reserveamerica.com. Sites are $22 per night for eight people. Credit cards are accepted. The maximum stay is 14 days.

Directions: From Port St. Joe, travel east on U.S. 98 to State Road 30. At the fork, veer right and proceed south on State Road C-30 for six miles, then turn right onto State Road 30-E and drive eight miles west to the park.

Contact: T. H. Stone Memorial St. Joseph Peninsula State Park, 8899 Cape San Blas Road, Port St. Joe, FL 32456, 850/227-1327, fax 850/227-1488, www.floridastateparks.org.

28 PRESNELL'S BAYSIDE MARINA AND RV RESORT

Scenic rating: 8

south of Port St. Joe

All sites in this 7.5-acre boating-oriented campground are on the waterfront, with sweeping views of St. Joseph Bay and St. Joseph Peninsula. Fishing guides, boat rentals, and charter services are available at the marina. You can swim in the bay, but the clear water is shallow and there's no real beach—just grass flats frequented by wading birds. An 18-hole golf course is located 0.25 mile away.

In the 1830s, this stretch of coastal highway was the most populous—and notorious—burg in all of Florida: the city of St. Joseph, population 12,000, is where the state's first constitution was penned. St. Joseph had a racetrack, nice hotels, bawdy houses, and a reputation as the "wickedest city in the Southeast." When a railroad linked it to the Apalachicola River, St. Joseph boomed, thanks to King Cotton. Its harbor was described as "a forest of spars and masts" because it was cluttered with ships transporting 150,000 bales of cotton a year. A catastrophe killed the townspeople of St. Joseph in 1841, when a South American sailing ship arrived with yellow fever in its hold. Within a few weeks, St. Joseph was a ghost town. Three years later, a hurricane-generated tidal wave washed away what was left.

After a century, commerce was resurrected thanks to a Savannah scientist named Dr. Charles H. Herty, who invented a cheap way to make newsprint, paper sacks, and corrugated boxes from the slash pine trees that grow like weeds in northwest Florida. U.S. 98 was lined with trailers and shacks sheltering laborers who built the first paper plant at Port St. Joe. The paper mill has closed, which is bad news for mill workers yet good news for campers. The pungent aroma that sometimes wafted through campsites on St. Joseph Bay was the perfume of wood-pulp brew—the smell of money.

RV sites, facilities: All 24 RV sites have water and electricity. On the premises are restrooms, showers, a boat ramp, a limited store, rental trailers, bait and tackle, boat rentals, and a small play area. Children are welcome. Leashed pets are permitted.

Reservations, fees: Reservations are required in July and August and recommended the rest of the year. Sites are $17–22 per night for four people, plus $2 for each additional person. Credit cards are accepted. Long-term stays are okay.

Directions: From Port St. Joe, drive one mile east on U.S. 98 to County Road 30-A. At the fork, veer right and proceed south on County Road 30-A (a.k.a. C30-A) for 2.1 miles to the park.

Contact: Presnell's Bayside Marina and RV Resort, 2115 County Road 30-A, Port St. Joe, FL 32456, 850/229-2710, www.presnells.com.

TALLAHASSEE

COURTESY OF VISIT FLORIDA

BEST RV PARKS AND CAMPGROUNDS

◖ Biking
Kelly's RV Park, page 103
Pine Creek Landing, page 105

◖ Most Unusual
Torreya State Park, page 91

Blessed with college-town charm and stately government buildings, Tallahassee is the state capital and home to Florida State University, famed for its football team the mighty Seminoles. But Tallahassee also plays center billing as one of Florida's most interesting regions for RVers.

It's the largest city in a widely diverse area that encompasses beachside haunts and fishing villages along the Gulf of Mexico, the sprawling Apalachicola National Forest, dozens of fishing lakes, the marshy Big Bend area, sparkling natural springs, and the mouth of the fabled Suwannee River. Mostly rural, and mostly undeveloped, many of Florida's finest natural attractions are here: bicycle trails, freshwater fishing, game-filled forests, and rivers beckoning canoeists and kayakers. Except for football weekends, Tallahassee remains largely undiscovered by the average Florida visitor. It's also supremely RV-friendly, with dozens of parks ranging from rustic to more-developed sites with heated swimming pools.

Scenic Highway U.S. 98 hugs the Gulf Coast near Apalachicola, famous for seafood, especially its oysters – don't pass through without slurping down a few. The teeming fish life and natural harbor is what drew Spanish explorer Hernando de Soto, who established a base of operations for a disastrous expedition from the Apalachicola River to Georgia, Alabama, and the Mississippi River, where de Soto, starving and sick, died. Apalachicola's next footnote in history came some 300 years later with the arrival of John Gorrie, a physician with a chilling legacy: He's credited with inventing air-conditioning. Near Apalachicola, St. George Island and Cape St. George are renowned for their award-winning white-sand beaches. The tourist season is generally reversed here, with most visitors coming during the summer months rather than in winter.

South of Tallahassee, RVers will enjoy visiting the Edward Ball Wakulla Springs State Park, which has one of the largest and deepest springs in the world. It's only one of dozens of springs dotted throughout the region, however; there are more springs near the towns of Madison and Mayo.

Crisscrossed by forest roads, the Apalachicola National Forest east of Tallahassee is an ideal place to spend a lazy weekend. Though popular with hunters, the hunting season is limited to only a few weeks in fall and winter. Nearby is the Natural Bridge State Historic Site, where a five-day battle raged in the final weeks of the Civil War.

Chattahoochee, in the northwest corner of the region, is the access point for Lake Seminole. The 37,500-acre reservoir is popular for boating, fishing, waterskiing, and swimming. Anglers may hook lunker, largemouth, scrappy hybrid, striped, and white bass, or catfish, crappie, and bream. Canada geese spend winter in the area.

The eastern edge of the region is bounded by the intriguing Suwannee River, which flows south to the Gulf of Mexico. All along the river, there are places to launch a canoe and paddle along white-sand bluffs under a thick wooden canopy of stately oak trees hung with Spanish moss.

© AVALON TRAVEL PUBLISHING, IN

1 EAST BANK CAMPGROUND, LAKE SEMINOLE

Scenic rating: 8

on Lake Seminole north of Chattahoochee

This park is actually in Georgia, but the easiest way to get to it is from Chattahoochee, Florida, and its boundary is only a couple of blocks north of the Sunshine State. An engineer's eye for detail is evident; each neatly kept campsite even has a special metal post for hanging camp lanterns, and one site (number 9) was designed for campers in wheelchairs. Sites are laid out in several pods on a gentle slope overlooking Lake Seminole, a 37,500-acre reservoir formed by damming the confluence of the Chattahoochee and Flint Rivers upstream of the Jim Woodruff Lock and Dam. Boating, fishing, waterskiing, and swimming are the things to do here. Anglers may hook lunker, largemouth, scrappy hybrid, striped, and white bass, or catfish, crappie, and bream. Canada geese spending winter in the area paddle around the edge of the lake near the campground.

RV sites, facilities: There are 68 gravel sites for RVs in this U.S. Army Corps of Engineers campground on Lake Seminole. Forty-one sites have 50-amp electrical service; the rest have 30-amp. Five sites are drive-through, and some are waterfront. Big rigs and slide-outs can be accommodated. An Internet connection, picnic tables, grills, fire rings, restrooms, showers, a dump station, laundry facilities, a boat ramp, shuffleboard, and horseshoe pits are on the grounds. The bathhouse and office are wheelchair accessible. Streets are paved. Children are welcome. Leashed pets are permitted.

Reservations, fees: Reserve your spot at least four days in advance of your arrival at 877/444-6777 or www.reserveusa.com. Rangers say, however, that there are almost always spots available, so reservations are not strictly necessary. Sites are $12–16 per night for up to eight people. Credit cards are accepted by the reservation system. The maximum stay is two weeks, although you may request a two-week extension.

Directions: In Chattahoochee, from the junction of U.S. 90 and State Road 269, drive four blocks west on U.S. 90 to Bolivar Street and look for the campground sign. Drive north on Bolivar Street for 1.4 miles to the campground entrance.

Contact: U.S. Army Corps of Engineers, Resource Management Office, Lake Seminole, P.O. Box 96, 2382 Booster Club Road, Chattahoochee, FL 32324, 229/662-2001. The campground phone number is 229/662-9273, www.sam.usace.army.mil.

2 TORREYA STATE PARK

Scenic rating: 10

north of Bristol

BEST (

Hiking is the favorite activity here. Perched atop 150-foot bluffs above the Apalachicola River, Torreya (pronounced "tory-ah") State Park is unique in Florida. In addition to the unusual terrain of deep ravines and hills, the park is noteworthy in that it supports trees and plants normally seen in Georgia's Appalachian Mountains. Wildlife and birds are plentiful, and at summer's end, the hardwood forest puts on a brilliant autumnal display. It's also one of just a few places in the world where the rare Torreya tree grows. Once common across the river bluffs, the Torreya is nearly extinct today because it is prone to at least 30 pathogens that attack just before it goes to seed. Only a few trees are left.

Also in the park is the Gregory House, an 1849 plantation home originally built across the river. (You can see a few specimens of the Torreya tree on either side of the entryway to the house.) The Civilian Conservation Corps, which built the park in the 1930s, moved the house—a feat that will boggle your mind. They dismantled the building, floated it across the river, and rebuilt it here. Earlier in history, the river bluffs were home to a Civil War gun battery, and archaeologists have found evidence of many Indian settlements.

The main campground is on top of one of the bluffs, and a few sites have sweeping views of the valleys beyond. Several short trails lead down to wooded ravines, good spots for exploring and picking up dead branches for your campfire. Take only fallen and dead limbs from the ground.

Torreya State Park is a great place to limber up for hiking in more hilly terrain out of state. Break in those boots on 15 miles of trails; Florida flatlanders will be startled by how steep those slopes are. Hike for 45 minutes or make a day out of it.

RV sites, facilities: There are 30 sites, half with 30-amp electricity and half with 50-amp. Each site has a picnic table, a grill, and a fire ring. Rigs up to 40 feet long can be accommodated. Park facilities include restrooms, showers, a dump station, hiking trails, and a museum. You can also rent a yurt (a type of circular tent), which has air-conditioning and heating. It sleeps five people. The bathhouse and picnic area are wheelchair accessible. Children are welcome. Pets are prohibited.

Reservations, fees: Reservations are recommended; contact ReserveAmerica at 800/336-3521 or reserveamerica.com. Sites are $12 per night for up to eight people. Credit cards are accepted. The maximum stay is 14 days.

Directions: From I-10 west of Quincy, take Exit 174 and head west on State Road 12 for about 11 miles. At County Road 1641, turn north and drive seven miles to the park. Or, from U.S. 20 in Bristol, drive north on State Road 12 for eight miles, turn left on County Road 1641, and drive seven miles west to the park. The route is well marked, with signs pointing the way.

Contact: Torreya State Park, 2576 Northwest Torreya Park Road, Bristol, FL 32321, 850/643-2674, www.floridastateparks.org.

3 CHATTAHOOCHEE/ TALLAHASSEE WEST KOA

Scenic rating: 6

off I-10 south of Chattahoochee

Convenient for overnight travelers and just 35 miles west of Florida State University's football stadium, this KOA also could become a base camp for exploring nearby attractions in Chattahoochee, such as Lake Seminole. Three Spanish missions were built here in the 1600s, and Native Americans were present as far back as 1450. Andrew Jackson was in command at a federal arsenal here during the Indian wars. That fortification later became a prison, then a mental institution. The Florida State Hospital is still a major employer. East of here is the town of Havana, Florida, which has antiques shops that draw hundreds of tourists every weekend. Note that the campground pool is open April 1–October 1. Firewood is offered free.

RV sites, facilities: There are 46 RV sites with water and 30-amp or 50-amp electric hookups, picnic tables, and grills. Drive-through sites are as long as 75 feet. A modem is available for dial-up Internet access. Restrooms, showers, laundry facilities, a dump station, a convenience store, a pool, a playground, a horseshoe pitch area, and cabins are available. The main building, pavilion, and restrooms (except showers) are wheelchair accessible. Children are welcome. Leashed pets are permitted.

Reservations, fees: Reservations are recommended. Sites are $23–29 per night for two people, plus $2 for each additional child or $3 per adult, and $3 for electricity. Credit cards are accepted. Long-term rates are available.

Directions: From I-10 at Chattahoochee, take Exit 166 southbound on County Road 270A and drive one mile to the park entrance on the east side of the road.

Contact: Chattahoochee/Tallahassee West KOA, 2309 Flat Creek Road, Chattahoochee, FL 32324, 850/442-6657 or 800/KOA-2153 (800/562-2153), www.koa.com.

❹ WHIPPOORWILL SPORTSMAN'S LODGE

Scenic rating: 4

on Lake Talquin south of Quincy

This tiny campground is part of a fishing- and hunting-oriented motel on Lake Talquin. Sites are shady and can accommodate rigs up to 40 feet long. Launch your fishing boat from the paved boat ramp; you can tie it up at the covered docks after your trip. Unpaved roads for exploring by bicycle surround the park. Pick up groceries in Quincy, which is 15 miles away; some limited supplies are available at the lodge. The restaurant hosts a shrimp boil every Friday night.

RV sites, facilities: There are seven RV sites with full hookups, electricity, and picnic tables. Restrooms, showers, laundry facilities, horseshoe pits, a boat ramp, boat and canoe rentals, cottage rentals, covered boat slips, a fishing pier, a convenience store, and a restaurant/waterfront pub are on-site. The fishing pier, stores, and restrooms are wheelchair accessible. Children are welcome. Leashed pets are permitted.

Reservations, fees: Reservations are recommended. Sites are $20 per night for two people, plus $5 for each additional person. Credit cards are accepted. The maximum stay is three months.

Directions: From I-10 at Quincy, take Exit 181 southbound on State Road 267 for eight miles. Turn east at Cook's Landing Road and drive three miles until the road dead-ends.

Contact: Whippoorwill Sportsman's Lodge, 3129 Cook's Landing Road, Quincy, FL 32351, 850/875-2605, fax 850/875-3345, email: fish-talquin@aol.com.

❺ PAT THOMAS PARK

Scenic rating: 7

on Lake Talquin south of Quincy

Tailored to overnight and short-term campers, this peaceful park is located on an oak-shaded hill sloping down to Lake Talquin, which surrounds it on three sides. Launch your fishing boat or canoe from the boat ramp near the campground. A full-time park ranger lives on the premises. Restaurants, supermarkets, and laundry facilities are available 10 miles north in Quincy. Bait and tackle and limited groceries can be obtained within one mile. The park is a popular daytime spot for locals all week long; they fish for the day at the piers, then go home, or hold family reunions and other gatherings in the picnic pavilion.

RV sites, facilities: This two-acre county park has 15 RV sites with full hookups and 30-amp electrical service. Lots vary in size, but big rigs can be accommodated. Three spots are drive-through. On the premises are showers, restrooms, picnic tables, grills, fishing piers, a dump station, a boat ramp, and a playground. Groceries and restaurants are five miles away. Most areas are wheelchair accessible. Children are welcome. Dogs are prohibited.

Reservations, fees: Reservations are recommended. Sites are $15 per night for two people, plus $1 extra for each additional person (small children are free). Credit cards are not accepted. The maximum stay is 14 days.

Directions: From I-10 at Quincy, take Exit 181 southbound on State Road 267 for nine miles. Turn east at the sign for Hopkins Landing and drive one mile until the road dead-ends at the park.

Contact: Pat Thomas Park, 949 Hopkins Landing Road, Quincy, FL 32351, 850/875-4544 or 850/875-8699.

❻ INGRAM'S MARINA

Scenic rating: 4

on Lake Talquin south of Quincy

If you're hooked on fishing, you'll appreciate this angler-oriented camp, which has sprawled over a hill on the edge of Lake Talquin for the past three decades. Interior roads are unpaved and uneven, but plenty of oak trees provide shade. Some boats can be docked in covered slips on a protected inlet. Bait and tackle and limited groceries are available here. It's near popular hunting areas.

RV sites, facilities: This fish camp has five RV sites available with 30-amp electricity, water, and sewer hookups. The other 50 sites are occupied by full-time residents or people who leave their trailers year-round. On the premises are showers, restrooms, cabin and boat rentals, a boat ramp, docks, groceries, bait and tackle, and laundry facilities. All areas of the park are said to be wheelchair accessible. Children are welcome. Leashed pets are permitted.

Reservations, fees: Reservations are recommended. Sites are $15 per night for two people, plus $1 for each additional person. Credit cards are accepted. Long-term stays are permitted.

Directions: From I-10 at Quincy, take Exit 181 southbound on State Road 267 for eight miles. Turn east at Cook's Landing Road and drive three miles until the road dead-ends at the park.

Contact: Ingram's Marina, 354 Lois Lane, Quincy, FL 32351, 850/627-2241.

⓮ HIGH BLUFF CAMPGROUND

Scenic rating: 8

on Lake Talquin south of Quincy

High Bluff Campground (formerly Joe Budd) is located near one of Florida's premier deer-hunting spots in the Joe Budd Wildlife Management Area, within the Lake Talquin State Forest. Hunters and anglers now tend to dominate the sole camping area—a mowed pine- and oak-dotted field on the shore of Lake Talquin. The campground was improved in recent years with the addition of vault restrooms, potable water, and 32 designated campsites. It is open year-round, not just during hunting season.

What sets Joe Budd Wildlife Management Area apart is its plentiful deer and the rolling hills

and creek bottoms that contrast with much of flat Florida. Boaters will notice less development surrounding the upper portion of 12-mile-long Lake Talquin, compared with the ample evidence of humans around the lower lake. As one of only two sizable reservoirs in Florida, 8,850-acre Lake Talquin offers rewards: largemouth and white bass, speckled perch, and bream. But watch out, or else your fishing line or boat motor—not the fish—may be what gets snagged. Dead standing trees jut hazardously from the water. The trees are remnants from when the Jackson Bluff Dam was built on the Ochlockonee River in 1927.

RV sites, facilities: A clearing by the lake with a fishing pier accommodates 32 self-contained camping units. Grills, fire rings, and picnic tables are provided. A county-run boat ramp is nearby. Children are welcome. Dogs are permitted on a leash.

Reservations, fees: Reservations are not accepted. Camping permits are not needed, but hunting requires a permit. Sites are $5 each. The maximum stay is 14 days in a 30-day period.

Directions: From I-10 west of Tallahassee, take Exit 192 and go west on U.S. 90 for 2.1 miles, then turn left at State Road 268. Travel 2.4 miles, passing Central Road and veering left onto Peters Road. After the pavement ends (in less than one mile), turn left at High Bluff Road. Continue 2.5 miles to the campground.

Contact: Lake Talquin State Forest, 856 Geddie Road, Tallahassee, FL 32304, 850/488-1871, fax 850/922-2107, www.fl-dof.com.

⓯ WILLIAM'S LANDING

Scenic rating: 6

on Lake Talquin near Tallahassee

Located four miles west of Coe's Landing (see next campground), this campground is slightly larger than that facility and has a recreation field. It's popular with large groups of picnickers. There's no dump station or electricity.

RV sites, facilities: There are 10 campsites for RVs. Drinking water is available, but there are no hookups. Facilities include restrooms, two picnic shelters, two fishing piers and boat docks, two fish-cleaning stations, and a boat ramp. Children are welcome. Leashed pets are permitted.

Reservations, fees: Reservations are not accepted. Camping is free. The maximum stay is 10 days or 30 days in a calendar year.

Directions: From Tallahassee, take State Road 263 to the intersection of State Road 20, then follow State Road 20 west for 11 miles. The park is at 951 William's Landing Road on the north side of the road, on Lake Talquin.

Contact: Leon County Parks and Recreation Department, 2280 Miccosukee Road, Tallahassee, FL 32308, 850/606-1470, fax 850/606-1471, www.co.leon.fl.us/parks/camping.asp.

9 COE'S LANDING

Scenic rating: 7

on Lake Talquin near Tallahassee

This is one of two RV campgrounds operated by Leon County along Lake Talquin, a haven for anglers just north of Apalachicola National Forest. (It's the only county park that accepts reservations, and park managers brag that each campsite has been located so that everyone has a view of the lake.) Most of the lakeshore is publicly owned and open to hikers. Talquin, which covers 8,850 acres, was formed by damming the Ochlockonee River in 1927. The dam broke once, in 1957, and was rebuilt. The lake is managed by the Florida Fish and Wildlife Conservation Commission, which stocks it with largemouth and striped bass, bluegill, and crappie. Swimming is prohibited.

Nearby is the northern starting point of the Tallahassee–St. Marks Historic Railroad State Trail, a 16-mile paved route for bicycling, in-line skating, horseback riding, and hiking. The trail follows an abandoned rail bed that was used to transport timber, cotton, and passengers to the Gulf of Mexico for 140 years. It begins at a parking lot at the intersection of U.S. 319 and State Road 363, and it ends in St. Marks at the edge of the St. Marks National Wildlife Refuge in Wakulla County. For bicyclists seeking a more rigorous challenge, turn off on a spur about 1.25 miles south of the Tallahassee end to the Munson Hills Off-Road Bicycle Trail through the Apalachicola Forest.

The Munson Hills are rolling sand dunes left from the shoreline one million years ago and now are rooted with longleaf pine forest. The sometimes-muddy bike trail dips through wetland hammocks of oak, cherry, and sassafras trees that are home to gopher tortoises, salamanders, deer, and the endangered eastern indigo snake. Bicyclists have two options: the 7.5-mile Munson Hills Loop or the Tall Pine Shortcut, which cuts the loop to 4.25 miles.

RV sites, facilities: There are 17 sites for RVs with electricity and water in this four-acre park. Facilities include restrooms, showers, a dump station, two picnic shelters, two fishing piers and boat docks, a fish-cleaning station, and a boat ramp. Children are welcome. Leashed pets are permitted.

Reservations, fees: Reservations are accepted; call 850/350-9560 or 866/350-9560. Camping is $12 per night. The maximum stay is 10 days or 30 days in a calendar year.

Directions: From Tallahassee, take State Road 263 to the intersection of State Road 20, then follow State Road 20 west for seven miles. The park is at 1208 Coe Landing Road on the north side of the road.

Contact: Leon County Parks and Recreation Department, 2280 Miccosukee Road, Tallahassee, FL 32308, 850/606-1470, fax 850/606-1471, www.co.leon.fl.us/parks/camping.asp.

10 BIG OAK RV PARK

Scenic rating: 4

in Tallahassee

"Very convenient," the management says of Big Oak. Indeed, this RV park puts you just 10 minutes from the governor's mansion and the nerve center of state government. Tallahassee is dotted with RV parks for that very reason; with a part-time legislature, don't be surprised if your neighbor with the big, flashy rig is a state senator on official business or a high-powered lobbyist here to buy a few rounds at Clyde's, Tallahassee's premier political watering hole.

Like most of Tallahassee, Big Oak is shaded by large trees, and it has the feel of bygone motor courts, which were popular before the advent of motel chains. From here, it's a short hike—across a busy highway—to fastfood restaurants, a couple of supermarkets, and an ATM. Just minutes away are a major shopping mall, movie theaters, and all the cultural fare and political intrigue of the Sunshine State's capital. The city has three marked scenic routes directing motorists along canopied roads and country lanes to museums and historic sites: the Native Trail, which takes about 4 hours, and the Cotton and Quail Trails, which take 3–3.5 hours each. For information and maps, call the Tallahassee Area Convention and Visitors Bureau at 800/628-2866.

RV sites, facilities: There are 72 RV sites with full hookups, 30/50-amp electricity, and cable TV; 12 are pull-through. A wireless Internet connection is available throughout the park. On the premises are restrooms, showers, laundry facilities, shuffleboard courts, and a horseshoe pit. Children are welcome. Leashed pets are permitted.

Reservations, fees: Reservations are accepted. Sites are $25 per night for two people, plus $2 for each additional person. Credit cards are accepted. Long-term rates are available.

Directions: From I-10 in Tallahassee, take Exit 199 onto U.S. 27 and drive 2.5 miles north to the park, on the west side of the road.

Contact: Big Oak RV Park, 4024 North Monroe Street, Tallahassee, FL 32303, 850/562-4660, www.bigoakrvpark.com.

11 LAKESIDE TRAVEL PARK AND CAMPGROUND

Scenic rating: 2

in Tallahassee

A laid-back spot on the western outskirts of Tallahassee, this 10-acre campground offers a small pond and oak-shaded sites. It's located near good fishing on Lake Talquin and the campuses of Florida State University and Florida Agricultural and Mechanical University. It's also within 0.5 mile of a Wal-Mart, fast-food restaurants, and, among other businesses, a car lot. The park has a split personality; permanent guests reside in one area while overnighters sleep in another. Plenty of open sites are usually available, except on big football weekends when the Florida State Seminoles play at home against their Gainesville rivals, the University of Florida Gators. About half the sites are occupied by full-timers.

RV sites, facilities: There are 65 RV sites with full hookups and a choice of 30-amp or 50-amp electrical service; 22 are pull-through. The park has restrooms, showers, laundry facilities, a dump station, and a fishing lake. Within 0.5 mile are a grocery store and restaurants. Children and leashed pets are welcome.

Reservations, fees: Reservations are taken. Sites are $28–34 per night for two people, plus $2 per extra person. Credit cards are accepted. Long-term rates are available.

Directions: From I-10 at Tallahassee, take Exit 196 onto State Road 263 (Capital Circle) and drive 1.5 miles south to U.S. 90. Turn west and drive one mile to the park. Alternatively, take I-10 Exit 192, then go east four miles on U.S. 90 to the park, at right.

Contact: Lakeside Travel Park and Campground, 6401 West Tennessee Street, Tallahassee, FL 32304, 850/574-5998.

12 TALLAHASSEE RV PARK

Scenic rating: 4

east of Tallahassee

This park on the east side of Tallahassee has easy access to the interstate and the city. Lighted, paved interior roads and big, grassy sites are comfortable for parking even the largest RVs. The park is shaded with large pines, magnolia, and dogwood, and is neatly landscaped with flowers and shrubs. Across the street is a nine-hole golf course and driving range. Visitors come from all over for the Florida Capitol, antiques shops, football games, and fishing on the coast. About 30 percent of the park is occupied year-round.

South of the park off U.S. 319 is Apalachicola National Forest and an attraction for Civil War history buffs: the Natural Bridge State Historic Site, where a five-day battle raged in the final weeks of the war. It ended with a rebel victory when a militia of old men and boys defeated seasoned Union troops, giving Tallahassee the distinction of being the only Confederate capital never to fall into Yankee hands. To get to the site, take U.S. 319 to State Road 363 and turn south. Continue four miles to Woodville, then turn east on Natural Bridge Road and drive six miles to the park. It's a great spot for picnics and for seeing Natural Bridge, where the St. Marks River disappears into a cavern and runs underground for 150 feet before resurfacing.

RV sites, facilities: This park has 66 gravel, drive-through RV sites with electricity, sewer, water, cable TV, and picnic tables; 23 have 30-amp electrical service, and 43 have 50-amp. Big rigs are welcome, as are slide-outs. Wireless Internet service is available throughout the park, including the campsites. On the premises are restrooms, showers, a dump station, a large recreation hall, and a pool. Groceries and restaurants are within 0.25 mile. Management says all areas are wheelchair accessible. Children are welcome. Leashed pets are permitted.

Reservations, fees: Reservations are recommended. Sites are $29–32 per night. Credit cards are accepted. Long-term rates are available.

Directions: From I-10 at Tallahassee, take Exit 209A onto U.S. 90 and drive 0.5 mile west to the park.

Contact: Tallahassee RV Park, 6504 Mahan Drive, Tallahassee, FL 32308, 850/878-7641, fax 850/878-7082, www.tallahasseervpark.com.

13 A CAMPER'S WORLD

Scenic rating: 3

near Monticello off I-10

Campers on the move will appreciate the easy interstate access this five-acre park has to offer. The sites are spacious and shaded by tall pines and landscaped with flowers and shrubs. It's far enough away from the highway to cut the traffic noise a few decibels. The exit also is not as congested as exits closer to nearby Tallahassee and Lake City.

RV sites, facilities: There are 29 RV sites with full hookups (30-amp and 50-amp service) and picnic tables; most are pull-through. Big rigs and slide-outs are welcome. On the premises are restrooms, showers, laundry facilities, a dump station, a pool, a playground, and pay-phone modem hookup for laptop computers. Children are welcome. Leashed pets are permitted.

Reservations, fees: Reservations are accepted. Sites are $25–28 per night for two people, plus $2.50 per additional person. Credit cards are accepted. Long-term rates are available.

Directions: From I-10, take Exit 225 north onto U.S. 19 and drive 0.2 mile to the park entrance on the west side of the road.

Contact: A Camper's World, 397 Campground Road, Lamont, FL 32336, 850/997-3300, email: acampersworld@aol.com.

14 TALLAHASSEE EAST KOA

Scenic rating: 6

south of Monticello off I-10

This wooded campground is convenient for travelers, who are welcomed with free cookies upon arrival and continental breakfast in the morning. Parking and hooking up are no hassle because nearly all the sites are pull-through. There's plenty of space for the kids to play, a pond to toss in a fishing line, rings to build campfires, and a game room with a fireplace. About 30 percent of the park is occupied by year-round residents.

RV sites, facilities: There are 75 pull-through RV sites with water, sewer and electric hookups, 65 of which have sewer connections. About two-thirds of the campsites have 30-amp electrical service, 25 sites have 50-amp. Picnic tables and grills are provided. A wireless Internet connection is available in the clubhouse. Facilities include restrooms, showers, a laundry room, a dump station, a convenience/country crafts store, a pool, a fishing pond, a game and meeting room, a playground, and rental cabins. Firewood, ministorage, and propane are available. The pool is available from late spring through the end of fall. Children are welcome. Leashed pets are permitted.

Reservations, fees: Reservations are taken. Sites are $30–32 per night for two adults, plus $2.50 for extra adults. Credit cards are accepted. Long-term rates are available.

Directions: From I-10 near Monticello, take Exit 225 onto U.S. 19 and head south for 0.25 mile. Turn right on County Road 158B (Nash Road) and drive 2.4 miles, then turn north on County Road 259 and drive 0.25 mile to the park.

Contact: Tallahassee East KOA, Route 5, P.O. Box 5160, Monticello, FL 32344, 850/997-3890 or 800/KOA-3890 (800/562-3890), fax 850/997-1509, www.koa.com.

15 MADISON CAMPGROUND

Scenic rating: 5

near Madison

Set in a wooded area near the Suwannee River, this campground is part of the Deerwood Inn motel complex, which has a pool with a luau hut, a floodlighted miniature golf course, one tennis court, and a game room with pool tables and video games. You're likely not to be crowded by other campers, the owners say, and the park's location near the interstate makes it an ideal stopover. Nearby is historic Madison, the county seat, where pre–Civil War cotton plantations once flourished. The explorer Hernando de Soto came through here in the 1590s, and a Spanish mission called Santa Helena de Machaba was founded northwest of the town. Madison County remains a quiet agricultural community.

RV sites, facilities: This park has 80 pull-through RV sites (39 with full hookups) and 10 tent-only sites set apart from the RVs. Water and 30-amp and 50-amp electricity are available. You'll find restrooms, showers, picnic tables, grills, some fire rings, a dump station, and laundry facilities. A recreation room, a pool, a playground, a game room, a miniature golf course, a tennis court, horseshoe pits, shuffleboard courts, and a volleyball area are available. Children are welcome. Leashed pets are permitted for a $2 fee.

Reservations, fees: Reservations are not necessary, unless you need 50-amp service. Sites are $20–25 per night per site. Credit cards are accepted. Long-term rates are available.

Directions: From I-10 east of Madison, take Exit 258 and head south on State Road 53 for 0.2 mile to the park.

Contact: Madison Campground, 155 Southwest Old Saint Augustine Road, Madison, FL 32340, 850/973-2504, fax 850/973-3805.

16 YOGI BEAR JELLYSTONE CAMP RESORTS

Scenic rating: 8

near Madison

Opened in 2000, this popular campground targets overnighters and destination travelers. It's a fun place for kids with lots for them to enjoy, including a 60-foot-high circular waterslide that speeds them down to a lake surrounded by a white-sand beach. The surroundings are wooded and natural, as befits this beautiful area of Florida. Giving a new meaning to "planned activities," this park holds paintball contests and the like.

RV sites, facilities: Campers can choose from 100 RV sites with full hookups, 30/50-amp electricity, picnic tables, and grills. Sixty-five sites are pull-through. Restrooms, showers, a dump station, laundry facilities, and telephone service are available. On the premises are three lakes, a pool, a playground, a campground store, a nature trail, a snack bar, boat rentals, a clubhouse, putt-putt golf, and a dog-walk area. Most areas are wheelchair accessible. Children are welcome. Leashed pets are permitted.

Reservations, fees: Reservations are recommended. Sites are $27–32 per night for two adults and two children, plus $5 per extra person. Credit cards are accepted. Long-term rates are available.

Directions: From I-10, take Exit 258 and drive south on State Road 53 about 150 yards. Turn right on Southwest Old Saint Augustine Road. Pass the Deerwood Inn; look for the Jellystone campground signs on the left.

Contact: Yogi Bear Jellystone Camp Resorts, 1151 Southwest Old St. Augustine Road, Madison, FL 32340, 850/973-8269 or 850/973-8546, fax 850/973-4114, www.jellystoneflorida.com.

17 JENNINGS OUTDOOR RESORT

Scenic rating: 3

off the northernmost exit in Florida on I-75

Jennings is a rural park with paved sites set among some oaks, convenient to the interstate. There is a fishing pond on-site (catch-and-release; no license required), and you can take out paddleboats and canoes. Most campers spend a night or two at this 30-acre park, although some stay for months. Drive just 10 miles and you can take a dip at Madison Blue Springs State Park (see listing in this chapter), one of the superfun, supercool, refreshing places in North Florida where clear water bubbles up from the earth. You also can reach the dark, mysterious Okefenokee Swamp in one hour or so. Stephen Foster Folk Culture Center State Park is about a half hour away. The biggest town nearby is Lake City, about 40 miles to the south. Osceola National Forest near Lake City is another place to explore. But the buzz is about the roller coasters found three highway exits north at the animal-oriented theme park Wild Adventures in Valdosta, Georgia. For hours, call 229/219-7080.

RV sites, facilities: This park has 102 pull-through RV sites with full hookups and 30/50-amp electrical service. On the premises are showers, restrooms, picnic tables, a dump station, a pool, a fishing pond, boat/canoe rentals, paddleboats, a recreation hall, a playground, horseshoes, shuffleboard, limited groceries, RV supplies, propane, and laundry facilities. Dial-up service is available in the laundry facilities. Restaurants are within four miles. Children are allowed, but the rules remind parents: "It is your responsibility to entertain and discipline your children. If you disagree, choose another campground." Leashed pets are permitted.

Reservations, fees: Reservations normally are not necessary. Sites are $24 per night for two people, plus $2 for each additional person over age four and $2 for cable TV. Credit cards are accepted. Long-term rates are available.

Directions: From Valdosta, Georgia, travel 18 miles south on I-75. If you are coming from the south, it's the last exit in Florida (Exit 467) onto State Road 143. The campground is right off the highway.

Contact: Jennings Outdoor Resort, 2039 Hamilton Avenue, Jennings, FL 32053, 386/938-3321, fax 386/938-3322, email: jor@alltel.net

18 SUWANNEE RIVER STATE PARK

Scenic rating: 10

northwest of the town of Live Oak at the confluence of the Suwannee and Withlacoochee Rivers

One feature of this 1,800-acre park is an overlook that offers a panoramic view of the Suwannee and Withlacoochee Rivers and surrounding wooded uplands. When the water is low, springs can be seen bubbling up from the riverbanks. Today the river is sentried by canoeists—the park is the starting point for the Suwannee River Canoe Trail, which flows to the Gulf of Mexico. Catfish, bass, and panfish can be pulled from the river. The campground is set in a densely wooded forest of slash pines, and at night the only sound you may hear is the lonesome wail of a freight train headed to the big city.

Established in 1936, Suwannee River State Park was one of the first parks in the state system, and it is steeped in American history. A short hike from the ranger station brings you to the ruins of earthworks built by Confederate soldiers to protect the railroad bridge over the river and trainloads of beef, salt, and sugar headed to rebels based in Georgia. Five thousand Union troops sent from Jacksonville to take the bridge were beaten back in a bloody five-hour face-off near Olustee on February 20, 1864—Florida's only major Civil War battle.

Later, paddle-wheel ferries plied these waters when the Suwannee was a commerce route, a highway to gulf ports for a prospering logging industry. The pioneer village of Columbus here was little more than the railroad bridge, a ferry landing, and a sawmill operated by George F. Drew, who became Florida's governor in 1876. All that's left of the settlement is the old Columbus Cemetery, which is accessible from a trail in the park. The disproportionate number of infants buried there is silent testimony to how tough it was to survive in the wilds of Florida.

RV sites, facilities: There are 30 campsites with 30-amp electricity and water, picnic tables, grills, and fire rings. A boat ramp, canoe rentals, a playground, and several short hiking trails are in the park. Children are welcome. Pets are permitted.

Reservations, fees: Reservations are recommended; contact ReserveAmerica at 800/336-3521 or reserveamerica.com. Sites are $15 per night for up to eight people. Credit cards are accepted. The maximum stay is 14 days.

Directions: From I-10 west of Live Oak, take Exit 275 northbound and drive six miles on U.S. 90 to the park, on the right side of the road.

Contact: Suwannee River State Park, 20185 County Road 132, Live Oak, FL 32060, 386/362-2746, www.floridastateparks.org.

19 SPIRIT OF THE SUWANNEE MUSIC PARK

Scenic rating: 8

north of Live Oak on the Suwannee River

This music-oriented campground is nestled on 800 acres of forest draped in Spanish moss. Among the things that make the place special are the three pickin' sheds used for impromptu jam sessions and the grassy meadow that becomes a stage for weekend rock-and-roll, blues, and bluegrass festivals, plus special activities for Halloween, Thanksgiving, and other holidays. A horse camping area is available, and there are 22 miles of trails for equestrians. The park is open to the public, but management is now selling memberships that include free camping and use of the park, park models, and wedding packages. Because it's so large and off the usual path for hurricanes, the park has served as a Red Cross evacuation center when storms threaten, once accommodating around 8,000 people.

An on-site concession rents bicycles and outfits canoeists for day trips or overnight paddling expeditions. Also available are about 18 miles of walking and bicycling trails along the Suwannee River, Rees Lake, and through the Bay Swamp. The restaurant features a Southern-style menu and holiday dinner specials. Square dancing, bingo, card playing, and Sunday church services are held in the common areas.

Nearby is Suwannee Spring. Sulfury water issues from this big hole in the ground, but it drew the likes of the Firestones and other rich Northerners who came to visit the large tourist hotels of the Jacksonville area at the end of the 1800s and the early part of this century. Smelly? Maybe. But people back then believed it could cure what ailed them, be it kidney problems, rheumatism, or gout. Railroad baron Henry Flagler built a spur route to bring the curious, making it one of Florida's earliest tourist attractions. Several hotels were built here, but the last one burned down in 1925. The Suwannee River Water Management District has purchased the land around the spring and is working to reverse erosion and other problems caused by years of overuse.

RV sites, facilities: This unusual campground has full-hookup sites for 700 RVs (100 more are set aside for members). Cable TV, picnic tables, grills, a pool, a river beach, a fishing dock, a game room, a boat ramp, a restaurant, an amphitheater, a music hall, an open-air concert stage, cabins, rental trailers, stables, canoe rentals, horseshoes, miniature golf, and nature trails are on-site. A horse camping area has 68 water-and-electric sites with easy access to rental stalls, stables, and pens. Children are welcome and are kept busy with crafts and other activities programs. Up to two pets under 20 pounds are allowed; they must be kept on a six-foot leash and are prohibited in concert areas.

Reservations, fees: Reservations are recommended two weeks in advance on holiday weekends and are accepted one year ahead for big events. Sites normally are $15 per night for four people, plus $2 per extra person. Camping rates rise during special events. Pets are prohibited in the campground during special events. Credit cards are accepted. Maximum stay is six months.

Directions: From I-75 north of Live Oak, take Exit 451 and drive 4.7 miles south on U.S. 129 to the park. Or, from I-10 at Live Oak, take Exit 283 and head 4.9 miles north on U.S. 129.

Contact: Spirit of the Suwannee Music Park, 3076 95th Drive, Live Oak, FL 32060, 386/364-1683 or 800/428-4147, fax 386/364-2998, www.musicliveshere.com.

20 STEPHEN FOSTER FOLK CULTURE CENTER STATE PARK

Scenic rating: 9

in White Springs on U.S. 41 by the Suwannee River

The Suwannee got its name from Seminole Indian words meaning "black, muddy water," but the river was made famous in the American standard "Old Folks at Home." The man who wrote the tune, Stephen Collins Foster, a Yankee from Pittsburgh, had little to do with the river other than liking its name. The popular composer had never actually seen the Suwannee, but it sounded better than South Carolina's Pee Dee River. Foster's family had lost their home there when he was a child, which left a lifelong impression of loss and longing. The story goes that Foster asked his brother for help in replacing the Pee Dee with a more lyrical river name. Many people today know Florida's state song as "Way Down Upon the Suwannee River."

The state park itself is way down upon the Suwannee River on 650 acres. It's one of the state's most unusual parks, combining outdoor recreation, American history, and cultural arts programs. A tribute to Foster, the state park has the feel of a well-manicured antebellum plantation, so often the setting for Foster's reminiscing lyrics. The idea for the Foster memorial originated with the son of Josiah K. Lilly, an Indiana pharmaceutical manufacturing tycoon. The land was donated to the state by Lillian Saunders, who was a local member of the Florida Federation of Music Clubs. It opened in 1950.

A museum on the grounds displays memorabilia of Foster's life, antique pianos, and mechanical dioramas depicting the themes of his other works, like "Camptown Races" and "Oh Susanna." A tube-bell carillon—touted as the world's largest—regularly chimes a repertoire of Foster favorites and echoes through the campground at 10 A.M., noon, 2 P.M., and 4 P.M. Tours are offered daily at 9 A.M., 11 A.M., 1 P.M., and 3 P.M. The state park hosts numerous events, such as the annual Florida Folk Festival, a Memorial Day weekend event featuring music, dance, crafts, food, and storytelling; a Christmas festival; and the "Jeannie" ball and women's vocal competition in fall, which takes its name from Foster's "Jeannie with the Light Brown Hair." The Nature and Heritage Tourism Center, offering information on travel and leisure destinations in Florida, is also on-site here, as is a gift shop and craft square, where artisans demonstrate their work throughout the year.

The state park makes a fine home base for exploring the picturesque countryside. White Sulphur Springs, on the riverbank at the Foster Center, has lured visitors since the 1700s, when Native Americans considered the sulfurous waters to be sacred and curative. In 1906, it was part of a spa that attracted Teddy Roosevelt and other famous tourists.

You'll find lots of shade under moss-draped oaks, and a bit of peace alongside the meandering Suwannee. Fishing is popular from the steep banks of the river, and a canoe launch allows easy access from within the park. Hiking is available along a 4.5-mile nature trail and a 4.5-mile section of the Florida National Scenic Trail that runs alongside the river. Mountain bikers have fun on the nature trail but are not allowed on the Florida Trail, which is reserved for hikers. Nearby are 33 miles of trails in the Big Shoals Public Lands. Big Shoals is a 3,700-acre preserve along the Suwannee River that features the only white-water rapids in the state. However, the water levels fluctuate, and during the dry months of winter, the water is too low for white water.

RV sites, facilities: The campground has 45 gravel campsites with water, 30-amp electricity, fire rings, grills, and picnic tables. Three sites have 50-amp plugs. Fourteen sites accommodate big rigs in pull-through sites. Restrooms, showers, laundry facilities, rental cabins, a canoe ramp, and a playground are available. Concession stands with snacks and souvenirs, craft shops, a museum, a carillon bell tower, and an amphitheater for musical events are situated within the park. Entry to the museum, carillon tower, and craft square is free for registered campers. Most areas are wheelchair accessible. Streets are paved. Groceries are four miles away, and restaurants are within two miles. Children are welcome. Pets are permitted.

Reservations, fees: Reservations are recommended; contact ReserveAmerica at 800/336-3521 or reserveamerica.com. The campground is open Memorial Day weekend for participants in the Florida Folk Festival only. Sites are $16 per night for up to eight people. Credit cards are accepted. The maximum stay is 14 days. Walk-in campers are accepted for a maximum two-day stay.

Directions: From Lake City, head north on U.S. 41 about 18 miles to White Springs. You'll see the entrance to the state park and culture center after you pass two traffic lights. From I-75, take Exit 439 eastbound on State Road 136. Travel three miles to U.S. 41 and turn north (left). The park is just ahead on the left. From I-10, take Exit 301 and drive north on U.S. 41 about nine miles to the park entrance on the left.

Contact: Stephen Foster Folk Culture Center State Park, P.O. Drawer G, White Springs, FL 32096, 386/397-2733 or 386/397-4331, www .floridastateparks.org.

21 SUWANNEE VALLEY CAMPGROUND

Scenic rating: 10

on the Suwannee River in White Springs

Here is a favored destination for RV caravans, camping clubs, and family groups that takes advantage of the spacious pull-through sites and a large recreation center for group activities. The campground is located on 36 oak-shaded acres on the banks of the Suwannee River and appeals to all age groups and types of campers. Off-road bicycling, canoeing, and hiking are nearby, and the Florida National Scenic Trail skirts the campground. There's a playground and wading pool for the kids, and the laundry room is equipped with many washers and dryers. A dog activity area allows you to let your pet off its leash to run and play. Steak and chicken cookouts are held every Saturday night.

RV sites, facilities: The campground has 119 pull-through sites with full hookups and grills. Sites have 30-amp electrical service, wireless Internet access, and "instant-on" telephone service that allows you to make toll-free and local calls. Other sites have 50-amp service and are suitable for big rigs. Restrooms, showers, a recreation hall, swimming and kiddie pools, horseshoe pits, basketball and shuffleboard courts, laundry facilities, canoe and kayak rentals, a dog activity area, rental cabins, and a convenience store are provided. The clubhouse is wheelchair accessible. Children are welcome, as are leashed pets.

Reservations, fees: Reservations are recommended. Sites are $25 per night for two people, plus $2 per extra person. Credit cards are accepted. Long-term rates are available.

Directions: From I-75, take Exit 439 and travel 2.5 miles east on State Road 136. Turn right just before a bridge onto White Springs Road. Go 0.1 mile, then turn left onto Stephen Foster Road and drive 0.5 mile to the park. Or, from I-10, take Exit 301 and drive eight miles north on U.S. 41. Turn left on State Road 136. Turn left after the bridge onto White Springs Road. Go 0.1 mile, turn onto Stephen Foster Road, and drive 0.5 mile.

Contact: Suwannee Valley Campground, 786 Northwest Stephen Foster Drive, White Springs, FL 32096, 386/397-1667 or 866/397-1667, fax 386/397-1560, www.suwanneevalleycampground.com.

22 KELLY'S RV PARK

Scenic rating: 6

near White Springs

BEST (

This adults-preferred campground is tidy, with paved streets and spacious, wooded sites on 20 acres. Visitors with pets in tow will find an area set aside for dog walking. A nature trail hooks up with the state's Gar Pond and Shoal Trails, which are excellent for hiking and off-road biking. A public boat ramp is within 0.5 mile of the campground. The clubhouse has a fire ring for communal use. Visitors come from all over the United States and Canada to "rest and relax."

RV sites, facilities: This park offers 56 RV sites with full hookups, 30/50-amp electrical service, concrete patios, and picnic tables. Thirteen sites are drive-through. Wireless Internet service is available at each campsite. RVs as long as 45 feet and slide-outs can be accommodated. On the premises are restrooms, showers, laundry facilities, a nature trail, horseshoe pits, and a clubhouse. The bathhouse, clubhouse, and office are wheelchair accessible. Groceries and restaurants are within 2 miles; malls and hospitals are 11 miles away. Children are welcome only for short-term visits or special occasions. Leashed pets (no attack breeds) are permitted.

Reservations, fees: Reservations are recommended November–March. Sites are $25 per night for two people, plus $2 for each additional person. Credit cards are accepted. Long-term rates are available.

Directions: From I-75, take Exit 439 and proceed east on State Road 136 into White Springs, then turn south on U.S. 41. The park is 1.5 miles down the road. Or, from I-10, take Exit 301 and drive 5.5 miles north on U.S. 41.

Contact: Kelly's RV Park, 142 Northwest Kelly Lane, White Springs, FL 32096, 386/397-2616, www.kellysrvpark.com.

23 CAMEL LAKE

Scenic rating: 7

south of Bristol in Apalachicola National Forest

Camping at the remote northwestern corner of Apalachicola National Forest is a great destination or starting point for backpackers because it has a trailhead for the Florida National Scenic Trail, which meanders east from here through the forest for about 60 miles. The site is in a grassy, open area dotted with longleaf pines, and slopes down to Camel Lake, which has a swimming area. Small boats without motors are permitted.

RV sites, facilities: Tent campsites with grills, picnic tables, and fire rings are available for self-contained RVs. There are no electrical or water hookups. Facilities include restrooms with flush toilets, hot showers, drinking water, a swimming beach with outdoor showers, a boat ramp, and a picnic area. Children are welcome. Pets must be leashed in the camping area.

Reservations, fees: Reservations are not accepted. Camping is $8 per night. Stays are limited to 14 days per month.

Directions: From Bristol, take State Road 12 south for 11 miles. Turn left on Forest Service Road 105 and drive two miles east to the park.

Contact: Apalachicola National Forest, Apalachicola Ranger District, P.O. Box 579, Highway 20, Bristol, FL 32321, 850/643-2282, www.southernregion.fs.fed.us/florida/recreation/apalachicola_rec.htm.

24 COTTON LANDING

Scenic rating: 6

west of Sumatra in Apalachicola National Forest

This campground offers a more rustic alternative to nearby Wright Lake, with fishing and boating on Kennedy Creek, which feeds into the Apalachicola River. See the trip notes for Wright Lake and Hickory Landing (campgrounds in this chapter) for a description of the area. Campers, be advised: There's no drinking water at Cotton Landing. Canoeing is not recommended because of the boat traffic on the Apalachicola River.

RV sites, facilities: This rustic camping area has room for about 10 tents or RVs. Camping is primitive; no drinking water or hookups are available. There are chemical toilets and a boat ramp. Children are welcome. Pets must be leashed in the camping area.

Reservations, fees: Reservations are not accepted. Camping is free. Stays are limited to 14 days per month.

Directions: From Sumatra, take County Road 379 northwest for 3.2 miles. Turn west on Forest Service Road 123 and continue 2.8 miles. Turn west on Forest Service Road 123B and drive 0.7 mile to the campground.

Contact: Apalachicola National Forest, Apalachicola Ranger District, P.O. Box 579, Highway 20, Bristol, FL 32321, 850/643-2282, www.southernregion.fs.fed.us/florida/recreation/apalachicola_rec.htm.

25 PORTER LAKE

Scenic rating: 7

south of Telogia in Apalachicola National Forest

Porter Lake is a good is on a short branch about 10 miles downstream from Pine Creek Landing (see listing in this chapter) on the west side of the river. This is also a trailhead for the Florida National Scenic Trail, which meanders through the national forest.

RV sites, facilities: The primitive camping area has room for about four tents and RVs. A hand pump for spring-fed drinking water and a non-flush vault toilet is provided. Children are welcome. Pets must be leashed in the camping area. Camping is not allowed during hunting season.

Reservations, fees: Reservations are not accepted. Camping is $3 per night. Stays are limited to 14 days per month.

Directions: From Telogia, drive south on County Road 67 for 16 miles, then turn east on Forest Service Road 13 and drive 3 miles to the campground.

Contact: Apalachicola National Forest, Apalachicola Ranger District, P.O. Box 579, Highway 20, Bristol, FL 32321, 850/643-2282, www.southernregion.fs.fed.us/florida/recreation/apalachicola_rec.htm.

26 WHITEHEAD LAKE

Scenic rating: 6

south of Telogia in Apalachicola National Forest

This is one of the larger primitive campgrounds on the Ochlockonee River's west bank, a good spot for fishing and launching boats, with no horsepower limit on boat motors. For campers traveling the river, it is 14 miles downstream from Pine Creek Landing and provides an alternative to making camp at Porter Lake, a few miles upriver.

RV sites, facilities: This primitive camping area has room for 10 tents or RVs. Sites have picnic tables and fire rings. Hand-pumped drinking water, chemical toilets, and a boat ramp are available. Children are welcome. Pets must be leashed in the camping area.

Reservations, fees: Reservations are accepted. Camping is $3 per night. Stays are limited to 14 days per month.

Directions: From Telogia, drive 16 miles south on County Road 67. Turn east on Forest Service Road 13 and drive 1.5 miles. Turn south on Forest Service Road 186 and drive 1.5 miles to the campground.

Contact: Apalachicola National Forest, Apalachicola Ranger District, P.O. Box 579, Highway 20, Bristol, FL 32321, 850/643-2282, www.southernregion.fs.fed.us/florida/recreation/apalachicola_rec.htm.

27 HITCHCOCK LAKE

Scenic rating: 6

south of Telogia in Apalachicola National Forest

This campground is touted for excellent fishing and boating on the Ochlockonee River. For canoe campers paddling downstream, it is located on the west side of the river, 27 miles from Pine Creek Landing, roughly across from Mack Landing on the east side.

RV sites, facilities: There are 10 primitive sites with no hookups or drinking water. The campground has a boat ramp. Children are welcome. Pets must be leashed in the camping area.

Reservations, fees: Reservations are not accepted. Camping is free. Stays are limited to 14 days per month.

Directions: From Telogia, drive south on County Road 67 for 23 miles, then turn east on Forest Service Road 184 and drive 1.5 miles to the campground.

Contact: Apalachicola National Forest, Apalachicola Ranger District, P.O. Box 579, Highway 20, Bristol, FL 32321, 850/643-2282, www.southernregion.fs.fed.us/florida/recreation/apalachicola_rec.htm.

28 PINE CREEK LANDING

Scenic rating: 5

in Apalachicola National Forest on the Ochlockonee River

BEST (

By RV standards, this is a rugged camping spot, set at the end of a dirt road with no drinking water, not even a communal spigot. The camp is popular with local hunters, who leave their trailers behind upon returning to the workaday world. But to the trained eye, the campground has superb potential: miles of logging trails for hiking and mountain biking in relative solitude except from November to January during hunting season. Some campsites are waterfront. The big plus of Pine Creek Landing is its boat ramp on the Ochlockonee River—a prime portal for canoeing to Ochlockonee River State Park through 50 miles of the vast Apalachicola National Forest. Established in 1936, the federal forest stretches 54 miles from Tallahassee and covers 631,260 acres of pineland, hardwood forest, hammocks, savannas, and dry ridges. Wildlife is as varied as the landscape: 190 species of birds, nine kinds of bats, coral snakes, various rattlers, alligators, flying squirrels, marsh rabbits, red and gray foxes, weasels, mink, otters, skunks, bobcats, deer, feral hogs, and, occasionally, a black bear. The Ochlockonee River slices the forest in two, with the Wakulla County District on the east side. Camping is not allowed during hunting season, roughly November–February. Most people here are locals.

From Pine Creek Landing, you can meander downstream with the river current pushing your canoe at two to three miles per hour, and wind up at Ochlockonee River State Park in two or three days without trying too hard. Possible obstructions include floating logs. Occasionally, the river is low in spots, requiring a portage. The best time for canoeing is from February through May, when the weather is cool and not too buggy. Camping is available at five established sites south of Pine Creek Landing, with two tucked away on creeks along the eastern riverbank. Both usually are marked on the river and are easily accessible from highways in Wakulla County. The other three sites are on the west bank, accessible from Liberty County.

RV sites, facilities: There are 10 primitive sites for tents and self-contained RVs up to 35 feet long or those with slide-out units. Bring water, food, and supplies. No facilities are available,

except for the boat ramp. Children are welcome. Pets should be leashed in the camping area.

Reservations, fees: Reservations are not accepted. Camping is free. Each site accommodates up to six people. The maximum stay is 14 days per month.

Directions: From Tallahassee, drive 18 miles west on State Road 20. At Bloxham, turn left on State Road 375 and go south for 12 miles. Head west on Forest Service Road 335/Piney Creek Road and drive 0.5 mile to the campground. The boat ramp is one mile west of the camp.

Contact: Apalachicola National Forest, Wakulla Ranger District, 57 Taft Drive, Crawfordville, FL 32327, 850/926-3561, fax 850/926-1904, www.southernregion.fs.fed.us/florida/forests/apalachicola.htm.

29 MACK LANDING

Scenic rating: 9

in Apalachicola National Forest near Sopchoppy

Mack Landing sits on a bluff in a hardwood forest about 27 miles downstream from Pine Creek Landing (see previous campground) and is popular with anglers. A steep, paved boat ramp leads to a creek that feeds into the Ochlockonee River, and space is available to tie boats to trees on the riverbank. The sites are casually laid out and spacious.

RV sites, facilities: The 10 primitive sites will accommodate tents or self-contained RVs up to 45 feet long and those with slide-outs. Each site has a picnic table and a fire ring, but no electricity. There are vault (nonflush) toilets, a communal water spigot, and a boat ramp. Groceries are 40 miles away; malls and hospitals are within 70 miles. Children are welcome. Pets should be leashed in the camping area.

Reservations, fees: Reservations are not accepted. Camping is $3 daily. The maximum stay is 14 days per month.

Directions: From Sopchoppy, drive west and then north on State Road 375 for 10 miles.

Turn left on Forest Service Road 336/Mack Landing Road and drive one mile west to the camp.

Contact: Apalachicola National Forest, Wakulla Ranger District, 57 Taft Drive, Crawfordville, FL 32327, 850/926-3561, fax 850/926-1904, www.southernregion.fs.fed.us/florida/forests/apalachicola.htm.

30 WOOD LAKE

Scenic rating: 6

in Apalachicola National Forest near Sopchoppy

This small campground located about 12 miles downstream from Mack Landing (see previous campground) provides anglers and boaters with a gently sloping ramp for launching into a creek that runs into one of the most interesting stretches, in terms of wildlife, of the Ochlockonee River, as it twists through Liberty and Franklin Counties, passing Ochlockonee River State Park some 10 miles downstream. The favorite activity is fishing, and most campers here are locals or visitors from other parts of Florida.

RV sites, facilities: These primitive sites will accommodate self-contained RVs up to 35 feet long, as well as slide-out campers. There are no amenities, electricity, or water, but a vault toilet is provided. The boat ramp may be unusable in low-water conditions. Groceries and restaurants are 20 miles away; hospitals and malls are 70 miles away. Children are welcome. Pets should be leashed in the camping area.

Reservations, fees: Reservations are not accepted. Camping is free. The maximum stay is 14 days per month.

Directions: From Sopchoppy, take U.S. 319 south for four miles. Turn west and then north on County Road 299 and drive three miles. Turn west onto Forest Service Road 338 and drive two miles to the camp.

Contact: Apalachicola National Forest, Wakulla Ranger District, 57 Taft Drive, Crawfordville, FL 32327, 850/926-3561, fax 850/926-1904, www.southernregion.fs.fed.us/florida/forests/apalachicola.htm.

31 WRIGHT LAKE

Scenic rating: 8

near Sumatra in Apalachicola National Forest

Set in tall pines on the west side of Apalachicola National Forest, this secluded park has spacious campsites beside a spring-fed lake lined with moss-draped cypress and live oak. Staffers consider it the KOA of the Apalachicola forest, thanks to its amenities compared with the typical primitive camps elsewhere in the forest. There's a beach for swimming and fishing, a lakeside picnic area, and an interpretive trail for hiking. The camping area is along the 31.5-mile Apalachee Savannahs Scenic Byway, which you can pick up in Sumatra by heading north on State Road 379. The highway, suitable for bicycling, is a showcase of flat and rolling terrain and wet lowlands abundant with magnolia, cypress swamps, and stands of native longleaf pine. Grassy savannas are speckled with wildflowers such as orchids, pitcher plants, and sundews. Stop often, keeping an eye out for red-cockaded woodpeckers, wild turkeys, bobcats, alligators, and possibly a black bear.

South of Wright Lake, off State Road 65 on Forest Service Road 129, is the Fort Gadsden Historic Site, overlooking the immense Apalachicola River, a waterway once plied by steamboats, ferries, and barges linking Georgia and Alabama to gulf ports. The fort is a nice stop for a picnic beside oaks covered with resurrection ferns. Interpretive exhibits, meanwhile, help resurrect the site's gruesome military history. The first fortification here was called Fort Blount, built by British troops. They abandoned the fort after the War of 1812, but not before helping a colony of Choctaw Indians and runaway slaves set up cannons to fire upon American warships. On July 24, 1816, the fort was attacked by troops under the command of General Andrew Jackson, who ordered the slaves returned to their "rightful owners." A red-hot cannonball hit the fort's gunpowder magazine, killing all but 60 of the 334 occupants, women and children included. Two of the uninjured survivors, one Native American and one black, were executed. Jackson rebuilt the fort while fighting Spanish forces in 1818. It was renamed for James Gadsden, an American diplomat and Jackson's aide-de-camp during the campaign. A Florida county also bears Gadsden's name.

RV sites, facilities: There are 18 sites with water, electricity, and fire pits for RVs or tents. Each site has a pad for an RV and a cleared area for a tent. The park has restrooms (with flush toilets), hot showers, a dump station, picnic tables, grills, and a swimming lake. A boat ramp is nearby at Hickory Landing. Children are welcome. Pets should be leashed in the park but can run free in the forest.

Reservations, fees: Reservations are not taken, but you can call the ranger district to see if a spot is available. The fee is $8 nightly. Credit cards are not accepted. The maximum stay is 14 days per month.

Directions: From Sumatra, take State Road 65 south for two miles. Turn west on Forest Service Road 101 and drive two miles. Turn north at the sign for the park and proceed 0.25 mile.

Contact: Apalachicola National Forest, Apalachicola Ranger District, P.O. Box 579, Highway 20, Bristol, FL 32321, 850/643-2282, www.southernregion.fs.fed.us/florida/recreation/apalachicola_rec.htm.

32 HICKORY LANDING

Scenic rating: 8

near Sumatra in Apalachicola National Forest

Hickory Landing is the no-frills neighbor of the Wright Lake campground, with secluded sites nestled in hickory trees and oaks. The landing has a mineral spring (by the boat ramp) but no showers, swimming, or electricity. The boat ramp opens onto Owl Creek, which feeds into the Apalachicola River. It's fine for powerboating and fishing, but not so great for canoeing because of the boat traffic.

RV sites, facilities: There are 10 primitive sites for tents and self-contained RVs. Drinking water is available, as are chemical toilets, picnic tables, grills, and a boat ramp. Children are welcome. Pets should be leashed in the camping area but can run free in the forest.

Reservations, fees: Reservations are not accepted. Camping is $3 per vehicle. The maximum stay is 14 days each month.

Directions: From Sumatra, take State Road 65 south for two miles. Turn west on Forest Service Road 101 and drive 1.5 miles, then turn south on Forest Service Road 101B and drive 1 mile to the landing.

Contact: Apalachicola National Forest, Apalachicola Ranger District, P.O. Box 579, Highway 20, Bristol, FL 32321, 850/643-2282, www.southernregion.fs.fed.us/florida/recreation/apalachicola_rec.htm.

33 GULF VIEW CAMPGROUND

Scenic rating: 8

near Eastpoint

The name says it all: Gulf View is a restful spot with a fabulous vista of St. George Island and the water. Its grassy campsites are shaded by towering slash pines on a gentle hill sloping down to the highway, and you can swim or fish from the seawall across U.S. 98 (although relatively few people do). The eight-acre park also is convenient to the resort community on St. George Island. Snowbirds dominate in winter, when license plates often hail from Ohio, Michigan, Indiana, New York, and Canada. About 30 percent of the park is occupied year-round, and there are some mobile homes on the site.

RV sites, facilities: Of the 45 sites with full hookups, about 30 are available for overnighters and seasonal visitors; most sites have picnic tables. Some have 20-amp electrical service; others have 30-amp. Restrooms, showers, and laundry facilities are available. Children are welcome. Leashed pets are permitted.

Reservations, fees: Reservations are suggested in winter. Sites are $22 per night for two adults and two children under age 12, plus $1 per additional person. Credit cards are not accepted. Long-term rates are available.

Directions: From Apalachicola, take U.S. 98 east for eight miles to the park.

Contact: Gulf View Campground, 897 U.S. 98, Eastpoint, FL 32328, 850/670-8970, fax 850/670-8857.

34 ST. GEORGE ISLAND STATE PARK

Scenic rating: 10

on St. George Island

This top-rated park sustained a great deal of hurricane damage in 2004 and 2005, and the campground is not open at this writing. For park updates or other information, call the John Gorrie Museum at 850/653-9347 or check the Florida State Parks website.

RV sites, facilities: Sixty sites have water and electricity, picnic tables, and campfire rings. The park has restrooms, showers, a dump station, two boat ramps, a boardwalk, and beaches. Children are welcome. Pets are allowed with proof of vaccination. Alcohol is not permitted.

Reservations, fees: Reservations are recommended; contact ReserveAmerica at 800/336-3521 or reserveamerica.com. Sites are $8–14 per night for four people, plus $2 for each additional person and $2 per pet. Credit cards are accepted. The maximum stay is 14 days.

Directions: From Apalachicola, take U.S. 98 east for six miles, then turn south on the St. George Island toll bridge. Drive eight miles to

the island traffic circle, then turn east on East Gulf Beach Drive. The park is located at the end of the road.

Contact: St. George Island State Park, 1900 East Gulf Beach Drive, St. George Island, FL 32328, 850/927-2111, fax 850/927-2500, www.floridastateparks.org.

35 CARRABELLE PALMS RV PARK

Scenic rating: 7

in Carrabelle

Gulf breezes kiss this well-kept, sunny campground, which was completely renovated in 2005. Across the road is a public beach for fishing and swimming in the gulf waters.

RV sites, facilities: RVs accepted at these 97 full-hookup sites with picnic tables. Restrooms, showers, a dump station, a small store, a modem hookup for laptop computers, and a recreation hall are available. A public beach is located across the street. Children are welcome. Leashed pets are permitted.

Reservations, fees: Reservations are recommended. Sites are $18.50–20.50 per night for two people, plus $2 per additional person. Credit cards are accepted. Long-term rates are available.

Directions: From Apalachicola, take U.S. 98 east for about 20 miles to Carrabelle Beach, then look for the park across from the beach.

Contact: Carrabelle Palms RV Park, 1843 Highway 98 West, Carrabelle, FL 32322, 850/697-2638, www.carrabellepalmsrvpark.com.

36 HO-HUM RV PARK

Scenic rating: 7

east of Carrabelle

For beachfront living, this three-acre park welcomes older RVers who can relax in their lawn chairs and gaze out over the water. The sites are numbered and laid out in rows on hard-as-a-rock shell roads along 400 feet of beachfront. All sites enjoy spectacular views of the gulf and are swept by sea breezes. The farthest your site can be is 250 feet from water's edge, but some sites are 15 feet away. Snowbirds come in winter, playing cards and bingo; in summer, the crowd turns to anglers. The adults-only park tends to be peopled by a few overnighters and mostly seasonal visitors who stay for a week or two or the entire winter. The proprietors report that their place is becoming increasingly popular among birders; migratory birds swoop onto an island one mile offshore. Campers pull their boats up on the sand, which also is fun for wading and shelling. At night, hook up the cable TV, if you must, but keep the volume low enough to hear the surf breaking on the shore.

RV sites, facilities: All 50 sites have full hookups with 30-amp electrical service, and some have picnic tables. On the premises are restrooms, showers, a recreation room, a 250-foot fishing pier, modem hookup for laptop computers in the laundry room, and cable TV. Children are not allowed. Leashed pets are permitted.

Reservations, fees: Reservations are recommended. Sites are $26 per night for two people, plus $2 for each additional person. Credit cards are accepted. Seasonal rates are available.

Directions: From Apalachicola, take U.S. 98 east for 22 miles to Carrabelle. The park is four miles east of Carrabelle, on the gulf side.

Contact: Ho-Hum RV Park, 2132 Highway 98 East, Carrabelle, FL 32322, 850/697-3926 or 888/88-HO-HUM (888/884-6486), www .hohumrvpark.com.

37 OCHLOCKONEE RIVER STATE PARK

Scenic rating: 9

south of Sopchoppy

Nestled between Apalachicola National Forest and the St. Marks National Wildlife Refuge,

this remote, 392-acre state park is an ideal base camp for exploring the vast northwest Florida wilderness on foot or via canoe. Bring plenty of bug repellent in summer; beware of ticks, chiggers, and wasp hives in low-hanging oak branches, and think twice about refilling your water tanks from the park's spigots—the well water, while potable, had a straw-colored tinge when I camped here (hence the park's Indian name: Yellow Water).

The place is teeming with wildlife, including deer, fox, squirrels, bobcat, and overly friendly raccoons. It's not unusual to see endangered red-cockaded woodpeckers, which nest in the upper cavities of old pines suffering from heart rot. The woods are periodically cleaned by controlled burning, which produces a bonus for nature lovers: explosions of wildflowers in summer months. The park also sports small grassy ponds, dense swampy bay heads, and oak thickets. From the park boat ramp, mariners can launch saltwater fishing trips to Ochlockonee Bay and the Gulf of Mexico, which are five miles downstream, or ply the Ochlockonee and Dead Rivers and Tide Creek in search of largemouth bass, bream, catfish, and speckled perch. (State fishing licenses are required.) For canoeists, the park marks the end of the Ochlockonee River Lower Canoe Trail, a 50-mile route along the Wakulla County line through Apalachicola National Forest.

RV sites, facilities: There are 30 campsites, all with water, picnic tables, fire rings, grills, and 30-amp electricity. Two have 50-amp service. Three sites are pull-through. Facilities include restrooms (wheelchair accessible), showers, a dump station, canoe rentals, and a boat ramp. Groceries and restaurants are within five miles. Malls and hospitals are 42 miles away. Children are welcome. Leashed pets are permitted with proof of rabies vaccination.

Reservations, fees: Reservations are recommended; contact ReserveAmerica at 800/336-3521 or reserveamerica.com. Sites are $16 per night for eight people. Credit cards are accepted. The maximum length of stay is 14 days.

Directions: From Tallahassee, take U.S. 319 south for 40 miles to Sopchoppy. Continue four miles south on U.S. 319 to the park, which is on the east side of the road.

Contact: Ochlockonee River State Park, P.O. Box 5, 429 State Park Road, Sopchoppy, FL 32358, 850/962-2771, fax 850/962-2403.

38 HOLIDAY PARK AND CAMPGROUND

Scenic rating: 6

in Panacea

This seaside resort is a straight shot from Tallahassee, with plenty of space for big RVs, including five pull-through sites. The park sports oak trees, waterfront sites, and fantastic views of the Gulf of Mexico and the Panacea bridge. An open-air pavilion and hefty barbecue pit are available for parties. You can walk to nearby seafood restaurants. There's a nice, quiet beach and a long pier jutting into Ochlockonee Bay where you can watch the sun set; a public boat ramp is nearby, and Wakulla Springs is a convenient drive away.

RV sites, facilities: This campground has 75 RV sites with full hookups, 30-amp and 50-amp electrical service, picnic tables, and cable TV. The clubhouse has a dial-up Internet connection. Facilities include restrooms, showers, a laundry room, a gift shop, a pool, a beach, a fishing pier, a recreation room, a playground, horseshoe pits, and shuffleboard and volleyball courts. All areas are said to be wheelchair accessible. Children are welcome. Leashed pets are permitted.

Reservations, fees: Reservations are accepted. Sites are $22–31 per night for two people, plus $5 for each additional person. Credit cards are accepted. Long-term rates are available.

Directions: From Tallahassee, take U.S. 319 south for 25 miles to the intersection with U.S. 98 in Panacea. Take U.S. 98 west for nine miles to the park.

Contact: Holiday Park and Campground, 14 Coastal Highway, Panacea, FL 32346, tel./fax 850/984-5757, www.holidaycampground.com.

39 NEWPORT RECREATION PARK

Scenic rating: 7

in Newport south of Tallahassee

Located off the beaten path, this no-frills campground makes a base for exploring the St. Marks River, spectacular Wakulla Springs, and the St. Marks National Wildlife Refuge, a 64,248-acre preserve that sprawls along 40 miles of Apalachee Bay and stretches from the Ochlockonee River (pronounced "o'clock-nee") on the west to the Aucilla River on the east. Its salt marshes, hardwood and pine forests, and palm and live-oak hammocks are popular for hiking, fishing, canoeing, mountain biking, and hunting. The park provides a camping destination for backpackers and bicyclists coming from Tallahassee. It is a few miles from the terminus of the Tallahassee–St. Marks Historic Railroad State Trail, a 16-mile paved route. For information, call the trail headquarters at 850/922-6007.

Downriver, where the St. Marks joins the Wakulla River, lies the San Marcos de Apalache State Historic Site, hallowed ground steeped in military lore. In 1528, Spanish explorer Panfilo de Narvaez arrived here from Tampa and built the first ships made by white men in the New World. His carpenters caulked their yellow-pine hulls with pitch and fiber from palmetto palm fronds. The vessels didn't get far. They sunk when de Narvaez tried to retreat to Mexico. (He was among the drowned.) In 1677, the Spanish considered the rivers' confluence a strategic location and built a pine fort, which promptly was sacked and burned by pirates.

A stone fort called San Marcos built in 1739 was occupied by both the Spanish and the British over the next 80 years, until Florida was ceded to the United States. In the 1850s, stone from the old fort was used to build a military hospital for victims of yellow fever. San Marcos also played a role, albeit minor, in the Civil War: It was taken by Confederate forces in 1861 and renamed Fort Ward, then blockaded by a Union squadron for the rest of the conflict. Today, a museum sits on the foundation of the old hospital; ancient Spanish and Confederate earthworks are visible at the site, as is a military cemetery.

Another nearby point of interest is Wakulla Springs, a three-acre wonder touted as one of the world's largest and deepest freshwater springs, with as much as a billion gallons a day flowing out. It's located in Edward Ball Wakulla Springs State Park, about 20 miles west of Newport, and can be viewed from glass-bottom boats. The spring is teeming with fish, and the mouth of a cavern yawns 100 feet below—complete with a few fossilized mastodon bones. The remains of nine other ice-age mammals have been discovered as far as 1,200 feet into the cave. Wakulla Springs has no camping facilities, but it's especially worth a side trip for bird lovers. During the winter, the park attracts thousands of migrating waterfowl, including American wigeon, hooded merganser, and American coot. Feathered locals include limpkin, purple gallinule, anhinga, and bald eagle. For more information, contact Wakulla Springs State Park at 550 Wakulla Park Drive, Wakulla Springs, FL 32305, 850/224-5950.

RV sites, facilities: There are 41 campsites, 15 suitable for self-contained RVs. Each site has a fire ring. Some sites have electricity and water. Park facilities include restrooms, showers, a dump station, and a boat ramp. All areas of this county park are said to be wheelchair accessible. Canoes and boats can be rented nearby. Children are welcome. Pets are permitted.

Reservations, fees: Reservations are recommended. Sites are $10–15 per night for up to five people. Credit cards are not accepted. Stays are limited to two weeks.

Directions: From Tallahassee, take State Road 363 south for 12 miles, then turn east on U.S. 98/319. Drive through Newport to the park.

Contact: Wakulla County Parks and Recreation Department, 79 Recreation Drive, Crawfordville, FL 32327, 850/926-7227, fax 850/926-5251. The park telephone is 850/925-4530.

40 ECONFINA RIVER RESORT

Scenic rating: 4

south of Lamont on the Gulf of Mexico

This private campground is next to the 3,377-acre Econfina River State Park's boat ramp and rents canoes so campers can explore it. About half the park is occupied by RVs that are used on weekends by their owners, chiefly anglers from southern Georgia. Overnighters stay in another area, sleeping beside two ponds. A six-unit motel and store are in the 27-acre park, but there's not much else around. In the state park, you'll find hiking and horseback trails, pine and oak forests, and a salt marsh. Upstream, the river, which flows almost two miles to the gulf, offers challenging canoeing waters on the stretch between Lamont and the County Road 257 bridge. Gnats can be a problem in this area, so come prepared. The park has a swimming pool that is open year-round, but the main attraction is fishing.

RV sites, facilities: There are 82 full-hookup gravel RV sites with a choice of 30-amp or 50-amp electrical service. All have picnic tables and fire rings. Facilities include restrooms, showers, a pool, a clubhouse, horseshoes, volleyball, a small playground, a store that sells ice, beer, fishing tackle, and limited groceries. Canoe rentals and a boat ramp are available. Children are welcome. Leashed pets are permitted.

Reservations, fees: Reservations are recommended. Full-hookup sites are $25 per rig for two people, plus $10 per extra person. Children under 12 camp for free. Credit cards are accepted. Long-term rates are available.

Directions: From Perry, drive west on U.S. Alt 27, crossing U.S. 19/98, at which point the highway changes names to become U.S. 98.

Head 22 miles west to County Road 14, turn south and go 6 miles until it ends at the park.
Contact: Econfina River Resort, 4705 Econfina River Road, Lamont, FL 32336, 850/584-2135, fax 850/838-2164.

41 PERRY KOA

Scenic rating: 5

south of Perry

Formerly known as Southern Oaks RV Park, this KOA campground is a good base camp for exploring the undiscovered Big Bend area, one of the few places in Florida without a convenient interstate highway. The major road that runs through this area is U.S. 19/98, going roughly east–west through Taylor, Dixie, and Levy Counties. Here in Perry, you'll be less than one hour's drive from the beach, freshwater and saltwater fishing, hunting grounds, and wilderness areas, as well as many historic and archaeological sites. Unspoiled rivers, many of them great for canoeing or houseboating, run south toward the gulf.

Begin your exploration of the area in Perry, which is known as the forest capital of Florida. More than 90 percent of the land in Taylor County is owned by the timber industry. Stop by the Forest Capital State Museum (850/584-3227) for a better understanding of the business and modern forest management practices; there's also a "Cracker" homestead typical of those where early settlers lived. (Crackers were so-called because they cracked whips to drive their cattle.)

RV sites, facilities: All 100 RV campsites have full hookups, 30/50-amp electrical service, wireless Internet connections, and optional cable TV and telephone service. On the premises are picnic tables, restrooms, showers, a dump station, horseshoe pits, a pool, a whirlpool tub with room for 12 people, fire rings, and laundry facilities. The bathhouse, laundry room, clubhouse, and store are wheelchair accessible.

Park models are for sale. Children are welcome. Leashed pets are permitted.

Reservations, fees: Reservations are recommended. Sites are $27–32 per night for two people, plus $3 for each additional person. Credit cards are accepted. Long-term rates are available.

Directions: From I-10 at Greenville, take Exit 241 and drive south on U.S. 221 for 23 miles to Perry. Continue south through Perry on U.S. 19/98 to the park.

Contact: Perry KOA, 3641 Highway 19 South, Perry, FL 32347, 850/584-3221 or 800/562-9864 (reservations only), www.perry-koa.com or www.koa.com.

42 TOWN AND COUNTRY CAMPER LODGE

Scenic rating: 3

south of Perry

Groceries and restaurants are available within one mile of this trailer park, which attracts mostly people who are visiting friends and family in Perry and visitors passing through. The campsites are grassy and have concrete patios. The Gulf of Mexico is 20 miles to the south. About half the park is occupied year-round.

RV sites, facilities: There are 25 RV sites in this park, which also has 29 mobile homes. All sites have full hookups, 30-amp electricity, cable TV, and telephone service. On the premises are picnic tables, restrooms, showers, rental trailers, and laundry facilities. The bathhouse and laundry room are wheelchair accessible. Children and leashed pets are welcome.

Reservations, fees: Reservations are not necessary. Sites are $11.50 per night for two people, plus $2 for each additional adult and $1 per child. Credit cards are not accepted. Long-term rates are available.

Directions: From the intersection of U.S. 19/98 and U.S. 27 in Perry, drive south on U.S. 19/98 for 2.5 miles to the park.

Contact: Town and Country Camper Lodge, 2785 Highway 19 South, Perry, FL 32348, 850/584-3095.

43 WESTGATE MOTEL CAMPGROUND

Scenic rating: 2

in Perry

Campers stay on pine-shaded acreage behind the motel, which is located in the town of Perry. Shopping is close by, and the motel pool and other facilities are available to guests of the RV park.

RV sites, facilities: The 60 RV sites have full hookups, electricity, cable TV, and picnic tables. Restrooms and showers are located in the motel building, as is a computer with Internet access. A pool, laundry facilities, a dump station, and RV supplies are available. Children are welcome. Leashed pets are permitted.

Reservations, fees: Reservations are not necessary. Sites are $21 per night for two people, plus $2 for each additional person and $2 for cable TV. Credit cards are accepted. Long-term rates are available.

Directions: From the intersection of U.S. 19/98 and U.S. 27 in Perry, drive south on U.S. 19/98 for one mile.

Contact: Westgate Motel Campground, 1627 South Byron Butler Parkway, Perry, FL 32348, 850/584-5235 or 888/703-7287, fax 850/584-3037, www.westgateusa.com.

44 THE RIVER RENDEZVOUS

Scenic rating: 8

east of Mayo

A spectacular canopy of old-growth oaks hung with lacy Spanish moss greets guests at The River Rendezvous, which caters to all kinds of campers and nature enthusiasts. Under new ownership since 2005, the park is being improved, with new full-hookup sites, a swim-

ming pool, a recreation room, and a synagogue. These are expected to be fully open by late 2006. Sites overlook the Suwannee River, which rings with the sounds of paddlers enjoying themselves on sunny weekends. Nearby are half a dozen springs and caverns suitable for experienced cave divers; Peacock Springs State Park is six miles north of Mayo.

Also worthy of note is Lafayette Blue Springs State Park. Set on a bluff on the Suwannee River, this park was undergoing renovations in 2006 after being acquired from the county by the state park system (386/294-1617).

RV sites, facilities: Forty RV sites are available with water, sewer hookups, and 30-amp electricity. On the premises are showers, restrooms, fire rings, a game room, a sauna and steam room, cabins, motel rooms, a hot tub, a boat ramp, boat and canoe rentals, a playground, horseshoes, volleyball, pavilions, pool tables, a restaurant, a spring for fishing and swimming, and laundry facilities. Children and leashed pets are welcome.

Reservations, fees: Reservations are recommended. Sites are $17 per night for two people, plus $2 per extra person. Credit cards are accepted. Long-term rates are available.

Directions: From Mayo, drive south on U.S. 27 for three miles. Turn left on Convict Springs Road. When the road turns to graded dirt (in about one mile), continue another mile to the park. Alternatively, from Branford, drive north on U.S. 27 for 12.7 miles. Turn right on Convict Springs Road. Proceed two miles to the park.

Contact: The River Rendezvous, 828 Northeast Primrose Road, Mayo, FL 32066, 386/294-2510 or 800/533-5276, fax 386/294-1133, www.theriverrendezvous.com.

45 GORNTO SPRINGS PARK

Scenic rating: 6

north of Old Town

Tucked on a rise of oak trees and saw palmetto, this out-of-the-way campground is one of three

Dixie County–operated parks on the west side of the Suwannee River. These parks are suitable for canoeists and people who want to get far away from city life. You can swim in the river or launch your canoe and paddle all the way to the Gulf of Mexico. Yes, there is a spring next to the riverbank at Gornto (sometimes spelled "Guaranto"), and swimmers in the hot summer months appreciate the cool water. The campground is not attended by any managers living on-site.

RV sites, facilities: This small, riverside county park has 24 campsites, some picnic tables, flush toilets (no showers), and a boat ramp. Electricity is available at 10 sites. Bring your own water. Children are welcome. Pets are prohibited, as are alcoholic beverages and firearms.

Reservations, fees: Reservations are not accepted. Sites are $12 per night. An attendant picks up the fee once a day. Credit cards are not accepted. The maximum stay is 14 days.

Directions: From U.S. 19/98 in Old Town, drive north on County Road 349 for 12 miles. Turn east on County Road 353, drive 0.5 mile past Rock Sink Baptist Church, make a sharp right, and follow the pavement until it ends. Continue on the lime-rock road about two miles to the park.

Contact: Dixie County Commissioner's Office, P.O. Box 2600, Cross City, FL 32628, 352/498-1239.

46 ORIGINAL SUWANNEE RIVER CAMPGROUND

Scenic rating: 8

east of Old Town

Tall oaks cast shade on this waterfront park, which is set on a small peninsula with canal access to the Suwannee River. Boats can be tied up near the campsites in protected waters; boat ramps are nearby. You can fish in the canal from the campground dock or toss in a line all around the 12.5-acre, horseshoe-shaped camp-

ground; it's nearly surrounded by water. Twenty sites are pull-through. The park offers plenty of space so you won't feel crowded next to your neighbor. Favorite things to do are fishing and enjoying the retirement years.

RV sites, facilities: Seventy sites with full hookups accommodate RVs, of which 20 sites are open for overnighters; the rest are year-round residents and snowbirds. Both 30-amp and 50-amp electrical service is available. Sites have picnic tables and fire rings, and some have grills. Dial-up Internet access is available in the office. Restrooms, showers, laundry facilities, a dump station, boat docks, and a clubhouse are available. Children are welcome. Small, leashed pets (no attack breeds) are permitted.

Reservations, fees: Reservations are recommended. RV sites are $21 per night for two people, plus $2 for each additional person. Kids under age six stay free. Credit cards are accepted. Long-term rates are available.

Directions: From Old Town, drive three miles south on U.S. 19/98. See the park just before you cross the river.

Contact: Original Suwannee River Campground, 28872 Southeast Highway 19, Old Town, FL 32680, 352/542-7680, fax 352/542-0046.

47 OLD TOWN CAMPGROUND 'N' RETREAT

Scenic rating: 6

south of Old Town

Owners Linda and Joe Navatto have made improvements to this oak- and pine-tree-shaded park that welcomes adult vacationers. Since purchasing the property in 1999, they have built two new bathhouses, added a miniature golf area and volleyball field, and upgraded the grounds. If a camper should have a sudden health problem, an emergency medical technician (Joe) may be available to assist. The park is situated just three miles from the Suwannee River. A favorite thing to do is to "enjoy the country quiet, sitting around a campfire." Most visitors come from Michigan, Ohio, and Canada.

RV sites, facilities: There are 35 RV grassy sites with 30-amp electrical service, water, fire rings, and picnic tables. Fifteen have sewer hookups. Sites averaging 40 by 100 feet accommodate the largest RVs and slide-outs on the market. Restrooms, showers, laundry facilities, cable TV, telephone service, a pavilion, miniature golf, a volleyball field, rental cabins, and horseshoe pits are available. Most areas are wheelchair accessible. Children under age 16 are not welcome. Leashed pets are permitted.

Reservations, fees: Reservations are recommended. Sites are $16 per night for two people, plus $3 per extra person. Credit cards are not accepted. Seasonal stays are allowed. Long-term rates are available.

Directions: From U.S. 19/98 in Old Town, drive about two miles south on County Road 349 to the campground on the east side.

Contact: Old Town Campground 'n Retreat, 2241 Southeast Highway 349, Old Town, FL 32680, 352/542-9500 or 888/950-2267, fax 352/542-9914, www.oldtowncampground.com.

48 HINTON LANDING

Scenic rating: 7

south of Old Town

Hinton Landing is the nicest of the three Dixie County parks west of the Suwannee. The river flows past your doorstep, perfect for canoeing, and the setting is wooded and peaceful. There's an open-air pavilion with three picnic tables on the high riverbank, a parking area for boat trailers, and two docks, including one that is wheelchair accessible. Don't expect fancy restrooms, though.

RV sites, facilities: This Dixie County park has 10 sites with nonpotable water, picnic tables, and flush toilets (no showers). Some sites have

electricity. Most of the park can be used by someone in a wheelchair, including the floating dock, county officials say. Bring drinking water. Children are welcome. Pets are prohibited, as are alcoholic beverages and firearms.

Reservations, fees: Reservations are not accepted. Sites are $12 per night. An attendant collects the fee once a day. Credit cards are not accepted. The maximum stay is 14 days.

Directions: From U.S. 19/98 in Old Town, drive three miles south on County Road 349. Turn east on County Road 346A and go two miles. Turn south on County Road 317 and drive 0.25 mile to the park.

Contact: Dixie County Commissioner's Office, P.O. Box 2600, Cross City, FL 32628, 352/498-1239.

49 SUWANNEE RIVER HIDEAWAY CAMPGROUND

Scenic rating: 8

south of Old Town

A 1,500-foot boardwalk that meanders through the wetlands and ends at the Suwannee River is the centerpiece of this park on 108 wooded acres. It's the perfect choice for the camper who needs more-developed amenities than Hinton Landing (see previous campground) but seeks the tranquillity and peace of being near the river and in the woods. A clubhouse built in 2005 offers space for socializing. Most visitors are from Michigan, New England, and the Southern states. Favorite things to do are bike riding, bird-watching, and fishing.

RV sites, facilities: There are 55 RV sites with full hookups, including 30-amp and 50-amp electrical service and cable TV. Rigs up to 50 feet long and slide-outs can be accommodated. Some sites have concrete patios and picnic tables. Restrooms, showers, laundry facilities, and telephone service are available. On the premises is a picturesque

1920s-style general store that sells ice, camping supplies, and souvenirs. The bathhouse and new clubhouse are wheelchair accessible. Grocery stores and restaurants are within three miles. Children are welcome. Leashed pets are permitted.

Reservations, fees: Reservations are recommended. Sites are $15–26 per night for two people, plus $2 per extra person over age 10. Fifty-amp service costs $2 additional. Credit cards are accepted. Long-term rates are available.

Directions: From U.S. 19/98 in Old Town, drive three miles south on County Road 349. Turn east on County Road 346A and go one mile to the park entrance on the right.

Contact: Suwannee River Hideaway Campground, P.O. Box 1135, Old Town, FL 32680, 352/542-7800, www.riverhideaway.com.

50 NEW PINE LANDING

Scenic rating: 4

south of Old Town

These tiny sites are clustered around a boat ramp on the Suwannee River in a wooded residential neighborhood of stilt homes. This park's single RV site is too small for most trailers; a county spokesperson estimates that the maximum length might be 24 feet. Come well stocked; groceries can be purchased about 15 miles to the northwest in Cross City or in Chiefland, 25 miles to the northeast. An attendant lives one block away.

RV sites, facilities: There are five sites for tents and one for a small RV, with electricity, picnic tables, and grills. Bring drinking water. Restrooms (no showers) and a boat ramp are available. Children are welcome. Pets are prohibited, as are alcoholic beverages and firearms.

Reservations, fees: Reservations are not accepted. Sites are $12 per night. An attendant picks up the fee once a day. Credit cards are not accepted. The maximum stay is 14 days.

Directions: From U.S. 19/98 in Old Town, drive five miles south on County Road 349. Turn east on New Pine Landing Road (just south of Old Pine Landing Road) and drive 1.5 miles to the campground.

Contact: Dixie County Commissioner's Office, P.O. Box 2600, Cross City, FL 32628, 352/498-1239.

51 YELLOW JACKET CAMPGROUND

Scenic rating: 10

south of Old Town

This enchanting 40-acre campground has been completely renovated since new owners bought the place in 2003. They call it an "oasis." Standing on the banks of the Suwannee in this shady, secluded campground, you'll see little but wilderness up and down the river for about a mile in either direction. You can fish for bass or bream in several private ponds or on the river; there are also 85,000 acres of public hunting lands adjacent to the park. The natural setting doesn't mean you go without amenities. The pool and spa are heated. Launch your boat from the parks' own ramp, which is set along 1,300 feet of riverfront. Campers tend to be families, and some bring bicycles to tool around the place. Sites 1–24 overlook the river. Although long-term rates are available, no permanent residents are parked here.

RV sites, facilities: The park offers 66 sites with sewer, water, and 20/30/50-amp electricity. Twenty sites are drive-through. Picnic tables, fire pits, restrooms, showers, cottages, a remodeled clubhouse, laundry facilities, a playground, boat and canoe rentals, waterfront decks, and a boat ramp are available. Sites have cable TV and there is a modem available in the clubhouse. The bathhouse, office, pool areas, and boat docks are wheelchair accessible. Groceries and restaurants are 10 miles away; malls and hospitals are within 40 miles. Children are welcome. Leashed pets of any size are permitted.

Reservations, fees: Reservations are recommended. Sites are $27–37 per night for two people, plus $6 for each additional person. Credit cards are accepted. Long-term rates are available.

Directions: From U.S. 19/98 in Old Town, drive south on County Road 349 for 9.1 miles. Turn left (east) at the sign and drive one mile to the park.

Contact: Yellow Jacket Campground, 55 Southeast 503rd Avenue, Old Town, FL 32680, 352/542-8365, www.yellowjacketcampground .com.

52 HORSESHOE BEACH PARK

Scenic rating: 9

on the Gulf of Mexico south of Cross City

Campsites are clustered around a sunny circular gravel drive overlooking the Gulf of Mexico in the little fishing community of Horseshoe Beach. Mudflats covered with old oyster shells make swimming difficult, but you'll have great views of the water and several uninhabited spoil islands (sandbars or oyster beds that are visible at low tide). One restaurant is in town; watch the shrimp boats head home every afternoon with their catch.

RV sites, facilities: All 14 RV sites in this Dixie County park have city water and electricity; a few have picnic tables. Restrooms with showers are available. Children are welcome. Pets are prohibited, as are alcoholic beverages and firearms.

Reservations, fees: Reservations are not accepted. Sites are $12 per night. An attendant picks up the fee once a day. Credit cards are not accepted. The maximum stay is 14 days.

Directions: From Cross City, drive south on County Road 351 for 15 miles. Turn right on Eighth Avenue in Horseshoe Beach and con-

tinue to the park, which is also called Butler Douglas Memorial Park.

Contact: Dixie County Commissioner's Office, P.O. Box 2600, Cross City, FL 32628, 352/498-1239.

53 SHIRED ISLAND PARK

Scenic rating: 9

on the Gulf of Mexico south of Cross City

Although not an island in the traditional sense of the word, Shired (pronounced "shirred") Island is surrounded by swamp and wetlands. At these prices, it offers one of the best deals in Florida for an island camping experience. The water vistas are spectacular; all around you are the marshy islands of the Lower Suwannee National Wildlife Refuge. Swim in the warm, shallow waters of the Gulf of Mexico but don't expect white-sand beaches; the sand is more coarse and dark along this stretch of the Big Bend. Many campers set up near one of the six covered picnic pavilions at this county park and use them as outdoor living rooms. A boat ramp is nearby. Bring everything you need because stores are 20 miles away in Cross City.

RV sites, facilities: There are 17 RV sites and five tent sites with nonpotable water, electricity, picnic tables, and grills. Restrooms with concrete floors accessible for wheelchairs are available, but not showers. Bring drinking water. Children are welcome. Pets are prohibited, as are alcoholic beverages and firearms.

Reservations, fees: Reservations are not accepted. Sites are $12 per night. An attendant picks up the fee once a day. Credit cards are not accepted. The maximum stay is 14 days.

Directions: From Cross City, drive south on County Road 351 for seven miles. At County Road 357, turn left (south) and go 11 miles to the park. Don't turn at the boat ramp.

Contact: Dixie County Commissioner's Office, P.O. Box 2600, Cross City, FL 32628, 352/498-1239.

54 MILLER'S MARINE CAMPGROUND

Scenic rating: 8

in Suwannee

There's an RV park here, but the real emphasis is on fishing and houseboating. Miller's Marine rents these floating homes (at least 44 feet long) so you can explore the marshes at the mouth of the Suwannee River where it empties into the Gulf of Mexico. Or travel upstream 70 miles to get a glimpse of what it may have been like when stern-wheelers cruised north at the turn of the 20th century. Fishing boats are also available; anglers catch drum, redfish, sea trout, and tarpon near East Pass. The campsites, which are barely large enough to accommodate a big rig, overlook a river marsh and a canal leading to the Suwannee. Covered boat docks are available at this 16-acre complex, but you are not permitted to park your boat trailer at your site. Most of the park's original 34 camping lots have been converted to condominium ownership.

RV sites, facilities: Eight sunny, grassy, drive-through sites are available with full hookups, 30-amp electricity, and cable TV. Restrooms, showers, a dump station, a marina, a boat ramp, cabins, houseboats, picnic tables, docks, fishing guide service, and boat rentals are available. A camp store sells ice, camping supplies, propane, snacks, souvenirs, and bait and tackle. Limited groceries are located within 1.5 miles. The office and store are wheelchair accessible. Streets are paved. Children are welcome. Leashed pets are permitted.

Reservations, fees: Reservations are recommended. Sites are $30 per night. Credit cards are accepted. Long-term rates are available.

Directions: From U.S. 19/98 in Old Town, drive south on County Road 349 for 23 miles to the park. Turn left at the bridge in Suwannee and follow the sign to Miller's Marine on Big Bradford Road.

Contact: Miller's Marine Campground, P.O. Box 280, Suwannee, FL 32692, 352/542-7349 or 800/458-2628, fax 352/542-3200, www .suwanneehouseboats.com.

GAINESVILLE

COURTESY OF FLORIDA STATE PARKS

BEST RV PARKS AND CAMPGROUNDS

◖ Biking
O'Leno State Park, page 130
Paynes Prairie Preserve State Park, page 132

◖ Equestrians
Otter Springs RV Resort, page 135

◖ Most Unusual
Tresca Memorial Park/
  Advent Christian Village, page 125
O'Leno State Park, page 130

◖ Natural Springs
Ichetucknee Springs Campground, page 128
Ginnie Springs Resort, page 129
Manatee Springs State Park, page 135
Otter Springs RV Resort, page 135

Unlike the towns near I-75, Gainesville has escaped much of the development that characterizes the more tourist-oriented parts of Florida. For RVers who are not in a hurry to get to points south, there's much to explore here, such as the east banks of the Suwannee River, historic Cedar Key, several first-rate natural springs, and dozens of great places for viewing wildlife.

Gainesville is home to the University of Florida, the nation's fourth-largest university and gridiron archrival of Florida State in Tallahassee. Its huge size (900 buildings on 2,000 acres, 48,000 students) greatly influences Gainesville, which has a laid-back collegiate feel and no other significant industries. A notable exception: In 1965, the world's first sports drink, Gatorade, was invented by UF researchers for use by the Gators football team. Royalties from the sale of the Gatorade formula help fund a plethora of other university research.

On the north side of town is Devil's Millhopper State Geological Site, a must-see with its 120-foot-deep sinkhole. Visitors can view plants and animals similar to those in the Appalachian Mountains while following the stairway to the bottom of the hole.

Just south of Gainesville, near Micanopy, is Paynes Prairie State Park. Once called the "great Alachua Savannah," wild bison roam its 22,000 acres but more commonly observed wildlife include sandhill cranes, hawks, and wading birds. RVers can spend the night in the state park's campground, or there's an overlook at a rest stop on I-75 for those just passing through.

Long before I-75 came through, the oldest federal highway or road in Florida passed near High Springs. The interstate was built in 1824 on the route taken by Franciscan missionaries in the 1590s. It was also one of the major north–south trails used by Florida Indians; Hernando de Soto was the first European to set foot on it back in 1539.

Ginnie Springs, just east of High Springs, covers 200 acres of wilderness along a two-mile stretch of the lazy Santa Fe River and includes seven bubbling crystal springs. The park hosts one of Florida's most attractive private campgrounds, Ginnie Springs Resort, offering everything from mountain biking to canoeing, kayaking, and diving. The black water of the Santa Fe continues through Ginnie Springs to nearby O'Leno State Park, meanders through the forest, then actually retreats underground at the "river sink," reappearing three miles later. Many nature trails follow the spot where it disappears.

For those more interested in riding the river than following it, Ichetucknee Springs State Park farther north is a center for the leisurely sport of river tubing, an endeavor that requires little in the way of skill, energy, or equipment – just an old inner tube or float for lounging.

Off the beaten path is the east side of Suwannee River, which flows from north to south into the gulf. Fishing is good along the riverbank for trout, bass, bream, and catfish. Along the river's edge, you may see alligators, turtles, herons, and the occasional manatee. You're more certain to see the elusive sea cow at Manatee Springs State Park, which also provides a fantastic swimming and snorkeling hole. The crystal-clear water bubbles to the surface here, before entering a 1,000-foot run to the Suwannee and the Gulf of Mexico, 23 miles downstream.

At the southern tip of the Gainesville area is Cedar Key, sometimes known as Margaritaville North. Reminiscent of Key West, quaint Cedar Key is home to a colony of artists and salty fishermen, as well as a history museum and plenty of seafood restaurants, art galleries, and the ubiquitous tourist shops.

If you're too weary to explore the Gainesville area, Lake City is a popular layover off I-75 and I-10 for travelers in a hurry to refuel, restock supplies, and reenergize before hitting the highway again in the morning.

GAINESVILLE

GEORGIA

FLORIDA

Osceola
National
Forest

JACKSONV

Osceola
National
Forest

see
Jacksonville
page 144

Live Oak

Dowling
Park

Lake City

Suwannee River

Branford

Lake Butler

Starke

see
St August
page 15

see
Tallahassee
page 90

High Springs

Alachua

GAINESVILLE

Hawthorne

Fanning Springs

Archer

Lochloosa
Lake

Orange
Lake

Lake
Oklawaha

Williston

see
Ocala
page 180

Lower
Suwannee
NWR

Otter Creek

Ocala

Rosewood

Goethe
State
Forest

Waccassassa

Bay Preserve

Cedar
Key

Waccassassa
Bay

State Park

G u l f

Yankeetown

Inglis

Hernando

o f

Crystal
River

M e x i c o

Homosassa
Springs

0   10 mi

0   10 km

AL   GA

Gulf
of
Mexico

1 TRESCA MEMORIAL PARK/ ADVENT CHRISTIAN VILLAGE

Scenic rating: 6

southwest of Live Oak

BEST (

The RV park here is part of Advent Christian Village, a 1,000-acre nondenominational retirement community set on the serene Suwannee River. But it is not strictly for seniors—there's also a church youth camp, and children are welcome in the campground. Outdoor recreation amenities abound, including hiking, fishing, and canoeing. There's also exercise equipment in the fitness center. The campground is oriented toward churchgoers, with conference facilities available for conventions, family celebrations, and personal retreats; alcoholic beverages are prohibited. Pastoral and counseling staff are on call. Each year, the village hosts a cultural series featuring theater, music, and dance. Most people staying in the park are building homes in the area.

RV sites, facilities: A retirement community, a youth-oriented church camp, and an RV campground all in one, this park offers 15 RV sites and limited tent-only sites. Eleven pull-through RV sites have full hookups (half are 30-amp and half are 50-amp) and cable TV; telephone service can be arranged. On the premises are restrooms, showers, a dump station, two pools, a boat ramp, a dock, canoe rentals, a playground, exercise equipment, horseshoe pits, shuffleboard and tennis courts, a volleyball area, a hiking trail, laundry facilities, and a medical clinic. A grocery store, a post office, a barbershop, and a beauty salon are on the property Twenty-four-hour security is provided. Children are welcome in the RV park. Pets are permitted.

Reservations, fees: Reservations are not usually necessary, but you can be assured of a spot by calling 800/371-8341. Sites are $19 per night for full hookups, $14 for dry camping. Long-term rates are available.

Directions: From I-10 west of Live Oak, take

Exit 258 southbound on State Road 53 for 17 miles to State Road 250. Turn east and drive three miles to the park.

Contact: Tresca Memorial Park/Advent Christian Village, P.O. Box 4320, Dowling Park, FL 32064, 386/658-5200 or 800/371-8341, fax 386/658-5279, www.acvillage.net.

2 LAKE CITY KOA NORTH

Scenic rating: 3

in northwest Lake City off I-10

Located on the outskirts of Osceola National Forest, this 20-acre park is grassy and mostly shaded. Still, it's convenient to the interstate, and you'll find the KOA amenities you've come to expect, plus free coffee in the morning. Additional features include a pool and two small ponds, where campers fish or feed ducks. The dirt interior roads lead to grassy sites and are named for alphabetical letters (B Road has no sewer hookups). It's about 3.5 miles to shopping and restaurants on U.S. 90 in Lake City.

RV sites, facilities: This park has 30 RV sites for overnighters and 20 available for seasonal visitors. Most sites have full hookups and 50-amp electrical service; the rest have water and 30-amp electricity. All sites have picnic tables. Cable TV and wireless Internet access is available. On the premises are restrooms, showers, laundry facilities, a pool, a playground, shuffleboard, volleyball, basketball, firewood, propane, and rental cabins. The swimming pool is open March 1–October 31. Children are welcome. Leashed pets are permitted.

Reservations, fees: Reservations are recommended for full-hookup sites with cable TV. Sites are $28–34 per night for two people, plus $2 per additional person over age three. Credit cards are accepted. Long-term rates are available.

Directions: From I-10, take Exit 301 onto northbound U.S. 441, then drive one mile to the park.

Contact: Lake City KOA North, 4743 North U.S. Highway 441, Lake City, FL 32055, 386/752-9131 or 800/562-9141, fax 386/529-9414, www.koa.com.

3 INN AND OUT CAMPGROUND

Scenic rating: 2

in Lake City off I-75

Lake City is a popular layover for traveling campers in a hurry to refuel, restock supplies, and reenergize before hitting the highway again in the morning. This park sits atop a hill overlooking the bustling intersection of I-75 and U.S. 90—convenient to restaurants, a large Wal-Mart shopping center, RV repair services, and even a bowling alley and movie theater. Two more perks are that Inn and Out has its own gas station and convenience store on the premises. For late-night arrivals, an attendant is on duty 24 hours. Grassy sites sit aside paved interior roads.

RV sites, facilities: There are 95 RV and tent sites with full hookups, 30-amp and 50-amp electrical service, and cable TV. Seventy-eight sites are pull-through. Restrooms, showers, laundry facilities, a dump station, a pool, a gas station, and a 24-hour convenience store are available. Children are welcome. Leashed pets are permitted.

Reservations, fees: Reservations are recommended but not always necessary. Sites are $25 per night. Credit cards are accepted. Long-term rates are available.

Directions: From I-75, take Exit 427 and head east on U.S. 90 for 0.25 mile, then turn south into the park.

Contact: Inn and Out Campground, 3010 U.S. 90 West, Lake City, FL 32055, 386/752-1648.

4 WAYNE'S RV RESORT

Scenic rating: 2

in western Lake City off I-75

This 40-acre park is convenient to the interstate as well as restaurants and suburban shopping centers on U.S. 90. If you dally on your way down the road, dip into the two swimming pools (one is a kiddie pool), let the kids burn off steam in the campground, and do your laundry. An "adult lounge" keeps nonparents secluded from the kids. About 80 percent of the sites are occupied year-round by local workers.

RV sites, facilities: Most of the 100 sites have full hookups, 30-amp electrical service, cable TV, and are pull-through. The park has a pool, a playground, volleyball, picnic tables, laundry facilities, limited groceries, propane, a dump station, restrooms, and showers. The restrooms, store, and pool area are wheelchair accessible. Children are welcome. Leashed pets are permitted.

Reservations, fees: Reservations are recommended. Sites are $22 per night for two people, plus $3 for each additional person and $3 for using air-conditioning or electric heaters. Credit cards are accepted. Long-term rates are available.

Directions: From I-75, take Exit 427 and head west on U.S. 90 for 0.2 mile to the third stoplight. Turn south on County Road 252B.

Contact: Wayne's RV Resort Inc., 427 Southwest County Road 252B, Lake City, FL 32024, 386/752-5721, fax 386/754-3864.

5 SLOW AND EASY LIVING RV PARK

Scenic rating: 10

southwest of Lake City off I-75

This small RV park offers "country living" within 15 minutes of shopping malls. Convenience to nearby state parks, rivers, and walking trails is another selling factor. Generally, visitors come from all over the United States and Canada to take part in Friday-night cookouts, potluck dinners, and domino games.

RV sites, facilities: Sixteen of the 20 full-hookup sites are drive-through. Ten sites have 30-amp electrical service, and six have 50-amp. Lots are 25 feet wide by 175 feet deep, accommodating large rigs. An Internet connection is available in the clubhouse. Picnic tables, restrooms, showers, and an animal run are on-site. All areas are wheelchair accessible. Children are welcome. Leashed pets are permitted.

Reservations, fees: Reservations are recommended. Sites are $18 per night for two people, plus $2 per extra person. Credit cards are not accepted. Long-term rates are available.

Directions: From I-75, take Exit 423 onto State Road 47 and drive southwest two miles. Turn left (south) on Southwest Walter Avenue and drive 2.75 miles (the road changes names to Southwest Old Wire Road). If your rig weighs more than eight tons, continue on State Road 47 to Highway 240. Turn left and drive one mile. Turn right on Old Wire Road and proceed 0.75 mile.

Contact: Slow and Easy Living RV Park, 929 Southwest Old Wire Road, Lake City, FL 32024, 386/755-4945 or 877/203-4125, fax 386/719-4446, email: halw38@aol.com

6 CASEY JONES CAMPGROUND

Scenic rating: 3

south of Lake City off I-75

The well-kept, grassy park has quick access to I-75. Restrooms are kept clean and stocked, and the proprietors are friendly and helpful. Overnighters may find this spot appealing because it's easy to get in and out of, but a remarkable number of snowbirds have decided to spend winters here on a sunny hill above the interstate. Asked why, one RVer in a new fifth wheel explained he'd had a heart attack on his last stay

here and spent a month in a hospital in nearby Lake City. After enduring another winter in the Northeast, his wife told him, "Let's just go back to Casey Jones."

RV sites, facilities: The campground has 69 pull-through RV sites with full hookups, 30-amp and 50-amp electrical service, cable TV, and a picnic table. Facilities include restrooms, showers, a laundry room, a dump station, and a recreation room. Restaurants and a convenience store are within 0.1 mile. Children are welcome, but the park tends to draw retirees. Leashed pets are permitted.

Reservations, fees: Reservations are recommended but not required. Sites are $20.50 per night. Credit cards are accepted. Long-term rates are available.

Directions: From I-75, take Exit 423 onto State Road 47 heading east for 0.1 mile. Turn north at the stoplight and travel 0.2 mile to the park.

Contact: Casey Jones Campground, 185 Southwest Arrowhead Terrace, Lake City, FL 32024, 386/755-0471 or 800/226-5559.

7 LAKE CITY RV PARK

Scenic rating: 1

south of Lake City off I-75

This one-acre park provides a shady layover for interstate travelers, but there are no restrooms or showers. Groceries, restaurants, and laundry facilities are available off the interstate wthin two miles of the campground. About half the park is occupied year-round.

RV sites, facilities: Five sites have full hookups, 50-amp electrical service, and cable TV. A dump station is available, but there are no restrooms or showers, so campers must be self-contained. Children are welcome. Leashed pets are permitted.

Reservations, fees: Reservations are not necessary. Sites are $17 per night. Credit cards are not accepted.

Directions: From I-75, take Exit 427 and head east on U.S. 90 to U.S. 41. Drive two miles south to the campground.

Contact: Lake City RV Park, 2463 Southwest Main Boulevard, Lake City, FL 32025, 386/755-0110.

8 E-Z STOP RV PARK

Scenic rating: 1

south of Lake City off I-75

Guests at this pine- and oak-shaded park enjoy some easy pull-through sites big enough to accommodate 42-foot rigs, as well as convenient access to gas stations and restaurants. Lots of overnighters stay here, but long-term campers toss horseshoes, play basketball, use the grill, or browse the aisles of antiques at the shops next door. About half the occupants live here year-round.

RV sites, facilities: Half of these 25 RV sites are pull-through, full-hookup spots with 30-amp and 50-amp; the rest have water and electricity only. Lots are about 70 feet deep. Restrooms, showers, picnic tables, horseshoes, basketball, a barbecue area, and a dump station are available. Need a haircut? A barbershop and beauty salon are on the premises. Children are welcome. Leashed pets are permitted.

Reservations, fees: Reservations are not necessary. Sites are $17–20 per night for two people, plus $2 per additional person. Credit cards are not accepted. Long-term rates are available.

Directions: From I-75, take Exit 414 southbound onto U.S. 41 for 0.1 mile, then turn west on Howell Street and proceed 500 feet to the park.

Contact: E-Z Stop RV Park, 181 Southwest Howell Street, Lake City, FL 32024, 386/752-2279.

9 ICHETUCKNEE SPRINGS CAMPGROUND

Scenic rating: 9

near Fort White off I-75

BEST (

Rustic, forested Ichetucknee Springs Campground covers 20 acres, complete with a tavern serving up pizza, nachos, and other munchies. The emphasis is on family fun; there's even an annual New Year's Eve party. Groups can rent the entire campground during off-season, and some visitors stay here while their homes are being built nearby. But the main attraction is next door: Ichetucknee Springs State Park, a hot spot for the leisurely sport of river tubing. Deepwater springs pump 233 million gallons a day into the Ichetucknee River, creating a gin-clear waterway so remarkable that the main spring was declared a National Natural Landmark in 1972. The waters draw thousands to the state park each year for tubing, an endeavor that requires little in the way of skill, energy, or equipment—just an old inner tube or float for lounging. You'll drift 3.5 miles past limestone outcrops under a canopy of oak and cypress. Occasionally, an alligator or snake can be spotted, and caution is advised. Tubing is permitted from 8 A.M. until sunset.

Launch at one of three drop sites: at the north entrance, the south entrance, or a midpoint drop-off open only at peak periods. From the south entrance, the river ride lasts 60–90 minutes. A free shuttle tram, which operates May–September, returns tubers to the starting point. The ride from the north entrance is the longest lasting—from two to three hours—and so popular that the park limits the trip to 750 tubers a day. Return shuttle service also is available. Inner tubes can be rented at the campground and dropped off at the end of the ride.

A few pointers: Start early to avoid the crowds. Stick together because it's easy to get separated. Children and nonswimmers should wear flotation vests. Bring along a pair of old sneakers or other footwear for the walk to the shuttle trams. A few rules: Food, drink, alcohol, tobacco, and disposable items are prohibited on the river. Climbing and jumping from riverbanks, trees, and docks is strictly forbidden. Respect the environment and your fellow tubers—avoid stirring up the river bottom with swim fins.

RV sites, facilities: There are 14 RV sites with 30-amp electricity and water in this 20-acre wooded park. Five sites are drive-through. Restrooms, showers, a dump station, a tavern, two game rooms, a volleyball field, a basketball court, and horseshoe pits are on-site. The campsites, bathrooms, showers, and tavern/restaurant are wheelchair accessible. Canoes, inner tubes, and snorkeling equipment may be rented. Groceries and stores are 15 miles away. Children are welcome. Leashed pets are permitted.

Reservations, fees: Reservations are recommended. Sites are $10 per night for two people, plus $4 for each adult and $5 for electricity. Credit cards are not accepted.

Directions: From I-75 southbound, take Exit 423 onto State Road 47 and drive south for 14 miles to Elim Church Road/County Road 238. Turn west and drive 3.5 miles to Breckenridge Lane. Turn right at the park. From I-75 northbound, take Exit 399 onto U.S. 441, then merge with U.S. 27 North for 2.5 miles and go west on Elim Church Road. Go west for 3.5 miles to Breckenridge Lane and look for the park sign on your right.

Contact: Ichetucknee Springs Campground, 245 Southwest Breckenridge Lane, Fort White, FL 32038, 386/497-2285.

🔟 GINNIE SPRINGS RESORT

Scenic rating: 10

near High Springs

BEST (

For active campers, this is one of Florida's most attractive campgrounds, offering everything from mountain biking to canoeing, kayaking, and diving. The park covers 200 acres of wilderness along a two-mile stretch of the lazy Santa Fe River and includes seven crystal springs, all bubbling away at a constant water temperature of 72°F. Rent or bring your own rubber raft (get free air refills here) for a refreshing hourlong float down the Santa Fe on a hot summer day. For really adventurous visitors, the park offers instruction in underwater cavern and cave exploration.

RV sites, facilities: There are 92 RV sites with water and electricity; half have 50-amp service. All sites have picnic tables and grills. Rigs up to 40 feet long can be accommodated. Group sites are available. Restrooms, showers, laundry facilities, a restaurant, two rental cottages, five covered picnic pavilions each located next to a spring, beach-style volleyball courts, a playground, firewood, and a country store are located on the premises. The bathhouses are heated during the winter. Also available is a full complement of recreational sports services, including scuba diving and underwater cave exploration for certified divers. Canoes, kayaks, inner tubes, and diving equipment can be rented here. Groceries and restaurants are eight miles away. Children are welcome. Pets are not permitted.

Reservations, fees: Reservations are highly recommended. Sites are $32 per night for two people and $16 for each additional person. Younger children camp for free. Electricity costs an additional $6 per site. Credit cards are accepted.

Directions: From I-75, take Exit 399 onto U.S. 441 five miles north to the town of High Springs. At the first stoplight in High Springs (at the Hardee's), turn left. Continue through the next stoplight, at the center of town, and go approximately 0.5 mile farther to the turnoff for County Road 340/NE 182nd Avenue. (You will see a sign on top of a pole indicating that this is the turnoff for Ginnie, Blue, and Poe Springs.) Turn right onto County Road 340 and go approximately 6.5 miles, to the sign indicating the turnoff to Ginnie Springs (NE 60th Avenue).

Turn right and drive approximately one mile to the Ginnie Springs entrance.

Contact: Ginnie Springs Resort, 7300 Northeast Ginnie Springs Road, High Springs, FL 32643, 386/454-7188, fax 386/454-2085, www .ginniespringsoutdoors.com.

11 O'LENO STATE PARK

Scenic rating: 10

north of High Springs off I-75

BEST (

Always magical, this place is especially so in the cooler months when it's quiet and uncrowded. The park encompasses 6,400 acres of hardwood forest flush with deer and other wildlife, miles of service roads great for mountain biking, and a historic wooden suspension bridge built by the Civilian Conservation Corps in the 1930s. The black-water Santa Fe River meanders through the forest, then actually goes underground at the "river sink" and reappears three miles later. Hike along one of the many nature trails to the spot where it disappears, but don't expect drama; the water gathers in a wide lake and seeps into the ground so slowly that algae grows across the top.

You can swim or canoe on the river, a tributary of the Suwannee; canoes are available for rent. Rangers say the river is an unpredictable fishing spot, but you may see alligators and turtles while trying your luck. Campsites are split between two areas: the Dogwood Camp and the Magnolia Camp. The heart of the park is an assortment of 1930s-era buildings and newer cabins at the point where the bridge crosses the river. Near this spot in the mid-1800s stood a lumber town perhaps called Keno (as in the game of chance) and later known as Old Leno. All that remains is a mill dam and an old road. Groceries, laundry facilities, and restaurants are available six miles from the park.

RV sites, facilities: This state park campground has 61 sites with water, 30/50-amp electricity, picnic tables, grills, and fire rings. Restrooms,

showers, a dump station, a playground, and hiking and horseback-riding trails are available. Children are welcome. Pets are prohibited.

Reservations, fees: Reservations are accepted. Sites are $15 per night for up to eight people. Credit cards are accepted. Maximum stay is 14 days.

Directions: From I-75 southbound, take Exit 414 onto U.S. 441 and drive five miles south to the park. From I-75 northbound, take Exit 399 onto U.S. 441 and drive 15 miles west and north to the park.

Contact: O'Leno State Park, Route 2, P.O. Box 1010, High Springs, FL 32643, 386/454-1853, www.floridastateparks.org.

12 HIGH SPRINGS CAMPGROUND

Scenic rating: 9

east of High Springs near I-75

With tall oaks, a natural setting, and a secluded location, this place will remind you more of a state park than a privately operated campground. Sites are shaded and thoughtfully laid out; 18 are pull-through, and even big rigs can be accommodated. About one-third of the park is occupied by year-round residents. This makes a good overnight spot for I-75 travelers—indeed, most guests are overnighters—but it's also a good base for exploring High Springs' antiques shops, the museums of Gainesville 17 miles to the south, and the O'Leno, Ichetucknee Springs, and Paynes Prairie State Parks. Groceries and restaurants are located within four miles of here. The campground is located on the oldest federal highway or road in Florida, built in 1824 on the route taken by Franciscan missionaries in the 1590s. (Three of the missions they built were within 15 miles of this campground.) It was also one of the major north–south trails used by Florida Indians; Hernando de Soto became the first European to set foot on it back in 1539.

RV sites, facilities: There are 45 RV sites with

full hookups and 30-amp electrical service; most have concrete picnic tables and fire rings. Restrooms, showers, laundry facilities, a dump station, a pool, and a playground are available. All areas are said to be wheelchair accessible. Streets are paved. Children are welcome. Leashed pets are permitted.

Reservations, fees: Reservations are not necessary. Sites are $22 per night for four people, plus $2 for each additional person. Credit cards are not accepted. Long-term rates are available.

Directions: From I-75 north of Alachua, take Exit 404 and drive west on County Road 236 for 0.1 mile. Turn north onto Old Bellamy Road and drive 1,000 feet to the campground, on the left.

Contact: High Springs Campground, 24004 Northwest Old Bellamy Road, High Springs, FL 32643, 386/454-1688, www.highsprings-campground.com.

13 BRADFORD MOTEL AND CAMPGROUND

Scenic rating: 2

north of Starke

This urban park is set in a partially wooded area behind a motel and near restaurants and shops; about half the sites are occupied year-round. Just north of the campground is the little burg of Lawtey. Drive slowly because it's known as a speed trap. Starke is a good starting point for exploring this off-the-tourist-track area, which is famous for extra-sweet strawberries, timber (half of Bradford County is heavily forested), lake fishing, hunting, and agriculture. Outside Florida, Starke may be more familiar as a newspaper dateline when there's an execution at the Florida State Prison in Raiford. On execution days, reporters and protesters pour into Starke, the nearest big town.

RV sites, facilities: There are 28 full-hookup campsites, including 8 that are drive-through. RVs up to 35 feet long can be accommodated. Restrooms, showers, a laundry room, and a

dump station are on the grounds. Restaurants and shops are within 0.5 mile. The bathhouse is wheelchair accessible. Children and leashed pets are welcome.

Reservations, fees: Reservations are recommended. Sites are $20 per night for two people, plus $3 for each additional person. Credit cards are accepted. Long-term rates are available.

Directions: From I-75, take Exit 414 northbound on U.S. 441 for 0.25 mile. Turn east on State Road 238 and drive 13 miles to the town of Lake Butler. Continue east on State Road 100 for 15 miles into Starke. Turn north on U.S. 301; the park is on the north side of town.

Contact: Bradford Motel and Campground, 1757 North Temple Avenue, Starke, FL 32091, 904/964-5332, fax 904/964-2026.

14 KINGSLEY BEACH RV PARK AND RESORT CAMPGROUND

Scenic rating: 9

near Lawtey next to Camp Blanding Wildlife Management Area

Kids love this place. Not only is there a swimming beach in spring-fed Kingsley Lake, there are opportunities for waterskiing, fishing, and boating. Kingsley Lake is a two-mile-long lake that is so round that it used to be called the Silver Dollar. Hunters drive a short distance east to stalk turkey, deer, and other animals in season at the 55,195-acre Camp Blanding Wildlife Management Area.

RV sites, facilities: There are 360 sites with full hookups. Restrooms, showers, a store, a restaurant, a boat ramp, and a game room with pool tables and weekend entertainment are available. There is no swimming pool, but the beach more than suffices. Snorkeling and scuba equipment, paddleboats, and kayaks are for rent. Children and leashed pets are welcome.

Reservations, fees: Reservations are recommended. Sites are $35–45 a night for up to six people; there is a $10 charge for each additional person. Long-term visitors are encouraged.

Directions: From Green Cove Springs, travel 18 miles west on Highway 16. The park is just past Camp Blanding Wildlife Management Area.

Contact: Kingsley Beach RV and Resort Campground, 6003 Kingsley Lake Drive, Starke, FL 32091, 904/533-2006, fax 904/533-9333, www.kingsleybeach.com.

15 STARKE KOA

Scenic rating: 6

south of Starke

This KOA offers easy access to several fishing lakes nearby and to Gainesville, Jacksonville, and Kingsley Lake. The owners, the four-generation Steffen family, have a full schedule of activities planned for their guests, including bingo, potluck dinners, Sunday-morning breakfasts, and hobo-stew dinner around the campfire. Nearly 75 people came for turkey and all the trimmings on one recent Thanksgiving Day. Note that the pool is not open January–March. The Starke golf course is nearby, but the favorite things to do are going to the local flea markets and out to eat. Restaurants are within less than a mile.

While you're in Starke, don't miss visiting the Camp Blanding Museum and Memorial Park, which displays weapons and World War II artifacts in a refurbished barracks and recalls a turning point in local history: Starke was pretty sleepy until the Second World War—it had only 2,000 residents when the National Guard camp east of here was expanded to accommodate 90,000 GIs. Also in Starke are several restored turn-of-the-20th-century homes and commercial buildings; pick up a driving brochure from the Starke-Bradford County Chamber of Commerce. The chamber also can provide brochures detailing fishing at the Camp Blanding

Fish Management Area, Lake Santa Fe, Lake Hampton, Lake Altho, and Sampson and Rowell Lakes.

RV sites, facilities: There are 127 sites (about 25 percent are occupied year-round) with full hookups, 30-amp and 50-amp electrical service, cable TV, and picnic tables. RVs up to 48 feet long and slide-outs can be accommodated. Restrooms, showers, laundry facilities, a pool, a recreation hall, and a store are available. The clubhouse, restrooms, and recreation hall are wheelchair accessible. Children are welcome. Leashed pets are permitted.

Reservations, fees: Reservations are recommended. Sites are $28–35 per night for two people, plus $3 for each additional person. Rates are likely to be higher during the annual Gatornational drag races in March. Credit cards are accepted. Long-term rates are available.

Directions: From the intersection of U.S. 301 and State Road 100 in Starke, drive south on U.S. 301 for 1.5 miles to the campground.

Contact: Starke KOA, 1475 South Walnut Street, Starke, FL 32091, 904/964-8484 or 800/KOA-8498 (800/562-8498), www .starkekoa.com.

16 PAYNES PRAIRIE PRESERVE STATE PARK

Scenic rating: 10

near Micanopy south of Gainesville

BEST (

Would you ever expect to see bison in Florida? At Paynes Prairie, wild bison still roam this 22,000-acre park, once called the "great Alachua Savannah." Wildlife more commonly observed are sandhill cranes, hawks, and wading birds. Hook up with a ranger-led nature walk, or venture out on one of the many trails. Foot traffic only is allowed on the 2.5-mile La Chua Trail and the short (0.3-mile) Wacahoota Trail. Hikers, mountain bikers, and horseback riders share the path as they travel through 6.5 miles of shady hammock, pine flat woods, and old fields on the Chacala Trail. At Cone's Dike, hikers and mountain bikers have access to the 8.24-mile trail that heads out into the marsh; wear a hat because there is no shade. Cyclists can also use the paved park road from the campground to the visitors center, where an observation tower provides views of the vast prairie.

Anglers and canoeists have access to Lake Wauberg at a boat ramp near the camping area. Common catches are bream, bass, and speckled perch. On the north side of the park at the Boulware Springs Trailhead is the terminus for the 17-mile Gainesville-to-Hawthorne walking, biking, and horseback-riding trail. The campground is 10 miles south of Gainesville, home to the University of Florida and the Florida Museum of Natural History. Don't miss seeing Devil's Millhopper State Geological Site on the north side of town. There's a 120-foot-deep sinkhole with a stairway to the bottom; on the way down, you'll see plants and animals similar to those in the Appalachian Mountains.

RV sites, facilities: There are 35 RV sites, all with water and 30-amp electricity. Picnic tables, lantern posts, grills, fire rings, a dump station, a boat ramp, a visitors center with an observatory, and 25 miles of hiking, horse-back-riding, and bicycling trails are in the park. The campground and visitors center are wheelchair accessible. Children are welcome. Pets are prohibited.

Reservations, fees: Reservations are recommended; contact ReserveAmerica at 800/336-3521 or reserveamerica.com. Sites are $15 per night for up to eight people. Credit cards are accepted. The maximum stay is 14 days.

Directions: From I-75, take Exit 374 eastbound for 0.5 mile to U.S. 441 in Micanopy. Turn north on U.S. 441 and drive 0.6 mile to the park.

Contact: Paynes Prairie Preserve State Park, 100 Savannah Boulevard, Micanopy, FL 32667, 352/466-3397, fax 352/466-4297, www.floridastateparks.org.

17 RANCH MOTEL AND CAMPGROUND

Scenic rating: 2

in Hawthorne

Close to everything and friendly are how the owners of this motel/RV park complex describe their property. The motel has only 12 rooms, so the RV park is a dominant feature, not an afterthought. With 15 fishing lakes within three miles, the park attracts anglers and seasonal visitors.

RV sites, facilities: There are 30 RV sites (12 pull-through) with full hookups and 5 with water. All have 30-amp electricity and picnic tables. Restrooms, showers, laundry facilities, cable TV, and telephone service are available. Most areas are wheelchair accessible. Children are welcome. Leashed pets are permitted.

Reservations, fees: Reservations are recommended. Sites are $18 per night. Credit cards are accepted. Long-term rates are available.

Directions: From the intersection of U.S. 301 and State Road 20 in Hawthorne, drive 0.75 mile south on U.S. 301 to the park.

Contact: Ranch Motel and Campground, P.O. Box 806, 8010 Southeast U.S. Highway 301, Hawthorne, FL 32640, 352/481-3851, fax 352/481-3562.

18 TWIN LAKES FISH CAMP

Scenic rating: 4

just north of Cross Creek, halfway between Gainesville and Ocala

Located on Cross Creek, which flows into Lake Lochloosa and Orange Lake, the campground attracts anglers interested in catching specks. You also can photograph an eagle on the wing or watch a sunset over the water. Cross Creek is famous as the home of Marjorie Kinnan Rawlings, Pulitzer Prize–winning author of *The Yearling*. You can tour the home at the Marjorie

Kinnan Rawlings State Historic Site, 1.5 miles from the campground. The Cracker-style house comprises three separate structures connected by screen porches and open verandas, all designed to take advantage of cooling breezes. The house is closed to the public on Mondays, Tuesdays, and Wednesdays and during August and September. Restaurants are nearby, and the Yearling Restaurant, which is 0.5 mile from the park, offers a variety of dishes from seafood to venison. The park is near the rails-to-trails bike path and Micanopy's fall antiques and arts-and-crafts festivals.

RV sites, facilities: The 15 RV sites have full hookups and 30-amp electricity. RVs up to 36 feet long and slide-outs can be accommodated. Picnic tables, restrooms, showers, a dump station, laundry facilities, cabins, and snacks are available. All areas of the park are said to be wheelchair accessible. Children are welcome. Leashed pets are permitted.

Reservations, fees: Reservations are recommended. Sites are $15 per night for two people, plus $2 for each additional person. Credit cards are not accepted. Long-term rates are available. The campground is closed Christmas Day, Easter weekend, and Thanksgiving Day.

Directions: From I-75, take Exit 374 eastbound for 0.5 mile on County Road 346 into Micanopy. Continue east for five miles until County Road 346 dead-ends at County Road 325. Turn south and drive three miles. The campground is one mile north of the hamlet of Cross Creek.

Contact: Twin Lakes Fish Camp, 17105 South County Road 325, Hawthorne, FL 32640, 352/466-3194.

19 ELITE RESORTS AT LITTLE ORANGE LAKE

Scenic rating: 6

south of Hawthorne

Set on 800-acre Little Orange Lake, this resort boasts a 130-foot fishing pier and water sports.

Formerly the Gator Landing Golf Club and Campground, the park was acquired in 2005 by the Elite Resorts chain, and improvements are planned. The park is closed as of May 2006, but may reopen sometime in 2007; call ahead for updated information.

RV sites, facilities: All sites have water and electricity, and some have full hookups. Oversized sites are 40 by 70 feet. Restrooms, showers, a dump station, a pool, a dock, a lake, a dog-walk area, and a boat ramp are on the premises. Children are welcome. Leashed pets up to about 50 pounds are permitted; no rottweilers, Doberman pinschers, or pit bulls are allowed.

Reservations, fees: Reservations are recommended. Sites are $14–20 per night for two people, plus $1 per extra person and $1 for 50-amp service. Rates are subject to change. Credit cards are not accepted. Long-term stays are allowed.

Directions: From the intersection of U.S. 301 and State Road 20, drive south on U.S. 301 across the railroad tracks. Take the first left and go 1.3 miles on Holden Park Road.

Contact: Elite Resorts at Little Orange Lake, 8815 Holden Park Road, Hawthorne, FL 32640, 352/481-5547 or 352/685-1900, www.eliteresorts.com.

20 HART SPRINGS GILCHRIST COUNTY PARK

Scenic rating: 9

near Trenton

Bordering this sprawling 400-acre park is the Suwannee River, a beautiful spot with bubbling springs and a beach for swimming and snorkeling. Fishing is good along the riverbank for bass, bream, and catfish; there's also a boat ramp. A 0.5-mile-long boardwalk that is wheelchair accessible meanders along the river's edge for a view of alligators, turtles, herons, and the occasional manatee. The campground is nestled under spreading oaks. The park is staffed around the clock by an attendant who lives here.

RV sites, facilities: There are 70 full-hookup RV sites with 30/50-amp electricity. Restrooms, showers, volleyball courts, a boat ramp, a snack bar, playground, and both open-air and closed pavilions for group activities are available. Most areas are wheelchair accessible. Children are welcome. Pets are allowed. Alcohol is prohibited.

Reservations, fees: Reservations are not necessary. Sites are $20 per night for four people, plus $2 for each additional person. Credit cards are not accepted. Long-term rates are available.

Directions: From I-75 north of Gainesville, take Exit 387 onto State Road 26 and drive west for 32 miles, through Trenton, then turn right on County Road 232 and head north for 4 miles. Turn left (west) on County Road 344 for 0.7 mile to the park.

Contact: Hart Springs Gilchrist County Park, 4240 Southwest 86th Avenue, Bell, FL 32619, 352/463-3444, www.hartsprings.com.

21 MANATEE SPRINGS STATE PARK

Scenic rating: 10

near Chiefland west of U.S. 19/98

BEST (

One of the gems of Florida's state park network, Manatee Springs encompasses 2,373 acres of heavily wooded hammock dressed in Spanish moss beside the lower Suwannee River. A nature trail and boardwalk lead to the scenic, meandering waterway; at the end is a boat dock, a launch pad for canoeing and fishing expeditions. And more natural wonders await within the park's boundaries: Manatee Springs is a fantastic swimming and snorkeling hole where 117 million gallons of crystal-clear water bubble to the surface every day, then wash down a 1,000-foot run to the Suwannee and the Gulf of Mexico, 23 miles downstream. Occasionally, manatees can be seen from the banks, especially during the winter months. Certified divers can

explore underground caverns that link a series of sinkholes. Divers must register at the ranger station. More than eight miles of trails for hikers and mountain bikers wind through the park. Keep on the lookout for red-shouldered hawks and have an ear cocked at night for the eerie hoots of barred owls. Just one word of warning about this pretty place: Ticks and chiggers can be a nuisance during the summer months. First aid is available at the ranger station.

RV sites, facilities: The park has 94 sites with water, 30-amp electricity, fire grills, and picnic tables. Two of the sites are 50-amp. RVs up to 35 feet long can be accommodated. On the premises are showers, restrooms, a dump station, playgrounds, a snack bar, a canoe rental concession, nature trails, horseshoe pits, and volleyball courts. The docks, bathhouse, office, and store are wheelchair accessible. Golf, groceries, restaurants, and laundry facilities are located within six miles. Children are welcome. Pets are allowed with proof of vaccination.

Reservations, fees: Reservations are recommended; contact ReserveAmerica at 800/336-3521 or reserveamerica.com. Sites are $16 per night for up to eight people. Credit cards are accepted. The maximum stay is 14 days.

Directions: From U.S. 19/98 in Chiefland, turn west on State Road 320 and drive six miles to the park.

Contact: Manatee Springs State Park, 11650 Northwest 115th Street, Chiefland, FL 32626, 352/493-6072, fax 352/493-6089, www.floridastateparks.org. Additional information can be obtained from Suwannee Basin GEOpark, 11650 Northwest 115th Street, Chiefland, FL 32626, 352/493-6072.

22 OTTER SPRINGS RV RESORT

Scenic rating: 10

northwest of Fanning Springs

BEST (

Otter Springs is a lovely place that boasts one mile of frontage on the east bank of the

Suwannee River and two natural springs. These 820 acres of woods have access to the Suwannee River for boating, canoeing, bird-watching, and fishing. One spring empties into the Suwannee after a mile-long run through the park; the other is about 30 yards in size. New owners have made vast improvements; the park had been closed for more than five years and reopened in 2005. The word is not out yet, so you can be among the first to tell your friends. The park is equestrian-friendly, and the owners allow people to ride their horses on the trails.

RV sites, facilities: There are 110 drive-through RV sites with sewer hookups, water, and 50-amp electricity, of which 10 only have water and electric. Most have fire rings and picnic tables. Even the largest RVs can be accommodated. You can access the Internet in the office. There are restrooms, showers, laundry facilities, a pool, a lodge with a wraparound porch, cabin rentals, a boat launch, and a dock for small boats, canoes, or kayaks. A store that sells ice and limited supplies, a game room, a screened picnic pavilion, a pool, a playground, and canoe rentals are on-site. The lodge and the pool area are wheelchair accessible. Groceries are 10 miles away in Chiefland, and restaurants are within 4 miles in Fanning Springs. Children are welcome. Leashed pets (no attack dogs) are permitted.

Reservations, fees: Reservations are not necessary. Sites are $20 per night for a family of four people, plus $3 for electricity and $4 for each additional person. Credit cards are not accepted. Long-term rates are available.

Directions: From the intersection of U.S. 19/98 in Fanning Springs, drive east one mile on State Road 26. At State Road 232, turn left on Southwest 70th Street and continue about one to the entrance.

Contact: Otter Springs RV Resort, 6470 Southwest 80th Avenue, Trenton, FL 32693, 352/463-0800 or 800/883-9107, fax 352/463-0575, www.otterprings.com.

23 BREEZY ACRES CAMPGROUND

Scenic rating: 4

near Chiefland on Alternate U.S. 27

This tranquil, sunny park in the countryside caters to seniors, with coffee-and-doughnut socials on Saturday mornings and cozy potluck dinners on Wednesday nights. Other favorite things to do are enjoying the peace and quiet.

RV sites, facilities: You'll be out in the country sleeping at one of the park's 50 large, grassy RV sites with full hookups. Eight sites have 50-amp electrical service, and the rest have 30-amp. On the premises are showers, restrooms, laundry facilities, a dump station, a recreation room, horseshoe pits, and shuffleboard courts. The bathhouse, clubhouse, and office are wheelchair accessible. Children are permitted for short visits. Leashed pets are allowed.

Reservations, fees: Reservations are recommended. Sites are $14 per night for four people, plus $1 for each additional person and $1 for using air conditioners. Credit cards are not accepted. Long-term rates are available.

Directions: From U.S. 19/98 in Chiefland, turn east on Alternate U.S. 27 and drive seven miles to the park.

Contact: Breezy Acres Campground, 10050 Northeast 20th Avenue, Chiefland, FL 32626, 352/493-7602.

24 SHELL MOUND COUNTY PARK

Scenic rating: 9

outside Cedar Key

This little treasure is a favorite for locals and is often overlooked by travelers exploring nearby Cedar Key. Here you can camp beneath gnarled oaks in the heart of the Lower Suwannee River National Wildlife Refuge, a 52,000-acre parcel of dry scrub, bottomland hardwoods, cypress swamp, and coastal marshes. It is teeming with more than 250 species of birds, reptiles, and mammals, including American bald eagles, eastern indigo snakes, Atlantic Ripley turtles, gopher tortoises, bobcats, red foxes, and white-tailed deer. The refuge stretches for 26 miles along the Gulf of Mexico and offers plenty of paved roadways, scenic overlooks, and trails for animal lovers who want to observe wildlife. For more information, contact the refuge manager at 352/493-0238 or see detailed maps and trail guides at http://lowersuwannee.fws.gov. Adjacent to the nine-acre campground is a prehistoric Indian mound. Throughout the park you'll have spectacular views of the gulf and marshes.

RV sites, facilities: Eight RV sites have water, electricity, picnic tables, and campfire rings. Restrooms, showers, a boat ramp, and a dump station are available. Children are welcome. Leashed pets are permitted. Alcohol is forbidden.

Reservations, fees: Sites are first-come, first-served. The fee is $5 per night for two people, plus $1 for each additional person. Credit cards are not accepted. Stays are limited to seven days.

Directions: From U.S. 19/98 at Otter Creek, turn southwest on State Road 24, drive 22 miles to County Road 347, and turn right. Drive 2.3 miles north to County Road 326 and turn left, then proceed 3.2 miles west to the campground. The park address is 17650 SW 78th Place, Cedar Key, FL 32625.

Contact: Levy County Parks and Recreation Department, P.O. Box 248, Bronson, FL 32621, 352/486-5127.

25 CEDAR KEY SUNSET ISLE PARK

Scenic rating: 6

in Cedar Key

Shady sites and beguiling sunsets on a marsh at the edge of the Gulf of Mexico are featured at

this campground behind the Sunset Isle Motel. It's just 1.3 miles from the center of Cedar Key, so you could cycle, walk, or take a street-worthy golf cart into town.

Cedar Key, also known as Margaritaville North, is a colony of artists and salty fishermen who would make balladeer Jimmy Buffett feel right at home. Reminiscent of Key West, quaint Cedar Key is home to a history museum and plenty of seafood restaurants, art galleries, and, yes, touristy T-shirt shops—it's just a lot less crazy and crowded than its sister city in the Florida Keys.

Like Key West, Cedar Key is steeped in seafaring lore. Spanish colonists built fortifications near the existing city, and Cedar Key was a bustling port and railroad terminal up until the Civil War. Until the turn of the 20th century, it prospered by harvesting slabs of cedar for pencils, until all the cedars were felled. Now fishing and tourism are mainstays of the economy. Offshore, accessible only by boat, is the Cedar Keys National Wildlife Refuge, a dozen islands that host a seabird rookery and an 1850s lighthouse. Rental boats are available at the downtown marina. To the south, the 30,000-acre Waccasassa Bay State Preserve, also accessible only by boat, offers more opportunities for fresh- and saltwater fishing, bird-watching, and canoeing—or for simply savoring unspoiled vistas of windswept black rush marsh and cypress hammocks; for information, call 352/543-5567. Little has changed since the 18th century, when pirate Jose Gasparilla plied the currents offshore, plundering Spanish merchant ships. Legend has it that he buried treasure a dozen miles north of here, at the mouth of the Suwannee River.

RV sites, facilities: There are 53 RV sites with full hookups, 30-amp and 50-amp electrical service, concrete patios, and picnic tables. RVs up to 52 feet long can be accommodated. Lots are long and narrow at 100 by 20 feet. Three sites are pull-through. Restrooms, showers, a recreation room, and a pool are available, as are motel rooms. You can fish from five docks, or watch the sunset; one dock even has a fireplace. Children are welcome. Leashed pets are permitted.

Reservations, fees: Reservations are recommended. Sites are $25–35 per night for two people, plus $5 for each additional person. Credit cards are accepted. Long-term rates are available.

Directions: From U.S. 19/98 at Otter Creek, turn west on State Road 24 and drive 24 miles. The park, which is part of a motel facility, is on the north side of State Road 24 as you enter Cedar Key.

Contact: Cedar Key Sunset Isle Park, P.O. Box 150, Cedar Key, FL 32625, 352/543-6124, www.cedarkeyrv.com.

26 RAINBOW COUNTRY RV CAMPGROUND

Scenic rating: 7

in Sumner off U.S. 19/98

You'll find a mix of sunny and shaded sites at this family-oriented campground, which is located just five miles from the beaches, docks, restaurants, and shopping in the historic village of Cedar Key. Next door is an antiques shop, bait, tackle, and groceries. Perched on the edge of expansive wildlife preserves, this is a perfect spot for artists and shutterbugs whose favored subjects are panoramas of marshland dotted with palms. About 20 percent of the park is occupied by year-round residents. Favorite things to do are fishing, hunting, shelling, shopping, and relaxing.

RV sites, facilities: This park has 62 RV sites, 42 with full hookups. Ten sites have 50-amp electrical service, and the rest have 30 amp. Each site has a concrete patio, a fire ring, and a picnic table. RVs up to 45 feet long and slide-outs can be accommodated. On the premises are showers, restrooms, a dump station, laundry facilities, limited groceries, rental campers, a community kitchen with potluck dinners, a game room, a recreation room, boccie ball (lawn bowling), horseshoes, and basketball hoops. The bathhouse, clubhouse, office,

and store are wheelchair accessible. Children are welcome. Leashed pets are permitted.

Reservations, fees: Reservations are recommended. Sites are $17 per night for two people, plus $2 for each additional person. Kids under three are free. Credit cards are accepted. Long-term stays are allowed.

Directions: From U.S. 19/98 at Otter Creek, turn southwest on State Road 24 and drive 14 miles to the campground.

Contact: Rainbow Country RV Campground, 11951 Southwest Shiloh Road, Cedar Key, FL 32625, 352/543-6268, www.rainbowcampground.com.

27 SHADY OAKS CAMPGROUND

Scenic rating: 2

south of Otter Creek off U.S. 19/98

Shady Oaks is described as "edge of woods quiet," which aptly sums up this place on the road to Cedar Key. The campground is wooded and grassy, with deer and wild turkeys occasionally wandering through. Like the critters, you are on your own: Select a site, slip $10 in the self-service payment box, hook up your rig, and kick back. "Just holler" across the fence if you want to meet owner Wayne Fouts. There are no restrooms, and the nearest phone is 0.75 mile away at Martin's convenience store on the corner of State Road 24 and U.S. 19/98, which is open 6 A.M.–6 P.M. daily except Monday.

RV sites, facilities: The 13 RV sites have full hookups and picnic tables. There are no restrooms or showers. The closest groceries and restaurants are 13 miles north in Chiefland. Children are welcome. Leashed pets are permitted.

Reservations, fees: Reservations are not necessary. Sites are $15 per night. Credit cards are not accepted. Long-term rates are available.

Directions: From U.S. 19/98 in Otter Creek, turn west on State Road 24 and drive 0.75 mile to the campground.

Contact: Shady Oaks Campground, 440 Southwest 3rd Street/P.O. Box 184, Otter Creek, FL 32683, 352/486-3236.

28 VILLAGE PINES CAMPGROUND

Scenic rating: 5

on U.S. 19/98 north of Inglis

Snowbirds flock to this park each winter to find peace and shade under the pines. It is close to the Gulf Hammock Wildlife Management Area and Goethe State Forest, a 48,000-acre tract of longleaf pine flat woods laced with roads and trails for hiking and horseback riding. For state forest information, call 352/447-2202. Groceries and restaurants are available seven miles away in Inglis.

RV sites, facilities: There are 30 RV sites with full hookups, electricity, and picnic tables; half are pull-through. On the premises are restrooms, showers, laundry facilities, a dump station, a recreation room, horseshoe pits, and shuffleboard courts. Children are allowed. Leashed pets are permitted.

Reservations, fees: Reservations are not necessary. Sites are $9 per night for two people, plus $1 for each additional person and $2 for using air conditioners or electric heaters. Credit cards are not accepted. Long-term rates are available.

Directions: From Inglis, on U.S. 19/98, drive seven miles north to the campground. Look for the covered wagon out front.

Contact: Village Pines Campground, 8053 Southeast 140th Lane, Inglis, FL 34449, 352/447-2777.

29 BIG OAKS RIVER RESORT AND CAMPGROUND

Scenic rating: 7

Between Inglis and Crystal River

These wooded three acres in this campground offer direct access to the Withlacoochee River for canoeing, fishing, and just enjoying the view. Saltwater fishing is just 7.5 miles downstream at the Gulf of Mexico.

RV sites, facilities: There are 21 full-hookup RV sites with water and electricity for overnighters and seasonal visitors. Restrooms, showers, laundry facilities, and cable TV are available. On the premises are a pool, a boat ramp, a dock, canoe rentals, cabins, and a dog-walk area. Also for rent are kayaks, bicycles, pontoon boats, inner tubes, and johnboats. A recreation hall offers darts, games, TV, and other entertainment. Children are welcome. Leashed pets are permitted.

Reservations, fees: Reservations are recommended. Sites are $25 per night for two people, plus $1.50 per extra person. Credit cards are accepted. Long-term rates are available.

Directions: From Inglis, drive south on U.S. 19 to the outskirts of town. Turn west on West River Road to the park entrance.

Contact: Big Oaks River Resort and Campground, 14035 West River Road, Inglis, FL 34449, 352/447-5333, fax 352/447-4125, www.bigoaksriverresort.com.

30 B's MARINA AND CAMPGROUND

Scenic rating: 5

west of Yankeetown

The only campground in Yankeetown that fronts on the Withlacoochee River, this park is just three miles from the Gulf of Mexico. With an emphasis on kayaking and fishing, this campground is decidedly water oriented. Fishing guides and charters are available. "We want you to come back and tell us some good fish tales," say the owners.

RV sites, facilities: There are 15 RV sites for overnighters and 15 for seasonal visitors. All have full hookups and a choice of 30-amp or 50-amp electrical service. Restrooms, showers, laundry facilities, a boat ramp, a dock, kayak and pontoon boat rentals, and a dog-walk area are provided. Children are welcome. Leashed pets ("good dogs only") are permitted.

Reservations, fees: Reservations are recommended. Sites are $25 per night for two people, plus $2.50 per extra person. Credit cards are not accepted. Long-term rates are available.

Directions: From Yankeetown, drive west on County Road 40 to 66th Street, where you'll see a sign for the park. Turn left on 66th Street and continue to Riverside Drive. Turn right and go one block to the park entrance on the river.

Contact: B's Marina and Campground, 6621 Riverside Drive, Yankeetown, FL 34498, 352/447-5888, fax 352/447-3177, www.bmarinacampground.net.

31 CATTAIL CREEK RV PARK

Scenic rating: 8

in Yankeetown

This friendly, well-kept campground has plenty of shade and paved roads that are great for little kids on skates and bikes. The pool is the social center of the park, although every now and then the party shifts to the recreation hall for a "wingding" potluck supper and dance. Fishing is the favorite pastime; a nearby county boat ramp and several marinas provide access to the Gulf of Mexico and estuaries in the Gulf Hammock Wildlife Management Area, havens for redfish, sea trout, flounder, and drum. The campground has fish-cleaning tables set aside for successful anglers and holds "fish lie fabrication classes" for those who come back empty-handed. The management also sponsors community fish fries and contests.

RV sites, facilities: There are 72 RV or tent sites with full hookups, picnic tables, and cable TV (long-term only). Both 30-amp and 50-amp electrical sites are available. On the premises are restrooms, showers, laundry facilities, a dump station, a pool, and a recreation hall. The restrooms are wheelchair accessible. Children and leashed pets are welcome.

Reservations, fees: Reservations are recommended. Sites are $25 per night for two people, plus $2 for each extra person. Credit cards are not accepted. Long-term rates are available.

Directions: From U.S. 19/98 in Inglis, turn west on County Road 40 and drive three miles to the campground.

Contact: Cattail Creek RV Park, 41 Cattail Lane, Yankeetown, FL 34498, 352/447-3050, www.cattailcreekrvpark.com.

JACKSONVILLE

BEST RV PARKS AND CAMPGROUNDS

◖ **Families**
Flamingo Lake RV Resort, page 146

◖ **Most Unusual**
Hidden River Resort, page 153

◖ **Publicly Managed
 Beachfront Campgrounds**
Huguenot Memorial Park, page 148
Kathryn Abbey Hanna Park, page 149

For many RV travelers, the first stop in Florida
is near Jacksonville – the largest city in the United States, if
counting by acreage. Rich in history, the area boasts great
beaches, unspoiled forests, city attractions, full-service RV
parks, and rustic campgrounds in beautiful settings. If driving
from the Northeast on I-95, pull over at the official "Welcome
to Florida" visitors center for a free glass of fresh orange juice –
it's a tradition. You'll also receive an official state highway
map.

This part of Florida was first settled by Europeans in 1513.
A few years later, the French built the first Protestant colony
in America at Fort Caroline. There, about 140 French colonists
were killed when Spanish soldiers swept down on their fort
in 1565. It was the first decisive battle fought by Europeans
for American soil and set into motion a chain of events that
left Florida in Spanish hands for years. Today a replica of the
fort, with French flags flying above cannons, stands on the
banks of the St. Johns River.

The river divides downtown Jacksonville, where skyscrap-
ers (mostly insurance businesses) rise on both banks. For
river views in a citified setting, Jacksonville Landing is an
entertainment center with boat docks, restaurants, and shopping (management says parking RVs is no problem, though
you can't stay overnight). Sightseeing includes touring the
Anheuser-Busch Brewery and Jacksonville Zoo, watching the
Jaguars play NFL football, and taking the kids to Adventure
Landing, an amusement park in Jacksonville Beach with miniature golf courses, a go-cart track, and a laser-tag arena.

To camp near the beach, head for Huguenot Memorial
Park, surrounded by three bodies of water: the Fort George

Inlet, the St. Johns River, and the Atlantic Ocean. From the beach, you're likely to see huge ships headed to Mayport Naval Air Station, where ship tours are available most weekends. This base is the third largest in the country. North of Jacksonville Beach is Fort Clinch, named for a commander who fought in the Second Seminole War in the 1840s.

You may be sorry if you don't make time to explore the five-square-mile Talbot Islands State Parks, especially Big Talbot Island State Park where huge, bleached, fallen tree trunks give the shore a spooky feel. Nearby attractions include the George Crady Bridge Fishing Pier and the historic Ribault Club (newly restored in 2005) at Fort George Island Cultural State Park. Don't miss a visit to Florida's oldest plantation—the former home of Zephaniah Kingsley. The plantation is part of the National Park Service's 46,000-acre Timucuan Ecological and Historic Preserve.

The Jacksonville area is also home to the 200,000-acre Osceola National Forest, where the campground at Ocean Pond is highly recommended. The Battle of Olustee, Florida's only major battle during the Civil War, was fought in this forest where some 3,000 soldiers lost their lives. Confederate soldiers headed off a Sherman-style invasion of Florida, which served as the Confederacy's breadbasket. Each February, on the second weekend of the month, reenactors dressed in Union and Confederate garb come here to light cannons, ride cavalry horses, and the like.

For a special side trip, cross the St. Marys River to get to the Cumberland Island National Seashore in Georgia. Wild horses roam the northern stretches of the island, and a couple of old mansions can still be viewed along its beaches.

1 FORT CLINCH STATE PARK

🥾 🛶 🏊 🚤 🐕 🚶 🚐 ⛺

Scenic rating: 10

on the Atlantic Ocean at Florida's northeastern tip

You can fall asleep to the sound of ocean waves crashing near your sandy campsite. The ride to the park is a study in contrasts, as you pass neat shops and Victorian homes in old-town Fernandina Beach, as well as huge power plants. But the key attraction is the park.

The campground is set where the St. Marys and Amelia Rivers come together to form Cumberland Sound, the border between Florida and Georgia. You have a choice of two camping areas: 21 unshaded, sandy sites are near the ocean, and 41 others are in a shady coastal hammock of big, beautiful oaks and cedars on the Amelia River. Both are outstanding in their own way. Fireflies might flicker like Christmas lights at dusk in the shady "river campground," where you will feel more sheltered from other campers thanks to at least some native brush providing a screen. At the beach sites, you'll be closer to other campers. But it's hard to beat waking up to feel the sea breeze and see the pink fingers of dawn reaching over the Atlantic and the nearby dunes. Raccoons can be a manageable but irksome problem at the river sites (tip: keep food and coolers in the car).

Anglers use a fishing pier to catch whiting, red bass, and sheepshead, while windsurfers take to the Amelia River, also known as the Intracoastal Waterway. The beach is popular among sunbathers and swimmers. Nearby in town are rental canoes and kayaks, a boat ramp, tennis and volleyball courts, and saltwater fishing charters. At the park, nature lovers have two hiking trails to choose from: a loop that leads through a wooded area and around man-made Willow Pond, or a shorter path near the park's namesake fort that passes through a hammock en route to the Intracoastal Waterway.

Even if you have a passing interest in history, don't miss the centerpiece of the two-square-mile park—the fort. Named for a commander who fought in the Second Seminole War in the 1840s, Fort Clinch was only partially finished when the Civil War commenced in 1861. Because no Yankee troops were around, the Confederates quickly took over the place. By early the following year, though, with the coastal islands to the north in Federal hands, the Confederates abandoned the fort as indefensible, and Union troops moved in soon thereafter. The fort never was completed because construction of its masonry walls was outpaced by the development of new and better cannons.

For the best reenactment, visit on the first weekend of each month and take a nighttime candlelight tour that conjures up images of the Union and Confederate soldiers who battled on these very grounds. During the summer, candlelight tours also are held on the second and third weekends of the month (call for reservations). In May, a special full-garrison reenactment by Union soldiers takes place, then the fort is turned over to the Confederates in October.

For a special side trip, cross the St. Marys River to get to the Cumberland Island National Seashore in Georgia. Wild horses roam the northern stretches of the island, and a couple of old mansions can still be viewed along its beaches. An eerie island attraction is the ruins of Dungeness, the stately home of the Carnegie family. "It sort of reminds you of Tara from *Gone with the Wind*—after it burned down," says a friend.

To get to Cumberland Island, use your own boat to cross the St. Marys River. An alternative is to drive 40 miles to the town of St. Marys, Georgia, and catch a ferry from there. To do this, head west on Highway A1A from Fort Clinch's campground through Fernandina Beach to northbound I-95. Cross the Florida/Georgia border. At the first exit, Highway 40, go east to the town of St. Marys. There, catch a ferry to Cumberland Island, which is just across the Cumberland Sound from Fort Clinch State Park. For more information, call the national seashore at 912/882-4335.

RV sites, facilities: Sixty-two sites of varying

sizes are available in two sections, all offering water and 30-amp electric hookups and campfire rings. RVs up to 40 feet long and slide-outs can be accommodated at some sites. Restrooms, showers, a dump station, laundry facilities, firewood, and a playground are available. Groceries, LP gas, restaurants, and bait are available within five miles. The bathhouse, fishing pier, and store are wheelchair accessible. Children are welcome. Leashed pets are permitted with proof of current rabies vaccination.

Reservations, fees: Reservations are highly recommended; contact ReserveAmerica at 800/336-3521 or reserveamerica.com. Sites are $24 per night for up to eight people. You should also call the park to see if a site is available that is large enough to accommodate your RV. Credit cards are accepted. Stays are limited to 14 days.

Directions: From I-95 north of Jacksonville, take Exit 373 and go 15 miles east on Highway A1A, passing through the town of Fernandina Beach along the way. Turn right at Atlantic Avenue. Proceed two miles to the park, on the left.

Contact: Fort Clinch State Park, 2601 Atlantic Avenue, Fernandina Beach, FL 32034, 904/277-7274, www.floridastateparks.org.

❷ BOW AND ARROW CAMPGROUND

Scenic rating: 3

on U.S. 17 south of Yulee

Back before I-95 was built, the road in front of this five-acre park, U.S. 17, was the region's main route into Florida. But today that highway is much less used, although still fairly busy. The sites—some sandy, some grassy—are set back from it quite a ways. So this park is quiet, and it's shady with oaks and pines. Most people here are stopping through or visiting local relatives.

RV sites, facilities: The park offers 56 full-hookup RV campsites, 24 of them pull-through, and 10 with 50-amp electrical service. Each site has a picnic table and 30-amp electricity. A laundry room, restrooms, showers, LP gas, a pool, cable TV, and telephone hookups are available. Children are permitted for overnight visits. Leashed pets are allowed.

Reservations, fees: Reservations are recommended. Sites are $25 per night for two people, plus $3 per extra person. Credit cards are accepted. Long-term stays are okay.

Directions: From I-95 north of Yulee at Exit 373, drive three miles east on Highway A1A to U.S. 17. Turn right and go south for two miles to the campground.

Contact: Bow and Arrow Campground, 598 U.S. 17, Yulee, FL 32097, 904/225-5577, fax 904/225-9233.

❸ FLAMINGO LAKE RV RESORT

Scenic rating: 7

off I-295 northwest of downtown Jacksonville

BEST (

Visitors at this family-oriented campground, which is located a quick hop off I-295, have two places to swim: the pool at the park's eastern end or the 17-acre lake on the western end. Much of the action is at the lake, which has a nice beach with lounging chairs. Gas grills, a pavilion, picnic tables, and a deck are near the shore, where some anglers wet a line. Kids will prefer heading to the east side, though, for the basketball courts, volleyball nets, playground, and pool. This is one of the closest campgrounds to the Anheuser-Busch Brewery on Main Street near the Broward River (tours are available). It also offers the quickest access to the Jacksonville Zoo.

RV sites, facilities: All 152 RV sites (33 pull-through) have full hookups with 30-amp or 50-amp electrical service and cable TV. Paved roads with a speed limit of five miles per hour pass the well-tended campsites. For the best lake views, ask about sites 10–22. Sites 78–98 form a semicircle around the playground, pool, some shaded tables, and a volleyball net on the opposite side of the park. No bicycles are allowed on the beach or sidewalks. Facilities include a pool, a game room, a playground, volleyball, basketball, a bonfire area, a fishing lake, an adult recreation room, a beach, a pavilion with gas grills, and nature trails. Showers, restrooms, a dump station, pay phones, cable TV, LP gas, and a laundry room are also available. A wireless Internet connection is available in the park. Alcoholic beverages must be contained in cups. Parents need to supervise their children at all times. Leashed dogs under 30 pounds are permitted, but they must use the two dog-walk areas and refrain from barking.

Reservations, fees: Reservations are recommended. Sites are $35 per night for two people, plus $3 for each additional person. Credit cards are accepted. Long-term rates are available.

Directions: From Jacksonville, take I-95 north to I-295 (Exit 362B). Head west to the first exit (Exit 32, Lem Turner Road), then drive north a short distance to Newcomb Road. Turn left. You'll soon see the campground.

Contact: Flamingo Lake RV Resort, 3540 Newcomb Road, Jacksonville, FL 32218, 904/766-0672, www.flamingolake.com.

❹ LITTLE TALBOT ISLAND STATE PARK

Scenic rating: 10

in Fort George on the Atlantic Ocean east of Jacksonville

Ideal for nature lovers and beachgoers, sun-washed Little Talbot Island is the only place you can camp in the sprawling complex of natural areas known as the Talbot Islands State Parks. At Little Talbot, you can hike and bike through maritime forests or boat through salt-marsh areas (rental canoes are available from an outfitter one mile north of the park; call 904/251-0016). You also can cross the dunes

that protect the island from the Atlantic Ocean to swim or fish for flounder, redfish, bluefish, striped bass, and sheepshead.

The packed-dirt campsites are fairly close together. Some are screened from neighbors by at least limited brush. Still, the island is remote, so it's not difficult to find solitude. Little Talbot's hiking trails span more than four miles and reward walkers with more solitude than found at many state parks. Try to spot otters, rabbits, or bobcats as you explore. Bird-watchers admire the bald eagles and songbirds, which are among the nearly 200 species of birds identified here.

Be sure to explore other portions of the five-square-mile Talbot Islands State Parks. At Big Talbot Island State Park, huge, bleached fallen tree trunks have become improbably large pieces of driftwood that give the shore a surreal, almost spooky feel. Look for birds along the five marked hiking trails that crisscross the sprawling 2,000-acre day-use area. Also nearby are the George Crady Bridge Fishing Pier, the equestrian-oriented Pumpkin Hill Creek Preserve State Park, and the newlyrestored historic Ribault Club at Fort George Island Cultural State Park.

A little farther north, Amelia Island State Park also offers a taste of "The Real Florida," resembling as closely as possible the Florida that European explorers found when they arrived some 500 years ago. It's a fishing spot, but some people hike along the beach or bird-watch. You can also rent horses to explore the beach. For $45 (age 13 and up only; weight limit 230 pounds), you can saddle up at the Kelly Seahorse Ranch concession in the park. Hourly rides leave at 10 A.M., noon, 2 P.M., and 4 P.M. Check in 30 minutes prior to your ride. For information, call 904/491-5166.

Finally, don't miss a visit to Florida's oldest plantation—nearby Kingsley Plantation, the former home of cotton and sugar planter Zephaniah Kingsley. Get good directions from Little Talbot Island State Park so that you can easily locate the plantation, which is tucked far back from a long dirt road where the bent arms of oak trees converge overhead to form a canopy. Kingsley was a slave trader who married a teenage slave named Anna, then freed her. She went on to own a five-acre farm on the eastern bank of the St. Johns River. She burned it down and fled when Confederates from Georgia threatened to return her to slavery. If you tour the fancy plantation house, you'll notice it faces the river instead of the entrance road. The reason: Rivers were the highways of the day back then. The plantation is part of the National Park Service's 46,000-acre Timucuan Ecological and Historic Preserve; call 904/251-3537 for more information. Also nearby is the Fort George State Cultural Center (see *Huguenot Memorial Park* in this chapter).

RV sites, facilities: These 35 water-and-30-amp electric sites are for RVs; about one-third can fit rigs up to 30 feet long. Two sites are pull-through, and two spots are wheelchair accessible. Each site has a picnic table, a grill, and a fire ring. Canoe rentals, a playground, a nature trail, bike rentals, guided interpretive programs (usually Saturday afternoons), and volleyball entertain campers. Showers, restrooms, a dump station, a small boat ramp, and a laundry room are available. A bird sanctuary is located on nearby Fort George Island. Groceries, restaurants, and bait are located within five miles. Children are allowed. Leashed pets with rabies tags are permitted; no pets may go on the beach.

Reservations, fees: Reservations are recommended; contact ReserveAmerica at 800/336-3521 or reserveamerica.com. Fees are $19 per night for up to eight people. The maximum length of stay is 14 days.

Directions: From I-95 in Jacksonville, take Exit 358A and go east on Heckscher Drive/State Road 105 for 22 miles to the park entrance at right.

Contact: Little Talbot Island State Park, 12157 Heckscher Drive, Jacksonville, FL 32226, 904/251-2320, fax 904/251-2325, www.floridastateparks.org.

5 HUGUENOT MEMORIAL PARK

Scenic rating: 8

on the Atlantic Ocean east of Jacksonville

BEST (

Broad beaches seem to span as far as the eye can see at this 450-acre park surrounded by three bodies of water: Fort George Inlet, the St. Johns River, and the Atlantic Ocean, stretching to 26,000 feet of beachfront. These sandy campsites have no shade, but they're great for passing a few days if you like beach settings. There's a magical quality; although the view from many Florida beaches inevitably includes high-rises or houses, here you'll see just sand and the Atlantic Ocean in the easternmost reaches of the park. Vehicles are permitted on the beach. Bring your own gear to snorkel or windsurf.

Although lacking water and electric hookups, these RV sites have the advantage of being reasonably close to some Jacksonville-area highlights. The nearest is the worthwhile Talbot Islands State Parks (see *Little Talbot Island State Park* in this chapter). The campground is also 10 miles from the Jacksonville Zoo and just down the road from the Fort George State Cultural Center, where you can take a 4.4-mile self-guided history tour by foot or car. Moss-draped oaks shade much of the route. Fort George Island has been continuously inhabited for some 5,000 years. Early Indian occupants shucked oysters and tossed them into piles, which today are up to 65 feet tall and are covered by sand and dirt, making this the highest coastal elevation south of North Carolina's Outer Banks.

RV sites, facilities: There are 68 sites, each with a picnic table, a fire ring, and a grill. Water and electricity are not available. Restrooms, showers, a dump station, and a store are on the premises. The restrooms and store are wheelchair accessible. Boat rentals and charter fishing are in the park. Two waterfront shelters with picnic tables and grills can be rented for $21 per day. Personal watercraft riding, windsurfing, and kite surfing are allowed. Laundry facilities are located eight miles away. Restaurants and bait are available within three miles. Children must be supervised by adults. Two leashed pets are allowed per campsite.

Reservations, fees: Reservations are accepted. Sites are $8 per night for up to six people. Credit cards are accepted. Stays are limited to 15 days out of any given 45 days.

Directions: From I-95 in Jacksonville, take Exit 358A and go east on Heckscher Drive/State Road 105 for 20 miles. The park is on the right side of the road, one mile past the ferry slip.

Contact: Huguenot Memorial Park, 10980 Heckscher Drive, Jacksonville, FL 32226, 904/251-3335, fax 904/251-3019, www.coj .net/Departments/Parks+and+Recreation.

6 CARY STATE FOREST

Scenic rating: 7

north of Baldwin

The three campsites here—set amid pine flat woods that provide only moderate shade—are used mostly by Boy Scouts and people who like to ride their horses through these 3,400 wooded acres. A network of nature trails leads through the flat woods and connects with a boardwalk that winds through a dark cypress swamp. Horseback riders and long-distance hikers may wish to range along a network of forest roads and trails stretching eight miles. There's also a 1.2-mile nature trail. Over a few weekends in fall and winter, the forest is open to archers and hunters bearing muzzle-loading guns. A picnic pavilion sits near the camping area (campers must call ahead for a permit), along with a wildlife-observation tower and interpretive signs. Look for deer, wild turkeys, bobcats, and elusive black bears.

RV sites, facilities: An indeterminate number of campers can be accommodated at a single camping area of three primitive sites located in the forest. Drinking water, restrooms, and showers are available. Supplies and other conveniences can be obtained one mile away in Bryceville or

seven miles south in Baldwin. Children are allowed. Leashed pets are permitted.

Reservations, fees: Reservations are required. Camping is $5 per night; you must obtain a permit by calling 904/266-5021. Day visitors are on the honor system and pay $2 per car.

Directions: From Baldwin, drive north on U.S. 301 for about seven miles. Look for the forest on your right, 0.25 mile north of the Bryceville Fire Station. The campsites are on the forest's main entrance road. From the town of Callahan, drive south on U.S. 301 for 15 miles. The entrance is 1.5 miles south of the forestry district office.

Contact: Cary State Forest, Florida Division of Forestry, 7465 Pavilion Drive, Bryceville, FL 32009. Forest district office: 904/266-5022; Cary State Forester/camping permits: 904/266-5021, www.fl-dof.com/state_forests/cary.html.

7 KATHRYN ABBEY HANNA PARK

Scenic rating: 8

on the Atlantic Ocean in Atlantic Beach east of Jacksonville

BEST (

This oceanfront gem—named for a historian who served on the Florida Board of Parks and Historical Places in the 1940s—is one of Jacksonville's most popular parks, and for good reason. These 450 acres offer something for almost everyone. The more adventurous may want to trek through 15 miles of off-road trails on mountain bikes tailored for beginners or advanced riders. Hikers and bicyclists (helmets are required) each enjoy their own narrow, woodsy nature trails that encircle a 60-acre freshwater lake, where anglers can try their luck for catfish. If you prefer saltwater fish, then head to the county-run park's 1.5-mile-long beach of grayish-tan sand. Lifeguards watch over ocean swimmers from Memorial Day to Labor Day. From the beach, you're likely to see huge ships headed to nearby Mayport Naval Air Station, where ship tours are available most weekends; call 904/270-NAVY (904/270-6289). Hanna Park is about seven miles from Adventure Landing, a pirate-themed family entertainment center with go-carts, laser tag, a water park, and other activities.

For nature lovers and history buffs, this is the closest campground to the National Park Service's Fort Caroline National Memorial. There, approximately 140 French colonists were killed when Spanish soldiers swept down on their fort just after dawn in September 1565. It was the first decisive battle fought by Europeans for American soil and set into motion a chain of events that left Florida in Spanish hands for years to come. Today a replica of the fort, with French flags flying above cannons, stands on the banks of the St. Johns River. You can also hike the pretty Old French Trail, which runs through a remnant of the maritime hammock forest that once covered most riversides in northeast Florida. Just down the road from Fort Caroline is the National Park Service's Theodore Roosevelt Area of the Timucuan Ecological and Historic Preserve. There, you can hike the Willie Browne Trail (named for the former landowner who bequeathed these woods to the public), passing underneath mossy trees and a Confederate soldier's grave en route to the old Willie Browne homestead.

RV sites, facilities: Several loops of campsites are set on either side of a crooked main campground road. The sandy/gravel campsites are irregularly spaced, so don't expect the manicured feel of a modern private campground. There are 278 full-hookup RV sites with water and 30-amp electrical service. For recreation, there's a hiking trail, 15 miles of single-track bicycle trails, a playground, and a fishing lake. Showers, restrooms, picnic areas, a dump station, log cabins (for rent), and a laundry room are available. Groceries and restaurants are located within a 0.5 mile-drive throughout the town of Atlantic Beach, which surrounds Hanna Park. The beach, lake, and six campsites are wheelchair accessible. Children under the age of eight must be supervised by adults

while swimming. Two leashed pets are permitted per campsite.

Reservations, fees: Reservations are recommended but are usually not necessary. Sites are $34 per night for six people. Credit cards are accepted. The maximum stay is 15 days within a 45-day period.

Directions: From I-95 in Jacksonville, take Exit 344 and drive east for about five miles on J. T. Butler Boulevard. Turn left at St. Johns Bluff Road and head north. In about six miles, turn right at Atlantic Boulevard/Highway 10. Continue seven miles, crossing the Intracoastal Waterway. Turn left at Mayport Road/Highway A1A. Turn right on Wonderwood Drive to enter the park, which is just south of the Mayport Naval Air Station.

Contact: Kathryn Abbey Hanna Park, 500 Wonderwood Drive, Jacksonville, FL 32233, 904/249-4700, fax 904/247-8688, www.coj .net/Departments/Parks+and+Recreation.

8 EAST TOWER

Scenic rating: 7

within Osceola National Forest

At East Tower you'll camp amid some of the most wildlife-rich acreage in the state. It's not uncommon to come across deer and turkeys or even to hear the rat-a-tat-tat of an endangered red-cockaded woodpecker. In drier sandy areas, look for gopher tortoises lumbering home to their sandy burrows.

This campground primarily is designed for hunters, as evidenced by the sign on a caged pen here: "Lost dogs." Sometimes, people in pursuit of big hairy beasts with the aid of their own smaller hairy beasts notice that their four-legged helpers have vanished. But the dogs usually come back, and fellow hunters place the pooches in these cages to await their masters' return. East Tower is on the middle prong of the St. Marys River (which leads eventually to Jacksonville and splits Georgia from Florida), offering freshwater anglers a place to fish. Mountain bikers will enjoy the backcountry roads in these parts.

RV sites, facilities: About 50 RVs tents can be accommodated at this primitive camping area. Flush toilets and drinking water are provided, but no electricity. Children are welcome. Leashed pets are permitted.

Reservations, fees: Reservations are not accepted. Camping is free. Stays are limited to 14 days in any 30-day period, except during hunting season.

Directions: From Lake City, take U.S. 441 north to County Road 250 and turn right. Head east about 23 miles. Make a right onto Forest Service Road 202 and continue a short distance to the camp.

Contact: Osceola National Forest, U.S. 90, P.O. Box 70, Olustee, FL 32072, 386/752-2577, www.r8web.com/florida/forests/osceola.htm.

9 WEST TOWER

Scenic rating: 8

western Osceola National Forest

The national forest system of horseback-riding and bicycling trails is centered on this rustic, no-frills crash pad for outdoorsy types. It's also the main place to camp with your horse. The idea isn't to while away time at the dirt-road camping area in the shadow of a forest lookout tower. Instead, you should get out and explore.

From here you can traverse some 50 miles of horse trails, which also are open to backcountry mountain bikers. For beginning riders, the Green Trail is a quick five-mile jaunt on mostly main roads (be on the lookout for vehicles). If you're riding after heavy rains, stick to the Red Trail, a 20-miler through pine flat woods and a few cypress sloughs. A cutoff allows you to reduce the Red Trail to just 10 miles.

Another 20-mile route is the Blue Trail, which offers the added enticement of the western border of the Big Gum Swamp Wilderness, a 13,640-acre

area with no roads at the heart of the national forest that is least disturbed by humans. The Gold Trail, which is approximately 16 miles long, passes through two bay swamps. Avoid this route in wetter periods, particularly if you are an inexperienced rider. Check the bulletin board near the stables at West Tower for further information.

Hunters tend to use these campsites from mid-November to mid-January. Wear bright orange clothing while hiking to avoid being mistaken for game.

RV sites, facilities: Up to 75 people can be accommodated at this primitive camping area. The only facilities are drinking water, flush toilets, and horse stalls. There is no electricity. Children are welcome. Leashed pets are permitted.

Reservations, fees: Reservations are not accepted. Camping is free. Stays are limited to 14 days in any 30-day period, except during hunting season.

Directions: From Lake City, take U.S. 441 north about four miles. Turn right onto Forest Service Road 233 and go about 5.5 miles east until you see the camp.

Contact: Osceola National Forest, U.S. 90, P.O. Box 70, Olustee, FL 32072, 386/752-2577, www.r8web.com/florida/forests/osceola.htm.

10 OCEAN POND CAMPGROUND

Scenic rating: 9

on the northeast end of Ocean Pond in Osceola National Forest

This shady, placid campground sits right beside Ocean Pond, which, at 1,760 acres, is quite a large "pond." It's one of the most popular within Florida's national forests, and the scenery partly explains why. Among other reasons are the sandy beach and the fact that you can keep your boat at your site if you get lucky.

The sites are mostly screened from each other by brushy vegetation, so you're likely to enjoy some privacy. Many sites—most of them under tall, moss-draped pines—face the pretty, round pond. You can swim in a roped-off area in front of the campground.

Boating, fishing, canoeing, and waterskiing are popular at Ocean Pond. If you're into a nice day hike, follow the Florida National Scenic Trail, which passes by the campground, through the outback. Head south for 5.6 miles, passing some smaller sinkholelike ponds along the way until you reach the trailhead at the Olustee Battlefield historic site. There, approximately 5,000 Johnny Rebs held off a larger force of Federals during the Civil War, preventing a Sherman-style invasion of Florida, which served as the Confederacy's breadbasket. Hunting in the forest also is popular, although it is restricted in the area immediately around Ocean Pond. Most hunters camp nearby in the far more primitive Hog Pen Landing site (see next campground) and nine primitive hunt camps. During hunting season, camping is allowed only at Ocean Pond and at the designated hunt camps.

RV sites, facilities: There are 66 sites, including 19 lots with water and 30-amp electricity, 27 sites with water only, and 20 primitive sites for self-contained RVs. The nonprimitive sites are placed on paved roads; the primitive sites are on gravel spurs. Each has a lantern post, a picnic table, and a fire ring. Big RVs can be accommodated at most sites. Facilities include a boat ramp, a swimming area, restrooms, a dump station, and showers. Sites 32–45 are closest to the swimming beach. Sites 1–19 are the most developed. There's a convenience store five miles away in Olustee, but you'll have to drive to Lake City for major supply refills and restaurants. Children and leashed pets are permitted.

Reservations, fees: Reservations are not accepted. Sites are $8–18 per night for up to five people. Stays are limited to 14 days between May 1 and September 30, and to 30 days between October 1 and April 30.

Directions: From Lake City, drive east on U.S. 90 for 14 miles. After you pass the ranger's office and the convenience store in the town of Olustee, turn left onto County Road 250A. Follow this road north about four miles to the campground.

Contact: Osceola National Forest, U.S. 90,

P.O. Box 70, Olustee, FL 32072, 386/752-2577, www.r8web.com/florida/forests/osceola.htm.

11 HOG PEN LANDING

🏃 🏊 🚤 🎣 🐾 🚐 ⛺

Scenic rating: 6

north of Ocean Pond in Osceola National Forest

Here is a tranquil, rustic retreat on the north side of Ocean Pond, with sites set underneath pines and a few oaks. In late fall and early winter, you're likely to share the place with hunters in search of deer, wild hogs, bobcats, and other game. In spring, turkey hunters turn up. It's possible to fish in the freshwater lake from the shore, but you'll do better if you have a boat.

Olustee Beach is worth a visit for a picnic and a walk down an interpretive boardwalk to the site of the long-gone, turn-of-the-20th-century Russell Eppinger sawmill. The trail follows an old tram road that was used to carry trees from the forest to the sawmill. Back then, workers made about $2 per day for cutting 15 cross ties. Not far away is the Olustee Battlefield historic site. The Florida National Scenic Trail passes near here for plentiful hiking opportunities.

RV sites, facilities: This primitive camping area accommodates up to 30 people. Chemical toilets and a boat ramp are available. You won't find drinking water or any other facilities. Water can be obtained four miles away at the developed Ocean Pond Campground. Children are welcome. Leashed pets are permitted.

Reservations, fees: Reservations are not accepted. The cost is $2 per vehicle. Stays are limited to 14 days in any 30-day period, except during hunting season.

Directions: From Lake City, head east on U.S. 90 about 10 miles. Turn left onto Forest Service Road 241, go about three miles north to Forest Service Road 241A, and turn right into the campground.

Contact: Osceola National Forest, U.S. 90, P.O. Box 70, Olustee, FL 32072, 386/752-2577, www.r8web.com/florida/forests/osceola.htm.

12 HIDDEN RIVER RESORT

Scenic rating: 8

north of Macclenny just across the state line

BEST (

Although technically located in Georgia, this 88-acre nature-oriented, nudist park on the St. Marys River is just across the water from Florida. Bring your own horse and ride on the trails that meander through the woods and along the river. The wooded campsites offer privacy. Family groups are welcome; a 60- by 30-foot pavilion provides gathering space. The "Nudie Blues" music festival is held each year on the last weekend in April.

RV sites, facilities: This is a nudist resort that brags there is absolutely no pavement to be seen, so "you can take off your shoes and wiggle your toes." Absolutely prohibited are any kind of glass containers in the park. There are 26 drive-through RV sites with full hookups (half with 30-amp service, half with 50-amp). Picnic tables, restrooms, showers, and a dump station are available. On the premises are a pool, a hot tub, horseback-riding and hiking trails, and a pavilion. The bathhouse is wheelchair accessible. Children are welcome. Leashed pets are allowed, as are horses.

Reservations, fees: Reservations are recommended. Sites are $45 per night for two people, plus $15 per extra person and $5 for 50-amp electricity. Credit cards are not accepted. Stay as long as you wish.

Directions: From I-10, take Exit 335 at Macclenny northbound on State Road 121 and drive seven miles. Cross three bridges at the St. Marys River and the Georgia state line and immediately turn left on State Road 185. Drive 8.5 miles to Reynolds Bridge Road and turn left (this is the only paved road). The park entrance is ahead about 2,000 feet on the left.

Contact: Hidden River Resort, 9988 County Road 120, Sanderson, FL 32087, 912/843-2603, www.hiddenriverresort.com.

13 WHITEY'S FISH CAMP

Scenic rating: 4

on Swimming Pen Creek south of Orange Park

Diners have pulled up in everything from little boats to limousines to eat the alligator-tail appetizers and secret-recipe fried catfish at Whitey's restaurant overlooking Swimming Pen Creek. The popularity of the all-you-can-eat catfish spread is credited with spawning this three-acre campground. Here, oaks shade RV sites and campers launch boats for free to try for snook (particularly in winter) on the St. Johns River. Brackish Swimming Pen Creek meanders into Doctors Lake and the St. Johns. Dogs occasionally accompany their masters at the restaurant deck, and female diners have arrived in swimsuits. Don't try the latter; although Whitey's is casual, sunbathers must slip on shirts. About 25 percent of the park is occupied year-round. Historic St. Augustine is about 35 miles away.

RV sites, facilities: All 44 RV sites have full hookups and 20/30/50-amp electrical outlets. RVs up to 40 feet long and slide-outs can be accommodated. Boat rentals, a boat ramp, charter fishing, a restaurant, and a snack bar are available. Showers, restrooms, picnic tables, a dump station, bait, tackle, and a laundry room are on-site. An 18-hole golf course and grocery stores are located two miles away. Children are welcome. Leashed pets are permitted.

Reservations, fees: Reservations are not necessary. Sites are $22 per night for two people, plus $1 per extra person. Credit cards are accepted. Long-term rates are available.

Directions: From I-295 in Orange Park, take Exit 10 and go south on U.S. 17/Roosevelt Boulevard for about five miles. Turn west (right) at County Road 220. Proceed about two miles to the campground entrance.

Contact: Whitey's Fish Camp, 2032 County Road 220, Orange Park, FL 32073, 904/269-4198, www.whiteysfishcamp.com.

ST. AUGUSTINE

BEST RV PARKS AND CAMPGROUNDS

It's hard to believe, but Spanish soldiers and missionaries were setting up house in St. Augustine two generations before the famished Pilgrims landed at Plymouth Rock. St. Augustine was founded in 1565 and served as Spain's capitol for its Florida colony. Today, the biggest reminder of Florida's first conquerors are the massive walls of the nearby Castillo de San Marcos fort, which is still standing and open to visitors. (Similar in style to fortresses built by the Spaniards in their conquest of the Caribbean, the fort was completed 100 years after St. Augustine's founding.) The nation's oldest city, St. Augustine charms visitors with its colorful heritage, amazing beaches, and nature-oriented retreats.

St. Augustine is a supremely pedestrian-friendly city, with restaurants, shops, and quaint watering holes. In fact, the city's cobblestoned historic district may have more tourist attractions than any other place outside of the Orlando/Disney area: sightseeing trains, Ripley's Believe It or Not!, Potter's Wax Museum, the "oldest store" museum," the oldest wooden schoolhouse, an old jail, the purported Fountain of Youth, ghost tours, an alligator farm, Florida's first lighthouse, the "oldest house," and horseback carriage rides. The World Golf Hall of Fame is a duffer's dream, with exhibits about the great players and history of the game. And yes, there are two golf courses, both 18-hole championship, par-

72 courses offering five sets of tees. Each golf cart has a global positioning system.

Be sure to also take in the spires of nearby Flagler College, which owns the former Ponce de Leon Hotel, an architectural jewel that was once a luxury hotel in the early 20th century. Across the street from the college at Memorial Presbyterian Church, you can see the tomb of Henry Flagler, the railroad tycoon who forever transformed Florida by building a railroad that reached the Florida Keys.

The magnificent Bridge of Lions (undergoing a multiyear renovation project) leads from downtown St. Augustine to Anastasia Island. On the island is Anastasia State Park, popular for its coastal camping at the edge of the Atlantic Ocean. It gets rave reviews for its beach, windsurfing, fishing, and swimming. For a short walk, hit the 0.25-mile quarry trail just inside Anastasia park's entrance to see where Spaniards mined the Castillo de San Marcos' walls.

For RVers requiring more comforts than the state parks provide, there are a few more developed parks near the beach, such as Bryn Mawr Ocean Resort, Ocean Grove RV Resort, Beverly Beach Camptown, and Flagler by the Sea.

Southwest of St. Augustine are vast acres of unspoiled woods on both sides of the St. Johns River as it flows southward into 100-acre Lake George. The fishing is great here, particularly for anglers looking for bass.

ST AUGUSTINE

see
Jacksonville
page 144

Lakeside

301

Starke

21

16

Glen Cove
Springs

1

21

Mike Roess Gold
Head Branch
State Park

Keystone
Heights

100

Georges
Lake

17

20

19

21

Welaka

Satsuma

22-23

Palatka

San Mateo

Georgetown

27-28

24

25

29

Hammond

Lake

George

Ocala

National

Lake George
State Forest

Crescent
Lake

26

Lake
Disston

17

Pierson

see
Ocala
page 180

0   5 mi

0   5 km

19

Forest

40

De Leon
Springs

Jacksonv
Beach

Ponte Ver
Beach

Palm Valley

Guana
River
State
Park

95

1

A1A

South Ponte
Vedra Beach

St Augustine

3-4

5-6

7

8

St Augustine Be

9-11

12-14

16

207

St Johns River

2

2

Crescent Beach

ATLANTI

15

OCEAN

Palm Coast

16-17

Beverly Beach

Bunnell

Flagler Beach

18

20

19

A1A

Ormond-by-
the-Sea

Ormond Beach

see
Daytona Beach
page 212

Tiger Bay

State Forest

Daytona Bea

AL   GA

Gulf
of
Mexico

1 MIKE ROESS GOLD HEAD BRANCH STATE PARK

Scenic rating: 10

northeast of Keystone Heights

BEST (

You'll walk along rolling, sandy hills where plants are somewhat sparse and the sun can get hot. But then the remote, three-square-mile park delivers its surprise: a wet minicanyon, Florida-style. Water pours freely from a ridge, carving a ribbon of lush greenery. It slices the wilderness lengthwise and cools hikers hugging the ravine-bottom stream. It's an unusual sight for mostly griddle-flat Florida.

Among the park's three camping areas, the pine-dotted open expanse of Sandhill Camp is the sunniest. The soft hills are ancient sand dunes—that's right, the sea was much higher back then, aeons ago. To the south, the gnarly branches of deep-ridged oaks provide some shade at Turkey Oak Camp. Picnic tables and a public parking area for day-use visitors are near Turkey Oak. The southernmost part of the park, Lakeview Camp, has a campfire circle at the edge of the park's largest lake, Big Lake Johnson, where anglers try for bass, speckled perch, and bream.

Five miles of hiking trails wind through this gem of a park, which was built by the Civilian Conservation Corps. The circular Loblolly Trail passes beneath the sparse branches of the park's largest loblolly pines and ends at a mill site. The shortest trail, Fern Loop, starts at the precipitous ravine stairway and passes the head-spring of the Gold Head Branch stream. Long ago, the Downing and Burlington narrow-gauge railroad transported logs through the current-day park. Today, you can hike or ride a bike along the former railroad route. Take a dip at the swimming beach in Little Lake Johnson. On some nights, the park offers stargazing and moonlit walks. Camp Blanding, which once was a training ground for the U.S. Army, is a sprawling presence across the street; its museum is about eight miles from the park.

RV sites, facilities: The 73 sites have water, and all but 11 have 30-amp electric hookups. Four have 50-amp electrical service. RVs as large as 40 feet long can be accommodated; four sites are drive-through. You'll find plenty of elbow room. Each campsite has a picnic table, a grill, and a fire ring. Recreational offerings include canoe and bicycle rentals, volleyball, and four hiking trails. Showers, restrooms, lakefront cabins, and a dump station are available. Laundry facilities, restaurants, groceries, and bait are available within 6–8 miles. Children are welcome. Leashed pets are permitted with proof of vaccination.

Reservations, fees: Reservations are recommended; contact ReserveAmerica at 800/336-3521 or reserveamerica.com. Sites are $16 per night for up to eight people. Credit cards are accepted. Length of stay is limited to 14 days.

Directions: From I-295 at Jacksonville, take Exit 12 and drive south for about 30 miles on Blanding Boulevard/State Road 21 to the park on the left.

Contact: Mike Roess Gold Head Branch State Park, 6239 State Road 21, Keystone Heights, FL 32656, 352/473-4701, www.floridastateparks.org.

2 PACETTI'S MARINA RV PARK AND FISHING RESORT

Scenic rating: 7

on the St. Johns River west of St. Augustine

BEST (

This historic wooded campground on the St. Johns River has lots of huge oak trees and is great for freshwater-fishing enthusiasts who would like to spend a few days relaxing. A tackle shop, gas docks, a boat ramp, a marina, and live bait are among the 25-acre campground's most prominent amenities, but there's plenty to do onshore. The World Golf Village and PGA Tours, Jacksonville, and St. Augustine are nearby, and the ocean is just 20 minutes away. Owners Pinkham and Linda Pacetti also offer square dances, bingo, and campfires. A 200-seat restaurant has inside and outside dining and live entertainment on weekends. A recreation hall offers TV and video games, and there are motel units for the noncampers in your party. The Pacettis are the third generation of their family to own this park, which was established in 1929.

RV sites, facilities: This park has 147 gravel-surface, full-hookup RV campsites (30 pull-through) and 25 tent sites. Some sites have picnic tables; all have 30-amp and 50-amp electrical service. RVs as large as 45 feet are welcome here. Recreational offerings include a recreation room, a playground, a game room, shuffleboard, fishing guide services, a bait and tackle shop, and horseshoes. On the premises are showers, restrooms, a dump station, rental cabins, a motel, a boat ramp and dock, groceries, a restaurant, a camp store, a large pavilion, and laundry facilities. Restrooms are wheelchair accessible. Children are welcome. Leashed pets are permitted.

Reservations, fees: Reservations are recommended. Sites are $28–32 per night for four people, plus $2 for each extra person over age four. Credit cards are accepted. Long-term stays are okay.

Directions: From I-95 near St. Augustine, take Exit 318 and proceed west along State Road 16 for 12 miles to the campground.

Contact: Pacetti's Marina RV Park and Fishing Resort, 6550 State Road 13 North, St. Augustine, FL 32092, 904/284-5356, fax 904/284-2369, www.pacettirv.com.

3 STAGECOACH RV PARK

Scenic rating: 2

Just off I-95 west of St. Augustine

This might make a good stopover for people flying by on I-95, and there's even a small playground with swings and a basketball court to burn off some steam. It's also convenient to downtown St. Augustine attractions seven miles away. In fact, most of the people staying here are tourists. Campsites are grassy, measuring 45 by 60 feet, and each site has some trees.

RV sites, facilities: This park offers 80 full-hookup RV sites (60 pull-through) with 30-amp and 50-amp electrical service. Roads are paved. RVs as long as 60 feet can be accommodated. A recreation room, a small playground, a basketball court, a camp store, restrooms, showers, picnic tables, a dump station, and a laundry room are available. Internet access is available in the office. A cluster of fast-food places and convenience stores are within 0.1 mile, and two outlet malls are about 0.5 mile away. Management says most of the facilities are wheelchair accessible. Well-behaved children and small, leashed pets are permitted.

Reservations, fees: Reservations are recommended. Sites are $28–30 per night for two people, plus $2 per extra person age four and older. Credit cards are accepted. Long-term stays are okay.

Directions: From I-95 and State Road 16 at Exit 318, turn left at the Denny's onto County Road 208. Drive west for 0.3 mile and look for the campground on your left.

Contact: Stagecoach RV Park, 2711 County Road 208, St. Augustine, FL 32092, 904/824-2319.

4 COOKSEY'S RV PARK

Scenic rating: 2

Just off I-95 west of St. Augustine

Cooksey's RV Park (formerly State Park Campgrounds of America) is a convenient place for folks passing through on I-95, although most people at this adult-oriented park stay year-round. You'll have a concrete pad and easy access to historic downtown St. Augustine. And since all the sites are drive-through, you don't have to worry about backing up with your RV.

RV sites, facilities: All 50 full-hookup RV sites

are pull-through; they have 30- and 50-amp service and concrete patios. A recreation room, showers, restrooms, picnic tables, and a laundry room are provided. Telephone service and cable TV are available from the appropriate utility company. Management says that the office, bathrooms, and laundry (renovated in 2005) are wheelchair accessible. Groceries are three miles away. Children are allowed. A dog-walk area is provided for leashed pets.

Reservations, fees: Reservations are recommended. Sites are $26 per night for two people, plus $3 per person over age 12 or $1 per younger child. Credit cards are not accepted. Dogs under 20 pounds are permitted. Tents are prohibited. Long-term stays are okay.

Directions: From I-95, take Exit 318 and proceed east along State Road 16 for two miles. The park is on the south side of the road.

Contact: Cooksey's RV Park, 1425 State Road 16, St. Augustine, FL 32095, 904/824-4016.

5 NORTH BEACH CAMP RESORT

Scenic rating: 8

on Highway A1A north of St. Augustine

"Sunrise on the ocean, sunset on the river, and a bit of Olde Florida in between" is a slogan of this 60-acre RV park, which extends from the ocean to the Intracoastal Waterway. Large oaks and myrtle trees add to the park's appeal. Aside from the ocean access, the location is great: North Beach is just about as close to the downtown historic section of St. Augustine as are the Beachcomber Outdoor Resort and Anastasia State Park campgrounds (see listings in this chapter). Trees separate campsites, but campers will appreciate the pool and hot tub. Rent a boat here, or fish off a dock. The park has 1,000 feet of riverfront. Only 10 percent of the sites are occupied by year-round residents. In summer, activities center on the beach, pool, and fishing; in winter, visitors fill their days with potluck dinners, bingo, and typical snowbird entertainment.

RV sites, facilities: This park has 130 level, gravel sites with full hookups. Each site has a picnic table. Most sites have 30-amp hookups, and the rest have 50-amp service. Although the trees provide shade at most sites, privacy varies depending on the location. A pool, a hot tub, a recreation room, a playground, boat rentals, horseshoes, shuffleboard, volleyball, basketball, limited winter activities, and a camp circle for gatherings entertain campers. Firewood is available for use in the fire circle. Showers, restrooms, limited groceries, a boat ramp, a dock, a restaurant, a dump station, telephone hookups, bait, cable TV, and a laundry room are available. Internet access is available in the office. Improvements planned at this writing include a wireless network for the entire campground, as well as 100-amp electrical service. The restroom, office, ocean deck, lobby, and pool are wheelchair accessible. Children and leashed pets are welcome.

Reservations, fees: Reservations are recommended. Sites are $43 per night for two people, plus $3 for each additional person. Credit cards are accepted.

Directions: From downtown St. Augustine, drive about five miles north on Highway A1A.

Contact: North Beach Camp Resort, 4125 Coastal Highway, St. Augustine, FL 32095, 904/824-1806 or 800/542-8316, fax 904/826-0897, www.northbeachcamp.com.

6 BEACHCOMBER OUTDOOR RESORT

Scenic rating: 7

across from the Atlantic Ocean in Vilano Beach

An ultracivilized RV park, this whirlpool-tub–equipped resort is across the street from the Atlantic Ocean. A 1,015-foot pier stretches west into the Intracoastal Waterway, making it a fine place to watch a sunset and wet a fishing line. Across the street, the white-capped ocean waves lap onto the beach. There, campers swim, surf-cast, and snorkel. The campground boasts "private ocean beach access," though, legally speaking, all beaches in Florida are public up to the high-tide line.

RV sites, facilities: Beachcomber features 140 full-hookup RV sites (12 are drive-through) with 30-amp electrical service. RVs up to 40 feet long and pull-out units can be accommodated. Palm trees provide a bit of shade. About 65 percent of the park is leased to year-round residents. Restrooms, a pool, a hot tub, a shuffleboard, a playground, a barbecue area, a pier, two laundry rooms, two bathhouses, a clubhouse with Internet connection, and a dump station are available. Bait, tackle, and charter fishing services are available nearby. Laundries, restrooms, and the recreation pavilion have wheelchair access. Children under 12 must be adult-supervised at the pool. At the pier, kids under 14 must be supervised. Pets must be leashed.

Reservations, fees: Reservations are required. Sites are $32 per night. Credit cards are accepted for transactions of $100 or more. It's a private membership resort, so nonmembers may stay a few days as "guests." Monthly leases and RV storage are available.

Directions: From downtown St. Augustine, head north on San Marco Avenue, following it about one mile before the road turns right to become the San Marco Bridge. Turn left onto Highway A1A. The campground is about one mile up the road, on the left.

Contact: Beachcomber Outdoor Resort, 3455 Coastal Highway, St. Augustine, FL 32095, 904/824-9157, fax 904/829-9252.

◨ ANASTASIA STATE PARK

🚶 🚲 ⛵ 🎣 🛶 🏠 🏇 ♿ 🚐 ⛺

Scenic rating: 10

in St. Augustine

BEST (

By far a favorite campground for many visitors, this 1,500-acre, state-run heaven seems to send just about everyone home raving about the beach, coastal camping, and windsurfing, fishing, and swimming in the Atlantic Ocean. The sunny park has one of the nicest and least-developed stretches of beachfront around. Of course, that means you won't have the place to yourself.

Moss-draped oaks help shade the camping area, which is separated from the ocean by a central park road, the slowly flowing Salt Run Lagoon (often dotted with windsurfers riding the surface), a marsh, and a barrier island. Although not located directly on the beach, you can still be lulled to sleep by the sounds of the ocean. Campfire-circle programs are offered in summer. A self-guided nature loop trail links two camping areas and leads through sand dunes covered by oaks, magnolias, and red bay trees.

This campground is the closest available to the magnificent Bridge of Lions, the impressive entrance to the historic district of downtown St. Augustine, the nation's oldest city. Spanish soldiers and missionaries were setting up housekeeping here two generations before famished Pilgrims landed at Plymouth Rock. Today, the biggest reminder of Florida's first conquerors are the massive walls of the nearby Castillo de San Marcos fort, which is still standing and open to visitors.

For a short walk, hit the 0.25-mile quarry trail just inside Anastasia park's entrance to see where Spaniards mined the fort's walls in the 1500s. The soft, porous limestone filled with shells and coral is known as "coquina" (or "tiny shells" in Spanish). One of the quarry pits has been turned into an amphitheater just outside the park.

You can rent a canoe or sailboard for a leisurely ride on Salt Run Lagoon. While bicycling on the sun-washed park roads in summer, remember to wear sunscreen. Look for the ruby-throated hummingbird (a summer resident) or the awkwardly beautiful and endangered wood stork (which lives here year-round), among the many birds known to use the park.

All of that aside, the main reason many campers stay here is found outside the park: St. Augustine's historic district. Most tourists spend some time knocking around the sidewalk cafes and shops of the old Spanish quarter, centered on St. George Street. But the walkable district also features the nation's oldest store, house, and school, plus modern attractions such as the Alligator Farm, Potter's Wax Museum, and Ripley's Believe It Or Not Museum. Be sure also to take in the spires of nearby Flagler College. Across the street from the college at Memorial Presbyterian Church, you can see the tomb of Henry Flagler, the railroad tycoon who forever transformed Florida by building a railroad that reached the Florida Keys.

RV sites, facilities: Each of the 104 sites has a picnic table, a grill, a fire ring, water, and 30-amp electricity. All spots require backing up. Privacy is good, with 10-foot to 40-foot spacing between campers. Several campsites are wheelchair accessible. Canoe rentals, windsurfing lessons and rentals, a playground, a 1.5-mile interpretive nature trail, horseshoes, and a camp circle for gatherings entertain campers. Showers, restrooms, a dump station, bait, beach chair and umbrella rentals, and a laundry room are available. Groceries and restaurants are located within 1.5 miles. Children are welcome. Pets are allowed with proof of vaccination; they are not permitted on the beach.

Reservations, fees: Reservations are recommended; contact ReserveAmerica at 800/336-3521 or reserveamerica.com. Sites are $23 per night for eight people. Credit cards are accepted. Stays are limited to 14 days.

Directions: From I-95 at Exit 311, go east on State Road 207, then turn right onto County Road 312. Turn north on Highway A1A. The park is 1.5 miles ahead on the right.

Contact: Anastasia State Park, 1340-A Highway A1A South, St. Augustine, FL 32084, 904/461-2033, fax 904/461-2006, www.floridastateparks.org.

🎱 ST. AUGUSTINE BEACH KOA

Scenic rating: 6

in St. Augustine Beach

Stroll just 0.75 mile along a walking/biking path and you'll be enjoying the sound of ocean waves lapping the sands of St. Augustine's beaches. Fishing without a license for bass and bream is allowed in the campground's three-acre lake, but only with artificial lures and only catch-and-release. Many a camper is more interested in hopping onto the KOA's daily shuttle to St. Augustine's historic district than hanging out here to swim in the campground pool. Some campsites are sunny, but others are shaded. The sites on Shark Fin Drive back up to a shopping plaza. The sites on Fisherman's Way are probably the most pleasant because they face the freshwater lake.

RV sites, facilities: Twenty tent campsites are set apart from 92 paved RV sites (60 pull-through). All RV sites have full hookups; more than half have 50-amp electrical service, and the rest have 30-amp. Each site has a picnic table. A walking/biking path, a fishing lake, a pool, paddleboats, a playground, horseshoes, winter activities, and daily shuttle service to the city's historic area are among the amenities. Showers, restrooms, a dump station, 22 rental cabins, snacks, limited groceries, firewood, cable TV, and a laundry room are available. Propane gas is available at the front entrance. You can walk to restaurants, a shopping center, and tennis courts. Most areas of the park are wheelchair-accessible. Kids and leashed pets are welcome. Stay as long as you like.

Reservations, fees: Reservations are recommended. Sites are $40–48 per night for two adults, plus $5 for each additional adult. Children up to 17 are not charged. Credit cards are accepted. Long-term stays are okay.

Directions: From I-95 at Exit 311, drive three miles north on State Road 207 to State Road 312. Turn right and go four miles east to Highway A1A, then turn right, heading south. Stay in the right lane for one block. Turn right on Pope Road.

Contact: St. Augustine Beach KOA, 525 West Pope Road, St. Augustine, FL 32080, 904/471-3113 or 800/562-4022, fax 904/471-1715, www.staugustinekoa.com.

⁹ INDIAN FOREST CAMPGROUND

Scenic rating: 5

in St. Augustine

Shaded by oak and maple trees, this park also boasts good sight lines for satellite TV dishes. It's only 3.75 miles from the St. Augustine city limits. In spite of its proximity to the city, the campground is sometimes visited by deer at the half-acre pond, where you can try your luck catching bass and bream. Some campsites are grassy, others are gravel. The ocean is six miles east. St. Augustine's historic district is a little closer.

RV sites, facilities: There are 105 RV sites (39 are pull-through) with 30-amp and 50-amp electrical service and picnic tables. Rigs up to 40 feet long can be accommodated. Pick from shady or sunny sites; most have full hookups. About 30 percent of the park is occupied by year-round residents, and many seasonal visitors return every winter. Horseshoes, a dump station, cable TV at 58 sites, wheelchair-accessible restrooms, propane gas, and laundry rooms are available. A modem is available in the office if you want to check your email or surf the Web. RVs can be stored here in the off-season. Groceries and restaurants are within 0.25 mile. Tents, weapons, firearms, and fireworks are prohibited. Children are welcome; however they must be under supervision at all times. Leashed pets are permitted, but aggressive breeds (defined by management as rottweilers, pit bulls, Dobermans, and wolf hybrids) are verboten.

Reservations, fees: Reservations are essential in winter and for evening arrivals in summer. Sites are $27–31 per night for two people, plus $2 for each additional person. Fifty-amp electrical service and cable TV are each $2 extra. Credit cards are accepted.

Directions: From I-95 at Exit 311, drive two miles east on State Road 207 to the campground entrance.

Contact: Indian Forest Campground, 1505 State Road 207, St. Augustine, FL 32086, 904/824-3574 or 800/233-4324.

¹⁰ SHAMROCK CAMPGROUND

Scenic rating: 2

south of St. Augustine on U.S. 1

Almost all of your neighbors will be retirees and local workers who stay at Shamrock's grassy, level, shaded sites year-round. Shaded by magnolias, oaks, and sabal palms, Shamrock nonetheless isn't a retreat far from urban life. A Wal-Mart is just 1.5 miles away, and a trip to the convenience store simply requires walking to the front of the campground and crossing busy U.S. 1. The inland park is located some five miles from the beach and from St. Augustine's downtown historic district.

RV sites, facilities: Shamrock has 38 full-hookup sites (3 are pull-through) with 30-amp electrical service. Showers, restrooms, a laundry room, rental trailers, propane sales, cable TV, and telephone service are available. Limited groceries are across the street; restaurants are one mile away. Children are permitted for short stays. Leashed pets under 30 pounds are allowed.

Reservations, fees: Reservations are advised since most sites are leased. Sites are $30 per night. Credit cards are not accepted. Adults may stay long-term.

Directions: From I-95 at Exit 318, go east on State Road 16 to U.S. 1, then drive seven miles south to the campground entrance at right.

Contact: Shamrock Campground, 3575 U.S. 1 South, St. Augustine, FL 32086, 904/797-2270.

11 ST. JOHNS RV PARK

Scenic rating: 2

Just east of I-95 south of St. Augustine

Weekend afternoons can be a noisy affair here-abouts because this campground shares 77 acres with a flea market located next door. Still, it's an easy detour off I-95. The park is split in two: One section is for campers; the other, dotted with pine trees, is for residents living in 50 trailers. At the park's 10-acre lake, some people fish from a gazebo. Beaches and St. Augustine's historic district are about five miles away.

RV sites, facilities: Fifteen pull-through RV sites are available for overnighters and snow-birds; the rest are full-timers over age 50 or local residents. Seven sites have full-hookups; three have 50-amp service, and the rest have 30-amp. Restrooms, showers, a dump station, a laundry room, a fishing lake, and limited RV supplies are available. Management says showers and laundry facilities are wheelchair accessible. A golf course, restaurants, and groceries are located within three miles. RV storage is available. Children must be attended at all times; this is primarily a retiree-oriented destination. Leashed pets are permitted.

Reservations, fees: Reservations are recommended. RV sites are $21–29 per night. Add $2 per extra person. Credit cards are accepted. Long-term rates are available.

Directions: From I-95 at Exit 311, head east for 200 feet on State Road 207. The campground is next to a flea market.

Contact: St. Johns RV Park, 2493 State Road 207, St. Augustine, FL 32086, 904/824-9840.

12 OCEAN GROVE RV RESORT

Scenic rating: 8

near the Atlantic Ocean south of St. Augustine

Pleasantly windy describes this barrier island campground, which backs onto the Intracoastal Waterway. On the other side, the Atlantic Ocean is just a 400-yard walk away, presenting opportunities for swimming, fishing, and snorkeling. The 20-acre resort appeals to families pining for a fun beach vacation, as well as snowbirds and visitors from Canada. But there's plenty to do in the park, as well. The owners also have an RV sales and service center next door.

A generous three-quarters of the park is shaded by laurels and live oaks. Anglers can launch their watercraft from the campground's boat ramp leading into the Intracoastal Waterway, also known in these parts as the Matanzas River. Downtown St. Augustine's historic district is about six miles away.

RV sites, facilities: The 198 full-hookup RV sites (about 40 pull-through) are set apart from the 20 tent sites. Each site has a picnic table, and a few sites have fire rings. Thirty sites have 50-amp service; the rest are 30-amp. Two pools, a hot tub, an exercise room, horseshoes, shuffleboard, a kiddie pool, a playground, a game room, cabins and park model rentals, and winter activities including basketball entertain campers. Showers, a recreation room, an outdoor pavilion, a laundry room, bait and tackle, firewood, cable TV, a boat ramp, and wheelchair-accessible restrooms are available. Internet access is available in the office; the owners plan to put in a wireless network throughout the park. About 10 percent of the park is occupied by year-round residents, and some park models are already rented. Groceries and a restaurant are within 0.25 mile. Children are welcome. Leashed pets are permitted.

Reservations, fees: Reservations are recommended. Sites are $43 per night for six people, plus $2 for each additional person and $1 for cable TV. Credit cards are accepted. Long-term stays are okay.

Directions: Take Highway A1A south from St. Augustine for nearly seven miles to the campground.

Contact: Ocean Grove RV Resort, 4225 Highway A1A South, St. Augustine, FL 32084, 904/471-3414 or 800/342-4007, fax 904/471-3590, www.oceangroveresort.com.

13 BRYN MAWR OCEAN RESORT

Scenic rating: 7

on the Atlantic Ocean south of St. Augustine

It's billed as the only RV park directly on 700 feet of beach in St. Augustine, and a sandy beach is indeed what you get at close proximity. These 20 or so sun-drenched acres are geared toward RVers who want to camp near the ocean with many of the comforts of home. You'll walk across the sand dunes on one of four wheelchair-accessible boardwalks to get to the water. A security gate controls access to the well-maintained, ownership park, where roads subject to a speed limit of five miles per hour have names like Sea Otter (closest to the beach) and Sea Nettle. If you get tired of fishing, swimming, bodysurfing, and snorkeling in the Atlantic Ocean, you can plunge into the park pool. Don't expect a beach party: Alcoholic beverages are not allowed on the shore.

In park lingo, "beachfront" campers enjoy the best view, beating out "oceanfront" (second-best) or "oceanside" (third-best) campsites. Other campers will see neighboring RVs but will still feel a sea breeze. If you don't want to camp near the entrance, avoid sites 67– 69 and 239–241. All lots are individually owned but can be rented when not occupied. Some units in the resort are park models. The campground is about eight miles south of the downtown historic district of St. Augustine (see *Anastasia State Park* in this chapter).

RV sites, facilities: All 135 paved RV sites have full hookups; about half have 50-amp electrical service, and 65 are pull-through. The sites closest to the beach are 219–238. In return for sleeping near the beach dunes, though, all pedestrian traffic to the ocean passes near those sites and across the four boardwalks. RVs up to 45 feet long and pull-outs can be accommodated. Shade and elbow room between sites is minimal. A pool, an activity center, an adult center, shuffleboard, horseshoes, a play-ground, basketball courts, lighted tennis courts, restrooms, cable TV, snacks, ice, rental trailers, and a laundry room are available. Children are welcome, but parents are responsible for their conduct. Leashed pets are permitted and should use the dog walk north of the propane tank.

Reservations, fees: Reservations are strongly recommended, particularly in winter. Call two months ahead to reserve a park-owned trailer ($91–94 nightly). Regular campsites vary seasonally $46–56 per night for four people, plus $5 for each additional guest or visitor, and $1 per pet. Credit cards are accepted. Long-term stays are okay.

Directions: From I-95 at Exit 305, go east on State Road 206 for six miles to Highway A1A. Turn left, heading north. The campground is three miles ahead to the right. From St. Augustine, take Highway A1A south about eight miles to the campground on the left.

Contact: Bryn Mawr Ocean Resort, 4850 A1A South, St. Augustine, FL 32080, 904/471-3353, fax 904/471-8730, www.brynmawroceanresort.com.

14 PEPPERTREE BEACH CLUB RESORT

Scenic rating: 6

on Highway A1A south of St. Augustine

PepperTree is as much a village as it is an RV resort. Streets are paved and lighted. Lawn maintenance is available, as is cable TV, for long-term visitors. It's reminiscent of many of Florida's established retirement communities. Along with shuffleboard and horseshoes, visitors can take advantage of darts, a big-screen TV, and a fireplace, found in the clubhouse.

The wee grass lawns separating the well-tended, 30- by 80-foot campsites are sunny and open. Catch-and-release fishing for bass and bream is available at a park lake, where you might even see otters. You can walk two blocks to the beach, and will find tennis courts about one mile away. St. Augustine's historic district is about seven miles north.

RV sites, facilities: PepperTree offers 12 sites for RVs, as well as rentals of park-owned homes known as "park units" and sales of lots. About 25 percent of the park is occupied by year-round residents. Each site has a concrete patio and picnic table, full hookups, and 50-amp electrical service. A pool, a fishing deck, shuffleboard, horseshoes, basketball, darts, two fishing ponds, and a clubhouse entertain campers. Showers, restrooms, a dump station, cable TV, and a laundry room are available. Many areas, including a ramp at the pool, are wheelchair accessible. Kids must be supervised when swimming or fishing; tents are prohibited. RV storage is minimal, due to the sale of an adjacent property. Leashed pets are allowed.

Reservations, fees: Reservations are recommended, particularly in February and March. Sites are $42 per night for two people, plus $3 per additional person and $1.50 for cable TV. Credit cards are accepted. Long-term rates are available.

Directions: From I-95 at Exit 305, go east on State Road 206 for six miles to Highway A1A. Turn left, heading north. The campground is about 1.25 miles ahead on the left. From St. Augustine, take Highway A1A south about seven miles to the campground on the right.

Contact: PepperTree Beach Club Resort, 4825 Highway A1A South, St. Augustine, FL 32084, 904/471-5263 or 800/325-2267, www.sabeach-rentals.com.

15 FAVER-DYKES STATE PARK

Scenic rating: 10

on Pellicer Creek off U.S. 1 south of St. Augustine

In this canoeist's delight, you will discover aquatic trails leading through a landscape that has changed little since Spanish explorers first set foot here. In fact, the main body of water in the 1,608-acre park, Pellicer Creek, is named for Francisco Pellicer, who received a land grant from the king of Spain when the Spanish flag still flew over Florida.

A four-mile canoe trail, which is easy enough for beginners, can be traversed against the weak current. That way, you can make it a loop trip instead of leaving your car at one end of the creek and arranging for a ride back to camp. Call ahead to reserve a park canoe, which rents for $8 for the first two hours, plus $3 for each hour thereafter. Daily rentals are $20.

The sandy/grassy campsites aren't as picturesque as the surroundings. Landlubbers can use the short hiking trail along Pellicer Creek and Rootan Branch. A second, short nature trail leads through the high, dry pinelands near the creek. Swamps, marshes, and elevated pinelands are among the mosaic of natural Florida habitats that enrich this park with such wildlife as otters, alligators, deer, wild turkey, and a variety of birds. Look for bald eagles, which aren't uncommon.

Anglers can launch into the creek and try their luck with trout, flounder, or redfish (live shrimp are the best bait, as is true in most coastal fishing locations). The creek contains both saltwater and freshwater habitats, depending on how far you travel. Currents are mild to medium, changing with the tides.

RV sites, facilities: These 30 sites for RVs or tents have water and 30-amp electricity but no sewer hookups. Each site has a picnic table, a grill, and a fire ring. One site is paved for wheelchair access. Most of the grassy or sandy sites can accommodate rigs up to 35 feet long; call the park if your unit is larger. All sites require the driver to back in. A primitive youth camping area provides simple facilities for up to 100 people. Canoe rentals, a playground, a nature trail, a boat ramp, a dump station, showers, and wheelchair-accessible restrooms are available. Children are welcome. Pets are not allowed.

Reservations, fees: Reservations are recommended; contact ReserveAmerica at 800/336-3521 or reserveamerica.com. Sites are $15 per night for eight people. Credit cards are accepted.

The maximum stay is 14 days, or 42 days during a six-month period.

Directions: From I-95 at Exit 298, go north on U.S. 1. On the right side of the road, you will see BP and Texaco gasoline stations. Turn right and follow the signs to the park.

Contact: Faver-Dykes State Park, 1000 Faver-Dykes Road, St. Augustine, FL 32086, 904/794-0997, fax 904/794-1378, www.floridastateparks.org.

16 FLAGLER BY THE SEA

Scenic rating: 7

on the Atlantic Ocean north of Flagler Beach

BEST (

If you're looking for a relaxing beach experience with easy access to tourist attractions in St. Augustine (about 22 miles) or Daytona Beach (25 miles), this ocean-side campground may do the trick. These few acres of beach also are near the residential community of Palm Coast, a place designed mostly for upscale retirees. Some campers swim and fish at the beach. For the best views, consider "oceanfront deluxe" sites, but the other sites are a short hop to steps that lead across the sand dunes and to the beach.

RV sites, facilities: There are 31 full-hookup campsites (15 pull-through) with 30-amp electrical service. Showers, restrooms, and cable TV are available. Groceries, restaurants, and shops are within walking distance. Children are allowed. Leashed pets are permitted and should use a pet walk along Highway A1A. Tents are prohibited.

Reservations, fees: Reservations are recommended. Sites are $30–50 per night for two people, plus $5 for each additional person. Rates are higher on holiday weekends. Credit cards are accepted. Long-term stays are okay.

Directions: From I-95 near Flagler Beach, take Exit 284 and go three miles east on State Road 100. Turn left onto Highway A1A. The campground is four miles ahead.

Contact: Flagler by the Sea, 2982 North Oceanshore Boulevard, Flagler Beach, FL 32136, 386/439-2124, fax 386/439-1666.

17 BEVERLY BEACH CAMPTOWN

Scenic rating: 7

on the Atlantic Ocean in Beverly Beach

BEST (

Sun worshippers, this 1,500-foot stretch of oceanfront is for you. One of few campgrounds directly overlooking the sand, Beverly Beach Camptown is located in along a relatively uncrowded beach, although some home subdivisions are crowding in around it. The RVs actually sit on top of the seawall above the ocean, and the most choice sites are numbered 1–67. Other RVers who keep their windows open certainly can fall asleep to the sound of rolling waves. But outdoors, "beach-view" campers are likely to be surrounded on three sides by RVs; Highway A1A is the western border.

Head north a few miles past the hamlet of Painter's Hill if you want to enjoy deserted oceanfront. Early-morning beach walks at the campground are popular, with patrons enjoying the burnt-orange and purple of the sun breaking over the Atlantic. Some campers wet a fishing line in the surf. Drunkenness is forbidden, and quiet time starts at 10 P.M. For day trips to area historic sites, St. Augustine is about a 30-minute drive away. Closer to home are the Bulow Plantation (see *Bulow Plantation Resort* in this chapter) and Washington Oaks State Gardens (see *Gamble Rogers Memorial State Recreation Area* in this chapter).

RV sites, facilities: All 130 RV sites have full hookups; none are drive-through. About two-thirds have 50-amp service; the rest are 30-amp. Rigs up to 45 feet long and slide-out units can be accommodated. Although sites are plenty long, elbow room is more scarce. A cafe, showers, restrooms, bait, tackle, a gift shop, a convenience store, cable TV, and a laundry room are available. Shopping is available within four miles. Most of the campground is wheelchair-accessible, except for the beach steps. Children are welcome but must be supervised by adults. Pets must be leashed.

Reservations, fees: Reservations are recommended. Sites vary seasonally $48–66. Rates are for two people, plus $5 per extra person age 12 and older. Credit cards are accepted. Long-term rates are available.

Directions: From I-95 near Flagler Beach, take Exit 284 and go three miles east on State Road 100. Turn left onto Highway A1A. Look for the campground three miles ahead to your right, on the beach.

Contact: Beverly Beach Camptown, 2816 North Oceanshore Boulevard, Beverly Beach, FL 32136, 386/439-3111 or 800/255-2706, www.beverlybeachcamptown.com.

18 GAMBLE ROGERS MEMORIAL STATE RECREATION AREA

Scenic rating: 10

on the Atlantic Ocean south of Flagler Beach

BEST (

A seemingly endless breeze wafts through the beachfront campsites of this 145-acre state park named for the late Gamble Rogers, the "Florida Troubadour" who chronicled the state's history and lore in folk songs before drowning in the ocean. The sun-washed campsites, composed of compressed coquina rock, overlook the beach where Rogers died.

For respite from the sun at this pretty picnic spot, a 20-minute nature trail near the park's entrance leads through a coastal scrub habitat of low-lying magnolia, oak, cedar, and sabal palms on the west side of the highway. Pick up an interpretive brochure at the entrance station to recognize the plants.

Bring your own boat or canoe to use the boat launch. Anglers go after trout, redfish, and flounder at the Intracoastal Waterway, located on the park's west side. Surfcasting at the beach may yield pompano, whiting, drum, or, at certain times of the year, bluefish.

For a pleasant day trip, the landscaped grounds of Washington Oaks State Gardens are about 13 miles north on Highway A1A. For my money, its nature trails outshine the gardens. You may be alone—or nearly so—on the Bella Vista and Mala Compra Trails. They take in a section of increasingly rare mature coastal hammock, as well as dense canopied coastal scrub and an estuarine tidal marsh. Bicyclists may join hikers on two other trails: the now-abandoned Old Highway A1A and the Jungle Road portion of the Bella Vista Trail. Call 386/446-6780. Nearby sites of interest include St. Augustine's historic district, within a 30-minute drive of Gamble Rogers. Nine miles away is the Bulow Plantation State Historic Site (see next campground).

RV sites, facilities: Thirty-four campsites have water and electrical service; call to see if 50-amp sites are available. The hard-packed sandy sites vary in size, but are generally 20–30 feet wide with shrubs between them. If you have a larger unit, call the park to see if a site is available. Each spot has a picnic table, a grill, and a fire ring. The beachfront sites are numbered 1–23, plus 25, 27, 29, 31, 33, and 34. A nature trail, a boat launch, showers, restrooms, and a dump station are available. Three accessible campsites, the restrooms, the picnic pavilion, a grill, a picnic table, and a beach ramp are wheelchair accessible. A public golf course is less than 0.5 mile away. Children are welcome. Leashed pets are permitted with proof of current rabies vaccination.

Reservations, fees: Reservations are recommended; contact ReserveAmerica at 800/336-3521 or reserveamerica.com. Sites are $25 per night for eight people. Credit cards are accepted. The maximum stay is 14 days.

Directions: From I-95 near Flagler Beach, take Exit 284 and go three miles east on State Road 100. Turn right at Highway A1A and look for the campground about three miles south of Flagler Beach.

Contact: Gamble Rogers Memorial State Recreation Area, 3100 Highway A1A, Flagler Beach, FL 32136, 386/517-2086, www.floridastateparks.org.

19 BULOW PLANTATION RESORT

Scenic rating: 8

east of I-95 and west of Flagler Beach

Although parts of this sprawling, 90-acre RV and park model community are sunny, much of it is shaded by the huge old oaks that define Florida's most beautiful woodlands. Visitors fish from canals, while others explore via rented canoes or bicycles. This park has become popular for rallies and gatherings during Daytona's Bike Week in March and other festivals. About half the park is occupied by park models and year-round residents.

The full-service park is practically next door to the ruins of a worthwhile yet little-visited attraction: Bulow Plantation Ruins State Historic Site. Once one of Florida's most prosperous sugar plantations, the place was destroyed during the Seminole Indian Wars. Now all that is left of the gracious mansion and plantation are the towering coquina-rock ruins of the sugar mill, several wells, a springhouse, and the crumbling foundation of the mansion. It looks sort of like a medieval castle in ruins (albeit a small one). Interpretive signs explain how the 1830s plantation functioned, and some mill machinery can be seen.

For a six-mile (one-way) day hike, follow the Florida National Scenic Trail from the plantation to Bulow Creek State Park in Ormond Beach. The route will take you through jungly forest, salt marsh, and pine flat woods. It's real Old Florida, which is increasingly difficult for modern-day vacationers to experience. Bring mosquito repellent. Consider skipping a hike in summer.

RV sites, facilities: All 350 RV campsites (most pull-through) have full hookups with 30 or 50-amp service. RVs as long as 60 feet can be accommodated, as can slide-out units. A pool, horseshoes, shuffleboard, and a 6,000-square-foot recreation hall with raised stage entertain campers. Showers, restrooms, a dump station, a restaurant/pub, rental cabins, cable TV, a convenience store, and a laundry room are available. Most areas of the park are wheelchair accessible. Children and pets are permitted.

Reservations, fees: Reservations are recommended. They are required during special events ($50 nightly, plus $25 per extra person). Sites normally are $31–39 per night for two people, plus $2 for each additional person. Credit cards are accepted. Long-term stays are okay.

Directions: From I-95 near Flagler Beach, take Exit 284 and go east on State Road 100 to the traffic light. Turn right onto Old Kings Road. Proceed three miles to the campground entrance.

Contact: Bulow Plantation Resort, 3345 Old Kings Road South, Flagler Beach, FL 32136, 386/439-9200 or 800/782-8569, fax 386/439-6757, www.mhchomes.com.

20 HOLIDAY TRAVEL PARK

Scenic rating: 5

off I-95 southwest of Flagler Beach

You're right next to I-95, which is great if you just want a quick place to stop for the night. If you like to fish, you might ask for a spot on Marco Polo Road, which is right across from the campground lake. The busiest area of the park is near the pool, tennis courts, and bathhouse. Three spots are right next to the pool: sites 117, 118, and 119. For longer-term stays, you could find comparably priced campgrounds nearby in woodsier settings or directly on the beach. What you're mainly buying here is convenience, although there is a bulletin of planned activities hanging in the office to help keep campers entertained. The campground is close to the Bulow Plantation Ruins State Historic Site (see *Bulow Plantation Resort* in this chapter). The nation's oldest city, St. Augustine, is within a half-hour drive.

RV sites, facilities: This co-op park has 65 RV sites, 7 of which offer full hookups; the rest have water and 20-amp or 30-amp electricity. Ten spots are pull-through. Some of the RV owners leave their rigs on-site year-round; others allow their lots to be rented out. About 40 percent of the park is occupied throughout the year. The roomy sites vary in size, accommodating rigs up to 50 feet long. One site is wheelchair accessible. Recreational offerings include adult and kiddie heated pools, a playground, tennis courts, a recreation hall, shuffleboard, and fire rings. Showers, restrooms, a dump station, picnic tables, and a laundry room are available. Campers 18 and younger are welcome but must be accompanied by an adult at the pool. Leashed pets are permitted.

Reservations, fees: Reservations are advised. Nightly fee for two people normally is $22–28 for RV sites, but will be higher during special events. Add $6 per extra person over age 12; $3 for kids ages 6–12. Credit cards are accepted.

Directions: From I-95 at Exit 278, go west on Old Dixie Highway. Make an immediate right turn into the gas station. Follow its road to the back to enter the campground.

Contact: Holiday Travel Park, 2261 South Old Dixie Highway, Bunnell, FL 32110, 386/672-8122, fax 386/437-8432.

21 RODMAN RESERVOIR

Scenic rating: 8

on the Rodman Reservoir south of Palatka

Once the domain of only primitive campers, significant improvements have been made here, making it a good place to stay for anglers. The Rodman Reservoir is considered one of the better fishing spots around. However, the campground here is also popular with snowbirds in the know during the winter.

The campground is not far from what some environmentalists refer to as "that damn dam." But don't let that deter you; there's plenty of wildlife and lots of things to do if you enjoy the outdoors. A little explanation about the contro-

versy: In the 1960s, with the communist threat of the Cuba–Soviet Union axis lurking just 90 miles south of Florida, some bright people got the idea to cut a waterway, à la Panama Canal, across central Florida. The idea was to offer ship traffic a route sheltered from the possibly problematic Straits of Florida. And so, voila! Let's just gouge a big canal through the middle of the state, using the Ocklawaha River as part of the pathway, the engineers and hydrologists thought. Little did they know that a decades-long fight to scotch the plan would ensue, led mostly by the Gainesville-based Florida Defenders of the Environment. The reason: It would have turned the gently meandering Ocklawaha into a series of ponds, much like the Rodman Reservoir you see here. A dam was built to stop up the river at this point, although environmentalists intervened during the Nixon administration to halt construction of the rest of the project.

Today, this big lake of a "river" is a unique place to stay. However, it remains controversial, with environmentalists trying to return it to its natural state, and bass fishers and other residents of the area fighting them bitterly every step of the way to keep it as a reservoir.

You're likely to see bald eagles soar overhead, and you'll definitely have great access to excellent bass fishing. Probably the most popular activity is fishing; there is no shortage of places to wet a line. The boat dock connects to a small island in the reservoir.

The campsites are sandy, only semishaded, and set amid pine trees. Good side trips are Ravine State Gardens or the open-air farmer's market in Palatka. For waterfront views of the barge canal, choose site numbered 59–68.

RV sites, facilities: There are 68 sites, of which 8 are drive-through. Forty-two sites have water and electricity, including 30-amp and 50-amp service. Grills, 12 picnic tables, eight picnic shelters, a dump station, a boat dock, a boat ramp, and wheelchair-accessible restrooms with showers are available. Grocery stores, laundry, and other supplies are less than 10 miles away in

Palatka. Children under 15 must be accompanied by an adult. Leashed pets are permitted.

Reservations, fees: Reservations are not taken. Sites are $17 per night for those with water and electricity; primitive sites are $10 per night. Credit cards are not accepted. The maximum stay is 14 days in a 30-day period but can be extended at the discretion of the gate tender or park ranger. Campers can use the boat launch free; others pay $3.

Directions: From Palatka, take State Road 19 south about 12 miles, crossing the bridge over the Cross Florida Barge Canal, then turn right to head west for 2.5 miles on Rodman Dam Road. Turn right onto Rodman Dam Access Road, which leads to the campground.

Contact: Florida Greenways and Trails, Department of Environmental Protection, 8282 Southeast Highway 314, Ocala, FL 34470, 352/236-7143 or 386/326-2846, www.dep .state.fl.us/gwt.

22 SHELL HARBOUR RESORT

Scenic rating: 6

on the St. Johns River in Satsuma

Part of a resort complex that includes a motel, cabins, a restaurant, and a bar, this park is set on 15 wooded acres along the St. Johns River. Don't be surprised to see at least two dozen peacocks running around the property. With an 800-foot-long dock and 1,600 feet of river shoreline, the campground can accommodate a huge number of anglers. The waterfront restaurant has banquet facilities and makes for a great spot to watch the sun set.

RV sites, facilities: There are 28 RV sites (some full-hookup). On the premises are restrooms, showers, a dump station, a heated pool, a boat ramp, a dock, horseshoes, volleyball, a restaurant, snacks, a rental cabin, motel-style rooms, a laundry room, and a bar with a pool table, darts, and a big-screen TV. Groceries are about two miles away. Children and leashed pets are welcome.

Reservations, fees: Reservations are recommended. Sites are $10–15 per night. Credit cards are accepted. Long-term stays are okay.

Directions: From Palatka, take U.S. 17 south about 15 miles into Satsuma. Head west (right) on County Road 309 for about two miles until you see Shell Harbour Road. Turn right. The campground is just ahead.

Contact: Shell Harbour Resort, 140 Shell Harbour Road, Satsuma, FL 32189, 386/ 467-2330.

23 ACOSTA CREEK HARBOR

Scenic rating: 6

north of Welaka

Majestic oak trees and fragrant citrus trees shade this lovely riverfront location on the St. Johns. Popular with anglers and boaters, the four RV sites are part of a large-boat marina with 40 slips and rental cottage complex built on the grounds of a turn-of-the-20th-century home. A boat ramp is one mile away. What to do here? Fish and relax with the view of the river.

RV sites, facilities: There are four full-hookup sites available for RVs with concrete patios and 30-amp and 50-amp electrical hookups. Each has picnic tables, cable TV, and concrete pads. Restrooms, showers, and laundry facilities are available. On the premises are a pool, boat docks, cabins, cottages, a ship store with ice, and efficiencies. The restrooms and pool are wheelchair accessible. Restaurants are 3 miles away, and groceries 15 miles. Children are welcome, but most campers are adults, and about half the park is occupied by year-round residents. Leashed pets are permitted.

Reservations, fees: Reservations are recommended. Sites are $25 per night. Credit cards are accepted. Long-term rates are available.

Directions: From the north, take U.S. 17 south to Satsuma. Turn right on County Road 309 and drive 3.5 miles to Acosta Creek Drive. Turn right and go to the end of the road. From Crescent City on U.S. 17, turn left on County Road 308 to Fruitland. Turn on County Road 309 and proceed to Welaka. Drive two more miles and turn left on Acosta Creek Drive.

Contact: Acosta Creek Harbor, 124 Acosta Creek Drive, Satsuma, FL 32189, 386/467-2229, www.acostacreek.com.

24 CRESCENT CITY CAMPGROUND

Scenic rating: 6

near Lake George on U.S. 17 south of Palatka

Several oaks lend shade to this 10-acre country campground, located near the bass-fishing waters of Crescent Lake and Lake George. A small creek runs through the park, where some campsites have concrete pads, while others are gravelly or grassy. All sites have concrete patios. Although overnighters use the park, it's more likely to be filled with vacationers who stay longer and participate in potluck suppers and other planned activities.

RV sites, facilities: There are 82 full-hookup RV sites (20 pull-through) with 20-amp, 30-amp, and 50-amp electrical service and cable TV. Park models are available for rent year-round or short-term. Restrooms, showers, a dump station, a laundry room, a recreation room, a pool, a playground, a hiking trail, lighted shuffleboard courts, horseshoes, telephone hookups, fire rings, LP gas sales, and campsite picnic tables are available. Groceries, a restaurant, and bait are about one mile away. Most areas are wheelchair accessible. Children and leashed pets are permitted.

Reservations, fees: Reservations are recommended in season. Sites are $24–29 per night for two people, plus $3 per extra person. Rates are $5 higher during Race Week (February) and Bike Week (March). Credit cards are accepted. Long-term stays are okay.

Directions: From Palatka, take U.S. 17 south about 20 miles. Look for the campground about one mile north of Crescent City.

Contact: Crescent City Campground, Route 2, P.O. Box 25, Crescent City, FL 32112, 386/698-2020 or 800/634-3968, www.crescentcity-ampground.com.

25 LEONARD'S LANDING LAKE CRESCENT RESORT

Scenic rating: 6

in Crescent City

BEST (

Lake Crescent is famed for bass and crappie fishing, and most visitors here are focused on angling. At 16,000 acres, the lake is one of the largest in the state and is 13 miles long and 2 miles wide. This campground (part of the Lake Crescent Motel and Resort) claims to offer the best lake access, with an on-site boat ramp, a dock, and a bait and tackle shop. Sites are sunny and have lake views; about half are occupied by long-term residents.

RV sites, facilities: This 27-unit park has 5 sites for overnighters and 21 for seasonal visitors; tents are allowed. All sites have water and electricity (22 have full hookups), picnic tables, grills, cable TV, and optional phone service. Restrooms, showers, a dump station, a heated pool, a recreation room, a boat ramp, a dock, bait and tackle, a restaurant and pub, a snack bar, and a motel are on the premises. A grocery store is across the street. Children are welcome. Small leashed pets are permitted.

Reservations, fees: Reservations are recommended. Sites are $25 per night for two people, plus $3 per extra person. Credit cards are accepted. Stay as long as you like.

Directions: From U.S. 17 in Crescent City, drive east on Grove Avenue when you see the sign for Lake Crescent Motel and Resort, across the street from Miller's Supervalue grocery store.

Contact: Leonard's Landing Lake Crescent Resort, 100 Grove Avenue, Crescent City, FL 32112, 386/698-2485, www.lakecrescent.com.

26 BULL CREEK CAMPGROUND

Scenic rating: 5

at Dead Lake west of Flagler Beach

Anglers arrive by boat, car, or seaplane to sleep at these waterfront sites that offer easy access to two lakes—Dead Lake and Crescent Lake. The focus of the rustic six-acre campground is water: A guide service helps anglers track down crappie and bass. Waterskiing and a protected cove for boaters round out the water-oriented amenities, including a marina and boat docks.

RV sites, facilities: There are 50 campsites for RVs up to 36 feet long, each with a picnic table and full hookups (but no cable TV). A boat ramp, boat rentals, a restaurant, showers, restrooms, cottages, cabins, horseshoes, bait and tackle, firewood, limited groceries, and a laundry room are available. Management says most of the park is wheelchair accessible. Children and leashed pets are permitted.

Reservations, fees: Reservations are recommended. Sites are $21 per night for two people, plus $3 for each additional person over age 12. Credit cards are accepted. Long-term rates are offered.

Directions: From I-95 near Flagler Beach, take Exit 284 and drive about six miles west on State Road 100. Turn left at State Road 305. Proceed about four miles south to State Road 2006, turn right, and continue four miles to the campground where the road dead-ends at Dead Lake.

Contact: Bull Creek Campground, 3861 County Road 2006, Bunnell, FL 32110, 386/437-3451.

27 HARLEY PAIUTE'S CAMPGROUND AND MARINA

Scenic rating: 7

near Georgetown

Located in a back-to-nature setting on the St. Johns River, this park has a boat ramp with river access. It attracts nature-loving campers,

anglers, and snowbirds, but motorcyclists are welcome, too. Watch the sun set over the Ocala National Forest across from the riverbank. An 18-hole golf course is across the street. You'll find good hiking three miles away in the Welaka State Forest, and Daytona is about an hour's drive.

RV sites, facilities: Platted on a narrow strip of land that runs down to the boat dock on the river, there are 46 RV sites with water and 50-amp electricity. Some sites have picnic tables, grills, cable TV, and phone service available. About half the sites are open for overnighters. Restrooms, showers, laundry facilities, a boat ramp, a dock, a dog-walk area, cabin rentals, and a clubhouse are on the premises. Children are welcome. Leashed pets are permitted.

Reservations, fees: Reservations are recommended. Sites are $20 per night for two people, plus $2 per extra person. Credit cards are accepted. Long-term rates are available.

Directions: From Satsuma at U.S. 17, drive south on County Road 309 for 11 miles. The park is on the river across from the Live Oak Golf Course.

Contact: Harley Paiute's Campground and Marina, 1269 County Road 309, Crescent City, FL 32112, 386/467-7050, www.harleypaiute.com.

28 GEORGETOWN MARINA AND LODGE

Scenic rating: 5

on Lake George in Georgetown

The lure here is fishing for the big bass that inhabit 11-mile-long Lake George. In fact, this quiet, out-of-the-way campground/marina/fish camp boasts, "See what a fish camp should be!" It's located on the St. Johns River at the mouth of Lake George. Largemouth bass are the main game fish, yet some anglers also go after striped bass, bream, shellcracker, catfish, or speckled perch. Efficiency apartments are available, in case you have guests. Retirees are the main patrons of these semishaded camping sites, which are set among pines. Other parts of the park are shaded by large oaks.

RV sites, facilities: All 33 full-hookup sites are for RVs, and 8 are pull-through. Each site has a concrete patio. Electrical service is rated 20-amp, 30-amp, and 50-amp. Slide-outs and rigs as long as 60 feet can be accommodated. About 65 percent of the park is occupied by permanent residents. Restrooms, showers, a dump station, a boat ramp, boat slips, charter fishing, horseshoes, cable TV, a laundry room, and a wheelchair-accessible fishing dock are available. Planned activities include potluck dinners, cookouts, bingo, and car trips to local malls. Groceries and a restaurant are located within one mile. Children and leashed pets are permitted.

Reservations, fees: Reservations are recommended. Sites are $25 per night for two people, plus $2 for each extra person. Credit cards are accepted. Long-term stays are okay.

Directions: From Palatka, take U.S. 17 south about 15 miles into Satsuma. Turn right on County Road 309 and proceed about 16 miles into Georgetown. When you pass the only yield sign in Georgetown, continue about one mile. The marina and lodge are on the right.

Contact: Georgetown Marina and Lodge, P.O. Box 171, 1533 County Road 309, Georgetown, FL 32139, 386/467-2002 or 866/325-2003, email: georgetownmarina@gbso.net.

29 PINE ISLAND CAMPGROUND AND MARINA

Scenic rating: 3

on Lake George west of Seville

If you like fishing, you'll like these four rustic acres on the shores of 100-square-mile Lake George. The grassy campsites and cabins are most popular among anglers seeking bass in the 72°F lake waters and with hunters hot on the trail of deer, turkey, hogs, and ducks. Much of the park is occupied by full-timers.

RV sites, facilities: The 29 campsites are for RVs up to 32 feet long. Sixteen have full hook-ups; the rest have water and 30-amp electricity. On the premises are showers, restrooms, cabin rentals, a boat ramp, a marina, boat slips, fishing guide services, a game room, a nature trail, horseshoes, a snack bar with ice, bait and tackle, a recreation room, propane gas tank exchange, and laundry facilities. Most of the park is wheelchair accessible. A convenience store is located within four miles. Children and leashed pets are allowed.

Reservations, fees: Reservations are recommended. Sites are $9.50–12 per night for two people, plus $1 for each additional person. Credit cards are not accepted. Long-term stays are okay.

Directions: Drive north on U.S. 17 from Barberville. When you reach the hamlet of Seville, head west on County Road 305/Lake George Road, passing through the Lake George Conservation Area. The road ends at Pine Island Marina.

Contact: Pine Island Campground and Marina, 1600 Lake George Road, Seville, FL 32190, 386/749-2818.

OCALA

BEST RV PARKS AND CAMPGROUNDS

☪ Fishing
Chassahowitzka River Campground
and Recreation Area, page 191
Parramore's Fantastic Fish Camp
and Family Resort, page 203

☪ Golf
Grand Lake RV and Golf Resort, page 181

☪ Most Luxurious
Grand Lake RV and Golf Resort, page 181

☪ Most Unusual
Rock Crusher Canyon RV and Music Park, page 190

☪ Natural Springs
Rainbow Springs State Park, page 191
Salt Springs Recreation Area, page 194

The Ocala area is a bit off the well-beaten

path that leads most visitors to Orlando, even though I-75 slices right through it. This is horse country. You'll see gently rolling hills of green grass, white rail fences, and glossy-coated thoroughbreds frolicking in the pastures. The Florida Horse Park, which opened in late 2005, plays host to competition and trail riding, as well as other equestrian events and tours. The Ocala area may be a bit underappreciated (take that as a cue that the winter crowds may be a bit thinner). Still, Ocala and its surroundings are well worth exploring.

A tourist attraction with a long history is the Silver Springs theme park. Famed for its glass-bottom boat rides that allow you to peer into crystal-clear water, it's a mix of environmental attractions as well as more traditional theme-park fare, such as concerts, boat and auto shows, festivals, and a gondola ride 80 feet above the springs. Henry Ford, Thomas Edison, and thousands of others have visited this theme park, which today includes animals from six continents, a petting zoo, and picnic areas on its 350 acres. Even Tarzan swung around here long ago – actually, it was actor Johnny Weissmuller shooting a 1939 Tarzan film across the street at the 780-square-foot cavern of Silver Springs. Also across the street is Wild Waters, a six-acre water park.

One of Florida's newest full-service, publicly owned camping parks is at Silver River State Park, practically next door to Silver Springs. With gravel-pad RV sites and paved roads, this is a state park with private-park class. A bonus: Look for otters in early morning along the Silver River, reached via a short walking trail. Anglers, hikers, mountain bikers, and seasonal hunters can drive a short distance east from the campground to popular Ocala National Forest, one of three federally run forests in Florida.

Alexander Springs, where there's a canoe run, picnic area, and nature trails, hosts another popular campground. The surrounding Ocala National Forest is one of the state's last bastions of the Florida black bear, although you're more likely to glimpse a wild turkey or a deer scampering away in the distance. Farther south is Mount Dora, a quaint historic town set on a big lake with a historic inn, lots of great restaurants, art galleries, and antiques shops.

If you're in the mood to see more natural art, head west to the Gulf of Mexico where you can see a manatee up close. At Homosassa Springs State Wildlife Park, a rehabilitation center for manatees who were born in captivity or orphaned or injured in the wild, an underwater observatory lets visitors observe them eye to eye. The manatees share the grounds with wood ducks, flamingos, birds of prey, herons, egrets, alligators, snakes, hippopotamuses, black bears, white-tailed deer, and river otters.

1 SPORTSMAN'S COVE ON ORANGE LAKE

Scenic rating: 4

at Orange Lake in McIntosh

As the name suggests, anglers use this campground as a launchpad for a day of snagging panfish and bass at Orange Lake and Lake Lochloosa. But it's convenient to the interstate for overnighters, and a good base camp for visiting Gainesville or Silver Springs. Oak trees and lake views are the reward for staying here, as well as the quiet. Instead of a monotonous blue sea that stretches hypnotically to the horizon, this scene is broken up by islands—Redbird Island is up ahead, and to the right are Hixon, Bird, and McCormick Islands. Lake levels have been variable in recent years; however, at this writing, the lake is "beautiful and the crappie are jumping in the boat. You'll have no problem reaching the limit," says the manager. Under new ownership since 2005, this retiree-oriented community of grassy canal-side campsites also has wintertime activities to keep campers entertained. Some of the sites are occupied by year-round residents, but most visitors come for three- to six-month stays.

RV sites, facilities: All 49 full-hookup campsites have 30-amp or 50-amp electrical service. Cabins, cable TV, showers, restrooms, a dump station, a boat ramp, boat slips, a recreation room, and laundry facilities are available. Children are welcome. Leashed pets are permitted but must use the dog walk on the park's east side.

Reservations, fees: Reservations are recommended. Sites are $18 per night for two people, plus $1.50 for each additional person. Long-term rates are available. Credit cards are not accepted.

Directions: From I-75 at Exit 368, take County Road 318 east for two miles to U.S. 441. Turn left. Continue three more miles north, passing State Road 320, and turn right at Avenue F, which is at the second blinking light. The campground entrance is ahead.

Contact: Sportsman's Cove on Orange Lake, 5423 Avenue F (mailing address: P.O. Box 107), McIntosh, FL 32664, 352/591-1435.

2 GRAND LAKE RV AND GOLF RESORT

Scenic rating: 8

on Orange Lake in the town of Orange Lake

BEST (

A nine-hole championship golf course greets RVers as they drive into this supermanicured resort, which sprawls on a hill overlooking Orange Lake. If golf isn't your game, you'll find world-class bass fishing in the lake and three separate gathering places for socializing; parimutuel betting is available at the jai alai fronton (arena) next door. The management boasts that this is one of the top-rated RV parks in the nation; however, as of this writing a park-model community was being developed and lots are for sale. Shade is minimal in most of the park, but some sites have panoramic views of the lake. Be careful with children around the lake; they are not allowed near it because of alligators.

RV sites, facilities: These 239 full-hookup RV sites overlook Orange Lake and have 30/50-amp electrical service. Some sites are grassy; "super" sites have concrete patios. Large RVs and slide-outs can be accommodated, and many sites are pull-through. A nine-hole golf course, a driving range, a pool, a clubhouse, a TV room, shuffleboard, exercise trails, golf lessons, and fishing lessons entertain campers. Showers, restrooms, a dump station, a boat dock, a pier, a barbecue pit, park models, and laundry facilities are available. All areas are wheelchair accessible. Children must be adult-supervised when at the pool, fishing, or near the pier. Leashed pets must walk in the open field or on the edge of the road.

Reservations, fees: Reservations are recommended. Sites are $31–35 per night. Credit cards are accepted. Long-term rates are available.

Directions: From I-75 at Exit 368, take County

Road 318 east for about two miles, crossing U.S. 441. Turn left (north) on the road next to Ocala Jai Alai to get to the campground.

Contact: Grand Lake RV and Golf Resort, P.O. Box 370/4555 West Highway 318, Orange Lake, FL 32681, 352/591-3474 or 800/435-2291, www.grandlakeresort.com.

3 ENCORE RV PARK–OCALA

Scenic rating: 10

off I-75 between Gainesville and Ocala

Set amid the sprawling ranches of horse country, this immaculate RV resort with a heated pool is surprisingly wooded and parklike. Paved roads wind past concrete-pad campsites with patios. Many campers stay for the season, but the park's location near the interstate makes it a good option for overnight travelers as well. The pool is an impressive sight for a campground swimming hole: The blue waters and encircling patio are surrounded by towering moss-draped oaks that provide some shade. Within a short drive is Orange Lake, famed for bass fishing, and the historic towns of McIntosh and Micanopy, which have quaint antiques shops.

RV sites, facilities: There are 140 full-hookup RV sites (45 pull-through) with 30/50-amp electrical service. The park describes itself as modem-friendly. A pool, horseshoes, shuffleboard, showers, restrooms, a dump station, firewood, cable TV, telephone hookups, laundry facilities, and two recreation halls with kitchens are available. Planned activities include tai chi, aerobics, and fishing outings, plus the usual array of card games, potlucks, movies, and so forth. Supermarkets and restaurants are within six miles. Children are welcome. Leashed pets are permitted, but they must use the wooded dog walk on the park's east side.

Reservations, fees: Reservations are recommended. Sites are $28 per night. Credit cards are accepted. Long-term rates are available.

Directions: From I-75 at Exit 368, turn west

onto County Road 318. Go 200 yards, turn left (south) on Highway 225, and continue 0.5 mile to the entrance on the left.

Contact: Encore RV Park—Ocala, 16905 Northwest Highway 225, Reddick, FL 32686, 352/591-1723 or 877/267-8737, fax 352/591-2842, www.rvonthego.com.

4 OAK TREE VILLAGE CAMPGROUND

Scenic rating: 5

west of Ocala

This park, a quick hop off I-75, feels almost like a subdivision, albeit a tree-shaded one. Row after row, street after street, campers are lined up 14 abreast, all parked diagonally on paved, 10-mph streets that are straight as arrows. When the pool is crowded, floats and tubes are forbidden. Most campsites at the 40-acre park are shaded (hence the park's name). Campsites 7–14 are closest to the laundry facilities, pool, and playground. Sites 104 and 105 flank the showers. Anglers, hikers, mountain bikers, and hunters can head about 15 miles east to Ocala National Forest. For a joyride, head west from the campground on U.S. 27. In about one mile you'll begin to see would-be champion horses grazing on the pretty rolling hills of some of the area's fabled horse farms. Double Diamond Farm is one of several in the region that permits visitors (1 P.M.–4 P.M. weekdays); call 352/237-3834.

RV sites, facilities: There are 137 pull-through RV sites (70 with full hookups with 30-amp electrical service. A pool, a playground, horseshoes, shuffleboard, racquetball, a party room, tennis, and winter social programs entertain campers. Showers, restrooms, picnic tables, a dump station, and laundry facilities are available. Management says restrooms and the recreation room are wheelchair accessible. Groceries are within 1 mile, and a restaurant is 0.25 mile away. Children under 12 must be adult-supervised at the pool and recreation area. All pets—even cats—must be leashed.

Reservations, fees: Reservations are not necessary. Sites are $15.50–18 per night for two people, plus $1.75 for each additional person. Major credit cards are accepted. Long-term stays are okay.

Directions: From I-75 at Ocala, take Exit 354 onto U.S. 27 heading west and turn right almost immediately at Blitchton Road. Proceed 0.25 mile to the campground.

Contact: Oak Tree Village Campground, 4039 Northwest Blitchton Road, Ocala, FL 34482, 352/629-1569.

5 ARROWHEAD CAMPSITES AND MOBILE HOME PARK

Scenic rating: 4

west of Ocala

This campground is a quick detour from I-75 for weary travelers on the road to Disney, and certainly the park borrows from that proximity in describing itself as a "convenient good neighborly park." About 40 percent of the park is occupied by year-round residents. Most seasonal visitors are from the Midwest and New York. They stay here in the winter months to play shuffleboard, partake in planned activities such as bingo, coffee klatches, dinners, and dances.

RV sites, facilities: Most of the 128 RV sites have full hookups, picnic tables, and drive-through access. Thirty-three sites have 50-amp service, the rest are 30-amp. The shady, level sites average 20 by 50 feet in size. They can accommodate 40-foot-long RVs and slide-outs. Internet service is available in the office. A pool, a playground, an exercise room, horseshoes, shuffleboard, a recreation room, a camp circle, and a wintertime activity schedule entertain campers. Showers, restrooms, firewood, cable TV, and laundry facilities are available. A camp store sells snacks, camping supplies, and propane gas. Most areas are wheelchair ac-

cessible. Groceries and a restaurant are within 300 feet. Children are permitted. Leashed pets are accepted.

Reservations, fees: Reservations are recommended in winter. Nightly fee for two people in an RV is $21. Add $1 per extra person. Major credit cards are accepted. Long-term rates are available.

Directions: From I-75 at Ocala, take Exit 354 onto U.S. 27 heading west, then turn left onto Northwest 38th Avenue. The campground is 250 feet ahead.

Contact: Arrowhead Campsites and Mobile Home Park, 1720 Northwest 38th Avenue, Ocala, FL 34482, 352/622-5627, email: shan1234@earthlink.net.

6 HOLIDAY TRAV-L-PARK

Scenic rating: 2

off I-75 in Ocala

Snowbirds fleeing blustery northern temperatures like to park big rigs at this 9.5-acre park, but it's also a convenient stop from I-75. Long-term visitors spend many a winter hour engaged in park activities such as bingo, suppers, and group barbecues, or visiting the Silver Springs theme park or nearby flea markets. Row after row, 12 to 13 campers are parked diagonally along ruler-straight streets. Oaks shade some grassy/sandy sites, but others are sunny. About half the lots are occupied year-round, and your neighbors will include families, seasonal vacationers, and working people, as well as repeat visitors who return year after year.

For a pleasant ride, go west along the rolling terrain of U.S. 27 to pass would-be champion thoroughbreds at some of the region's horse farms. To watch equestrian training activity at Ocala Breeders' Sales Company and Training Center, show up before 10 A.M.; call 352/237-2154. Some anglers, hikers, mountain bikers, and seasonal hunters come here to be just 20 miles from Ocala National Forest.

RV sites, facilities: There are 106 full-hookup RV sites (all with 30-amp electrical service and picnic tables), of which 102 are pull-through. More than 50 sites have 50-amp service. The grassy, mostly shady, level sites are 30–35 feet wide and 65 feet long. Some sites allow for satellite dish setup; cable TV is included in the nightly fee. A wireless network for accessing the Internet is available in some areas of the park. A pool, a playground, a horseshoe pit, shuffleboard, a recreation room, and winter activities entertain campers. Showers, restrooms, picnic tables, a dump station, a store with ice, snacks, propane and camping supplies, cable TV, telephone hookups, and laundry facilities are available. Restaurants, groceries, malls, and hospitals are within three miles. All areas of the park are wheelchair accessible. Children must be accompanied by an adult at the pool. Leashed dogs should use the dog walk or fenced dog run near the 100 row. The management is superstrict about cleaning up after your dog; in fact, you must carry a visible pick-up bag or other device whenever you walk your dog.

Reservations, fees: Reservations are recommended, particularly in winter. Sites are $24 per night for two people, plus $2 for each additional person and $1.50 for using 50-amp electricity. Credit cards are accepted. Long-term rates are available, and the maximum length of stay is indefinite.

Directions: From I-75 at Exit 352, take State Road 40 west 0.25 mile to the park on the right.

Contact: Holiday Trav-L-Park, 4001 West Silver Springs Boulevard, Ocala, FL 34482, 352/622-5330 or 800/833-2164, www.holidayrvocala.com.

7 MOTOR INNS MOTEL AND RV PARK

Scenic rating: 2

off I-75 in Ocala

Convenience is the main attraction here, though the park prides itself on being clean and quiet. RVs are somewhat surrounded, with a handful of mobile homes to the north and two motel buildings and a fruit stand to the south. I-75, which leads vacationers to Disney World, Tampa, or even Michigan, is just one block west. A paved road with a 10-mph speed limit passes the partially shaded sites. About 15 percent of the park is occupied by year-round residents in mobile homes. Most visitors are over 55, though families are welcome. Free coffee is available in the office.

RV sites, facilities: Most of the 80 sites available for RVs have full hookups, with a choice of 30-amp or 50-amp electrical service. Sites are grassy and level, measuring about 30 feet wide by 60 feet deep, and they can accommodate the largest RVs (up to 50 feet long) and slide-outs. Sunny sites allow for setup of satellite dishes. A pool, showers, restrooms, a dump station, ice, cable TV, and laundry facilities are available. Groceries, malls, and restaurants are within three miles. All areas are wheelchair accessible. Kids must be supervised at all times. Small, leashed animals are permitted, but pooches must use the park's dog walk.

Reservations, fees: Reservations are recommended, particularly in winter. Sites are $26 per night. Credit cards are accepted. Long-term rates are available.

Directions: From I-75 at Exit 352, take State Road 40 east for one block to the campground.

Contact: Motor Inns Motel and RV Park, 3601 West Silver Springs Boulevard, Ocala, FL 34475, 352/629-6902, fax 352/629-2530.

8 THE SPRINGS RV RESORT

Scenic rating: 5

near the Silver Springs nature theme park in Silver Springs

Although you certainly may lounge around the sunny Olympic-sized pool or in the 17,000-square-foot clubhouse, at least some campers prefer spending daylight hours three blocks away at Silver Springs, a 350-acre nature theme park with animal shows and picnic areas. Also within blocks of here is Wild Waters, a six-acre water park. The 52-acre campground bills itself as "the land of sunshine." Stay at one of these open, unshaded concrete-pad and grassy sites and you'll probably agree.

RV sites, facilities: All 618 pull-through RV sites have full hookups with 30-amp and 50-amp electrical service. For recreation, there's a pool, horseshoes, tennis, shuffleboard, social programs, a wheelchair-accessible clubhouse, a card room, and a poolroom. Showers, restrooms, cable TV, some telephone hookups, and laundry facilities are available. Restaurants are located within blocks of here. Children are welcome. You must walk leashed pets outside the park.

Reservations, fees: Reservations are recommended. Sites are $25 per night for two people, plus $2.50 for each additional person. Credit cards are accepted. Long-term rates are available.

Directions: From I-75 at Exit 352, take State Road 40 east for about eight miles to 52nd Court. Turn left. The campground is ahead.

Contact: The Springs RV Resort, 2950 Northeast 52nd Court, Silver Springs, FL 34488, 352/236-5250, www.rvresorts.com.

9 SILVER SPRINGS CAMPERS GARDEN

Scenic rating: 5

opposite the Silver Springs theme park in Silver Springs

Tarzan swung through this neighborhood long ago. Actually, it was actor Johnny Weissmuller shooting the 1939 film *Tarzan Finds a Son* across the street at the 780-square-foot cavern of Silver Springs—Florida's original tourist attraction. Henry Ford, Thomas Edison, and thousands of others have visited the theme park, which today offers glass-bottom boats, animals from six continents, a petting zoo, and picnic

areas on its 350 acres. Also across the street is Wild Waters, a six-acre water park. The proximity of these attractions make the campground popular with families, seasonal visitors over age 55, and repeat customers. About 60 percent of the sites are occupied by full-time residents. In the wintertime, visitors play bingo and shuffleboard, and they go to parties, Silver Springs, and concerts nearby.

The bent branches of deep-furled oaks help shade some campsites at the 15.5-acre campground, but others are sunny and open. Just downstream at Silver River State Park, a hiking trail winds beneath fan-leafed sabal palms and shiny-leaf magnolias. If you go, look for otters in early morning along the Silver River, reached via the trail. Anglers, hikers, mountain bikers, and seasonal hunters can drive a short distance east from the campground to Ocala National Forest.

RV sites, facilities: Nearly all the 199 full-hookup RV sites are pull-through. All have 30-amp electrical service, and 75 have 50-amp hookups. Rigs up to 45 feet long and slide-outs can be accommodated. Dial-up Internet access is available in the clubhouse. A pool, a playground, a horseshoe pit, a shuffleboard court, a wintertime activity schedule, and a clubhouse entertain campers. Showers, restrooms, a dump station, picnic tables, cable TV, telephone hookups, laundry facilities, and a small store with propane, ice, and camping supplies are available. Most areas of the park are wheelchair accessible. A restaurant is located next door, and groceries are within two blocks. Children are welcome, but not for long-term stays. Leashed pets are permitted.

Reservations, fees: Reservations are recommended in winter. Sites are $27 per night for two people, plus $1.50 for each additional person, $2.50 for cable TV, and $2.50 when using air conditioners or heaters. Credit cards are not accepted. Long-term rates are available.

Directions: From I-75 at Exit 352, take State Road 40 east for about eight miles. The campground is opposite the Silver Springs nature theme park.

Contact: Silver Springs Campers Garden, 3151 Northeast 56th Avenue, Silver Springs, FL 34488, 352/236-3700 or 800/640-3733, www.campersgarden.com.

10 SILVER RIVER STATE PARK

🏃 🚲 🚐 🐴 ♿ 🚙 ⛺

Scenic rating: 10

east of Ocala and south of Silver Springs

Wow! Dozens of springs, 14 distinct plant communities, and 10 miles of river frontage dot these 5,000 breathtaking acres. "People rave about this place," says one of the park rangers. Canoe or kayak on the Silver River; there are two launching points. One is outside the park at the foot of the Ocklawaha Bridge on State Road 40; the other is in the park at the end of the River Trail (you'll have to portage your canoe 0.6 mile from the parking lot). A concessionaire rents kayaks.

Opened in 1995, this park is popular with families, seasonal visitors, and locals. Bicyclists bomb around on a 5.6-mile trail or meander around on the paved roads. Hiking trails lead to a sinkhole and to the river. There's also a museum focusing on nature and Native American culture, as well as a "Cracker village" with houses, a church/school, a cane-syrup boiler, and a blacksmith's shop. The park is also a hot spot for stargazing, bird walks, and annual festivals, such as the Country Cracker Days, held the second week of November. The Silver Springs theme park is next door to the park; a Wal-Mart is about a mile away.

RV sites, facilities: The campsites are divided into two loops, the Sharpe's Ferry camping area (near the museum and closest to the trail heads) and the Fort King camping area. There are 59 gravel, level sites with picnic tables, water and electricity, grills, and fire rings. Big rigs and slide-outs are welcome. Six sites have 50-amp electrical service; the rest have 15/30-amp hookups. Sites are spacious, and there is a mix of sunny and shady spots. Drive-through spots

can be found at 22 sites. Restrooms, showers, a dump station, laundry facilities, and cabin rentals are available. Restaurants and groceries are within one mile. The park office, bathhouses, museum, and playground are wheelchair-accessible. Children are welcome. Leashed pets are permitted.

Reservations, fees: Reservations are recommended; contact ReserveAmerica at 800/336-3521 or reserveamerica.com. Sites are $21 per night for six people. Major credit cards are accepted. The maximum length of stay is 14 days.

Directions: From the intersection of State Road 40 and State Road 35 in Silver Springs, drive south on State Road 35 one mile.

Contact: Silver River State Park, 1425 Northeast 58th Avenue, Ocala, FL 34470, 352/236-7148, www.floridastateparks.org.

11 OCALA RV CAMP RESORT

🏊 🐴 🎣 🚐

Scenic rating: 8

off I-75 south of Ocala

Ducks flapping their wings at the two park ponds and the graceful springtime sight of blooming magnolias lend atmosphere to this 20-acre wooded retreat just off I-75. The oak- and magnolia-shaded grassy/sandy campsites tend to fill up pretty quickly in winter, so call ahead. The attraction for couples and families is plunging into the pool or heading to the game room after a long day of interstate driving or taking in area attractions. The Silver Springs nature theme park is less than one-half hour east. Ocala National Forest is farther east. For a joyride, head west on U.S. 27 to pass would-be champion horses grazing on the rolling hills of some of the region's more than 1,000 horse farms.

RV sites, facilities: Under new ownership since 2005, this was formerly a KOA. The new owners have expanded the number of sites to 200, added landscaping, and upgraded electrical service and the overall look of the park. The 200 RV sites have full hookups with 30-amp and

50-amp electrical services available. Each site has a picnic table. For recreation, there's a pool, a hot tub, a sauna, a kiddie pool, a game room, a playground, a TV lounge, a horseshoe pit, a shuffleboard court, a volleyball net, a recreation room, a basketball court, and wintertime social activities. Facilities include showers, restrooms, a convenience store, a dump station, cabins, cable TV, and a laundry room. Twenty-five restaurants are within two miles. Children are welcome. Leashed pets are permitted.

Reservations, fees: Reservations are recommended. Sites are $30–35 per night for two people. Add $8 for each additional adult, $4 per extra child age four and older. Credit cards are accepted. Long-term stays are okay, but there are no mobile homes on-site.

Directions: From I-75 at Exit 350, take State Road 200 west to 38th Avenue. Turn right. The campground is 0.5 mile ahead at left, next to the Disney Information Center.

Contact: Ocala RV Camp Resort, 3200 Southwest 38th Avenue, Ocala, FL 34474, 352/237-2138 or 866/858-3400, fax 352/237-9894, www.ocalarvcampresort.com.

12 CAMPER VILLAGE OF AMERICA

Scenic rating: 3

off I-75 south of Ocala

With four shopping plazas, a mall, and two movie theaters within one mile of here, you have all the comforts of home. Still, to the other side of the campground, horse farms dominate. This adult-oriented, family-run campground aims to create a small-town, familiar feel by scheduling numerous wintertime activities, including dancing, musical performances, bus trips to nearby attractions, and potluck dinners. Each morning, free coffee is brewed at the office of this lighted park with paved roads. There's not a lot of landscaping, so campsites tend to be open and sunny.

RV sites, facilities: The park offers 250 full-hookup RV sites (several pull-through), of which 75 percent have 30-amp electrical service and the rest 50-amp. About 150 sites are filled by park models or permanent residents. For recreation, there are shuffleboard courts, horseshoe pits, winter activities, and a 400-person-capacity recreation hall. Showers, restrooms, a dump station, telephone hookups, laundry facilities, and free cable TV are available. Within one mile you'll find four supermarkets, a hospital, and nearly 40 restaurants. The recreation hall, restrooms, and office are wheelchair accessible. Children are permitted for short stays. Leashed pets are accepted.

Reservations, fees: Reservations are recommended in winter. Sites are $22 per night for two people, plus $1.50 per additional person. Use of air conditioners or electric heaters costs $2.25 each night. Credit cards are not accepted. Long-term stays are okay.

Directions: From I-75 at Exit 350, take State Road 200 west for 1,000 feet to the campground.

Contact: Camper Village of America, 3931 Southwest College Road, Ocala, FL 34474, 352/237-3236, email: campervill@earthlink.net.

13 CRYSTAL ISLE RV RESORT

Scenic rating: 10

west of Crystal River

Located on a canal with access to the Crystal River, this resort owned by the Encore chain offers lots to do, including fishing, boating, social activities, sports, and even tennis. But the location makes it ideal as a base camp for those who want to explore local sights. Manatees are a top tourist draw, with several local tours offering trips to see the 200 lumbering sea cows that spend their winters in the spring-fed, 72°F waters of the Crystal River. Spectacular diving springs, famous around the world for their purity and clarity, are within four miles.

King Spring, near the Plantation Inn and Golf Resort (352/795-4211) down the road from the RV resort, is 75 feet across and drops 30 feet to a cavern. If you didn't bring your diving gear, you can rent snorkel or scuba equipment from many local dive shops.

RV sites, facilities: This 30-acre RV resort has 250 full-hookup sites (6 pull-through) with 30/50-amp electrical service and cable TV. Restrooms, showers, picnic tables, grills, fire rings, laundry facilities, a heated pool, a hot tub, a dump station, a recreation room, a playground, horseshoes, shuffleboard, tennis, basketball, volleyball, a boat ramp, boat docks, fishing lake, and a store are on the premises. Children and leashed pets are welcome.

Reservations, fees: Reservations are recommended. Sites are $28–32 per night. Major credit cards are accepted. Long-term stays are okay.

Directions: From U.S. 19 in Crystal River, drive four miles west on State Road 44/Fort Island Trail to the park, on the right.

Contact: Crystal Isle RV Resort, 11419 West Fort Island Trail, Crystal River, FL 34429, 352/795-3774 or 888/783-6763, fax 352/795-4897, www.rvonthego.com.

14 QUAIL ROOST RV CAMPGROUND

Scenic rating: 4

north of Crystal River

For the retired snowbird who likes conveniences in a more natural setting, this well-maintained park may fit the bill: Some sites are set under trees, and some are out in the open. The main roads are paved. Visitors tend to be repeat customers over 55 who come from all areas of the United States. Social programs in winter include bingo, cards, games, campfires, dinners, and darts. Asked what the favorite thing to do, the owners answered, "Talk!" Pick up major supplies in Crystal River or Dunnellon,

both 7.5 miles away. Only 1 percent of the park is occupied year-round.

RV sites, facilities: This adults-preferred park has 72 full-hookup sites with picnic tables and telephone and cable TV access. The level, grassy or gravel lots measure about 32–40 feet wide by 40 feet deep. More than 40 sites have 50-amp electrical service; the rest have 30-amp. Half are pull-throughs and can accommodate the largest RVs, even triple slide-outs. Swim in the heated pool, or set up your satellite dish. Internet access is available at some sites and in the clubhouse. Restrooms, showers, laundry facilities, picnic tables, shuffleboard, horseshoes, boccie ball (lawn bowling), basketball, a pool table, wintertime social programs, and a recreation room are available. Two restaurants are within walking distance. The clubhouse, bathhouse, and office are wheelchair accessible. Streets are paved. There are no facilities for children, however they are allowed for short visits. No dogs are allowed November–April.

Reservations, fees: Reservations are recommended. Sites are $27 per night for two people, plus $1 for each additional person. Credit cards are not accepted. Long-term stays are allowed.

Directions: In downtown Crystal River, from the intersection of U.S. 19 and County Road 495, drive northwest on the county road for 7.5 miles to the park, at right.

Contact: Quail Roost RV Campground, 9835 North Citrus Avenue, Crystal River, FL 34428, 352/563-0404, www.quailroostcampground.com.

15 LAKE ROUSSEAU RV AND FISHING RESORT

Scenic rating: 6

Between Crystal River and Dunnellon

Bass fishing is primo on Lake Rousseau, and a fishing guide is on-site. Land-bound campers will also enjoy views of its sparkling waters. Nestled amid oaks draped with Spanish moss, the campground is home to a mix of year-round residents in mobile homes, travelers in all manner of rigs, and anglers. Some sites are on the water; you may share your bit of lakefront with the ducks. The park is out in the countryside but not prohibitively far from attractions such as Homosassa Springs State Wildlife Park, golf courses, beaches, Silver Springs, and Weeki Wachee Spring. About 10 percent of the park is occupied year-round. Most visitors come from Ohio, Indiana, and Michigan, but you'll also find locals making this their base camp. Planned activities include bingo, potluck dinners, luaus, day trips, and fishing tournaments.

RV sites, facilities: Park your RV on one of 123 grassy sites with full hookups, concrete patios, and picnic tables. Wireless Internet access, telephone service, and cable TV are available at your site. About 20 sites are available for overnighters, and 60 for seasonal visitors. Rigs up to 40 feet long and slide-outs can be accommodated. Two sites are pull-through. Restrooms, showers, laundry facilities, a pool, a recreation room with planned activities during the winter season, boat docks, a boat ramp, boat rentals, rental cabins, a store, propane gas, and horseshoes are on-site. The restrooms, office, and recreation hall are wheelchair accessible. Streets are paved. Groceries and restaurants are five miles away. The park store sells ice, camping supplies, snacks, fishing tackle, and bait. Adults are preferred. Children are allowed for stays up to one month. Leashed pets (no attack dogs) are welcome.

Reservations, fees: Reservations are recommended. Sites are $24–27 per night four people. Cable TV costs $2.50. Boat launches are free for campers. Boat dockage is available for an extra charge. Credit cards are accepted. Long-term rates are available.

Directions: From the town of Crystal River, drive north on U.S. 19 for six miles. Turn east on State Road 488 and continue four miles. Turn north on Northcut Avenue (watch for the campground sign) and proceed 1.3 miles

until the road dead-ends at the campground. From Dunnellon, at the intersection of U.S. 41 and State Road 488, drive five miles west on State Road 488 to Northcut Avenue and proceed as above.

Contact: Lake Rousseau RV and Fishing Resort, 10811 North Coveview Terrace, Crystal River, FL 34428, 352/795-6336 or 800/561-CAMP (800/561-2267), fax 352/564-4287, www.lakerousseaurvpark.com.

16 CAMP 'N' WATER OUTDOOR RESORT

Scenic rating: 7

south of Homosassa Springs

Secluded but not isolated, this 13-acre, well-shaded park is on the banks of the Homosassa River. The resort is oriented to boaters as well as campers: There are 28 boat slips in the marina, and the fishing grounds of the Gulf of Mexico are just five miles away. Anglers from all over the world flock to the Crystal River area for sportfishing. Sea trout and redfish are plentiful in near-shore waters, and the magnificent silver tarpon is abundant farther out. Don't miss a visit to nearby Homosassa Springs State Wildlife Park (352/628-2311), where you can see a manatee up close. The park, previously a private zoo and tourist attraction, is a rehabilitation center for manatees who were orphaned or injured in the wild and for those born in captivity. It claims to be the only center in the world where you can view these gentle creatures every day of the year. An underwater observatory lets visitors observe them eye to eye. You can also see wood ducks, flamingos, birds of prey, herons, and egrets on the grounds. Alligators, snakes, hippopotamuses, black bears, white-tailed deer, and river otters are among the other residents.

RV sites, facilities: There are 76 RV sites with full hookups, 30-amp and 50-amp electrical service, and cable TV; some have telephone access.

Most sites are pull-through and have concrete patios. Restrooms, showers, picnic tables, grills, a dump station, laundry facilities, a dining area, rental cabins, and an adult TV room are available. You'll also find a playground, a pool, basketball and shuffleboard courts, horseshoes, a boat ramp, a fish-cleaning station, park model rentals, canoes for rent, and a marina. The bathrooms and clubhouse are wheelchair accessible. A supermarket is five miles away. Children and leashed pets are welcome.

Reservations, fees: Reservations are advised. Sites are $28 per night for four people, plus $2.50 for each additional person up to a party of six. Credit cards are accepted. Long-term rates are available.

Directions: From Crystal River, drive south on U.S. 19 for 7.3 miles to County Road 490A/West Halls River Road and turn west. Drive 0.5 mile, turn south (left) on Fishbowl Drive, and follow to Mason Creek Road. Turn left. Go one mile to Garcia Road, turn right onto Garcia. Continue four blocks to Priest Lane. Turn right, and follow signs to the park.

Contact: Camp 'N' Water Outdoor Resort, 11465 West Priest Lane, Homosassa, FL 34448, 352/628-2000, fax 352/628-0066, email: campnwater@mindspring.com.

17 TURTLE CREEK RV RESORT

Scenic rating: 7

south of Homosassa Springs

You can cast your line into Turtle Creek from the bank of this campground, but the wintertime action tends to take place indoors. Planned seasonal activities run the gamut, from ladies' luncheons, holiday dinners, and potluck feasts to crafts, exercise classes, card tournaments, and boat tours. There's even a bowling league, plus line dancing and country music shows performed by campers (bring your instrument). A short distance upriver is the Homosassa Springs State Wildlife Park (described in previous camp-

ground); six miles downriver is the Gulf of Mexico. Sites are oversized, big enough for large RVs. Folks are friendly; a nice widow brought me home-baked cookies one night.

RV sites, facilities: All 225 sites have full hookups, cable TV, 30-amp electrical service, and picnic tables. Some have 50-amp electricity, and around 10 sites are pull-through. Internet connection is available in the office. Restrooms, showers, laundry facilities, a dump station, a pool, a recreation pavilion, pool tables, fishing from the bank, horseshoes, shuffleboards, and rental units are available. The restrooms, office, recreation hall, and laundry are wheelchair accessible. Children are welcome. Leashed pets are permitted.

Reservations, fees: Reservations are recommended. Sites are $25 per night for two people, plus $2 per additional adult and $2 for children. Credit cards are accepted. Long-term rates are available.

Directions: From Crystal River, drive south on U.S. 19 for 7.3 miles to County Road 490A/West Halls River Road and turn west. Drive 0.5 mile to Fishbowl Drive, turn south, and go 1.5 miles.

Contact: Turtle Creek Campground, 10200 West Fishbowl Drive, Homosassa Springs, FL 34448, 352/628-2928 or 800/471-3722, fax 352/628-6964, email: turtlecreek@gowebco.com.

18 ROCK CRUSHER CANYON RV AND MUSIC PARK

Scenic rating: 10

east of Crystal River

BEST (

Want to see headline artists like Willie Nelson, Hootie and the Blowfish, Pat Boone, the Oak Ridge Boys, Three Dog Night, or Faith Hill? This 60-acre RV park is part campground, part concert venue. There's live entertainment every weekend in a garden pavilion, plus outdoor concerts in an amphitheater that seats 7,000. For show information, call 352/795-1313 or visit www.rockcrushercanyon.com. The RV park itself has much to recommend, set in a wooded area not far from the Withlacoochee State Forest. Rallies and caravans are welcome. The park was opened in 2001, and the grounds are kept immaculate, even to the point of reseeding the RV sites when the grass gets eroded. Don't worry about noise from the concerts; they are usually over by 10 P.M.

RV sites, facilities: There are 398 full-hookup RV sites with 50-amp electrical service, cable TV, instant phone service, and grassy pads. Sites are wooded. Restrooms, showers, laundry facilities, a heated pool, a whirlpool tub, a fitness station, a restaurant, and a recreation hall are provided. The concert area is set apart from the RV park. Children are welcome. Leashed pets are permitted.

Reservations, fees: Reservations are recommended. Sites are $35 per night for two people, plus $2 per extra person. Credit cards are accepted. Long-term rates are available.

Directions: In Crystal River, from State Road 44 and U.S. 19, drive south on U.S. 19 about two miles to the Home Depot and intersection with Venable Road. Turn left on Venable Road and go west about 3.5 miles. At Rock Crusher Road, turn south and drive 0.5 mile to the park.

Contact: Rock Crusher Canyon RV and Music Park, 275 South Rock Crusher Road, Crystal River, FL 34429, 352/795-3870, www.rc-crvpark.com.

19 CHASSAHOWITZKA RIVER CAMPGROUND AND RECREATION AREA

Scenic rating: 8

south of Homosassa Springs

BEST (

The shady campground gets hard use during holidays and weekends, but the location can't be beat and it's well worth a visit. Campers can launch their boats or canoes from the boat ramp near Chassahowitzka Spring. The waterway flows

southwest to the Gulf of Mexico, with dozens of creeks and crystal-clear springs offering tempting side trips along the way. Be sure to rinse your boat motor and trailer thoroughly afterward to remove all weed fragments and to prevent the spread of weeds to other bodies of water. Canoes and small flat-bottomed boats can be rented at the campground. Nearby is the Chassahowitzka National Wildlife Refuge, a swampy coastal area that's popular among area anglers for both freshwater and saltwater fishing.

RV sites, facilities: There are 40 sites with sewer hookups and 30/50-amp electricity. Restrooms, showers, laundry facilities, a camp store, and a boat ramp are available. Canoes and johnboats are for rent. Alcoholic beverages are prohibited. Children are welcome. Leashed pets are permitted with proof of rabies vaccination.

Reservations, fees: Reservations are accepted. Sites are $18–20 per night for two people, plus $3 for each additional person above age six. Credit cards are accepted. Maximum stay is six months.

Directions: From the intersection of U.S. 19 and County Road 480 south of Homosassa Springs and Crystal River, drive west on County Road 480/Miss Maggie Drive for 1.7 miles until the road ends at the campground.

Contact: Chassahowitzka River Campground and Recreation Area, 8600 West Miss Maggie Drive, Homosassa, FL 34448, 352/382-2200. Citrus County Parks and Recreation Office, P.O. Box 1439, Crystal River, FL 34423-1439, 352/795-2202, http://bocc.citrus.fl.us/parks/parks_recreation.htm

20 RAINBOW SPRINGS STATE PARK

Scenic rating: 9

near Dunnellon

BEST (

Rainbow Springs is the state's third-largest spring, pumping 600 million gallons of sparkling water a day. The surroundings are so breathtaking that a hotel was built near the spring in the 1890s. In the 1930s, private developers made it a tourist attraction that operated for four decades. The state, in conjunction with the Marion County parks department, acquired the park in 1989, and later acquired the previously privately operated campground (ergo, a swimming pool). Today, the main part of the park has azalea gardens, an amphitheater, and picnic grounds that are popular for group events. Avoid holidays, when the park gets crowded. You can rent canoes and kayaks to drift downstream; note that there is no shuttle service to bring you back to the campground. Strap on a snorkel mask and explore the crystalline waters near the swimming area in the campground.

The campground and the main part of the park are on opposite sides of the river; to reach the main part, you'll have to paddle up the river or drive several miles. As you paddle, you'll be able to peer deep into the water and even see boils where the water bubbles up below you from the sandy floor. Dark green water plants wave in the stream. It's a hypnotic experience. The campground is divided into two areas: a more wooded loop near the picturesque Rainbow River and a sprawling sunny field without trees near the office. You may think you're in two different parks. Each has its pros and cons. The wooded section is prettier, but can be crowded and noisy on weekends; the field accommodates large RVs and is near the swimming pool.

RV sites, facilities: The 93 RV sites have water and 30-amp electricity; 40 have sewer hookups. Sites vary in size, but some will accommodate slide-outs and bigger rigs. Restrooms, showers, picnic tables, fire rings, grills, laundry facilities, a dump station, a playground, a pool, canoe rentals, and a recreation hall are provided. Also for rent are inner tubes and diver-down flags; however, shuttle service is not provided for those who float too far down the river. Some groceries are available in the camp store, along with ice, firewood, and souvenirs. The restrooms, pool

area, office, and store are wheelchair accessible; some streets are paved. Children are welcome. Pets are permitted in the campground with proof of vaccination.

Reservations, fees: Reservations are recommended; contact ReserveAmerica at 800/336-3521 or reserveamerica.com. Sites are $19 per night for eight people. Credit cards are accepted. Stays are limited to 14 days.

Directions: From I-75 south of Ocala, take Exit 341 onto State Road 484 west for 19 miles. At Southwest 180th Avenue Street (west of the airport), turn north and drive past a high school. Drive 2.5 miles to the entrance, on the west side.

Contact: Rainbow Springs State Park, 18185 Southwest 94th Street, Dunnellon, FL 34432, 352/489-5201, fax 352/465-7209, www.floridastateparks.org.

21 OCALA RANCH RV PARK

Scenic rating: 6

off I-75 south of Ocala

Winter campers and overnight travelers flock to this renovated park, where amenities include a "doggie bath" and a pool for your pet, a "free-range Doggie Corral," and pet-sitting services. The park boasts that it is one of the few RV parks in the nation that has a cardiac defibrillator on-site. There's a 24-hour security patrol, and wireless Internet service is available throughout the park. Visitors tend to be snowbirds from the Midwest and Canada, as well as families. It's also convenient to the interstate.

RV sites, facilities: Among the 160 RV sites, 60 are pull-through. All have full hookups and telephone availability. There are 54 sites with 30-amp electrical service and 100 with 50-amp hookups; each has a picnic table. Big rigs can be accommodated, and sites are as large as 40 by 50 feet. Facilities include a heated pool, a spa, walking paths, and a community center building. Showers, restrooms, and laundry facilities are available. During the winter season, you'll find the usual planned activities such as bingo, boccie ball (lawn bowling), and horseshoes, but also monthly CPR classes. You can hook up to the Internet at the clubhouse or at your site on a wireless network. Shopping, restaurants and the Florida Horse Park are within five miles. All areas are said to be wheelchair accessible. Children are welcome. Pets are allowed.

Reservations, fees: Reservations are recommended. Sites are $29 per night for two people, plus $2 for each additional person. Major credit cards are accepted. Long-term stays are okay.

Directions: From I-75 at Exit 341, take County Road 484 west for 0.5 mile to the park on the right.

Contact: Ocala Ranch RV Park, 2559 Southwest Highway 484, Ocala, FL 34473, 352/347-4008 or 877/809-1100, www.ocalaranchrv.com.

22 SOUTHERN SUN RV AND MOBILE HOME PARK

Scenic rating: 3

Just south of Belleview

Call early if you want a spot at this sunny, sleepy 10-acre RV park. When contacted one November, the place already was booked up until March and had a wait list of six parties. Retirees tend to dominate the clientele, and they come back year after year. These grassy lots are sizable at 30 by 50 feet. They're set back from cars zipping by on U.S. 441 and County Road 25, and the park can't be seen from the highway.

RV sites, facilities: All 45 RV sites have full hookups with 30-amp or 50-amp electrical service and a picnic table; an additional 18 mobile homes are on-site. Internet connection is available in the office. Horseshoes, showers, restrooms, a recreation room, cable TV, telephone hookups, and laundry facilities are available. Management says the clubhouse, showers, and laundry room are wheelchair accessible. Children are allowed for short visits. Small, leashed pets under 15 pounds are permitted.

Reservations, fees: Reservations are recommended. Sites are $20 per night for two people, plus $2 for each additional person. Credit cards are not accepted. Long-term rates are available.

Directions: From Belleview, go south on U.S. 441 a short distance to County Road 25A. Turn left at Southeast 69th Terrace, the first driveway on your left.

Contact: Southern Sun RV and Mobile Home Park, 11665 Southeast 69th Terrace, Belleview, FL 34420, 352/245-8070, fax 352/245-8070.

23 OCKLAWAHA RV PARK AND CANOE OUTPOST

Scenic rating: 8

on the Ocklawaha River near Ocala National Forest

Canoeing beneath the moss-draped trees flanking the 110-mile-long Ocklawaha River is something bored office workers might daydream about as they wait for five o'clock to roll around. Paddlers in spring and fall wind through narrow waterways lined with gnarly cypress, swamp maple, and sabal palm—the fan-leafed state tree. Along the way, an early morning mist rises over spring-fed streams. The river widens into lily-pad-filled ponds in some places. Bobcat, deer, and Florida black bears live in the surrounding forest.

Adventure-seekers tend to be drawn to this seven-acre campground, where canoes rent for $35 daily and campsites fill up fast, except in summer. Some seasonal campers have stayed here at least three consecutive winters. Anglers can launch at the boat ramp to go after some 100 species of fish in the Ocklawaha, or take advantage of the park's catch-and-release fishing pond. RV sites are shady or sunny. Proprietor Larry Reiche contends there are no mosquitoes to speak of and the canopy of trees makes riverfront canoe-in camping comfortably cooler in summer. Hikers may see deer or wild turkeys along the nearby Cross Florida Greenway, which long ago was meant to become a barge canal gouged through the belly of Florida, almost like the Panama Canal, linking the Atlantic Ocean and the Gulf of Mexico. A welcome center for the Cross Florida Greenway and Ocala National Forest is at the corner of County Road 316 and Highway 40.

RV sites, facilities: There are 12 full-hookup RV sites with electricity. A catch-and-release fishing pond, a small playground, a recreation room, showers, restrooms, snacks, a boat ramp, limited camping and fishing supplies, a dump station, cabin rentals, and canoe and kayak rentals are available. Children are welcome. Dogs may chase a ball in a large field but must be leashed elsewhere, including along the park's dog walk.

Reservations, fees: Reservations are recommended for canoeing or camping. Nightly fee is $21 for four people. Add $3 for each additional person. A pet deposit of $50 is required. Overnight primitive canoe/camping trips are $95 per rental canoe per day, plus transportation ($20–45). Or bring your own canoe and just pay for the shuttle. Credit cards are accepted. Long-term stays are okay.

Directions: From I-75 at Exit 352, take State Road 40 east about 10 miles through Ocala and Silver Springs. Turn left at County Road 315 and proceed 12 miles north to County Road 316. Turn right. The campground is about four miles ahead at the Ocklawaha River. Turn left before the bridge, and follow to the camp store, located near where the road's pavement ends.

Contact: Ocklawaha RV Park and Canoe Outpost, 15260 Northeast 152nd Place, Fort McCoy, FL 32134, 352/236-4606, www.out-postresort.com.

24 LAKE DELANCY EAST CAMPGROUND

Scenic rating: 3

in northern Ocala National Forest

The Florida National Scenic Trail passes through this rustic, no-frills campground, of-fering you an opportunity to scale the rolling, sandy, pine-studded hills that dominate the sunny northern part of the forest. You also can try your hand at fishing in the shallow freshwater lake next to the campground, which basically is little more than a clearing in the woods and is dominated by hunters during prescribed seasons. Please note: The Lake Delancy West Campground nearby is designated for motorcyclists, horseback riders, and all-terrain vehicle camping.

RV sites, facilities: This primitive camping area can accommodate 29 self-contained RVs. Vault toilets, hand-pumped drinking water, fire rings, grills, and several picnic tables are available. There are no showers. Children are welcome. Leashed pets are permitted.

Reservations, fees: Reservations are not accepted, nor are credit cards. Sites are $6 per night. The maximum stay is 14 days in any 30-day period.

Directions: From Ocala, take State Road 40 east about 12 miles. Turn left onto County Road 314 and continue northeast about 15 miles. Turn left (north) onto Forest Service Road 88 and go about nine miles, then turn right (east) onto Forest Service Road 75 and look for the campground on the right. If you reach State Road 19, you've gone too far.

Contact: Ocala National Forest, Lake George Ranger District, 17147 East State Road 40, Silver Springs, FL 34488, 352/236-0288 or 352/625-2520.

25 SALT SPRINGS RECREATION AREA

Scenic rating: 9

in northeastern Ocala National Forest

BEST (

The big attraction here is the natural springs, called Salt Springs, but not salty the way ocean water is. Instead, it's tinged with calcium, sodium, potassium, and other minerals, yet still is clear enough to make swimming or snorkeling pleasant. Flowing at a speedy rate of 53 million gallons per day, the spring was treasured by Native Americans and was said to have medicinal value, with each of the five boils supposedly curing different ailments. It's even been said that these waters were the legendary Fountain of Youth. When President Roosevelt designated the Ocala National Forest in 1908, hardy travelers braved difficult roads to take a dip.

Canoeists follow the spring's run to Lake George (rental canoes are available nearby), while anglers snag bass at Florida's second-largest lake. Motorboats can be rented at Salt Springs Marina and Landing; call 352/685-2255.

There's good hiking nearby along the Salt Springs Trail, a three-foot-wide dirt path that cuts a two-mile loop through sand-pine scrub, slash-pine flat woods, bayheads, cypress, and clusters of oak trees. The trail leads to an observation platform on the Salt Springs Run, a nice place to picnic in cooler months. For a longer hiking challenge, try the sandier, more open portion of the Florida National Scenic Trail that runs nearby. The Bear Swamp Trail boardwalk winds for 1.5 miles past some huge cypress trees.

The campground itself is sort of bowl shaped, leading down to the springs. Big shady oaks as well as some sand pine and longleaf pine dot the grounds. The RV sites are grassy, and primitive sites are sandy. If you bring horseshoes or a basketball, you can use them at facilities here. Salt Springs is actually a small town in the woods where you can get pizza, seafood, or a square meal at various restaurants, or mail a postcard at the local post office. Campers are a mix of locals, anglers, families, and tourists from as far away as Germany, the United Kingdom, and Alaska. Planned activities such as bingo, potluck dinners, and day trips to local attractions are available in the winter months (October–April).

RV sites, facilities: There are 103 full-hookup RV sites (back-in only) with full hookups and 20/30/50-amp electrical service. In addition, there are 54 primitive sites for self-contained

campers. Rigs as large as 40 feet and slide-outs can be accommodated. Each site has a picnic table, a grill, and a fire ring. On the premises are restrooms, showers, a dump station, a small store, a recreation barn, and a picnic area. You can swim in the springs. The bathhouse, office, and store are wheelchair accessible. Streets are paved. A camp store offers ice, camping supplies, snacks, and souvenirs. Groceries and restaurants are within one mile. Malls and hospitals are 24–30 miles away. Children and leashed pets are welcome. Pets are not allowed in the day-use area (the spring). Note that checkout time is 1 P.M.; if you stay longer, you will be charged a day-use fee. The campground gate is locked around sunset.

Reservations, fees: Reservations are recommended; call 877/444-6777 or go online at www.reserveusa.com. Full-hookup sites are $20 per night for five people and two vehicles, plus $5 for electricity; primitive sites are $14 for five people and two vehicles. The charge for an extra person is $4. Credit cards are accepted. Maximum stay is two weeks during summer (April–October) and six months in winter.

Directions: From Ocala, take State Road 40 east 11 miles. At County Road 314, turn northeast and drive 16 miles. At State Route 19, drive 0.25 mile and look for the campground on the right.

Contact: Salt Springs Recreation Area, Ocala National Forest, 14152 State Road 19 North, Salt Springs, FL, 32134. Mailing address: c/o American Land and Leisure, P.O. Box 5358, Salt Springs, FL 32134, 352/685-2048 or 352/685-2674.

26 ELITE RESORTS AT SALT SPRINGS

Scenic rating: 9

in northeastern Ocala National Forest

This wooded 70-acre campground fronts onto Little Lake Kerr, where you can fish or rent pontoon boats from the park. It's one of the more deluxe RV-oriented parks in the Ocala National Forest and is located 300 yards from the Salt Springs. In the recreation hall, you'll find bingo twice weekly, dances on Saturday nights, and myriad other activities. A modem is accessible here, too, if you need to check your email. Vacation homes and lots are for sale.

RV sites, facilities: There are 470 RV sites available for overnighters, of which 50 can be used for seasonal stays. All have full hookups, picnic tables, and cable TV. RVs as large as 45 feet can be accommodated, and eight sites have 50-amp electrical service. Restrooms, showers, a dump station, laundry facilities, and telephone service are available. On the premises are a pool, a sandy beach, a boat ramp, a dock, a clubhouse, propane gas sales, horseshoe pits, volleyball and shuffleboard courts, tennis courts, a dog-walk area, a shopping center with two restaurants, 40 cottages for rent, nature trails, and miniature golf. Most areas are wheelchair accessible; all roads are paved. Children are welcome. Leashed pets are permitted.

Reservations, fees: Reservations are recommended but usually are not necessary. Sites are $32 per night, plus $3 for 50-amp electricity, $5 for each additional person, and $5 for pull-through sites. Credit cards are accepted. Long-term rates are available.

Directions: From Ocala, take State Road 40 east about 12 miles to County Road 314. Turn left and drive 18 miles north to the campground. At State Road 19, turn north and go one mile to the park. From I-95 in Daytona, take Exit 88 westbound 25 miles on State Road 40 to State Road 19. Turn north and drive 17 miles to the park.

Contact: Elite Resorts at Salt Springs, 25250 East County Road 316, Salt Springs, FL 32134, 352/685-1900, fax 352/685-0557, www.eliteresorts.com.

27 FORE LAKE CAMPGROUND

Scenic rating: 8

on Fore Lake in western Ocala National Forest

If you don't mind the lack of electricity, you'll while away the time amid picturesque live-oak hammocks and pines beside a pretty freshwater lake. Fishing and swimming in 77-acre Fore Lake are popular pursuits here at one of the forest's most popular lake-area campgrounds (Juniper Springs, Salt Springs, and Alexander Springs are more popular). You may also launch a canoe if you bring one. The green, pleasant campground is only a 15-minute drive from the Silver Springs nature theme park (see *Silver Springs Campers Garden* campground in this chapter), and just minutes away from fine nature trails at Lake Eaton.

RV sites, facilities: All seven RV sites have picnic tables, grills, and concrete patios, but no electricity. One site is drive-through. RVs up to 30 feet long can be accommodated. Restrooms with flush toilets, hot showers, and drinking water are available, as are a picnic shelter and pay phone. There are no showers, dump stations, or other facilities. Campfires are permitted inside fire rings. The bathhouse is wheelchair accessible. Children and leashed pets are welcome.

Reservations, fees: Reservations are not taken. Sites are $10 per night for five people. Credit cards are not accepted. The maximum stay is 30 days.

Directions: From Ocala, take State Road 40 east about 12 miles. Turn left onto County Road 314 and continue northeast about six miles until you see the entrance on the left.

Contact: Ocala National Forest, Lake George Ranger District, 17147 East State Road 40, Silver Springs, FL 34488, 352/236-0288 or 352/625-2520.

28 LAKE EATON CAMPGROUND

Scenic rating: 5

on Lake Eaton in western Ocala National Forest

Oaks and pines tower over this small campground at the southern end of idyllic Lake Eaton. The fishing pier and boat launch are pluses for those who want to stick close to camp; however, you should not miss the opportunity to explore some really interesting hiking terrain nearby. Head back out to County Road 314A and continue north approximately two miles to County Road 314. Turn right (heading east), then make another right onto the dirt road that comes up next, Forest Service Road 86. When that curves around to the left, turn right (south) onto Forest Service Road 79. Whew! All the maneuvering is worth it, though, because you will find two first-class hiking trails that are accessible, short, and interesting enough even for people who aren't into hiking for the sheer pleasure of it.

One favorite is the Lake Eaton Sinkhole Trail, which is actually a network of trails totaling 2.2 miles. The big feature, as you might imagine, is the sinkhole. A mere half-mile hike brings you to an observation deck that allows you to peer into this dark, cool hole spanning 450 feet across and reaching a depth of 80 feet. By all means, take the last few steps and follow the boardwalk and stairs leading down into the sinkhole.

The other trail is the Lake Eaton Loop Trail. It provides access through a slightly inclined forest slope to the lake's northeast shore. Passing over mulch and yellow-red sand, you'll walk through an area where you will encounter odd, dwarflike oaks and the pointy fronds of saw palmetto. Altogether, you can see more than a half dozen natural communities ranging from the dry xeric hammocks filled with sand to the lake itself. Animals of note include the osprey, deer, wild turkey, and scrub jay. People who are interested in rare plants should keep an eye out for the scrub milkwort, scrub buckwheat, and scrub morning glory.

RV sites, facilities: Four RV sites are available for rigs up to 30 feet long and slide-outs. There is no electricity. On the premises are picnic tables, vault toilets, hand-pumped drinking water, a boat ramp, fire rings, and a fishing pier. A few spaces will accommodate RVs up to 35 feet. Children are welcome. Leashed pets are permitted.

Reservations, fees: Reservations are not accepted, nor are credit cards. Sites are $6–8 per night for up to five people. The maximum stay is 14 days in any 30-day period.

Directions: From Ocala, take State Road 40 east for approximately 17 miles, turning left onto County Road 314A about 5 miles after entering the forest. Head north for five miles, then turn right (east) onto Forest Service Road 95. After just 0.5 mile or so, turn left onto Forest Service Road 96A. Drive about one mile north to the campsites.

Contact: Ocala National Forest, Lake George Ranger District, 17147 East State Road 40, Silver Springs, FL 34488, 352/236-0288 or 352/625-2520.

29 HOPKINS PRAIRIE

Scenic rating: 4

in central Ocala National Forest

Camp in an oak hammock next to a wet prairie and a shallow lake. You can try your luck fishing there. If you decide to boat, bring a canoe or craft with a motor of no more than 10 horsepower. The Florida National Scenic Trail passes near here.

RV sites, facilities: The camping area has 21 sites with fire rings, lantern posts, and picnic tables, plus some undeveloped sites. Drinking water is available from a hand pump. Vault toilets are provided. Children and leashed pets are permitted.

Reservations, fees: Reservations and credit

cards are not accepted. Sites are $6 per night for up to five people. The maximum stay is 14 days in a 30-day period.

Directions: From Ocala, take State Road 40 east about 32 miles. Turn left on State Route 19 and go about eight miles north to the campground entrance on the left.

Contact: Ocala National Forest, Lake George Ranger District, 17147 East State Road 40, Silver Springs, FL 34488, 352/236-0288 or 352/625-2520.

30 WILDERNESS RV PARK ESTATES

Scenic rating: 6

at the western edge of Ocala National Forest

The meandering, tree-flanked Ocklawaha River is only steps from this 39.5-acre wooded campground, so it's no wonder that bass anglers launch boats at the nearby county boat ramp to try their luck in the sun-dappled waters. Canoeists on the lookout for deer and turkeys peer into the passing woods as they paddle along the river. For a picnic lunch, consider a takeout pork sandwich from Roger's Bar-B-Que, down the street on East State Road 40. It's next door to an Ocala National Forest Visitor Center, where you can pick up forest maps.

Of the paved or gravelly/grassy sites, some are shady, but others are sunny. The park's wintertime activities include bingo, cards, dances, and crafts, and favorite pastimes are walking, biking, boating, and playing horseshoes and shuffleboard. RV sites are laid out along roads like city blocks, and about 25 percent of the park is occupied by year-round residents. Most visitors are from Canada, Illinois, and Wisconsin. Kayaks and canoes are for rent. The park changed hands in 2005, and the new owners were planning to make improvements as of this writing.

RV sites, facilities: This park has more than

300 full-hookup RV sites (of which half have 30-amp electrical service, and the rest have 50 amp). Each site has a picnic table and a concrete patio. Slide-outs and rigs longer than 40 feet are welcome. A pool, a hot tub, a playground, a nature trail, a horseshoe pit, shuffleboard, a game room, a camp circle, volleyball, and winter activities entertain campers. Showers, restrooms, a dump station, cabins, laundry facilities, and canoe rentals are available. Internet access is available in the clubhouse. Streets are paved, and the bathhouse, clubhouse, office, and pool area are wheelchair accessible. A camp store sells ice and propane, and there is a restaurant on the premises. Within 0.5 mile are a boat ramp, a restaurant, bait, and firewood. Groceries can be purchased four miles away. Children are welcome. Leashed pets should use the dog walk in back.

Reservations, fees: Reservations are recommended in winter. Sites are $25 per night for two people, plus $5 for each extra person, $2 for cable TV, and $1 for pets. Credit cards are not accepted.

Directions: From I-75 at Exit 352, take State Road 40 east for about 12 miles. The park is on the left, just beyond the Ocklawaha River Bridge.

Contact: Wilderness RV Park Estates, 10313 East State Road 40, Silver Springs, FL 34488, 352/625-1122 or 352/625-1911.

31 WHISPERING PINES RV PARK

Scenic rating: 6

in western Ocala National Forest

This nine-acre, pine-dotted campground (formerly Forest Cove Campground) offers sun-dappled campsites near several lakes in the surrounding national forest. Under new ownership since March 2003, the neatly kept park has 80 percent of its sites available to visitors; the rest are occupied year-round. Most visitors are families and tourists from the Northeast and Canada. Juniper Springs Recreation Area, a popular picnic spot, is about 13 miles east. From November through April, visitors enjoy planned activities such as bingo, potluck dinners, shuffleboard, horseshoes, campfires, games, and casino outings. Favorite activities are playing cards and visiting nearby flea markets. The Silver Springs nature theme park is about five miles west. The Atlantic Ocean and Gulf of Mexico are about one hour's drive in either direction.

RV sites, facilities: There are 65 grassy full-hookup sites (19 pull-through). One site has 50-amp electrical service; the rest are 30-amp. Each site has a picnic table. Average site size is 30 by 70 feet, and rigs as long as 45 feet or slide-outs are welcome. Sites 22–36 are pull-through. Most sites have cement patios. You can hook up to the Internet in the office; long-term visitors can arrange for DSL service at their site by contacting the local provider. A group barbecue/campfire area, a recreation hall, horseshoes, and shuffleboard entertain campers. Showers, restrooms, two dump stations, laundry facilities, a car wash area, and tire-air machine are available. Propane delivery to your site can be arranged. A convenience store is about one mile away; a supermarket is within five miles. Children are allowed for two-week stays. Leashed pets are permitted.

Reservations, fees: Reservations are accepted. Sites are $17 per night for two people, plus $2 per extra person and $1 per night for cable TV. Credit cards are not accepted. Long-term rates are available.

Directions: From I-75 at Exit 352, take State Road 40 east for 14 miles to Piney Path Road/Northeast 118th Avenue. Turn right. At 19th Street, turn right. When you reach 115th Avenue, turn left (south).

Contact: Whispering Pines RV Park, 1700 Northeast 115th Avenue, Silver Springs, FL 34488, 352/625-1295, email: whisperingpines-rvpark@yahoo.com.

32 BEN'S HITCHING POST

Scenic rating: 4

in western Ocala National Forest

This adults-only park is the closest private campground to the Ocala National Forest Visitor Center Northeast. Some campsites are open and grassy, but trees help shade others. As much as picnickers like to relax at Juniper Springs Recreation Area, about 13 miles west, or spend the day at the Silver Springs nature theme park, 4–6 miles to the east, this campground makes sure its guests stay busy: Potluck dinners, bingo, and campfires are among the activities on the schedule.

RV sites, facilities: This adult-oriented park offers 46 full-hookup RV campsites (some pull-through) with 30-amp electricity. For recreation, there's a pool, a hot tub, shuffleboard, horseshoes, wintertime planned activities, a recreation hall with a fireplace, game tables, and exercise equipment. Showers, wheelchair-accessible restrooms, picnic tables, telephone hookups, firewood, and laundry facilities are available. Restaurants are within one mile. Children are not permitted. Pets are allowed.

Reservations, fees: Reservations are recommended. Sites are $20 per night for two people, plus $3 per extra person. Credit cards are accepted. Long-term rates are available.

Directions: From I-75 at Exit 69, take State Road 40 east for 14 miles to Piney Path Road/Northeast 115th Avenue. Turn right. The campground is 50 feet ahead.

Contact: Ben's Hitching Post, 2440 Northeast 115th Avenue, Silver Springs, FL 34488, 352/625-4213, fax 352/625-0020.

33 LAKE WALDENA RESORT

Scenic rating: 8

in western Ocala National Forest

Check out the wintertime activities posted on the bulletin board: exercise at 9 A.M., bowling at 10 A.M., and bingo at 7 P.M.—and that's just one day. Activities vary daily at this 35-acre campground and may include singing hymns on Sunday or going to a potluck dinner on Saturday. Campers' birthdays and anniversaries are also noted so you can pass along your best wishes.

The park is surrounded by the Ocala National Forest. Paved roads lead to several tree-shaded campsites that border nature preserves or Lake Waldena, where anglers, boaters, and swimmers head. Don't fish in the lake's roped-off area, though, because that's for swimmers. To sleep closest to Lake Waldena, try sites 2–13. A semitropical environment—unusual for national forests—is located 13 miles east at Juniper Springs Recreation Area. The Silver Springs nature theme park is eight miles west of the campground. About 20 percent of the sites are occupied year-round.

RV sites, facilities: All 105 campsites have full hookups with electricity, a concrete slab, and a picnic table. There are 82 sites with 30-amp service and 23 sites with 50-amp. Some sites are pull-through. Shuffleboard, horseshoes, pool tables, a television, winter activities, a playground, boat rentals, a swimming lake, and a recreation hall entertain campers. Showers, restrooms, firewood, telephone hookups, park model sites, and laundry facilities are available. A wireless Internet connection is online in the office. Groceries and the nearest restaurant are about three miles away. The bathhouse and clubhouse are wheelchair accessible. Streets are paved. Kids under 12 must be accompanied by an adult in common areas. Pets should be tied up within your campsite and leashed during walks.

Reservations, fees: Reservations are advised. Sites are $20 per night for two people, plus $2 for each additional person. Credit cards are not accepted. Long-term rates are available.

Directions: From I-75 at Exit 352, take State Road 40 east for about 17 miles through Ocala. (Lake Waldena Resort is eight miles east of the Silver Springs theme park.)

Contact: Lake Waldena Resort, 13582 East Highway 40, Silver Springs, FL 34488, 352/625-2851 or 800/748-7898, fax 352/625-7069, www.lakewaldena.com.

34 ROBIN'S NEST RV PARK

Scenic rating: 4

in western Ocala National Forest

This no-frills, over-55 campground at the western edge of the Ocala National Forest attracts retirees who pay by the year or month and enjoy wintertime activities such as ice-cream socials and darts. Most come from New England and Canada. The Silver Springs nature theme park is a short drive to the east. The national forest's popular Juniper Springs Recreation Area is about 10 miles east. About 25 percent of the park is occupied year-round. Although there is an abundance of planned activities in the clubhouse, the favorite thing to do is talking to other visitors. "We have a wonderful group of people," says the manager.

RV sites, facilities: Only self-contained rigs are accepted at these 51 level, grassy full-hookup sites, which are split between 30-amp and 50-amp electrical service. Big rigs are welcome. No showers or restrooms are provided. An exercise room, wintertime planned activities (bingo, potlucks, dances, day trips, crafting), laundry facilities, and a ramp for airboats are available. An Internet connection is available in the office. Groceries and restaurants are within two miles. Snacks and bait are within 0.25 mile. Children are not allowed. Leashed pets are permitted.

Reservations, fees: Reservations are recommended. Sites are $16 per night for two people, plus $2 per extra person. Credit cards are not accepted. Long-term rates are available.

Directions: From I-75 at Exit 352, take State Road 40 east about 20 miles to enter Ocala National Forest and the town of Lynne. Turn right at the campground sign. Proceed to the hilltop and turn right. Go one block, then turn left into the park.

Contact: Robin's Nest RV Park, 13400 Northeast 1st Street Road, Silver Springs, FL 34488, 352/625-3090.

35 MILL DAM LAKE RESORT

Scenic rating: 7

in Ocala National Forest

Under new ownership since 2005, this sunny mobile-home/camping community on Mill Dam Lake is popular with boaters, all-terrain vehicle enthusiasts, families, and seasonal visitors. Only self-contained RVs are welcome. Bring your own small boat and launch it at the lake. Anglers try for largemouth bass, bream, catfish, perch, and specks at this huge lake, which is at least 200 acres in size. Or they cross State Road 40 to fish at Halfmoon Lake. Mill Dam Beach is within walking distance. The surrounding national forest is one of the state's last bastions of the Florida black bear, although you're unlikely to see one of the nocturnal creatures. Instead, while hiking any of the 68 miles of the Florida National Scenic Trail that span the national forest, you might glimpse a wild turkey or a deer scampering away in the distance.

RV sites, facilities: All 16 gravel or grassy campsites have water and 50-amp electrical hookups; 7 sites are drive-through. RVs up to 40 feet long and slide-outs can be accommodated. Adjacent but separate is a mobile-home park with 138 lots. Cabins, a screened pavilion, shuffleboard, horseshoes, laundry facilities, showers, restrooms, picnic tables, a snack bar, and a restaurant are available. The camp store also sells groceries, propane, fishing tackle, and bait. Shopping is 12 miles away. Children are welcome. Pets must stay out of the lake and be leashed at all times. The maximum stay is six months.

Reservations, fees: Reservations are advised; there is a 25 percent nonrefundable deposit. Sites are $18 per night for two people, plus $2 per additional adult. Pets are accepted by prior arrangement; a onetime pet fee is $30.

Major credit cards are accepted. Long-term rates are available.

Directions: From I-75 at Exit 352, take State Road 40 east about 21 miles through Ocala and past the Silver Springs nature theme park to the campground entrance. The campground is four miles east of County Road 314A.

Contact: Mill Dam Lake Resort, 18975 East State Road 40, Silver Springs, FL 34488, 352/625-4500, fax 352/625-4506, www.milldamlake.com.

36 LAKE BRYANT PARK

Scenic rating: 4

on Lake Bryant in Ocklawaha

Dirt roads lead through this wooded campground/mobile-home park, where launching at the boat ramp for a day of fishing on Lake Bryant is the focus for anglers. It's the only public boat launch in the area, the owners say. Some rustic campsites are fairly sunny, although most have at least a little shade. Forty-five mobile homes share the property, and some long-term campers spend the year here. It's primarily an adult park.

RV sites, facilities: The 84 campsites (some pull-through) have sewer hookups and 30/50-amp electrical service. Trailer rentals, a boat ramp, bait, a general store, showers, restrooms, and cable TV (long-term campers only) are available. Kids and small leashed pets are permitted.

Reservations, fees: Reservations are recommended. Sites are $24 per night for four people, plus $2 per extra person. Credit cards are accepted. Long-term rates are available.

Directions: From I-75 at Exit 352, take State Road 40 east about 24 miles, passing the Silver Springs nature theme park, a high bridge, and County Road 314A. Approximately 2.5 miles past County Road 314A, turn right between the church and convenience store. The campground is 2.5 miles ahead.

Contact: Lake Bryant Park, 5000 Southeast 183rd Avenue Road, Ocklawaha, FL 32179, 352/625-2376 or 888/807-4858, fax 352/625-5676.

37 JUNIPER SPRINGS RECREATION AREA

Scenic rating: 9

near Juniper Springs in central Ocala National Forest

Situated beside two springs that pour forth 13 million gallons of crystal-blue water each day, this site is a contender for the most popular campground in the forest. Of course, the presence of warm showers and other amenities such as concession-stand food doesn't hurt. This campground has been highly rated by several organizations, so be sure to make reservations.

The campsites are sufficiently sheltered from one another by generous shrubs and a campground setup that utilizes paved, curving roads to help provide privacy. Hiking is available on the Florida National Scenic Trail, which runs through the campground and north into the Juniper Prairie Wilderness. A short interpretive nature trail also wends its way along the creek. Canoeing is popular. There is a security gate that is closed at night.

RV sites, facilities: Juniper Springs has three campground loops with 79 campsites, about half of them pull-through. Sites have picnic tables, grills, fire rings, and lantern posts. There are no hookups. Hot showers, restrooms, a concession stand, hiking trails, canoe rentals, laundry facilities, a modem hookup at a pay phone, a convenience store, and a dump station are available. The day-use buildings are wheelchair accessible. Restaurants and shopping are within 10 miles. Children, leashed pets, and campfires are allowed.

Reservations, fees: Reservations are recommended; contact ReserveAmerica at 800/336-3521 or reserveamerica.com. They must be made at least four days in advance of your stay. Sites are $19 per night for five people. Credit cards are accepted. The maximum stay is 14 days in any 30-day period.

Directions: From Ocala, take State Road 40 east about 28 miles. Look for the entrance road on your left.

Contact: Juniper Springs Recreation Area, 26701 East State Road 40, Silver Springs, FL 34488, 352/625-0546, www.camprrm.com.

38 ST. JOHNS RIVER CAMPGROUND

Scenic rating: 6

west of Astor Park

Large, shaded sites and centralized location make this new park a gem. Clean and modern facilities, huge oak trees, and nearby access to fishing on the St. Johns River are just part of the attraction; the campground is also fairly close to Daytona Beach. Marinas and restaurants are 200 yards away.

RV sites, facilities: Of a total of 60 sites, 30 are available for overnighters and seasonal visitors. All RV sites have full hookups and picnic tables; some have grills and cable TV. Restrooms, showers, laundry facilities, a clubhouse, cabin rentals, and shuffleboard courts are available. Children are welcome. Small, leashed pets are permitted.

Reservations, fees: Reservations are recommended. Sites are $20 per night for two people, plus $3 per extra person. Credit cards are accepted. Long-term rates are available.

Directions: From I-95, drive west on State Road 40 for 28 miles. The park is on the right side, 0.25 mile from the St. Johns River Bridge.

Contact: St. Johns River Campground, 1520 State Road 40, Astor, FL 32102, 352/749-3995, fax 352/759-3419, www.stjohnsrivercampground.com.

39 PARRAMORE'S FANTASTIC FISH CAMP AND FAMILY RESORT

Scenic rating: 6

on the St. Johns River south of Lake George

BEST (

As the campground's largemouth bass logo suggests, probably the biggest draw here is the lure of good fishing, followed closely by the chance to see wild animals such as deer and, if you're lucky, bobcats. A fishing guide and boat rentals are available, as are docks, a boat ramp, and bait and tackle. The sunny, grassy campsites provide a decent base of operations for those who want easy access to various pursuits in this slow-paced part of the state. About half the 33-acre, semishady resort is occupied by year-round residents. It is located across the river from Ocala National Forest and, should you tire of the campground pool, it is quite close to the swimming and hiking opportunities at Alexander Springs (see listing in this chapter). The park is only about six miles from the Pioneer Arts Settlement, where reenactors of pioneer life produce arts and crafts. Festivals are held at the arts settlement twice a year in fall and spring. At nearby Spring Garden Ranch, restaurant patrons can look through windows to watch trotter horses train every morning during winter.

RV sites, facilities: There are 72 full-hookup sites for RVs with 30-amp electrical service; 45 have 50-amp. Each site has a picnic table and fire ring, and some have grills. Rigs up to 45 feet long and slide-outs can be accommodated. Wireless Internet service is available in the clubhouse. A pool, boat and canoe rentals, a playground, snorkeling, paddleboats, an exercise room, a game room, tennis, and volleyball entertain campers. On the premises are restrooms, showers, a boat ramp, a dock, a dump station, groceries, bait, tackle, cabin rentals, and laundry facilities. Cable TV, phone service, and firewood are available. The camp store sells ice, camping supplies, groceries, snacks, and souvenirs. All areas are wheelchair accessible, and streets are paved. A restaurant is about two miles away. Children and leashed pets are welcome.

Reservations, fees: Reservations are recommended. Sites are $32–35 per night for two adults, plus $2 for each additional adult and $1 for each child. Credit cards are accepted. Long-term rates are available.

Directions: From I-95 at Exit 268, go west on State Road 40. About two blocks short of the St. Johns River, turn right (north) onto Riley Pridgeon's Road. After one mile, turn left onto South Moon Road, which leads west to the park entrance.

Contact: Parramore's Fantastic Fish Camp and Family Resort, 1675 South Moon Road, Astor, FL 32102, 386/749-2721 or 800/516-2386, fax 386/749-9744, www.parramores.com.

40 ASTOR LANDING CAMPGROUND AND MARINA

Scenic rating: 7

on the St. Johns River south of Astor

People arrive by boat and by car to camp at these 11 rustic acres on the west bank of the St. Johns River and Lake Dexter, where the owners have recently invested in a boat ramp and other amenities. Outdoorsy folks use the tree-shaded spot as a base for hunting, swimming, hiking, and bicycling at Ocala National Forest, the park's neighbor across the street. Anglers fish for bass and specks at the St. Johns River. It's a good location for all sorts of outdoor activities, and the park welcomes family reunions and other groups. Houseboats are for rent (call 352/759-3300), but there's lots to do in this decidedly marine-oriented park.

RV sites, facilities: All 50 sites have full hookups with electricity. Boat slips with 30-amp and 50-amp shore power and water hookups, dockside sewage pump-out, a boat ramp, canoe rentals, a fishing pond, showers, restrooms, a picnic area, a general store, laundry facilities, and a dump station are available. Groceries and a restaurant are about five miles away in Astor. Children and pets are permitted.

Reservations, fees: Reservations are suggested. Sites are $28 per night for a family of four. Credit cards are accepted. Long-term rates are available.

Directions: From I-75 at Exit 352, drive about 40 miles east on State Road 40 through Ocala, Silver Springs, and Ocala National Forest. Turn right at Alco Road, one mile west of the St. Johns River. Continue four miles as the road veers left to the riverside camp.

Contact: Astor Landing Campground and Marina, 25934 Holmar Drive, Astor, FL 32102, 352/759-2121, www.astorlanding.com.

41 WILDWOODS CAMPGROUND

Scenic rating: 6

near Astor in the Ocala National Forest

All travelers are welcome at this fishing-oriented park near the St. Johns River and Lake George, a sleepy area that has not changed much in recent years. Practice your casting in the fishing pond on the premises. You'll find both sunny and shady spots here. About 75 percent of the park is occupied year-round. Your neighbors will be a mix of seasonal tourists, families, anglers, and working people. Top on the list to do are fishing and boating.

RV sites, facilities: There are 72 large campsites with full hookups for RVs up to 45 feet long and slide-outs. Most sites have 30-amp electrical service; a few have 50-amp. Internet access is available in the office. Restrooms, showers, laundry facilities, cable TV, telephone service, and propane are available. On the premises are a clubhouse with planned activities, shuffleboard courts, and a dog-walk area. The bathhouse, clubhouse, and office are wheelchair accessible, and streets are paved. Groceries and restaurants are within 2 miles; malls and hospitals are 25

miles away. Children are welcome. Leashed pets are permitted.

Reservations, fees: Reservations are recommended. Sites are $21 per night for two people, plus $1.50 per extra person. Credit cards are not accepted. Long-term rates are available. Stay as long as you wish.

Directions: From I-95 in Ormond Beach, take Exit 268 and go west 30 miles on State Road 40 the park. From I-75 at Exit 352, go east on State Road 40 for 30 miles.

Contact: Wildwoods Campground, 22113 State Road 40, Astor, FL 32102, 352/759-3538.

42 ALEXANDER SPRINGS CAMPGROUND

Scenic rating: 9

in southeastern Ocala National Forest

The clear, 72°F water flowing out of this spring at the rate of 80 million gallons daily makes this a very pleasant place to spend a hot summer day. Swimming and snorkeling are popular pursuits (equipment can be rented here), and certified divers may scuba dive. The sandy beach sets it apart from the forest's other popular springs—Juniper Springs. Canoe rentals are available, and many campers make the seven-mile trip down the spring's run. Archaeologists say the area around the springs has been inhabited for more than 1,000 years. You can hike about one mile along an interpretive trail that explains how early inhabitants, the Timucuan Indians, used native plants. A spur trail leads to a nearby section of the Florida National Scenic Trail, which leads over sandy, pine-covered hills. I spotted a baby wild hog there, just one of the wildlife species, including deer and black bear, said to abound here.

Look for otters along the spring's run and gopher tortoises in the sandy hills nearby. The campground is open, covered mostly with pines. It offers less privacy than many spots in the national forest, but it's still pleasant. Mountain bikers enjoy the Paisley Woods biking trail, a 22-mile loop that connects Alexander Springs with the Clearwater Lake campground, passing mostly through pine-dotted hills. Visitors here are a mix of seasonal tourists, anglers, and families who enjoy swimming and canoeing.

RV sites, facilities: There are 67 level, paved sites for self-contained campers in slide-outs or RVs up to 40 feet long. No electrical hookups are available. Sites are shady and have picnic tables, fire rings, and grills. On the premises are restrooms, showers, a dump station, a concession stand, a swimming area, hiking trails, and an amphitheater. A camp store sells ice, camping supplies, some groceries, snacks, and souvenirs. Canoes are for rent. Most areas are wheelchair accessible. Children and leashed pets are permitted.

Reservations, fees: Reservations are taken; call 877/444-6777. Sites are $17 per night for five people. Major credit cards are accepted. Stays are limited to 14 days in summer and six months in winter.

Directions: From Ocala, take State Road 40 east about 26 miles to State Road 19. Turn right and continue about eight miles south. Make a left, heading east, on County Road 445 (not 445A). Look for the entrance to the campground about five miles ahead on the left.

Contact: Alexander Springs Campground, Ocala National Forest, 49525 County Road 445, Altoona, FL 32702, 352/669-3522. Or write to RRM Regional Office, 26701 East Highway 40, Silver Springs, FL 34488, 352/625-0546, fax 352/625-0712, www.camp rrm.com.

43 OCALA FOREST CAMPGROUND

Scenic rating: 9

in southeastern Ocala National Forest

It would be hard to accidentally stumble upon the Skorski family's out-of-the-way private campground within Ocala National Forest.

Area attractions are canoeing at the forest's Juniper Springs Recreation Area 12 miles away, and the antiques shops of Mount Dora 17 miles away. But there's lots to do in the park, from boating and bicycling, to bingo, card games, shuffleboard, dances, parties, and potluck dinners. The owners say it's quiet and relaxing. About 10 percent of the park is occupied by year-round residents, but park models are for sale in an area set apart from the RV section. Most seasonal visitors come from the north, but the customer mix varies from locals to working people, families, and retirees. A long oval island of RVs forms the center of this thumb-shaped campground. To sleep closest to the pool (and dog walk), try sites 1–11. To border stands of trees, ask about sites 69–95.

RV sites, facilities: There are 125 campsites (about half are pull-through) with 30-amp service. Lots are 30 by 50 feet with concrete patios and picnic tables. Sewer hookups are available at sites 1–68, and sites A–H. Slide-outs and rigs as long as 45 feet can be accommodated. A pool, horseshoes, shuffleboard, a recreation hall, bike rentals, winter activities, a game room, a playground, and a pool table entertain campers. There are showers, restrooms, a dump station, a camp store with ice, snacks, propane and souvenirs, a park model section, and laundry facilities are available. Wheelchair-accessible areas are the clubhouse, office, store, and pool area, and some of the streets are paved. The park also has a boat ramp and docks. Groceries, restaurants, shopping, and hospitals are about 15 miles away. Young children must be adult-supervised. Leashed pets must use the eastern-border dog walk.

Reservations, fees: Reservations are recommended. Sites are $17 per night for two people, plus $3 for each additional person and $2 for use of air conditioners or electric heaters. Credit cards are accepted. Long-term rates are available.

Directions: From Umatilla, go north on State Road 19, then turn left at County Road 42. The campground is ahead to your right.

Contact: Ocala Forest Campground, 26301 Southeast Highway 42, Umatilla, FL 32784, 352/669-3888.

44 LAKE DORR CAMPGROUND

Scenic rating: 4

in southern Ocala National Forest

Extremely tall, straight pines provide reasonable shade from the sun for these sandy campsites, which are set within a forest where fire has beaten back much of the understory of saw palmetto. That means you won't enjoy a whole lot of privacy. The following could apply to many areas of the forest, but it should be reiterated: Stay away from the clusters of saw palmetto because they can harbor rattlesnakes. Fishing and waterskiing are popular at nearby Lake Dorr, where you also can swim at a sandy beach. Canoes share the lake with buzzing motorboats—after all, this is one lake where there is no limit on how much horsepower your boat can pack. Hikers can pick up the Florida National Scenic Trail a few miles up State Road 19 at Alexander Springs.

RV sites, facilities: All 34 campsites have picnic tables, fire rings, and grills. No hookups or pull-through sites are available. RVs up to 34 feet long can be accommodated; a few sites will allow slide-outs. Drinking water, restrooms, hot showers, picnic tables, boat docks, and two boat ramps are provided. Groceries and restaurants are within three miles. Children and leashed pets are welcome.

Reservations, fees: Reservations are not taken. Sites are $8 per night for five people. Credit cards are not accepted. Stays are limited to 14 days.

Directions: From Deland, go west on County Road 42 for 24 miles. Turn right and head north on State Road 19 about three miles. Look for the entrance to your right.

Contact: Ocala National Forest, Seminole Ranger District, 40929 State Road 19, Umatilla, FL 32784, 352/669-3153, www.fs.fed .us/rb/florida.

45 CLEARWATER LAKE RECREATION AREA

Scenic rating: 8

in southeastern Ocala National Forest

Set in an oak hammock on the shores of Clearwater Lake, this beautiful campground is one of the few National Forest campgrounds that accepts reservations. Swimming, fishing, and canoeing are possible in the lake, but motorboats are banned. Mountain bikers can follow the Paisley Woods biking trail, a 22-mile loop that connects Alexander Springs with the Clearwater Lake campground, passing mostly through pine-dotted hills. Canoes are for rent in the campground. Visitors here come from all over the world.

Hikers can stay busy for quite a while here. Consider the Florida National Scenic Trail, which passes through a section of woods that was burned out a few years ago but is now regenerating. By all means, though, don't miss the nearby St. Francis Interpretive Trail, which passes through riverine swamp, pine flat woods, oak hammock, bayhead swamp, and open flat woods. Keep your eye out for red-tailed hawks and pileated woodpeckers. If you're up to a seven-mile round-trip hike, consider trekking to the former town of St. Francis, once a bustling citrus and timber port on the St. Johns River. After steamboats were replaced by railroads as the main form of transport, St. Francis faded away and eventually was overtaken by the forest. With the aid of a pamphlet available at the trailhead, you can pick out markers of the onetime civilization, including an old levee built to flood a field so rice could be grown. To reach the trailhead, take County Road 42 east a few miles from the campground, turn left (north) on Forest Service Road 542, and look for signs.

Access to the forest's hiking and biking trails is restricted during hunting season, which generally runs mid-November–early January. Check with the Forest Service for exact dates.

RV sites, facilities: The campground is laid out in two loops, with sites 1–23 closest to the beach and lake. Keep in mind that this is also near the day-use area so it may be busy at times. All 42 campsites have picnic tables, fire rings, and grills. Water is available, but there's no sewer or electric service. On the premises are flush toilets, showers, a dump station, a swimming beach, and hiking trails. Firewood is for sale in the park. Children and leashed pets are permitted.

Reservations, fees: Reservations are accepted; call 877/444-6777. Sites are $14 per night for five people. Credit cards are accepted. Stays are limited to 14 days.

Directions: From DeLand, take County Road 42 west about 15 miles to the hamlet of Paisley. Look for the campground entrance ahead on the left.

Contact: Ocala National Forest, Seminole Ranger District, 40929 State Road 19, Umatilla, FL 32784, 352/669-3153, www.fs.fed .us/rb/florida.

DAYTONA

COURTESY OF DAYTONA BEACH AREA
CONVENTION & VISITORS BUREAU

BEST RV PARKS AND CAMPGROUNDS

❮ Families
Sunshine Holiday Daytona RV Resort, page 213

❮ Fishing:
Highbanks Marina and Camp Resort, page 218

❮ Most Unusual:
Sunny Sands Nudist Resort, page 213

T

Daytona's claim to fame is racing, and it
revels in its celebration of the automobile. The beaches are
comprised of hard-packed sand – hard enough to support
the weight of a car – which auto-racing enthusiasts found
ideal for setting land-speed records as early as 1903. You'll
recognize their names: Messieurs Ford, Chevrolet, Olds, and
Packard were all here to test their inventions. NASCAR, the
sanctioning body for stock-car racing, set up shop in 1947.
The Daytona International Speedway provided a track where
spectators could watch their favorite drivers compete, and
events are still held here, most famously the "great American
race" known as the Daytona 500.

The area offers lots to do for all ages. Though some RVers
spend the winter months here escaping the chilly North, Daytona tends to be a family-oriented and destination vacation
spot. Even kids can become motorheads at Atlantic Race
Park, a go-cart track, and Daytona USA, which has racing
simulator rides and other interactive attractions. The Richard
Petty Driving Experience and Speed Park Motorsports puts
adults in the driver's seat. Aside from car fans, motorcycle
enthusiasts flock to Daytona for special events, such as Bike
Week (a 10-day festival and race, usually held in March), and
Biketober Fest in the fall.

Other attractions in the Daytona area include 17 world-class
golf courses, the Daytona Beach Boardwalk, Oceanwalk Village,
Daytona Lagoon entertainment park, six miniature golf courses,
parasailing, a skate park, an ice arena, laser tag, fishing charters,
paddle-wheel boat tours, and of course, the beach itself. You
can drive on it except for when turtles are nesting.

If you tire of all things automotive, head to Ponce Inlet to
climb to the top of the well-preserved Ponce de Leon Inlet
Light Station. At 175 feet, it is the nation's second-tallest light-

house. Farther north, Bulow Creek State Park, a little-used, out-of-the-way slice of natural Florida, is open for day visits. Bulow Creek hosts the Fairchild Oak, which sprang up from an acorn about 800 years ago. Several hiking trails lead through the gorgeous Florida backcountry.

Inland fishing is excellent throughout the area, whether you choose lakes, rivers, or salt marshes. Brackish-water catches include snook, redfish, flounder, and speckled trout. Anglers with freshwater fishing licenses can find bass, bluegill, shell-crackers, and specks.

Don't leave the area without heading west to visit DeLeon Springs State Park. The 0.5-mile nature trail there is pleasant for even the least-rugged visitor. At one time, elephants, giraffes, and other circus creatures would pad down the route annually when the trail led to a railroad siding where the Clyde Beatty Circus unloaded each year for its winter respite. Swim in the springs, where 19 million gallons of water bubble out of the earth every day.

Be sure to check out the manatees at Blue Spring State Park, near Orange City. When it's cold, you may spot 60 or so at a time in the 72°F waters flowing from the park's namesake spring. The endangered sea cows generally congregate November–March. History-minded visitors should check out the park's waterfront Thursby House, a two-story wooden house built in 1872 atop a mound of snail shells deposited by Timucuan Indians. The Thursby House has been visited by everyone from Union gunboat crews to U.S. presidents over the years.

If you're visiting Daytona Beach in the winter months or during special events, reservations are highly recommended at any campground. This area is also popular during spring break, when space near the beach is at a premium.

DAYTONA

see St Augustine page 158

see Ocala page 180

see Orlando page 228

see Space Coast page 326

Lake George

Pierson

Barberville

De Leon Springs State Park

Lake Dias

De Leon Springs

Lake Woodruff

Ocala

National

Forest

De Land

Orange City

De Bary

Deltona

Lake Monroe

Lake Ashby

Lake Jessup

Lake Harney

Gulf

of

Mexico

AL GA

Tiger Bay

State

Forest

Holly Hill

Daytona Beach

Port Orange

New Smyrna Beach

Ormond

ATLANT

OCEAN

Flagl Beach

Jo Anne Beach

Ormond-b the-Sea

Mosquito Lagoon

Indian

River

0   5 mi
0   5 km

© AVALON TRAVEL PUBLISHING,

1 SUNNY SANDS NUDIST RESORT

Scenic rating: 3

east of Pierson

BEST

You're way out in the boondocks here. As if that weren't enough to ensure privacy, the place is fenced and gated. The park should rightfully be called a "clothing-optional" rather than "nudist" resort. You can wear clothes anywhere you'd like except the swimming pool and hot tub, and on cold days you'll find that almost everyone has a stitch of clothing on somewhere. The 45-acre park is heavily shaded with live oaks and, according to the management, features a laid-back lifestyle targeted at families. About 60 families or couples live here permanently in mobile homes. Bring your own canoe to paddle on the small lake or head a few miles away to catch bass in Lake George. Sites along Lakeshore Drive overlook tiny Crystal Lake. At Sunny Sands, nights are generally quiet, but there are some social events such as bingo, dances, happy hours, and spaghetti and chili cook-offs.

RV sites, facilities: This clothing-optional resort has 14 sites for RVs, 13 with full hookups with 30-amp electrical service; 1 site has 50-amp. RVs up to 45 feet long and slide-outs can be accommodated. On the premises are restrooms, showers, laundry facilities, a nine-hole chipping course, basketball, volleyball, horseshoes, a pool, a hot tub, a one-mile-long walking trail, a restaurant and bar (open on weekends only), and a *pétanque* court (French-style bowling). Cable TV and telephone service are available in the rental trailers. Restaurants and limited groceries are about 2 miles away; a grocery store is within 15 miles. Malls and hospitals are 30 miles away. The bathhouse, clubhouse, office, and pool area are wheelchair accessible. Children are welcome, but single adults must be members of the Kis-

simmee-based American Association of Nude Recreation or the Naturist Society based in Oshkosh, Wisconsin. One leashed cat or dog is allowed per site.

Reservations, fees: Reservations are recommended, particularly in the winter months. Sites are $40 per night for two people, plus $14 per extra person. Single campers are asked to phone before visiting. Credit cards are accepted. Long-term rates are available.

Directions: From I-95 at Exit 268, head west on State Road 40 for about 18 miles. In Barberville, turn right onto U.S. 17 and go about five miles north to the town of Pierson. Turn east (right) onto Washington Avenue. Follow it 1.25 miles to Turner Road, where you'll turn left. When the road curves to the right, you'll be within one block of the resort's gate. Continue, then look to the left for the resort gate and telephone.

Contact: Sunny Sands Nudist Resort, 502 Central Boulevard, Pierson, FL 32180, 386/749-2233, fax 386/749-0240, www.sunnysands.com.

2 SUNSHINE HOLIDAY DAYTONA RV RESORT

Scenic rating: 9

in Ormond Beach

BEST

Set in an area of pine flat woods nine miles from the ocean, this park is ideal if you want a clean, resort-style camping experience far removed from the spring-break atmosphere of Daytona Beach. Many sites are at least partially shaded, thanks to a towering forest of ruler-straight pine trees. If you're just passing through, this is an excellent choice: It's just off the highway, and you'll probably find what you need right at the resort, which has 351 RV sites and 100 tent sites. In winter, there are planned activities geared toward retirees fleeing cold winters: bingo, dances, exercise classes, coffee klatches, and card parties. But bikers do show up during Daytona's famed

Bike Week. A perky staff aims to adhere to the park's "fun and friendly service" mantra, and an example is their name for those giant umbrellas you see scattered around the park—they're "fun-brellas." It's convenient to Tomoka Basin GeoPark (see listing in this chapter) and the Bulow Plantation Ruins State Historic Site (see *Bulow Plantation Resort* in the *St. Augustine* chapter).

RV sites, facilities: There are 335 RV sites (250 full-hookup, 219 pull-through). For entertainment, try the golf driving nets, *pétanque* (French-style bowling), horseshoes, miniature golf, racquetball, basketball, shuffleboard, sand volleyball, boccie ball (lawn bowling), tennis courts, the playground, the pool, or winter activities. Facilities include restrooms, showers, picnic tables, a convenience store, a dump station, cable TV hookups, and laundry facilities. Restaurants are within one mile, and groceries are about five miles away. The 80-acre park is broken into two circles of campsites, one devoted to overnight guests, the other mainly for permanent residents and overflow campers. At the center of the camper-oriented circle is a swimming pool, a store, a laundry room, and a campground office. To sleep around this hub of activity (and its parking area), try sites 1–12. You'll pay the highest fee for these "super sites," as they're called. For canal-side spots, request from among sites 384–390. Children and leashed pets are permitted.

Reservations, fees: Reservations are necessary January–March and are recommended at other times of the year. Sites are $32–38 per night for two people, plus $2 daily if you want to hook up to cable TV. Credit cards are accepted. Long-term rates are available.

Directions: From I-95 at Exit 273, head north on U.S. 1 for 0.5 mile to the park entrance on the right.

Contact: Sunshine Holiday Daytona RV Resort, 1701 North U.S. 1, Ormond Beach, FL 32174, 386/672-3045 or 877/277-8737, fax 386/672-3026, www.rvonthego.com.

3 TOMOKA BASIN GEOPARK

Scenic rating: 10

at the Halifax River north of Ormond Beach

Set at the confluence of the Tomoka and Halifax Rivers, this 10,000-acre state park incredibly started out as a simple sandbar between the two rivers but today is a lush forest of large oaks, shady hammocks, and saltwater marshes. Here, Timucuan Indians built a village they dubbed Nocorroco long before a wealthy Scotsman named Richard Oswald transformed it into the Mount Oswald Plantation. Oswald arrived after the American Revolution and proceeded to grow sugar, rice, and indigo, a plant used to make a blue dye popular at the time. (Visit the park museum to learn more about the history of the place.)

A 0.25-mile nature trail leads from the park museum through a shady coastal hammock to a picnic area. Rental canoes allow visitors to explore the rivers and salt marshes, which still teem with the fish that originally attracted the Timucuans. Brackish-water catches include snook, redfish, flounder, and speckled trout. Rangers say the best bait is live shrimp.

The park is a short drive from the Atlantic Ocean and is close to Bulow Creek State Park, a little-used, out-of-the-way slice of natural Florida open for day visits. At Bulow Creek, you'll find the Fairchild Oak, which sprang up from an acorn about 800 years ago. Today its heavy, gnarly branches, covered in resurrection ferns, dip all the way to the ground. (Don't climb on them, please.) The oak is named for David Fairchild, a botanist who loomed large in Florida's history around the turn of the 20th century. Several hiking trails lead through the gorgeous Florida backcountry, including a six-mile hike along the Florida National Scenic Trail from Bulow Creek State Park to the Bulow Plantation Ruins State Historic Site (see *Bulow Resort Campground* in the *St. Augustine* chapter).

RV sites, facilities: The sandy landlocked campsites are set along three circles. You'll enjoy at least some privacy from neighbors, thanks to the oaks and palms that help divide camping spots. There are 100 sites with water and 30-amp electricity for RVs (up to 34 feet long and 11 feet in height). Five sites have 50-amp service. Each site has a picnic table, a grill, and a fire ring. On the premises are restrooms, showers, a dump station, a recreation room, a boat ramp, firewood, canoe and kayak rentals, and a playground. A camp store sells ice, camping supplies, snacks, souvenirs, bait, and tackle. Groceries, restaurants, and laundry facilities are within six miles. The park's museum, docks, bathhouse, office, store, and picnic shelters are wheelchair accessible, as are four campsites. Children are welcome. Pets are permitted with proof of vaccination against rabies.

Reservations, fees: Reservations are recommended; contact ReserveAmerica at 800/336-3521 or reserveamerica.com. Rates are $20 per night for up to eight people. Credit cards are accepted. The maximum stay is 14 days.

Directions: From I-95 at Exit 268, go east on State Road 40 to North Beach Street. Turn left and drive 3.5 miles north to the park entrance.

Contact: Tomoka Basin GeoPark, 2099 North Beach Street, Ormond Beach, FL 32174, 386/676-4050, www.floridastateparks.org.

4 HARRIS VILLAGE AND RV PARK

Scenic rating: 6

in Ormond Beach

Open October–April, this sunny, over-55 park has a preference for motor homes and describes itself as "a nice little place for quiet people." Still, things can get busy during special events in the Daytona area, such as Bike Week, Speed Weeks, and Biketoberfest (bikes meaning motorcycles), so be sure to call ahead. Daytona Beach's International Speedway is 20 minutes away. About 10 percent of the sites are occupied year-round.

RV sites, facilities: There are 20 RV sites of varying sizes, with 10 available for overnighters and 10 for seasonal visitors. RVs up to 40 feet long can be accommodated. Each site has full hookups, 30/50-amp electrical service, picnic tables, concrete patios, and cable TV. An Internet connection is available in the office. Restrooms, showers, laundry facilities, and rental cabins are available. The office is wheelchair accessible. Streets are paved. RV supplies, stores, and restaurants are within 0.5 mile. Children are not welcome. One small leashed pet is permitted; barking dogs will not be tolerated, and the management must preapprove all pets.

Reservations, fees: Reservations are required. Sites are $35–66 per night for two people, plus $5–15 per extra person. Rates are higher during special events. Credit cards are accepted. Long-term rates are available.

Directions: From I-95, take Exit 273 southeast four miles on U.S. 1 to the park.

Contact: Harris Village and RV Park, 1080 North U.S. 1, Ormond Beach, FL 32174, 386/673-0494, fax 386/672-5716, www.harrisvillage.com.

5 INTERNATIONAL RV PARK AND CAMPGROUND

Scenic rating: 6

in Daytona Beach

Opened in 2001, this park built on what was once vacant land is convenient to beaches, Daytona's International Speedway, and other tourist attractions. It attracts people of all ages—from snowbirds to race fans. Sites are extra large, accommodating rigs up to 40 feet long. Favorite things to do are relaxing, fishing, and going to the beach.

RV sites, facilities: All 200 sites have full hookups, 30/50-amp electrical service, concrete patios, and picnic tables. At 35 by 90 feet, these are some of the largest sites I've seen in a developed campground, and they were planned that way. Other sites are 30 by 45 feet, and 14 are drive-through. Restrooms, showers, laundry facilities, a pool, a clubhouse, horseshoe pits, shuffleboard courts, a dog-walk area, and a putting green are available. All areas are wheelchair accessible. Streets are paved. A camp store sells ice, camping supplies, and snacks. Groceries, restaurants, malls, and hospitals are within five miles. Children are welcome. Leashed pets are permitted.

Reservations, fees: Reservations are recommended. Sites are $30 per night for two people, plus $2 per extra person. Credit cards are accepted. Long-term rates are available. The maximum length of stay is six months.

Directions: From I-95, take Exit 261 onto U.S. 92 and travel west 1.1 miles to the park.

Contact: International RV Park and Campground, 3175 West International Speedway Blvd., Daytona Beach, FL 32124, 386/239-0249, www.internationalrvdaytona.com.

6 HIGHLAND PARK FISH CAMP

🚴 🎣 🚐 🐕 🚙 ⛺

Scenic rating: 3

northwest of DeLand by the Lake Woodruff
National Wildlife Refuge

This rustic place has a great location. The oak-shaded and sunny campsites at this 33-acre fish camp give anglers access to the St. Johns River and Lake Woodruff (and the surrounding wildlife refuge) via the Norris Dead River. For hikers, these grassy campsites also are the closest available to two sets of trails, one at Lake Woodruff National Wildlife Refuge and another at DeLeon Springs State Park.

At the wildlife refuge (next door), there are three short nature trails and a much longer circuit of about 6.5 miles that leads bicyclists and hikers through woods and atop dikes built to hold in man-made freshwater lakes. Anglers can buy tackle and live bait at the fish camp to try their hand here. Visit in fall or winter to see abundant waterfowl and wading birds. Any time of the year, keep an eye out for otters, bobcats, deer, and other wild animals, particularly early or late in the day. Florida black bears live in the refuge but are rarely seen. To get to the refuge, head north on Grand Avenue to Mud Lake Road, where you will see refuge headquarters. Proceed down Mud Lake Road to a parking area to find the hiking trails. For refuge information, call 386/985-4673.

In recent years, the fish camp has started attracting bluegrass music fans who, a couple times a week or so in winter, put on impromptu pickin's. Snowbirds tend to be devoted anglers, though, so the camp offers an occasional fish fry.

RV sites, facilities: There are 55 full-hookup sites, five water-and-electric sites, and an indeterminate number of primitive spots. On the premises are showers, restrooms, a dump station, firewood (at times), cabin rentals, horseshoes, a boat ramp, charter fishing services, motorboat and rowboat rentals, a limited store, bait, tackle, and a dock. Restaurants and a grocery store are located within three miles. Children and leashed pets are welcome.

Reservations, fees: Reservations are recommended but are not always necessary. Sites are $16 per night for two people, plus $2 per additional adult. If you want to turn on your air conditioner, a $2 daily fee applies. Credit cards are accepted. Long-term stays are okay.

Directions: From central DeLand, take State Road 44/New York Avenue west to Grand Avenue. Turn right, heading north. Grand Avenue will dogleg, merging for a time with Minnesota Avenue to head west and then turn north again. Stay on Grand Avenue as you pass the landfill and Humane Society Road on the right. Not far past that, turn left onto Highland Park Road. Follow it 1.5 miles to the fish camp.

Contact: Highland Park Fish Camp, 2640 West Highland Park Road, DeLand, FL 32720, 386/734-2334 or 800/525-3477, fax 386/943-9681, www.hpfishcamp.com.

7 BLUE SPRING STATE PARK

Scenic rating: 9

west of Orange City

At any time of year this well-used picnic spot is worth a visit, but show up when it's cold for a better shot at getting a gander at lots of manatees—maybe 60 of them, like on the day I visited. Endangered sea cows congregate generally November–March in the 72°F waters flowing from the spring for which the park is named. From the boardwalk above the clear blue waters it's easy to see their whiskers and the outlines of their dark, blubbery bodies.

You can't take motorboats up the Blue Spring Run, but you can swim there. Canoeing, swimming, and scuba diving may be restricted in certain areas if manatees are present, yet you always can enjoy these activities somewhere in the vicinity. Rental canoes give visitors access to the St. Johns River and Lake Beresford, where anglers with freshwater fishing licenses find bass, bluegill, shellcrackers, and specks.

Regular campsites are in a sun-dappled pine forest not far from the spring. Hikers and backpackers traverse a four-mile trail that tends to flood in summer and fall (bring hiking boots). The trail straddles pine flat woods and marsh, ending in a lush oak hammock where four primitive campsites tend to be dry even when the trail is under water.

History-minded campers should check out the park's waterfront Thursby House, a two-story wooden house with double verandas and a real Old South feel. The pioneer Thursby family built it in 1872 atop a mound of snail shells deposited by Timucuan Indians, who made the snails a staple of their diet hundreds of years before. Union gunboat crews and U.S. presidents are among the visitors who have arrived at the Thursby House over the years.

RV sites, facilities: This state park offers 51 gravel sites, all with 30/50-amp electricity, water, picnic tables, and grills. Sites are on the small side; RVs up to 30 feet long can be accommodated. On the premises are restrooms, showers, picnic tables, a dump station, rental cabins, a fishing pier, covered pavilions, and canoe rentals. A boat ramp for small boats is nearby. A park concession stand sells snacks and some groceries. Restaurants, groceries, and laundry facilities are about two miles away. Groceries and restaurants are within five miles. Children are welcome. Leashed pets are permitted with proof of current rabies vaccination.

Reservations, fees: Reservations are recommended; contact ReserveAmerica at 800/336-3521 or reserveamerica.com. Sites are $20 per night for up to eight people. Credit cards are accepted. Maximum stay is 14 days.

Directions: From I-4, take Exit 114 and follow the signs south on 17-92 to Orange City, about 2.5 miles. Make a right onto West French Avenue and drive until it ends at the campground. The park is about two miles west of City Hall.

Contact: Blue Spring State Park, 2100 West French Avenue, Orange City, FL 32763, 386/775-3663, fax 386/775-7794.

8 DELAND/ORANGE CITY KOA

Scenic rating: 4

in Orange City

Birders might spy hawks, woodpeckers, or other birds in the oaks dotting this family-run park, where sandy interior roads lead to shady, sandy sites, most of them with patios. Children's activities are sometimes scheduled on holiday weekends. There's also a swimming pool, a game room, a playground, and the like. Leave the campground by day to enjoy area highlights such as nearby Blue Spring State Park, Hontoon Island State Park, and DeLeon Springs State Park. It's also close to the St. Francis Interpretive Trail.

RV sites, facilities: There are 150 RV sites (70 pull-through) with picnic tables, water, and 30-amp electricity hookups; 130 have full hookups. Some sites have 50-amp service. On the premises are showers, restrooms, a dump station, a recreation room, a pool, a playground, a game room, horseshoes, volleyball, basketball, limited groceries, a restaurant, and laundry facilities. Firewood is available. A grocery store is a five-minute drive away. Children and leashed pets are welcome.

Reservations, fees: Reservations are necessary in February and March. Sites are $25–40 per night for two people, plus $2.50 for each additional adult. For electricity, the fee is $3; add sewer for $2 more. Credit cards are accepted. Long-term stays are okay.

Directions: From I-4 at Exit 114, travel west on State Road 472 for 1.5 miles to Minnesota Avenue. Turn left. The campground is about 0.25 mile ahead.

Contact: DeLand/Orange City KOA, 1440 East Minnesota Avenue, Orange City, FL 32763, 386/775-3996 or 800/KOA-7857 (800/562-7857), www.koa.com.

9 HIGHBANKS MARINA AND CAMP RESORT

Scenic rating: 7

on the St. Johns River in DeBary

BEST (

Like most campgrounds along the St. Johns River, this one is geared toward anglers who go after bass, shellcracker, catfish, and other freshwater prizes. Big oaks, interspersed with magnolias, shade parts of these 25 acres. The management employs a full-time recreation director year-round, so don't be surprised to find an ice-cream social on Saturday evening or bingo on weekends. Kids can fish at the park's small-fry fishing pond and take a two-hour nature cruise on the park's tour boats to see alligators and other wildlife. Half of the campers live permanently at the grassy/concrete-pad sites. They enjoy a pool for swimming and 0.5 mile of riverfront for strolling. Hiking trails are nearby. This campground is only a few miles from Blue

Spring State Park and, by boat, Hontoon Island State Park. It's also pretty close to DeLeon Springs State Park and Ocala National Forest.

RV sites, facilities: All 221 full-hookup sites are for RVs up to 40 feet long. Six sites are pull-through. To camp nearest to the St. Johns River, ask about Cypress Lane sites 107–130. To stay beside the fishpond, request sites 38–64 on Hickory and Live Oak Drives. Charter fishing services, wildlife boat tours, rental boats, billiards, a playground, a game room, horseshoes, shuffleboard, a recreation room, and a full-time recreation director entertain campers. On the premises are showers, restrooms, firewood, a 72-slip marina, a boat ramp, bait and tackle, limited groceries, picnic tables, a dump station, rental RV cabins, a snack bar, laundry facilities, and a restaurant. Management says the main bathhouse and clubhouse are wheelchair accessible. Children are welcome but may stay only two weeks. Two small- to medium-size pets are allowed per site.

Reservations, fees: Reservations are recommended and are accepted up to two months in advance. Sites are $30–40 per night for two people, plus $5 for each additional person. Credit cards are accepted. Adults are welcome for long-term stays.

Directions: From I-4 at Exit 104, head north on U.S. 17/92 into DeBary. At the second light, turn left onto Highbanks Road. Go 2.5 miles west to the campground and marina.

Contact: Highbanks Marina and Camp Resort, 488 West Highbanks Road, DeBary, FL 32713, 386/668-4491, fax 386/668-5072, www.campresort.com.

10 ORANGE CITY RV RESORT

Scenic rating: 7

off I-4 in Orange City

This is part of a much larger complex of manufactured homes with suburban-style carports on mowed lots. Most of the sites are snagged by people who live here year-round (20 percent), or for the winter season, taking advantage of the park's arts-and-crafts classes, dances, parties, and special outings. Many guests spend some time across the street sipping coffee at a diner, frequenting a shopping center, or taking in movies at a theater. Guests also have access to an 18-hole wooded golf course, which surrounds the RV parks. Park models are for sale.

RV sites, facilities: All 521 full-hookup spots have 30-amp electrical service (125 have 50-amp). Twenty sites are pull-through. A wireless Internet network is available in the park. For entertainment, there's golf, miniature golf, a billiards room, a picnic pavilion, horseshoes, boccie ball (lawn bowling), a large heated pool, a whirlpool tub, a kiddie pool, planned activities, and the game room. Facilities include restrooms, showers, picnic tables, laundry facilities, and a convenience store. The clubhouse and pool area are wheelchair accessible. Streets are paved. Groceries are within two miles. Children are welcome. Leashed pets are allowed.

Reservations, fees: Reservations are recommended. Sites are $27–33 per night for two people, plus $2 for each additional person. Credit cards are accepted. Long-terms stays are okay.

Directions: From I-4 at Exit 114, head west on State Route 472 (Howland Avenue) to the traffic light. Turn left on Route 4101 and drive one mile. At Graves Avenue, turn left and drive one block to the park.

Contact: Orange City RV Resort, 2300 East Graves Avenue, Orange City, FL 32763, 386/775-2545 or 866/786-0139, fax 386/775-1517, www.orangecityrvresort.com.

11 LAKE MONROE PARK AND CAMPGROUND

🛶 🚐 🐕 🎣 ♿ 🚐 ⛺

Scenic rating: 8

on the St. Johns River south of DeBary

Renovated in 2004, this small, oak-shaded campground is in a county-run park where Lake Monroe runs into the St. Johns River, a habitat for alligators (don't feed them). It's shady, and you'll often get a breeze off the lake. Saw palmettos between the sites help provide some privacy. Your neighbors may be snowbirds or construction workers who toil up the road a little way; because it's just off the interstate, this campground may make a convenient stop in a pretty spot. Although anglers catch bluegill and speckled perch from the pier, most guests use this campground as an inexpensive springboard for trips to Orlando, Disney World, Daytona Beach, or Ocala National Forest. Even closer are Blue Spring State Park and Hontoon Island State Park, as well as DeLeon Springs State Park.

RV sites, facilities: This park, just 0.5 mile off the interstate, offers 44 spots for RVs, all with water and electricity. On the premises are restrooms, showers, a dump station, picnic tables, grills, fire rings, two boat ramps, a playground, a picnic pavilion, and a wheelchair-accessible floating dock and fishing pier. A restaurant and groceries are about one mile away. Children and leashed pets are permitted.

Reservations, fees: Reservations are recommended. From April 1 through August 31, rates are $10 per night for two people, plus $2 for each additional person and $2 for electricity. From September 1 through March 31, the rate rises to $15. During special events, rates are higher. Credit cards are not accepted. Stays are limited to two weeks, or three weeks if no one is waiting for a site.

Directions: From I-4 at Exit 104, head north on U.S. 17/92. Cross the St. Johns River and you'll see the park on your right. If eastbound on I-4, take Exit 52; at the end of the ramp, turn left and proceed to U.S. 17/92, then turn north (left) on U.S. 17/92.

Contact: Lake Monroe Park and Campground, 975 South U.S. 17/92, DeBary, FL 32713, 386/668-3825. Or write to Volusia County Leisure Services, 202 North Florida Avenue, DeLand, FL 32720, 386/736-5953, www.volusia.org/parks/camping.htm.

12 PARADISE LAKES TRAVEL TRAILER PARK

Scenic rating: 4

south of Deltona

This family-run campground is set in an oak forest next to a small lake with a swimming beach where anglers try to catch bass. Most campsites are sandy, although a few are grassy. If you want to canoe or go out in a johnboat, bring your own; no motorized watercraft are allowed on the lake. Most campers are senior citizens who stay only during the winter months. Some weekend regulars leave their trailers on-site and pay $50 per month for the privilege. Although campsites 1–40 are termed "lakeside," sunbathers may prefer sites 11–20 to be closest to the beach.

RV sites, facilities: The park offers 170 full-hookup sites with 30-amp electrical service and picnic tables. Seven sites are pull-through. On the premises are restrooms, showers, a dump station, laundry facilities, a playground, horseshoes, and a limited convenience store that sells ice and camping supplies. Groceries and restaurants are about two miles away. Children are permitted for one-week stays only. Leashed pets are allowed in the camping area but are forbidden at the beach and the grassy beachfront.

Reservations, fees: Reservations are recommended October–April but are not necessary at other times. Sites are $22 per night for two people, plus $2 for each additional person and $2 for electricity. Credit cards are not accepted. Long-term rates are available.

Directions: From I-4 at Exit 53, head east on DeBary Avenue/Doyle Road for about four miles. You'll see the park on the right.

Contact: Paradise Lakes Travel Trailer Park, 1571 Doyle Road, Deltona, FL 32725, 386/574-2371.

13 ORANGE ISLES CAMPGROUND

Scenic rating: 6

in Port Orange

One big plus in winter is that you can pick oranges and grapefruit from the trees growing in this renovated 17-acre campground, although some visitors are more interested in jumping into the 50-foot-long swimming pool. The large, shaded campsites are about 2.5 miles from the Atlantic Ocean and just around the corner from the Port Orange Sugar Mill Ruins (see next campground). It's close to Daytona's International Speedway and is popular during Bike Week and other festivities.

RV sites, facilities: There are 350 full-hookup sites for RVs. Each site has a picnic table. On the premises are showers, restrooms, a dump station, a log cabin recreation room, a pool, a playground, shuffleboard, horseshoes, and laundry facilities. Restrooms and showers are wheelchair accessible, according to management. Groceries and restaurants are within one mile. Children are permitted. Leashed pets are allowed.

Reservations, fees: Reservations are recommended. Sites are $25–78 per night for two people, plus $5 for each additional person (except kids under 12). Rates are higher during special events. Credit cards are accepted. Long-term stays are okay.

Directions: From I-95 at Exit 256, go east on State Route 421/Dunlawton Avenue about three miles to Nova Road. Turn north and look for the park on the left.

Contact: Orange Isles Campground, 3520 South Nova Road, Port Orange, FL 32119, 386/767-9170.

14 NOVA FAMILY CAMPGROUND

Scenic rating: 5

in Port Orange

Amid the big oaks shrouded in Spanish moss, you'll occasionally hear owls hooting at night. Weddings and family reunions sometimes are held in the log cabin recreation hall, and special events include hayrides, pig roasts, canoe trips, and karaoke nights. About 10 percent of the park is occupied year-round. This is an adult park, but families are welcome for short-term stays. Log cabins are for sale.

RV sites, facilities: There are 269 grassy sites with full hookups, cable TV, and 30-amp or 50-amp electrical service. RVs up to 35 feet long and slide-outs can be accommodated. Ten sites are pull-through. Picnic tables and grills are available at some sites. An Internet connection is available in the clubhouse. On the premises are showers, restrooms, fire rings, a dump station, a recreation room, a pool, horseshoes, shuffleboard, a game room, rental cabins, limited groceries, snacks, and laundry facilities. Children are welcome for stays of less than 21 days. Pets are permitted, for a daily fee.

Reservations, fees: Reservations are recommended. Sites are $28 per night for two people, plus $3 for each additional person over age 10, $2 for pets. Rates increase during special events such as Bike Week. Credit cards are accepted. Long-term rates are available.

Directions: From I-95 at Exit 256, go east on State Route 421/Dunlawton Avenue through two stoplights to Clyde Morris Boulevard and turn left. Continue north through two more lights to Herbert Street, then turn right. The park is 0.25 mile ahead.

Contact: Nova Family Campground, 1190 Herbert Street, Port Orange, FL 32119, 386/767-0095, fax 386/767-1666, www.novacamp.com.

15 DAYTONA BEACH CAMPGROUND

Scenic rating: 6

in Port Orange

Although it is dubbed Daytona Beach Campground, this 17-acre park actually is in the quieter neighboring city of Port Orange. The sunny campsites are set in a neighborhood located just a few miles from the Daytona Beach Regional Airport and the Daytona International Speedway. Although overnighters appreciate that fact, patrons also include seasonal residents who enjoy holding bingo games, potluck dinners, and dances away from the bustling throng of oceanside Daytona Beach. Like all campgrounds in the area, this place is extremely popular during certain times February–April, starting with Bike Week and lasting through spring break. For day trips, drive about six miles to swim in the Atlantic Ocean instead of the park's pool. About 10 percent of the park is occupied year-round.

RV sites, facilities: Twenty of the 180 sites are drive-through. All have 30-amp electrical service, and 24 have 50-amp. Each site has a picnic table and a concrete patio. RVs up to 45 feet long and slide-outs can be accommodated on lots averaging 30 by 80 feet. On the premises are restrooms, showers, a dump station, a recreation room, a pool, a playground, shuffleboard, horseshoes, basketball, and laundry facilities. Cable TV is available. Management says all areas are wheelchair accessible. Streets are paved. Groceries, snacks, and a restaurant are within walking distance. Children and leashed, attended pets are welcome.

Reservations, fees: Reservations are required. Sites are $27–30 per night for two people, plus $5–10 for each additional person. Credit cards are accepted. Long-term rates are available.

Directions: From I-95 at Exit 260A, proceed east on State Road 400 for about 2.5 miles to Clyde Morris Boulevard. Turn right and continue about three miles south to the campground on the left.

Contact: Daytona Beach Campground, 4601 South Clyde Morris Boulevard, Daytona Beach, FL 32119, 386/761-2663, fax 386/761-9187, www.rvdaytona.com.

16 ROSE BAY TRAVEL PARK

Scenic rating: 5

at Rose Bay in Port Orange

Popular with Canadians and Northerners who escape frigid temperatures by spending winters on Rose Bay, inland from the Atlantic beach, the 37-acre park gets crowded with all manner of folks during Bike Week in spring and Race Week in winter. Besides bingo and potluck dinners, some winter residents enjoy fishing in the park's small brackish lake. About 40 percent of the park is occupied year-round.

RV sites, facilities: All 307 full-hookup sites can accommodate RVs up to 40 feet long and slide-outs. Ten sites have 50-amp electrical service, and 290 have 30-amp. To sleep closest to the waterfront recreation area at the tip of this long, narrow RV park, ask about campsites 300–305. To be closest to the boat launch and dock, try sites 283–289 or 227–231. The pool and recreation room are at the opposite end of the park near campsite 78. On the premises are restrooms, showers, a dump station, laundry facilities, picnic tables, a pool, shuffleboard and *pétanque* courts, a dock, a boat ramp, and a recreation room. Cable TV and telephone service are available. Groceries and restaurants are within 0.2 mile. All areas are wheelchair accessible. Children are allowed on a short-term basis. Pets must be kept on three-foot leashes.

Reservations, fees: Reservations are recommended. Sites are $30 per night for two people, plus $5 for each additional person. Credit cards are accepted. Adults are welcome for long-term stays.

Directions: From I-95 at Exit 256, take State Road 421 east for three miles to Nova Road. Turn right and head south. The campground is about 5 miles ahead on the right, 0.5 mile west of U.S. 1.

Contact: Rose Bay Travel Park, 5200 South Nova Road, Port Orange, FL 32127, 386/767-4308, fax 386/767-7060.

17 NEW SMYRNA BEACH RV PARK AND CAMPGROUND

Scenic rating: 6

west of New Smyrna Beach

Swimmers have their choice of aquatic venues: the campground pool or the Atlantic Ocean five miles away, where you can drive on the hard-packed sand (except when the nests of endangered sea turtles are present). Some shell-rock or grassy sites are sunny, whereas others enjoy shade from magnolias, oaks, or palms. Indeed, 25 acres of this 30-acre park are dotted with trees, and sites are scattered throughout. Expect little privacy, though, because sites are right next to each other with little or no brush to separate them. During some holiday periods, children's activities are organized here, but retirees dominate November–April, when activities trend toward bingo, potluck dinners, and dances. It's about 20 miles to the Merritt Island National Wildlife Refuge, heading south. Daytona International Speedway is about 20 miles north.

RV sites, facilities: There are 208 sites with full hookups and 30-amp or 50-amp electrical service, cable TV, Internet access, and picnic tables. On the premises are showers, restrooms, a dump station, a recreation room, cabin rentals, a pool, a playground, a game room, miniature golf, horseshoes, shuffleboard, limited groceries, and laundry facilities. Restaurants and bait are within five miles. The showers and store are wheelchair accessible, according to management. Children and leashed pets are welcome.

Reservations, fees: Reservations are recommended. Sites are $24–27 per night (higher during special events) for two people, plus $3 for each additional adult. Credit cards are accepted. Long-term stays are okay.

Directions: From I-95 at Exit 249, go east on State Road 44 to Old Mission Road. Turn right and continue 1.5 miles south to the campground on your right.

Contact: New Smyrna Beach RV Park and Campground, 1300 Old Mission Road, New Smyrna Beach, FL 32168, 386/427-3581 or 800/928-9962, email: beachcamp@beach-camp.net.

18 SUGAR MILL RUINS TRAVEL PARK

Scenic rating: 5

west of U.S. 1 in New Smyrna Beach

At this shady campground where anglers catch mullet and catfish from the banks of the brackish fishing hole, the owners have taken some pains to preserve native Florida vegetation. The full-hookup grassy campsites along Quail Hollow Drive tend to enjoy the most shade from palms, pines, and oaks. Camping spots farther from the center of the park can be quite sunny because they're in the garden section, where small hibiscus bushes dominate. Don't expect to see a sugar mill. The park gets its name from the nearby Sugar Mill Ruins Historic Site, a small, sleepy, wooded, Volusia County–run park. It serves as a reminder of the Second Seminole War, when Indians clashed with settlers who moved into the area to grow sugar and indigo, a plant valued for its role in making a then-popular blue dye. You can picnic at tables near the decaying stone walls of the mill, now being overcome by sabal palms and other native vegetation. Elsewhere, the quaint commercial district of New Smyrna Beach is sort of a quiet cousin of Daytona Beach. For now, at least, it's far enough removed from Daytona that it doesn't get quite the crowds, except for spillover business during the festivals in Daytona Beach.

RV sites, facilities: There are 117 RV full-hookup sites with 30-amp and 50-amp electrical service; many are pull-through. Sites are lined up, as many as 21–25 abreast, along straight, 5-mph roads whose names conjure up natural images—Jack Rabbit Run, Raccoon Road, Armadillo Drive. To sleep nearest to the pool (and the entrance-area laundry room), ask about full-hookup sites 47–50. On the premises are showers, restrooms, a dump station, laundry facilities, a recreation room, a convenience store, a pool, volleyball, basketball, a playground, horseshoes, and canoe rentals. Children must be adult-supervised at the pool. Leashed pets must use the designated dog walk.

Reservations, fees: Reservations are recommended except in summer. Sites typically are $25–33 per night for two people, plus $5 for each additional adult. Credit cards are accepted. Long-term rates are available.

Directions: From I-95 at Exit 249, head east on State Road 44. Turn right onto Old Mission Road. In about 0.25 mile, look for the faux waterwheel marking the campground entrance on the right.

Contact: Sugar Mill Ruins Travel Park, 1050 Old Mission Road, New Smyrna Beach, FL 32168, 386/427-2284, fax 386/428-8521, www.sugarmilltravelpark.com.

ORLANDO

COURTESY OF VISIT FLORIDA

BEST RV PARKS AND CAMPGROUNDS

This is it — you've arrived at Florida's most popular tourist area, the home of Mickey Mouse. In 1971 Walt Disney World opened in what was then a remote, undeveloped area southwest of Orlando; since then this region has been transformed into a sprawling leisure-oriented destination known the world over. Constantly renewing itself, Walt Disney World is a mega-adventure with sights, sounds, and experiences for all age groups.

For RVers, the center of the Disney experience is the top-rated Fort Wilderness Campground, which is located on the property. Not only do visitors avoid the traffic jams of plebeian cars coming into the park, they get free transportation into the park by shuttle bus, boat, or monorail. The recreational opportunities alone are mind-boggling: swimming, fishing, waterskiing, and canoeing on the property's lakes, as well as biking, tennis, horseback riding, and a two-mile nature trail. Children are thrilled by nightly campfire visits from Disney characters, Disney movies, a petting farm, and pony rides. Air-conditioned bathrooms and heated swimming pools lend a very polished feel to this "campground."

Fort Wilderness sets the standard for dozens of other RV parks around Disney — and there's something to be said for staying outside the park. The Orlando area is also home to dozens of other attractions: Universal Studios theme park, Sea World, and Wet 'n' Wild, just to name a few.

The RV parks in Orlando can be roughly divided into three types: the Disney-oriented family destinations, the "snowbird" communities where winter visitors congregate for months at a time, and the nature-focused campgrounds that offer everything from fishing and hiking to bike riding and bird-watching.

Most ubiquitous are the adult-preferred parks that cater

to Northerners looking to get out of the cold. Here, RVers stay for six months, availing themselves of the popular "6/6" plan, which allows them to leave their rig on-site half the year to avoid paying high lodging taxes. Interior street names can give you a clue to where most visitors are from (one park that caters to Canadians has street names like Bruins Drive, Maple Leaf Drive, and Canadiens Drive). Many visitors return year after year to the same park and stay in touch with each other via a park newsletter.

These parks are often organized for socializing. Potluck dinners, line dancing, exercise classes, bingo, crafts, horseshoes, shuffleboard, movies, and day trips to other shopping and entertainment venues are popular activities. The larger parks go even further by hiring full-time activity directors. Visitors can expect on-site activities and amenities such as wood-carving classes, computer lessons, gardening clubs, motorcycle clubs, mini-sailboat races, tennis courts, concerts, golf courses, restaurants, hair salons, libraries, and even a post office.

For campers who prefer a less-citified experience, state parks and some private parks offer quick access to nature. The Withlacoochee River has miles of undeveloped cypress-lined riverbank to canoe or fish. Bicyclists shouldn't miss the 46-mile Withlacoochee State Trail, a paved route that follows an old railroad bed. The trail begins in Citrus County near Dunnellon and travels south through Hernando County and the Withlacoochee State Forest, ending in northern Pasco County. At Wekiwa Springs State Park, a natural spring delights swimmers, snorkelers, and paddlers while its run to the Wekiva River is a wonderful route to canoe or kayak in a bit of natural Florida that is being rapidly surrounded by the creep of suburbia.

ORLANDO

see Daytona page 212

see Ocala page 180

See "Walt Disney World and Vicinity" Map

see Tampa page 354

see St Petersburg page 340

Gulf of Mexico

Tampa Bay

De Land
Deltona
De Bary
Sanford
Oviedo
Chuluota
Winter Park
ORLANDO
Apopka
Sorrento
Mount Dora
Tavares
Leesburg
Bushnell
Brooksville
Inverness
Homosassa Springs
Spring Hill
Hudson
Dade City
Zephyrhills
Land O'Lakes
Kissimmee

Lake Woodruff
Lake Monroe
Lake Comc
East Lake Tohopekaliga
Lake Tohopekaliga
Lake Apopka
Lake Eustis
Lake Harris
Lake Weir

Withlacoochee State Forest
Withlacoochee State Forest
Withlacoochee State Forest

10 mi
10 km

© AVALON TRAVEL PUBLISHING,

WALT DISNEY WORLD AND VICINITY

LAKELAND/
SEBRING

see
Space Coast
page 326

see
Lake Okeechobee

see
Tampa
page 354

Yeehaw Junction

192

441

157

139

Alligator
Lake

192
441

138

140

Cypress
Lake

Lake
Tohopekaliga

Lake
Marion

Lake
Hatchineha

Lake
Rosalie

Lake
Pierce

Kissimmee
State Park

152-154

Lake
Kissimmee

155-156

Tiger
Lake

151

Kissimmee

Kissimmee Prairie
Preserve State Park

River

Lake
Weohyakapka

174

Lake
Arbuckle

Lake Wales
Ridge State
Forest

60

Spring
Lake

98

Avon Park

Sebring

64

17

168-173

27

98

163-167

146-150

27

134-137

Davenport

92

27

133

Cypress Gardens

17 92

131-132

Winter
Haven

141-145

Lake Wales

17

98

Lake
Hancock

125-128

Lakeland

129-130

98

Bartow

17 98

17 98

Fort Meade

17

98

64

66

5 mi

5 km

0

0

162

Zolfo Springs

158-161

Wauchula

64

Mulberry

37

62

60

674

© AVALON TRAVEL PUBLISHING,

1 RIVERSIDE LODGE

Scenic rating: 6

east of Inverness
See map page 228

Want to settle in for a while in a pretty wooded setting with great fishing? Sites are nestled under tall oaks and palms next to the Withlacoochee River and near the Withlacoochee State Trail, which is a good route for bicycling. Bass anglers and canoeists think the area is paradise. About 10 percent of the park is occupied by year-round residents, a figure that will increase because park models are for sale. Karen and Hardy van Niersen bought the park in 2003 and have been steadily converting this vintage fish camp into a resort. A small island is visible from the campground. Explorers are welcome but cautioned against feeding the alligators—good advice anywhere there is freshwater.

RV sites, facilities: This 49-unit park has 19 RV sites with full hookups and 30/50-amp electrical service. Two sites are drive-through. Rigs up to 40 feet can be accommodated. Sites 29–33 overlook the river, and several other sites overlook a creek. On the property are a bathhouse with showers (added in 2005), laundry facilities, a wheelchair-accessible recreation lodge, cabin and boat rentals, a picnic and party pavilion, a swing set, a fishing pier, and a boat ramp. You can connect to the Internet via dial-up modem in the clubhouse. Planned activities are not available. A restaurant is across the street, and grocery stores are four miles away. Children are welcome. Leashed pets under 20 pounds are permitted.

Reservations, fees: Reservations are recommended. Sites are $25–35 per night for two people, plus $5 per extra person. Credit cards are accepted. Long-term stays are okay.

Directions: From Exit 329 on I-75, take State Road 44 west 8.5 miles toward Inverness.

Contact: Riverside Lodge, 12561 East Gulf to Lake Highway, Inverness, FL 34450, 352/726-2002, www.riversidelodgerv.com.

2 TRAIL'S END CAMP

Scenic rating: 6

near Floral City
See map page 228

If you're lucky enough to get a campsite at this heavily wooded mobile-home park on the Withlacoochee River, you'll have views of miles of undeveloped cypress-lined riverbank. "Once you're in the campground, you are in the woods," says the management. Paddle your canoe, or fish from the dock. You're pretty much surrounded by wilderness. The river's headwaters are in northern Polk County at Green Swamp, the same place that gives rise to the Hillsborough, Ocklawaha, and Peace Rivers. Don't confuse it with the river of the same name in northern Florida. The waters are colored dark by the tannins and organic acids seeping from surrounding cypress swamps and pinewoods. If you brought your bicycle, don't miss the 46-mile Withlacoochee bike trail, which is within 10 minutes of the park. Some nature trails are nearby in the Withlacoochee State Forest. The campground's location in Floral City is ideal for exploring the nearby Withlacoochee State Forest and historic Fort Cooper State Park. It tends to be favored by retirees, hunters, and anglers who leave their trailers year-round. About 90 percent of the sites are permanently occupied.

RV sites, facilities: This 65-acre campground has 20 full-hookup RV sites for overnighters, one of which is drive-through. Half the sites have 30-amp electrical service; the other 10 have 50-amp. The roads are not paved, and the sites are grassy. Restrooms, showers, picnic tables, fire rings, a playground, a fishing pier, boat docks, a gun range, rental cabins, an archery range, rental canoes and rowboats, and horseshoe pits are available. A camp store sells beer, wine, and groceries. Children and leashed pets are welcome.

Reservations, fees: Reservations are not necessary. RV sites are $16 per night for four people.

Credit cards are accepted. Stay as long as you wish.

Directions: From I-75, take Exit 314 and drive west on State Road 48 for 10 miles to Trail's End Road. Turn north and go four miles to the river.

Contact: Trail's End Camp, 12900 Trail's End Road, Floral City, FL 34436, 352/726-3699.

🖪 MOONRISE RESORT

Scenic rating: 6

between Floral City and Inverness

See map page 228   **BEST (**

This campground is part of a quiet five-acre community of rental cabins and mobile homes on the shores of Tsala Apopka Lake. You can rent a boat or canoe and explore the 9,000-acre body of water, which is actually a chain of connected lakes. The park rents johnboats, larger motorboats, canoes, and paddleboats by the hour, day, or week. Cast your line from the dock, or sit on the benches and watch the water. Throughout the park are cypress trees and oaks hung with frilly Spanish moss that trails down from the branches. Pick up supplies in Floral City or in Inverness, which is five miles north. The Withlacoochee State Trail is nearby, and the northern terminus of this 46-mile bicycling, horseback-riding, and walking trail begins in Citrus County near Dunnellon and travels south through Hernando County and the Withlacoochee State Forest, ending in northern Pasco County. Access points are scattered along the route, which parallels U.S. 41 along the northern half and the Withlacoochee River in the southern half. The trail, formerly a railroad right-of-way, is paved; equestrians use a parallel sandy path.

RV sites, facilities: The park has 12 RV sites with full hookups and 30-amp electrical service; cable TV and telephone service are available for long-term visitors. RVs up to 30 feet long can be accommodated; note that there are

no drive-through sites. Each site has a patio, and elbow room between sites averages 15 feet on either side. Nearly the entire park is occupied by year-round residents. Restrooms, showers, picnic tables, a dump station, a recreation room, laundry facilities, shuffleboard courts, horseshoe pits, a boat ramp, fishing docks, and rental cottages are on the property. Children and leashed pets are welcome.

Reservations, fees: Reservations are recommended. Sites are $25 per night for two people, plus $1 for each additional person. Credit cards are not accepted. Long-term rates are available. The minimum stay is two nights; on holiday weekends, it's three nights.

Directions: From I-75, take Exit 314 and drive west on State Road 48 for approximately 12 miles until you reach Floral City. One block before you arrive at the big intersection with U.S. 41, turn north on Old Floral City Road, which parallels U.S. 41. Drive 1.5 miles, turn east on Moonrise Lane, and continue 0.25 mile to the park entrance. Or, from the intersection of U.S. 41 and County Road 39A/Gobbler Road, drive east for one block to Old Floral City Road, then turn south and drive one mile to Moonrise Lane.

Contact: Moonrise Resort, 8801 East Moonrise Lane, Lot 18, Floral City, FL 34436, 352/726-2553 or 800/665-6701, www.moonriseresort .com.

🖪 RECREATION PLANTATION RV RESORT

Scenic rating: 8

in Lady Lake

See map page 228   **BEST (**

As the name suggests, an active social lifestyle is what campers get in this country setting designed for adults. Events noted on the clubhouse bulletin board may range from 8:30 A.M. exercises to 7 P.M. card games or bingo in winter, so you may need your alarm clock to keep up. Some sort of activity is scheduled for most hours by the full-time winter-activities director. A trio of 18-hole golf courses is located within three miles.

About half of the campsites form concentric circles around the park's central attractions—a clubhouse, a heated pool, a spa, and sports courts. The minimum 65- by 35-foot lots tend to be sunny with token, well-kept bushes and lawns that give the park a residential atmosphere. Kids may feel out of place around the middle-aged and retiree crowd, if only because rules forbid them from using the hot tub, exercise equipment, and pool tables. Full-time residents live at about 300 lots sprinkled throughout the park.

RV sites, facilities: These 850 full-hookup sites are grassy and average 35 by 65 feet in size. All have sewer hookups, 30/50-amp electrical service, picnic tables, and Internet access. Another Internet connection is available in the clubhouse. Recreational offerings include a pool, a spa, two clubhouses (one is wheelchair accessible), an exercise room, billiards, planned activities, shuffleboard, boccie ball (lawn bowling), tennis, horseshoes, and table tennis. Showers, restrooms, a post office, cable TV access, telephone hookups, and laundry facilities are available. Children may camp for up to two weeks at this otherwise adult-oriented park. Leashed pets are permitted but should be walked around the retention pond and attended at all times.

Reservations, fees: Reservations are suggested. Sites are $33 per night for two people, plus $4 for each additional person. Credit cards are accepted. Long-term rates are available.

Directions: From Leesburg, drive about seven miles north on U.S. 27. Turn left on County Road 466. The park is on the right, 0.5 mile west of the turnoff.

Contact: Recreation Plantation RV Resort, 609 County Road 466, Lady Lake, FL 32159, 352/753-7222 or 800/448-5646, www.recreationplantation.com.

5 BLUE PARROT CAMPING PARK

Scenic rating: 5

in Lady Lake

See map page 228

Convenience and relaxation are the standout features at this park. Besides teeing off for free at the park's par-3, nine-hole golf course, visitors can swim in the heated pool, share potluck dinners, attend Bible studies, play bingo (in winter), learn to quilt and sew, and take part in other activities organized by a resident association.

La Plaza Grande shopping center and an RV hand-wash business are nearby, so expect a suburban experience. Most of the concrete-pad or grassy sites along the lighted, paved streets are devoted to retirees who spend months at the 80-plus-acre park. Overnighters are relegated to a small area close to County Road 25. Located in sleepy Lake County, which is marked by rolling hills and 1,400 named lakes, the camp could serve as a crash pad for bass anglers.

RV sites, facilities: All 452 full-hookup sites (17 pull-through) at this retiree-oriented park are for RVs up to 44 feet long. A golf course, a pool, billiards, a recreation room, horseshoes, shuffleboard, and social programs entertain campers. Showers, restrooms, a convenience store, a Sunday chapel, cable TV, telephone service, and laundry facilities are available. Children may stay short-term. Leashed pets must use the designated dog walks.

Reservations, fees: Reservations are recommended. Sites are $27 per night for two people, plus $2.50 for each additional person. Credit cards are accepted. Long-term rates are available.

Directions: From County Road 466/Lemon Street in Lady Lake, drive a short distance northwest on U.S. 27/441 to the cutoff for County Road 25. Take County Road 25 north to the park entrance on your right.

Contact: Blue Parrot Camping Park, 40840 County Road 25, Lady Lake, FL 32159, 352/753-2026, fax 352/753-8383, www.rvresorts.com.

6 SUNSHINE MOBILE HOME PARK

Scenic rating: 2

south of Lady Lake

See map page 228

Visitors are outnumbered by residents of the 70 mobile homes at this age-55-plus park, but overnighters can join along in winter activities or take a dip in the pool all the same. That would include breakfasts, potluck dinners, card games, and Bible study. The grassy/concrete-pad RV sites are set on 11 acres about three miles due north of Lake Griffin State Park. Paddlers and bass anglers launch into 14-square-mile Lake Griffin. This growing region of Florida is characterized by lake-dotted countryside surrounded by grassy, rolling hills that were citrus groves before freezes drove the industry to warmer climes. Disney World and other Orlando-area attractions are about one hour south.

RV sites, facilities: This age-55-and-older park has 20 full-hookup RV sites (two pull-through) with picnic tables and 50-amp electric service. Lots have concrete pads set under oak trees and vary in size, but average around 20 by 70 feet. Also inside the park are 70 mobile homes. A pool, an exercise room, horseshoes, shuffleboard, winter social programs, and a wheelchair-accessible recreation hall entertain campers. Showers, restrooms, and laundry facilities are available. Children are not allowed. Leashed pets are permitted.

Reservations, fees: Reservations are suggested. Sites are $20 per night for two people, plus $2 for each additional person and $1 if you use air conditioners or electric heaters. Credit cards are not accepted. Long-term stays are okay.

Directions: From County Road 466 in the town of Lady Lake, drive south on U.S. 27/441 to Griffin View Drive. Turn left (east). The park is 0.5 mile ahead at Sunshine Boulevard.

Contact: Sunshine Mobile Home Park, 401 Sunshine Boulevard, Lady Lake, FL 32159, tel./fax 352/753-2415.

7 LAKE GRIFFIN STATE PARK

Scenic rating: 8

in Fruitland Park

See map page 228

Largemouth bass are the goal of anglers at 14-square-mile Lake Griffin, although bluegill and specks make respectable consolation prizes. Bird-watchers, on the other hand, remark that the rookery, which resounds with a cacophony of bird chatter, is their favorite part of the 500-acre park. Actually, the most unusual facet of this park may be the "floating islands." See the marsh between Lake Griffin and its uplands? Sometimes chunks break off from that marshy mat of soil and roots, and they float like icebergs toward the lake.

I once spent a New Year's Eve watching the stars, but the traffic getting to the park can be congested. Campers sleep under oaks, and the sites are lovely. Bring mosquito repellent in summer. All sites—most sandy, some with pads—have a picnic table, a grill, and a fire ring for roasting marshmallows. As at most other state parks, campers are set apart from day-use areas such as the 0.75-mile nature trail. Look for otters, rabbits, and raccoons during your stay. Canoeists and boaters use a ramp at the head of a 0.25-mile canal leading to Lake Griffin. Ocala National Forest is nearby.

RV sites, facilities: The 40 sites have water and 30-amp electric hookups. Ten spots have 50-amp power, and eight sites are pull-through. Each site has a picnic table, a grill, and a fire ring. On the premises are showers, restrooms, a dump station, a boat ramp, a dock, canoe rentals, a playground, a nature trail, horseshoe and volleyball areas, and laundry facilities. Three campsites, the pavilion, the restrooms, and fishing dock have wheelchair access. A restaurant, bait, and groceries are available within one mile. Children are welcome. Leashed pets are allowed.

Reservations, fees: Reservations are recommended; contact ReserveAmerica at 800/336-3521 or reserveamerica.com. Sites are $17 per night for four people. Credit cards are accepted. The maximum stay is 14 days.

Directions: From Leesburg, drive about two miles north on U.S. 441/27. The park is on the right side of the road.

Contact: Lake Griffin State Park, 3089 U.S. 441/27, Fruitland Park, FL 34731, 352/360-6760, fax 352/360-6762, www.floridastate-parks.org.

8 PINE ISLAND CAMPGROUND AND FISH CAMP

Scenic rating: 3

at Lake Griffin east of Lady Lake

See map page 228

Bass is king at this remote retreat near the mouth of the Ocklawaha River at the northwestern end of Lake Griffin. Bream, catfish, and crappie also lurk in the sizable lake. Owner Len Garner and Captain Joe Hammond have more than 25 years of experience to help anglers seek out the prize that some people mount on their walls—bass. If you don't like to fish or motor around in a boat, look elsewhere for a spot to set up camp.Oaks shade each rustic campsite. About one-third of the lots are occupied year-round. The park has been under new ownership as of mid-2005 and they have given the park a facelift with paint and good cleaning.

RV sites, facilities: Thirty-three sites have full hookups, 30/50-amp electricity, and picnic tables. Ten sites are pull-through. RVs up to 45 feet long can be accommodated. The sites vary in size; Average site size is 20 by 40 feet, but some are larger. For recreation, there's a fishing guide, boat rentals, 57 covered boat stalls, a boat ramp, and campfire areas. You can even rent a pontoon boat that accommodates parties of 20. The fish cleaning station is enclosed. No pool, shuffleboard, or other activities are offered. Boat and trailer storage is on-site. Showers, restrooms, a dump station, laundry facilities, and a camp store that sells the basics, plus bait

and tackle, are available. Children are welcome. Pets must be leashed.

Reservations, fees: Reservations are not taken. Sites are $35 per night. Credit cards are accepted. Long-term rates are available.

Directions: From U.S. 27 in Lady Lake, drive east on County Road 466/Lemon Street to the stop sign. Turn left and follow Lake Griffin Road about five miles to the campground entrance.

Contact: Pine Island Campground and Fish Camp, 6808 Lake Griffin Road, Lady Lake, FL 32159, 352/753-2972.

9 MORGAN'S MOBILE HOME PARK AND FISH CAMP

Scenic rating: 2

on Lake Griffin in eastern Fruitland Park

See map page 228

At this 15-acre, laid-back RV park/fish camp on Lake Griffin, anglers of all ages launch their boats to pursue bass and bream or to spot alligators, herons, and the occasional otter. Many visitors here are locals who rent by the week or visitors who have relatives in the immediate area.

RV sites, facilities: All 58 full-hookup sites have 30-amp electrical service. Six spots are drivethrough. About 20 percent are occupied by year-round residents. Recreation options include a boat ramp and dock, sightseeing boat tours, and a recreation room. It's one of the few marinas on the lake that sell gasoline, the owners say. Showers, restrooms, a dump station, bait and tackle, and laundry facilities are available. You can access the Internet on a limited basis in the office. A camp store sells snacks and many varieties of alligator souvenirs. Groceries can be purchased one block from here. A restaurant is one mile away. Children are permitted, but the park is geared toward retirees. Small, leashed pets are allowed.

Reservations, fees: Reservations are not necessary. Sites are $18 per night for two people, plus $3 for each additional person. Credit cards are not accepted. Long-term rates are available.

Directions: From the intersection of U.S. 27 and U.S. 441 in Leesburg, drive north on U.S. 27. At the third stoplight, turn right. The park entrance is 1.5 miles ahead on Picciola Road.

Contact: Morgan's Mobile Home Park and Fish Camp, 04056 Picciola Road, Fruitland Park, FL 34731, 352/787-4916.

🔟 TILLIS HILL

♿ 🚐 ⛺

Scenic rating: 8

in the Withlacoochee State Forest Citrus Tract south of Inverness

See map page 228   **BEST (**

Both families and organized equestrian groups enjoy this campground, which serves as a base camp for dozens of miles of horseback-riding trails through the sandy, rolling terrain of the state forest. Ride for the day on forest roads or on trails weaving through the pinewoods, which sprawl over 41,000 acres. (The Citrus Tract is the largest of the five sections of the Withlacoochee State Forest.) There's also a two-day horseback trail with a primitive camping zone called Perryman Place that can accommodate 100 people; be sure to bring water because there are no facilities. Organized groups need to have a permit for all activities in the forest.

RV sites, facilities: Targeted to horseback riders, this state forest campground has 37 sites with water, 50-amp electricity, picnic tables, grills, and fire rings. There's also a 20-stall horse stable, a dining hall with a kitchen, a large open-air picnic shelter, and a barbecue pit. Restrooms, showers, and a dump station are provided. The bathhouse is wheelchair accessible. Groceries are 20 miles away; gas and convenience stores are within 13 miles. Children are welcome, but pets are prohibited.

Reservations, fees: Reservations are required. Sites are $13 per night for five people, plus $3 for each horse stall. The dining hall can be rented for a fee, depending on the size of the group. Credit cards are not accepted.

Directions: From Inverness, drive 10 miles south on U.S. 41 to County Road 480. Turn right and drive eight miles west. Turn north on Forest Road 13 and drive three miles to the campground.

Contact: Withlacoochee State Forest Recreation Visitors Center, 15003 Broad Street, Brooksville, FL 34601, 352/754-6896 or fire dispatch 352/754-6777. For reservations, call 352/344-4238 or visit www.fl-dof.com.

🔟🔟 HOLDER MINE

Scenic rating: 8

in the Withlacoochee State Forest Citrus Tract south of Inverness

See map page 228

Holder Mine is so named because there were once phosphate mines in the area. In fact, a pit created by the mining operation remains near the campground, which has oversized sites in a pine forest. There's deep water at the bottom of the pit, and curious anglers have been known to catch fish here, although swimming is prohibited and probably not a good idea for scofflaws. This is also a staging area for hikers on the Florida National Scenic Trail (46 miles long) and for horseback riders exploring the forest. A watering area for horses is provided, as is a place to tie them up while riders use the restrooms. The forest roads are also available for bicyclists.

RV sites, facilities: You'll find 27 campsites with water, 50-amp electrical service, picnic tables, grills, and fire rings. Rigs up to 40 feet long are welcome. Wheelchair-accessible restrooms, showers, and a dump station are available. Groceries are within seven miles. Children are welcome. Leashed pets are allowed.

Reservations, fees: Reservations are not taken. Sites are $13 per night for five people. Credit cards are not accepted. This campground is open only on weekends (from noon Friday to noon Monday) and holidays.

Directions: From the junction of State Road 44 and State Road 581 on the west side of

Inverness, drive five miles south on State Road 581 to the campground entrance.

Contact: Withlacoochee State Forest Recreation Visitors Center, 15003 Broad Street, Brooksville, FL 34601, 352/754-6896 or fire dispatch 352/754-6777, www.fl-dof.com.

12 MUTUAL MINE RECREATION AREA

Scenic rating: 9

in the Withlacoochee State Forest Citrus Tract south of Inverness

See map page 228

Self-contained campers are well separated from their neighbors in this secluded pine flat-wood forest that's remote enough to escape urban traffic and noise. The Florida National Scenic Trail can be accessed from here by walking 1.5 miles west of the campground. An abandoned mining pit is nearby; most of the water has leached out, and it's only about 10 feet deep. Nonetheless, swimming is prohibited. You'll have to pick up supplies in Inverness because there's not much in the way of civilization around here.

RV sites, facilities: There are 13 sites with water, picnic tables, grills, and fire rings. Flush toilets are available, but there are no showers. Nor is there electricity. The sites are gravel or grassy; none are drive-through. Rigs up to 40 feet long can be accommodated. A dump station and a youth camping group are also on-site. Children are welcome. Pets and alcohol are prohibited.

Reservations, fees: Reservations are not taken. Sites are $10 per night for five people. Credit cards are not accepted. This campground is open only on weekends (from noon Friday to noon Monday) and holidays.

Directions: From the junction of State Road 44 and State Road 581 on the west side of Inverness, drive eight miles south on State Road 581 to the campground entrance on the west side of the highway.

Contact: Withlacoochee State Forest Recreation Visitors Center, 15003 Broad Street, Brooksville, FL 34601, 352/754-6896 or fire dispatch 352/754-6777, www.fl-dof.com.

13 IDLEWILD LODGE

Scenic rating: 5

at Lake Panasoffkee southwest of Wildwood

See map page 228

A four-acre, lakeside campground, Idlewild Lodge has lots of trees and borders a wooded area. The main activity here is fishing on Lake Panasoffkee. The whole region is pretty laid-back, and this small campground is located at the even quieter north end of the lake. The RV sites, with 12- by 30-foot concrete pads, are set behind 10 cottages that front the solar heated pool. Don't forget to pack your swimsuit; park rules forbid swimmers to wear shorts or cutoffs.

RV sites, facilities: Ten sites are available for RVs. Hookups include sewer and 30/50-amp electrical service. Park on concrete pads under the oaks. On the premises are restrooms, showers, laundry facilities, a dump station, some picnic tables, rental efficiencies, bait, tackle, a boat ramp, a pool, horseshoes, basketball, shuffleboard, a camp store with snacks, and boat rentals. Groceries and restaurants are about two miles away. Children and small leashed pets are permitted.

Reservations, fees: Reservations are recommended. Sites are $21 per night for two people, plus $5 for each extra person. Credit cards are not accepted for overnight stays. Long-term stays are okay.

Directions: From I-75 at Exit 321, head west on County Road 470 for about five miles. Turn right onto County Road 400. The campground is one mile ahead.

Contact: Idlewild Lodge, 4110 County Road 400, Lake Panasoffkee, FL 33538, 352/793-7057, www.idlewildlodge.com.

14 PANA VISTA LODGE

Scenic rating: 5

at the Outlet River southwest of Wildwood

See map page 228   BEST (

You'll find this charmingly rustic park at the mouth of what's known as the Outlet River, a stream that connects the popular boating and bass-fishing waters of Lake Panasoffkee to the Withlacoochee River. The park sees all kinds of visitors: overnighters, snowbirds, and Floridians who leave their rigs on-site to use on the weekends. About half the park is occupied by year-round residents. Fishing for bass, perch, and shellcrackers is the favorite occupation, and competitive types can participate in the occasional fishing contest.

RV sites, facilities: There are 70 full-hookup RV sites with picnic tables and 30/50-amp service. Six sites are drive-through. On the premises are restrooms, showers, a dump station, grills, fire rings, rental cabins, mobile homes, a bait and tackle shop, a boat ramp, and boat and canoe rentals. Groceries and restaurants are within two miles. Children are welcome. Small leashed pets are permitted.

Reservations, fees: Reservations are recommended. Sites are $20 per night for two people, plus $1 for each additional person. Credit cards are accepted. Long-term stays are okay.

Directions: From I-75 at Exit 321, drive almost five miles west on County Road 470. Turn right at County Road 421 (you'll see a sign for the lodge).

Contact: Pana Vista Lodge, 3417 County Road 421, Lake Panasoffkee, FL 33538, 352/793-2061, fax 352/793-5683, www.panavista.qsy.com.

15 TURTLEBACK RV RESORT

Scenic rating: 6

off I-75 southwest of Wildwood

See map page 228

Set on a creek that leads to the popular bass-fishing waters of 27-square-mile Lake Panasoffkee, this wooded park offers campsites that are grassy and mostly shaded for its clientele, which tends to stay for winter. Fish from the dock or from a boat. If you don't own a boat or a canoe, you can rent one here. For visitors who couldn't care less about fishing, try the heated pool or year-round planned activities such as bingo games, dancing, and potluck dinners. Most folks are over 55 and are repeat visitors from places like Michigan and Indiana.

RV sites, facilities: There are 138 RV sites (100 full-hookup, 15 pull-through) in this park, which is 70 percent occupied year-round. Fifteen sites have 50-amp service. Sites vary in size and are laid out irregularly in the woods, not subdivision-style in a row. Each site has a picnic table. A pool, boat and canoe rentals, a playground, a recreation hall, pool tables, horseshoes, two shuffleboard courts, and a nature trail are on the premises. Restrooms, showers, a dump station, laundry facilities, LP gas sales, rental cabins, a boat ramp, telephone service, cable TV, and social activities are available. There's a wireless Internet connection available near the office. Management says all facilities are wheelchair accessible. Groceries and restaurants are within one mile. Children and pets are permitted.

Reservations, fees: Reservations are recommended. Sites are $28 per night for two people, plus $5 for each additional person. Credit cards are not accepted. Long-term stays are okay.

Directions: From I-75 at Exit 321, head west for 0.75 mile to the campground on the left.

Contact: Turtleback RV Resort, 190 County Road 488, Lake Panasoffkee, FL 33538, 352/793-2501 or 800/887-8525.

16 COUNTRYSIDE RV PARK

Scenic rating: 5

off I-75 southwest of Wildwood

See map page 228

This park in a quiet, rural area is good for a quick stopover if you're traveling on I-75. It's also not far from the local focus of interest: Lake Panasoffkee, or any of the creeks leading to the watery domain of anglers and boaters. To paddle a 10-mile stretch of the nearby Withlacoochee River, try renting a canoe from Nobleton Boat Rentals; call 352/796-7176 or 800/783-5284. During the winter, park activities include bingo, potluck dinners, cards, music around the bonfire, horseshoes, shuffleboard, and a coffeehouse. Oak trees provide some shade and atmosphere. About have the sites are occupied year-round. Most visitors are retirees from the Midwest and Canada.

RV sites, facilities: The camp has 64 full-hookup sites, of which 15 are pull-through (more if the park is not crowded). Almost all have 30/50-amp electrical outlets; five have just 30-amp. On the premises are restrooms, showers, a dump station, a laundry room, a recreation hall, and a game room. Firewood is available, and a boat ramp accessing the Withlacoochee River and Lake Panasoffkee is just three miles away. Management says all buildings are wheelchair accessible. Campground roads are black-topped. Groceries and restaurants are about two miles away. Children are welcome on a short-term basis. Pets are allowed.

Reservations, fees: Reservations are recommended. Sites are $23 per night for two people, plus $2 for each additional person and $2 for using air conditioners or electric heaters. Credit cards are not accepted. Long-term stays are okay for adults.

Directions: From I-75 at Exit 321, drive west on County Road 470. In less than one mile, bear left on County Road 489, which leads to the park.

Contact: Countryside RV Park, 741 County Road 489, Lake Panasoffkee, FL 33538, 352/793-8103, email: countrysidervpark@cfl.rr.com.

17 WILDWOOD KOA

Scenic rating: 6

off I-75 in Wildwood
See map page 228

Perhaps the best thing about this KOA is that it's right off the interstate, making it easier to get to Disney-area attractions, Ocala National Forest, or the Withlacoochee State Forest in short order. If you're tired of the pool, try the miniature golf course or hot tub. Only 2 percent of the occupants stay here year-round; the rest are through-travelers and seasonal visitors.

RV sites, facilities: There are 108 full-hookup sites (76 pull-through, 20 with 50-amp service). Each site has a picnic table. RVs up to 45 feet long can be accommodated on sites that average 52 by 21 feet. On the premises are restrooms, showers, a dump station, a pool, a hot tub, a playground, miniature golf, horseshoes, shuffleboard, a camp store with limited groceries, and laundry facilities. Firewood is available. Restrooms and the recreation hall are wheelchair accessible. Restaurants are located within walking distance; a grocery store is three miles away. Pets and children are allowed.

Reservations, fees: Reservations are recommended. Sites are $33–48 per night for two people, plus $3 for each additional person. Credit cards are accepted. Long-term stays are okay.

Directions: From I-75 at Exit 329, drive 300 yards east on State Road 44.

Contact: Wildwood KOA, 882 East State Road 44, Wildwood, FL 34785, 352/748-2774 or 800/562-3272 (reservations only), fax 352/748-6832, www.floridawildwoodkoa.com.

18 LAKE DEATON RV PARK

Scenic rating: 3

at Lake Deaton east of Wildwood
See map page 228

At this wooded adult park, some campers fish in 1.5-mile-wide Lake Deaton or head for three major golf courses nearby. Others like to bicycle down the back roads to Wildwood. If you don't have any fishing luck at Lake Deaton, try a more noted bass-fishing spot—Lake Okahumpka—on the other side of State Road 44. This campground is favored by snowbirds looking for a quiet, out-of-the-way RV park, somewhat isolated from The Villages, a huge retirement community that is being built nearby. Just 10 percent of the park is occupied by year-round residents.

RV sites, facilities: This retiree-oriented park offers 81 full-hookup RV sites (two pull-through). Lots are 20 by 45 feet and vary from grassy to paved surfaces. On the premises are restrooms, showers, a dump station, a boat ramp, a dock, a clubhouse, horseshoes, and laundry facilities. Ask about wireless Internet access. Restrooms and the clubhouse have wheelchair-accessible ramps. Groceries and restaurants are within six miles. Children are permitted only for two weeks. Two small pets are allowed.

Reservations, fees: Reservations are recommended. Sites are $21 per night for two people, plus $2 for each additional person. Credit cards are not accepted. Long-term stays are okay.

Directions: From I-75 at Exit 329, drive eight miles east on State Road 44. Turn left onto State Road 44A and then make an immediate right turn onto County Road 146 and proceed about two miles to the park.

Contact: Lake Deaton RV Park, 4855 County Road 146, Wildwood, FL 34785, 352/748-2397.

19 HOLIDAY TRAVEL RESORT

Scenic rating: 9

in Leesburg

See map page 228

Indoor pools are rare at Florida camping parks, but here adult swimmers can float on their backs and gaze up at a blue sky through a row of skylights in a modern, bright-white building, or peer out the broad glass doors to see RVs parked in the distance. Outdoors, another pool is open to kids as well as adults. This 200-plus-acre park is massive: Beyond a security gate, the paved park roads lead to a sprawling resort with 935 sites, of which 185 sites are for short-term campers. The rest are for RVs planning to stay a while. A social director plans activities for not one, but four, recreational buildings. Boaters can access Lake Harris from here.

A retired and semiretired crowd is targeted by management, but kids can take advantage of the miniature golf course and other amenities by camping short-term. Bring your own boat to launch from a campground ramp into a canal leading to the bass-fishing waters of Lake Harris. A nine-hole chip-and-putt golf course has artificial turf. Palms, native pines, and other trees lend shade to portions of the park, but several gravel or grassy RV sites bear the brunt of the sun's forceful rays. Only 16 percent of occupants live here year-round, though the park has committed about 80 percent of its space to long-term seasonal visitors.

RV sites, facilities: There are 185 full-hookup, pull-through sites with 30-amp electrical service for RVs up to 40 feet long. All sites have picnic tables. Another 750 sites are set aside for long-term or seasonal stays, and these have 30/50-amp service. RV storage is available in the off-season. A chip-and-putt golf course, a miniature golf course, two pools, four recreation rooms, a playground, a hot tub, billiards, a softball field, eight horseshoe pits, 14 shuffleboard courts, four lighted tennis courts, two volleyball courts, and winter social programs entertain campers. Showers, restrooms, a marina, a boat ramp, 210 boat slips, a dock, a dump station, groceries, bait and tackle, laundry facilities, propane gas, and a poolside restaurant are available. An Internet connection is available in one of the rec halls. Groceries are within one mile in Leesburg. An activities director organizes live music, the wood shop, ceramics, and T-shirt painting. Church services and a post office are also on-site. The recreation buildings and showers are wheelchair accessible. Children may camp up to two weeks at this otherwise adult-oriented park. Leashed pets must use the designated dog walk.

Reservations, fees: Reservations are recommended. Sites are $32 per night for two people, plus $3 per extra person and $2 for cable TV. Credit cards are accepted. Long-term rates are available.

Directions: From Leesburg, drive south on U.S. 27 for three miles. Turn west at County Road 33 and proceed one mile to the park.

Contact: Holiday Travel Resort, 28229 County Road 33, Leesburg, FL 34748, 352/787-5151 or 800/428-5334, fax 352/787-1052, www .holidaytravelresort.com.

20 RIDGECREST RV RESORT

Scenic rating: 6

south of Leesburg

See map page 228

Half of 30-acre Ridgecrest RV Park is devoted to retirees in mobile homes, and the other half is set up for RV campers aged 55 and up. The result is a residential feel at this park, located about two miles from the bass-fishing waters of Lake Harris. Some campsites are grassy, and others have concrete pads. A January antiques fair and a March art festival entertain folks in the city of Leesburg, but some overnighters may be more interested in Disney World, which is 36 miles away. Most visitors are repeat campers who come back year after year.

RV sites, facilities: There are 155 full-hookup RV sites (10 pull-through), of which 145 have 50-amp electrical service. Some sites have picnic tables. Lots average around 25 by 40 feet, with a mix of grassy and concrete slab surfaces. A heated pool, a hot tub, a recreation hall, shuffleboard, a library, a camp circle for gatherings, winter social programs, a game room, and an exercise room entertain campers. Showers, restrooms, a dump station, rental park models, telephone hookups, propane, and laundry facilities are available. You'll find groceries one mile away and a restaurant within five miles. A golf course is next door. Children are allowed, but not encouraged. Pets under 20 pounds are permitted.

Reservations, fees: Reservations are recommended. Sites are $25 per night for two people, plus $2 for each additional person. Credit cards are not accepted. Long-term stays are okay.

Directions: From Leesburg, travel five miles south on U.S. 27 to the park entrance.

Contact: Ridgecrest RV Resort, 26125 U.S. 27 South, Leesburg, FL 34748, 352/787-1504.

21 TRIMBLE PARK

Scenic rating: 6

by Lake Beauclaire near Mount Dora

See map page 228

Set beside serene Beauclaire and Carlton Lakes, this 71-acre, county-run park is well removed from the hustle and bustle of Orlando and technically is in the town of Tangerine (despite the Mount Dora address). It's geared toward locals, but vacationers passing through are welcome to set up camp at the grassy sites, which are shaded by oak trees. Bird-watching and picnicking are popular pursuits, and fishing is possible from lakeside docks. A short nature trail provides about 15 minutes of diversion for hikers, threading through a forest studded with moss-covered oaks. Birds you may see include bald eagles, osprey, woodpeckers and hawks.

RV sites, facilities: All 15 sites have 30-amp electricity, picnic tables, grills, and fire rings. Two sites are drive-through. Trees and plants separate the sites from each other. Big rigs are welcome. There are no sewer hookups. On the premises are restrooms, showers, a dump station, a boat ramp, and a playground. The bathhouses are wheelchair accessible. Groceries, restaurants, and laundry facilities are a three-mile drive away in Mount Dora. Children are welcome. Pets and alcohol are prohibited.

Reservations, fees: Reservations are recommended. Telephone reservations are not accepted; you must make them in person at the park. Sites are $8–18 per night. Credit cards are not accepted. Stays are limited to 14 days.

Directions: From Apopka, head north on U.S. 441 about seven miles. Turn left onto Earl Wood Road, which will turn into Trimble Park Road. The campground is two miles ahead.

Contact: Trimble Park, 5802 Trimble Park Road, Mount Dora, FL 32757, 352/383-1993, http://parks.orangecountyfl.net.

22 LAKE HARRIS RESORT

Scenic rating: 7

near Lake Harris south of Tavares

See map page 228   BEST (

This park (formerly Fisherman's Cove RV Resort) bills itself as a luxury golf, marina, and RV resort community. About half the campsites back onto a par-3, nine-hole golf course that overlooks tree-lined Lake Harris. The lake provides a pretty backdrop for golfers and fertile fishing grounds for anglers seeking bass and catfish. The blue waters are reachable by boat via a canal from the campground boat ramp. Other amenities include a 120-slip marina and dry storage for 160 boats, a six-unit hotel, villa rentals, park models, and a post office. About 10 percent of the park is occupied by full-time residents. Most visitors are over 55, though in the summertime, you may find some children staying here.

Expect plenty of sunshine, although there are a few palm and oak trees to frame the view of the lake. Some of the pricier sites overlook the golf course and Lake Harris. West of the golf course are the heated pool and recreation hall, where volunteers organize potluck dinners, worship services, coffee klatches, and other entertainment. Nearby is historic Mount Dora, home to antiques shops and good restaurants. Disney World is about 45 miles away.

RV sites, facilities: All 330 full-hookup sites are for RVs up to 40 feet long. Forty-five sites have 50-amp service. Some sites are grassy; others have concrete pads. Recreation options include a nine-hole, par-3 golf course, a pool, horseshoes, shuffleboard, two activity lodges, and organized events. Showers, restrooms, a boat ramp, a 120-slip marina, park-model rentals, a small motel, a dump station, propane gas, and laundry facilities are available. Internet access is available in the library/mail-room building near the pool. Most of the park is accessible to wheelchairs, and streets are paved. Children under age 16 must be adult-supervised at the pool. Leashed, attended pets are permitted.

Reservations, fees: Reservations are recommended. Sites are $29–40 per night for two people, plus $10 per extra person. Credit cards are accepted. Long-term rates are available.

Directions: From Tavares, drive 2.5 miles south on State Road 19/Duncan Drive to the campground entrance on your right.

Contact: Lake Harris Resort, 29115 Eichelberger Road, Tavares, FL 32778, 352/343-1233 or 800/254-9993, www.lakeharrisresort.com.

23 HOLIDAY MOBILE PARK

Scenic rating: 2

at Lake Eustis in Tavares

See map page 228

Campers are outnumbered by residents living at the 40 RV spaces and 159 mobile homes, leaving a handful of sunny, gravel lots for short-term stays. At least in winter, boat slips are hard to come by at the marina. Nearly the entire park is filled with full-timers or repeat visitors who have been coming here for two decades.

RV sites, facilities: This age-55-and-up park has full-hookup sites with 30-amp electrical service for RVs up to 35 feet long; three are drive-through. A pool, a clubhouse, shuffleboard, a lakeside picnic area, and a jam-packed activity schedule entertain campers. Showers, restrooms, a marina, a dump station, and laundry facilities are available. Shopping and restaurants are within walking distance, though many visitors ride their bikes. Children are allowed to visit. Pets are prohibited.

Reservations, fees: Reservations are recommended. Sites are $20 per night for two people. Credit cards are not accepted. Long-term rates are available.

Directions: From the intersection of State Road 19/Duncan Drive and U.S. 441/Burleigh Bou-

levard in Tavares, continue northeast on U.S. 441 for about one mile to the RV park.
Contact: Holiday Mobile Park, 561 East Burleigh Boulevard, Tavares, FL 32778, 352/343-2300.

24 PALM GARDENS

Scenic rating: 4

at the Dead River north of Tavares
See map page 228

Boating is the name of the game at this tree-dotted over-55 mobile-home community on the Dead River, linking you to a chain of lakes. If you don't bring your own watercraft, rent one here ($50 and up for a half day for a 14-footer, or $100 for a half day on a 21-foot pontoon boat). Tour the Dead River, which river flows for about two miles before joining seven-mile-long Lake Eustis, then the bigger fishing waters of Lake Harris. Indeed, boaters and anglers who stay at these paved RV spots can explore thousands of acres of waters hereabouts, including Little Lake Harris and the Dora Canal, which leads to Lake Dora. Mount Dora's antiques shops, boutiques, and many restaurants are close by. Disney World is about 45 miles away. About 20 percent of the park is occupied year-round, and about 100 lots are taken by mobile homes.

RV sites, facilities: The park offers 15 pull-through RV sites with full hookups and 30-amp electrical service. Lots vary in size, but some can accommodate RVs up to 40 feet long. A camp circle for gatherings, showers, a dump station, restrooms, 14 rental cottages, bait, tackle, laundry facilities, snacks, a boat dock, boat rentals, a restaurant, and a lounge are available. The recreation room is available only to mobile-home owners, not RV visitors. Children are welcome. Leashed pets are permitted in the camping area but not the rental cottages.

Reservations, fees: Reservations are advised. Sites are $15 per night for two people, plus $5 for each additional person. Credit cards are accepted. Long-term rates are available.

Directions: From Tavares, drive one mile north on U.S. 441 to the park entrance on the right.
Contact: Palm Gardens, 11801 U.S. 441, Tavares, FL 32778, 352/343-2024, fax 352/342-5516, www.palmgardensmarina.com.

25 WOODS-N-WATER TRAILS RV COMMUNITY

Scenic rating: 4

on Lake Saunders west of Mount Dora
See map page 228

A gazebo sits at a point stretching into tree-lined Lake Saunders, where boaters from the 17-acre adult park can tool around. From another nearby point, picnickers can look onto the calm one-square-mile lake. Campers tend to spend months at this country-atmosphere community, so it may be difficult to get a reservation if you wait to call between November 1 and March 15. About half the park is occupied year-round. Although Disney World and other Orlando-area attractions are about one hour to the south, Floridians familiar with this region and the February Mount Dora Art Festival think two words whenever Mount Dora is mentioned: "antiques" and "art."

RV sites, facilities: This adults-only park has 136 grassy, full-hookup RV sites with concrete patios and driveways. Both 30-amp and 50-amp sites are offered. RVs up to 40 feet long and slide-outs can be accommodated at the roomy 40- by 60-foot lots. For recreation, there's a pool, horseshoes, shuffleboard and boccie ball (lawn bowling) courts, volleyball, a nature walk, a boat ramp, and an activities hall with volunteer-organized activities such as line dancing, dinners, quilting, and craft making for charities. Once a month, all the men cook breakfast for everyone. Showers, restrooms, a dump station, and laundry facilities are available. The clubhouse and restrooms are wheelchair accessible. Children are permitted with overnight campers or those staying less than two weeks. Kids should be supervised at all times. Leashed pets are permitted at designated campsites at the park's northern end and must use the bordering dog walk.

Reservations, fees: Reservations are required. Sites are $25 per night. Credit cards are not accepted. Long-term rates are available.

Directions: From Eustis, exit on U.S. 441 south to State Road 19A. At Bay Road, turn right and drive 0.25 mile to the park.

Contact: Woods-n-Water Trails RV Community, 1325 North Bay Road, Mount Dora, FL 32757, 352/735-1009, www.woods-n-water-trails.com.

26 HAINES CREEK RV VILLAGE

Scenic rating: 5

on Haines Creek east of Leesburg

See map page 228

A campground gazebo and boardwalk overlook Haines Creek, and boaters can tie up at a 650-foot dock. On the banks, anglers try to snag bream and other fish—as do a few long-legged wading birds at creekside. Paved, lighted streets curve past gravel and grassy campsites, a few sporting RVs with attached screen patios. Although you technically could take day trips to Disney World or other Orlando-area attractions farther south, that isn't the focus of this relaxed lake region where the action revolves around boating, fishing, and, to a lesser extent, canoeing. Tree-lined Haines Creek leads west to Lake Griffin and east to Lake Eustis, and anglers can take advantage of the camp's private docks and boat ramp to get to bass country. About half the park is occupied long-term. Guests run the clubhouse, and they have decided on "lights off" at 9 P.M.

RV sites, facilities: RVers can choose from 40 of 86 full-hookup sites (1 is pull-through). The rest of the lots have park models on them. Each RV site is spacious enough to park an extra car or boat and has a picnic table. Almost all spots have 50-amp service. The facility includes a boat ramp, private docks, horseshoes, and a recreation hall. Showers, restrooms, a dump station, and laundry facilities are available. The restrooms, recreation hall, and laundry room are accessible to wheelchairs. Groceries and bait can be purchased across the street. Restaurants are three miles away. Most areas of the park are wheelchair accessible. Roads are paved. Children and guests are welcome for up to one month. Leashed pets are permitted.

Reservations, fees: Reservations are recommended. Sites are $22–25 per night for two people, plus $1 for each additional person and $1 for pets. Credit cards are not accepted. Senior citizens are welcome to stay long-term.

Directions: From U.S. 27 in Leesburg, drive south on U.S. 441 about four miles. At the traffic signal, turn left onto County Road 44. Drive five miles and turn left into the campground before you reach the Haines Creek bridge.

Contact: Haines Creek RV Village, 10121 County Road 44 East, Leesburg, FL 34788, 352/728-5939, fax 352/728-5798.

27 SOUTHERN PALMS RV RESORT

Scenic rating: 7

in northern Eustis

See map page 228

In summer, families stake out the grassy campsites and two swimming pools at this 100-plus-acre park, part of the Manufactured Homes Communities Inc. chain. In winter, retired Northerners predominate, attracted by bingo, pancake breakfasts, and other entertainment. Lighted, paved streets lead past the quite-sunny RV sites where mowed lawns and, in some cases, trailer skirts lend a residential touch. A handful of camping spots are near a pond where visitors catch minnows to use for bait at bass lakes found 10 minutes away in Tavares. (In fact, there are some 1,400 named lakes in Lake County.) Disney World and other Orlando-area attractions are about one hour south. Bring an umbrella or hat. Although pines and palms are scattered around the park, they provide relatively little shade. The park also has 320 park model homes.

RV sites, facilities: All 950 full-hookup sites have 30-amp or 50-amp electrical services. RVs up to 42 feet long can be accommodated. Sites are level and grassy, ranging in size from 20 by 40 feet to 40 by 60 feet. Three clubhouses, two pools, two hot tubs, shuffleboard, horseshoes, boccie ball (lawn bowling), and winter social programs entertain campers. An activities director organizes shows, painting classes, choirs, and many other things to do. Showers, restrooms, a dump station, cable TV, telephone hookups, exercise rooms, and three laundry facilities are available. Within one mile are groceries, bait, and restaurants. Most areas are wheelchair accessible. Children are welcome. Leashed pets are permitted.

Reservations, fees: Reservations are recommended. Sites are $31 per night for two people, plus $2 for each additional person. Credit cards are accepted. Long-term stays are the norm.

Directions: From State Road 44/Orange Avenue in Eustis, turn north on State Road 19/Grove Street. In about 0.5 mile, veer left onto County Road 44 and follow it nearly 0.5 mile. The park is on the right before the intersection with County Road 452.

Contact: Southern Palms RV Resort, 1 Avocado Lane, Eustis, FL 32726, 352/357-8882 or 800/277-9131, fax 352/357-2155, www .southernpalmsrv.com.

activities are boating, fishing, and shopping at local flea markets. To the south, Eustis hosts a folk festival in December, a jazz festival in March, and April's Lake County Fair. Disney World and other Orlando-area attractions are about one hour's drive to the south.

RV sites, facilities: This age-55-plus park offers 50 full-hookup RV sites (20 pull-through). Each site has a picnic table. Half the roomy sites (40 by 60 feet) have 50-amp electrical service; the rest have 30-amp. About half the park is taken up with park models and full-timers. A pool, a hot tub, a recreation hall, and winter social programs entertain campers. Showers, restrooms, a dock, a boat ramp, a dump station, firewood, and laundry facilities are available. Management says all areas are wheelchair accessible. Streets are paved. Groceries, bait, and a restaurant are located within 1.5 miles. Children are allowed to visit. Pets are prohibited.

Reservations, fees: Reservations are recommended. Sites are $20 per night for two people, plus $5 for each additional person. Credit cards are not accepted. Long-term rates are available.

Directions: From the intersection of State Road 44/Lakewood Avenue and State Road 19 in Eustis, drive about 2.5 miles north on State Road 19 to the park entrance. The campground is halfway between Eustis and Umatilla.

Contact: Lakeside RV Park, 38000 State Road 19, Umatilla, FL 32784, 352/669-4418, fax 352/669-5113, email: bonniemccain4@ cs.com.

28 LAKESIDE RV PARK

Scenic rating: 6

on Lake Smith south of Umatilla

See map page 228

Although Lake Smith isn't large enough to be named on a state map, the bass anglers who set up camp here (mainly retirees) don't seem to mind. About 60 percent of the sites in this park are occupied year-round. Visitors hail from Florida and the Northeast, and their favorite

29 OLDE MILL STREAM RV RESORT

Scenic rating: 7

on Lake Pearl in Umatilla

See map page 228

This spotlessly clean and manicured campground is set on 127 acres on Lake Pearl, and the owners say the park is "Florida's best-kept secret." A curving, heated pool overlooks the blue waters of the 100-acre lake, where boaters search for bass. The sizable sunny sites (40 by 60 feet) are big enough so that if you have two or three slide-outs, you won't feel stuck on top of your neighbor. Around 80 percent of the visitors here are staying for six months, so you'll have plenty of time to get to know one another.

RV sites, facilities: This adults-only park offers 303 large RV sites with sewer hookups, 50-amp electrical service, large concrete patios, and telephone access. Each site has a picnic table. Six sites are drive-through. For entertainment, there's a pool, a driving range, miniature golf, a barbecue picnic area, horseshoes, shuffleboard, wintertime social activities, and a wheelchair-accessible, 800-square-foot recreation hall. Showers, restrooms, three dump stations, and laundry facilities are available. Groceries and a restaurant are across the street. You must be at least 25 years old to camp, but children may visit guests. Pets must be leashed and walked in the mowed field.

Reservations, fees: Reservations are recommended. Sites are $29 per night for two people, plus $3 for each additional person. Credit cards are accepted. Long-term rates are available. The maximum length of stay is eight months.

Directions: From Orlando, drive northwest on U.S. 441 to State Road 19. Turn right, heading toward Umatilla. Continue about 10 miles to the park entrance on the right, south of State Road 42.

Contact: Olde Mill Stream RV Resort, 1000 North Central Avenue, Umatilla, FL 32784, 352/669-3141 or 800/449-3141, www.oldemillstreamrv.com.

30 KELLY PARK

Scenic rating: 7

at Rock Springs in Apopka

See map page 228   BEST (

Each minute, more than 26,000 gallons of cool, crystal-clear water pour out of a cave to form Rock Springs, which is the main attraction of this 245-acre county park. Swimming, tubing, and snorkeling in the cool, natural spring waters are favored activities. You can rent an inner tube just outside the park for $5 per day, and float nearly a mile downstream. Fishing is not allowed. The picnic pavilions and two miles of hiking trails also are popular. The camping sites—concrete pad and shell rock—are set in a shady forest.

RV sites, facilities: This county-run park has 21 RV sites (1 pull-through) with 30-amp electricity and water hookups. There are no sewer hookups. Each shaded site has a picnic table, a fire ring, and a grill. Campsites are mostly shell rock with concrete pads; they vary in length from 35 to 70 feet, accommodating the largest RVs on the road. On the premises are showers, restrooms, a dump station, a playground, a nature trail, volleyball, and snacks. Festivals, environmental displays, and other community activities are held throughout the year. The restrooms, boardwalks, pavilions, and ramp to the swimming area are wheelchair accessible. Groceries, restaurants, and laundry facilities are within five miles. Children are allowed. Pets and alcoholic beverages are prohibited.

Reservations, fees: Reservations are recommended, but you must make them in person. Sites are $15 per night for up to four people, plus $3 for electricity. The maximum stay is 14 consecutive days.

Directions: From Orlando, take U.S. 441 northwest into Apopka. Turn right (north) on Park Avenue (Rock Springs Road). Proceed six miles to the end, then bear right onto Kelly Park Road. The park is at the end of the road.

Contact: Kelly Park, 400 East Kelly Park Road, Apopka, FL 32712, 407/889-4179, fax 407/889-3523, www.orangecountyparks.net.

31 TWELVE OAKS RV RESORT

Scenic rating: 5

off I-4 west of Sanford

See map page 228

The crooked branches of oaks and bristly pines help shade some of the campsites at this nearly

30-acre park that's a quick hop off I-4 but primarily caters to longer-term RVers. Other campsites are sunny. Despite the heated swimming pool and the shuffleboard court, some visitors are more interested in other things: shopping malls nearby and Disney World, which you'll find about 30 miles south of here. The park has a few sites available for overnighters or new snowbirds staying for the season. About half the park is occupied by RVers living here year-round, including retirees, snowbirds, and local workers.

RV sites, facilities: Among these 247 full-hookup, concrete-pad RV sites (about 35 pull-through), 20 are available for overnighters and 45 are for seasonal stays. Sites have full hookups and 30/50-amp electricity. RVs as large as 42 feet can be accommodated. A pool, two recreation halls with planned activities, shuffleboard, horseshoes, a playground, long-term storage, social programs, a dog walk, and a picnic shelter are available. Showers, restrooms, two dump stations, a small store that sells minimal camping supplies, and two laundry facilities are on the premises. Grocery stores are within 0.5 mile. Internet access is available in the office. The recreation halls, laundry buildings, office, and restrooms are wheelchair accessible. Children are allowed. Leashed pets under 20 pounds are permitted.

Reservations, fees: Reservations are recommended. Sites are $28 per night for two people, plus $2 for each additional person. Credit cards are accepted. Long-term stays are okay.

Directions: From Orlando, take I-4 north to State Road 46 (Exit 101BC). Drive two miles west to the park.

Contact: Twelve Oaks RV Resort, 6300 State Road 46 West, Sanford, FL 32771, 407/323-0880 or 800/633-9529, fax 407/323-0899.

32 TOWN AND COUNTRY RV RESORT

Scenic rating: 4

off I-4 west of Sanford

See map page 228

Mainly snowbird retirees and motor-home club members pull into this 30-acre community's paved roads to arrive at grassy campsites and concrete patios shaded by oak, palm, and pine trees. Although anglers can head three miles to the St. Johns River or two miles to Lake Monroe, some campers prefer to stay right here on two-lane Orange Boulevard and spend some time socializing. In winter, campers break bread together at numerous organized dinners and take trips to craft shows and flea markets. About half the park is occupied year-round. Nearby are several miles of hiking and canoe trails at Wekiwa Springs State Park. The Sanford Historic District is about 5 miles east, and Disney World is about 30 miles south.

RV sites, facilities: All 300 grassy RV sites have full hookups, 30/50-amp electrical service, concrete pads, and picnic tables. Six sites are pull-through with water and electricity only. Lots average 25 by 40 feet, accommodating rigs up to 45 feet long. Bingo, a swimming pool, a pool table, a recreation room, shuffleboard, horseshoes, and winter activities entertain campers. Showers, restrooms, a dump station, propane gas, and laundry facilities are on the premises. Management says all areas are wheelchair accessible, with ramps at each building. A mall, restaurants, and bait are available two miles away, and groceries are within one mile. Children are allowed for overnight stays or short vacations but not long-term. Leashed pets are permitted.

Reservations, fees: Reservations are required in winter. Sites are $30 per night for two people, plus $2 for each additional person. Credit cards are accepted. Long-term rates are available.

Directions: From Orlando, take I-4 north to State Road 46 (Exit 101C). Go west about one mile to Orange Boulevard, then turn right. The park is about one mile ahead on the right.

Contact: Town and Country RV Resort, 5355 Orange Boulevard, Lake Monroe, FL 32747, 407/323-5540, fax 407/321-4495, www.town-andcountryrvresort.com.

33 WEKIVA FALLS RESORT

Scenic rating: 6

on the Wekiva River east of Sorrento

See map page 228

Swimmers plunge into the springs where prehistoric sharks and elephant-like mastodons standing nine feet tall lived thousands of years ago. It's the kind of place where your children can let their imaginations run wild: Cave divers have uncovered shark teeth dating back at least 10 million years from the caverns beneath the swimming-beach area. And a mastodon jawbone with teeth was found here quite accidentally during a cleanup of the spring boil (the spot where the most water surges out of the ground).

RV sites, facilities: All 786 RV sites offer full hookups and electricity. A fishing pier, sightseeing cruises, rental canoes, and hiking trails entertain campers. On the premises are showers, restrooms, a marina, more than 200 picnic tables, a dump station, limited groceries, and laundry facilities. Children are welcome. Pets are prohibited.

Reservations, fees: Reservations are recommended. Sites are $18 per night for two people, plus $9 for each additional person older than 12 or $6 for campers aged two to 11. Electricity costs $2 extra. Credit cards are not accepted. Long-term rates are available.

Directions: From I-4 at Exit 101C, drive about six miles west on State Road 46 to Wekiva River Road. Turn left there and go 1.25 miles south to the campground entrance.

Contact: Wekiva Falls Resort, 30700 Wekiva River Road, Sorrento, FL 32776, 407/830-9828 or 352/383-8055.

34 WEKIWA SPRINGS STATE PARK

Scenic rating: 10

at Wekiwa Springs north of Apopka

See map page 228   **BEST (**

This is one of the most popular and well used of Florida's state parks, and for good reason. Wekiwa Springs pumps about 42 million gallons of cool, clear water daily to the delight of swimmers, snorkelers, and paddlers. Its run to the Wekiva River and ultimately the St. Johns River is a wonderful route to canoe or kayak in a bit of natural Florida that is being rapidly surrounded by the creep of suburbia. Tall oaks lend shade to campsites, which give visitors a good base for seeing natural Florida. Some campers hike on the 13.5-mile Sand Lake Trail or the shadier 5.3-mile Volksmarch Trail. Bicyclists are limited to paved roads within the 10-square-mile park and some of the hiking trails. The equestrian crowd can set out on eight miles of trails set largely along backcountry roads, and stop to water horses at Camp Big Fork (where horse camping is allowed for a fee). The horse trails are divided into two loops and are used by hikers and park staff. Keep your eye out for black bears because this park not far south of Ocala National Forest is one of the bruins' southernmost outposts in the region; periodically, the shy, nocturnal mammals turn up in the backyards of suburbanites whose homes are quickly clogging this once-peaceful swath of the Sunshine State.

RV sites, facilities: Sixty shell-pad sites with 30-amp electricity and water are offered. Each site has a picnic table, a grill, and a fire ring. Like most state parks, these sites vary in size to fit into the natural environment. These range from 25 by 55 feet to 30 by 60 feet. On the premises are restrooms, showers, a dump station, snacks, and canoe and kayak rentals. The rentals are handled by a concessionaire (407/880-4110 or 407/884-4311); two-hour fees range from $12 for canoes to $15 for a kayak, and shuttle service is available. Horseshoes, a playground, and a volleyball court are in a picnic area. Management says all park buildings and two sites (Numbers 30 and 60) are accessible to wheelchairs. Groceries, restaurants, and laundry facilities are within four miles of the park. Two golf courses are within one mile. Children are welcome. Leashed pets with proof of rabies vaccination are permitted. Firearms and alcohol are prohibited.

Reservations, fees: Reservations are recommended; contact ReserveAmerica at 800/336-3521 or reserveamerica.com. Sites are $20 per night for eight people. Pet fee is $2 daily. Credit cards are accepted. Maximum stay is 14 days.

Directions: From Orlando, take I-4 northeast to Exit 94. Head west on State Road 434 for about one mile to Wekiwa Springs Road. Turn right and continue 5.5 miles to the campground.

Contact: Wekiwa Springs State Park, 1800 Wekiwa Circle, Apopka, FL 32712, 407/884-2008, fax 407/884-2014, www.floridastateparks.org.

35 HOLIDAY SPRINGS RV RESORT

Scenic rating: 2

southwest of Brooksville

See map page 228

This clean park has an eight-acre lake for fishing and boating and an unusual 100-by-200-foot spring-fed natural swimming pool whose temperature stays at 75°F year-round. A short nature trail leads from the lake to the spring. Management works extra hard at security, parking patrol cars with dummies near the entrance and keeping doors to common areas locked at times. The park, "a semiretirement community," caters to the 55-plus age group, and about 35 percent of the sites are occupied year-round. In winter, you'll find the traditional planned activities, such as bingo, cards, and so forth.

RV sites, facilities: There are 30 RV sites in this 235-unit mobile-home community that accommodates rigs up to 40 feet long. Sewer hookups,

30-amp and 50-amp electrical service, cable TV and telephone access, picnic tables, laundry facilities, a dump station, recreation rooms, a 40- by 80-foot dance hall, shuffleboard courts, a boat dock, and rental trailers are available. Roads are paved, and sites have cement slabs. Twelve sites are drive-through. The park may allow families with small children for overnight stays but primarily is interested in people age 55 and over driving newer RVs. One small pet is permitted per site.

Reservations, fees: Reservations are not necessary. Sites are $35 per night for two people, plus $2 for each additional person. Credit cards are not accepted. Long-term rates are available.

Directions: From the junction of U.S. 19 and State Road 50, drive seven miles south on U.S. 19. The park is on the northwest side of the intersection of U.S. 19 and County Road 578/County Line Road.

Contact: Holiday Springs RV Resort, 138 Travel Park Drive, Spring Hill, FL 34607, 352/683-0034, www.holidayspringsrvresort.com.

36 MARY'S FISH CAMP

Scenic rating: 3

on the Mud River west of Weeki Wachee

See map page 228

You'll find this quiet, secluded park tucked into an almost junglelike thicket of trees on the Mud River, a tidal watercourse that joins the scenic Weeki Wachee River 2.5 miles away. It's ideal for canoeists, anglers, and boaters (the river has gulf access); a few brave sailors have even been known to come up the river when the water was high. A boat ramp is nearby at Bayport. You can also fish from the campground docks. Mullet is a particular delicacy, and there is a lot of pride and discussion on how to cook it properly. To keep a "nice, quiet, family atmosphere," management does not permit alcohol or use of foul language in the park. About half the sites are occupied year-round. Some visitors (mostly from Michigan) have been coming here every winter for 15 years or more. Activities are not formally organized; rather, the occasional cookout or potluck dinner breaks up the fishing.

RV sites, facilities: There are 26 sites with full hookups and 30-amp electrical service. Restrooms, showers, picnic tables, three rental cabins, and boat docks on the Mud River are available. The restroom is wheelchair accessible. Absolutely no alcohol or profanity are allowed. Restaurants and shopping are within four miles. Children are welcome but not pets.

Reservations, fees: Reservations are recommended. Nightly fee for two people is $18. Add $1.50–2.50 for each additional person. Credit cards are not accepted.

Directions: From U.S. 19 and State Road 50 in Weeki Wachee, drive four miles west on Cortez Boulevard (Highway 550). Look for the park sign at Mary's Fish Camp Road and drive 0.25 mile south.

Contact: Mary's Fish Camp, 8092 Mary's Fish Camp Road, Weeki Wachee, FL 34607, 352/596-2359, fax 352/596-5562.

37 CHIEF ARIPEKA TRAVEL PARK

Scenic rating: 2

west of Spring Hill
See map page 228

Close to shopping and restaurants, the RV park is nonetheless secluded and far from noise and traffic. Oversized lots of crushed white rock accommodate big rigs. There's not much to do in the park, but within a couple of miles are the deep-sea fishing charters and marinas of Hernando Beach. The community of Aripeka is a fishing village today, but in the 1920s it was quite the fashionable vacation resort.

RV sites, facilities: All 28 RV sites have sewer hookups. Ten sites have 50-amp service; the rest have 30-amp. Restrooms, showers, and a dump station are provided. A wheelchair-accessible ramp leads to the bathhouse. The park is oriented toward retirees and snowbirds. Children may visit adult campers. Pets are permitted.

Reservations, fees: Reservations are recommended. Sites are $23 per night for two people, plus $1 for each additional person. Fifty-amp electrical service costs $2 per night extra. Credit cards are not accepted. Long-term stays are permitted.

Directions: From U.S. 19 and County Road 595 in Spring Hill, drive west on County Road 595 for two miles. The park is on the south side of the road.

Contact: Chief Aripeka Travel Park, 1582 Osowaw Boulevard, Spring Hill, FL 34607, 352/686-3329.

38 CAMPER'S HOLIDAY TRAVEL PARK

Scenic rating: 6

southeast of Brooksville
See map page 228

This countryside park with a 13-acre fishing lake offers large sites set in a gridlike fashion. The RV section adjoins the park's 300 retirement-camper condominium lots, and campers may use all of the common areas. Don't feed or approach the alligators you may see on Sparkman Lake. Note that boat motors are limited to three horsepower. A convenience store is next door to the park, and a gatehouse keeps out curiosity seekers. It's too remote from the interstate for overnight campers who don't plan ahead, and reservations are absolutely required for winter stays. About 75 percent of the visitors stay 3–6 months; no year-round residents are located in the RV section. Popular activities are quilting, card games, bingo, shuffleboard, and horseshoes.

RV sites, facilities: All 67 RV sites have full hookups and cable TV and telephone access. They are black-topped with grassy sides. Twelve sites have 50-amp service; the rest have 30-amp. RVs as long as 45 feet are welcome. Restrooms, showers, picnic tables, laundry facilities, a dump station, a pool, a recreation room, shuffleboard courts, and a playground are on the premises. Roads are paved. Most common areas are wheelchair accessible. Shopping and restaurants are within 15 miles. Children are allowed. One leashed pet is permitted per site.

Reservations, fees: Reservations are recommended. Sites are $28 per night for two people, plus $2 for each additional person. Add $2 for using 50-amp electricity. Credit cards are not accepted. Campers must be vacationers or retired snowbirds.

Directions: If driving south on I-75, take Exit 301 and drive west on State Road 50 into Brooksville. At the intersection with Emerson Road/County Road 581, turn south for 5.5 miles. Stay on that road all the way to the park; it winds around. Look for the park sign at left. If driving north on I-75, take Exit 285 onto County Road 52 and drive west. Turn north on County Road 581 and drive five miles. The park is just past the intersection with Hayman Road/County Road 576.

Contact: Camper's Holiday Travel Park, 2092 Culbreath Road, Brooksville, FL 34602, 352/796-3707, fax 352/796-6232.

39 TOPICS RV COMMUNITY

Scenic rating: 4

south of Brooksville

See map page 228

Set on a hill in the open countryside, the Topics RV and park-model community has unusually large sites at 40 by 100 feet. Loads of social activities are planned during the winter months, including golf leagues (ending the season with a competition), monthly ladies' and men's luncheons at local restaurants, a mixed bowling league, and a year-end festival with free food and drink. The Blue Tees driving range is across the street, and many golf courses are nearby. About half the sites are occupied by year-round residents, and park models are for sale. The park also is convenient to Weeki Wachee Spring, one of the longest-lived tourist attractions in Florida. In fact, no one can travel across the

state without seeing the billboards for Weeki Wachee's "mermaid" theater, which, since 1947, has featured underwater ballet performed by women wearing fishtail costumes. There's also a bird-of-prey show, a petting zoo, and a wilderness river cruise. If that's not enough, next door is Buccaneer Bay, a water park with flume and tube rides, beaches, and picnic areas. Just to the east of the park is the little Slovakian farming community of Masaryktown, founded in 1925 and named after Garrigue Masaryk, the first president of Czechoslovakia.

RV sites, facilities: The 40-acre, 231-unit, adults-only park has large RV sites with sewer hookups, cable TV, and telephone access. Internet connectivity is available at the campsites. Twenty-one sites have 50-amp electrical service; the rest have 30 amps. Restrooms, showers, laundry facilities, a clubhouse with kitchen facilities, shuffleboard courts, a dump station, and a heated pool are available. All areas are wheelchair accessible. Children are not allowed. Two leashed pets are permitted per site.

Reservations, fees: Reservations are required. Sites are $33 per night for two people, plus $3 for each additional person. Credit cards are accepted. Seasonal visitors are preferred.

Directions: From U.S. 41, drive two miles west on County Road 578/County Line Road. Or, from U.S. 19, drive eight miles east on County Road 578/County Line Road.

Contact: Topics RV Community, 13063 County Line Road, Spring Hill, FL 34609, 352/796-0625, fax 352/796-0282, email: topics@mhchomes.com.

40 GULF COAST RESORT

Scenic rating: 5

east of Hudson

See map page 228

Nudists will find a relaxed, friendly, rustic setting with lots of trees, say the managers of this eight-acre, clothing-optional park. RVs up to 45 feet in length are welcome. About 15 percent of the sites are occupied year-round. Dominoes, bingo, tennis, shuffleboard, and card games are popular in the wintertime. Most visitors are snowbirds here to soak up the rays.

RV sites, facilities: There are 78 grassy RV sites with sewer hookups; 20 sites are pull-through. Thirty-amp electrical service is provided at 60 sites, and 50-amp at 18 sites. Picnic tables, restrooms, showers, laundry facilities, a dump station, a pool, a recreation hall, tennis courts, horseshoes, shuffleboard, *pétanque* (French-style bowling) courts, a camp circle, a small restaurant, and rental trailers are on-site. The restaurant and clubhouse are wheelchair accessible. Children are welcome. Leashed pets are permitted.

Reservations, fees: Reservations are required. Sites are $20–60 per night for two people, plus half the camping fee for each additional person. Credit cards are accepted. Long-term stays are okay.

Directions: From U.S. 19 in Hudson, drive two miles east on County Road 578/County Line Road. At East Road, turn south and continue two miles. Look for the campground's six-foot sign on a fence.

Contact: Gulf Coast Nudist Resort, 13220 Houston Avenue, Hudson, FL 34667, 727/868-1061, www.gulfcoastresort.com.

41 FRONTIER CAMPGROUND

Scenic rating: 3

west of Brooksville

See map page 228

Near the campground office is a small, open-air gathering place called "Liar's Corner," presumably reserved for anglers bragging about their catch of the day. With little screening between the sites, however, neighbors will know the real truth. Populated by snowbirds and permanent residents, this fenced park is close to doctors' offices, auto-repair outfits, and a Wal-Mart. About 40 percent of the sites are occupied year-round, and visitors tend to return year

after year. Motorbikes are allowed in the park only for registered camper transportation to their sites—an important point to remember if the Croom Motorcycle Area campground in the Withlacoochee State Forest is full and you have visitors.

RV sites, facilities: There are 118 full-hookup RV sites in this community of 66 mobile homes. Since most of the campers here are repeat visitors from Canada and the Northeast, space is limited. Half the sites have 50-amp electrical service; the rest have 30-amp. Seventy sites are drive-through. Each spot has a patio and a picnic table. Restrooms, showers, laundry facilities, a dump station, an adult recreation hall, a pool, horseshoe pits, shuffleboard courts, and a playground are provided. Roads are paved. Most of the park is wheelchair accessible. Shopping and groceries are within three miles. Children are welcome. One small dog or cat is permitted on each lot; pets must not be kept outside.

Reservations, fees: Reservations are accepted. Sites are $23 per night for two people, plus $1 for each additional person. No credit cards are accepted. Long-term stays are allowed.

Directions: From Brooksville, drive west on State Road 50 for five miles.

Contact: Frontier Campground, 15549 Cortez Boulevard, Brooksville, FL 34613, 352/796-9988.

42 BRENTWOOD LAKE CAMPING

Scenic rating: 2

north of Brooksville

See map page 228

Secluded from the highway on a wooded hill, the campground is perched on high ground overlooking a private lake stocked with bass, catfish, and bream. Tall oaks provide shade and atmosphere. In the center is a grassy field for outdoor games. Grocery stores, restaurants, and a golf course are within two miles. Children are welcome, although most people staying here are retirees. "Spend a little time or a lifetime," say the owners, Laine and Elaine Brayko. "People of all ages are welcome." During the winter months, activities are planned for each day. Favorites are cards, crafts, Bible study, horseshoes, shuffleboard, potluck dinners, and pancake breakfasts.

RV sites, facilities: There are 64 RV sites with water and 30-amp electricity; 60 have sewer hookups. Eight sites are drive-through. RVs as long as 40 feet can be accommodated. Restrooms, showers, picnic tables, a dump station, laundry facilities, a recreation room, shuffleboard courts, and horseshoe pits are available. The restrooms and recreation hall are wheelchair accessible, as is the office. Children are allowed. Small leashed pets are permitted.

Reservations, fees: Reservations are not necessary. Sites are $17 per night for two people, plus $2 for each additional person. If you use air-conditioning or electric heaters, there is an additional charge of $2 per unit. Credit cards are not accepted. Long-term rates are available.

Directions: From Brooksville, drive north on U.S. 41 for 3.2 miles. Turn west onto Ancient Trail, a gravel road, and go 0.2 mile to the campground.

Contact: Brentwood Lake Camping, 11089 Ancient Trail, Brooksville, FL 34601, 352/796-5760, www.brentwoodlakecamping.com.

43 CLOVER LEAF FOREST RV PARK

Scenic rating: 6

in Brooksville

See map page 228

A sign at the entrance states: "Welcome back, winter residents. We missed you." What are they coming back to? A shaded, wooded setting of slash pines and leafy oak trees and neatly kept campsites with concrete patios. Another unusual feature is the indoor swimming pool, whirlpool tub, and sauna. Believe it or not, it can easily get too cold for outdoor swimming in upper Florida, although, of course, everything's

relative. The RV park is next door to a mobile-home community, and many campers stay for the season or year-round. Only 5 percent of visitors make this their home for less than a month. Favorite activities in the winter season are arts and crafts, carving, bingo, sewing, horseshoes, and swimming.

RV sites, facilities: All 277 RV sites have sewer hookups and 20/30/50-amp electrical outlets. Restrooms, showers, laundry facilities, picnic tables, an indoor and an outdoor pool, a recreation room, shuffleboard, a billiards and card room, horseshoe pits, cable TV access, and telephone service are available. Most areas are wheelchair accessible; in fact, there is a lift in and out of the pool, plus ramps to the club-house, bathhouse, and office. You can access the Internet in the office. Propane can be delivered to your site on a weekly basis. Children may stay up to two weeks as guests of their grandparents. Leashed pets are permitted.

Reservations, fees: Reservations are recommended. Sites are $28–32 per night for two people, plus $1 per extra person. Credit cards are accepted. Long-term rates are available.

Directions: From I-75 at Exit 301, go west 10 miles on State Road 50, which merges into State Road 50A. Turn right (north) onto State Road 41. Look for the park one mile ahead, across the street from an elementary school.

Contact: Clover Leaf Forest RV Park, 910 North Broad Street, Brooksville, FL 34601, 352/796-8016 or 877/796-5381, fax 352/796-5381, email: cnichols@hometownamerica.net.

44 HIDDEN VALLEY CAMPGROUND

Scenic rating: 4

east of Brooksville

See map page 228

Enormous live-oak trees provide a pretty, leafy canopy over this rustic, family-friendly campground, a longtime family operation where the owner raised his children. About 40 percent of the occupants live here year-round. Most of the folks here are snowbirds and retirees. One attraction nearby in Brooksville is Roger's Christmas House Village, a garden complex of five historic houses where various vendors sell gifts. Also in Brooksville, you'll find grocery stores and plenty of fast-food restaurants, mostly on the south side of town along U.S. 41.

RV sites, facilities: All 64 RV sites have full hookups and cable TV access. Eight sites earmarked for long-term visitors have 50-amp electrical service; the rest have 30 amps. Rigs up to 40 feet can be accommodated. Two spots are large enough for 45-foot RVs. Most sites are shaded with picnic tables and concrete pads. Restrooms, showers, picnic tables, laundry facilities, a communal fire pit, a playground, a recreation hall, horseshoe pits, and shuffleboard courts are provided on the property. Groceries are within four miles. Families with children are welcome. Leashed pets are allowed.

Reservations, fees: Reservations are not necessary. Sites are $22 per night for two people, plus $2 for each additional person. A surcharge of $2 per day applies if you use air-conditioning or an electric heater. Credit cards are accepted. Long-term stays are permitted.

Directions: From I-75, take Exit 301 and drive west for approximately seven miles on State Road 50 to the campground entrance. Or, from Brooksville, drive 2.5 miles east on State Road 50.

Contact: Hidden Valley Campground, 22329 Cortez Boulevard, Brooksville, FL 34601, 352/796-8710.

45 LAKESIDE MOBILE MANOR

Scenic rating: 2

in Brooksville

See map page 228

Coffee and doughnuts are served to guests at this RV park on Saturday mornings, but if that's not enough to get you going, cast your line in a four-acre fishing lake and try your luck. Most campers here are snowbirds staying for six months, availing themselves of the popular "6/6" plan, which allows you to leave your RV on-site after you head back north. Popular activities are birding, fishing, bingo, crafts, horseshoes, and dominoes. A wooded area nearby is home to a pair of eagles and a flock of wood storks.

RV sites, facilities: Targeting snowbirds, this 14-acre lakefront mobile-home park has 73 spaces, with 35 available for RVs. Sewer hookups, 30-amp electrical service, cable TV and telephone access, and picnic tables are provided at each site. There are no showers. Campers under age 55 are not welcome. The recreation hall is wheelchair accessible. One leashed pets weighing less than 30 pounds is permitted per site.

Reservations, fees: Reservations are recommended. Sites are $22 per night for two people, plus $3 per extra person. Credit cards are not accepted. Long-term stays are okay; stay for six months and leave the RV for the rest of the year for free.

Directions: From downtown Brooksville, travel one mile north on U.S. 41. The park entrance is at the intersection of the highway and Croom Road.

Contact: Lakeside Mobile Manor, 1020 Lakeside Drive, Brooksville, FL 34601, 352/796-4600.

46 BIG OAKS RV PARK

Scenic rating: 3

south of Brooksville

See map page 228

Set in the countryside, this adult park caters to overnighters as well as snowbirds. It's within one hour's drive of Busch Gardens, Weeki Wachee Spring, Sea World, Disney World, the Gulf of Mexico, and Roger's Christmas House Village. The latter is a fanciful Victorian year-round place where six houses are each decorated with their own Christmas theme. Golf, fishing, bowling, shopping, restaurants, and flea markets are within 10–15 minutes. Sites are large and grassy. They're also shady, except for the two treeless sections of pull-through spaces.

RV sites, facilities: The park has 110 sites with full hookups and concrete pads. Sixty sites are drive-through. Restrooms, showers, laundry facilities, a pool, a clubhouse, shuffleboard courts, horseshoes, and a dump station are on the premises. Rental trailers are available. Children are permitted to visit only. One small leashed pet per site is permitted.

Reservations, fees: Reservations are recommended. Sites are $25 per night for two people, plus $2 for each additional person. Credit cards are not accepted. Long-term stays are okay.

Directions: From Brooksville at State Road 50, drive south on U.S. 41 for eight miles. Or, from I-75, take Exit 285 onto County Road 52 and drive west. Turn north on U.S. 41 and drive five miles.

Contact: Big Oaks RV Park, 16654 U.S. 41, Spring Hill, FL 34610, 352/799-5533, www.bigoakspark.com.

47 TRAVELERS REST RESORT

Scenic rating: 7

off I-75 west of Dade City

See map page 228

Long-legged egrets and blue herons swoop into the three lakes of this wooded resort set in the rolling hills of Florida's citrus and cattle ranching country. But it's no shrinking violet of a place—not with wood carving, a gardening club, a motorcycle club, minisailboat races, a restaurant, a post office, a library, a fire department, and several social programs planned by a full-time activities director. And let's not forget the USGA-rated nine-hole golf course, two tennis courts, a shuffleboard "plaza," and an auditorium that seats 600 people. You'll likely be parked on a hill, where there's room for 60 rigs. The age-55-plus community is near the Pioneer Museum and antique malls.

RV sites, facilities: The mobile-home/RV-park community has 647 sites, of which about 60 spots

with full hookups are for RVs. Only self-contained, hard-sided, factory-made RVs are allowed. All sites have 20/30/50-amp plugs. A heated pool, a spa, a nine-hole golf course, three recreation buildings, two tennis courts, table tennis, shuffleboard, and boccie ball (lawn bowling) are on-site. Cable TV, telephone access, restrooms, showers, laundry facilities, limited supplies, propane, a dump station, and Internet access are available. Groceries and restaurants are within 12 miles. Children are welcome to visit for no more than 30 days. Pets must be leashed.

Reservations, fees: Reservations are recommended. Sites are $27 per night. Credit cards are accepted. Long-term stays are okay for adults.

Directions: From I-75, take Exit 293 and drive 0.24 mile west. Turn south on County Road 577 and continue one mile. At Johnston Road, turn west and go one mile to the park.

Contact: Travelers Rest Resort, 29129 Johnston Road, Dade City, FL 33523, 352/588-2013, fax 352/588-3462, www.travelersrestresort.com.

48 BUTTGENBACH MINE CAMPGROUND

Scenic rating: 7

in the Croom Tract of Withlacoochee State Forest

See map page 228   BEST (

Nearby is the Croom Motorcycle Area, which is nirvana for motorcyclists, dirt bikers, and all-terrain cycle fans. The motorcycle area sets aside 2,600 acres for cyclists to rev their engines and roar around the forest. The result is a kind of dusty moonscape of denuded trails, lonely trees with all the soil eroded around their roots, and a noise level to rival the Grand Prix. Decades ago, the terrain had been damaged already by phosphate mining operations, borrow pits dug to build the interstate highway, and cyclists during a time when their activities were not regulated and they were free to roam. By setting aside this land, the state confines the motorcycles to one area. Bikers from as far north as Canada come to use the "training pit," a crater-sized sandy valley with plenty of bumps for getting airborne. An "inexperienced rider area" is near the campground. There's also a day-use area with picnic tables, water, restrooms, and parking. Bikers must purchase permits in person at the entrance gate; credit cards are not accepted. All cycles must be trailered in; however, you are allowed to ride your vehicle in low gear from the campground to the riding area. No bicycling is allowed. If the campground is full, then try the nearby Silver Lake Recreation Complex or Tall Pines RV Park.

RV sites, facilities: All 50 sites in this state forest campground have 50-amp electricity. RVs up to 40 feet long can be accommodated. Water, restrooms, showers, grills, fire rings, picnic tables, and a dump station are available. The bathhouse is wheelchair accessible. Children are welcome. Pets are prohibited. Alcoholic beverages are not allowed.

Reservations, fees: Reservations are not accepted. Sites are $13 per night for five people. Up to five people, using one RV, are permitted per site. Larger groups need to get a permit. Credit cards are not accepted.

Directions: From I-75, take Exit 301 westbound on State Road 50 and drive 0.1 mile. Turn north onto Western Way; the forest entrance is just ahead. Buttgenbach Mine Campground is four miles north of the entrance. Be sure your gear is tied securely because the dirt road is pitted and bumpy.

Contact: Withlacoochee State Forest Recreation Visitors Center, 15003 Broad Street, Brooksville, FL 34601, 352/754-6896 or fire dispatch 352/754-6777, www.fl-dof.com.

49 SILVER LAKE CAMPGROUND

Scenic rating: 9

in the Croom Tract of Withlacoochee State Forest, Silver Lake Recreation Complex

See map page 228

Silver Lake gets much use from locals and savvy folks during the summer, but it can be nearly deserted weekdays in winter. It's also convenient

to I-75, a fact that campers on the road may not realize. Interstate noise is the only drawback; otherwise, the campground would be nearly perfect. It overlooks Silver Lake, which is really a broad area on the Withlacoochee River; your neighbors in the campground may be canoeists passing through. The woods are thick and shady, and cypress trees with peculiar-looking root knobs erupting from the ground line the bottomlands near the lake. More than 30 miles of hiking trails are in the surrounding forest. The wonderful paved bicycle trail called the Withlacoochee State Trail is just a few minutes away from the campground access road. The trailhead at Ridge Manor is about three miles north. Note that mountain bikes are restricted to forest roads and the approved off-road trails; hiking trails are for foot traffic only. The local health department has banned swimming in the river as a potential health hazard because of bacteria, but the truth is that people do go for dips at will.

RV sites, facilities: Twenty-three campsites have water, 50-amp electricity, grills, fire rings, and picnic tables. Restrooms, showers, a dump station, and a boat ramp are available. RVs up to 44 feet can be accommodated. The bathhouses are wheelchair accessible, but the roads are not paved. Children are welcome. Pets are allowed. Alcohol is prohibited.

Reservations, fees: Reservations are not taken. Sites are $13 per night for five people. Up to five people, using two tents or one RV, are permitted per site. Groups require a permit. Credit cards are not accepted.

Directions: From I-75, take Exit 309 eastbound on State Road 50 for 0.75 mile. Turn north at the traffic light; the highway is marked as Croom Rital Road on the north side and Kettering Road on the south side, but just follow the signs for the Withlacoochee State Trail. Drive 3.5 miles. Just before the interstate overpass, turn east into the Silver Lake complex. This is the first campground on your left.

Contact: Withlacoochee State Forest Recreation Visitors Center, 15003 Broad Street, Brooksville, FL 34601, 352/754-6896 or fire dispatch 352/754-6777, www.fl-dof.com.

50 CYPRESS GLEN CAMPGROUND

Scenic rating: 9

in the Croom Tract of Withlacoochee State Forest, Silver Lake Recreation Complex

See map page 228

Set in a mixed forest of pines and hardwoods, the campground slopes toward Silver Lake, where there's a small beach and a far-off view of the interstate bridge. Sites are generously spaced, and the forest creates lush shade. The hiking trails begin at Silver Lake Campground down the road; bicycles are allowed on forest roads. Just north of the Silver Lake area is a canoe outfitter: Nobleton Boat and Canoe Rental (352/796-7176). Anglers regularly catch all kinds of bass, panfish, and catfish in the river.

RV sites, facilities: The largest of the three campgrounds in this state forest complex, Cypress Glen has 43 sites with piped water and 50-amp electricity. Large RVs (as long as 44 feet) are welcome, but the roads are not paved. Restrooms, showers, picnic tables, grills, and fire rings are provided. The bathhouse is wheelchair accessible. Children and pets are welcome; no alcohol, please.

Reservations, fees: Reservations are not taken. Sites are $13 per night for five people. Up to five people, using one RV, are permitted per site. Groups need a permit. Credit cards are not accepted. This campground is open only on weekends (from noon Friday to noon Monday) and holidays.

Directions: From I-75, take Exit 309 eastbound on State Road 50 for 0.75 mile. Turn north at the traffic light; the highway is marked as Croom Rital Road on the north side and Kettering Road on the south side, but just follow the signs for the Withlacoochee State Trail. Drive 3.5 miles. Just before the interstate overpass, turn east into the Silver Lake complex.

This is the second campground on your left, about 0.8 mile from the turn.

Contact: Withlacoochee State Forest Recreation Visitors Center, 15003 Broad Street, Brooksville, FL 34601, 352/754-6896 or fire dispatch 352/754-6777, www.fl-dof.com.

51 CROOKED RIVER CAMPGROUND

Scenic rating: 9

in the Croom Tract of Withlacoochee State Forest, Silver Lake Recreation Complex

See map page 228

You'll find more level, open sites here than in the other campgrounds in this forest complex, making it a better choice for self-contained RVers. Many sites overlook the Withlacoochee River, which at this point becomes a narrow, winding course with coffee-colored waters. Steps lead down to the river's edge.

RV sites, facilities: All 26 sites have water, picnic tables, grills, and fire rings but no electricity. Restrooms and showers, which are wheelchair accessible, are available. Roads are not paved. Children are welcome, but pets and alcoholic beverages are prohibited.

Reservations, fees: Reservations are not taken. Sites are $10 per night for five people. Up to five people, using two tents or one RV, are permitted per site. Groups need a permit. Credit cards are not accepted.

Directions: From I-75, take Exit 309 eastbound on State Road 50 for 0.75 mile. Turn north at the traffic light; the highway is marked as Croom Rital Road on the north side and Kettering Road on the south side, but just follow the signs for the Withlacoochee State Trail. Drive 3.5 miles. Just before the interstate overpass, turn east into the Silver Lake complex. This is the third campground on your left, about 1.2 miles from the main entrance.

Contact: Withlacoochee State Forest Recreation Visitors Center, 15003 Broad Street, Brooksville, FL 34601, 352/754-6896 or fire dispatch 352/754-6777, www.fl-dof.com.

52 TALL PINES RV PARK

Scenic rating: 3

near Brooksville

See map page 228

This 5.5-acre park is right off I-75 and gets overflow use from the all-terrain- vehicle and motorbike users of the Croom Motorcycle Area in the state forest less than one mile away. Don't be concerned about the motorcyclists; they're more Nickelodeon types than Hell's Angels, with brightly colored racing silks, expensive gear, and miniature motorbikes for their kids. Nearby are all the usual interstate stops: restaurants, fast food, gas stations, and even tourist information; a big grocery store and a shopping center are within walking distance. You can stay as long as you like, as do the 60 percent of year-round residents.

RV sites, facilities: Fifty sites have full hookups and electrical service (18 have 50-amp plugs). A few sites can accommodate large RVs. Restrooms, showers, laundry facilities, a dump station, and a wheelchair-accessible recreation hall are provided. Shopping and groceries are within two blocks. Children are welcome. Leashed pets are permitted.

Reservations, fees: Reservations are not necessary. Sites are $22 per night for two people, plus $3 per extra person. Credit cards are accepted. Long-term stays are okay.

Directions: From I-75, take Exit 301 eastbound on State Road 50 for 0.1 mile. Watch for the park driveway on the north side of the road, between the Waffle House and the Racetrac station.

Contact: Tall Pines RV Park, 30455 Cortez Boulevard, Brooksville, FL 34602, 352/799-5587, email: tallpinesrvpark@yahoo.com.

53 THE OAKS CAMPGROUND

Scenic rating: 4

in Bushnell

See map page 228

Most folks come for the season, enjoying music-oriented activities and all manner of dancing, bingo, exercise programs, bus tours, craft and quilting classes, and nondenominational Sunday school and Bible study. But the theme here is music. "There's always something musical going on," the owners say. Jam sessions and choir practices are held each week; a piano bar offers crooners the chance to entertain. Indoors or out, you might find a spontaneous sing-along. Tastes are eclectic, from country music and Broadway tunes to swing. Tampa, Walt Disney World, and other Central Florida attractions are within a one-hour drive. The park is for visitors age 55 and up. There's a Wal-Mart across the street.

RV sites, facilities: This 530-unit community is laid out subdivision-style and features 100 sites for overnighters. Fifty sites are pull-through. Big rigs can be accommodated. All sites have full hookups with 30-amp or 50-amp electrical service, picnic tables, cable TV, and wireless Internet access. Park models are for sale. Restrooms, showers, a dump station, laundry facilities, a pool, spa, a recreation and entertainment hall, meeting rooms, horseshoe pits, and boccie ball (lawn bowling) and shuffleboard courts are on the premises. Most areas are wheelchair accessible, and streets are paved. Children are permitted for short visits only. Leashed pets are allowed.

Reservations, fees: Reservations are recommended. Sites are $27 per night, plus $2 for cable TV. Credit cards are accepted. Stay as long as you wish. Long-term rates are available.

Directions: From I-75, take Exit 314 and drive east 0.25 mile on State Road 48.

Contact: The Oaks Campground, 5551 Southwest 18th Terrace, Bushnell, FL 33513, 352/793-7117, fax 352/793-7792, www.oaksrv.com.

54 SUMTER OAKS RV PARK

Scenic rating: 3

south of Bushnell

See map page 228

With planned activities keeping visitors busy November–March, this Escapees RV Club membership park is open to nonmembers only as space is available.

RV sites, facilities: There are 99 RV sites that have concrete patios, 30-amp or 50-amp electrical service, and sewer hookups. Fifteen are pull-through. Restrooms, showers, laundry facilities, a pool, a clubhouse, shuffleboard courts, a snack bar, propane gas, and a store are on the premises. All areas are wheelchair accessible. Children are permitted for short visits. Pets are permitted.

Reservations, fees: Reservations are recommended. Sites are $25 per night for two people, plus $1 per extra person. Credit cards are accepted.

Directions: From I-75, take Exit 309 and drive east 1.5 miles on County Road 673.

Contact: Sumter Oaks RV Park, 4602 County Road 673, Bushnell, FL 33513, 352/793-1333.

55 RED BARN RV RESORT

Scenic rating: 5

off I-75 in Bushnell

See map page 228

Under new ownership since 2005, the park is big-rig friendly and near shopping; there's a Wal-Mart across the street. This is the closest campground to the Dade Battlefield Historic Site, where Major Francis Dade and his troops were massacred three days after Christmas in 1835 by Seminole Indians dead-set against being moved to Oklahoma. "Have a good heart. Our difficulties and dangers are over now," Dade said shortly before the battle, believing his soldiers had passed the most likely spots for an Indian ambush. "And as soon as we arrive at Fort King you'll have three days to rest and keep Christmas gaily." You can walk along the old Fort King Military Road, the route the soldiers took from Fort Brooke (now Tampa) to Fort King (now Ocala). Make sure to stop at the visitors center that dissects the battle's action. The battle is reenacted during one weekend each December.

RV sites, facilities: This retiree-oriented community has 397 full-hookup RV sites. Most sites are pull-through, and some have picnic tables. A pool, a recreation room, horseshoes, shuffleboard, and winter social programs entertain campers. On the premises are restrooms, showers, a recreation room, and laundry facilities. Shopping is available within two miles. Management says all areas are wheelchair accessible. Children are permitted. Pets are allowed.

Reservations, fees: Reservations are recommended. Sites are $36 per night for two people, plus $2 per extra person and $2 for cable TV. If you're a first-time visitor, ask for a special daily rate of $30. Credit cards are accepted. Long-term stays are okay.

Directions: From I-75 at Exit 314, drive east on State Road 48. You will see the park almost immediately.

Contact: Red Barn RV Resort, 5923 Southwest 20th Drive, Bushnell, FL 33513, 352/793-6065 or 352/793-6220.

56 SEVEN ACRES RV PARK

Scenic rating: 1

north of Dade City on U.S. 301

See map page 228

Although it's located on busy U.S. 301, this park is quiet and favored by long-term RVers, snowbirds, and people living in manufactured homes. During the winter season, planned activities include country-western concerts.

RV sites, facilities: There are 160 grassy RV sites with full hookups, 30/50-amp electrical service, and telephone access. Five sites are pull-through. RVs up to 40 feet long and slide-outs can be accommodated on sites that average 30 feet wide by 65 feet long. The recreation hall, laundry, and bathrooms are wheelchair accessible. About 80 percent of the sites are occupied by full-timers. Groceries are within four miles. Children and small pets are permitted.

Reservations, fees: Reservations are not necessary. Sites are $15 per night, plus $2 for electricity. Credit cards are not accepted. Long-term stays are okay.

Directions: From Dade City, drive three miles north on U.S. 301 to the park on the west side of the road.

Contact: Seven Acres RV Park, 16731 U.S. 301, Dade City, FL 33525, 352/567-3510, email: 7acresrv@wmconnect.com.

57 WITHLACOOCHEE RIVER PARK

Scenic rating: 9

east of Dade City

See map page 228

As one of the few areas in Pasco County that has not been developed for farming or commercial uses, this park is a gem. An expansion for RV use was planned by summer 2006, but as of this writing construction had not yet begun. You may see bald and golden eagles, owls, deer, wild hogs, alligators, blue indigo snakes, armadillos, and more. The campground makes a good base for hiking the 13 miles of nature trails here or for canoe trips on the Withlacoochee River. There's also a two-mile bike path. Fish off the dock on the river, not on the riverbank; it's adjacent to the canoe launch. Note that you'll have to carry your canoe 100 feet from the parking area to the launch.

The park also offers a 40-foot observation tower, picnic shelters, playground, a recreation field, and a taste of life from the 19th century—you'll see a reconstructed 1800s fort, a primitive log cabin, and Indian villages. The campground is part of the 260-acre county-run park in the larger wilderness area operated by the Southwest Florida Water Management District.

RV sites, facilities: Twenty-four RV sites with

electricity and water are planned for some point in the future. As of this writing, there was a small primitive campground for tenters only. The nearest groceries are five miles away in Dade City. Children are welcome. Leashed pets are permitted.

Reservations, fees: Call for the latest information.

Directions: From Dade City, take State Road 533 to River Road and turn right (east). Follow the road about five miles to Auton Road, then turn right (south) and go to the park entrance.

Contact: Withlacoochee River Park, 12929 Withlacoochee Boulevard, Dade City, FL 33525, 352/567-0264 or 352/521-4104 (tel./fax). Information is also available from the East Pasco Parks and Recreation Department, 36620 State Road 52, Dade City, FL 33525, 352/521-4182.

58 CLERBROOK RESORT

Scenic rating: 9

in Clermont

See map page 228   BEST (

You can't do this place justice by calling it an RV park, not with its library, post office, beauty salon, barbershop, country-club amenities, and, oh yes, obvious devotion to golf. Osprey and long-legged wading birds sometimes look onto the 18-hole, par-67 golf course from surrounding wetlands and lakes. If golfers somehow lose a club, they can order a customized replacement from the park's pro shop and ask the golf pro for tips to try out at the putting green or driving range.

Clearly, the idea is to leave your grassy, sunny RV site at this 287-acre resort each morning and take part in everything else it offers: 13 shuffleboard courts, three pools, four hot tubs, and more. Anglers try for bass and catfish at ponds and at any of the region's chain of 17 lakes including Lake Harris, a boating and waterskiing spot. A full-time activities director also keeps campers moving with square dancing lessons, bingo, and a host of events in the three clubhouses. For a day trip, try Disney World, Sea World, or other Orlando-area attractions. The park is so huge that it's laid out like a town with several subdivisions or neighborhoods. About 430 sites have park models on them.

RV sites, facilities: There are 1,253 sites, of which 850 full-hookup sites are for RVs up to 40 feet long. All have 50-amp electrical service. Six sites are drive-through. Each site has a picnic table. Internet access is available at the clubhouse in the "Lifestyles" and "Cross Roads" areas. For recreation, there's a golf course, three pools, three hot tubs, a playground, an exercise room, a driving range, a putting range, horseshoes, lighted shuffleboard courts, a softball field, a game room, tournament pool tables, and winter social programs. BYOB ("Bring your own bottle") for happy hour in the club house every Wednesday in the wintertime. For rallies or group retreats, the resort offers a reception and meeting rooms. Showers, restrooms, villa rentals, a dump station, cable TV, and three laundry facilities are available. The golf pro shop sells coffee, snacks, and candy, but there's also a major grocery store and restaurants within one mile or so. Management says all areas are wheelchair accessible. Children are welcome, though it's primarily an over-55 group. Leashed pets are permitted.

Reservations, fees: Reservations are required. Sites are $29–31 per night. Credit cards are accepted. Long-term rates are available.

Directions: From Florida's Turnpike west of Winter Garden, take Exit 289 and drive south on U.S. 27 for about two miles. The park is on the east side.

Contact: Clerbrook Resort, 20005 U.S. 27, Clermont, FL 34711, 352/394-5513 or 800/440-3801, fax 352/394-8251.

59 TORCHLITE RV AND MOBILE HOME PARK

Scenic rating: 2

south of Clermont
See map page 228

The 39 grassy/concrete-pad RV sites are set on 13 shaded acres near department stores, grocer-

ies, and shopping centers. Fifty-four mobile homes are also in this park, and space for travelers is scarce; 85 percent of the lots are taken by year-round residents. Local bass anglers head west to Lake Louisa, one of 13 lakes linked together by an officially designated "Outstanding Florida Water"—the Palatlakaha River. To swim, fish, or canoe, try the lake's namesake state park at Louisa's southwestern corner off U.S. 27, seven miles south of State Road 50; call 352/394-3969.

RV sites, facilities: There are 30 sites with 30-amp electrical service and 9 with 50-amp for RVs up to 40 feet long. Each site has a picnic table and full hookups. Shuffleboard and a recreation room entertain campers. Showers, restrooms, a dump station, and laundry facilities are available. Groceries are 4.5 miles. Bathhouses, laundry facilities, and the recreation hall are wheelchair accessible. Children and people of all ages are welcome to camp but may not reside in mobile homes. Leashed pets are permitted.

Reservations, fees: Reservations are recommended. Sites are $15–20 per night for two people, plus $1 for each additional person. Credit cards are not accepted. Long-term rates are available.

Directions: From State Road 50 in Clermont, drive 3.5 miles south on U.S. 27. You'll see the park entrance on the right.

Contact: Torchlite RV and Mobile Home Park, 10201 U.S. 27 South, Clermont, FL 34711, 352/394-3716.

60 LAKE LOUISA STATE PARK

Scenic rating: 8

south of Clermont
See map page 228   BEST (

One of the newest additions to the Florida State Park system, this campground opened in 2003 with fanfare that called it a "world-class" park. Indeed, it offers spectacular recreation, with six lakes and rolling hills for horseback riding and hiking (although you may have to wait a few years for the planted landscape to grow to full regalia). Swim or catch some rays on the sandy beach at Lake Louisa, or canoe and kayak on Dixie Lake; the park has a small ramp there and on Lake Hammond. RVers can fish in four of the lakes, but gas-powered engines are not allowed. A public boat ramp is outside the park on the west side of Lake Louisa on Hull Road. There are 15 miles of equestrian trails and 20 miles of hiking paths. The park is a popular site for marathons, triathlons, and equestrian events held by Orlando area clubs.

RV sites, facilities: The camping areas are arranged in three loops. The 60 sites have water and 30/50-amp electrical service; 15 have sewer hookups. Each site has a picnic table, a grill, and a fire ring. On the premises are showers, restrooms, a dump station, two fishing piers, three docks, a pavilion, an amphitheater, and rental cabins. The restrooms and three campsites have wheelchair access. Groceries are within three miles. Children are welcome. Leashed pets are allowed.

Reservations, fees: Reservations are recommended; contact ReserveAmerica at 800/336-3521 or reserveamerica.com. Sites are $21 per night for four people. Credit cards are accepted. The maximum stay is 14 days.

Directions: From Clermont, drive south seven miles on State Road 50.

Contact: Lake Louisa State Park, 7305 U.S. 27, Clermont, FL 34714, 352/394-3969, www .floridastateparks.org.

61 THOUSAND TRAILS ORLANDO

Scenic rating: 8

south of Clermont

See map page 228

Part of the Thousand Trails national campground membership club, this 255-acre resort (or "preserve," as the marketing folks call it) targets Disney World and theme-park-destination campers, families, and full-timers. Disney World is just

nine miles away, but there's plenty to do in the campground, too. On the premises is a 60-acre, spring-fed lake with fishing, rowboats, and canoeing options. Teens can play video games in the game room, and playgrounds occupy the younger set. Entertainment is presented weekly in the recreation hall. Activities directors lead campers in arts and crafts, line dancing, and the like; they also plan children's activities. If you invite friends or family who don't camp, they can rent one of the 30 on-site trailers to round out your party.

RV sites, facilities: In this membership park, RVs and tents can be accommodated on 734 sites, all of which have picnic tables and grills. Restrooms, showers, a dump station, and laundry facilities are available. Amenities include a pool and spa, a boat ramp and dock, canoe rentals, miniature golf, a recreation hall, playgrounds, nature trails, shuffleboard and tennis courts, a video and game room, horseshoe pits, a campground store, rental trailers, and propane gas sales. Most areas are wheelchair accessible. Children are welcome. Leashed pets are permitted.

Reservations, fees: Reservations are recommended, especially during the busy season from December 19 through March 31. Call 90 days in advance for reservations during this high-demand period. Trial memberships are available for one weekend. Credit cards are accepted.

Directions: From Clermont, drive 13 miles south on U.S. 27. From Kissimmee, drive west on State Road 192 eight miles to U.S. 27; turn north on U.S. 27 and drive two miles.

Contact: Thousand Trails Orlando, 2110 U.S. 27 South, Clermont, FL 34711, 352/394-7575 or 800/723-1217, www.1000trails.com.

62 ORLANDO WINTER GARDEN RV RESORT

Scenic rating: 5

in Winter Garden

See map page 228

All the streets in this 30-acre community are paved, and about 85 percent are shaded by oaks and many orange trees. There are four bathhouses, two laundry rooms, and an adult lounge. When guests don't drive 30 minutes to Disney World or other theme parks (back roads near the park get you there with less traffic), they enjoy swimming in the two heated pools and biking around the park. For an alternate, head to a nearby favorite of bicyclists, joggers, and inline skaters—the West Orange Trail, two miles west of Florida's Turnpike at the Lake/Orange County line. The trail links Apopka, Clarcona, Winter Garden, and other points; for details, call West Orange Trail at 407/654-1108. About one-third of the park is occupied by year-round residents.

RV sites, facilities: The 376 sites for RVs have full hookups, 50-amp electrical service, cable TV, and picnic tables. Sites 1–26 and 57–85 are drive-through. RVs as large as 45 feet and slide-outs can be accommodated. Internet access is available in the clubhouse. Two pools, a playground, a recreation room, horseshoes, shuffleboard, an adult lounge, cable TV, and winter social programs entertain campers. On the premises are restrooms, showers, a dump station, and laundry facilities. Management says the pool, laundry room, and restrooms are wheelchair accessible. A restaurant and groceries are across the street. Children and leashed pets are permitted.

Reservations, fees: Reservations are recommended. Sites are $34 per night for two people, plus $3.50 for each additional person. Credit cards are accepted. Long-term rates are available.

Directions: From Florida's Turnpike at Exit 267, take Colonial Drive/State Road 50 west for two miles to the campground at right.

Contact: Orlando Winter Garden RV Resort, 13905 West Colonial Drive, Winter Garden, FL 34787, 407/656-1415, fax 407/656-0858.

63 STAGE STOP CAMPGROUND

Scenic rating: 6

in Winter Garden

See map page 228

These 22 acres of grassy sites are set alongside a major highway 10 miles west of Orlando, where about 20 percent of the land is occupied by year-round residents. Some sites overlook a small lake and pinewoods, but shopping centers are across the street and next door. Most visitors are retirees. One unusual feature is the Olympic-sized swimming pool, although guests also can take advantage of horseshoes, shuffleboard, and badminton. Disney-area attractions are about 30 minutes away.

RV sites, facilities: Fifty-amp electrical service is available at 80 of the 248 full-hookup sites; the rest have 30-amp. Each has a concrete patio and picnic table. About 30 sites are pull-through, and big rigs are welcome. Streets are paved. Sites are 25 feet wide, varying in depth from 50 to 60 feet. A pool, horseshoes, shuffleboard, a playground, badminton, winter activities, restrooms, showers, a convenience store with RV supplies, and laundry facilities are available. Management says the clubhouse and restrooms are wheelchair accessible. Children and pets are permitted.

Reservations, fees: Reservations are recommended in winter. Sites are $25 per night for two people, plus $4 for each additional person. From May 1 through September 30, there is an additional electric fee of $1.50 per day. Credit cards are accepted. Long-term stays are okay.

Directions: From Florida's Turnpike (northbound), take Exit 267 and travel 2.5 miles west on State Road 50 to the campground. If you're traveling southbound on the turnpike, get off at Exit 272 and drive 2.5 miles east on State Road 50 to the campground.

Contact: Stage Stop Campground, 14400 West Colonial Drive, Winter Garden, FL 34787, 407/656-8000, fax 407/656-3840.

64 WOODLANDS LUTHERAN CAMP

Scenic rating: 6

in Montverde

See map page 228

No, you don't have to be of the Lutheran faith to camp in these 180 acres of woods and horse pastures. Your religion isn't an issue, though available space may be the challenge. Woodlands Lutheran Camp attracts retirees for winter-long visits and families for shorter vacations spent around the heated pool and along wooded trails for hikers, mountain bikers, and horseback riders. However, space is somewhat limited by park models, cabins, and a retreat center.

Trees help shade the sandy campsites, but the true attraction is the surroundings: Guests enjoy free use of canoes in which they can paddle around two small park lakes, stopping now and then to fish. For better-known bass waters, travel about 10 miles north to Little Lake Harris and adjoining 7-mile-wide Lake Harris. East of the little community of Montverde looms eight-mile-long Lake Apopka, a popular place to watch sunsets from the eastern lakeshore. (Early risers might consider viewing sunrises from Lake Apopka's western border.) Disney World is about a one-half-hour drive away.

RV sites, facilities: All 201 sites have full hookups and a picnic table. RVs up to 35 feet long can be accommodated. A pool, a playground, horseback trails, horseshoes, shuffleboard, tennis, basketball, volleyball, a softball field, and winter social programs are available. Showers, restrooms, a dump station, a recreation room, four rental cabins, snacks, firewood, and laundry facilities are on the premises. A 24-hour supermarket is within five miles. Families with children usually stay short-term. Leashed pets are permitted.

Reservations, fees: Reservations are recommended, particularly in winter. Sites are $24 per night for four people, plus $2 per extra adult

and $2 for using air conditioners. Credit cards are accepted. Season-long stays are okay.

Directions: The campground is on County Road 455, two miles north of State Road 50/West Colonial Drive. From Florida's Turnpike at Exit 272, go west 2.5 miles to County Road 455. Turn right. Continue less than two miles to the campground.

Contact: Woodlands Lutheran Camp, 15749 County Road 455, Montverde, FL 34756, 407/469-2792, fax 407/469-4742, www.woodlandscamp.com.

65 MAGNOLIA PARK

Scenic rating: 4

on Lake Apopka west of Apopka

See map page 228

Orange County promotes this 56-acre park/campground as a place that features spectacular sunsets on the county's largest lake (33,000 acres). And that much is true; the sunsets over Lake Apopka are simply gorgeous. What they don't tell you is that Lake Apopka was once fouled by runoff from nearby vegetable farms. Years of work are still going on to bring the lake back to a healthful state, and the water quality is said to be improving to the point you can even fish in it. The state has purchased 33,000 acres on the north side as a kind of huge water filter, which also protects it from development. The park is shaded by oak, magnolia, and hickory trees. Anglers who bring a boat can make a run down toward Winter Garden and try their luck, or work their way up into the canals on the lake's north side to fish for specks or catfish before returning to the gravel campsites.

RV sites, facilities: All 18 sites at this county-run park have 30-amp electricity, cement pads, water, picnic tables, and fire rings. Sewer hookups are not available. RVs as long as 40 feet can be accommodated on wood sites that vary in size from 30 to 40 feet wide by 60 to 80 feet deep. On the premises are restrooms, showers, a dump station, a boat ramp, and a playground. The restrooms and sites 15 and 16 are wheelchair accessible. Groceries, restaurants, and laundry facilities are within five miles. Children are welcome. Pets are permitted in the camping area, but not in the general park or playground. Alcohol is prohibited.

Reservations, fees: Reservations are recommended; they must be made in person. Sites are $13–18 per night, depending on your age and county residency. Credit cards are not accepted. Maximum stay is 14 days.

Directions: From Apopka, head south on County Road 437/Ocoee-Apopka Road. Turn right onto Binion Road, which leads to the campground.

Contact: Magnolia Park, 2929 Binion Road, Apopka, FL 32703, 407/886-4231, www.orangecountyparks.net.

66 SUN RESORTS

Scenic rating: 8

west of Apopka
See map page 228

Targeted to families and adult visitors, this park does a nice job of separating overnighters and seasonal vacationers from permanent residents in a 110-acre wooded condominium park. It also has emphasized a balance of maintaining a mix of shaded areas and tree-limb clearance in the RV area. The Y-shaped pool is one of the largest in an RV park, with 100,000 gallons of water with Olympic-sized swimming lanes and a poolside stage for entertainment and shows. A kiddie pool is next to the big pool. A park model area with about 800 manufactured homes is set apart from the overnighters so you have more of an RV park feel. Shopping and restaurants are nearby, and Walt Disney World is a 25-mile ride. You can make a day trip out of it. Manufactured homes and lots are for sale or rent.

RV sites, facilities: There are 108 RV sites (45 pull-through), and most have 30-amp elec-

trical service. Six sites have 50-amp service, for which there is an additional fee. Sewer hookups can be found at 74 sites, while 34 have just water and electricity. Rigs up to 40 feet can be accommodated on lots varying in size from 35 or 40 feet wide and 60 feet deep. All sites have picnic tables; some have cable TV. A wireless Internet network is available at the trading post and at campsites near it. Restrooms, showers, laundry facilities, a pool, a trading post/store with limited groceries, a snack bar, miniature golf, propane gas sales, a recreation hall with planned activities, a dog-walk area, and shuffleboard courts are on the premises. Entertainment includes volleyball, basketball, billiards, bingo, holiday events, water aerobics, a kiddie pool, and a playground. Five RV sites, the bathhouses, the office, the recreation hall, and laundry and trading post areas are wheelchair accessible. Grocery stores and shopping are within five miles. Children are welcome, though wintertime guests tend to be snowbirds and summertime visitors are families. Leashed pets are permitted.

Reservations, fees: Reservations are recommended. Sites are $28 per night for two adults and three children, plus $5 per additional person and $2 for 50-amp electrical sites. First-time visitors should ask about special rate offers. Credit cards are accepted. Long-term rates are available.

Directions: From the Florida Turnpike, take Exit 267A to 429 North. Turn right on West Road (Exit 26). At Clarcona-Ocoee Road, turn left and go 3.2 miles. Turn north on Apopka Vineland Road and drive 1.8 miles to the park on the left. From I-4, take Exit 92 onto Semoran Boulevard and drive west 6.5 miles. Turn south on Sheeler Road and proceed 2.8 miles. At Clarcona-Ocoee Road, turn left and drive 0.2 mile to the resort.

Contact: Sun Resorts, 3000 Clarcona Road, Apopka, FL 32703, 407/889-3048, fax 407/889-0887, www.sunrvresorts.net.

67 CLARCONA HORSEMAN'S PARK

Scenic rating: 6

in Apopka

See map page 228   **BEST (**

Saddle up! This 40-acre park with access to the 22-mile West Orange Trail equestrian path was created for horseback riders, but anyone can camp here if space is available. The campground primarily accommodates equestrians participating in myriad competitions and shows, or those who want to take their mounts on the adjoining trail. Operated by Orange County, the park also has a go-cart track for Quarter Midget Racing. A manager lives on the property; office hours are 7 A.M.–6 P.M. daily, but the park is open 24 hours. Since it's on the show circuit, you may hear your neighbors leaving at 3 A.M. to get to the next stop.

RV sites, facilities: There are 28 campsites for RVs or tents; each has water and electricity. Restrooms, showers, horse barns, bleacher seating, judging towers, and dressage show rings are on the premises. Children are welcome. Leashed pets are permitted.

Reservations, fees: All sites are first-come, first-served. Sites are $15 per night for two people, plus $3 for electrical service. Credit cards are not accepted. The maximum stay is two weeks.

Directions: From I-4, take Exit 80B onto U.S. 441/Orange Blossom Trail and drive northbound to Apopka, about 13 miles. Turn west on Apopka-Vineland Road/County Road 435 and drive four miles. Turn right on McCormick Road and proceed 0.5 mile. Turn right on Damon Road to the park.

Contact: Clarcona Horseman's Park, 3535 Damon Road, Apopka, FL 32703, 407/886-6255 or 407/886-9761 if horse shows are in progress, fax 407/886-2142, www.orangecountyparks.net.

68 BILL FREDERICK PARK AND POOL AT TURKEY LAKE

Scenic rating: 7

in west Orlando

See map page 228

A very unusual addition to this popular, shady, wooded city-run park is the Children's Farm, which re-creates a nostalgic look at Florida's rural life. Seven miles of nature trails meander through the live-oak hammock and cattail marshes, and bicyclists can cover three miles of trails before returning to their asphalt campsites. Picturesque enough to be used for the occasional wedding, the park is a local favorite for weekend picnics, as families stake out the 125 picnic tables, 77 barbecue grills, and 15 picnic shelters. Swimmers plunge into a pool overlooking Turkey Lake. A 200-foot-long fishing pier aids freshwater anglers. What's remarkable is that this little nature spot is just about 1 mile from Universal Studios, 5 miles from International Drive, and 15 miles from Disney-area attractions.

RV sites, facilities: There are 36 full-hookup RV sites with 30/50-amp electrical outlets. Each site has a picnic table and a grill. A pool, three playgrounds, a nature trail, disc golf, volleyball, cabins, restrooms, showers, a dump station, and laundry facilities are on the premises. Groceries and restaurants are about one mile away. The restrooms, laundry, and picnic areas are wheelchair accessible. Children are welcome. Leashed pets are permitted.

Reservations, fees: Reservations are recommended on weekends and holidays; the camping area is full almost every weekend. Nightly fee for four people is $18 (full hookups), plus $2.50 for each additional person. Credit cards are accepted. Stays are limited to 29 days.

Directions: Head west from downtown Orlando on the East–West Expressway/State Road 408. Exit at Hiawassee Road. Go south 3.5 miles to the campground.

Contact: Bill Frederick Park and Pool at Turkey Lake, 3401 South Hiawassee Road, Orlando,

FL 32835, 407/299-5594 or 407/299-5581, www.cityoforlando.net.

69 LAKE MILLS PARK

Scenic rating: 6

east of Casselberry near Chuluota

See map page 228

No large RVs can be accommodated at this rural nature park—just small trailers or pop-up campers that set up in a grassy clearing. Towering oak trees said to be 150 years old, pine forests, and a mixed hardwood swamp remind you of how Florida used to look. Carry-in boats or canoes can head out on the lake, but fishing and motorized vessels are prohibited. This pretty 50-acre county park also has a day-use area with volleyball, a playground, and a jogging trail, but campers tend to be Scouts in a walk-in group campsite or families.

RV sites, facilities: There are 12 primitive sites (no water, no electricity, no dump station) with picnic tables. Restrooms and showers are provided. In the park are a boardwalk, playground, a jogging and fitness trail, sand volleyball courts, an amphitheater, and picnic pavilions. Children are welcome. Pets are not allowed.

Reservations, fees: A camping permit is required; call the park at 407/788-0609 for details. The fee is $5 per person, or $20 for the park's single group site. Credit cards are not accepted. The maximum stay is seven days.

Directions: From County Road 415/Chuluota Road in the town of Chuluota, drive east on Lake Mills Road about 0.25 mile. Turn north on Tropical Avenue and proceed a short distance to the park.

Contact: Lake Mills Park, 1301 Tropical Avenue, Chuluota, FL 32766, 407/788-0609. Or, contact the Seminole County Parks and Recreation Department, 1101 East 1st Street, Sanford, FL 32771, 407/788-0405, www.co.seminole.fl.gov.

70 CHRISTMAS AIRSTREAM PARK

Scenic rating: 5

in Christmas east of Orlando

See map page 228   BEST (

Although the name might mislead you, you don't have to arrive in one of those now-fashionable orbs of silver known as an Airstream to camp at the concrete pad/gravel sites in this rustic 18-acre park. Any RV will do. The flat, wooded park is about 20 miles from the Kennedy Space Center, and about 50 miles from Disney-area attractions. You'll also be just a few miles from the St. Johns River and the St. Johns River National Wildlife Refuge. You can hike through the wildlife refuge or tour it by car. Also close by is the Fort Christmas Historical Park and Museum, where you can see how early settlers lived in this part of Florida during the Second Seminole War of the 1830s and 1840s. A replica fort and other displays are featured. Generally speaking, this sleepy part of Florida is skipped by out-of-towners except at Christmastime when people travel for hours to the post office here to have their greeting cards postmarked "Christmas, FL." About 10 percent of the lots in this park are occupied year-round.

RV sites, facilities: All of the 165 grassy RV sites have full hookups and 30-amp electrical service, and a few have 50-amp. More than 120 sites are pull-through, and RVs as long as 45 feet can be accommodated. However, rigs with slide-outs must be approved by the management in advance, and pop-up campers are prohibited. Roads are crushed shell and dirt; some sites have concrete pads. Picnic tables are provided. Internet connections are available in the clubhouse. A pool, a playground, three recreation rooms, a camp circle for gatherings, winter recreation programs organized by volunteers, restrooms, showers, dump stations, telephone service, and laundry facilities are available. Two meeting halls are offered for camper rallies. Shopping is 8 miles away in Titusville or 15 miles away in Orlando. Management says the rec halls and restrooms are wheelchair accessible. Children are welcome, though most visitors are snowbirds. Two leashed pets are permitted per site; aggressive breeds are prohibited.

Reservations, fees: Reservations are necessary in winter. Sites are $25 per night for four people, plus $5 for each additional person. Credit cards are accepted. Long-term rates are available.

Directions: From I-95, take Exit 215 and drive eight miles west on State Road 50 to the park. If you're traveling on I-4, use Exit 83B and drive 18 miles east on State Road 50 to the park.

Contact: Christmas Airstream Park, 25525 East Colonial Drive, Christmas, FL 32709, 407/568-5207, www.christmasairstreamrvpark.com.

71 WINTER PARADISE RV PARK

Scenic rating: 3

north of Hudson Beach
See map page 228

Whether for golfing, boating, fishing, visiting the beach, shopping, or relaxing by the pool, this park is centrally located, just three miles from the Gulf of Mexico in a busy suburb with plenty of entertainment. The area has many seafood and ethnic restaurants, as well as chain-operated eateries. Favorite things to do include water aerobics in the pool, bingo, and other fun organized by a year-round activities director.

RV sites, facilities: Most sites at this 302-unit RV park have full hookups and 30-amp electrical service; a few are drive-through. Forty sites have 50-amp service. RVs as large as 45 feet long can be accommodated. Heavier units can be parked on gravel sites. Other spots are grassy with concrete patio slabs. Restrooms, showers, laundry facilities, a dump station, shuffleboard courts, horseshoe pits, a pool, and a recreation building with billiard tables and a library are provided. Propane delivery is available. The clubhouse,

office, and laundry room are wheelchair accessible. Roads are paved. Shopping and restaurants are within three miles. Children are welcome. Pets are allowed; dog walks are on two sides of the park.

Reservations, fees: Reservations are recommended. Sites are $35 per night. Credit cards are accepted. Long-term stays are okay.

Directions: From Hudson, drive 2.5 miles north on U.S. 19 to the park, at the corner with Denton Avenue.

Contact: Winter Paradise RV Park, 16108 U.S. 19, Hudson, FL 34667, 727/868-2285 or 800/328-0775, www.chateaucomm.com.

72 SEVEN OAKS TRAVEL PARK

Scenic rating: 3

in Hudson
See map page 228

Although located smack-dab in the middle of the urbanized Gulf Coast, this 297-unit adult park has a semirural setting in an area of rolling hills. It's just east of the major thoroughfare at 17 feet above sea level, which means it's probably secure from high water if you leave your RV parked here long-term. Beaches are three miles away. Two-thirds of the residents stay here year-round. Planned activities in the wintertime include cruises, potluck dinners, bingo, and shuffleboard.

RV sites, facilities: This adults-only park has 120 RV sites with full hookups to accommodate rigs up to 40 feet long. Half have 30-amp service; the rest have 50-amp. Most sites have concrete patios or are paved. Restrooms, showers, laundry facilities, a pool, shuffleboard courts, a recreation hall, horseshoe pits, and propane gas are available. The clubhouse, pool, office, and bathhouse are wheelchair accessible. Children are welcome to stay two weeks at a time. Leashed pets are permitted.

Reservations, fees: Reservations are recommended. Sites are $25 per night for two people, plus $3 for each additional person.

Credit cards are not accepted. Long-term stays are okay.

Directions: From Hudson, drive 1.5 miles north on U.S. 19. Turn east on Bolton Avenue in town and continue 0.7 mile to the park on the north side.

Contact: Seven Oaks Travel Park, 9207 Bolton Avenue, Hudson, FL 34667, 727/862-3016, www.7oakstravelpark.com.

73 SHADY ACRES MOBILE HOME AND RV PARK

Scenic rating: 3

north of Hudson

See map page 228

About 20 percent of the sites are occupied year-round at this mobile-home park located off a six-lane highway. Head to the recreation hall for bingo, coffee, doughnuts, cookouts, and potluck dinners. The beach is one mile away. Supermarkets, doctors' offices, and a hospital are conveniently close.

RV sites, facilities: This 72-unit urban mobile-home community with a recreation hall, laundry facilities, and restrooms has 25 roomy full-hookup RV sites, of which 9 are drive-through. Twenty sites have 30-amp electrical service, and four have 50-amp. RVs up to 37 feet can be accommodated. Cable TV and telephone access are available, and the rec hall and restrooms are wheelchair accessible. Picnic tables and a fire ring round out the picture. upermarkets, doctors' offices, and a hospital are within 0.4 mile. Children are welcome. Small pets are allowed.

Reservations, fees: Reservations are recommended. Sites are $20 per night. Overnighters must check out by 10 A.M. Credit cards are accepted. Long-term rates are available.

Directions: From the junction of State Road 52 and U.S. 19, drive two miles north on U.S. 19.

Contact: Shady Acres Mobile Home and RV Park, 14417 U.S. 19 North, Hudson, FL 34667, 727/868-9589.

74 GULFBREEZE RV PARK

Scenic rating: 2

north of Hudson

See map page 228

The park targets long-term visitors for, as they say, "a week, a month, forever." It's set on a hill in a quiet residential area with plenty of trees, yet is still close to shops and restaurants. About half the occupants live here year-round. In winter, snowbirds and retirees enjoy pancake breakfasts, spaghetti dinners, crafts, golf and bowling leagues, deep-sea fishing charters, and line dancing. A "get acquainted" coffee is held every Wednesday.

RV sites, facilities: There are 147 RV sites with full hookups, 50-amp electrical service, and telephone and cable TV access. Most sites are grassy and average 30 by 50 feet in size. RVs up to 40 feet long and slide-outs can be accommodated. Restrooms, showers, laundry facilities, picnic tables, a dump station, a pool, a recreation hall with Internet access, horseshoe pits, and shuffleboard courts are on the premises. Streets are paved, and the clubhouse and bathhouse are wheelchair accessible. Children are welcome. Leashed pets are permitted.

Reservations, fees: Reservations are not necessary. Sites are $20 per night for two people, plus $3 for each additional person. Credit cards are accepted. Long-term RVers are preferred.

Directions: From the junction of State Road 52 and U.S. 19, drive five miles north on U.S. 19. Turn east at Bolton Avenue (look for the Chevron sign) and go two blocks.

Contact: Gulfbreeze RV Park, 9014 Bolton Avenue, Hudson, FL 34667, 727/862-6826.

75 LAKEWOOD TRAVEL PARK

Scenic rating: 2

in Hudson

See map page 228

Backing up to a country meadow and overlooking a pond, this suburban park contains a mix of sunny and shady spots. The atmosphere is friendly and homey, with some 70 percent of the residents living here year-round. It may be hard to find a spot in winter, when many campers opt for the $295 monthly rate. Within a few miles are gulf beaches, Tarpon Springs, Weeki Wachee, nature parks, and golf courses.

RV sites, facilities: Of the 88 lots, about 40 RV sites are available to visitors. They have 30-amp electrical service, full hookups, and optional cable TV and telephone service. Restrooms, showers, laundry facilities, and an activities building are provided. The park caters to retirees staying one month at a time. Children are welcome for short-term visits. Pets are allowed.

Reservations, fees: Reservations are not necessary. Sites are $20 per night for two people, plus $2 for each additional person and $1 for pets. Credit cards are not accepted.

Directions: From U.S. 19 in Hudson, drive east on State Road 52 for 4.5 miles.

Contact: Lakewood Travel Park, 11517 State Road 52, Hudson, FL 34669, 727/856-1306.

76 BARRINGTON HILLS RV RESORT

Scenic rating: 7

in Hudson

See map page 228

Targeting active retirees, this RV park is centrally located to shopping and the Gulf of Mexico. Sometimes known as Sunburst, the park is part of the Equity Lifestyle Properties chain, which also owns the Encore parks. During the winter, a full schedule of planned activities helps seasonal visitors socialize and get to know each other.

RV sites, facilities: There are 390 RV sites, among which 20 are pull-through. Rigs up to 45 feet long can be accommodated. All sites have full hookups, 50-amp service, picnic tables, cable TV, and telephone service available. Wireless Internet access is available at

two-thirds of the resort; be sure to ask if you want one of these spots. Restrooms, showers, a dump station, laundry facilities, a pool, a clubhouse, horseshoe pits, shuffleboard courts, a billiards room, and a golf net are on the premises. Children are welcome. Leashed pets are permitted.

Reservations, fees: Reservations are recommended. Sites are $26 per night. Credit cards are accepted. Long-term rates are available.

Directions: From the intersection of U.S. 19 and State Road 52 in Hudson, drive north on U.S. 19 for 2.5 miles. Turn east on New York Avenue and drive 1.4 miles to the park.

Contact: Barrington Hills RV Resort, 9412 New York Avenue, Hudson, FL 34667, 727/868-3586 or 877/287-2757, fax 727/863-7259, www.rvonthego.com.

77 GROVE RIDGE ESTATES

Scenic rating: 3

south of Dade City on U.S. 98

See map page 228

Horses graze near this neatly kept park located adjacent to an orange grove, unless the bulldozers get to it. The country setting offers plenty of wide-open spaces for those who crave the outdoors, but stores and other conveniences are nearby in Dade City. About half the sites are occupied year-round. Park models are for sale.

RV sites, facilities: This adults-only RV resort accepts self-contained rigs at least 20 feet long at the 256 full-hookup sites with 50-amp electrical service. Sites are 30 by 50 feet, and rigs up to 42 feet long can be accommodated. Laundry facilities, shuffleboard courts, horseshoe pits, a recreation hall, a pool, telephone service, and rental trailers are available. There is no bathhouse. The clubhouse is wheelchair accessible and has an Internet connection. Children are not allowed except for brief visits. One pet under 25 pounds is permitted per site.

Reservations, fees: Reservations are recommended. Sites are $25 per night for two people, plus $2 for each additional person. Credit cards are not accepted. Most campers are retirees staying for the winter season.

Directions: From I-75, take Exit 285 eastbound 10 miles on State Road 52 to Dade City. Turn south on U.S. 301/U.S. 98 and go through town. At the point where U.S. 98 veers off toward Lakeland, keep traveling on U.S. 98. Drive 0.5 mile southeast to the park.

Contact: Grove Ridge Estates, 10721 U.S. 98, Dade City, FL 33525, 352/523-2277, www.bel-aireresorts.com.

78 COUNTRY AIRE ESTATES

Scenic rating: 4

south of Dade City

See map page 228

Groceries and restaurants are nearby, and antiques hounds will find plenty of shops to browse in Dade City. Social activities are held year-round at this park, where the vast majority of the 68 lots are owned by residents, leaving about 18 sites open to people passing through in winter. There's a two-acre pond for those anglers inclined to try their luck. Most people here hail from Michigan, Ohio, Pennsylvania, New York, New Jersey, and Canada.

RV sites, facilities: Catering to RVers age 55 and older, this hillside park with a total of 68 units has about 18 sites with sewer hookups, 30/50-amp electrical service, and picnic tables available for short-term visitors. The maximum size RV that can be accommodated is 38 feet. Some sites are waterfront. Restrooms, showers, picnic tables, laundry facilities, a heated pool, a clubhouse, horseshoe pits, shuffleboard courts, telephone service, and cable TV are available. Groceries and restaurants are within one mile. All areas are wheelchair accessible. Families with children are permitted to stay a couple of nights in summer; children are not accepted at other times. Pets under 15 pounds are permitted.

Reservations, fees: Reservations are recom-

mended. Sites are $25 per night for two people. Credit cards are not accepted. Long-term rates are available.

Directions: From downtown Dade City, drive south on U.S. 301 for three miles, turn east on McDonald Road near the city limits, just before the Wal-Mart shopping center, and go 0.2 mile.

Contact: Country Aire Estates, 38130 McDonald Road, Dade City, FL 33525, 352/567-3630, www.premiercm.com.

79 MORNINGSIDE RV ESTATES

Scenic rating: 4

on the south side of Dade City

See map page 228

This snowbird-oriented resort with a gated entrance is within walking distance of two large shopping centers. Shade in the RV park is minimal. About 25 percent of the residents stay here year-round. Favorite activities include euchre (a card game) and ice-cream socials.

RV sites, facilities: The 55-and-older park has 399 sites with full hookups, 50-amp electrical service, free cable TV, and telephone access. Restrooms, showers, a dump station, a heated indoor pool, two clubhouses, two laundry facilities, horseshoe pits, and shuffleboard courts are provided. Lots are 36 by 60 feet, and a few have concrete slabs. The recreation hall, pool, and pool hall are wheelchair accessible. Groceries and shopping are within 0.25 mile. Pets are prohibited.

Reservations, fees: Reservations are recommended. Sites are $30 per night for two people, plus $1 for each additional person. Credit cards are not accepted. Long-term rates are available.

Directions: From downtown Dade City, drive south on U.S. 301 for three miles, turn east on McDonald Road near the city limits, just before the Wal-Mart shopping center, and go 0.2 mile.

Contact: Morningside RV Estates, 12645 Morning Drive, Dade City, FL 33525, 352/523-1922, morningrv@aol.com.

80 MANY MANSIONS RV PARK

Scenic rating: 3

south of Dade City

See map page 228

Surrounded by dwindling citrus groves and open pastureland, this park is located in the country yet is just five minutes from shopping, dining, and downtown Dade City. Planned activities include bingo, cards, pokeno, and cookouts, as well as weekly evening church services. Sites are laid out neatly in subdivision style, with straight roads; most spots are not back-to-back. About half the units are occupied year-round.

RV sites, facilities: This adults-oriented RV park has 235 grassy, full-hookup sites with optional telephone service and cable TV access. RVs up to 40 feet long can be accommodated. Sites average 30 by 50 feet. Restrooms, showers, laundry facilities, a dump station, a camp circle, and a clubhouse with Internet access are available. The clubhouse, bathhouse, and laundry facilities are wheelchair accessible. Streets are paved. Some trailers are available for rent. Children may camp short-term only. Small pets are permitted on a leash.

Reservations, fees: Reservations are recommended. Sites are $24 per night for two people, plus $3 for each additional person. Credit cards are not accepted. Long-term rates are available.

Directions: From Dade City, drive south on U.S. 301/98. When U.S. 98 forks south on the edge of town, continue on U.S. 98 for three miles. Take the Richland exit to County Road 35A, turn right and go one mile to Stewart Road. Turn left (east) at the park entrance.

Contact: Many Mansions RV Park, 40703 Stewart Road, Dade City, FL 33525, 352/567-8667 or 800/359-0135.

81 CITRUS HILL PARK AND SALES

Scenic rating: 3

between Dade City and Zephyrhills

See map page 228

As the name implies, the trailer park is on a hill in what used to be orange grove country before freezes forced the citrus industry to look south to warmer points. Activities within the park include a golf league, bingo, crafts, bunco, euchre, church services, special dinners and socials, and a weekly coffee hour. Grocery stores, restaurants, and five golf courses are within five miles. There are no facilities for children. About 15 percent of the occupants stay here all year long, and most visitors return year after year from places like Canada, Indiana, and Michigan.

RV sites, facilities: This retiree-oriented park has 183 spots with full hookups and telephone and cable TV access, of which 45 are for RVs up to 40 feet long. Restrooms, showers, picnic tables, laundry facilities, a recreation hall, horseshoe pits, shuffleboard courts, a post office, and planned social activities are provided. The clubhouse is wheelchair accessible. Children are welcome to visit their grandparents for two weeks. Leashed pets are allowed.

Reservations, fees: Reservations are required. Sites are $24 per night for two people, plus $2 for each additional person. Credit cards are not accepted. Stays of up to seven months are okay. Long-term rates are available.

Directions: From Dade City, drive six miles south on U.S. 98. The park is on the east side of the road.

Contact: Citrus Hill Park and Sales, 9267 U.S. 98, Dade City, FL 33525, 352/567-6045, fax 352/567-3119, www.bel-aireresorts.com.

82 FOREST LAKE RV RESORT

Scenic rating: 5

north of Zephyrhills

See map page 228

This sparkling-clean park maintains it is "your year-round vacation home," and fewer than half of the sites are open for seasonal campers. Interior street names attest to the park's affinity for Canadian campers: for example, Bruins Drive, Maple Leaf Drive, and Canadiens Drive. The location is close to Gulf of Mexico beaches and Central Florida attractions, including baseball spring training, dog and horse racing, and Seminole bingo. Planned activities, such as ice-cream socials, make sure the residents have fun if they care to stay onsite most of the time. It's also a popular spot for camping rallies.

RV sites, facilities: The RV resort/mobile-home park has 124 sunny lots with concrete slabs for RVers (out of a total of 274). Sites have sewer hookups, 30/50-amp electrical service, and telephone and cable TV access. Lots are 30 by 50 feet, on average, and they can accommodate RVs up to 40 feet long. Restrooms, showers, laundry facilities, a dump station, six shuffleboard courts, four lighted horseshoe pits, a recreation hall, a pool, and a spa are on the premises. The pool area and clubhouse are wheelchair accessible. Shopping and golf courses are within eight miles. Children are not welcome except when visiting residents for less than two weeks. Small pets are permitted on a leash.

Reservations, fees: Reservations are recommended. Sites are $24 per night. Credit cards are accepted.

Directions: From I-75, take Exit 279 and drive 12 miles east on State Road 54 to the intersection with U.S. 301. The park is on the south side of the highway, east of the intersection.

Contact: Forest Lake RV Resort, 41219 Hockey Drive, Zephyrhills, FL 33540, 813/782-1058 or 800/283-9715, fax 813/788-5246, www .forestlake-estates.com.

83 WATERS EDGE RV RESORT

Scenic rating: 4

north of Zephyrhills

See map page 228

Set on 20 acres with tall oak trees, Waters Edge is located far enough away from town to enjoy a rural neighborhood setting but still be within a few minutes of shopping, restaurants, and a hospital. Paved interior roads lead to grassy back-in sites; few are shady. Social activities in winter include bingo, billiards, card games, and exercises in the pool. About 20 percent of the park is occupied year-round.

RV sites, facilities: This adult park has 70 RV sites with full hookups and cable TV and telephone access. Sites average 25 by 50 feet. Restrooms, showers, laundry facilities, a dump station, a pool, a clubhouse, horseshoe pits, and shuffleboard courts are on-site. The park caters to retirees who stay seven months out of the year and store their RVs on-site the rest of the time. Children may visit park residents for up to two weeks. Leashed pets are permitted.

Reservations, fees: Reservations are recommended. Sites are $25 per night for two people, plus $2 for each additional person. Credit cards are not accepted.

Directions: From Zephyrhills, drive one mile north on U.S. 301. Turn east onto Pretty Pond Road and go 0.5 mile to the stop sign at Wire Road. Head north on Wire Road for 0.25 mile to Otis Allen Road, then turn east and continue 0.5 mile to the entrance.

Contact: Waters Edge RV Resort, 39146 Otis Allen Road, Zephyrhills, FL 33540, 813/783-2708 or 800/471-7875, www.bel-aire resorts.com.

84 BAKER ACRES RV RANCH

Scenic rating: 4

on the north side of Zephyrhills

See map page 228

Nondenominational church services are held each Sunday in the recreation hall. Other activities include dances, a singles club, exercise classes, ceramics, crafts, sewing, wood carving, quilting, bowling, cards, bingo, and field trips. The pool is heated. In the card room, residents play cribbage, euchre, pinochle, and more. The park is part of the Bel-Aire Resorts group. More than half the park is occupied year-round.

RV sites, facilities: Among 355 sites, 60 are available for RVs. They have sewer hookups, 50-amp electricity, telephone service and cable TV available. About half have concrete pads. Average site size is 30 by 40 feet. RVs up to 40 feet long can be accommodated. Restrooms (but no showers), laundry facilities, shuffleboard and boccie ball (lawn bowling) courts, horseshoe pits, a recreation hall, a card room, and a pool are on the premises. RVs must be at least 20 feet long (up to a maximum of 35 feet) and must be less than 10 years old. Management says all areas of the park are wheelchair accessible. Shopping, groceries, and restaurants are within one mile. Children are not welcome except for short visits. Leashed pets under 25 pounds are permitted.

Reservations, fees: Reservations are recommended. Sites are $25 per night for two people, plus $2 for each additional person. Credit cards are not accepted. Long-term rates are available.

Directions: From Zephyrhills, drive one mile north on U.S. 301. Turn east onto Pretty Pond Road and go 0.5 mile to the stop sign at Wire Road. Head north on Wire Road to the park entrance.

Contact: Baker Acres RV Ranch, 7820 Wire Road, Zephyrhills, FL 33540, 813/782-3950 or 800/741-7875, fax 813/783-3406, www.bel-aireresorts.com.

85 QUAIL RUN RV PARK

Scenic rating: 6

west of Zephyrhills in Wesley Chapel

See map page 228

"No rig is too big," brag the managers. Tall oaks shade this gated RV park, which is close enough to I-75 to be a practical overnight refuge. You

might spot a flock of sandhill cranes on the rolling hills nearby or even in the park. A golf course, tennis courts, and a driving range are within one mile, but the park is a nice stopping place for interstate drivers. About a third of the park is occupied by year-round residents.

RV sites, facilities: All 147 grassy RV sites have sewer hookups, 30/50-amp electrical service, and telephone access. Lots vary in size, but the average is 20 by 50 feet. Some have cement patios and are pull-through. A pool, a playground, a volleyball field, horseshoes, shuffleboard, restrooms, showers, a computer room, picnic tables, propane gas, and a dump station are provided. Internet access via wireless network is available in the park. The camp store sells ice, some groceries, snacks, and beer. Management says the bathhouse, recreation hall, laundry, and office are wheelchair accessible. Families with children are welcome for short stays, although the park tends to attract full-time RVers and retirees. Leashed pets under 35 pounds are permitted. Only two pets are allowed per site, and attack breeds are prohibited.

Reservations, fees: Reservations are recommended. Sites are $30 per night for two people, plus $5 for each additional person. Credit cards are accepted. Long-term stays are allowed.

Directions: From I-75, take Exit 279 westbound on State Road 54 0.5 mile. At Old Pasco Road, turn north and drive two miles.

Contact: Quail Run RV Park, 6946 Old Pasco Road, Wesley Chapel, FL 33544, 813/973-0999 or 800/582-7084, www.quailrunrv.com.

86 ENCORE RV PARK– TAMPA NORTH

Scenic rating: 6

north of Lutz

See map page 228

In winter, snowbirds thaw out in the solar-heated hot tub and swimming pool and catch some rays on the pool deck. Set on 28 acres across from a Wal-Mart and near other shopping, the community offers comfortable amenities for those who like this style of vacation. Park models are for sale, as well. A 17-acre fishing lake keeps anglers busy; a gazebo looks out over it. It's a bustling place in winter, when the park population swells to 550 and an activities director arranges special events, parties, tournaments, and dances. About 25 percent of the people live here year-round, conveniently close to Busch Gardens, numerous Disney-area attractions, Crystal Springs, the Hillsborough River, several lakes, and Gulf Coast beaches. Big-rig sites are available.

RV sites, facilities: All 256 grassy sites have sewer hookups, 50-amp electrical service, paved patios, wireless Internet access, and telephone availability. Sites vary in size, but some will accommodate RVs up to 40 feet long and slide-outs. None are drive-through. A heated pool, a whirlpool tub, a recreation center, horseshoes, shuffleboard, billiards, a game room, restrooms, showers, a dump station, picnic tables, propane, park model sales, and laundry facilities are on the premises. An activities director organizes dances, dinners, games, and crafts from October through April. Across the street is a shopping center with a supermarket, restaurants, a pharmacy, a Wal-Mart, and hair salons. Most areas are wheelchair accessible with ramps. Children are permitted. Pets must be leashed.

Reservations, fees: Reservations are recommended. Sites are $31 for two people. Add $5 for each additional person. Credit cards are accepted. Monthly rates are available.

Directions: From I-75, take Exit 279 and drive 8.2 miles west on State Road 54. The resort is at left, near the corner of U.S. 41.

Contact: Encore RV Park—Tampa North, 21632 State Road 54, Lutz, FL 33549, 813/949-6551 or 800/879-2131, fax 813/949-4921, www.equitylifestyle.com.

87 LAKE COMO CLUB

Scenic rating: 5

on U.S. 41 north of Tampa

See map page 228   BEST (

Lake Como Club has all of the amenities of a fancy RV park: three clay tennis courts, a heated swimming pool, a hot tub, a sauna, a golf driving range, an archery range, planned activities in the recreation hall, and fishing and boating on a 35-acre lake with a sandy beach. The major difference? This has been a nude recreation community since 1940. In fact, Pasco County claims to have more nudist resorts than any other place in Florida—even a nudist housing development.

RV sites, facilities: This family nudist resort has 75 RV sites. All have water and 30-amp electricity. Two sites have 50-amp service, and 38 have sewer hookups. A couple of sites are drive-through. About one-third of the park is occupied year-round. On the premises are restrooms, showers, a dump station, a pool, a boat ramp, a dock, a playground, a volleyball field, laundry facilities, and motel rooms. Most of the visitors are from Canada or from the local nudist club. Planned activities include karaoke, *pétanque* (French-style bowling), boccie ball (lawn bowling), bingo, and potluck dinners. Internet access is available in the library. The RV sites, restrooms, and showers are wheelchair accessible. Children are welcome. Leashed pets are permitted.

Reservations, fees: Reservations are required. Sites are $30–36 per night for two people, plus one half the camping fee for each additional person. For 50-amp electrical service, the fee is $2.50 per night. Credit cards are accepted.

Directions: From I-75, take Exit 275 and drive west on State Road 56 for one mile. At State Road 54, bear west five more miles. At the intersection with U.S. 41, turn south and drive one block to Leonard Road, where you will turn west. Drive 0.5 mile to the park.

Contact: Lake Como Club, 20500 Cot Road, Lutz, FL 33549, 813/949-1810 or 877/TRY-LAKE (877/879-5253), fax 813/949-4937, www.lakecomoresort.com.

88 SWEETWATER RV PARK

Scenic rating: 4

south of Zephyrhills

See map page 228

Like most Zephyrhills parks, this one caters to retired RVers who like to spend several months at a time in Florida. It's part of a chain of nine parks in this area, including Baker Acres, Blue Jay, Citrus Hill, Glen Haven, Grove Ridge, Rainbow Village, Southern Charm, Water's Edge, and Big Tree. Yearly rates ($1,380) are for seven months' occupancy and five months' storage, allowing residents to avoid paying sales tax on their rent. The park is surrounded by a wooden fence. About 10 percent of the lots are occupied year-round.

RV sites, facilities: This 289-unit, snowbird-oriented mobile home and RV park offers full hookups, restrooms, showers, telephone availability, cable TV, and laundry facilities. Two hundred sites have 30-amp electrical service; the rest are 50-amp. Your RV must be self-contained. Lots average 30 feet wide by 50 feet deep, and RVs up to 40 feet long and slide-outs can be accommodated. None of the sites are drive-through. A recreation hall, shuffleboard and boccie ball (lawn bowling) courts, horseshoe pits, and table tennis and pool tables are provided. Most areas are wheelchair accessible. Streets are paved. Campers age 50 and up are preferred, although children may stay for up to two weeks. Pets are permitted in the designated pet section.

Reservations, fees: Reservations are recommended. Sites are $24 per night for two people, plus $2 for each additional person. Credit cards are not accepted. Long-term rates are available.

Directions: From U.S. 301 just south of Zephyrhills, turn west on Chancey Road and drive 0.25 mile.

Contact: Sweetwater RV Park, 37647 Chancey Road, Zephyrhills, FL 33541, 813/788-7513, www.bel-aireresorts.com.

89 SETTLER'S REST RV PARK

Scenic rating: 3

south of Zephyrhills

See map page 228

Seasonal visitors flock here each winter to escape the chilly North, and most of them return year after year to this 350-unit adult community. Just 14 sites are available for overnighters. About 15 percent of the units are occupied year-round. Also on the premises are park models, which are for sale. This family-owned park has a homey atmosphere. The visitors have their own form of government and raise funds each year to make improvements to the park; for example, they bought an organ for their church services. The church has a Methodist affiliation.

RV sites, facilities: RVs as long as 40 feet can be accommodated at the 14 RV sites open for overnighters. The rest of the sites are for long-term visits. Sites are split evenly between 30-amp and 50-amp electrical service. Sites are shady and average 30 by 60 feet in size. All have sewer hookups, picnic tables, cable TV, and phone service available. Restrooms, showers, a dump station, laundry facilities, and a recreation hall are in the park. The clubhouse and showers are wheelchair accessible. Children are welcome as visitors only. Leashed pets are permitted.

Reservations, fees: Reservations are advised. Sites are $32 a night for two people, plus $2 per extra person. Credit cards are not accepted. Long-term (up to six months) or seasonal stays are encouraged.

Directions: From U.S. 301 just south of Zephyrhills, turn west on Chancey Road and drive about 0.25 mile.

Contact: Settler's Rest RV Park, 37549 Chancey Road, Zephyrhills, FL 33541, 813/782-2003.

90 SOUTHERN CHARM RV RESORT

Scenic rating: 5

south of Zephyrhills
See map page 228

Most sites are occupied by RVs parked year-round in this 48-acre, supermanicured mobile-home resort with a total of 500 spaces. Trees are sparse, although some sites overlook a lake. Lighted, paved roads lead to sites, some with trees. If you like golf, many challenging courses are located within an easy drive. Unusual wintertime activities include pool exercises, wood carving, and a kitchen band.

RV sites, facilities: At this adults-only park, 200 RV lots have full hookups, 30/50-amp electrical service, optional telephone service, and cable TV access. None of the sites are drive-through. Sites are 35 by 50 feet. The maximum length of vehicle that can be parked here is 40 feet, and slide-outs are permitted. An Internet connection is available in the office and the clubhouse. Facilities include a recreation hall with a large stone fireplace, shuffleboard courts, horseshoes, planned activities, laundry facilities, a post office, a pool room, a whirlpool tub, and a heated pool. RVs must be in excellent condition and at least 20 feet long. Small pets are permitted in the designated pet section.

Reservations, fees: Reservations are recommended. Sites are $25 per night for two people, plus $2 for each additional person. Credit cards are not accepted. Long-term rates are available.

Directions: From U.S. 301 just south of Zephyrhills, turn west on Chancey Road and drive 0.5 mile to Autumn Palm. The resort is just ahead, at right.

Contact: Southern Charm RV Resort, 37811 Chancey Road, Zephyrhills, FL 33541, 813/783-3477 or 800/471-7875, fax 813/783-3406, www.bel-aire resorts.com.

91 GLEN HAVEN RV AND MOBILE PARK

Scenic rating: 4

south of Zephyrhills
See map page 228

Glen Haven is one of several retirement-oriented parks along this road. Grocery stores and restaurants are within three miles in Zephyrhills. About 70 percent of this park is populated with park models, though just a few are occupied year-round.

RV sites, facilities: This mobile-home community/RV park has 218 concrete-pad sites with full hookups, 30/50-amp electricity, optional telephone service, cable TV access, and cement slabs. RVs up to 40 feet long can be accommodated. Average lot size is 35 by 50 feet. Restrooms, showers, a whirlpool tub, a pool, horseshoe pits, shuffleboard courts, an exercise room, a clubhouse with Internet connection, propane gas, and laundry facilities are provided. Activities include the usual pancake breakfasts, dances, and ice-cream socials, but also a computer club with software classes. Most areas are wheelchair accessible. Campers must be 55 or older, though children may visit for a short time. Leashed pets under 25 pounds are permitted.

Reservations, fees: Reservations are recommended. Sites are $35 per night for two people, plus $2 for each additional person. Credit cards are not accepted. Long-term stays are okay.

Directions: From the south side of Zephyrhills, drive south on U.S 301/County Road 41 to the intersection with Chancey Road. Turn west on Chancey Road and go one mile.

Contact: Glen Haven RV and Mobile Park, 37251 Chancey Road, Zephyrhills, FL 33541, 813/782-1856 or 800/362-5181, fax 813/783-3132, www.bel-aireresorts.com.

92 WHITE'S RV PARK

Scenic rating: 4

south of Zephyrhills

See map page 228

Set on 18 acres, this family-owned and -operated park offers lots of planned activities for its retired clientele, which hails from the northeast and central part of the United States. A golf course, grocery stores, and restaurants are close. Favorite things to do are bingo, cards, euchre, potluck dinners and breakfasts, dances, church activities, crafts, and off-site trips.

RV sites, facilities: This 55-and-older park has 270 concrete-pad RV sites with full hookups, 30/50-amp electrical plugs, picnic tables, and telephone service available. Lots range in size from 30 to 32 feet wide by 50 feet deep. None of the sites are drive-through. An Internet connection is available in the clubhouse. Restrooms, showers, a dump station, laundry facilities, a pool, a recreation room, billiard tables, and shuffleboard courts are on the premises. A golf course, grocery stores, and restaurants are within three miles. Management says all areas are wheelchair accessible. Children are permitted for short visits only. Pets are allowed.

Reservations, fees: Reservations are recommended. Sites are $18 per night for two people, plus $1 for each additional person. Credit cards are not accepted. Long-term stays are okay.

Directions: From U.S. 301 just south of Zephyrhills, turn west on Chancey Road and drive 0.5 mile. The park is on the south side of the road.

Contact: White's RV Park, 37400 Chancey Road, Zephyrhills, FL 33541, 813/783-1644, email: whiterv374@aol.com.

93 HUNTER'S RUN RV RESORT

Scenic rating: 4

south of Zephyrhills

See map page 228

Planned social activities are held during winter in the recreation hall. The community offers retirees a relaxing winter with lots of opportunities to make friends. Of the 309 sites, many are occupied by park models. During the winter season, visitors enjoy live bands every Saturday, line dancing, church services on Sunday, ice-cream socials, bingo, potluck dinners, breakfasts, cruises, and casino trips. The owners say their park is different because it's in the countryside, yet close to everything.

RV sites, facilities: All 309 sites have sewer hookups, 30-amp electricity, telephone service and cable TV access. About 40 sites have 50-amp service. RVs up to 35 feet long can be accommodated. Restrooms, showers, a dump station, laundry facilities, shuffleboard and boccie ball (lawn bowling) courts, horseshoe pits, a recreation hall with Internet connection, a pool, a spa, a sauna, and an exercise room are on the premises. Shopping and groceries are within two miles. Most areas are wheelchair accessible, and streets are paved. Campers must be 55 or older, although children are allowed to visit for up to two weeks. Small pets are permitted on a leash.

Reservations, fees: Reservations are recommended. Sites are $24 per night for two people, plus $2 for each additional person. Credit cards are not accepted.

Directions: From the south side of Zephyrhills, drive south on U.S 301/County Road 41 to the intersection with Chancey Road. Turn west and go 1.2 miles to the park, near the corner of South Allen Road.

Contact: Hunter's Run RV Resort, 37041 Chancey Road, Zephyrhills, FL 33541, 813/783-1133.

94 PALM VIEW GARDENS

Scenic rating: 4

south of Zephyrhills

See map page 228

This sprawling and well-manicured park on a corner of a major highway is somewhat exposed to the road. Trees are minimal, but most RVers in Zephyrhills don't seem to mind, and about two-thirds of the park is occupied year-round. Bench seating overlooks the stocked fishing lake, and the paved, lighted interior roads lend themselves to bicycling. Social activities are held during the season in two spacious recreation halls. The oversized pool is heated during the cooler months.

RV sites, facilities: The adults-only park has 525 sites with full hookups, 30-amp electrical service, concrete patios, and telephone and cable TV access. Sites are a roomy 30 by 90 feet, with 10 feet of buffering between neighbors. The management creates a directory of its visitors so they can stay in touch with each other when they go back home to places like Michigan, New York, or Canada. Restrooms, showers, laundry facilities, a dump station, a pool, two recreation halls with kitchens, horseshoes, championship shuffleboard courts, and a fishing lake are provided. Most areas are wheelchair accessible, and streets are paved. Children may visit tenants for no longer than two weeks. Leashed pets are permitted.

Reservations, fees: Reservations are recommended. Sites are $23 per night for two people, plus $2.50 for each additional person. Credit cards are accepted. Long-term stays are preferred.

Directions: From State Road 54 and U.S. 301 in Zephyrhills, turn south on U.S. 301 and drive two miles to the park. Gall Boulevard is the same as U.S. 301.

Contact: Palm View Gardens, 3331 Gall Boulevard, Zephyrhills, FL 33541, 813/782-8685, www.rvresorts.com.

95 HAPPY DAYS RV PARK

Scenic rating: 5

west of Zephyrhills
See map page 228

Churches, a shopping center, and other points of interest are close to this park. There's even a bus stop nearby. Planned activities, such as exercise and crafts classes, fashion shows, games, bingo, and Sunday church services, are held in winter. The recreation hall has a dance floor, a stage, and an electronic bingo scoreboard; the smaller lodge has a workshop area for hobbies. About half the park is occupied by park models.

RV sites, facilities: All 300 lots have sewer hookups and 20/30-amp electrical outlets; 150 sites are available for RVs. Rigs up to 40 feet in length can be accommodated. Restrooms, showers, laundry facilities, a dump station, shuffleboard courts, horseshoe pits, a recreation hall, two pool tables, cable TV, and a heated pool are available. The streets are paved, and the laundry and clubhouse are wheelchair accessible. This is an age-55-and-over park; children are not permitted except for short visits. Leashed pets under 20 pounds are allowed in one area of the park.

Reservations, fees: Reservations are recommended. Sites are $22 per night for two people, plus $2 for each additional person. Credit cards are accepted. Long-term stays are permitted.

Directions: From State Road 54 and U.S. 301 in Zephyrhills, drive west on State Road 54 for about 0.5 mile. Turn south on Allen Road (by the convenience store). The park is ahead within 0.5 mile, just past the shopping center.

Contact: Happy Days RV Park, 4603 Allen Road, Zephyrhills, FL 33541, 813/788-4858.

96 ANDY'S TRAVEL TRAILER PARK

Scenic rating: 2

west of Zephyrhills
See map page 228

Ready for a Saturday-night bonfire? This retirement-oriented snowbird park boasts a very active social schedule, with barbecues, coffee hours, potluck dinners, bingo, cards, video nights, and more. About 10 percent of the park is occupied by year-round residents. Favorite things to do? "Walk, talk, and enjoy life."

RV sites, facilities: Designed for the winter visitor, the park has 75 full-hookup sites for snowbirds, and six spots for overnighters. All have picnic tables, 30-amp electrical service, and concrete patios. Lots vary in size; in fact, all are different, the owners say. Some sites can handle large rigs and slide-outs. An Internet connection is available in the office. Restrooms, showers, a wheelchair-accessible clubhouse, shuffleboard courts, and a dog-walk area are on-site. The bathhouse and clubhouse are wheelchair accessible. Streets are paved. Groceries and restaurants are within 0.5 mile. Adults over 55 are preferred; children are not allowed. Leashed pets under 12 pounds are permitted.

Reservations, fees: Reservations are recommended. Sites are $20 per night for two people, plus $2 per extra person. Credit cards are not accepted. Long-term rates are available.

Directions: From I-75, take Exit 279 and drive east on State Road 54 for 10 miles.

Contact: Andy's Travel Trailer Park, 37707 State Road 54, Zephyrhills, FL 33541, 813/782-3843, email: jodyr@3oaks.com.

97 JIM'S RV PARK

Scenic rating: 3

west of Zephyrhills

See map page 228

Catering to retired snowbirds who like to stay put for the season, the park has a volunteer committee that organizes a full array of winter activities, such as bingo, crafts, potluck suppers, dances, bowling parties, and golf outings. Within one mile are shops, restaurants, a library, banks, and video rentals. Flea markets abound in the area.

RV sites, facilities: The adults-only park has 147 sites (more than 60 percent are occupied year-round) with sewer hookups. Half have 30-amp electrical service, the rest have 50-amp. Slide-outs and 45-foot-long RVs can be accommodated on lots that average 30 by 60 feet. Sites are sunny and paved. Restrooms,

showers, laundry facilities, a dump station, shuffleboard and horseshoe courts, a recreation hall, and a pool are on the premises. The bathhouse, pool area, and recreation hall are wheelchair accessible. Children may visit campers for up to two weeks. One small, leashed pet is permitted per unit.

Reservations, fees: Reservations are recommended. Sites are $22 per night for two people, plus $1 for each additional person. Credit cards are not accepted. Long-term stays are okay.

Directions: From I-75, take Exit 279 and drive east on State Road 54 for nine miles.

Contact: Jim's RV Park, 35120 State Road 54 West, Zephyrhills, FL 33541, 813/782-5610.

98 RALPH'S TRAVEL PARK

Scenic rating: 4

west of Zephyrhills

See map page 228

Canadians get a warm welcome at this sprawling wooded park, which has full-service amenities, plus a car wash area. Gas and food stores are located next door. Owners claim it has the largest swimming pool in the Zephyrhills area.

RV sites, facilities: There are 100 RV sites available with full hookups and 30/50-amp electrical service in this 402-lot snowbird retreat, where folks return year after year. About half the units are occupied year-round. Restrooms, showers, laundry facilities, a pool, shuffleboard courts, horseshoe pits, two recreation halls, and a workshop are available. The recreation halls, laundry room, and restrooms are accessible to wheelchairs. Campers must be 50 or older. Pets under 25 pounds are allowed. Aggressive breeds are prohibited

Reservations, fees: Reservations are recommended. Sites are $19 per night for two people, plus $1 for each additional person. Credit cards are not accepted. Long-term stays are the norm.

Directions: From I-75, take Exit 279 and go six miles east on State Road 54 to the park, which

is on the corner of Morris Bridge Road across the street from the Home Depot.
Contact: Ralph's Travel Park, 34408 State Road 54 West, Zephyrhills, FL 33543, 813/782-8223 or 866/234-2056, email: ralphs33543@aol.com.

99 HILLCREST RV RESORT

Scenic rating: 4

on the west side of Zephyrhills
See map page 228

Extra-large lots accommodate residents in this sunny park-model/RV retreat, which caters to seasonal visitors and retirees, about half of whom live here year-round. The management of the 40-acre resort prides itself on keeping the premises neat and orderly. RVs must be modern and well maintained; rules are strict regarding maintenance of the lots. In the wintertime, an activities director organizes weekly shows, golf, game nights, men's and women's billiards, a jam session every Wednesday, aerobics in the pool, and Crime Watch meetings once a month.
RV sites, facilities: There are 496 full-hookup sites with 30/50-amp electrical service and telephone availability, of which 200 are available for RVs. Restrooms, showers, two laundries, a dump station, a pool, and two clubhouses are provided; many areas are wheelchair accessible. Internet access is available in the clubhouse. Grocery stores and restaurants are within one mile. Children are not welcome except for brief visits. Leashed pets are permitted.
Reservations, fees: Reservations are recommended. Sites are $25 per night for two people, plus $2 for each additional person.
Directions: From I-75, take Exit 279 eastbound on State Road 54 for 10 miles. After passing the Winn-Dixie, go 0.5 mile farther, turn south on Lane Road, and proceed to the park.
Contact: Hillcrest RV Resort, 4421 Lane Road, Zephyrhills, FL 33541, 813/782-1947 or 800/992-8735, email: hillcrestrv@verizon.net.

100 LEISURE DAYS RV RESORT

Scenic rating: 3

west of Zephyrhills
See map page 228

Staying at this sunny, landscaped, retiree-oriented park puts you close to fishing waters, tennis courts, golf courses, shopping, and Central Florida attractions. Social programs are held from November through mid-April; among them are planned campfires, bingo, crafts, card parties, pancake breakfasts, and dances. The pool is heated.
RV sites, facilities: This park has 41 RV sites with full hookups for overnighters, cable TV, and telephone access. They accommodate rigs up to 37 feet in length. Restrooms, showers, laundry facilities, a pool, an activity center, horseshoe pits, and shuffleboard courts are available. All units must be self-contained. There are 200 additional sites for long-termers. All areas are wheelchair accessible. An age-55-and-older park, Leisure Days permits children as visitors and for short periods only. Leashed pets under 25 pounds are allowed.
Reservations, fees: Reservations are recommended. Sites are $14.50 per night. Credit cards are not accepted. Long-term stays are okay.
Directions: From I-75, take Exit 279 and drive east on State Road 54 for six miles. Turn south on Morris Bridge Road and drive one block.
Contact: Leisure Days RV Resort, 34533 Leisure Days Drive, Zephyrhills, FL 33541, 813/788-2631, fax 813/715-7617.

101 ORLANDO SOUTHEAST/ LAKE WHIPPOORWILL KOA

Scenic rating: 7

on Lake Whippoorwill east of Orlando
See map page 228

These mostly grassy sites are set amid palm trees alongside fishable 350-acre Lake Whippoorwill in the rural eastern section of Orange County. A hairdresser is available in winter, when the place fills up with snowbirds who enjoy pancake breakfasts, potluck dinners, and bingo at the 40-acre park. Swimming, boating, fishing, and waterskiing are popular. The management says it's about a 20-minute drive to Disney-area attractions and 35 minutes to Cape Canaveral. Many people live here on a semipermanent basis.

RV sites, facilities: There are 120 RV sites (all full-hookup with 30/50-amp electrical service; 22 are pull-through. Each site has a picnic table. Rigs up to 45 feet long and slide-outs can be accommodated. Sites vary in size from 15 feet wide and 25–45 feet deep. Cable TV and telephone service are available. A pool, a recreation hall, a hot tub, canoe rentals, a playground, horseshoes, shuffleboard, and volleyball entertain campers. On the premises are restrooms, showers, a boat ramp, a dock, a dump station, cabin rentals, laundry facilities, limited bait and tackle, and a gift shop and store. The recreation hall, pool, and convenience store are wheelchair accessible. Restaurants and groceries are within two miles. Children and leashed pets are welcome.

Reservations, fees: Reservations are recommended. Sites are $37–47 per night for two people, plus $2–3 for each additional person. Credit cards are accepted. Long-term stays are okay.

Directions: From Orlando, take State Road 528/the Bee Line Expressway east about 10 miles to State Road 15/Narcoossee Road, then go south for five miles to the park.

Contact: Orlando Southeast/Lake Whippoorwill KOA, 12345 Narcoossee Road, Orlando, FL 32827, 407/277-5075 or 800/999-5267, www.whippoorwillkoa@piorl.com.

102 MOSS PARK

Scenic rating: 7

near Lake Hart southeast of Orlando

See map page 228

Boating, hiking, and wildlife observation are the most popular activities at this 2.5-square-

mile county campground, which is favored by locals. The heavily wooded shell-rock sites, each with a picnic table, a grill, and a fire ring, are nestled between Lake Hart and Lake Mary Jane, both of which are popular for swimming and fishing. It's adjacent to the 1,800-acre Split Oak Forest Mitigation Park, where you'll find several hiking trails. Hurricanes in 2004 blew away more than 400 trees, so the park is less shady these days.

Look for sandhill cranes, deer, wild turkeys, wood storks, and fox squirrels—a remarkable array when you consider how close you are to Orlando. When the Moss family donated the land to Orange County in 1930, it was known as "Bear Island," but you won't see any bears today. Canoeing, kayaking, waterskiing, and windsurfing are possible on the lakes if you bring your own equipment. A three-mile nature trail and several more miles of hiking trails will please day hikers. This park is 25 miles from Disney-area attractions. Park rangers live on-site.

RV sites, facilities: The county-run campground offers 54 hard-shell sites with 30/50-amp electric service and piped water. Sites 1–4, also designated as multifamily sites for a maximum of 12 people per site, are pull-through. Sites 5 and 6 are wheelchair accessible. Each site has a picnic table, a grill, and a fire ring. Facilities include restrooms, showers, two dump stations, two boat ramps, a beach, hiking trails, playgrounds, pavilion rentals, softball field, and volleyball. Management says the restrooms are wheelchair accessible. Children are welcome. Pets are prohibited. Absolutely no alcohol is allowed; the rule is enforced with a $500 fine and/or six months in jail.

Reservations, fees: Reservations must be made in person. Pay by cash or check when you make the reservation 45 days in advance, and you must stay a minimum of two nights. Telephone reservations are not accepted. Sites are $14–19 per night. Credit cards are not accepted. Stays are limited to 14 days.

Directions: Take State Road 528/Bee Line

Expressway east from Orlando International Airport about three miles. At Exit 22, head south on Narcoossee Road/State Road 15 for 2.5 miles, then turn left onto Moss Park Road. From State Road 417/Greenway Expressway, take Exit 22 onto Narcoossee Road and go north one mile to Moss Park Road.

Contact: Moss Park, 12901 Moss Park Road, Orlando, FL 32812, 407/273-2327, fax 407/249-4498, www.orangecountyparks.net.

103 EAST LAKE FISH CAMP

Scenic rating: 3

on East Lake Tohopekaliga south of Orlando
See map page 228

Not for nothing is the main road through the park known as Big Bass Road. This place on four-mile-wide East Lake Tohopekaliga is designed for anglers, but the airboat rides are also a big attraction. You'll find a kidney-shaped pool and a barnyard with donkeys, geese, and ducks. Some families camp here even if they're not after bass, specks, or shellcrackers, but the vast majority of visitors are snowbirds. You may be able to get a shady spot, but about one-third of the sites are sunny. Permanent residents take up about 40 percent of the spots, and there's a restaurant on-site with all-you-can eat buffets on weekend nights.

RV sites, facilities: There are 263 grassy full-hookup RV sites (about 35 pull-through) with concrete pads. Fifty lots have 50-amp electrical service; the rest have 30-amp. RVs up to 40 feet long and slide-outs can be accommodated at the grassy sites, which vary in size. Facilities include restrooms, showers, a dump station, gasoline and LP gas sales, laundry facilities, picnic tables, cabin rentals, a pool, a restaurant, boat rentals, fishing guide services, bait and tackle sales, a boat ramp, and tennis courts. The camp store sells beer, ice, and fishing tackle. Management says the bathhouse and camp store are wheelchair accessible. Children and pets are permitted.

Reservations, fees: Reservations are not accepted. Nightly fee for two people is $20 for an RV site. Add $1 per extra person. Credit cards are accepted. Long-term rates are available.

Directions: From the Central Florida Greenway/Highway 417, take Exit 17 and drive south on Boggy Creek Road for about five miles. Turn right onto Fish Camp Road and continue south to Big Bass Road, which leads through the park.

Contact: East Lake Fish Camp, 3705 Big Bass Road, Kissimmee, FL 34744, 407/348-2040, fax 407/348-7797, email: eastlake@concentric.net.

104 THE FLORIDIAN RV RESORT

Scenic rating: 7

south of Orlando on the Orange/Osceola County line
See map page 228

This large, 140-acre gated park is next to a mobile-home park run by the same folks who manage the campground. Some college students live in the campground; the rest are retirees staying year-round or those who park their RVs under the 6/6 plan that allows them to leave their rigs in the park during hot months. During the busy winter season, campers enjoy dances, play bingo and card games, organize tennis teams, and attend periodic on-site health fairs. If you bring a boat or canoe, you can launch from the park into Fells Cove, which leads to East Lake Tohopekaliga. Bathrooms are within easy walking distance on lighted paths from the water-and-electric sites. The campground is about 20 miles from Walt Disney World.

RV sites, facilities: The campground offers 457 grassy RV sites (about 350 full-hookup) with concrete slabs. RVs up the 40 feet long can be accommodated. On the premises are restrooms, showers, a dump station, laundry facilities, picnic tables, a playground, a recreation hall, a hot tub, a boat ramp and dock, volleyball, shuffleboard, and tennis courts. The clubhouse has an atrium seating area where you can access the Internet, TV and card rooms, and billiards. Many areas have wheelchair access. Streets are paved. Children and small pets are allowed.

Reservations, fees: Reservations are recommended in January, February, and March. Sites are $32 per night for two people, plus $1 for each additional person age six and older. Credit cards are accepted. Long-term rates are available.

Directions: From Orlando, take State Road 15/Narcoossee Road south 150 miles to State Road 530. The campground is at the intersection of State Roads 530 and 15.

Contact: The Floridian RV Resort, 5150 Boggy Creek Road, St. Cloud, FL 34771, 407/892-5171, www.florida-rv-parks.com/index.html.

105 ELITE RESORTS AT CITRUS VALLEY

Scenic rating: 5

in Clermont within 10 miles of Disney World

See map page 229

Proximity to Disney World—less than 10 miles away—may be the biggest selling point of this place. And that's what is happening: New owners in 2005 converted the campground to a condominium RV park, and lots are for sale for year-round occupancy. Still, as the conversion goes on, overnighters may find a spot here. Anglers can head to little Hancock Lake, perhaps the closest of the region's plentiful (mostly small) lakes. Local bass anglers prefer 3,634-acre Lake Louisa, located about six miles north of the park as the crow flies. Picnicking and swimming at Lake Louisa State Park requires a longer drive, yet you may get to see alligators and deer at the 1,790-acre parcel of land, which is home to 10 types of biological communities, including scrubland, a black-water stream, and upland hardwoods. Call the state park at 352/394-3969.

RV sites, facilities: Of the 378 sites, most have full hookups, 30/50-amp electrical service, and wireless Internet access. A pool, a playground, horseshoes, shuffleboard, a pool table, a rec-

reation hall, and seasonal planned activities entertain campers. Showers, restrooms, a dump station, trailer rentals, cable TV, telephone hookups, and laundry facilities are available. All areas are said to be wheelchair accessible. Shopping, groceries and restaurants are within two miles. Children are welcome. Pets must be leashed.

Reservations, fees: Reservations are recommended. Sites are $30–34 per night for two people, plus $3 for each additional person. Credit cards are accepted.

Directions: From I-4 at Exit 64B in Kissimmee, take U.S. 192 west. Turn north onto U.S. 27 and continue 2.5 miles to the park on your right.

Contact: Elite Resorts at Citrus Valley, 2500 U.S. 27 South, Clermont, FL 34714, 352/394-4051 or 877/369-0004, www.eliteresorts.com.

106 DISNEY'S FORT WILDERNESS CAMPGROUND

Scenic rating: 10

on the grounds of Walt Disney World

See map page 229   **BEST (**

At this gem of a park, the 700 acres of lush wilderness stand out as the sole campground located on the Disney resort property, with full access to Disney World by land, water, or monorail. Guests enjoy complimentary transportation throughout the Walt Disney World Resort. For a campground, the recreational opportunities are mind-boggling: Swimming, fishing, waterskiing, and canoeing are popular at lakes on the property, and golf courses are nearby. Biking, tennis, horseback riding, and hiking on a two-mile nature trail are available. Children's activities include a nightly campfire visit by Disney characters, Disney movies, a petting farm, and pony rides.

The park, which has paved sites with separate gravel sitting areas, is highly recommended to parents. This is camping with a very polished feel, including air-conditioned bathrooms and heated swimming pools. Of course, you pay for the amenities. Still, the price is no more than you'd expect to pay to stay in most of the mid- to low-priced motels in the area. Plan on waiting quite awhile if you're checking in at a busy time. An hour-long wait is not unusual, but arriving early in the day helps. The busy times of year are generally in summer and around major holidays, although things can get busy at any time.

RV sites, facilities: The 694 full-hookup RV sites have 30-amp and 50-amp service, picnic tables, and grills. A pool, charter fishing, boat and canoe rentals, paddleboats, a playground, game rooms, a nature trail, golf and miniature golf, a driving range, horseshoes, shuffleboard, tennis, volleyball, hayrides, horseback riding, a petting farm, dinner shows, and pony rides entertain guests. On the premises are restrooms, showers, a dump station, groceries, laundry facilities, and restaurants. Management says the restrooms and transportation to other facilities on the Disney property are wheelchair accessible. Cable TV is available at some RV sites. Children are welcome. Leashed pets are restricted to full-hookup sites.

Reservations, fees: Reservations are recommended. Sites vary in price depending on the time of year from $39 to $92 per night. Credit cards are accepted. Long-term stays are okay.

Directions: From I-4, take Exit 67 onto State Road 536 westbound and follow signs to the campground entrance.

Contact: Disney's Fort Wilderness Campground, 4510 North Fort Wilderness Trail, Lake Buena Vista, FL 32830, 407/824-2900 or for reservations, 407/939-6244, fax 407/824-3508, www.disney.com.

the park to enjoy yourself; it's a self-contained recreation place for all ages. Pools, tennis courts, planned activities, and views of 160-acre Lake Davenport offer relaxation after a day in the theme parks. It's all done in the first-class manner that this chain of parks is known for. About 10 percent of the park is occupied by year-round residents.

RV sites, facilities: There are 467 sunny RV sites (70 pull-through). RVers have picnic tables, paved pads, and patios with 30/50-amp electrical hookups available, plus cable TV and telephone service. Rigs up to 45 feet long can be accommodated. Internet connection is available at the clubhouse. Restrooms, showers, laundry facilities, two heated pools, a whirlpool tub, a playground, tennis courts, sand volleyball, a basketball court, horseshoe pits, shuffleboard courts, a recreation center, a fitness center, a mail center, and golf nets are on the premises. Groceries and shopping are within 0.2 mile. Most areas are wheelchair accessible. Children are welcome. Leashed pets are permitted.

Reservations, fees: Reservations are recommended. Sites are $39–46 per night for two people, plus $5 for each extra person. Credit cards are accepted. Long-term rates are available.

Directions: From I-4 westbound, take Exit 64B, drive west about five miles on U.S. 192/Irlo Bronson Highway to the park entrance on the left. Eastbound from I-4, take U.S. 27 north to U.S. 192; turn east and go 0.25 mile. The resort will be on the right.

Contact: Lake Magic RV Resort, 9600 Irlo Bronson Highway, Clermont, FL 34714, 863/420-1300 or 888/558-5777, fax 863/420-1400, www.rvonthego.com.

107 LAKE MAGIC RV RESORT

Scenic rating: 10

four miles west of Disney World

See map page 229 BEST (

Just four miles from Walt Disney Resort, this park (formerly known as Encore) is convenient to shopping and restaurants. You won't have to leave

108 TROPICAL PALMS FUNRESORT

Scenic rating: 8

off U.S. 192 near Disney World

See map page 229

A fair supply of palms, pines, and other trees shade the sites at this resort, but you can get a sunny spot if that's what you're after. The 60 acres located behind a Days Inn motel are shared by campers and people renting cottages, but no year-round residents. A full-sized, somewhat Y-shaped heated pool is open 24 hours, and sunbathers lounging around its patio can gaze at a pleasant green backdrop of palms, tall pines, and shade trees. But the main benefit of staying here is that you're within a few minutes of the major Central Florida attractions. You can even walk to the Old Town entertainment district, which has 80 shops, restaurants, and rides. Two championship golf courses and Pirate's Cove adventure golf are nearby.

RV sites, facilities: There are 525 roomy RV sites (425 full-hookup, 200 pull-through) large enough to accommodate huge rigs and slide-outs. Both 30-amp and 50-amp electrical service is provided. Each site has a picnic table. The office has an Internet connection. A pool, a kiddie pool, a playground, a cafe, basketball hoops, a game room, shuffleboard, a recreation room, horseshoes, and a sand volleyball court entertain campers. A shuttle bus, store with camping supplies, snacks, laundry facilities, restrooms, showers, a dump station, cable TV, telephone hookups, a business center, discounted attraction tickets, rental cottages, rental suites, rental park models, and a poolside cafe are available. The bathhouse and one of the cottages are wheelchair accessible. Restaurants and shops are located within walking distance. Children and leashed pets are welcome.

Reservations, fees: Reservations are recommended. Sites are $25–49 per night. Credit cards are accepted. Stays are limited to 30 days.

Directions: From I-4 at Exit 64A, head east one mile on U.S. 192/Irlo Bronson Highway, then turn right on Holiday Trail. Follow it south to the campground, which is located behind Old Town.

Contact: Tropical Palms Fun Resort, 2650 Holiday Trail, Kissimmee, FL 34746, 407/396-4595 or 800/64-PALMS (800/647-2567), fax 407/396-8938, www.tropicalpalmsrv.com.

109 SHERWOOD FOREST RV RESORT

Scenic rating: 7

on U.S. 192 near Disney World

See map page 229

Like numerous campgrounds in the area, the big attraction of Sherwood Forest is its proximity to the many Disney-area attractions. Staying here puts you about four miles from the main gate to Disney World. Parts of the sprawling, manicured community have oaks and pines. Paved roads lead from the security gate to the campsites—most grassy, some sunny. Parents are welcome to bring the kids; they can send them to the playground while they head to the small on-site lake (no fishing) or heated pool. About half the park is occupied year-round by park models. The clubhouse is big enough to seat at least 200.

RV sites, facilities: All 512 full-hookup sites (375 pull-through) have 30-amp or 50-amp electrical service; about half are available for tourists. Most sites have a picnic table. Sites 31–40 overlook the lake. A pool, a hot tub, putt-putt golf, a fitness room, a library, a post office, a financial center, horseshoes, tennis, shuffleboard, a clubhouse, and winter social programs are on the premises. Volunteers organize activities such as bingo, potluck dinners, and casino trips. On the premises are restrooms, showers, a dump station, laundry facilities, trailer rentals, and limited groceries. The office has an Internet connection. Restaurants and shopping are within 0.2 mile. Management says the restrooms and camp store are wheelchair accessible. Children are welcome. Two pets under 30 pounds each are permitted per site.

Reservations, fees: Reservations are recommended. Sites are $38–43 per night for two people, plus $1.50 for each extra person. Credit cards are accepted. Long-term rates are available.

Directions: From I-4 at Exit 64A, head east on U.S. 192/Irlo Bronson Highway nearly three miles to the campground.

Contact: Sherwood Forest RV Resort, 5300 West Irlo Bronson Highway, Kissimmee, FL 34746, 407/396-7431 or 800/548-9981, fax 407/396-7239, www.mhchomes.com.

110 KISSIMMEE/ORLANDO KOA

Scenic rating: 6

off U.S. 192 in Kissimmee, east of Disney World

See map page 229 **BEST (**

This KOA is tucked just off the busy main drag—U.S. 192—about five miles from Walt Disney World. The eight-acre park has a pool and grassy or gravel sites with shade. Some sites designated as "deluxe" have patio furniture (not just picnic tables) and come with a bundle of firewood for the "chiminea" firepot; they are also pull-through and you park your rig on a concrete pad instead of gravel or grass. It's a real RV park; there are no full-time occupants.

RV sites, facilities: The camp has 96 full-hookup RV sites with 20/30/50-amp electrical outlets and cable TV. Each has a picnic table and campfire. Sites vary in size; some are as deep as 80 feet and can accommodate huge RVs or slide-outs. On the premises are restrooms, showers, a dump station, a pool, a playground, a basketball court, rental bikes, a convenience store with firewood and 'smores ingredients for your campfire, propane, and laundry facilities. Internet connection is available via wireless network throughout the park, and there's also a stand-alone Internet room. Roads are paved, and most areas of the park are said to be wheelchair accessible. You can select your own site before settling in; the park management will drive you through to inspect the sites first. Groceries and restaurants are within one mile. Children and pets are welcome.

Reservations, fees: Sites are $45–79 for two people, $6 for each additional adult, and $3 for children. Credit cards are accepted. Stays are limited to six months.

Directions: The campground is off U.S. 192, between mile markers 12 and 13. Coming from the west on I-4, take Exit 192 five miles east on U.S. 192/Irlo Bronson Highway, passing Highway 535. Turn left at Seven Dwarfs Lane, then right on Happy Camper Place. If coming from the east on I-4, take Highway 535 to U.S. 192, and follow the directions starting with Seven Dwarfs Lane.

Contact: Kissimmee/Orlando KOA, 2644 Happy Camper Place, Kissimmee, FL 34746, 407/396-2400 or 800/562-7791, fax 407/396-7577, www.koa.com.

111 ORANGE GROVE CAMPGROUND

Scenic rating: 6

off U.S. 192 in Kissimmee, east of Disney World

See map page 229

Imagine waking up on a brisk winter morning, walking a few feet from your paved or grassy campsite, and plucking fresh oranges off a tree for breakfast. You can do it at this former orange grove, where campers can savor tangerines, grapefruits, lemons, and oranges for free. Onetime grove or not, trees—and therefore shade—are sparse. Play miniature golf on the premises, or drive a short distance to get in a round of the real thing. Most visitors are snowbirds, although a few families find their way here.

The 14-acre park is behind the Value Outlet Shops in the heart of Disney-area shopping and entertainment attractions. It's essentially around the corner from the Medieval Times dinner show and about five miles from the main gate to Disney World.

This is not camping in the get-back-to-nature sense. Your eyes will be assaulted whenever you venture far from the campground by the electric signs of T-shirt shops, restaurants, and the rest of the tourist traps packed chockablock along U.S. 192. But it is one of the more convenient spots to camp if you're making the rounds at Disney World.

RV sites, facilities: The park offers 177

full-hookup RV sites (4 drive-through). Thirty sites have 50-amp electrical service; 137 have 30-amp. Each site has a picnic table. The office has an Internet connection and a wireless network has been installed. A pool, miniature golf, a playground, horseshoes, shuffleboard, and winter social programs organized by volunteers entertain campers. On the premises are restrooms, showers, a dump station, laundry facilities, propane sales, and limited groceries (no bread or milk). Golf and restaurants are within one mile; groceries are two miles away. Most areas are wheelchair accessible. Children are welcome. Leashed, attended pets are permitted.

Reservations, fees: Reservations are recommended in winter. Sites are $30–35 per night for two people, plus $1 for each additional person over the age of three. Credit cards are accepted. The maximum length of stay for new visitors is six months, though about 25 percent of the sites are occupied by year-round residents.

Directions: From I-4 at Exit 68, head east on State Road 535 for 2.5 miles. Turn south on U.S. 192/Irlo Bronson Highway and drive 3.5 miles to the stoplight with the Wal-Mart. Turn west on Old Vineland Road and proceed one mile to the campground on the right, behind the Kissimmee Manufacturers Outlet Mall. From Florida's Turnpike, take Exit 244 westbound to U.S. 192 for 6.75 miles. Turn right at Old Vineland Road and drive one mile to the park on the right side.

Contact: Orange Grove Campground, 2425 Old Vineland Road, Kissimmee, FL 34746, 407/396-6655.

112 GREAT OAK RV RESORT

Scenic rating: 6

in Kissimmee, six miles east of Disney World

See map page 229

If you want to sleep closest to the well-used swimming pool or the restrooms, ask for a spot in section C. Although some families vacation here (a pediatric clinic is conveniently located next door), the typical campers at Great Oak RV Resort are snowbird couples who might like to take part in bingo, potluck suppers, or trips to the bowling alley during the winter months. About 20 percent of the sites are occupied year-round. Disney World is about six miles from these grassy campsites with concrete patios—some with shade and others in the sunshine. About 4 miles away is a Kissimmee city park on 11-mile-long Lake Tohopekaliga, where fishing, boating, and picnicking are popular pursuits.

RV sites, facilities: The gated park offers 196 grassy full-hookup RV sites (10 pull-through). Each site has a picnic table and a concrete patio. Shade is minimal. Rigs up to 38 feet long can be accommodated; lots are 26 feet wide by 28–40 feet deep. All sites have 30/50-amp electrical outlets. On the premises are restrooms, showers, a dump station, a heated pool, horseshoes, shuffleboard, a playground, and laundry facilities. In season (November–April 1), planned activities include group meals, trips, bingo, and a "senior Olympics" sports contest in March. Management says the office, showers, and recreation hall are wheelchair accessible. Groceries and restaurants are within two miles. Children are welcome, but not pets.

Reservations, fees: Reservations are recommended. Sites are $26 per night for two people, plus $2 for each additional person. Credit cards are accepted. Long-term rates are available.

Directions: From I-4, take Exit 68 and proceed east on U.S. 192/Irlo Bronson Highway for five miles. Turn right on Bass Road (the first street past the Wal-Mart). Continue about 0.75 mile to Yowell Road. Turn right. You'll soon see the campground.

Contact: Great Oak RV Resort, 4440 Yowell Road, Kissimmee, FL 32741, 407/396-9092, fax 407/396-9093.

113 MILL CREEK RV RESORT

Scenic rating: 1

in Kissimmee, east of Disney World

See map page 229

This may not be the ideal vacation spot, with 75 percent of its occupants being full-time campers, families, and students attending the Motorcycle and Marine Institute of Orlando. But if you needed a place to stay, it's about 13 miles from the entrance to Disney World and about 3 miles from the bass-fishing waters of 11-mile-long Lake Tohopekaliga. In spring, the Houston Astros play exhibition games a short drive away at 5,130-capacity Osceola County Stadium (1000 Bill Beck Boulevard). For tickets, call 407/839-3900.

RV sites, facilities: This park offers 157 full-hookup RV sites (3 pull-through). Twelve have 50-amp electrical service; the rest have 30-amp. Rigs up to 45 feet long can be accommodated on some of the larger sites. Restrooms, showers, laundry facilities, a pool, a recreation hall, shuffleboard, horseshoes, cable TV, propane, and telephone service are available. Management says restrooms, the clubhouse, and laundry facilities are wheelchair accessible. Groceries and restaurants are within one mile. Children are allowed. Small pets under 20 pounds are okay.

Reservations, fees: Reservations are recommended. Sites are $30 per night for two people, plus $1 for each additional person. Credit cards are accepted. Long-term rates are available.

Directions: From I-4 at Exit 68, head east on U.S. 192/Irlo Bronson Highway about 10 miles to Michigan Avenue/Highway 531. At the bowling alley, turn left (north). Proceed about two miles to the park.

Contact: Mill Creek RV Resort, 2775 Michigan Avenue, Kissimmee, FL 34744, 407/847-6288.

114 PONDEROSA RV PARK

Scenic rating: 7

off U.S. 192 east of Kissimmee

See map page 229

The Houston Astros' spring training home and Osceola Heritage Park rodeo arena and expo center are across the street from this snowbird- and family-oriented park, where the sparse needles of pine trees partially shade some camping spots (other sites are sunny). The 15-acre park is about 3 miles northeast of a Kissimmee city park, where you can fish, boat, and picnic, at the north end of 11-mile-long Lake Tohopekaliga. It's also close to the four-mile-wide bass-fishing waters of East Lake Tohopekaliga. But to answer the kids' question, the campground is about 15 miles northeast of Disney World. About 65 percent of the park is occupied by year-round residents, and most winter months are sold out far in advance. To secure a reservation during the season, you'll have to call before June. In summer, it's easier to get a site.

RV sites, facilities: Of the 180 shady or sunny RV sites, all have full hookups and 30-amp or 50-amp electrical service, 2 are pull-through, and most have concrete pads. For recreation, there's a heated pool, a recreation room, a playground, horseshoes, shuffleboard, basketball, and winter social programs planned by a paid activities director. Restrooms, showers, a dump station, laundry facilities, and a wireless Internet network are available. Management says the restrooms, recreation hall, and other buildings are wheelchair accessible. Streets are paved. Groceries are within one mile. Children and pets (no pit bulls) are permitted. Campfires are forbidden.

Reservations, fees: Reservations are highly recommended for winter stays. Sites are $29 per night for two adults, plus $2 for each additional person. Credit cards are accepted. Stay as long as you like.

Directions: From I-4 at Exit 64A, head east on U.S. 192/Irlo Bronson Highway to Boggy Creek Road. Turn left and proceed about one mile north to the park.

Contact: Ponderosa RV Park, 1983 Boggy Creek Road, Kissimmee, FL 34744, 407/847-6002, fax 407/847-2400, www.ponderosarvpark.com.

115 FLORIDA CAMP INN

Scenic rating: 6

southwest of Disney World on U.S. 27, north of Davenport

See map page 229

Bring sunscreen if you plan to lounge around the patio of the heated pool or spend a lot of time outdoors at this sun-drenched community located about a 12-mile drive from Disney World. A few bushes and trees separate the grassy campsites. You'll be certain to meet your neighbors, even if you don't attend the organized winter dances and sing-alongs. About two-thirds of the park is occupied by year-round residents, and a mobile-home section is on the north side of the park. Pet sites are grouped together near the entrance and on the eastern border.

From the air, this grid-pattern park appears to be a sea of white RVs with clumps of shade trees at the center. Beyond its borders, broad expanses of dirt fields are broken up by green dots of citrus trees planted in straight rows. Campers tend to spend months here and are asked to follow the 33 park rules. Among them: Follow the 9.75 mph speed limit on park roads, use power tools between 10 A.M. and 3 P.M. only, and ride your bike only during daylight hours.

RV sites, facilities: There are 503 full-hookup sites, most with 30-amp electrical service. Sixteen have 50-amp hookups. RVs up to 40 feet long can be accommodated at the sites, which average 40 by 60 feet in size. Sites are grassy with cement pads. Some lots are drive-through, though availability varies seasonally. A pool, a recreation hall, shuffleboard, a dump station, grills, four bathhouses, cable TV, ice cream, ice, snacks, and laundry facilities are available. The bathhouses and clubhouse are wheelchair accessible. Children are permitted. Leashed pets

are permitted for overnight, but not monthly, stays and must use the dog walk between the fence and the highway.

Reservations, fees: Reservations are recommended. Monthly and seasonal campsites are first-come, first-served, although reservations can be made for stays of four months or more. Sites are $17 per night for two people, plus $2 for each additional person. Credit cards are not accepted. Long-term rates are available.

Directions: From I-4 at Exit 55, drive 4.5 miles north on U.S. 27 to the park on your left.

Contact: Florida Camp Inn, 9725 U.S. 27 North, Davenport, FL 33837, 863/424-2494, fax 863/424-3599, www.floridacampinn.com.

116 WALLABY RANCH FLIGHT PARK

Scenic rating: 6

southwest of Disney World

See map page 229   **BEST (**

This hang-glider park is included as an inducement for those free spirits out there who might want to try something completely new while camping their way across Florida. "The Best Place on Earth to Fly Hang Gliders" is how the 200-acre former cattle ranch bills itself. And darned if it doesn't attract hang gliders from all over. RVs should be self-contained as there are no hookups.

The focus of the ranch is a 120-acre, level field of green grass, which is free of debris and power lines. With six "aerotugs" available, veteran hang gliders won't have to wait long to get in the air. Novices are welcome, too. The park promises a safe, enjoyable training session. Back on the ground, members of your party who are not interested in hang gliding can swim in a pool, enjoy woodsy hiking or mountain biking trails, or scale the climbing wall.

RV sites, facilities: An indeterminate number of campsites are available; you do not have to be a hang glider to stay here. The owners welcome the curious adventurers who wander

in now and then (and discover a new hobby along the way).

Reservations, fees: Reservations are not accepted nor are they necessary for hang gliders using the park's facilities. Camping is $5 (subject to change). Hang-gliding rides are $20 each. Novices can go up with an instructor in a tandem flight and learn to hang glide for $95 a flight.

Directions: From Kissimmee, take I-4 south to U.S. 27 (Exit 55). Head north for 1.5 miles. Turn left at Dean Still Road. Look for the ranch 1.7 miles ahead on the left.

Contact: Wallaby Ranch Flight Park, 1805 Dean Still Road, Wallaby Ranch, FL 33837-9358, 863/424-0070, www.wallaby.com.

117 FORT SUMMIT KOA CAMPING RESORT

Scenic rating: 8

off I-4 south of Disney World

See map page 229   BEST

Don't be confused by the name. This is not Disney World's famed Fort Wilderness Campground, but Disney World is definitely the focus for staying here. Set behind a Best Western motel that shares ownership with the RV park, this sunny, palm-dotted campground nonetheless caters to the theme-park crowd by offering free shuttle rides to Disney World, which is seven miles northeast. The grassy sites with concrete patios are large. Expect to have a good view of neighboring RVs (which is par for the course this close to Disney). Scattered native palms provide token shade. Grass, not privacy hedges, is the preferred landscaping.

In a region often dominated by retirees, parents may breathe a sigh of relief here. A fenced low-impact playground, video games, a wading pool, and a heated pool with plenty of lounge furniture keep young campers entertained. So can the park's car rentals, if you want to drive the family to Sea World or Universal Studios, about 20 minutes away.

RV sites, facilities: There are 249 full-hookup RV sites (80 pull-through) with 30/50-amp electrical service, concrete pads, picnic tables, brick campfire pits, and grills. A large heated pool, a wading pool, a sundeck, a recreation room, a playground, a game room, an exercise room, basketball, volleyball, pool tables, and social programs entertain campers. Wireless Internet connections are available near the store and in the pool area. Showers, restrooms, rental cabins, a dump station, a "fully stocked" convenience store with beer, wine, supplies, souvenirs and groceries, snacks, laundry facilities, car rentals, cabins, cable TV, telephone hookups, and free Disney World shuttles are available. Planned activities are on tap in the winter months. The store and restrooms are wheelchair accessible. A restaurant is within walking distance. Children are welcome. Leashed pets are permitted.

Reservations, fees: Reservations are not necessary. Sites are $34–63 per night for two people, plus $4 for each additional person. Credit cards are accepted. Long-term rates are available.

Directions: From I-4 at Exit 55, go south on U.S. 27 about 0.1 mile; turn right on Frontage Road and go two blocks. The park is behind the Best Western Motel.

Contact: Fort Summit KOA Camping Resort, 2525 Frontage Road, Davenport, FL 33837, 863/424-1880 or 800/424-1880, fax 863/420-8831, www.fortsummit.com.

118 DEER CREEK RV GOLF RESORT

Scenic rating: 8

off I-4 south of Disney World

See map page 229   BEST

With names like Arnold Palmer Drive and Jack Nicklaus Lane in one of the park's lot-ownership sections, it's clear that the most unusual amenities aren't the two-story poolside clubhouse or even the five heated pools. Instead, golf is king. It would be hard to find a Florida RV destination more focused on golf than this one, with a lighted driving range, a pro shop, a putting green, and a hilly, 18-hole golf course.

The RV portion of this manicured, 200-acre residential-style retirement community welcomes families, while the huge park-model sections are for people over age 55. The mostly sunny RV campsites sit about 35–40 feet apart on what is known as the Lake Wales Ridge (elevation 150 feet above sea level, once a long island in a much deeper ancient sea). As you drive through this complex of park models and RVs to get to your paved campsite, you'll go up one major hill to approach the RV section. Some sites are on one side of the hill; others are on the descent. Disney World is about 10 miles north.

RV sites, facilities: One hundred of the 861 lots are for RVs and have picnic tables, full hookups, and 30/50-amp electrical outlets. RVs must be self-contained and use sewer hookups. Rigs up to 45 feet can be accommodated on sites varying in size but averaging 40 by 80 feet. A golf course, a driving range, a pro shop, pools, a spa, a playground, a game room, horseshoes, shuffleboard, basketball, tennis, volleyball, billiards, and organized activities (usually in winter) entertain campers. Two hired activities directors organize casino trips, cruises, golf tournaments, bingo, dances, and crafts classes. Showers, restrooms, park-model rentals, a snack bar, a restaurant/lounge, cable TV, LP gas sales, and laundry facilities are available. Groceries are within 0.5 mile. The clubhouse and bathhouse are wheelchair accessible. Children are welcome. Pets are permitted.

Reservations, fees: Reservations are recommended in winter. The rate is $40–45 per night for two people, plus $10 per extra person. Credit cards are accepted. Long-term stays are okay.

Directions: From I-4 at Exit 55, drive one mile south on U.S. 27 to the park on your left.

Contact: Deer Creek RV Golf Resort, 42049 U.S. 27 North, Davenport, FL 33837, 863/424-2839 or 800/424-2931, fax 836/424-3336, www.deercreekrv.com.

119 MOUSE MOUNTAIN RV AND MOBILE HOME RESORT

Scenic rating: 7

south of Disney World

See map page 229

Many campers here are planning to go to Disney World, which is located a mere six-mile drive north past citrus groves and tiny Reedy Lake (on the left). The sunny or somewhat shaded, grassy campsites and accompanying paved patios are set on a hill, which in flat Florida passes for a "mountain" (hence the park's name). A plus: The family-managed spot is set a respectable distance from the neon signs and multiple lanes of U.S. 192, where many bargain-hunting, Disney-bound motel guests end up. About one-third of the park is occupied by year-round residents in mobile homes. In winter, you'll find mostly snowbirds, and in summer, the park is popular with families.

RV sites, facilities: There are 260 full-hookup RV sites (12 pull-through) with 30-amp and 50-amp electrical service and concrete patios. Rigs up to 40 feet long can be accommodated. Sites are a mix of gravel and grass. A heated pool, a playground, horseshoes, shuffleboard, practice putting greens, a recreation hall, and winter activities entertain campers. A paid activities director organizes concerts, square dancing, clogging, and bingo. Restrooms, showers, a dump station, snacks, propane, cable TV, laundry facilities, and a pet walk are available. You can hook up your laptop in the office to pick up your email. Groceries are within one mile. The bathhouse, recreation hall, laundry area, and office are wheelchair accessible. Children and leashed pets are permitted.

Reservations, fees: Reservations are recommended. Sites are $25–28 per night for two people, plus $1.50 for each additional person. Credit cards are accepted. Long-term rates are available.

Directions: From I-4, take Exit 58 onto State Road 532/Osceola Polk Line Road. Drive east

1.6 miles just past the light. The park is on the right.

Contact: Mouse Mountain RV and Mobile Home Resort, 7500 State Road 532/Osceola-Polk Line Road, Davenport, FL 33896, 863/424-2791 or 800/347-6388, fax 863/420-9104, www.mousemountainrv.com.

LAKEWOOD RV RESORT

Scenic rating: 6

south of Disney World

See map page 229

Many campers leave their rig on-site when they head home for spring and summer, and on about half the sites are mobile homes. The grounds support 482 sunny or shady sites—221 in a park-model section and most others used by long-term residents accustomed to the routine of 3 P.M. daily garbage pickups (except Sundays). The 30- by 40-foot pool sits closest to campsites A6–A8 in the grid-pattern portion of the park, where every street is accorded an alphabetical letter. So to sleep near the pool, ask for a site in the lower end of the alphabet; section R is farthest away, at the back of the park. Overnight spaces during the winter months are limited and do not accommodate RVs more than 33 feet long.

RV sites, facilities: There are 175 full-hookup sites (many pull-through) with 30-amp electrical service. For recreation, there's a pool, a playground, horseshoes, shuffleboard, a recreation hall, and wintertime planned activities. Restrooms, showers, a dump station, and laundry facilities are available. Children under 12 must be adult-supervised at the pool. Leashed, attended pets under 30 pounds are permitted and must use the designated dog walk.

Reservations, fees: Reservations are recommended. Sites are $29–38 per night for two people, plus $2 for each additional person. Credit cards are not accepted. Long-term rates are available.

Directions: From I-4 at Exit 58, go east on State

Road 532/Osceola/Polk Line Road less than one mile to the park on the right side. The park is just beyond a traffic light.

Contact: Lakewood RV Resort, 7700 Osceola/Polk Line Road, Davenport, FL 33896, 863/424-2669, fax 863/424-6229, email: lakewoodfl@earthlink.net.

PARADISE RV RESORT

Scenic rating: 4

four miles west of Disney World

See map page 229

This park has an unusual amenity for its denizens: an underground shelter in case of tornadoes or threatening weather. The RV spots aren't shaded, although the grassy tent sites are. RV sites are set diagonally on 20- by 40-foot concrete pads separated by grass. Many campers stay for extended periods in winter, and some live at the nine-acre park year-round, congregating at the TV and card room to socialize.

RV sites, facilities: There are 115 full-hookup RV sites (5 pull-through) with 50-amp electrical service, concrete patios, and picnic tables. For recreation, there's a recreation room, horseshoes, a campfire area, a playground, and basketball hoops. Restrooms, showers, a dump station, LP gas sales, limited groceries, a laundry room, cable TV, telephone hookups, and an underground storm shelter are available. Management says the restrooms and showers are wheelchair accessible. Restaurants are about four miles away. Children and leashed pets are welcome.

Reservations, fees: Reservations are recommended. Sites are $20 per night for two people, plus $1.50 for each additional person over age three. Credit cards are not accepted. Long-term stays are allowed.

Directions: From I-4 at Exit 64B, head west on U.S. 192/Irlo Bronson Highway. Turn left onto County Road 545/Old Lake Wilson Road and proceed 3.5 miles south, passing under I-4. The campground is on the left.

Contact: Paradise RV Resort, 725 South Old Lake Wilson Road, Kissimmee, FL 34747, 407/396-7711, fax 407/396-2506, www.snow-fresh.com/page26.html.

21 PALMS RV RESORT

Scenic rating: 6

seven miles south of Disney World

See map page 229

A small alligator in the fishpond certainly intrigues out-of-state visitors, but an even bigger attraction of these 30 secluded acres is the short seven-mile drive to Disney World. Not only for campers who want to lounge around a solar-heated pool, this park offers a free Nautilus fitness center with an unusual pitch: "Take a healthy break. Relax and enjoy our facilities while you strengthen, firm, and tone your body." Paved roads lead to the level RV sites and concrete patios. A few palm trees dot the lots, although the surrounding land is woodsy. About one-third of the park is occupied year-round. In winter, the park plays host to snowbirds. Summer visitors include families and temporary workers.

RV sites, facilities: This all-ages park has 94 paved RV sites with full hookups, 50-amp electrical service, and concrete patios. About half are pull-through. RVs up to 40 feet long can be accommodated. A pool, a fitness center, horseshoes, shuffleboard, a pool table, a recreation hall, and activities planned by volunteers keep campers entertained. Restrooms, showers, a dump station, picnic tables, TV hookups, propane, rental park models, propane, and air-conditioned laundry facilities are available. The office, laundry room, and bathhouse are wheelchair accessible, and the streets are paved. Children are welcome. Inquire about pet restrictions.

Reservations, fees: Reservations are· recommended. Sites are $20 per night. Credit cards are accepted.

Directions: From Orlando, take I-4 to U.S.

192 (Exit 64B). Go west nearly three miles, passing the Disney World entrance, to State Road 545. Turn left. Continue five miles to Polk County Road. Turn left. The park is two miles ahead. From Tampa, take I-4 to Polk County Road (Exit 58) and go about two miles east to the park.

Contact: 21 Palms RV Resort, 6951 Polk County Road, Davenport, FL 33837, 407/397-9110.

123 RV CORRAL

Scenic rating: 2

south of Disney World on U.S. 17/92

See map page 229

All ages are welcome at this 25-acre park, where about 70 percent of the sites are occupied year-round. It's located about 11 miles south of Disney World in a rapidly developing area. Most visitors hail from Florida or the Midwest.

RV sites, facilities: There are 29 full-hookup RV sites (four pull-through) with concrete patios; most have picnic tables and 30-amp electrical service. Eight lots have 50-amp service. Wheelchair-accessible showers, restrooms, and laundry facilities are available. Streets are paved. A supermarket and restaurant are about four miles away, but you can pick up snacks in the park. Adults are preferred. Leashed, attended pets are allowed.

Reservations, fees: Reservations are recommended. Sites are $20 per night for two people, plus $2 for each additional person. Credit cards are not accepted. Long-term rates are available.

Directions: From I-4 at Exit 58, go left on Osceola Polk Line Road. Turn right on U.S. 17/92 and drive four miles south. The park is ahead at right.

Contact: RV Corral, 4141 U.S. 17/92 North, Davenport, FL 33837, 863/420-2181, email: conrad20015@cs.com.

124 THREE WORLDS RV AND MOBILE HOME RESORT

Scenic rating: 6

on U.S. 17/92 south of Disney World

See map page 229

Country living is the catchphrase at this 120-acre rural home of preserved wooded areas and three small fishing lakes, yet the park is not far from two major tourist attractions: Sea World is about 18 miles away, while the I-4 exit to Disney World is 11 miles off. (Also about 18 miles away, Cypress Gardens, a 70-year-old park best known for its water-ski exhibitions and beautiful grounds hosted by "Southern belles" dressed in long gowns.) Many retirees treat the place like a second home and spend entire winters at the grassy/concrete-pad sites.

The typically sunny campsites sit along curvy roads in an amoeba-shaped section dotted with pines and sabal palms. To sleep apart from most RVs, ask for one of the 12 lake-view spots at the northwest corner of the RV recreational area. Farther east, sites east of the heated pool also enjoy the relative seclusion of having no neighbors to the back. You'll just need to walk a couple of blocks to attend dances and other activities at the 5,000-square-foot lakeside clubhouse, shared with residents of the park's 64 mobile homes (situated to the east of RVs) and 66 park models (set to the west).

RV sites, facilities: This park has 247 full-hookup sites for RVs (5 pull-through). A pool, a recreation hall, shuffleboard, horseshoes, social programs, billiards, and a miniature golf course provide entertainment. Showers, restrooms, a dump station, trailer rentals, cable TV, a country store, and laundry facilities are available. Management says the showers, bathhouse, recreation hall, and pool area are wheelchair accessible. A supermarket and restaurant are about seven miles away in Haines City. Families with small children may camp up to two weeks. Leashed pets under 30 pounds are permitted.

Reservations, fees: Reservations are not necessary. Sites are $28 nightly for two people, plus $2 for each additional person. Credit cards are accepted. Adults may stay long-term.

Directions: From I-4 at Exit 58, drive east to U.S. 17/92. Turn south and proceed 4.5 miles. The park is ahead at left.

Contact: Three Worlds RV and Mobile Home Resort, 3700 U.S. 17/92 North, Davenport, FL 33837, 863/424-1286 or 888/293-3020, fax 863/424-3877.

125 LAKELAND RV RESORT

Scenic rating: 7

off I-4 in Lakeland

See map page 230

This manicured 24-acre resort is a convenient stop off I-4. It's near little Lake Deeson, which is stocked with bass, catfish, and bluegill. A heated pool and wintertime activities such as bingo, card nights, and arts classes entertain campers. However, the park's paved interior roads with streetlights are also used for in-line skating, walking, or bicycling. About 30 percent of the park is occupied by year-round residents, and park models are for sale. Theme parks in Tampa and Orlando are about 30 minutes from the grassy and paved sites (most with patios). A sound wall along I-4 shields the park from highway noise. The Detroit Tigers play spring training games down the road off State Road 33; call 863/686-8075 for game information.

RV sites, facilities: There are 230 full-hookup sites (100 pull-through) for RVs as large as they come. All have 30-amp electrical service; 190 have 50-amp. Each has a picnic table, a concrete patio, and a fire ring. The roomy lots are typically 33 feet wide by 80 feet deep. "Super-size" sites are 100 feet deep. If you travel with a satellite dish, ask for a less-shady site. A wireless Internet network is available at each lot, as well as in the office. For recreation, there's a pool, a spa, a kiddie pool, a clubhouse, free paddleboats, rental boats, a stocked lake, a playground, horseshoes, miniature golf, table tennis, basketball, seasonal activities, shuffleboard, and a children's playroom. Also on the premises are showers, restrooms, LP gas sales, a dump station, a screened pavilion, rental cabins, a camp store, an on-site video/book library, a 3,000-square-foot screened pavilion, two kitchens, laundry facilities, and a dog-washing station (you do the washing). Management says most areas are wheelchair accessible. Streets are paved. Groceries, a restaurant, and bait are available within a five-minute drive. Children are welcome. Leashed pets are permitted.

Reservations, fees: Reservations are accepted except in January, February, and March, when sites are first-come, first-served. Sites are $36 per night for two people, plus $2.50 for each additional person and $2 for 50-amp electrical service. Credit cards are accepted. Long-term stays are okay.

Directions: From I-4, take Exit 33 and drive about one mile northeast on State Road 33/County Road 582 (Socrum Loop) to Old Combee Road. Turn right and proceed 0.25 mile to the campground, on the right.

Contact: Lakeland RV Resort, 900 Old Combee Road, Lakeland, FL 33805, 863/687-6146 or 888/622-4115, www.lakelandrvresort.com.

126 TIKI VILLAGE CAMPGROUND

Scenic rating: 5

off I-4 in Lakeland
See map page 230

An RV dealer and one of Florida's largest malls (Lakeland Mall) are within walking distance when you stay at Tiki Village, a fast stop off I-4. Still, you may see tigers, as in the Detroit Tigers, play spring training games nearby at Joker Marchant Stadium, 2301 Lakeland Hills Boulevard; call 863/686-8075 for game information. Despite the winter social programs and the swimming pool, you're getting convenience here: Tampa and Orlando theme parks are only about 30 minutes away by car. The two fishponds are a plus, especially for families with

kids in tow (though they are limited to short-term stays). The park is favored by adults, repeat visitors, and working people.

RV sites, facilities: All 203 full-hookup, 30/50-amp sites are for RVs up to 45 feet long and slide-outs. Twenty are pull-through. Some lots have concrete patios. A pool, a recreation room, a play area, horseshoes, shuffleboard, and winter activities entertain campers. On the premises are showers, restrooms, snacks, LP gas sales, and laundry facilities. A camp store sells snacks, camping supplies, and souvenirs. A wireless Internet network is planned. Streets are crushed blacktop asphalt. The bathhouse, clubhouse, office, and pool area are wheelchair accessible. Groceries, restaurants, malls, and hospitals are within two miles. Children are welcome to visit for short-term stays. Two small pets are permitted per site.

Reservations, fees: Reservations are recommended. Sites are $32 per night for two people, plus $3 for each additional person. Credit cards are accepted. Yearly rates are available.

Directions: From I-4, take Exit 32 and drive one block north on U.S. 98 to Crevasse Street. Turn right and proceed about 0.25 mile to the entrance, on the left.

Contact: Tiki Village Campground, 905 Crevasse Street, Lakeland, FL 33809, 863/858-5364 or 863/858-8217, fax 863/853-9446, www.tikivillage.net.

127 LELYNN RV RESORT

Scenic rating: 3

in Polk City
See map page 230

Although children are allowed, this RV park is decidedly retiree- and snowbird-oriented, with planned activities during the winter months, such as bingo, potluck dinners, crafts, dancing, games, and exercise. The park boasts of a quiet setting, where campers can watch the sun set over Lake Agnes. Fishing and boating are options, too. About 40 percent of the park is occupied by year-round residents, including working people.

RV sites, facilities: Of the 369 sites, most are available for seasonal visitors and 15 for overnighters; 9 are pull-through. All have full hookups, 50-amp service, concrete patios, and picnic tables. A wireless Internet connection is available in the office. Restrooms, showers, a dump station, laundry facilities, and, for long-termers, telephone service are available. On the premises are a pool, a boat ramp, a dock, propane gas sales, shuffleboard courts, a dog-walk area, and a recreation room. All areas are wheelchair accessible. Children and small pets are permitted.

Reservations, fees: Reservations are recommended. Sites are $30 per night for two people, plus $4 per extra person. Credit cards are not accepted. Long-term or seasonal stays are allowed.

Directions: From I-4, take Exit 44 and drive north on State Road 559 for one block to the park.

Contact: LeLynn RV Resort, 1513 State Road 559, Polk City, FL 33868, 863/984-1495, fax 863/984-0257.

128 LAKE JULIANA BOATING AND LODGING

Scenic rating: 4

at Lake Juliana north of Auburndale

See map page 230

In a region normally focused on retirees, families can take solace in knowing that this five-acre fish camp has a swimming beach, pool, volleyball net, and toddler-oriented play center. Bass fishing nonetheless remains the key attraction for campers at these grassy/concrete-pad sites. A canal links nearly two-mile-long Lake Juliana with smaller Lake Mattie, giving anglers and water-skiers 2,100 watery acres to explore. This area is still relatively undeveloped, so you'll find a countryside setting. This being Florida, that could change at any time, but the park prides itself on its natural setting.

Campers are somewhat outnumbered by mobile-home residents at this small complex, where the family atmosphere comes with rules that Mom and Dad would approve of: Eat in the picnic area, not at the pool; and no foul language, please. Disney World, Sea World, and Busch Gardens are within 45 miles. Park models are for sale.

RV sites, facilities: All 10 full-hookup, grassy, sunny sites are for RVs up to 40 feet long. They have 50-amp electrical service and cable TV. On the premises are a pool, an adult swing, a wheelchair-accessible recreation room, a volleyball net, a playground, restrooms (no showers), a dump station, rental cottages, cabins, a boat ramp, covered boat slips, boat rentals, a tanning bed, a toddler play area, limited groceries, a picnic area, bait, tackle, cable TV, and laundry facilities. Restaurants are three miles away. Children must be adult-supervised at the pool and pier. Leashed, attended pets are permitted.

Reservations, fees: Reservations are recommended. Sites are $27 per night for two people, and $5 per extra person. Credit cards are accepted. Long-term rates are available.

Directions: From I-4, take Exit 44 and drive south less than one mile on State Route 559. Turn right onto Lundy Road and proceed to the complex at Lake Juliana.

Contact: Lake Juliana Boating and Lodging, 600 Lundy Road, Auburndale, FL 33823, 863/984-1144, http://lakejuliana.tripod.com.

129 VALENCIA ESTATES

Scenic rating: 2

on U.S. 98 south of Lakeland

See map page 230

Palm trees dot this age 55-and-older park, where residents of the 86 mobile homes outnumber RVers at the 30 grassy/concrete-pad campsites. The full schedule of winter activities includes Bible study, crafts, card nights, bingo, bowling, golf and pool leagues, as well as weekly coffees, monthly potlucks, and twice-monthly pancake-and-sausage breakfasts. Most visitors hail from Michigan, Indiana, New York, and Canada. Favorite things to do? Walk and talk.

Lakeland doesn't usually jump to mind when one considers Florida's prime tourism spots, but this way station of a city between Tampa and Orlando hosts the Detroit Tigers for spring-training games in March. It's a good home base for the Florida Aquarium or pier in St. Petersburg, as well as Disney World and Historic Bok Sanctuary in Lake Wales. For a pretty walk, park four miles away at Florida Southern College, whose buildings at Ingraham Avenue and Lake Hollingsworth Drive were designed by Frank Lloyd Wright. Then circle the lake fronting the college—Lake Hollingsworth. You'll pass the Lakeland Yacht and Country Club along the way.

RV sites, facilities: At this age-55-plus park, all 30 full-hookup sites will accommodate RVs up to 39 feet long. Electrical service is 30-amp. A dump station and laundry facilities are provided. Showers and restrooms are available in the clubhouse. A pool, three lighted shuffleboard courts, winter programs, and a clubhouse entertain campers. Cable TV and telephone hookups are available. The bathhouse, clubhouse, and pool area are wheelchair accessible. Streets are paved. A restaurant and groceries are within two miles. Children are prohibited. Leashed pets up to 45 pounds are allowed.

Reservations, fees: Reservations are recommended, and they are a must for the winter season because most tenants return year after year. Sites are $23 per night for two people, plus $10 per extra person. Credit cards are not accepted. Long-term rates are available.

Directions: From East Main Street in Lakeland, drive 3.5 miles south on U.S. 98. The park entrance is on the right. From I-4, take Exit 27 to State Road 570 (Polk Parkway) west. Exit on U.S. 98 at Bartow and drive 0.5 mile north to the first left turn.

Contact: Valencia Estates, 3325 Bartow Road/ U.S. 98, Lakeland, FL 33803, 863/665-1611 or 800/645-9033, fax 863/667-3698, email: mfeldm3402@aol.com.

130 SANLAN RANCH CAMPGROUND

Scenic rating: 10

on U.S. 98 south of Lakeland

See map page 230   BEST (

More than 90 types of birds have been spotted at this notable private recreation area, which covers more than one square mile. Still, golfers tend to prefer walking from their grassy campsites to the adjacent Bramble Ridge Golf Course, where the driving range was voted best in the county by locals. A private camper entrance leads to the par-72, 18-hole course, where Sanlan guests receive a discount. The adjacent wooded 600 acres were once a phosphate mine, resulting in an abundance of trails and wildlife.

Look for alligators and ducks while paddling along the park's canoe trails or walking along three wooded hiking trails (a total of seven miles). A cacophony of bird chatter in winter enlivens a pensive stop along the two-mile-long Rookery Trail, near Banana Lake. A boat ramp provides access to Banana Lake, one of three park lakes. The park isn't only about wilderness activities, though; bingo games and potluck dinners are held in winter at the 200-person-capacity recreation hall, and aquacize sessions are sometimes offered at one of the three solar-heated pools. Joggers follow a three-mile shady trail around the golf course.

Lakefront campsites have no utilities, just tables. At sites along the camping circle, there are no sewer hookups. If you prefer big sites, note that the "ranch-view" sites are smaller than regular full-hookup sites. Park models are for sale.

RV sites, facilities: More than 500 sites and a primitive group camping area are for RVs up to 50 feet long or tents. Three pools, a wading pool, 18 lighted shuffleboard courts, a lighted golf driving range, a playground, horseshoes, two recreation halls, three nature trails, and winter activities entertain campers. Facilities include restrooms, showers, a dump station, a modem hookup to check email, and laundry facilities. Children are permitted. Two pets are allowed per site.

Reservations, fees: Reservations are recommended. Sites are $21.50–40 per night for two people, plus $2.50 for each additional person. No more than five people are permitted per site. Families with children are limited to 14 days. Pet fee is 50 cents daily. Credit cards are accepted. Long-term rates are available.

Directions: From East Main Street in Lakeland, drive 3.5 miles south on U.S. 98 to the park, which is on the right side of the road. Or, from the Polk County Parkway (State Road 520), take Exit 10 southbound on U.S. 98. Drive 0.25 mile to the park on the west side of U.S. 98.

Contact: Sanlan Ranch Campground, 3929 U.S. 98 South, Lakeland, FL 33813, 863/665-1726 or 800/524-5044, www.sanlan.com.

131 OAK HARBOR

Scenic rating: 7

on Lake Lowery west of Haines City

See map page 230

You'll pass citrus groves—and perhaps the aroma of sweet blossoms—on the approach to this off-the-beaten-path lakefront park, where clumps of tall, lanky palms and brushy oaks lend a woodsy feel. Bass anglers, water-skiers, and swimmers share the calm blue waters of nearly two-mile-long Lake Lowery here. Many campers spend entire winters at these grassy campsites with concrete patios, while other folks live in the 65-acre park's 70 mobile homes and park models. Although the private park enjoys admirable shade from its overstory of trees, there is comparatively little eye-level brush separating camping spots. This is a gathering spot for seaplane and floatplane rallies.

RV sites, facilities: There are 110 RV sites with full hookups and 30/50-amp electrical service. A recreation room, winter social programs, showers, restrooms, picnic tables, a dump station, a boat ramp, and laundry facilities are available. A restaurant and a bait shop are three miles away. Groceries are within five miles. Children and leashed pets under 40 pounds are permitted.

Reservations, fees: Reservations are recommended. Sites are $22 per night for two people, plus $2 for each additional person. Prices include your own boat dock. Credit cards are not accepted. Long-term stays are okay.

Directions: From U.S. 27 in Haines City, drive 4.5 miles west on U.S. 17/92. Turn right at Experiment Station Road. Cross the railroad tracks, then turn right at Old Haines City/Lake Alfred Road. Continue 1.5 miles. Turn left on Lake Lowery Road. The park is ahead at right.

Contact: Oak Harbor, 100 Oak Harbor, Haines City, FL 33844, 863/956-1341 or 877/956-1341, fax 863/956-1341, www.oakharbor-rv.com.

132 CENTRAL PARK OF HAINES CITY

Scenic rating: 7

off U.S. 27 in Haines City

See map page 230

With morning newspaper delivery and daily garbage pickup service, snowbirds don't escape civilization—they embrace it in this rapidly developing region of the state. Many retirees from the Northeast and Canada spend entire winters here, some taking advantage of cards, darts, bingo, exercises, and Sunday church services in the park's recreation hall. Oaks shade some campsites, which are set block-style in single and double rows. Some sites are at waterfront. This is an over-age-55 park where most people are staying for the winter season.

RV sites, facilities: The 351 full-hookup sites are for RVs up to 50 feet long and slide-outs. Fourteen sites are pull-through. One-hundred sites have 50-amp electrical service; the rest have 30-amp. All have a picnic table and a concrete patio. Lots average 30 feet wide by 60 feet deep. An Internet connection is available in the office. For recreation, there's a pool, a recreation hall, horseshoes, shuffleboard, boccie (lawn bowling) courts, and winter activities. Showers, restrooms, laundry facilities, rental cabins, propane, and camping supplies are available. All areas are wheelchair accessible. A shopping center is 0.25 mile away. An 18-hole golf course is one mile away. Children are permitted. Leashed pets must use two pet walks at park boundaries.

Reservations, fees: Reservations are not necessary. Sites are $25 per night for two people, plus $2 for each additional person. Credit cards are not accepted. Long-term stays are okay.

Directions: From I-4 at Exit 55, go south about 12 miles on U.S. 27. Turn right at Commerce Avenue, which is the second stoplight in Haines City (if you hit U.S. 17/92, you've gone too far). The park is ahead on the left.

Contact: Central Park of Haines City, 1501 Commerce Avenue, Haines City, FL 33844, 863/422-5322, www.centralparkofhaines city.com.

133 GREENFIELD VILLAGE RV PARK

Scenic rating: 3

off U.S. 27 in Dundee
See map page 230

In this region of rolling, citrus-dotted hills, the bigger towns of Lake Wales and Winter Haven (with their antiques shops) are better known than Dundee, a sleepy, wide spot in the road where these 104 concrete-pad RV sites are set. Swimming in the heated pool is a highlight at the grassy, flat park, which is kept neat as a pin. Oaks and palms provide some shade for campers, who often stay at least three months. Park models are for sale. Elsewhere, an 18-hole golf course is 0.2 mile away and locals fish at area lakes. The boat ramp to the biggest nearby body of water, Lake Hamilton, is up U.S. 27 about 3.5 miles northwest of the park. Historic Bok Sanctuary, an estate and gardens where 45-

minute carillon recitals are held daily at 3 P.M., is in Lake Wales (call 863/676-1408).

RV sites, facilities: This age-55-and-up park has 92 sites with full hookups, 30/50-amp electrical service, picnic tables for long-staying RVs or park models, and 12 sites with full hookups for overnighters. Rigs up to 45 feet in length can be accommodated. A pool, shuffleboard, a recreation hall, winter social programs, showers, restrooms, and free local calls are available. Management says the pool, laundry facilities, bathhouse, and recreation hall are wheelchair accessible. Groceries, a restaurant, and laundry facilities are within 0.25 mile. Children are not allowed. Aggresive dog breeds like rottweilers, pit bulls, and Doberman pinschers are prohibited; otherwise, pets are permitted.

Reservations, fees: Reservations are recommended. Sites are $45 per night, plus $4 per extra person and $2.50 for electricity. Credit cards are not accepted. Long-term rates are available.

Directions: From U.S. 27 at Dundee, drive west 0.1 mile on State Road 542. Turn left almost immediately into the park.

Contact: Greenfield Village RV Park, 1015 State Road 542 West, Dundee, FL 33838, 863/439-7409.

134 MERRY D RV SANCTUARY

Scenic rating: 6

southeast of Disney World
See map page 230

This 54-acre rural park bills itself as a "back-to-nature" campground where most sites are shaded and people who want a peaceful, quiet night after a hectic day at Disney World will be happy. Some folks stay here long-term, too. Paved interior roads lead to large sites—at least 50 by 80 feet for pull-through spots. In the busy winter season, campers can enjoy arts-and-crafts classes, card games, ice-cream socials, Bible study nights, and periodic group trips to casinos and other places. Fishing is possible in a small lake, but you'll have to travel about eight miles to get bait and tackle. The park is within a few miles of the main gate to Walt Disney World.

RV sites, facilities: There are 91 full-hookup sites with 50-amp electricity, cable TV, and telephone availability. Forty-two sites are pull-through. Each site has a picnic table. On the premises are restrooms, showers, a dump station, rental trailers, a recreation room, a playground, a nature trail, horseshoes, laundry facilities, and a long, narrow field that some campers have used as a golf driving range. Management says the restrooms and showers are wheelchair accessible. Groceries and restaurants are within two miles. Children and pets are permitted.

Reservations, fees: Reservations are required. Sites are $28 per night for two people, plus $2 for each additional person. Credit cards are accepted. Long-term stays are okay.

Directions: From U.S. 192 in Kissimmee, go south on U.S. 17/92 about three miles. Turn left at County Road 531/Pleasant Hill Road. Continue seven miles to the campground, at left.

Contact: Merry D RV Sanctuary, 4261 Pleasant Hill Road, Kissimmee, FL 34746-2933, 407/870-0719 or 800/208-3434, fax 407/870-0198, www.merryd.com.

135 ALOHA RV PARK

Scenic rating: 1

southwest of Kissimmee

See map page 230

In winter, you can pick oranges at this adults-preferred park, located within 15 miles of Disney World. Anglers may want to head about 5 miles east to fish for bass, specks, or catfish in 11-mile-long Lake Tohopekaliga. A good number of these paved campsites are taken by full-time or seasonal residents rather than overnighters, although campers may choose to spend only one night. Park rules tend to be geared toward full-time residents. Also, camp-

ers are asked to use the restrooms in their rigs. Winter residents take part in bingo games, shuffleboard, pancake breakfasts, and spaghetti dinners. About 55 percent of the sites are occupied year-round.

RV sites, facilities: Self-contained rigs are accepted at this adult-oriented park with 90 full-hookup, grassy RV sites (27 pull-through). Sixty sites have 30-amp electrical service; the rest have 50-amp. RVs up to 40 feet long and slide-outs can be accommodated. Each lot has a picnic table and a concrete patio. An Internet connection is available in the clubhouse. On the premises are restrooms, showers, laundry facilities, a pool, and a game room. Groceries and restaurants are about five miles away. The clubhouse and pool area are wheelchair accessible. Streets are paved. Children may camp on a short-term basis. Pets under 25 pounds are welcome.

Reservations, fees: Reservations are recommended. Sites are $29 per night for two people, plus $2 per extra person. Credit cards are not accepted. Long-term rates are available.

Directions: From Kissimmee, take U.S. 17/92 south about seven miles.

Contact: Aloha RV Park, 4648 South Orange Blossom Trail, Kissimmee, FL 34746, 407/933-5730.

136 RICHARDSON'S FISH CAMP

Scenic rating: 5

on Lake Tohopekaliga south of Kissimmee

See map page 230

The main reason to stay at this 6-acre camp is to venture out onto 23,000-acre Lake Tohopekaliga to fish for trophy bass, specks, and panfish. A fishing guide is available, as are boat docks, a boat ramp, and bait and tackle. This off-the-beaten-path spot on the lake's northeast shore emphasizes a laid-back lifestyle in a quiet setting shaded by large oak trees. Many patrons stay in air-conditioned rental cabins. A plus: One boat slip is included in the price of the campsites, which are sandy or grassy with concrete pads. The park also offers airboat rides. Most visitors are families, locals, and anglers.

RV sites, facilities: There are 16 full-hookup sites (12 pull-through) with 30-amp electrical service. Big rigs and slide-outs can be accommodated. The grassy sites are a mix of sun and shady, and some have concrete patios. On the premises are restrooms, showers, a dump station, a boat ramp, charter fishing services, a dock, covered slips, and laundry facilities. A camp store sells ice, snacks, and bait and tackle. Management says the dock behind the bait shop and office are wheelchair accessible. Children and pets are permitted.

Reservations, fees: Reservations are recommended. Sites are $28 per night for two people, plus $1 for each additional person and $1 for pets. Credit cards are not accepted. The maximum length of stay is six months.

Directions: From Kissimmee, take State Road 525/Neptune Road east for one mile. Turn right (south) onto King's Highway and travel 1.5 miles. Turn right onto Pine Island Road and drive 0.5 mile, then right again onto Scotty's Road. You'll be heading north at this point. Follow signs and take the road to the end about 0.25 mile.

Contact: Richardson's Fish Camp, 1550 Scotty's Road, Kissimmee, FL 34744, 407/846-6540.

137 SOUTHPORT RV PARK, CAMPGROUND, AND MARINA

Scenic rating: 7

south of Kissimmee on West Lake Tohopekaliga

See map page 230

Although this 25-acre park is plenty close to Disney World, most folks here are more interested in the boating, fishing, and wooded atmosphere on West Lake Tohopekaliga, which is known for world-class bass fishing. You get a free boat slip with each campsite. The clientele is a mix of families, anglers, and retirees.

RV sites, facilities: There are 53 full-hookup RV sites with electricity, picnic tables, and grills. Sites 28–37 overlook the lake, and two sites are wheelchair accessible. The campers' fishing area is separated from the boat slips so you're not apt to snag your line or tangle with a neighbor's boat lines. Restrooms, showers, a dump site, and laundry facilities are available. On the premises are a boat ramp, a dock, a fish-cleaning station, a clubhouse with planned activities in season, bait and tackle, a store, a snack bar, a horseshoe pit, a volleyball net, and a pavilion. Airboat tours leave every 30 minutes, and fishing guide service is available. Children are welcome. Leashed pets are permitted.

Reservations, fees: Reservations are recommended. Sites are $19–24 per night for two people, plus $2 per extra person. Credit cards are not accepted. Long-term rates are available.

Directions: From I-4, take Exit 64A east onto U.S. 192 about six miles. Turn south on Poinciana Boulevard between mile markers 10 and 11. Follow Poinciana Boulevard 18.5 miles until it crosses Pleasant Hill Road and dead-ends at Southport Park.

Contact: Southport RV Park, Campground and Marina, 2001 East Southport Road, Kissimmee, FL 34746, 407/933-5822, www.southportpark.com.

138 LAKE TOHO RV AND MOBILE HOME PARK

Scenic rating: 2

on Lake Tohopekaliga south of Kissimmee

See map page 230

This place was once known as Red's Fish Camp, which is why they sometimes answer the phone, "Reds!" Lacking amenities such as a pool or other diversions for children, Lake Toho Resort is favored mostly by a crowd interested in fishing or taking airboat rides on the lake. About half the residents live here year-round. Sites are grassy, and shade is fairly sparse unless you manage to get a site in the back row. You can fish from the bank of 11-mile-long Lake Tohopekaliga, but you'll probably have better luck if you bring your own boat (no rentals are available) and use the park boat ramp.

RV sites, facilities: This park has 250 full-hookup RV sites. Each site has a picnic table. Facilities include restrooms, showers, a dump station, laundry facilities, a boat ramp, and a restaurant that serves breakfast, lunch, and dinner. Management says all public areas are wheelchair accessible. Groceries are seven miles away. Children are welcome. Pets must be leashed.

Reservations, fees: Reservations are recommended in winter. Sites are $20 for two people, plus $2 per extra person. Credit cards are not accepted. Long-term stays are okay.

Directions: From I-4 at Exit 64A, head east on U.S. 192/Irlo Bronson Highway. Turn right at Kissimmee Park Road, at the first stoplight on the east side of town. The road dead-ends into the campground at Lake Tohopekaliga.

Contact: Lake Toho RV and Mobile Home Park, 4715 Kissimmee Park Road, St. Cloud, FL 34772, 407/892-8795.

139 CANOE CREEK CAMPGROUND

Scenic rating: 5

south of St. Cloud

See map page 230

Although it's called Canoe Creek Campground, there is no creek and no place to canoe in this rapidly developing area. You can stay here as long as you like, though. Some sites are grassy; others have concrete patios. For the most part, the place (and its four-foot-deep screened and heated pool) attracts senior citizens, but families are welcome. As for the puzzling name, Canoe Creek simply is the name of a creek that connects two nearby lakes—Cypress and Gentry. Disney-area attractions are about 25 miles away. About 20 percent of the park is occupied

year-round. Wintertime activities include golf outings, karaoke, country music, pokeno, and church services.

RV sites, facilities: These 178 full-hookup sites with picnic tables are for RVs. Most have 30-amp electrical service; 85 have 50-amp. Thirty-seven sites are pull-through. Big rigs and slide-outs can be accommodated. A therapy exercise pool, horseshoes, shuffleboard, and winter social programs entertain campers. On the premises are restrooms, showers, a dump station, trailer rentals, and laundry facilities. The recreation hall, pool area, and laundry facilities are accessible to wheelchairs. Streets are paved. Groceries are within two miles. Children and pets are permitted.

Reservations, fees: Reservations are recommended. Sites are $27–30 per night for two people, plus $2 for each extra person. Credit cards are not accepted. Long-term rates are available.

Directions: From St. Cloud, drive about six miles south on State Road 523 to the campground.

Contact: Canoe Creek Campground, 4101 Canoe Creek Road, St. Cloud, FL 34772, 407/892-7010 or 800/453-5268.

140 CYPRESS LAKE FISH CAMP AND RV

Scenic rating: 7

on Lake Cypress south of St. Cloud

See map page 230

Lake Cypress makes this remote RV park a picturesque place to stay where you're sure to see some interesting wildlife, including sandhill cranes, otters, and bald eagles. The main thing to do here is to ride airboats or fish for bass; some people also go after specks or bream. You don't have to be an angler to appreciate the place—just gazing out at the pretty blue waters of Lake Cypress is a treat. The park has been under new ownership as of mid-2005 and the proprietors will give you an airboat tour of the lake where you're likely to see bald eagles, alligators, and other wildlife. A boat launched here can make its way all the way to Lake Okeechobee and back, but not in one day. The sites are grassy and right near the lake's edge; most are sunny, but some are shaded by giant cypress trees. Disney World is about 30 miles north. About 10 percent of the park is occupied year-round.

RV sites, facilities: All 52 RV spaces have full hookups with a choice of 30-amp and 50-amp electrical service, concrete patios, picnic tables, and fire rings. On the premises are restrooms, showers, laundry facilities, a playground, a recreation room, rental cabins, a boat ramp, bait and tackle, snacks, gasoline sales, seven cabins, and basketball. Aviation fuel is also available for seaplanes. Management says the sites and restrooms are wheelchair accessible. You'll find groceries and restaurants within 10 miles. Kids and small pets are permitted.

Reservations, fees: Reservations are recommended, particularly in winter. Sites are $30. Credit cards are accepted.

Directions: From St. Cloud, take Highway 523/Canoe Creek Road south about 10 miles. Just after you pass under Florida's Turnpike, turn right onto Lake Cypress Road. Follow it to the end, where you'll find the campground.

Contact: Cypress Lake Fish Camp and RV, 3301 Lake Cypress Road, Kenansville, FL 34739, 407/957-3135, fax 407/892-3978.

141 GOOD LIFE RV RESORT

Scenic rating: 5

at Lake Garfield east of Bartow

See map page 230

Located along a divided highway east of the phosphate-mining town of Bartow, this sunny, retiree-oriented park is set on one-mile-wide Lake Garfield. Locals often use a boat ramp off Highway 60 to fish for bass and bream; however, visitors to this park are more interested in the planned activities, day trips, and theme-park visits. There's a nine-hole chipping course

between the RV section and the lake, but no beach; swimmers use a heated pool instead. The lake-view sites are taken by full-timers.

Mobile homes and long-term residents nearly dominate the 397 sites (about 125 are for RVs). Ruler-straight streets are laid out in a grid pattern and are named after states that are close to retirees' hearts: Ohio, North Carolina, New York, and so on. To avoid sleeping nearest to State Road 60, skip sites 101–199 and 140–150.

RV sites, facilities: This retiree-oriented park offers 125 RV sites with full hookups, 50-amp electrical service, and concrete patios measuring 20 by 35 feet. Lot size is 35 by 67 feet. A pool, a recreation hall, a golf course, shuffleboard, horseshoes, and winter activities entertain campers. Showers, restrooms, a dump station, and laundry facilities are available. The bathhouse, clubhouse, office, and pool area are wheelchair accessible. Streets are paved. Groceries and restaurants are within seven miles. Adults are preferred. Children under 17 must be adult-supervised at the pool, and their length of stay may be restricted. Pets are prohibited.

Reservations, fees: Reservations are recommended. Sites are $25 per night for two people, plus $1.50 per extra person. Credit cards are not accepted. Long-term rates are available.

Directions: From U.S. 98 in Bartow, drive east six miles on State Road 60, passing U.S. 17 and the Peace River. The park is ahead on the right.

Contact: Good Life RV Resort, 6815 State Road 60 East, Bartow, FL 33830, 863/537-1971, fax 863/537-2687.

142 CYPRESS GARDENS MOBILE HOME AND RV PARK

Scenic rating: 5

east of Winter Haven

See map page 230

"Lots of trees and wonderful people" is how the owners describe their adults-preferred park in this lake-dotted region west of Walt Disney World. Most visitors are snowbirds here for the winter months. Shopping and restaurants are close by. About two-thirds of the lots are taken year-round, and there are 143 mobile homes in a separate section. Repeat visitors are the rule, but openings do arise.

RV sites, facilities: There are 126 oversized RV sites with full hookups and picnic tables. About 80 percent have 30-amp electrical service, the rest have 50-amp. Big RVs can be accommodated, and many of the seasonal visitors build carports, awnings, or screen rooms onto their units. Restrooms, showers, laundry facilities, and telephone service are available. On the premises are a pool, a recreation hall with planned activities during the winter, shuffleboard courts, and a dog-walk area. A dial-up connection to the Internet is available in the recreation hall. Most areas are wheelchair accessible. Children are welcome to visit for short stays. Leashed pets are permitted (no attack breeds).

Reservations, fees: Reservations are recommended. Sites are $30 per night for two people, plus $2 per extra person. Credit cards are not accepted. Long-term rates are available.

Directions: From the intersection of U.S. 17 and State Road 542 in Winter Haven, go east on State Road 542 about 5.5 miles. When you reach the burg of Eastwood, turn right on Lake Daisy Road and go about one mile to the park.

Contact: Cypress Gardens Mobile Home and RV Park, 1951 Lake Daisy Road, Winter Haven, FL 33884, 863/324-3136, fax 863/318-9806.

143 HOLIDAY TRAVEL PARK

Scenic rating: 7

south of Winter Haven
See map page 230

Scrub oaks shade some sites at this 22-acre park, where half of the campers stay short-term, and the rest spend the entire winter. All campsites have 8- by 10-foot patios and are set diagonally along paved, ruler-straight, 5 mph roads. At the heart of

the park are the recreation halls for potluck dinners, arts and crafts, and the 25- by 50-foot pool near the entrance. Each Friday night, the park hosts a country-music concert and line dancing. The Cypress Gardens theme park is close by.

RV sites, facilities: Eighty RV sites for overnighters and 120 for seasonal visitors are available. Many are pull-through, and all have full hookups, 50-amp electricity, concrete pads, patios, and picnic tables. A heated pool, a game room, miniature golf, a playground, horseshoes, tennis, boccie ball (lawn bowling), shuffleboard, a recreation hall, and winter social programs entertain campers. Showers, restrooms, a dump station, firewood, a limited store, cable TV access, a kitchen, and laundry facilities are available. A restaurant is across the street, and groceries are one mile away. Children are welcome. Leashed pets under 20 pounds are okay.

Reservations, fees: Reservations are recommended. Sites are $24–36 per night, plus $4 for each additional person and $4 for pets. Credit cards are accepted. The maximum stay is six months.

Directions: From U.S. 27, drive one mile west on State Road 540 to the park entrance.

Contact: Holiday Travel Park, 7400 Cypress Gardens Boulevard, Winter Haven, FL 33884, 863/324-7400 or 800/858-7275 (for reservations), www.holidaytravelpark.com.

144 A-OKAY CAMPGROUND

Scenic rating: 2

near Eagle Lake south of Winter Haven
See map page 230

A citrus grove abuts this three-acre, adults-only park, where permanent residents live in 11 mobile homes and at some of the grassy RV sites equipped with concrete patios. Across the street to the north, Eagle Lake stretches about 1.5 miles. Not far south from the sun-dappled park is one-half-mile-wide Millsite Lake. You can fish for bass in this lake-dotted region. Favorite things to do are going to nearby theme parks, boating, and fishing. Most visitors come from Ohio and Michigan.

RV sites, facilities: All 21 full-hookup sites are for RVs up to 40 feet long. Sites have either 30-amp or 50-amp electrical service. Lots are 35 feet wide by 45 feet deep. Showers, restrooms, and a dump station are available. All areas are wheelchair accessible, according to management. One mile away are groceries, a restaurant, and laundry facilities. Children are not permitted, but they can visit campers here. Leashed pets are allowed.

Reservations, fees: Reservations are recommended in winter. Sites are $17 per night for two people, plus $2 for each additional person. Credit cards are not accepted. Long-term stays are okay for adults.

Directions: From Winter Haven, go south on U.S. 17, passing Highway 559. At Bartow Municipal Airport, turn right onto Spirit Lake Road. Continue less than two miles to Thornhill Road. Turn right. The campground is on the right at the junction with Crystal Beach Road.

Contact: A-okay Campground, 6925 Thornhill Road, Winter Haven, FL 33880, 863/294-9091.

145 LAKESHORE PALMS TRAVEL PARK

Scenic rating: 2

south of Winter Haven

See map page 230

Lakeshore Palms claims to be the closest RV park to the Cypress Gardens adventure theme park, famed for its water-ski shows and beautiful gardens. Indeed, from Lakeshore Palms, you can see the distant, towering spindle of the "Island in the Sky" sightseeing ride about 1.4 miles south. This all-ages park offers 40 grassy campsites fitted onto about two acres. A fence and hedges enclose the property, which overlooks 100-acre Lake Grass. Bass anglers and water-skiers find fun in the region's lakes.

Bicyclists pedal past orange groves and lakes east of the park on County Road 540A. Disney World is 33 miles north.

RV sites, facilities: There are 40 RV sites (32 full-hookup) and 8 with water and electricity. All have 30-amp electrical service. Fifteen sites are occupied year-round. In 2005 new owners began renovations to the property, which offers two boat docks, a screened pavilion, showers, restrooms, picnic tables, a dump station, a boat ramp, boat rentals, telephone hookups, and laundry facilities. Cable TV is reserved for monthly campers. A wireless Internet network is available in the recreation hall and in some areas of the park. Groceries and a restaurant are two miles away. Children are welcome. Quiet, leashed pets under 25 pounds are allowed.

Reservations, fees: Reservations are recommended. Sites are $22–26 per night for two people, plus $2 for each additional person. Credit cards are not accepted. Long-term stays are okay for adults.

Directions: Follow highway signs to Cypress Gardens; the campground is about two miles north of the park entrance. Or, from Winter Haven, take U.S. 17 south over the bridge past the Cleveland Indians spring-training ballpark and go to the next stoplight. Turn left onto County Road 655. Travel about two miles to the next stoplight. Turn left by the convenience store onto Eagle Lake Loop Road, which becomes Eloise Loop Road/County Road 540A. The campground is about two miles ahead on your right.

Contact: Lakeshore Palms Travel Park, 4800 Eloise Loop Road, Winter Haven, FL 33884, 863/324-1339, www.lakeshorepalms.com.

146 PARAKEET PARK

Scenic rating: 2

on South Scenic Highway (State Road 17) south of Lake Wales

See map page 230

On your approach to this 20-acre adults-preferred park, don't be surprised if you need to slow your speed to follow a truck laden with a heap of oranges. You're in the northern portion of Florida's fabled citrus belt. The park nonetheless has a residential feel: Campers are outnumbered by residents of the 103 mobile homes.

RV sites, facilities: All 25 full-hookup sites are for RVs up to 36 feet long and have picnic tables. Both 30-amp and 50-amp electrical service is available. A pool, a game room, shuffleboard, and winter activities in the wheelchair-accessible clubhouse entertain campers. Showers, restrooms, a dump station, cable TV, telephone hookups, and laundry facilities are available. Groceries and a restaurant are within two miles. Children may camp only on a short-term basis. Small pets are permitted.

Reservations, fees: Reservations are recommended. Sites are $20 per night for two people, plus $1 for each additional person and $2 for using electric heaters or air-conditioning. Credit cards are not accepted. Long-term rates are available.

Directions: From Lake Wales, drive 2.4 miles south on South Scenic Highway/State Road 17 to the park.

Contact: Parakeet Park, 2400 Parakeet Park Boulevard, Lake Wales, FL 33859, 863/676-2812.

147 LAKE WALES CAMPGROUND

Scenic rating: 6

south of Lake Wales

See map page 230

Oaks and the sparse needles of pine trees lend shade to some grassy campsites at this busy winter spot, but other sites are sunny. A shaded walkway leads through a flower garden, and a small natural pond adds to the scenery of the 14-acre, renovated park, which also features an indoor shuffleboard court and indoor, heated pool. Nearby are the Historic Bok Sanctuary, a hilly garden spot perfect for picnics at its 3 P. M. carillon recitals; and Le Chalet Suzanne, a noted gourmet restaurant. More than a few diners have landed private planes at the on-site airstrip to feast by candlelight on six-course

dinners. Favorite things to do in the park are "eat, talk, and shuffle," the managers say. Visitors come from all over the United States to participate in planned activities, including bingo, dances, potluck dinners, and day trips. They also enjoy the gym and listening to bands.

RV sites, facilities: There are 114 RV sites (50 pull-through) with full hookups, a choice of 30-amp or 50-amp electrical service, concrete patios, and picnic tables. A wireless Internet connection is available in the park. Shuffleboard courts, wintertime activities, and a wheelchair-accessible recreation room entertain campers. The recreation hall has a raised stage, a dance floor, a kitchen, and an entertainment center. Coffee is served every morning, and on Sundays there are church services. Showers, restrooms, and laundry facilities are provided on the grounds. The recreation room is also wheelchair accessible, and the park's roads are paved. Groceries and restaurants are within three miles. Children may camp for up to two weeks. Leashed pets are permitted.

Reservations, fees: Reservations are recommended. Sites are $24–26 per night for two people, plus $2 for each additional person. If you have more than one pet, another $1 fee is charged. Credit cards are accepted. Long-term stays are okay.

Directions: From State Road 60 at Lake Wales, drive three miles south on U.S. 27 to the park entrance.

Contact: Lake Wales Campground, 15898 U.S. 27, Lake Wales, FL 33859, 863/638-9011, fax 863/638-2873, www.lakewalescampgroundrvresort.com.

148 LAKEMONT RIDGE HOME AND RV PARK

Scenic rating: 4

in Frostproof

See map page 230

Retirees flock here each year from all over the United States and Canada to partake of a very busy social schedule planned by an activities director, such as exercises, dances, dinners, crafts, live entertainment, bingo, and seasonal events like holiday parties. There are also Sunday-morning church services. Favorite things to do are fishing, bike riding, and playing billiards and throwing horseshoes. A computer with Internet access is available in the recreation hall. About 35 percent of the park is occupied year-round, and there are two sections with park models and mobile homes. Additional land is set aside for future development.

RV sites, facilities: Among 265 full hookup RV sites, 142 have 30-amp electrical service and 110 have 50-amp. In 2005, 100-amp service was added to 100 sites. All have concrete patios and are paved. Big rigs can be accommodated on lots that are 35 feet wide and 78 feet long. An Internet connection is available in the clubhouse. Restrooms, showers, laundry facilities, a pool, a recreation hall, shuffleboard courts, cabin rentals, and a large fenced dog-walk area are on-site. All areas are wheelchair accessible. Groceries and restaurants are within 3 miles; malls and hospitals are 15 miles away. This tends to be an over-age-55 park. Leashed pets are permitted.

Reservations, fees: Reservations are recommended. Sites are $38 per night for two people. Credit cards are not accepted. Long-term rates are available.

Directions: From the intersection of County Road 630 and U.S. 27 in Frostproof, drive east on County Road 630 about 0.5 mile to the park on the right.

Contact: Lakemont Ridge Home and RV Park, 2000 Maine Street, Frostproof, FL 33843, 863/635-4472, fax 863/635-1627, email: lakemontridge@aol.com.

149 LILY LAKE GOLF RESORT

Scenic rating: 6

south of Frostproof

See map page 230　　　　　**BEST**

This manufactured-home community really can't be considered an RV park, per se. RVers

are welcome to rent a limited number of sites from owners of existing lots. The emphasis is on selling park models and "RV ports," which are manufactured homes with attached two-story garages for parking your RV. Of course, the amenities are spectacular. Campers can fish on Lily Lake and guests have free use of boats. The golf course is a major draw for the mostly retirement-age clientele.

RV sites, facilities: A limited number of RV sites (around 15) are available for rent from owners of lots at this sprawling manufactured-home community. Full hookups, 50-amp electrical service, cable TV, full security, and a clubhouse are available. (Pop-up campers and truck campers are prohibited.) On the premises are a heated pool, a golf course, a fishing lake, billiards, a dog-walk area, tennis and shuffleboard courts, and a recreation hall. All areas are wheelchair accessible. Children are not welcome. Leashed pets are permitted (limit of two).

Reservations, fees: Reservations are recommended. Sites are $30 per night for two people. Credit cards are accepted. Long-term stays are available.

Directions: From the intersection of U.S. 98 and U.S. 27, drive south one mile on U.S. 27. The resort is on the east side.

Contact: Lily Lake Golf Resort, 500 U.S. 27 South, Frostproof, FL 33843, 863/635-3685 or 800/654-5177, www.lilylake.com.

150 CAMP INN RESORTS

Scenic rating: 7

in Frostproof

See map page 230

Located down the road from the small Lake Wales Municipal Airport, an RV dealer, and other commercial establishments, this 85-acre park is big: Indeed, 45 campsites line up side by side at its widest point (Evergreen Circle). And the place has not one, but three, laundry rooms. Paved roads pass the grassy RV sites, where some campers spend months or even years.

Near the entrance on busy U.S. 27 are a

handful of water- and electricity-equipped sites, as well as two pools—one heated. Beyond that, a section of pull-through camping spots leads to eight shuffleboard courts and an 8,000-square-foot recreation hall at the park's center. Farther back, you'll find the bulk of the campsites—meaning most RVs are insulated from U.S. 27. To overlook an oval meadow, ask about sites on Laurel or Seagrape. For pull-through spots closest to a small lake (across a park road), consider sites B1, C1, D1, E5, E6, or E7.

RV sites, facilities: The 796 RV sites have full hookups with 30/50-amp electrical service; 190 are pull-through. There are picnic tables at each site. Two pools, a whirlpool, a game room, a recreation hall, shuffleboard, horseshoes, and winter social programs entertain campers. Showers, restrooms, a dump station, LP gas sales, and laundry facilities are available. Management says all areas are wheelchair accessible. A restaurant and groceries are within two miles. Children may camp on a short-term basis. Leashed pets should use the entrance-area dog walk.

Reservations, fees: Reservations are recommended. Sites are $22 per night for two people, plus $1 for each additional adult and $2 for cable TV. Credit cards are accepted. Long-term stays are okay for adults, preferably age 50 and up.

Directions: From State Road 60 in Lake Wales, turn south onto U.S. 27. The campground is eight miles ahead on the right side of the road.

Contact: Camp Inn Resorts, 10400 Highway 27, Frostproof, FL 33843, 863/635-2500 or 877/622-6746, fax 863/635-4822.

151 LAKE PIERCE ECO RESORT

Scenic rating: 10

between Haines City and Lake Wales on the north side of Lake Pierce

See map page 230

Fed up with big-city life, Frank Wezyk in 1999 sold his assets to create this 20-acre paradise on the north side of 4,000-acre Lake Pierce. Once a dilapidated trailer park, the place today is a jewel, where you can see wildlife close at hand (his feeding of the birds and fish, though of course not alligators, is something to see, and visitors are invited to join in), and just enjoy the outdoors. In fact, that's the kind of traveler Wezyk wants to visit the park, and he's worked hard to create an "ecological park." For example, a series of lights and mirrors under the 200-foot dock illuminate the fish and watery denizens. You can canoe, fish, hike, and bike around the area. The only thing you can't do is bring pets. They'll scare away the wildlife. A Vietnam veteran, Wezyk offers special rates for veteran's groups, car clubs, and Harley Davidson clubs.

RV sites, facilities: There are 15 RV sites with full hookups and 50 tent sites. Ten tent sites have water and electricity. All developed sites have picnic tables, grills, and cable TV. Restrooms, showers, laundry facilities, a nature trail, a fishing dock, canoe rentals, and shuffleboard courts are on the premises. Most areas are wheelchair accessible. Children are welcome. No pets, please.

Reservations, fees: Reservations are recommended. Sites are $20–25 per night for two people, plus $3 per extra person. Credit cards are not accepted. Long-term rates are available.

Directions: From the intersection of State Road 60 and U.S. 27 in Lake Wales, drive east on State Road 60 one mile. Turn north on U.S. Alternate 27/U.S. 17 and proceed 15 miles. Turn right on Tindel Camp Road and go one mile. At Lake Mabel Road, turn left and proceed to Canal Road one mile.

Contact: Lake Pierce Eco Resort, 3500 Canal Road, Lake Pierce, FL 33898, 863/439-2023, fax 863/439-6166, www.lakepierce.com.

152 LAKE KISSIMMEE STATE PARK

Scenic rating: 10

at Lake Kissimmee east of Lake Wales

See map page 230

This nearly eight-square-mile state park is famous for its weekend living-history demonstrations of an 1876 "cow camp." Just walk 50 yards from the parking lot to the 200-acre pen of scrub cows to swap stories around a campfire with a costumed ranger posing as a "cow hunter." Don't make reference to modern-day things such as MP3 players or cell phones, though, because the cowpoke will claim to not understand you. He'll instead hearken back to simpler days—when frontier cowboys herded cattle and, earlier, provided the Confederacy with much of its beef.

Campers relax north of the cow camp along two loops near an observation tower, where visitors climb three landings to gaze onto an expanse of prairielike pasture. Each shell-rock campsite is equipped with a grill, a picnic table, and a fire ring handy for building campfires to roast marshmallows by. Plentiful picnic tables sit at creekside or beneath the twisted branches of oaks elsewhere in the park.

Look for turkeys, bald eagles, deer, and a sea of pickerelweed stretching toward the horizon during walks along 13 miles of hiking trails. A short nature loop and two long loop trails that encompass much of the park—one north of Zipper Canal, the other south of it—are reachable from the marina-area concession stand north of the cow camp. Notice the park's varied landscape: wide-open wet prairies, sun-dappled pine flatlands, and shady hammocks with orchids and mosses. Bring mosquito repellent for a more pleasant walk.

A launch ramp leads boaters a short distance east to the park's namesake, Lake Kissimmee, where anglers try for specks, bass, and shellcrackers in Florida's third-largest lake. Canoeists who bring their own craft can paddle five to seven miles along a pretty loop starting at Zipper Canal and heading west (counterclockwise) to Lake Rosalie, Rosalie Creek, Tiger Lake, Tiger Creek, and the eastern corner of 47-square-mile Lake Kissimmee, before returning to the boat ramp. The placid waters you'll see here eventually flow south down the Kissimmee River to the Everglades and Florida Bay at the state's southern tip, some 200 miles distant. At night, you'll listen to the croaking of frogs, but on busy fishing weekends, the roar of far-off boat engines can also be heard. However, development is beginning to move in to this once-remote area.

RV sites, facilities: All 60 sites have water, 30-amp electricity, a picnic table, a grill, and a fire ring. A playground, nature trails, showers, restrooms, a dump station, and a 50-person-capacity youth camping area are available. Two campsites, the fishing pier, and restrooms are wheelchair accessible. Laundry facilities, a restaurant, snacks, and bait are within 5 miles, and groceries are 15 miles away. Kids are welcome.

Reservations, fees: Reservations are recommended; contact ReserveAmerica at 800/336-3521 or reserveamerica.com. Sites are $17 per night for up to eight people. Credit cards are accepted. The maximum stay is 14 days.

Directions: From U.S. 27 at Lake Wales, travel about nine miles east on State Road 60. Turn left at Boy Scout Road. After three miles, turn right at Camp Mack Road. The park is five miles ahead.

Contact: Lake Kissimmee State Park, 14248 Camp Mack Road, Lake Wales, FL 33853, 863/696-1112, www.floridastateparks.org.

153 CAMP MACK'S RIVER RESORT

Scenic rating: 8

at Lake Kissimmee east of Lake Wales

See map page 230   BEST (

Fish camps are usually not known for their amenities, but this one is deluxe and getting more so every year to fit "a fisherman's dream," as the managers put it. A pool, motel, and a clubhouse were built in the early 2000s, and the park added large sites for big rigs while retaining a wooded atmosphere. But the main deal is fishing, airboat riding, and boating on Lake Kissimmee and other nearby waters famed for bass. Lake Kissimmee State Park is nearby. About 8 percent of the park is occupied year-round.

RV sites, facilities: There are 150 RV sites with 30/50-amp electrical service, sewer hookups, concrete pads, and picnic tables. None of the sites are pull-through. Park models are being sold on the property, and cabins are for rent. Restrooms, showers, laundry facilities, a pool, a boat ramp, a fish-cleaning station, a clubhouse, bait and tackle, a store, and boat rentals are available. Most areas are wheelchair accessible. Streets are paved. Children are welcome. Leashed pets are permitted.

Reservations, fees: Reservations are recommended. Sites are $33 per night for four people, plus $2 per extra person. Additional fees are $2 for 30-amp electrical service, $3 for 50-amp, and $5 for cable TV. Credit cards are accepted. Year-round rates are available for visitors over 55 only.

Directions: From U.S. 27 at Lake Wales, travel about nine miles east on State Road 60. Turn left at Boy Scout Road. After three miles, turn right at Camp Mack Road. The park is six miles ahead.

Contact: Camp Mack's River Resort, 14900 Camp Mack Road, Lake Wales, FL 33898, 863/696-1108 or 800/243-8013, fax 863/696-1500, www.campmack.com.

154 THE HARBOR RV RESORT AND MARINA

Scenic rating: 6

on Lake Rosalie east of Lake Wales

See map page 230

If the boat ramp on seven-square-mile Lake Rosalie isn't enough to convince you, then the bass logo makes it clear: Fishing is popular at this

13-acre marina and RV park set in a relaxed, lake-dotted region. Many campers enjoy this park's tranquillity and the bright glow of the sun rising over the lake. For a lakeside camping spot, request sites 37, 54, 55, or 56. Lots 99–104 are secluded spots near the woods. About 8 percent of the park is occupied by full-timers.

Paved, 5 mph streets pass the grassy/concrete-pad sites, most of which are shaded by oaks. Outside the park, much of the land bordering the lake is undeveloped, making it easy on the eyes. Three miles away is the 1800s-style cow camp at Lake Kissimmee State Park (see listing in this chapter). Orlando-area theme parks are about 45 minutes north.

RV sites, facilities: There are 45 grassy or gravel full-hookup sites (10 pull-through). Seventeen sites have 50-amp electrical service; the rest have 30-amp. A wireless Internet connection is available in the clubhouse and in the office. The park caters to mix of seasonal visitors, baby boomers, and families. A pool, shuffleboard, and a recreation hall entertain campers. Showers, restrooms, laundry facilities, a marina, propane, rental cabins, a fishing guide, boat docks, a boat ramp, and boat rentals are available. Planned activities get started in November, with fishing and shuffleboard tournaments, dinners, art classes, church services, and day tours, to name just a few. Children are welcome. Pets are permitted.

Reservations, fees: Reservations are recommended in winter. Sites are $36 per night for two people, plus $3 for each additional person, $2 for using heaters or air conditioners, and $3 for cable TV. Credit cards are accepted. Long-term rates are available.

Directions: From U.S. 27 at Lake Wales, travel about 9.9 miles east on State Road 60. Turn left at Boy Scout Road. In 3.5 miles, turn right at Camp Mack Road. Continue 1.7 miles to the park entrance.

Contact: The Harbor RV Resort and Marina, 10511 Monroe Court, Lake Wales, FL 33898, 863/696-1194, fax 863/696-4000, www.harbor-rv-marina.com.

155 GRAPE HAMMOCK RV PARK AND MARINA

Scenic rating: 3

on the Kissimmee River east of Lake Wales

See map page 230

Fishing is the lure at this relaxed spot on the Kissimmee River. In inclement weather, die-hard anglers can cast lines from the riverbanks, but the usual routine is to head a short distance to the broad waters of Florida's third-largest lake—Lake Kissimmee. Campers have been known to bring back some big bass. In addition to fishing guides and boat rentals, you can arrange to take part in an alligator hunt in September (though the dates may change; hunts are regulated by the state of Florida). Call 863/676-3173. Also known as Grape Hammock Fish Park, these 21 acres are rustic and family-owned since 1950. Cabins sit beneath a canopy of oaks. Campsites are sandy or grassy, with some situated near the canal. Three-wheelers may ride slowly through the park to get to the main road. The owners report that the state of Florida purchased three surrounding fish camps in 2005, so the land is being preserved.

Professional guide Johnny Doub says the odds of catching a 10-pound bass are best from January until summer's end; call 800/826-0621. Campground motorboats rent for $90.

RV sites, facilities: There are 70 grassy, full-hookup RV sites, of which 5 have 50-amp electrical service, and the rest have 30-amp. Sites have concrete patios, picnic tables, and grills. Some are waterfront. A pool, shuffleboard, a recreation room, showers, restrooms, a dump station, cabin rentals, a boat ramp, a dock, boat rentals, airboat tours, houseboat moorings, bait, tackle, and laundry facilities are on the premises. Management says the recreation room and restrooms are wheelchair accessible. Groceries are 24 miles away; restaurants are within 12 miles. Children under 12 must be adult-supervised at the pool. Pets are welcome, but disruptive animals should be leashed.

Reservations, fees: Reservations are recom-

mended. Sites are $16–22 per night for two adults and two children, plus $1 per extra person and $2 for cable TV. Credit cards are accepted. Long-term rates are available.

Directions: From Lake Wales, travel 22 miles east on State Road 60. Turn left at Grape Hammock Road. The entrance is 1.25 miles ahead.

Contact: Grape Hammock RV Park and Marina, 1400 Grape Hammock Road, Lake Wales, FL 33853, 863/692-1500, www.grapehammock.com.

156 RIVER RANCH RV RESORT

Scenic rating: 10

on the Kissimmee River between Lake Wales and Yeehaw Junction

See map page 230   BEST (

Families like this deluxe spot. The buffet is a popular choice at this spectacular resort's restaurant, which is located across the driveway from the on-site airstrip. Kids stop to buy candy at the snack bar between bouts of combat in the game room, and a guard stands posted at the resort's long entranceway. It's a special spot. The setting is rustic and woodsy, right next to the Kissimmee River in a rural section of Florida, but don't even think about roughing it. Choose from a campsite in a shady Old Florida oak hammock or a sunny site next to the canal where you can dock your boat. Fish from a riverbank, or try for bass from your own johnboat or canoe. Fishing guide services are available nearby; inquire at the registration desk. On-site are a catch-and-release pond, a nine-hole golf course, a petting zoo, minigolf, and horseback riding. Try a short hike down the Florida National Scenic Trail next door at KICCO Wildlife Management Area. Or, take a drive over to Lake Kissimmee State Park and check out the historic cow camp.

RV sites, facilities: All 367 paved RV sites have 30/50-amp electricity, water, cable TV, wireless Internet access, concrete patios, fire rings, and picnic tables. Lots are 40–65 feet wide and 70–85 feet long, accommodating the largest RVs on the market. Facilities include restrooms, showers, a dump station, an airstrip, a restaurant, laundry facilities, a boat dock, hiking trails, a game room, a snack bar, limited bait and tackle sales, guided horseback rides on weekends, golf, tennis courts, and meeting rooms. Other entertainment includes rodeos, "gunslinger" shows, trap and skeet shooting and a gun range, a petting zoo, boat tours, airboat rides, and more. Many areas are wheelchair accessible. Streets are paved. Children and pets are permitted in the camping area but not in the resort's motel rooms.

Reservations, fees: Reservations are recommended. Sites are $40–50 per night for four people, plus $2 for each extra person. Credit cards are accepted. Long-term rates are available.

Directions: From Florida's Turnpike at Yeehaw Junction, take Exit 193 and travel west on State Road 60 about 25 miles, crossing the Kissimmee River, and look for the entrance ahead on the left. From Lake Wales, head east on State Road 60 about 25 miles and look for the entrance on the right before you reach the Kissimmee River.

Contact: River Ranch RV Resort, 24700 State Road 60/P.O. Box 30421, River Ranch, FL 33867, 863/692-1321, fax 863/692-9707, www.riverranchrv.com.

157 LAKE MARIAN PARADISE

Scenic rating: 3

on Lake Marian south of St. Cloud

See map page 230

Under new ownership since 2005, this fish camp–turned–nature resort values its natural setting, and the state's policy of preserving the acreage nearby in its pristine glory. Some retirees and a number of working people live at these sunny and shady sites full-time or at least long-term (about 70 percent of the park is occupied year-round). Visitors tend to be anglers, families, and repeat customers. The camp is set on Lake Marian, a 5,800-acre unspoiled lake. Besides fishing, you can hike in the wildlife management area, which seems to burst at the seams with critters compared with nearby urban Florida. There's also a par-27 golf course overlooking the lake. A restaurant is located in the nearby hamlet of Kenansville one mile away.

RV sites, facilities: All 57 full-hookup sites have full hookups, 30 or 50-amp electrical service, and picnic tables. A boat dock is included with your camping fee, and the waterfront sites are just steps away from the marina. Rigs up to 40 feet long and slide-outs can be accommodated. On the premises are restrooms, showers, a dump station, picnic tables, a boat ramp, efficiency motel rentals, laundry facilities, bait and tackle, a general store, and boat rentals. Planned activities are low-key bingo and potluck dinners; the favorite thing to do is fishing. Groceries are within three miles. The clubhouse and store are wheelchair accessible. Children may stay short-term. Pets are permitted, although management reserves the right to turn away pets that are troublesome.

Reservations, fees: Reservations are advised. Sites are $31–36 per night for two people, plus $3 for each additional person. Credit cards are accepted. Adults interested in long stays should inquire about monthly rates.

Directions: From St. Cloud, take Highway 523/Canoe Creek Road south about 32 miles. When you see Arnold Road, turn right, heading southwest, for 0.5 mile. It leads to the fish camp. If you reach the point where Highway 523 passes under Florida's Turnpike west of Kenansville, you've gone too far. If you're coming from southern Florida, take Florida's Turnpike to the Yeehaw Junction exit. Head north on U.S. 441 about 14 miles to Highway 523, turn left (west), and go about 3 miles to Arnold Road, where you'll turn left.

Contact: Lake Marian Paradise, 901 Arnold Road, Kenansville, FL 34739, 407/436-1464, www.lakemarian.com.

158 PIONEER CREEK RV PARK

Scenic rating: 7

off U.S. 17 south of Bowling Green
See map page 230

A socially active lifestyle is what you'll get at Pioneer Creek RV Park, which offers paved, lighted streets and clean RV sites where outdoor clotheslines are forbidden. From golf at 8:30 A. M. to pinochle in the smoke-free clubhouse at 7 P.M., the rotating schedule of winter activities can keep visitors busy in case the heated pool and woodworking shop aren't enough. Small mowed lawns and, in some cases, attached screen rooms lend a residential feel to the park. The favorite thing to do is socializing. RVs on Drum Drive and the northern portion of Arrowhead Loop back onto a conservation area that divides the park. Nearby is the Paynes Creek State Historic Site, where a Seminole Indian trading post once stood. Although life in this region of Florida is slow paced, you'll find that a Ford dealership, a citrus stand, a pet supply store, and other businesses down a ways on U.S. 17, in Wauchula, are reminders of urban life. Most visitors here are from the Midwest and New York.

RV sites, facilities: This park offers 377 full-hookup sites with 50-amp electrical service, concrete patios, and wireless Internet access. RVs up to 40 feet and slide-outs are welcome. A pool, a clubhouse, a woodworking shop, shuffleboard, horseshoes, pool tables, boccie ball (lawn bowling) courts, and planned wintertime activities entertain campers. Showers, restrooms, a dump station, picnic areas, winter church services, cable TV (long-term campers only), propane, and laundry facilities are available. All areas are wheelchair accessible. Groceries and restaurants are within three miles. Children are not allowed. Campers with pets sleep in a designated section; one leashed pet is permitted per site.

Reservations, fees: Reservations are suggested. Sites are $24 per night for two people, plus $2.50 per extra person. Credit cards are accept-ed. Long-term rates are available. The park's office is closed in summer.

Directions: From Main Street/State Road 64A in Wauchula, go north about six miles on U.S. 17 to Broward Street (just south of the Polk County line) to the park, on the right.

Contact: Pioneer Creek RV Park, 138 East Broward Street, Bowling Green, FL 33834, 863/375-4343, www.rvresorts.com.

159 WAGON WHEEL RV PARK

Scenic rating: 5

off U.S. 17 north of Wauchula
See map page 230

Located 50 miles from the beach in a citrus-dotted portion of the state often overlooked by tourists, the 20-acre, adults-only park is 0.5 mile off the main drag, U.S. 17. Retirees take part in wintertime social programs before retiring to their grassy RV sites with concrete patios. About half the park is occupied by full-time residents.

RV sites, facilities: This adults-only park has 265 full-hookup, 50-amp sites for RVs up to 40 feet long. Showers, restrooms, laundry facilities, a recreation room, horseshoes, shuffleboard, and winter social programs are available. A 0.5-acre lake is available for fishing. Management says all facilities are wheelchair accessible. Children are only permitted to visit park residents; campers must be at least 18. Leashed pets under 30 pounds are allowed; management must preapprove the breed.

Reservations, fees: Reservations are not necessary. Sites are $20 per night for two adults, plus $5 per extra person. Credit cards are not accepted. Long-term stays are encouraged.

Directions: From the junction of U.S. 17 and State Road 62 north of Wauchula, travel 0.5 mile north on U.S. 17 to Bostick Road. Turn left and continue 0.5 mile west to the park, on the right.

Contact: Wagon Wheel RV Park, 2908 Red Barn Lane, Bowling Green, FL 33834, 863/773-3157.

160 CRYSTAL LAKE VILLAGE RV AND MOBILE HOME PARK

Scenic rating: 7

off U.S. 17 north of Wauchula

See map page 230

Orange groves flank three sides of this 37-acre community, set in the sleepy inland region of Florida. Retirees escape cold northern winters by spending six months here, passing the time with square dances, arts and crafts, trips on the park's 29-passenger bus, and fishing at a three-acre stocked lake. Lighted streets and paved driveways lead up to the plentiful park models and the RV sites, some of which are shaded. If the 18-hole golf course located about 1.25 miles away doesn't fit the bill, then try another course 6 miles distant. Disney World is a long day trip to the northeast. More than 70 percent of the park is occupied year-round.

RV sites, facilities: Open to campers age 55 and over, this 360-site mobile-home/RV park offers more than 50 full-hookup sites with paved driveways and patios for RVs up to 48 feet long. All sites have 30/50-amp electrical service. Internet access is available in the clubhouse. Showers, restrooms, a pool, a hot tub, trailer rentals, horseshoes, shuffleboard, a recreation hall, billiards, planned activities, a fishing lake, and laundry facilities are provided. Management says all facilities are wheelchair accessible. A restaurant, groceries, and an 18-hole golf course are within 1.5 miles. Leashed pets are permitted.

Reservations, fees: Reservations are recommended. Sites are $20–25 per night for two people, plus $3 for each additional person and an additional charge for cable TV. Credit cards are accepted. Long-term rates are available.

Directions: From Wauchula, travel 3 miles north on U.S. 17 to Maxwell Drive, which is 0.25 mile south of State Road 62. Turn right onto Maxwell and continue east to the park.

Contact: Crystal Lake Village RV and Mobile Home Park, 237 Maxwell Drive, Wauchula, FL 33873, 863/773-3582 or 800/661-3582, fax 863/773-0410.

161 LITTLE CHARLIE CREEK RV PARK

Scenic rating: 5

at the Peace River north of Wauchula

See map page 230

Household garbage must be placed in dark-colored bags and recyclables in clear or white bags for the twice-weekly curbside pickup—a hint that this park prizes cleanliness and neatness. The attraction at this adult park is mixing with your neighbors at potluck dinners and organized games of pokeno, bingo, shuffleboard, and pool. For anglers, the lure is the Peace River, which is located just west of the RV park. Little Charlie Creek passes by here, too, to intersect with the Peace River. Keeping the peace is a good idea at the RV park, set in a sleepy section of Florida. Among the 31 park rules: Anything hung on a clothesline must be removed by 4 P.M., and lawn watering must be done early in the morning or late in the evening, and in moderation. Most people stay for winter, though there are a few full-timers. About 40 percent of the lots are occupied year-round.

RV sites, facilities: The adult-oriented park has 190 full-hookup sites with 50-amp electrical service and concrete patios. Six sites are drive-through. Showers, restrooms, laundry facilities, shuffleboard, horseshoes, planned activities, and a recreation hall are provided. Internet connections are available in the clubhouse. Visiting children must be accompanied by an adult while in the recreation center or other common areas. Leashed, immunized pets are permitted.

Reservations, fees: Overnighters are welcome but reservations are suggested. Sites are $30 per night for two people. Credit cards are accepted. Long-term rates are available.

Directions: From the intersection of U.S. 17 and Main Street in Wauchula, drive north on U.S. 17 about one mile. Turn right at REA Road at the Wal-Mart. Soon after, turn left onto Heard Bridge Road. Travel north about two miles, crossing the Peace River. The campground is to your right.

Contact: Little Charlie Creek RV Park, 1850 Heard Bridge Road, Wauchula, FL 33873, 863/773-0088, fax 863/773-2274.

162 PEACE RIVER PRESERVE

Scenic rating: 10

south of Wauchula

See map page 230   BEST (

With the Peace River running alongside and a campground boat ramp, anglers and boaters find this resort (formerly River Valley RV Resort) just their style, but so will families and campers with pets. This park is part of the Thousand Trails campground membership club, but trial offers are available to nonmembers. Part of the park has a wooded canopy, and children are welcome year-round. A playground, sand and grass volleyball areas, and a basketball court were added in 2005. A separate area of the park is set aside for older snowbirds. This park has much to offer for the camper who likes a nature-oriented setting with civilized amenities and lots of sports.

RV sites, facilities: This sprawling, 73-acre, all-ages resort has 454 sites laid out in neat suburb style. About 226 tents can be accommodated in a large field, as well. RV sites have full hookups and picnic tables; big rigs can be accommodated. Restrooms, showers, a dump station, laundry facilities, a heated pool, a snack bar, an activity center/lodge, a boat ramp, shuffleboard courts, propane gas sales, and a nature trail are on the premises. Many areas are wheelchair accessible. Children are welcome. Leashed pets are permitted.

Reservations, fees: Reservations are recommended. Trial memberships are available. Credit cards are accepted. Stay as long as you wish.

Directions: From Wauchula, drive two miles south on U.S. 17 to the resort, which is on the east side.

Contact: Peace River Preserve, 2555 U.S. 17 South, Wauchula, FL 33873, 863/735-8888, www.1000trails.com.

163 ADELAIDE SHORES RV RESORT

Scenic rating: 7

north of Avon Park

See map page 230

Under new ownership since 2005, this sunny lakeside retirement community offers social programs for residents and guests; they enjoy bingo, cards, parties, shows, trips, and cruises. Many campers are seasonal; Avon Park's population swells from 9,000 to 13,000 in winter. The RV resort is on a 96-acre lake, affording opportunities for fishing. The heated swimming pool and tennis courts are also popular. In the area, numerous golf courses are located within a 10-minute drive. About 25 percent of the sites are occupied year-round.

RV sites, facilities: This adults-only park offers 399 full-hookup sites; some have been sold for RVs or park models. Lots are 45 by 67 feet and all have 30/50-amp electrical service. Three sites are drive-through. A wireless Internet connection is available. On the premises are restrooms, showers, a dump station, two laundry facilities, a 5,000-square-foot clubhouse, trailer rentals, an Olympic-sized pool with tiki bar, a dock with boat slips, an exercise room, a dance floor, tennis courts, boccie ball (lawn bowling) courts, shuffleboard, horseshoes, a pool table, and a putting green. Cable TV (free) and telephone service are available. All areas are said to be wheelchair accessible. Groceries and restaurants are within one mile. Children are allowed for short visits. Pets are permitted.

Reservations, fees: Reservations are recommended. Sites are $28 per night for two people, plus $3 per extra person. Credit cards are not accepted. Stay as long as you like.

Directions: From Avon Park, travel north four miles on U.S. 27 to the park.

Contact: Adelaide Shores RV Resort, 2881 U.S. 27 North, Avon Park, FL 33826, 863/453-2226 or 800/848-1924, www.adelaideshores.com.

164 ORANGE BLOSSOM RV PARK

Scenic rating: 2

in Avon Park
See map page 230

The RV sites basically are an adjunct to the more-permanent mobile homes. Some residents like to fish at a small on-site lake. Unsurprisingly for this area of Florida, the park borders orange groves. Campers have a choice of sandy, concrete pad, and grassy sites. Shade is sparse. Most people stay two to three months in winter, but 20 percent of the sites are occupied year-round. Says the management: "We are an RV park, not a regular campground."

RV sites, facilities: There are 35 full-hookup sites with 50-amp electrical service, concrete patios, and wireless Internet access available for visitors. Rigs up to 45 feet long can be accommodated. On the premises are restrooms, showers, shuffleboard, and a recreation room with regularly scheduled church services. The bathhouse and clubhouse are wheelchair accessible. Streets are paved. Groceries, a restaurant, and laundry facilities are about two miles away. Children are not permitted except for shot stays. Leashed pets under 30 pounds are allowed.

Reservations, fees: Reservations are recommended. Sites are $19 per night for two people, plus $1 for each additional person. Credit cards are not accepted. Long-term rates are available.

Directions: From U.S. 27, take State Road 64/Main Street east through the town of Avon Park. After about two miles, turn left onto County Road 17A. drive about three miles and look for the park ahead on the left

Contact: Orange Blossom RV Park, 1400 County Road 17A North, Avon Park, FL 33825, 863/453-6052, fax 863/453-0301.

165 STEWARTS MOBILE VILLAGE

Scenic rating: 1

on U.S. 27 in Avon Park
See map page 230

For many visitors, this location's main appeal is its proximity to the RV repairs and service center on-site. RVs and tents are outnumbered by mobile homes at this small roadside park located down the street from Avon Park Municipal Airport. It's within walking distance of a shopping center. You also can cross the street to fish from the piers at 0.25-mile-wide Lake Onaka. About one-third of the park is occupied year-round.

RV sites, facilities: There are 10 full-hookup sites, of which seven have 30-amp electrical service, and the rest have 50-amp. Slide-out RVs can be accommodated. On the premises are restrooms, showers, a dump station, picnic tables, laundry facilities, rental trailers, and horseshoes. The restrooms and office are wheelchair accessible. Streets are paved. Children and pets are welcome.

Reservations, fees: Reservations are recommended. Sites are $20 per night for two people, plus $5 for each extra person. Credit cards are accepted. Long-term rates are available.

Directions: Take U.S. 27 south from Avon Park one mile to the campground.

Contact: Stewarts Mobile Village, 1116 U.S. 27 South, Avon Park, FL 33825, 863/453-3849 or 800/724-7502, www.stewartsmobilevillage.com.

166 REFLECTIONS ON SILVER LAKE

Scenic rating: 6

south of Avon Park
See map page 230

A "winter destination community" for the over-age-55 crowd, this family-owned park is divided into three areas: RVs, park models, and mobile homes. A full-time activities coordinator fills the hours for RVers who come from all over the Midwest and Canada to spend the season here. The park fronts onto Silver Lake for pretty views and fishing.

RV sites, facilities: There are 338 RV sites, of which 20 are available for overnighters. The majority of sites are occupied year-round or rented to tourists on an annual contract. All have full hookups and 30-amp electricity; 10 sites have 50-amp. None are drive-through, but 40-foot-long RVs and slide-outs can be accommodated. Sites are gravel, grassy, or paved, with concrete patios. Restrooms, showers, laundry facilities, a heated pool, fishing lake, a boat dock, two recreation halls, shuffleboard, *pétanque* (French-style bowling) and boccie ball (lawn bowling) courts, propane sales, and a dog-walk area are on-site. All areas of the park are wheelchair accessible. Groceries and hospitals are within 0.5 mile; restaurants and malls are 5 miles away. Children are allowed as guests visiting campers. Leashed pets are permitted.

Reservations, fees: Reservations are recommended. Sites are $25 per night for two people, plus $2 per extra person. Credit cards are accepted. Long-term rates are available.

Directions: From the intersection of U.S. 27 and State Road 64, drive south on U.S. 27 1.5 miles. The park entrance is across the street from South Florida Community College.

Contact: Reflections on Silver Lake, 1850 U.S. 27 South, Avon Park, FL 33825, 863/453-5756, fax (863)453-9468, www.reflectionsonsilver-lake.com.

167 LAKE BONNET VILLAGE

Scenic rating: 7

at Lake Bonnet south of Avon Park

See map page 230

This combination campground and mobile-home park is in a quiet, woodsy setting overlooking spring-fed 260-acre Lake Bonnet. Many sites are shady, and the view of the lake is pretty. Favored by retirees, this is a nice option for those who prefer a more nature-oriented setting. The

RV sites have concrete pads. Nearly half the sites are occupied by people who live here year-round, and a good portion of the rest stay here on a long-term basis. Lot purchases are encouraged. You can swim in the heated pool, relax in a hot tub, or go boating, fishing, or waterskiing on Lake Bonnet. Highlands Hammock State Park is about 15 miles away (see next campground). If you're feeling adventurous, check out the secluded hiking trails at the 106,000-acre Avon Park Air Force Range (call 863/452-4254), approximately 12 miles away.

RV sites, facilities: The 209 full-hookup RV sites have 30/50-amp electrical service and can accommodate vehicles up to 40 feet long. Five RV sites are pull-through. On the premises are restrooms, showers, a dump station, laundry facilities, picnic tables, a wheelchair-accessible recreation room, a pool, a hot tub, a boat ramp, a dock, boat and canoe rentals, a playground, horseshoes, shuffleboard, volleyball, and limited groceries. Children are welcome for up to one month. Pets are permitted.

Reservations, fees: Reservations are recommended. Sites are $30–35 per night for two people, plus $2 for each extra person and $1.50 for electricity. Credit cards are accepted. Long-term rates are available.

Directions: From Avon Park, take State Road 17 south about four miles to Lake Bonnet Road. Turn left and go about one mile east to the park.

Contact: Lake Bonnet Village, 2900 East Lake Bonnet Road, Avon Park, FL 33825, 863/385-7010, fax 863/402-0430, www.lakebonnetvil-lage.com.

168 HIGHLANDS HAMMOCK STATE PARK

Scenic rating: 10

west of Sebring

See map page 230

An occasional white-tailed deer may be seen munching in open fields at dusk here at one of

Florida's oldest state parks—one of my favorite campgrounds in the state. During the winter, you're nearly guaranteed to see large groups of deer at the historic homestead/grove area snacking on the still-producing citrus trees! The scenery is worth the somewhat-cramped-together official camping spots. This park offers nearly 10,000 acres of virgin hardwood forest with a cypress swamp, pine flat woods, sand pine scrub, scrubby flat woods, and marsh.

You're almost certain to see an alligator during your stay, and the lucky camper could encounter more elusive wildlife such as bobcats, otters, and owls. Opened in 1931, this gem was one of the four original parks in the state parks system, which was organized in 1935. A museum here recounts how the Civilian Conservation Corps helped build Florida's park system during the Great Depression.

Guided walks and tram tours offered by rangers are your best bet for viewing wildlife, but you also can choose from eight nature and mountain-biking trails that cover 11 miles. Horseback-riding trails are available, too. Riding rented bikes along a loop road is popular. Some nature trails traverse boardwalks in a gorgeous old cypress swamp and other wet areas, and dirt paths elsewhere lead through woods. RVs and tents in the regular campground are pretty much squeezed together.

RV sites, facilities: The campground has 138 sunny and shady RV sites with water and 30-amp electric hookups, picnic tables, and grills. Most of the sites are grassy or gravel. On the premises are restrooms, showers, a dump station, laundry facilities, grills, a camp store with ice, snacks, souvenirs and camping supplies, a recreation hall, playgrounds, nature trails, horseshoes, shuffleboard, bicycle rentals, and mountain-bike trails. The Hammock Inn, run by a concessionaire, offers breakfast, lunch, and dinner. Try the locally famous "wild orange" pies and milk shakes. In the winter months, campground hosts provide morning coffee socials, potluck dinners, and music around the campfire. There's also a tram tour. Manage-

ment says the museum, restrooms, and some trails have wheelchair access. Groceries and restaurants are about five miles away. Children and groups are welcome. Pets are allowed with proof of vaccination.

Reservations, fees: Reservations are recommended; contact ReserveAmerica at 800/336-3521 or reserveamerica.com. Sites are $20 per night for eight people. Credit cards are accepted. Stays are restricted to two weeks.

Directions: From U.S. 27 near Sebring, drive four miles west on County Road 634/Hammock Road to the park.

Contact: Highlands Hammock State Park, 5931 Hammock Road, Sebring, FL 33872, 863/386-6094, fax 863/386-6095, www.floridastateparks.org.

169 HIGHLAND WHEEL ESTATES RV/MOBILE HOME PARK

Scenic rating: 3

near Lake Jackson in Sebring

See map page 230

These shady oak- and pine-dotted lots are located across from 3,000-acre Lake Jackson, where locals scuba dive, snorkel, windsurf, fish, water-ski, and swim. The lake is a spectacular sight as you drive through Sebring, and on windy days, you'll see whitecaps whipping up across the waters. Catering to snowbirds age 50 and older, many of whom have been visiting the park for more than a decade, the park is close to historic downtown Sebring. There, you'll find a small community theater, an arts complex, a library, a civic center, and a YMCA. The campground is about one mile from a mall and not much farther from Highlands Hammock State Park.

RV sites, facilities: This adult-oriented park has 100 full-hookup RV sites with picnic tables. A heated swimming pool with therapy jets, clubhouse, horseshoes, billiards, a computer room, and winter social programs entertain campers. On the premises are restrooms, showers, a dump station, laundry facilities, and trailer rentals. Be sure to bring your own spoon and dish for the Sunday ice-cream socials. Other activities are water aerobics, arts and crafts, Bible study and church services, bunco, ladies billiards, and more. Management says the clubhouse is wheelchair accessible. Groceries are one mile away, and a restaurant is within walking distance. Visiting children are welcome. Pets are not allowed.

Reservations, fees: Reservations are recommended. Sites are $23 per night for two people, plus $2 for each additional person. Credit cards are not accepted. Long-term rates are available.

Directions: From the corner of U.S. 27 and Hammock Road in the center of Sebring, travel west on Hammock Road for a short distance.

Contact: Highland Wheel Estates RV/Mobile Home Park, 1004 Hammock Road, Sebring, FL 33872, 863/385-6232, www.hwepark.com.

170 LAKESIDE STABLES

Scenic rating: 3

in Sebring on Arbuckle Creek

See map page 230   BEST (

Equestrians will like this campground, which is part of a horse stable operation. It's located on Arbuckle Creek, and you can launch a canoe here or fish. But the emphasis is on horses, with breaking and training available, and mounts for sale. You can fish in the creek.

RV sites, facilities: There are 10 RV sites with full hookups. Restrooms, showers, horse stables, canoe rentals, and a dog-walk area are available. Children are welcome. Leashed pets are permitted.

Reservations, fees: Reservations are recommended. Sites are $25 per night for two people, plus $5 per extra person. Credit cards are not accepted.

Directions: From the intersection of U.S. 27 and U.S. 98 in Sebring, drive east on U.S. 98 to the park.

Contact: Lakeside Stables, 5000 U.S. 98, Sebring, FL 33876, 863/655-2252, fax 863/655-9525, www.horserentals.com/lakesidestables.html.

171 SEBRING GROVE RV RESORT

Scenic rating: 5

south of Sebring

See map page 230

Just 0.5 mile from Lake Jackson's swimming, fishing, and boating activities, Sebring Grove is convenient to shopping and restaurants. Planned activities, such as bingo, dinners, trips, and parties, keep guests busy. Sebring is a flourishing retirement community with one of the finest state parks in Florida nearby, Highlands Hammock State Park (see listing in this chapter). About 5 percent of the lots are occupied year-round, and the majority are rented to repeat visitors on a seasonal basis. Most people staying here are from Indiana, Michigan, Ohio, and New York.

RV sites, facilities: There are 20 full-hookup sites with 50-amp electrical service and concrete patios for overnighters in this 115-unit park. Six sites are pull-through. RVs up to 38 feet in length and slide-outs can be accommodated. Lots range in size 15–32 feet wide by 38 feet deep. Restrooms, showers, laundry facilities, telephone hookups, a pool, a clubhouse, shuffleboard courts, and a dog-walk area are available. The clubhouse is wheelchair accessible. Streets are paved. Groceries are within two miles; shops and restaurants are within one mile. Children may stay for short visits. Leashed pets are permitted; only one pet per lot.

Reservations, fees: Reservations are recommended. Sites are $25 per night for two people, plus $2 per extra person. Credit cards are not accepted. Long-term (up to six months) or seasonal stays are preferred.

Directions: From Sebring, drive south on U.S. 27 about two miles. If you pass U.S. 98, you will have gone too far.

Contact: Sebring Grove RV Resort, 4105 U.S. 27 South, Sebring, FL 33870-5599, 863/382-1660, fax 863/382-2565.

172 WHISPERING PINES VILLAGE

Scenic rating: 5

in Sebring

See map page 230

This place is one-third mobile homes and two-thirds RV sites, but the feeling is more residential than campground. Shaded by some palms and pines, it is one of the closest places to camp near notable Highlands Hammock State Park (see listing in this chapter). The park tends to attract people staying for winter, with just 10 sites available for overnighters. About 2 percent of the lots are occupied year-round. Most visitors hail from Indiana, Ohio, Pennsylvania, and Michigan, and they like each other so much that they hold an annual summer reunion in the northern states. Boating and fishing are possible one mile away at 3,000-acre Lake Jackson, but the favorite things to do are boccie ball (lawn bowling) and shuffleboard. Many activities are planned in the recreation hall, such as professional entertainment, trips, potluck dinners, and seminars. A mall and theaters are nearby, and downtown Sebring is three miles away.

RV sites, facilities: This retiree-oriented park has 155 full-hookup RV sites with 30-amp or 50-amp electricity. About 100 have picnic tables and 112 are drive-through. Lots range in size from 24 to 25 feet wide and 35 to 40 feet deep, accommodating a few 40-foot RVs. On the premises are restrooms, showers, laundry facilities, a wheelchair-accessible recreation room, trailer rentals, and horseshoes. Streets are paved. You will find groceries, malls, and restaurants within one mile. Children are allowed, but the park is geared toward retirees. Pets are prohibited, unless you are an overnight visitor staying with friends camped in the park.

Reservations, fees: Reservations are recommended. Sites are $28 per night for two people, plus $4 daily for each additional person. Credit cards are not accepted. Long-term rates are available.

Directions: From U.S. 27 near Sebring, drive west on County Road 634/Hammock Road for one mile to Brunn's Road. Turn right, heading north, and look for the campground 0.5 mile ahead on the left.

Contact: Whispering Pines Village, 2323 Brunn's Road, Sebring, FL 33872, 863/385-8806, www.snobhollow.com/wpines.

173 HIGHLAND OAKS RV RESORT

Scenic rating: 5

off U.S. 27 south of Sebring

See map page 230

Winter visitors from Canada and the United States flock to this RV park and mobile-home community in Central Florida to thaw out in the sun and get to know each other and the surrounding area. It doesn't have a pool, but it does have shuffleboard courts and a horseshoe pit. Fishing and waterskiing are possible at area lakes, and Highlands Hammock State Park is a short drive away. But the favorite thing to do is relaxing with neighbors in the sun.

RV sites, facilities: This adults-only park has 106 grassy, full-hookup RV sites with picnic tables, concrete patios, and 30-amp or 50-amp electrical service. The average site is 34 feet wide by 72 feet deep, accommodating large RVs and slide-outs. Sites are a mix of shade and sunshine. Connect to the Internet in the office. On the premises are restrooms, showers, laundry facilities, a recreation room, horseshoes, and shuffleboard. There is no dump station. Management says all facilities are wheelchair accessible. Cable TV and telephone service are available. Groceries can be purchased within five miles. One restaurant is across the road, and others are in town, about seven miles away.

Children are welcome only to visit park residents. Pets are permitted.

Reservations, fees: Reservations are recommended. Sites are $20.50 per night for two people, plus $2 for each extra person. Credit cards are not accepted. The maximum length of stay is six months; however, 10 percent of the resort is occupied year-round.

Directions: From the intersection of U.S. 27 and U.S. 98/State Road 66, turn onto U.S. 98 and drive about 0.25 mile. Turn left on County Road 17 North and drive about 0.5 mile. Turn left on 6th Street South and follow the paved road to the park entrance.

Contact: Highland Oaks RV Resort, 7001 Seventh Avenue West, Sebring, FL 33876, 863/655-1685, email: daveandsherrye@yahoo.com.

174 LAKE GLENADA RV PARK

Scenic rating: 3

south of Avon Park

See map page 230

Adults are preferred at this lakeside RV park in citrus and cattle country. You'll see huge trucks loaded with oranges driving past the park on their way to the citrus processing plants. The park has a boat ramp and access to fishing and boating on Lake Glenada.

RV sites, facilities: Out of a total of 202 RV sites with full hookups, about 150 are available for overnighters and 50 for seasonal visitors. Rigs up to 36 feet can be accommodated. Sites have concrete pads, picnic tables, and cable TV. Restrooms, showers, laundry facilities, a pool, a boat ramp, dock, recreation hall with planned activities, shuffleboard courts, and a dog-walk area are available. Children are not welcome. Small, leashed pets are permitted.

Reservations, fees: Reservations are recommended. Sites are $26 per night for two people, plus $2 per extra person. Credit cards are not accepted. Long-term rates are available.

Directions: From the intersection of State Road 64 and U.S. 27 in Avon Park, drive south on U.S. 27 about three miles to the park, on the east side.

Contact: Lake Glenada RV Park, 2525 U.S. 27 South, Avon Park, FL 33825, 863/453-7007, email: lgrv@strato.net.

SPACE COAST

© PETER TRITLEY

BEST RV PARKS AND CAMPGROUNDS

A roughly 72-mile sliver of territory stretching from Titusville to Melbourne, the Space Coast encompasses pristine Atlantic beaches, unparalleled boating and fishing, great seafood dining, and opportunities to view wildlife.

If you're fortunate, you may find yourself along Florida's Space Coast during a shuttle launch. If your timing is not so good, don't worry. The Kennedy Space Center Visitor Complex brings visitors up close and personal with the astronauts and technology that make it all happen. There's even an outdoor "rocket garden" with Apollo and Saturn spacecraft, an astronaut hall of fame, and bus tours of the space center.

If your visit coincides with a launch, those interested in rockets can get an official "launch viewing opportunity ticket" from NASA to see shuttle launches from inside the restricted area just seven miles away from takeoff. But the truth is that launches are visible throughout the area. Park your RV along U.S. 1 in Titusville, near the ocean at Cocoa Beach, or along State Road 528; several RV parks in this area also boast they are close to good viewing spots and will give campers specific directions. At Jetty Park, for example, campers can watch from a 500-foot-long fishing pier as the rockets rumble into the heavens. Other days, you can spot the Disney and Carnival cruise ships sail in on the jetty from Cape Canaveral.

The space center abuts Merritt Island National Wildlife Refuge, 219 square miles of mostly unspoiled Florida backcountry that will please casual hikers and thrill birders – at least 310 species of winged creatures have been spotted. Show up in January or February to watch tens of thousands of ducks and coots stopping to dine. Great bird-watching can also be found on the isolated beaches of the Canaveral National Seashore. Park rangers say 1,045 species of plants and 310 species of birds can be found on the barrier island.

Sebastian Inlet State Park is popular with surfers and boasts three miles of natural beaches and an inlet connecting the ocean and Indian River Lagoon. It's also paradise for anglers who take out their own boats, rent them from the park, or use the jetties to catch a vast array of fish. If it's summer, sign up for a ranger-guided nighttime turtle walk to watch sea turtles lumber onto the beach to dig holes in which they'll lay more than 100 eggs each. The park's Sebastian Fishing Museum highlights the area's history of commercial fishing. The McLarty Treasure Museum commemorates a Spanish fleet that was wrecked near here by a hurricane in 1715 while carrying gold and silver from Peru to Spain.

So how convenient is the Space Coast to Orlando? Theoretically, you could park your RV in this area and head 55 miles west for day trips to the theme parks, but it would be a long day. Best to save the Space Coast for when you can devote more time to its unique pleasures.

SPACE COAST

see
Daytona Beach
page 212

Deltona

Lake
Ashby

Lake
Monroe

Lake
Jessup

Lake
Harney

Oviedo

ORLANDO

ATLANTIC

OCEAN

Mosquito Lagoon

Scottsmoor

1

Turnbull

2

3-4 Mims

Titusville

5

6

JOHN F
KENNEDY
SPACE CENTER
(NASA)

Banana River

see
Orlando
page 228

Lake
Poinsett

9 Cocoa

Merritt
Island

7

8 Cape Canaveral

Rockledge

Cocoa Beach

Winder
Lake

10

11

Lake
Washington

12

Melbourne

Palm Bay

13

Indian River

14-15

16

Micco

17

see
Treasure Coast
page 424

Sebastian

0   5 mi
0   5 km

AL   GA

Gulf
of
Mexico

1 CRYSTAL LAKE RV PARK

Scenic rating: 4

off I-95 in Scottsmoor

A quick hop off I-95, this family-owned park's main attraction is looking skyward to watch NASA's thunderous space shuttle liftoffs. At other times, the key on-site entertainment is fishing at a three-acre lake, where you can catch bass and catfish, although you also may wet a line for saltwater species in the Indian River, three miles away. This is probably the closest private campground to the isolated beaches of the Canaveral National Seashore. During special events at Daytona Beach, such as Bike Week and Speed Weeks, the management says there's room here for a quiet night's sleep. (Bike week is usually held in March; Speed Weeks vary from year to year, but tend to fall in the early part of the year and in the summer.) It's also fairly close to the Merritt Island National Wildlife Refuge (see *Cape Kennedy KOA* in this chapter). Kennedy Space Center (321/452-2121) is about 30 miles from these grassy campsites, which are surrounded by a few maples, palms, and cedar trees. About 15 percent of the park is occupied by year-round residents.

RV sites, facilities: This park offers 60 full-hookup RV sites (44 pull-through), most with 30-amp electricity. Ten sites have 50-amp. RVs up to 45 feet long and slide-outs can be accommodated. The park has a wireless Internet network. On the premises are restrooms, showers, laundry facilities, picnic tables, a pool, a recreation hall, horseshoes, and shuffleboard. A convenience store is 1.5 miles away; groceries and restaurants are 7 miles. Children and leashed pets are welcome.

Reservations, fees: Reservations are recommended in winter. Sites are $24–30 per night for two people, plus $3 for each additional person. Credit cards are not accepted. Long-term rates are available.

Directions: From I-95, take Exit 231 and drive east 1,000 feet on State Road 5A/Stuckway Road. Look for the campground on the left behind Stuckey's.

Contact: Crystal Lake RV Park, 4240 Stuckway Road (or P.O. Box 362), Scottsmoor, FL 32775, 321/268-8555 or 888/501-7007, www.nbbd .com/crystallake.

2 WILLOW LAKES RV AND GOLF RESORT

Scenic rating: 6

in Titusville

BEST (

Willow Lakes is a deluxe ownership park that targets 55-plus RVers. It offers RV lots for overnighters, but many have already been sold for park models or seasonal visitors. Once built out, it may have more than 400 sites. Some lots are waterfront or golf-view, and you can watch space launches from the park. Your RV must be at least 22 feet long. As of this writing, a nine-hole golf course is scheduled to be expanded to 18 holes. All facilities are new; the park looks more like a fancy housing development than a campground.

RV sites, facilities: There are two areas, one for Class A motor homes only and one for Class C vehicles and fifth wheels. All sites are full hookup, with 30/50-amp electrical service, cable TV, and concrete pads. Restrooms, showers, a dump station, laundry facilities, and telephone service are available. On the premises are a heated pool, a recreation hall, a golf course, shuffleboard courts, and *pétanque* and boccie ball (lawn bowling) courts. Park models are for rent. This is an adults-only park, but children are allowed to visit Leashed pets are permitted.

Reservations, fees: Reservations are recommended. Sites are $35 per night. Credit cards are accepted. Long-term rates are available.

Directions: From I-95, take Exit 223 eastbound on State Road 46 to U.S. 1. Turn south and drive 0.5 mile to the park.

Contact: Willow Lakes RV and Golf Resort, 2199 North U.S. 1, Titusville, FL 32796, 321/269-7440 or 877/787-2751, www.willowlakes.com.

3 SEASONS IN THE SUN MOTORCOACH RESORT

Scenic rating: 10

in Mims

BEST (

Opened in 2002, this big-rig resort has 232 sites in a sunny, landscaped area of citrus trees and shady old oak hammocks. The owners say you can see space shuttle launches from within the park, and most tourist attractions are within easy driving distances.

RV sites, facilities: All 232 sites have full hookups with 20/30/50-amp electrical service, picnic tables, grills, cable TV, and telephone service connections. Restrooms, showers, a dump station, and laundry facilities are available. On the premises are a heated pool, a lap-swimming pool, whirlpools, lakes, a recreation hall with a fully equipped kitchen, exercise equipment, tennis and boccie ball (lawn bowling) courts, a reading library, shuffleboard courts, a dog-walk area, and a nature trail. A wireless Internet network is available throughout the RV section, plus a dial-up modem in the bathhouse. Most areas are wheelchair accessible. Children are welcome. Leashed pets are permitted.

Reservations, fees: Reservations are recommended. Sites are $33 per night for two people, plus $1.50 per extra person and $1.50 for electrical service. Credit cards are accepted. Long-term rates are available.

Directions: From I-95, take Exit 223 westbound on State Road 46 for 0.5 mile to the park.

Contact: Seasons in the Sun Motorcoach Resort, 2400 Seasons in the Sun Boulevard, Titusville, FL 32754, 877/687-7275, fax 321/385-0450, www.seasonsinthesunrvresort.com.

4 CAPE KENNEDY KOA

Scenic rating: 5

off I-95 west of Mims

The names of the paved streets—Michigan Avenue, Iowa Avenue, and Ontario Boulevard, for example—at this 14-acre park are a clue that the place is popular among snowbirds. These mostly shady, grassy spots, about 5 percent of which are occupied by permanent residents, are within one mile of an 18-hole golf course. Temperatures can dip to an average low of 48°F in winter, which explains the fireplace in the adult recreation room, where potluck dinners and bingo entertain visitors during the busy winter.

The campground is less than 20 miles from Kennedy Space Center, so periodically you'll hear the roar of NASA launches. But another big draw is that this is one of the closest parks to the Merritt Island National Wildlife Refuge—219 square miles of mostly unspoiled Florida backcountry that will please hikers or vacationers who prefer a casual walk in the woods. Try the 0.5-mile Oak Hammock Interpretive Trail, the 2-mile Palm Hammock Loop Trail, or the 5-mile Allan D. Cruickshank Loop Trail, which features an observation tower and leads to the Indian River. For a self-guided driving tour, pick up a pamphlet at the visitors center. Keep your eye out for birds—at least 310 species of winged creatures have been spotted. If you show up in January or February, you're likely to see tens of thousands of ducks and coots stopping to dine there. Call the refuge at 321/861-0667.

RV sites, facilities: These 150 sites have full hookups and picnic tables. Half of the sites have 30-amp electrical service; the other half have 50-amp. Big RVs are welcome; lots are up to 60 feet long. Forty sites are drive-through. A free wireless Internet network is available throughout the park. A pool, a playground, a game room, shuffleboard, horseshoes, a pool table, video games, and wintertime social programs entertain campers. On the premises are restrooms, showers, a dump station, laundry facilities, LP gas sales, a camp store, a picnic pavilion, rental cabins, and a lodge where functions are held. The bathhouse, clubhouse, store, and pool area are wheelchair accessible. Streets are paved. Children must be adult-supervised at the pool and play in designated areas. Leashed, attended, vaccinated pets are permitted and must use the perimeter dog walk.

Reservations, fees: Reservations are recommended. Sites are $27–30 per night for two people, plus $2 for each additional child and $3 per adult. Add $3.25 nightly for cable TV. Credit cards are accepted. Long-term rates are available.

Directions: From I-95, take Exit 223 and drive west on State Road 46 for 0.25 mile to the campground, on your left.

Contact: Cape Kennedy KOA, 4513 West Main Street, Mims, FL 32754, 321/269-7361 or 800/KOA-3365 (800/562-3365), fax 321/267-2417, www.koa.com.

5 THE GREAT OUTDOORS RESORT

Scenic rating: 10

off I-95 west of Titusville

BEST (

To call this a campground is a major understatement. Actually, it's a sprawling retirement community, complete with a post office, a beauty shop, and a golf cart showroom. Lots are for sale. It's also one of the few RV parks I know of that markets itself through a videotape and CD-ROM.

Located across the street from the St. Johns National Wildlife Refuge, the complex is huge—about 4.5 square miles. Facilities range from back-in RV sites to a full-scale retirement home for the non-RVer. An interesting innovation between those two extremes is the RV "port" or "executive suite," which looks sort of like a garage or carport. You can park your RV under its roof and feel more or less like you're in a regular home. Some have decks and screened porches. Others have three-bedroom homes with full kitchens built around them. Instead of adding a garage to the home, these folks have added homes to the garage.

The range of available activities is astounding: golfing at a par-71 course, playing tennis at four lighted courts, swimming in two pools, getting in a game of darts or billiards, participating in year-round organized activities such as arts-and-crafts classes, bicycling around the park, relaxing at the restaurant and lounge, exercising at the health club, or hiking on nature trails. You can even rent a golf cart. Anglers try for catfish, bass, and panfish in at least 20 stocked freshwater lakes on the property. The park emphasizes its array of resident wildlife, including deer, wild turkeys, bald eagles, quail, rabbits, and waterfowl. Kennedy Space Center is about 12 miles away.

RV sites, facilities: The campground has 110 full-hookup RV sites with 30/50-amp electrical service, a wireless Internet network, and picnic tables. All are for self-contained rigs at least 18 feet long. Sites vary in size but most are 40 by 80 feet and require backing in. On the premises are restrooms, showers, a dump station, laundry facilities, two pools, two hot tubs, a recreation room, an exercise room, shuffleboard, a golf course, tennis courts, groceries, and a restaurant. A camp store sells limited groceries, souvenirs, and camping supplies. Grocery stores and restaurants are within 0.5 mile. All areas are wheelchair accessible. This park permits children, but it targets older campers. Two dogs per site are allowed.

Reservations, fees: Reservations are recommended. Sites are $45 per night for two adults, plus $3 for each additional adult. To rent an RV port, add $10. Credit cards are accepted.

Directions: From I-95, take Exit 215 and head west on State Road 50 for 0.5 mile.

Contact: The Great Outdoors Resort, 125 Plantation Drive, Titusville, FL 32780, 321/269-5004 or 800/621-2267, fax 321/269-0694, www.tgoresort.com.

6 MANATEE HAMMOCK

Scenic rating: 9

on the Indian River in Titusville

BEST (

This lovely 26-acre spot on the Indian River is probably the closest, most nature-oriented campground from which to feel the ground rumble beneath your feet as you look skyward at the space shuttle blasting off from Kennedy Space Center less than 10 miles away. It's a wooded park, a pleasant piece of Old Florida preserved by the county government. The grassy or compacted-dirt campsites sit along narrow 5-mph roads marked by occasional tight turns that can challenge big rigs. Near the park's center sit many of its entertainment options: shuffleboard, a pool, and horseshoe pits. To the northeast, windsurfing and fishing are possible in the Indian River. You also can canoe or kayak (bring your own watercraft). Campfires are forbidden at individual campsites unless you rent a portable fire ring at $10 per stay. You can also use the public fire ring across the road from the east bathhouse if you're up for telling ghost stories late at night. Nearby is the Enchanted Forest Nature Center, which opened in 2002 (321/264-5192).

RV sites, facilities: There are 147 full-hookup RV sites (12 pull-through) and 35 sites with water and electricity only. Rigs up to 40 feet long can be accommodated. Each site has a picnic table. On the premises are restrooms, showers, a dump station, laundry facilities, a grill area, a pool, a small boat ramp, horseshoes, shuffleboard, volleyball, and a recreation hall. Management says the restrooms are wheelchair accessible. Children are welcome but must be adult-supervised. Two leashed, attended pets are permitted per RV.

Reservations, fees: Reservations are taken up to one year in advance but are not accepted for some spots. A two-night minimum payment is required before your reservation can be confirmed. Sites are $20–22 per night for six people. Credit cards are accepted. Long-term stays are okay.

Directions: From I-95, take Exit 215 and drive east on State Road 50 for three miles to U.S. 1. Turn right, heading south. Look for the park on your left, four miles beyond the turnoff.

Contact: Manatee Hammock, 7275 U.S. 1 South, Titusville, FL 32780, 321/264-5083, fax 321/264-6468, www.campingspacecoast.com.

7 JETTY PARK CAMPGROUND

Scenic rating: 10

in Cape Canaveral

BEST (

For spectacular views, check out Jetty Park. This 30-acre publicly owned park is best known as one of the great places to stand at a 500-foot-long fishing pier to watch NASA's space shuttle rumble into the heavens from Kennedy Space Center, about 10 miles away. Other days, campers can watch the Disney and Carnival cruise ships sail in on the jetty from Cape Canaveral; in fact, the park is operated by the Canaveral Port Authority. As one of the most popular parks in this area, the seaport officials in 2001 began undertaking improvements to Jetty Park, including upgrades to the roads, utilities, and other niceties (it's a 20-year project and still ongoing). Dolphins and manatees travel the waterway at times. In summer, you might notice sea turtles lumbering onto the beach to dig holes and plop as many as 200 eggs in their earthen "nests" at night.

The campsites—mostly sandy and grassy with precious little shade—are set back from the beach alongside the channel into Port Canaveral. Most spots are along two loops; restrooms, showers, and laundry facilities are at the center of each loop. To be closest to the beach, ask for sites 87–117.

RV sites, facilities: The camp has 150 sites (32 full-hookup with electricity), plus an overflow area. Each RV site has a grill and picnic table. On the premises are restrooms, showers, laundry facilities, a playground, a fishing pier, horseshoes, volleyball, bait and tackle, snacks, picnic pavilions, a dump station, and limited groceries. Management says the jetties and fishing pier are accessible to wheelchairs. A restaurant is within three miles. Children are welcome. Pets under 35 pounds are permitted in the campsites only.

Reservations, fees: Reservations are recommended; a two-day minimum stay is required for reserved sites. Sites are $25–31 per night for six people, plus $2 for pets. It costs $2 to make the reservation. Credit cards are accepted. The maximum stay is 21 days.

Directions: From I-95, take Exit 205 and follow the Bee Line Expressway/State Road 528 east. Exit at mile marker 54, enter Port Canaveral's South Cruise Terminal, then turn right onto George King Boulevard. Follow the signs to the campground, at 400 East Jetty Park Road.

Contact: Jetty Park Campground, 400 East Jetty Road, Cape Canaveral, FL 32920, 321/783-7111, fax 321/783-5005, www.portcanaveral.org.

8 MANGO MANOR

Scenic rating: 2

in Cape Canaveral

This is a quiet, no-frills place in an industrial section not particularly geared toward recreation. About half of the 20-acre facility is occupied by people (many of them retirees) who live year-round in mobile homes. Kennedy Space Center is about 10 miles from the sites—most paved, some grassy. A plus for water lovers: Ocean swimming and fishing spots are a little under one mile away.

RV sites, facilities: All 51 full-hookup sites in this park are for self-contained RV units up to 40 feet long. Most sites have 20/30/50-amp electrical hookups and concrete patios. There are no restrooms, showers, or cable TV; however, wheelchair-accessible laundry facilities and a dump station are provided. Children are welcome. One leashed pet per site is permitted.

Reservations, fees: Reservations are recommended; the park fills up early in winter. Sites are $35 per night for two people, plus $5 per extra person. Credit cards are not accepted. Long-term rates are available.

Directions: From I-95, take Exit 205 and follow the Bee Line Expressway/State Road 528 east to Port Canaveral. At the port, go right (south) on Highway A1A over the bridge to the traffic light. Turn left onto Central Avenue. Look for the park to your left, just past the lumberyard, at 8705 North Atlantic Avenue.

Contact: Mango Manor, 190 Oak Manor Drive, Cape Canaveral, FL 32920, 321/799-0741, fax 321/783-8671.

9 SON RISE PALMS

Scenic rating: 5

off I-95 west of Cocoa

This sunny and open park is a convenient place to pull off the highway for a night's rest. Geared to all ages, the campsites are relatively close to a nearly one-mile-long nature trail and a 20-acre lake. About 1 percent of the park is occupied year-round. Favorite things to do in winter are golf, fishing, flea-market shopping, and playing cards.

RV sites, facilities: The 91 full-hookup RV sites have a mix of 30-amp and 50-amp electrical service, concrete patios, and picnic tables. Sites vary in size, but a few sites will accommodate 40-foot rigs. On the premises are restrooms, showers, laundry facilities, a nature trail, horseshoes, rental units, and a pool. Management says the bathhouse and pool area are wheelchair accessible. Streets are paved. A supermarket is two miles away; restaurants are within three miles. Children are welcome. Nonaggressive, leashed pets under 35 pounds are permitted.

Reservations, fees: Reservations are recommended, particularly in winter. Sites are $40 per night for two people, plus $2 per additional adult, $1 per extra child. Credit cards are accepted. Maximum stay is unlimited.

Directions: From I-95, take Exit 201 and head west one short block on State Road 520 to Tucker Lane. Turn left, heading south for about 0.7 mile. The park is just ahead.

Contact: Son Rise Palms, 660 Tucker Lane, Cocoa, FL 32926, 321/633-4335, www.sonrisepalmsrvpark.com.

10 SPACE COAST RV RESORT

Scenic rating: 7

off I-95 south of Rockledge

This 22-acre park benefits from its location convenient to I-95 if you happen to be passing through and need a place to spend the night, or want to stay somewhat near a space launch. Fishing is possible in two small on-site ponds and in the nearby Indian River. If you're too pooped to drive nine miles to the Atlantic Ocean, you can swim in the park's heated pool or walk across the street to a golf course. To stay nearest to a long pond, ask for full-hookup sites E15–E24. Kennedy Space Center is about 15 miles away. Most visitors here are from the eastern seaboard and northern states. Favorite things to do in the park are socializing, walking, shopping, and sightseeing.

RV sites, facilities: There are 259 full-hookup RV sites (88 pull-through) with concrete patios and picnic tables. One-hundred sites have 30-amp electrical service, and 124 have 50-amp. A few have 100-amp service. RVs up to 45 feet long and slide-outs can be accommodated on sites that average 40 by 55 feet. On the premises are restrooms, showers, a dump station, LP gas sales, laundry facilities, rental cabins, a pool, a unisex beauty shop, a TV lounge, and shuffleboard. A camp store sells ice, camping supplies, and snacks. All areas of the park are wheelchair accessible. Children are welcome. Small, leashed, attended pets are permitted but must be transported to and from the designated pet-walk area.

Reservations, fees: Reservations are recommended in winter. Sites are $40 per night, plus $3 per extra person. Credit cards are accepted. Long-term rates are available.

Directions: From I-95, take Exit 195 and head north on Fiske Boulevard to Barnes Boulevard. Turn right (east). The campground is about 0.5 mile ahead.

Contact: Space Coast RV Resort, 820 Barnes Boulevard, Rockledge, FL 32955, 321/636-2873 or 800/982-4233, fax 321/636-0275, www.spacecoastrv.net.

11 CASA LOMA ESTATES

Scenic rating: 2

at the Indian River north of Melbourne

At this 55-plus mobile-home park located 300 yards from the Indian River, retirees count bingo, exercise classes, and potluck dinners among the highlights of a wintertime visit. Many visitors stay for winter or are retired military personnel who want to be near the base exchange and social milieu of Patrick Air Force Base. The grassy sites have concrete patios and asphalt driveways. The 21-acre park is on busy U.S. 1 and is a good 35-minute drive from the Kennedy Space Center. The ocean is about four miles away, across the nearby Pineda Causeway. About 10 percent of the park is occupied year-round.

RV sites, facilities: This adults-only park has 24 full-hookup RV sites, each with a picnic table and a concrete patio; all have 50-amp electricity. On the premises are restrooms, showers, a dump station, a recreation hall, a pool table, an indoor shuffleboard table, table tennis, horseshoes, shuffleboard, and laundry facilities. Management says the recreation room is wheelchair accessible. Streets are paved. A convenience store is next door. Groceries and restaurants are within two miles. Children are prohibited, except when visiting older family members. Pets are permitted.

Reservations, fees: Reservations are advised in winter. Sites are $30 per night. Credit cards are not accepted. Long-term rates are available.
Directions: From I-95, take Exit 191 and head east on Highway 509/Wickham Road. As soon as the road angles right to head south, turn left onto Suntree Boulevard. At U.S. 1, turn right and proceed less than one mile to the park, on the right.
Contact: Casa Loma Estates, 6560 North Harbor City Boulevard/U.S. 1, Melbourne, FL 32940, 321/254-2656.

12 WICKHAM PARK

Scenic rating: 7

west of U.S. 1 in Melbourne

BEST(

Not only can you horse around at Wickham Park, but you also likely will see horses in the stalls or along horse trails at the 400-acre local landmark. In far-flung Brevard County, this popular county-run picnic spot stands out because of its size and all that it offers, including archery, disc golf, a horse exercise area, and a 20-station, 1.5-mile-long workout trail. Visitors can jump into two sand-bottomed fishing lakes for a swim. They can hike through a honeycomb of nature trails on the park's east side or ride their own horses along trails on the west side. Bicyclists and in-line skaters take advantage of the wide, paved streets that circle the open, airy park. In the wintertime, planned activities, such as dances and potluck dinners are held. Favorite things to do in the park are exercise, Frisbee, golf, and letting the dogs frolic in the dog park.

The 88 grassy campsites are not too far removed from major streets, giving the place a suburban feel. The water- and 30-amp electricity-equipped grassy sites are set along two loops—Campground A (with about 55 sites) and smaller Campground B. If you want to roast marshmallows around a campfire, head to the fire pit in Campground A. Brush screens some of the 35- by 35-foot sites from neighboring campsites. All have picnic tables, and some are waterfront. The campground is busy in winter; the park's separate day-use areas are most popular in summer. The fishing waters of the Indian River are five miles away. Kennedy Space Center is about 35 miles distant.

RV sites, facilities: All 88 RV sites have water and electricity and are set apart from 22 primitive tent sites. Two man-made swimming lakes, a nature trail, an archery range, horseshoes, volleyball, a horse trail, ball fields, disc golf, a playground, restrooms, showers, a dump station, an amphitheater, picnic pavilions, horse stalls, a horse show ring, grills, picnic tables, and laundry facilities are available. Campground A has a fire pit. Management says the office and restrooms are wheelchair accessible. Streets are paved. Groceries and restaurants are within one mile. Children must be adult-supervised. Two leashed pets are permitted per site.
Reservations, fees: Reservations are accepted with a two-night minimum stay. Sites are $20 per night. Credit cards are accepted. The maximum stay is six months (for RVs).
Directions: From I-95, take Exit 183 and head east on State Road 516/Eau Gallie-Sarno Road to the third traffic light. Turn left on Wickham Road. Travel about 2.5 miles north to Parkway Drive, then turn right. The entrance is ahead on the left.
Contact: Wickham Park, 2500 Parkway Drive, Melbourne, FL 32935, 321/255-4307, fax 321/255-4343. Or contact the Brevard County Parks and Recreation Department, 8400 Forrest Avenue, Cocoa, FL 32922, 321/633-1874, fax 321/633-1850, www.campingspacecoast.com.

13 OUTDOOR RESORTS MELBOURNE BEACH

Scenic rating: 10

on Highway A1A in Melbourne Beach

One of the best things about this luxury RV resort is its proximity to the ocean and beach, which is just across Highway A1A, and to the Indian River nearby. You'll often feel a sea breeze here. The paved RV sites—with patios and a few sabal palms—are across the highway from a nicely landscaped beachside recreation complex that includes a 3,000-square-foot activity center and a palm-flanked ocean-view pool.

The 40-acre park isn't exactly a place for shrinking violets. You can swim in the ocean or in one of three pools, choose from six tennis courts or eight lighted shuffleboard courts, use the boat ramp to access the Indian River for boating or fishing, or drop a line off the 300-foot fishing pier. Bicyclists tool around the park or on a path that runs along Highway A1A. On summer nights, some guests watch sea turtles nest on the nearby beach. Kennedy Space Center is within a 45-minute drive.

RV sites, facilities: Amid this 576-unit community, there are a varying number of full-hookup sites available for overnight or seasonal RVs. Each site has a picnic table. On the premises are restrooms, showers, three pools, lighted tennis courts, a hot tub, an activities center, a health club, two clubhouses, a boat ramp, a dock, shuffleboard, and a laundry room. Planned activities are held during the winter months. A wireless Internet network is available in some parts of the park. Management says the buildings, bathhouse, and pool areas are wheelchair accessible. Children are welcome. Leashed, attended pets are permitted.

Reservations, fees: Reservations are recommended. Sites are $38–49 per night for four people, plus $2 for each additional person. Credit cards are accepted. Long-term stays are okay.

Directions: From I-95, take Exit 180 and travel east on State Road 192 to Highway A1A. Turn right (south). Look for the campground on the right in four miles.

Contact: Outdoor Resorts Melbourne Beach, 3000 Highway A1A South, Melbourne Beach, FL 32951, 321/724-2600 or 800/752-4052, fax 321/727-0175, www.outdoorresortsmelbournebeach.com.

14 ENCHANTED LAKES ESTATES

Scenic rating: 3

in Malabar

Mention the obscure town of Malabar and many Floridians will scratch their heads. But bring up the nearby Indian River, and they'll certainly know what you're talking about. A popular boating and fishing destination, the river is two miles east of the grassy/concrete-pad sites at this 28-acre park. The ocean is just two miles farther east as the crow flies, but you should expect to drive six miles north to a Melbourne causeway first to get there. This neatly kept, sunny RV park's "enchanted lake" has fountains and lush tropical landscaping. About 45 percent of the park is occupied year-round. Visitors come from Canada, New York, Maine, and Massachusetts, primarily.

RV sites, facilities: Of the 71 full-hookup RV sites, 65 are pull-through. Each site has 30/50-amp electricity, a concrete patio, and a picnic table. RVs up to 50 feet long and slide-outs can be accommodated. On the premises are showers, restrooms, a recreation hall, a heated pool, an exercise room, a pool table, laundry facilities, and planned activities. Cable TV and telephone service are available. Management says the recreation hall and office are wheelchair accessible. Streets are paved. A restaurant, groceries, and bait are available within two miles. Children are allowed. Leashed pets are permitted.

Reservations, fees: Reservations are recommended. Sites are $30 per night for two people, plus $5 for each additional person. Credit cards are not accepted. Long-term rates are available.

Directions: From I-95, take Exit 173 and travel east on State Road 514/Malabar Road for two miles. The park is next to Palm Bay Hospital.

Contact: Enchanted Lakes Estates, 750 Malabar Road, Malabar, FL 32950, 321/723-8847, fax 321/724-1102, www.enchantedlakes.net.

15 CAMELOT RV PARK

Scenic rating: 6

on U.S. 1 in Malabar

Finding out what activities are scheduled to take place at the recreation hall is as simple as turning on the free 40-channel cable TV service and tuning to Channel 5, the park's information station. Why would you need a TV channel to tell you what's happening? As many as 75 volunteers are organizing things to do, that's why. Beyond the entrance gates of the family-run park, paved roads lead to sunny spots equipped with concrete patios and picnic tables. Anglers and boaters can cross the street—well-traveled U.S. 1—to get to a dock on the Indian River. Many of the usual RV-park rules apply at this 20-acre RV/mobile-home destination, with two perhaps-welcome exceptions: You may wash your RV or car; and two vehicles, not one, may be parked at each site. Channel 15 on the cable TV service delivers information about NASA so you can monitor space launches at the Kennedy Space Center, about a 45-minute drive northeast. The park overlooks the Indian River Lagoon.

RV sites, facilities: Many of the 130 full-hookup sites with concrete pads are available for overnighting RVs, and 2 or 3 are taken by seasonal visitors. Thirty-amp and 50-amp electrical service, cable TV, and telephone service are available. Rigs up to 45 feet long can be accommodated. A recreation hall, a craft center, a fishing dock, shuffleboard, basketball, and winter activities entertain campers. Restrooms, showers, picnic tables, laundry facilities, and a dog-walk area are on-site. Most areas are wheelchair accessible. Children are allowed to visit, but this is primarily a 50-plus age park. Leashed, attended pets are permitted.

Reservations, fees: Reservations are recommended. Sites are $31–35 per night for two people, plus $5 for each additional adult. Credit cards are accepted. Long-term rates are available.

Directions: From I-95, take Exit 173 and travel 4.5 miles east on State Road 514/Malabar Road to U.S. 1. Turn right. The park entrance is about two blocks ahead at right.

Contact: Camelot RV Park, 1600 U.S. 1, Malabar, FL 32950, 321/724-5396, fax 321/724-9022, www.camelotrvpark.com.

16 LONG POINT PARK

Scenic rating: 7

at the Indian River in Melbourne Beach

Long Point is actually on an island, not a point. But that probably makes it all the more popular. Surrounded by the Indian River, this 60-acre, county-run camping park draws boaters, anglers, canoeists, and kayakers bound for the Indian River. Most of the grassy campsites are set around the park perimeter. Full-hookup sites are located at the center. As a brochure puts it, this place has two little lakes—one for swimming, and one for wildlife. To be closest to the swimming lake, ask about the water- and electricity-equipped sites numbered 14–22. Full-hookup sites are near the other lake. The park is just 1.5 miles from the quiet, slow-paced Sebastian Inlet State Park, on the Indian River.

RV sites, facilities: Fifteen sites have full hookups; 113 have water and electricity only. On the premises are showers, restrooms, a dump station, picnic tables, grills, fire rings (at waterfront sites), a one-lane boat ramp, a fishing pier, a playground, horseshoes, volleyball, and a laundry room. Management says the restrooms, pavilions, swimming pond, and playground are wheelchair accessible. Children are welcome. Two leashed, well-attended pets are permitted per site.

Reservations, fees: Reservations are accepted; but if you make a reservation, you are required to stay for at least two nights. There is a $12.50 cancellation charge if you change your mind 72 hours prior to check-in date. No refunds are given if you cancel within 72 hours. Sites are $23–25 per night, depending on the campsite services you need. Credit cards are accepted. The maximum stay is 180 days.

Directions: From U.S. 192 in Melbourne, go south approximately 17 miles on Highway A1A. Look for the turnoff to the park on the right about 1.5 miles north of Sebastian Inlet State Park.

Contact: Long Point Park, 700 Long Point Road, Melbourne Beach, FL 32951, 321/952-4532, www.campingspacecoast.com.

17 SEBASTIAN INLET STATE PARK

Scenic rating: 10

on the Indian River in Melbourne Beach

Surfers are fond of this popular state-run park, which boasts three miles of natural beaches and an inlet connecting the ocean and Indian River Lagoon. And it's paradise for anglers who take out their own boats, rent them from the park, or use the jetties to catch any of a vast array of fish attracted to the inlet.

Actually, the 379-acre park is different things to different people. Sunbathers favor a dip in the ocean. Picnickers stake out their favorite sun-washed spots (bring caps and sunscreen). Bicyclists who desire something more challenging than the park roads can head north for 14 miles along Highway A1A, stopping to enjoy numerous access points to the ocean. Snorkeling is also possible, but you should avoid the inlet itself, which has wicked currents. Instead, rangers recommend heading to the southern portion of the park to snorkel in the ocean; reefs are about 50 feet offshore.

Campsites overlook the Sebastian Inlet. You will enjoy relative peace away from the madding daytime crowds because you'll camp at the Indian River side of the park, not near the concession stand, ocean swimmers, surfers, or showers on the Atlantic side across Highway A1A.

Don't neglect the park's Sebastian Fishing Museum, which highlights the area's history of commercial fishing, or the McLarty Treasure Museum, recollecting the days hundreds of years ago when treasure-laden Spanish galleons would crash along this coast. The museum commemorates a Spanish fleet that was wrecked near here by a hurricane in 1715 while carrying gold and silver from Peru to Spain.

If you arrive in summer, sign up for a ranger-guided nighttime turtle walk to watch sea turtles lumber onto the beach to dig holes and lay as many as 200 eggs each. This park is one of my favorite campgrounds in Brevard County, but it's *way* down at the southeastern corner. Expect at least a 30-minute drive to Kennedy Space Center and Cocoa Beach. Still, if you want to see a slice of southern ocean-side Brevard in a more or less natural state, this is probably your best bet.

RV sites, facilities: All 51 sites are for RVs and tents, and all have water and 30-amp electricity. Each site has a picnic table, a grill, a fire ring, and a pad made of stabilized fill. Three sites have 50-amp electrical service. RVs up to 40 feet and slide-outs can be accommodated. On the premises are restrooms, showers, a dump station, a boat ramp, kayak and canoe rentals, a nature trail, a breakfast-and-lunch snack bar, and laundry facilities. Management says that restrooms, parking lots, docks, store, both museums and jetties, and the concession area are wheelchair accessible. A camp store sells ice, snacks, souvenirs, bait, and tackle. Groceries are 12 miles away. Children are welcome. Pets are allowed in designated areas.

Reservations, fees: Reservations are recommended; contact ReserveAmerica at 800/336-3521 or reserveamerica.com. Sites are $23 per night for eight people. Credit cards are accepted. The maximum stay is 14 days.

Directions: From U.S. 192 in Melbourne, travel approximately 22 miles south on Highway A1A. Look for the park about 1.5 miles south of Long Point Park. If you're traveling from Vero Beach, drive about 12 miles north on Highway A1A to the park entrance.

Contact: Sebastian Inlet State Park, 9700 Highway A1A South, Melbourne Beach, FL 32951, 321/984-4852, www.floridastateparks.org.

ST. PETERSBURG

BEST RV PARKS AND CAMPGROUNDS

《 Biking
Bay Aire RV Park, page 344

《 Equestrians
Jay B. Starkey Wilderness Park, page 342

**《 Publicly Managed
   Beachfront Campgrounds**
Fort de Soto Park Campground, page 350

If one of the reasons you've come to Florida

is to experience the beach, the St. Petersburg-Clearwater area will be to your liking. Bounded on the west by the Gulf of Mexico and on the east by Tampa Bay, the area offers 35 miles of first-rate, white sand beaches convenient to major tourist attractions. A number of RV parks offer easy access to both beaches and the Pinellas Trail, a 42-mile paved biking and walking path converted from an old railway. For the RV camper, this area is the best of all worlds.

The sparkling gulf waters are calm and tranquil most of the year, gently lapping the shoreline. Good roads and highways connect beachfront communities to theme parks, restaurants, and shopping. It's an easy 30-minute drive to most Tampa attractions, so the St. Petersburg area can make a great base camp for visiting Busch Gardens and other top spots.

Nearby points of interest include the Pinellas Trail bicycle and walking path, the Sunken Gardens, the Toronto Blue Jays spring training facilities, the municipal pier, the John's Pass Boardwalk, the Great Explorations Hands-on Museum, and the Florida Aquarium. Of special note is the Salvador Dali Museum, the world's largest collection of the artist's surrealist works, including several huge "masterwork" canvases. Originally a private collection, the art was moved from Cleveland to St. Petersburg by the owners in 1982.

On the northern edge of the peninsula is Tarpon Springs, a quaint, wooded community famed for its fishing, sponge docks, and numerous restaurants serving great seafood and Greek dishes. Early in the 20th century, many Greeks immigrated here and found work diving to the depths of the gulf in search of natural sponges; they built a thriving industry until bacteria contaminated the sponge beds in the 1940s. Sponge diving has made a comeback in recent years, but the real business of Tarpon Springs is tourism: sponge-diving exhibitions, sponge museums (including the aptly named Sponge-o-rama), and, of course, sponges for sale.

Fort de Soto, a county-run RV park and campground, offers the officially designated Number 1 beach in America. Almost all 235 sites are waterfront, and some have good views of St. Petersburg and the Gulf of Mexico. Due to its popularity, reservations are highly recommended.

Honeymoon Island State Park, north of Dunedin at the west end of State Road 586, is another top-ranked beach with four miles of sand and even a dog park. Though camping is not allowed here, it still makes for a great day trip. If you brought your boat, don't miss Anclote Key State Preserve. You'll have to anchor offshore and wade in or beach your boat on the sand. The effort is worthwhile, though. On the southern shore is a lighthouse built in 1887 that once guided shipping traffic with its 101-foot-high beacon. The island is a bird-watcher's delight; more than 43 species have been spotted, including the bald eagle.

Slightly more accessible is Caladesi Island State Park with 650 dry acres and 1,800 acres of mangrove flats and submerged lands. The beach is so beautiful that it's been ranked as one of the top 10 in the United States for nearly a decade. Walk the four miles of unspoiled beach in search of the perfect seashell or hike the island's nature trails. Those without access to a boat can use the ferry from Honeymoon Island to make a day trip out of it.

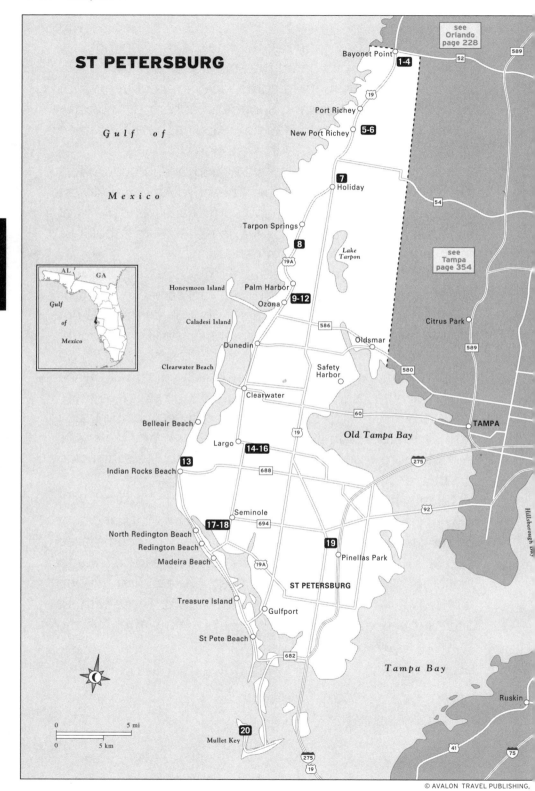

1 SUNDANCE LAKES RV RESORT

Scenic rating: 3

in Port Richey

This sunny and neatly kept community, which can accommodate rigs up to 40 feet long, is set back one block from a busy six-lane highway, but boasts four fishing lakes. Shopping centers are within walking distance and a flea market is next door. Five major golf courses are a short drive away. Tarpon Springs, Busch Gardens, Weeki Wachee Spring, Disney World, Epcot, the Salvador Dali Museum, and Homosassa Springs are easy day trips from the park. Hudson Beach is two miles away, and the beach at Green Key is four miles away. Complete medical facilities and churches are close by. With an 11,000-square-foot recreation hall, many visitors stay on-site for planned activities.

RV sites, facilities: Perfectly manicured, the park has a total of 523 concrete-pad sites with full hookups, 30/50-amp electrical service, and telephone access. Restrooms, showers, laundry facilities, a heated pool, tennis, a pool hall, a huge recreation hall with a sitting porch, shuffleboard, horseshoes, and four lakes are on the premises. Children are welcome for short stays, but there is no playground and management prefers campers 55 and older. Leashed pets under 25 pounds are permitted.

Reservations, fees: Reservations are recommended. Sites are $25 per night for two people, plus $2.50 for each additional person. Credit cards are accepted. Long-term rates are available. The resort targets Northerners age 55 and over who stay for the season, although overnighters are welcome.

Directions: From the junction of U.S. 19 and State Road 52, drive 300 yards south on U.S. 19. Turn west on Hachem Drive and continue into the park.

Contact: Sundance Lakes RV Resort, 6848 Hachem Drive, Port Richey, FL 34668, 727/862-3565, www.rvresorts.com.

2 SUNCOAST RV RESORT

Scenic rating: 4

north of New Port Richey

With tall pines casting sun-dappled shadows, you can hardly tell this RV resort is next to a mall and on a major highway. The managers guarantee in writing that restrooms will be clean, staff will be courteous, and the pool will be sparkling. It's near shopping, restaurants, and fishing and boating on the Gulf of Mexico. Planned activities are held in the winter months, with everyone pitching in to offer ideas or help. Choose between sunny and shady sites. About 25 percent of the park is occupied year-round.

RV sites, facilities: There are 165 RV sites with full hookups, 30/50-amp electrical service, and wireless Internet access. A pool, shuffleboard courts, horseshoe pits, a recreation hall, a pavilion with a fireplace, and laundry facilities are available. Shops and restaurants are within 0.2 mile. The laundry room and pavilion are wheelchair accessible. Children and leashed pets are welcome.

Reservations, fees: Reservations are recommended. Sites are $25 per night for two people, plus $3 for each additional person and $3 for using electrical service. Credit cards are accepted.

Directions: From the junction of U.S. 19 and State Road 52, drive 1.8 miles south on U.S. 19 to the park, on the east side of the road.

Contact: Suncoast RV Resort, 9029 U.S. 19, Port Richey, FL 34668, 727/842-9324 or 888/922-5603, www.suncoastrvresort.com.

3 OAK SPRINGS TRAVEL PARK

Scenic rating: 3

north of New Port Richey

Several small lakes are scattered throughout this huge adult travel resort, which is so big it has bicycle parking near the recreation hall to accommodate guests who want to cover a lot of ground on wheels. In winter, snowbirds pass the time with social activities such as line dancing, potluck dinners, ice-cream socials, exercise classes, parties, arts-and-crafts classes, and bingo. Church services are held here, too.

RV sites, facilities: For adults only, this 528-unit park has 200 RV sites with full hookups and 30-amp electrical service. Facilities include restrooms, showers, a pool, a horseshoe pit, a game room, shuffleboard courts, and a laundry room. Children are not welcome. Leashed pets are allowed.

Reservations, fees: Reservations are recommended. Sites are $25 per night for two people, plus $2.50 for each additional person. Credit cards are accepted. Long-term rates are available.

Directions: From the junction of U.S. 19 and State Road 52 in New Port Richey, drive two miles south on U.S. 19. At Jasmine Boulevard, turn west and go one block to the park entrance on Scenic Drive.

Contact: Oak Springs Travel Park, 10521 Scenic Drive, Port Richey, FL 34668, 727/863-5888, www.rvresorts.com.

☑ JA-MAR TRAVEL PARK

Scenic rating: 3

in Port Richey

Actually two resorts located 1,800 feet apart, this mobile-home/RV park welcomes overnighters, even though most people here are seasonal visitors. Planned activities—as many as 10 daily—include everything from Bible study to line dancing and euchre games. Bus trips are arranged to nearby attractions. Stores and restaurants are close by. Two ponds line the entrance drive; be careful when entering the park at night. One of the lakes is stocked for fishing.

RV sites, facilities: There are 400 lots with full hookups and 30/50-amp electrical service, with about half available for overnighters. Rigs up to 38 feet in length can be accommodated. Restrooms, showers, laundry facilities, a recreation hall, shuffleboard courts, lakes, and a pool are on the premises. All areas are wheelchair accessible. This is a 55-and-older park, but children may stay short-term. Leashed pets are permitted.

Reservations, fees: Reservations are recommended. Sites are $26 per night for two people, plus $2 for each additional person, $2 for 30-amp electrical service, and $3.50 for 50-amp service. Credit cards are not accepted. Long-term stays are allowed.

Directions: From U.S. 19 near Hudson, drive south to State Road 52. The park is on the west side of the road, just south of the intersection.

Contact: Ja-Mar Travel Park, 11203 U.S. 19, Port Richey, FL 34668, 727/863-2040, fax 727/862-8882, www.ja-mar-travelpark.com.

☑ JAY B. STARKEY WILDERNESS PARK

Scenic rating: 10

on the east side of New Port Richey

BEST (

Pop-up campers can get even here. Well, at least two of them. Sometimes pop-ups are not allowed in the more snooty RV parks, but in this beautiful nature park they are the only trailers permitted. Set on the edge of an urban area and upscale housing developments, this 8,700-acre public preserve is part of a wilderness tract originally owned by Jay B. Starkey, who bought the land in 1937 for cattle grazing. An environmental education center was built for meetings, exhibits, and nature training. Almost all the sites are for tents; only two can accommodate pop-up trailers. Picnic areas, pavilions, shelters, a paved bike trail, and 13 miles of hiking trails are in the park. Limited freshwater fishing is available along the Anclote and Pithlachasotee Rivers. The following are not allowed: alcoholic beverages, guns or trapping devices, collecting or removing plants or animals, swimming, canoeing or boating, digging, motorcycles, and all-terrain vehicles. The park has 10 miles of marked bridle paths designated for equestrian use. Horses must be trailered into the park, and each rider must carry proof of a current negative Coggins test.

RV sites, facilities: The main campground has 16 primitive sites for tents, including two for pop-up campers. Larger RVs and generators are not allowed. Facilities include restrooms, showers, picnic tables, grills, and fire rings. Large cabins are available for rent for $15 per night for eight persons; smaller cabins are $10 per night for four people. One cabin and the environmental education center are wheelchair accessible. Children are welcome. Pets are prohibited in the campground, though you may walk a dog on a six-foot leash elsewhere in the park.

Reservations, fees: Reservations are required for the main campground; they may be made up to 30 days in advance in person. Pop-up camper sites in the main area are $5 per night (a site accommodates up to eight people). Credit cards are not accepted. Stays are limited to seven days, with an extension available for a maximum of 14 days.

Directions: From I-75, take Exit 285 and drive west on State Road 52 for 21 miles. At Little Road, turn south and go six miles. Turn east onto River Crossing Boulevard and drive three miles to the park entrance. The drive winds through a residential development until it dead-ends at Wilderness Road. When coming from U.S. 19 in New Port Richey, take State Road 54 east for 2.5 miles to Little Road, then head north to River Crossing Boulevard. Drive three miles east to the park entrance.

Contact: Jay B. Starkey Wilderness Park, 10500 Wilderness Road, New Port Richey, FL 34656, 727/834-3247 or 727/834-3262, fax 727/834-3277. Or write to Pasco County Parks and Recreation Department, 7750 North Congress Street, New Port Richey, FL 34653.

6 ORCHID LAKE TRAVEL PARK

Scenic rating: 3

in New Port Richey

This quiet park is located on Orchid Lake near orange groves, upscale homes, shopping, and many golf courses. Social programs are held in the winter months.

RV sites, facilities: The 55-and-older, retiree-oriented park has 406 RV sites with full hook-ups, 30-amp and 50-amp electrical service, concrete patios, and telephone and cable TV access. Lots are 30 by 50 feet, accommodating RVs up to 40 feet long and slide-outs. None of the sites are drive-through. An Internet connection is available in the clubhouse. Restrooms, showers, a recreation hall, a card room, laundry facilities, a pool, horseshoe pits, and shuffle-board courts are provided. The clubhouse, office, and pool are wheelchair accessible. Streets are paved. Visiting grandchildren are welcome. Indoor cats are permitted; no dogs are allowed.

Reservations, fees: Reservations are recommended. Sites are $25 per night for two people, plus $2 for each additional person. Credit cards are not accepted. Long-term rates are available.

Directions: From I-75, take the exit to State Route 52 and go west to Little Road and proceed one mile to Arevee Drive. Turn west; the park is near the corner.

Contact: Orchid Lake Travel Park, 8225 Arevee Drive, New Port Richey, FL 34653, 727/847-1925.

7 HOLIDAY TRAVEL PARK

Scenic rating: 3

in Holiday north of Tarpon Springs

This is a convenient base for exploring Gulf Coast attractions, such as the sponge docks of Tarpon Springs four miles south. Rigs up to

40 feet long can be accommodated. At 7,000 square feet, the clubhouse has a seating capacity of 400, a poolroom, a card room, and a library. For those cool winter days, the pool is heated.

RV sites, facilities: The 613-unit park has 60 full-hookup RV sites with 50-amp electrical service(some pull-through). Wheelchair-accessible restrooms, plus showers, laundry facilities, a dump station, a pool, pet areas, and a recreation hall are provided. Rental trailers are available. There is a dial-up Internet connection in the clubhouse. The resort caters to 50-and-older travelers, but all ages are welcome. Leashed pets are permitted.

Reservations, fees: Reservations are not necessary. Sites are $30 per night for two people, plus $2 for each additional person. Credit cards are not accepted. Long-term rates are available.

Directions: From the intersection of U.S. 19 and State Road 54, drive 3.5 miles south on U.S. 19. The park is on the east side of the junction of U.S. 19 and Alternate U.S. 19.

Contact: Holiday Travel Park, 1622 Aires Drive, Holiday, FL 34690, 727/934-6782.

8 PALM HARBOR RESORT

Scenic rating: 3

in Palm Harbor

With just a few spots for overnighters, this trailer park and fish camp overlooks the Sutherland Bayou. Most folks here are anglers, and the park fills up fast for the entire winter. About one-third of this tiny park is occupied by year-round residents.

RV sites, facilities: There are 22 RV sites available with full hookups, 30/50-amp electrical service, and picnic tables. About half have concrete pads. Restrooms, showers, laundry facilities, and telephone service are available. On the premises are a pool, a boat ramp, a fish-cleaning station, a clubhouse, and a bait and tackle store. Children are welcome. Leashed pets are permitted.

Reservations, fees: Reservations are recommended. Sites are $30 per night for two people. Credit cards are accepted. Long-term rates are available.

Directions: From Palm Harbor, drive north on Alternate 19 North to the Crystal Beach area. Look for the park on the big curve between Tampa Road and Alderman Road.

Contact: Palm Harbor Resort, 2119 Alternate 19 North, Palm Harbor, FL 34683, 727/785-3402.

9 BAY AIRE RV PARK

Scenic rating: 5

in Palm Harbor

BEST (

Like most Florida RV campgrounds, this park wears two coats: In the wintertime, retirees migrate south to renew old acquaintances and participate in planned activities in the recreation hall. In the off-season, the demographics are more mixed, and the place is less crowded. Either time, the grassy park has a friendly, homey feel, with a blend of Australian pines, palm trees, tropical shrubs, and grass lawns and a gate for security. Across the street is the Pinellas Trail, a 42-mile paved biking and walking path converted from an old railway. This park also makes a good stopover for those who want to explore Tarpon Springs and its Greek village.

RV sites, facilities: This park has 151 RV sites, all with full hookups, 30-amp and 50-amp electricity, plus cable TV and telephone access. A limited number of sites are available for 40-foot rigs and slide-out trailers. On the premises are restrooms, showers, a recreation hall, a pool, shuffleboard courts, horseshoe pits, and laundry facilities. The recreation hall and restrooms are wheelchair accessible. This is primarily an adult park. Children are welcome only in the summer months up to October 1; after that, they can visit campers. Leashed pets are welcome.

Reservations, fees: Reservations are recommended November–April. Sites are $38 per night for two people, plus $2 for each additional person over the age of three. Cable TV, telephone, and 50-amp electrical service cost extra. Credit cards are accepted. RVers can stay as long as they like. Long-term rates are available.

Directions: From the intersection of Alternate U.S. 19 and State Road 584/Tampa Road, drive 1.4 miles north on Alternate U.S. 19. The park is on the east side of the road.

Contact: Bay Aire RV Park, 2242 Alternate U.S. 19, Palm Harbor, FL 34683, 727/784-4082, fax 727/784-9698 or 888/241-9090.

10 SHERWOOD FOREST RV RESORT

Scenic rating: 4

in Palm Harbor

Beach lovers will appreciate the park's proximity to Caladesi Island State Park and Honeymoon Island State Park. Ferry service is available to Caladesi Island from Honeymoon Island. The ferry leaves from the Honeymoon Island State Park Marina on the hour 10 A.M.–4 P.M. For ferry information, call 727/442-7433 or visit www.dolphinencounter.org. The sponge docks of Tarpon Springs and the antiques stores of downtown Dunedin are only minutes away. You can ride your bike on the Pinellas Trail, which passes within 100 feet of the campground. About 70 percent of the sites are occupied by year-round residents.

RV sites, facilities: Campers will find 104 grassy RV sites with full hookups, electricity, concrete patios, and picnic tables. Sites up to 45 feet long and slide-outs can be accommodated. One site is drive-through; the rest are back-in. On the premises are restrooms, showers, a clubhouse, a pool, and laundry facilities; all areas are said to be wheelchair accessible. Streets are paved. An Internet connection is available in the clubhouse. Children are welcome. Cats

and dogs under 35 pounds are permitted in a separate section.

Reservations, fees: Reservations are recommended. All sites are $45 per night for two people, plus $2.50 for each additional person. Credit cards are accepted. Long-term stays are okay.

Directions: From the intersection of Alternate U.S. 19 and State Road 586/Curlew Road, drive 0.8 mile north on Alternate U.S. 19 to the park on the west side of the road.

Contact: Sherwood Forest RV Resort, 175 Alternate U.S. 19 North, Palm Harbor, FL 34683, 727/784-4582, www.meetrobinhood.com.

11 CLEARWATER-TARPON SPRINGS KOA

Scenic rating: 6

in Palm Harbor

If you like KOA-style convenience and plan on doing a lot of sightseeing, then this vacation-oriented park may be for you. It's on a busy six-lane highway and is convenient to Tarpon Springs, the beaches at Dunedin, and Central Florida attractions such as Busch Gardens, Weeki Wachee, St. Petersburg museums and aquariums, and Ybor City. The pool is heated. Only 2 percent of the sites are occupied by year-round residents.

RV sites, facilities: There are 116 back-in RV sites with full hookups, 30-amp and 50-amp electrical service, wireless Internet access, concrete patios, and picnic tables. RVs up to 42 feet long and slide-outs can be accommodated. Sites vary in size. Restrooms, showers, laundry facilities, a dump station, a pool, and a recreation hall (with planned activities) are on the property. A separate wheelchair-accessible restroom is provided, and all other areas of the park, including the pool area, office, and store, are navigable for wheelchairs. Streets are paved. A camp store sells ice, camping supplies, snacks, and souvenirs. Groceries and restaurants are within one mile. Children are welcome. Leashed pets are permitted.

Reservations, fees: Reservations are recommended. Sites are $33–38 per night for two people, plus $1.50 for extra children under 17 and $5 for each additional adult. Use of air conditioners and electric heaters costs $4 per day. Credit cards are accepted. Long-term stays are okay.

Directions: From U.S. 19 and State Road 584/Tampa Road, drive 2.9 miles north on U.S. 19 to the park on the east side of the road.

Contact: Clearwater–Tarpon Springs KOA, 37061 U.S. 19 North, Palm Harbor, FL 34684, 727/937-8412 or 800/KOA-8743 (800/562-8743), www.koa.com.

12 DUNEDIN RV RESORT

Scenic rating: 7

in Dunedin

Targeted to the "active and adventurous," this immaculate park is near everything civilized as well as the ocean and beaches. For guests who enjoy biking and walking, the Pinellas Trail passes right by the park, where about 10 percent of the sites are occupied year-round. You're just three miles from the Caladesi Island ferry and Honeymoon Island State Park, the Toronto Blue Jays spring training facilities, Tarpon Springs sponge docks, antiques shops, flea markets, deep-sea fishing, and restaurants. Planned activities are held November 1–May 1. Visitors come from all over the United States, Canada, Germany, and the Netherlands.

RV sites, facilities: This 233-unit park has 81 RV sites available with full hookups, 30-amp and 50-amp electrical service, wireless Internet, concrete patios and picnic tables; 18 are pull-through. Lots vary in size, but some are 30 by 60 feet and can accommodate RVs up to 45 feet long and slide-outs. Restrooms, showers, a dump station, a recreation hall with big-screen TV and Internet hookup, a heated pool, a play-

ground, laundry facilities, and a clubhouse are provided. You'll also find shuffleboard courts, table tennis, foosball, volleyball, boccie ball (lawn bowling), and a playground. The mobile homes are separated from the RV area. All sites, one bathhouse, the laundry room, and the recreation room are wheelchair accessible. Streets are paved. Groceries and restaurants are within 0.5 mile. Children and leashed pets are welcome.

Reservations, fees: Reservations are recommended. Sites are $39–47 per night for two people, plus $4 for each additional person. Credit cards are accepted. Long-term rates are available.

Directions: From the intersection of Alternate U.S. 19 and State Road 586/Curlew Road in Dunedin, drive 0.5 mile north on Alternate U.S. 19 to the park.

Contact: Dunedin RV Resort, 2920 Alternate U.S. 19 North, Dunedin, FL 34698, 727/784-3719 or 800/345-7504, www.campingfriend.com/dunedinrvresort.

13 INDIAN ROCKS TRAVEL PARK

Scenic rating: 2

in Largo

An 18-hole golf course is within walking distance of this RV park. Best of all, though, this open and sunny park is just 1.5 miles east of the beach. The place is oriented to retirees who spend winter in Florida, so expect organized activities. About 80 percent of the park is occupied year-round.

RV sites, facilities: There are 35 RV sites with full hookups, 30-amp electrical service, and access to cable TV and telephone service in this 175-unit retirement trailer park. Lots are 25 by 50 feet, and rigs up to 40 feet long can be accommodated. On the premises are restrooms, showers, a dump station, a pool, a recreation room, shuffleboard courts, and laundry facilities. An Internet connection is available in the clubhouse. The office, clubhouse, and pool area are wheelchair accessible. Streets are paved. Families with small children may stay only for short visits. Pets are prohibited.

Reservations, fees: Reservations are recommended. Sites are $27 per night for two people, plus $3 for each additional person. Credit cards are accepted. Long-term stays are okay.

Directions: From the intersection of U.S. 19 and State Road 688/Ulmerton Road, drive west on State Road 688 for 11 miles. At Vonn Road, turn right and continue 0.3 mile north to the park at right.

Contact: Indian Rocks Travel Park, 12121 Vonn Road, Largo, FL 33774, 727/595-2228.

14 YANKEE TRAVELER RV PARK

Scenic rating: 7

in Largo

A maintenance crew works daily to keep up the park's neat appearance, and the managers live on-site to ensure that older RVers have everything they need for a relaxing vacation. The pool is heated, and social programs are held in winter. Among favorite activities are dances, bingo, potluck suppers, day trips, cards, art classes, pancake breakfasts, Bible study, swimming in the pool, and going to the beach. Under family ownership for more than two decades, this park intends to stay in the big leagues of snowbird destinations. About 90 percent of the lots are occupied year-round. As the owners say, "Luxury at your front door—the best of Florida in your back yard." Lake Seminole is three miles away for the anglers in the group.

RV sites, facilities: There are about 30 RV sites with full hookups for overnighters in this 211-unit park. All sites have 30/50-amp electrical service, sewer hookups, concrete patios, and picnic tables. Rigs up to 40 feet and slide-outs can be accommodated on lots averaging 30 by 60 feet. An Internet connection is available in the clubhouse. On the premises are restrooms, showers, a dump station, a pool, a whirlpool tub, a wheelchair-accessible recreation hall, horseshoe pits, shuffleboard courts, a dog-walk area, and laundry facilities. Streets are paved. Public parks, malls, and restaurants are within 0.1 mile. Campers must be over 55; children may visit them for short periods. Pets under 15 pounds are permitted.

Reservations, fees: Reservations are recommended. Sites are $25–30 per night for two people, plus $2 for each additional person. Credit cards are accepted. Long-term rates are available.

Directions: From I-275 southbound, take Exit 31B on Ulmerton Road west for 6.6 miles. The campground is on the left. Northbound, take Exit 30. Drive 1.5 miles northwest on State Road 686/Roosevelt Boulevard. At State Road 688/Ulmerton Road, turn west and drive 5.1 miles to the park on the south side of the road.

Contact: Yankee Traveler RV Park, 8500 Ulmerton Road, Largo, FL 33771, 727/531-7998, fax 727/373-0084, www.yankeetraveler.net.

15 VACATION VILLAGE/ SUNBURST

Scenic rating: 6

in Largo

Bingo, billiards, card games, and trips to the dog track entertain RVers at this park, part of the Encore chain. Stores, hair salons, an 18-hole golf course, restaurants, and shopping are within 0.5 mile.

RV sites, facilities: There are 288 full-hookup RV sites with cable TV. Rigs up to 45 feet long can be accommodated. Restrooms, showers, a dump station, laundry facilities, and telephone service are available. On the premises are a pool, a recreation hall with planned activities, horseshoe pits, shuffleboard courts, a billiards room, and a golf net. Children are welcome. Leashed pets are permitted.

Reservations, fees: Reservations are recommended. Sites are $20 and up per night. Credit cards are accepted. Long-term rates are available.

Directions: From I-275 southbound, take Exit 31B on Ulmerton Road West. The park is just past Roosevelt Road on the left.

Contact: Vacation Village, 6900 Ulmerton Road, Largo, FL 33771, 727/531-5589 or 877/297-2757, fax 727/531-0160, www .rvonthego.com.

16 BRIARWOOD TRAVEL VILLA

Scenic rating: 5

in Largo

You may forget you're in the city; when I was there, I was stunned to find such a pretty RV spot in an urban setting. Even though there's a bus stop at the front, this peaceful community is heavily wooded with hundreds of tall oak trees and winding paved roads that encircle little Lake Kathleen. "Sometimes I feel like I have my own little cabin out in the woods," says one resident, whose remarks are printed in the park brochure, and I concur. Some lots overlook the one-acre lake, and all sites have shade trees. Golf courses, groceries, a mall, and laundry facilities are nearby; the Pinellas Trail bike path is 0.5 mile away. RV and boat storage is available. About 85 percent of the park is occupied year-round.

RV sites, facilities: This adults-only park has 138 RV sites, most with full hookups and 30/50-amp electrical service. Cable TV and telephone service are available. On the premises are a dump station, a picnic shelter, horseshoe pits, shuffleboard courts, and a restaurant. Campers must be self-contained; there are no showers or restrooms. The nearest grocery store is 0.25 mile away. Children are permitted for short stays only; the park prefers campers who are over 55. Cats are welcome, but dogs are not allowed.

Reservations, fees: Reservations are not taken. Sites are $30 per night. Credit cards are not accepted. Long-term rates are available.

Directions: From the intersection of State Road 688/Ulmerton Road and Alternate U.S. 19/Seminole Boulevard in Largo, drive two blocks north on Seminole Boulevard. The park is on the west side.

Contact: Briarwood Travel Villa, 2098 Seminole Boulevard, Largo, FL 33778, 727/581-6694.

17 BICKLEY PARK

Scenic rating: 3

in Seminole

Concrete-pad sites accommodate rigs up to 35 feet long at this park set beside a busy highway. It's 1.5 miles from the beach and near golf courses, fishing, shopping, and churches. Bay Pines Veterans Hospital is one mile away. But what really keeps the same folks coming back winter after winter are the planned activities, such as potluck dinners, bingo, crafts, and parties. "We're just a friendly mom-and-pop place," says the manager. Most of the park is occupied by year-round residents in park models or other units.

RV sites, facilities: The 186-unit adults-only park has 150 paved RV sites available, with full hookups, 30-amp and 50-amp electrical service, and concrete patios. Lots are 38 or 40 feet wide by 30 feet, accommodating RVs up to 35 feet long and slide-outs. Restrooms, showers, shuffleboard courts, a clubhouse, and laundry facilities are provided. A wireless Internet connection is available in the clubhouse. Shopping is within 1.2 miles. All areas are wheelchair accessible. Children are not welcome. Leashed pets under 35 pounds are permitted.

Reservations, fees: Reservations are recommended. Sites are $40 per night for two people, plus $4 per extra person. Credit cards are accepted. Long-term rates are available.

Directions: From I-275, take Exit 28 and drive

nine miles west on County Road 694 (Gandy Boulevard/Park Boulevard) to Alternate U.S. 19 (Seminole Boulevard). Turn south and drive 1.5 miles to the park, which is on the west side between 54th and 57th Streets.

Contact: Bickley Park, 5640 Seminole Boulevard, Seminole, FL 33772, 727/392-3807 or 727/488-4618, www.bickleypark.com.

18 ST. PETERSBURG RESORT KOA

Scenic rating: 6

in St. Petersburg

A secluded family resort, this KOA offers large sites in a quiet oak- and palm-shaded setting adjacent to Boca Ciega Bay and two miles from Gulf of Mexico beaches. The bay provides boat access to the gulf waters. Among the activities for kids are video games, bike rentals, and miniature golf. Sites of interest nearby include the Pinellas Trail bike path, Busch Gardens, Sunken Gardens, the municipal pier, John's Pass Boardwalk, the Great Explorations Hands-on Museum, and the Florida Aquarium. Of special note is the Salvador Dali Museum (727/823-3767), the world's largest collection of the artist's surrealist works, including several huge "masterwork" canvases.

RV sites, facilities: The campground has 379 RV sites (87 pull-through) with full hookups, 30/50-amp electricity, and picnic tables. "Deluxe water's edge" sites have 50-amp service and overlook a mangrove-fringed bayou. Restrooms, showers, a dump station, a pool, a whirlpool tub, a boat ramp, docks, a playground, a game room, walking trails, horseshoe pits, shuffleboard and volleyball courts, laundry facilities, and a store are on the property. The stores, restrooms, recreation hall, pool, and pier are wheelchair accessible. Rental cabins are available. Children and leashed pets are welcome.

Reservations, fees: Reservations are recommended. Sites are $36–67 per night for two

people, plus $6 for each additional adult and $4 for children ages 4–17. The deluxe sites are $64–80 per night. Credit cards are accepted. RV campers can stay as long as they like. Long-term rates are available.

Directions: From I-275, take Exit 25 and drive 5.5 miles west on 38th Avenue North. Veer right onto Tyrone Boulevard/Bay Pines Boulevard and drive 1.5 miles to 95th Street, then turn north and continue 0.5 mile.

Contact: St. Petersburg Resort KOA, 5400 95th Street North, St. Petersburg, FL 33708, 727/392-2233 or 800/562-7714, fax 727/398-6081, www.koa.com.

19 ROBERT'S MOBILE HOME AND RV RESORT

Scenic rating: 4

in St. Petersburg

This 624-unit, neatly manicured mobile-home park draws older campers who appreciate the large RV sites shaded by oaks and pines. Social programs are held in winter; you can also play tennis or relax in the pool's spa.

RV sites, facilities: There are 427 RV sites with full hookups, 30/50-amp electrical service, cable TV, and available telephone service. On the premises are restrooms, showers, a dump station, a recreation room, a pool, a whirlpool tub, horseshoe pits, shuffleboard, volleyball and tennis courts, and laundry facilities. All areas are wheelchair accessible, and streets are paved. Older travelers are preferred, but children are allowed to visit for short periods. Pets under 40 pounds are permitted.

Reservations, fees: Reservations are recommended. Sites are $25–30 per night for two people, plus $3 for each additional person. Credit cards are accepted. Long-term rates are available.

Directions: From I-275, take Exit 28 and drive 1.3 miles west on County Road 694 (Gandy Boulevard/Park Boulevard) to the park.

Contact: Robert's Mobile Home and RV Resort, 3390 Gandy Boulevard North, St. Petersburg, FL 33702, 727/577-6820, www .robertsrv.com.

20 FORT DE SOTO PARK CAMPGROUND

Scenic rating: 10

on Pinellas Bayway South in Tampa Bay

BEST (

Not only is this park wooded and shady, but it also has great water views and abundant foliage screening campers from their neighbors. Guests are not allowed to swim in the waters off the campground, but there are two swimming beaches within the park. Like most great parks so close to a city, Fort De Soto draws a crowd on weekends, so consider making a reservation.

RV sites, facilities: This 235-site county campground is divided into two areas: one along a spit of land surrounded by water, the other fronting on the bay. Among them are 149 RV sites and 86 tent sites. Almost all sites are waterfront, and some have good views of St. Petersburg and the Gulf of Mexico. Most areas are wheelchair accessible. Sites 1–85 are designated for tent, van, and pop-up campers; the good news is that these are beautifully situated on the waterfront. The RV sites (86–233) are excellent, too. Water, 30-amp electricity, picnic tables, grills, restrooms, showers, a dump station, laundry facilities, a store, and two play areas are provided. A boat ramp is in the park. Alcoholic beverages are prohibited. Children are welcome. Previously prohibited, pets are now allowed on a trial basis in certain campsites only.

Reservations, fees: Reservations are recommended, though a number of sites are set aside for first-come, first-served campers. You can make reservations at the campground, by telephone, or online. Sites are $28 per night for six people. Credit cards are not accepted. The maximum stay is 14 days during any 30-day period between January and April; the rest of the year, you may extend your visit by 14 days depending on availability of campsites.

Directions: From I-275, take Exit 17 and drive two miles west on State Road 682, also known as U.S. 19 North/54th Avenue South/Pinellas Bayway. At Pinellas Bayway South, turn south and continue about three miles to the park.

Contact: Fort De Soto Park Campground, 3500 Pinellas Bayway South, Tierra Verde, FL 33715, 727/582-2267, www.fortdesoto.com.

TAMPA

COURTESY OF VISIT FLORIDA

BEST RV PARKS AND CAMPGROUNDS

(Biking
Alafia River State Park, page 361

(Fishing
Hide-A-Way RV Resort, page 363

(Golf
Hidden River Travel Resort, page 360

One of Florida's major destinations, Tampa is a thriving city built in a rough half circle around Tampa Bay. Three rivers — the Hillsborough, Alafia, and Little Manatee — flow into Tampa Bay, and the prettiest camping can be found along those waterways.

The Spanish explorers were here in the early 1500s, but they evidently did not have much interest in settling Tampa. It wasn't until 1845, when the Tampa Bay area became part of the United States, that it was recognized as a strategic location. One of the early developers of the area was Henry B. Plant, who brought a railroad along the Hillsborough River in 1884 and built fancy hotels to accommodate the passengers. Plant City, east of Tampa, is named in his honor, and it is the site of an annual strawberry festival that attracts thousands.

In the late 1880s, the Tampa neighborhood of Ybor City was home to more than 100 cigar factories that employed Cuban, Spanish, and Italian immigrants. (One of the best-known cigar slogans of the era was "Hav-a-Tampa.") The former "cigar capital of the world" is now a charming National Historic Landmark District with a vibrant nightlife featuring blues cafes, rock clubs, a microbrewery, and restaurants. The Ybor City Museum State Park, housed in an old bakery, explores the area's past and includes a restored cigar worker's home on the grounds.

Today, Tampa is one of the fastest-growing communities in Florida, with a big-city skyline overlooking the water and the seventh-largest commercial seaport in the nation. It's also home to the sprawling MacDill Air Force Base, which supports United States military operations around the world. The Gasparilla Pirate Fest, held each February, commemorates pirates that once patrolled the waters near here, looking for ships to plunder. It begins with an "invasion" of Tampa Bay by an authentic-looking pirate ship under full sail, accompanied by scores of modern boats who pretend to take over. Most visitors, whether they be nuclear families or grandparents seeking to entertain the grandkids, will likely be drawn to the enormous Busch Gardens theme park. The area's major tourist attraction, it has eight roller coasters, numerous children's educational activities, more than 2,700 animals, and a petting zoo.

RV overnighters and rally groups are welcome at Rally Park, northeast of Tampa. Part of a 104-acre RV-oriented shopping center, the park includes the Lazy Days Super Center and a Camping World store. There's a full-time coordinator to help plan group events and a banquet kitchen that can serve as many as 600 people. Of course, if you want to kick the tires of a new RV, this is the place.

Most of the RV parks in the Tampa area are inland along the rivers. One of the most attractive is the lushly forested Hillsborough River State Park, farther northeast. Developed by the Civilian Conservation Corps during the 1930s, the park features eight miles of nature trails, a huge spring-fed swimming pool, and canoeing on one of the few rivers in the state with Class II rapids. At Fort Foster, visitors can reserve space on a tour where sometimes volunteers don period dress to reenact fort life in the 1830s.

TAMPA

❶ HILLSBOROUGH RIVER STATE PARK

Scenic rating: 10

north of Thonotosassa and south of Zephyrhills

Like most of the Florida parks developed by the Civilian Conservation Corps during the 1930s, Hillsborough River State Park is a jewel. The river flows through a lush forest of pines and oaks, its waters dark with tannin. Canoeing is great because this is one of the few rivers in the state with Class II rapids. There are eight miles of nature trails, and a huge man-made, spring-fed swimming pool draws crowds of bathers on hot summer days. You can also tour Fort Foster (by reservation only); sometimes, volunteers clad in period dress enact what life was like in the fort in the 1830s when its role was to protect a military road during the Indian wars. Bicycles and canoes are available for rent; you're not allowed to take rental canoes on the rapids. The campground is thoughtfully arranged in three loops, so there's a feeling of privacy and seclusion. Visitors come from all over the United States, as well as Germany and England. Pick up supplies in Thonotosassa or Zephyrhills, 6–8 miles away.

RV sites, facilities: There are 114 sites with water and electricity (no sewer hookups). Seventy-one sites have 30-amp service, and 43 have 50-amp. RVs up to 40 feet long and slide-outs can be accommodated. Picnic tables, grills, fire rings, restrooms, showers, a dump station, a pool, canoe rentals, hiking trails, a historic fort, horseshoe pits, a snack bar, and laundry facilities are available. A camp store sells ice, snacks, and souvenirs. Campsites, picnic areas, and the pool are wheelchair accessible. Streets are paved. Children are welcome. Leashed pets are permitted in the Hammock Circle camping area with proof of vaccination.

Reservations, fees: Reservations are recommended; contact ReserveAmerica at 800/336-3521 or reserveamerica.com. Sites are $22.40 per night for up to eight people. Credit cards are accepted. The maximum stay is 14 days.

Directions: From I-75, take Exit 265 and drive east on State Road 582/Fowler Avenue for 1.2 miles. At U.S. 301, turn north and drive 12 miles to the park. From I-4, take Exit 7 onto U.S. 301 and drive 13 miles north to the park.

Contact: Hillsborough River State Park, 15402 U.S. 301 North, Thonotosassa, FL 33592, 813/987-6771, fax 813/987-6773, www.floridastateparks.org.

❷ HAPPY TRAVELER RV PARK

Scenic rating: 6

east of I-75 in Thonotosassa

Leafy trees shadow many of the sites in this all-ages RV-oriented park, which claims to be the closest campground to Busch Gardens, the zoo and roller coaster attraction. The Big Top Flea Market is across the street, and plenty of shops and restaurants are nearby. But what really puts the 28-acre park on the map is its next-door neighbor, Canoe Escape (813/986-2067). Campers can get discounts to paddle rental canoes on the beautiful Hillsborough River. Paved interior roads lead to sites that are grassy or dirt; a few are concrete. About 25 percent of the park is occupied year-round. Favorite things to do are "making friends," which is made easier through the planned activities (bingo, day trips, and shows) held in the park during the winter season. Visitors come from all over the world. Although you're only 12 miles from downtown Tampa, you'll see lots of birds and wildlife.

RV sites, facilities: This adult park has 220 full-hookup sites with 30/50-amp electrical service. A wireless Internet network is available in the clubhouse and in other parts of the park. On the premises are restrooms, showers, a dump station, a pool, a clubhouse, tennis, shuffleboard, horseshoes, table tennis, and laundry facilities. Restaurants are within 0.2 mile. The clubhouse, bathhouse, and store are wheelchair accessible. All ages are welcome, but no one under age 21 can stay longer than two weeks. Leashed, nonaggressive pets are allowed.

Reservations, fees: Reservations are recommended. Sites are $22–25 per night for two people, plus $1 for each additional person, $2 for electricity, and $2 for cable TV. Credit cards are accepted. Long-term rates are available.

Directions: From I-75, take Exit 265 onto Fowler Avenue and go 0.5 mile east to the park, at the corner of Walker Road.

Contact: Happy Traveler RV Park, 9401 East Fowler Avenue, Thonotosassa, FL 33592, 813/986-3094 or 800/758-2795, fax 813/986-9077, www.happytravelerrvpark.com.

3 CAMP LEMORA RV PARK

Scenic rating: 6

in Thonotosassa

Much of the park is open to the sun, with plenty of space for big RVs, and a little creek runs down the back of the property. The owners describe the place as a quiet, relaxing nature park close to springs, a river, and a lake, with an area for hiking nearby. In the winter months, this park is often fully booked by seasonal visitors. Favorite things to do are "getting together and having fun." Planned activities are held from late October through late April, and most visitors come from all over the United States and Canada.

RV sites, facilities: This 302-slot RV park has 150 sites available for overnight campers; the rest are occupied by winter residents. Full hookups, 30-amp electrical service, and picnic tables are available. Some sites have concrete patios. Sites average 40 by 50 feet, accommodating RVs up to 40 feet long and slide-outs. On the premises are restrooms, showers, a dump station, a pool, horseshoe pits, shuffleboard courts, a general store, and laundry facilities. A camp store sells ice, camping supplies, and limited groceries. Restaurants, grocery stores, and other shops

are within 11 miles. Most areas are wheelchair accessible, and streets are paved. Children are welcome. Leashed pets are allowed.

Reservations, fees: Reservations are recommended. Sites are $24 per night for two people, plus $2 for each additional person. Credit cards are not accepted. Long-term rates are available.

Directions: From I-75, take Exit 265 and drive east on State Road 582/Fowler Avenue for 1.2 miles. At U.S. 301, turn north and drive eight miles to the park. From I-4, take Exit 7 onto U.S. 301 and drive north for 1.5 miles. Or, from I-4 at Exit 6, drive north on U.S. 301 for 12.5 miles.

Contact: Camp Lemora RV Park, 14910 Dead River Road, Thonotosassa, FL 33592, 813/986-4456.

4 SOUTHERN AIRE

Scenic rating: 6

in Thonotosassa

Rigs up to 40 feet long can be accommodated on the manicured grounds of this countryside park. A sunny, Olympic-sized, heated pool, neatly tended shuffleboard courts, and a large private lake keep snowbirds busy during the winter. Park models are for sale.

RV sites, facilities: This park has 450 sites with full hookups, 30/50-amp electricity, plus cable TV, picnic tables, and telephone service. On the premises are restrooms, showers, a recreation hall, a pool, a whirlpool tub, horseshoe pits, shuffleboard courts, and laundry facilities. Children and pets are permitted.

Reservations, fees: Reservations are not necessary. Sites are $24 per night for two people, plus $2.50 for each additional person. Credit cards are accepted. Long-term rates are available.

Directions: From I-4, take Exit 10 and drive north on County Road 579 for four miles. Turn right on Florence Avenue and drive 0.1 mile east to the park.

Contact: Southern Aire, 10511 Florence Avenue, Thonotosassa, FL 33592, 813/986-1596, www.rvresorts.com.

5 RALLY PARK

Scenic rating: 4

northeast of Tampa

This is part of a 104-acre RV-oriented shopping center, the Lazy Days Super Center (formerly Lazy Days RV Resort), with more than 1,100 new and used rigs on display and a Camping World store where you can pick up needed supplies. Overnighters and rally groups are welcome, and there's a full-time coordinator to help plan group events. The banquet kitchen can serve as many as 600 people. Of course, if you want to kick the tires of a new RV, this is the place.

RV sites, facilities: There are 300 RV sites with full hookups, 50-amp electricity, high-speed Internet access, concrete pads, and picnic tables. Rigs up to 45 feet can be accommodated. Restrooms, showers, laundry facilities, a dump station, a screened and heated pool, a 12,000-square-foot recreation hall, a computer room with Internet access, tennis courts, and horseshoe and shuffleboard courts are on the premises. A Cracker Barrel restaurant is part of the complex. All areas are wheelchair accessible. Included with the price of your site is breakfast and lunch Monday–Saturday, cable TV, and the morning newspaper. Children are welcome. Leashed pets are permitted.

Reservations, fees: Reservations are recommended. Sites are $20 per night. Credit cards are accepted. The maximum stay is two weeks.

Directions: From I-4 north of Tampa, take Exit 10 northbound on County Road 579 for 0.2 mile to the Lazy Days Super Center.

Contact: Rally Park, 6210 County Road 579, Seffner, FL 33584, 813/246-4777 or 800/905-6627, fax 813/246-5504, www.lazydays.com.

6 TAMPA EAST RV RESORT

Scenic rating: 8

near Dover

Convenient to the interstate and to Tampa attractions 12 miles west, this enormous park (actually two parks combined into one) attracts retirees and families on vacation. Some visitors head to Busch Gardens theme park, one of the nation's largest zoos. It has more than 2,700 animals, lots of children's educational activities, and a petting zoo, as well as the world's two tallest inverted roller coasters. In winter, the RV park largely becomes a snowbird park, and social programs include music jamborees, dances, line dancing, potlucks, and parties. RVs up to 45 feet long can be accommodated. This is a good place to stay when attending RV shows nearby. Interior paved roads lead to a mixture of sites, some grassy and sunny, others shell-carpeted and shaded by palms. Some sites have patios.

RV sites, facilities: All sites are full-hookup with 30/50-amp electrical service, wireless Internet access, and concrete patios. Picnic tables, restrooms, showers, laundry facilities, a dump station, three swimming pools, a heated spa, a playground, horseshoes, two recreation halls, fishing ponds, propane, a camp store, and shuffleboard are available. Restaurants and shops are a 10-minute drive away. Children are welcome. Leashed pets are permitted.

Reservations, fees: Reservations are recommended. Sites are $27–43 per night, higher during special events. Credit cards are accepted. Long-term stays are okay.

Directions: From I-4, take Exit 14. Drive south about one-eighth of a mile to the park at right.

Contact: Tampa East RV Resort, 4630 McIntosh Road, Dover, FL 33527, 813/659-2504 or 866/786-6298, fax 813/659-2171, www.tamparvresort.com.

7 BAY BAYOU RV RESORT

Scenic rating: 5

west side of Tampa

Free coffee and snacks are served each morning to wintertime campers, who also enjoy a full menu of planned activities in the 6,000-square-foot recreation hall, including ice-cream socials, potluck dinners, bingo, card games, poker, and special outings. Sites are grassy, oversized, and shady with paved access roads. Some even overlook a creek. The modern, free-form pool is heated during the cooler months, and the whirlpool tub is kept at the same temperature as the pool. About 25 percent of the park is occupied year-round.

RV sites, facilities: All 241 RV sites in this adult-oriented park have full hookups and 30-amp electrical service; 166 have 50-amp. Concrete patios and picnic tables are on hand. RVs up to 45 feet long and slide-outs can be accommodated on sites averaging 40 by 50 feet. A wireless Internet connection is available in the clubhouse and in the park. On the premises are restrooms, showers, a dump station, a pool, a whirlpool tub, shuffleboard courts, and laundry facilities. A camp store sells ice, camping supplies, and snacks. Kayaks are for rent. Groceries and restaurants are within one mile; malls and hospitals are within four miles. All areas are wheelchair accessible. Children are permitted for a maximum of 30 days. One leashed dog under 30 pounds is allowed per site.

Reservations, fees: Reservations are recommended. Sites are $36–39 per night for two people, plus $4 for each extra person. Credit cards are accepted. Long-term rates are available.

Directions: From I-275, take Exit 50 and drive west on Busch Boulevard for 0.1 mile. At Florida Avenue, turn left and drive 0.5 mile south. At Waters Avenue, turn and travel west for 10 miles to Country Way Boulevard. Turn south and drive 0.25 mile. Turn west on Memorial Highway and drive 0.8 mile to the park. From I-4 going west, take Exit 7 onto Hillsborough Avenue (U.S. 92). Drive west through Tampa for 17 miles. At County Way Boulevard, turn north and drive 0.5 mile to Memorial Highway. Turn west on Memorial Highway 0.8 mile to the park.

Contact: Bay Bayou RV Resort, 12622 Memorial Highway, Tampa, FL 33635, 813/855-1000, fax 813/925-0815, www.baybayou.com.

8 CITRUS HILLS RV PARK

Scenic rating: 3

east of Brandon

This quiet, shady park is family-owned and has a relaxing atmosphere. About half of the sites are sunny; oaks lend shade to the rest. It's a retiree magnet in winter, when bingo and potluck dinners are among activities. The park is close to several Tampa attractions, including Ybor City, a worthwhile stop. At the turn of the 20th century, Ybor City was home to more than 100 cigar factories that employed Cuban, Spanish, and Italian immigrants. Today, the National Historic Landmark District is celebrated for its charm and its vibrant nightlife featuring blues cafes, rock clubs, a microbrewery, and restaurants—the most famous being the Columbia, which serves authentic Spanish cuisine. Explore the area's past as the "cigar capital of the world" at the Ybor City Museum State Park (813/247-6323), housed in an old bakery with a restored cigar worker's home on the grounds. Now you know where "Hav-a-Tampa" came from.

RV sites, facilities: All 220 RV sites have full hookups, 30/50-amp electrical service, and cable TV. More than half are permanent residents. No sites are pull-through. On the premises are picnic tables, restrooms, showers, and a 6,000-square-foot recreation hall with planned activities, such as bingo and cards. Restaurants and a supermarket are one mile away. The park targets retired travelers, but there are no age restrictions. Small pets are allowed.

Reservations, fees: Reservations are not necessary. Sites are $18 per night for two people, plus $3 for each additional person. Credit cards are not accepted. Long-term rates are available.

Directions: From I-75, take Exit 257 and drive east on State Road 60 about two miles to the park on the east side of Brandon.

Contact: Citrus Hills RV Park, 5311 State Road 60 East, Dover, FL 33527, 813/737-4770, www.citrushillsrvpark.com.

9 LITHIA SPRINGS PARK

Scenic rating: 8

southeast of Brandon

For scenic beauty, this park is beautiful, but some of the facilities need modernization. Still, camping is a first-come, first-served deal at this popular 160-acre Hillsborough County park, so you'll have to register early on holiday weekends. The oversized sites are shaded by a jungle of scrub oak trees. Each year, some 200,000 people come from all over to swim in the 72°F spring, which has been fenced off and resembles a municipal pool. A lifeguard is on duty on winter weekends, and everyone is ordered out of the water every hour or two for safety checks. You can canoe and fish in the Alafia River, but swimming is banned by the health department.

RV sites, facilities: There are 40 sites with water, 30-amp electricity (6 with 50-amp), picnic tables, grills, and fire rings. Some sites will not fit RVs because of low-hanging trees; others can accommodate rigs up to 38 feet long. Restrooms, showers, a dump station, horseshoe pits, a canoe launch, and a playground are on the property. Groceries and restaurants are within two miles. Children are welcome. Leashed pets are permitted.

Reservations, fees: Reservations are not taken. Campsites are $16 per night for eight people. Credit cards are not accepted. The maximum stay is 14 days at a time, or 90 days in a year.

Directions: From I-75, take Exit 257 and drive east on State Road 60 for two miles. At County Road 640/Lithia Road, turn right and drive south to the park.

Contact: Lithia Springs Park, 3932 Lithia Springs Road, Lithia, FL 33547, 813/744-5572. Hillsborough County Parks and Recreation Administrative Office: 1101 East River Cove Street, Tampa, FL 33604, 813/975-2160, www.hillsboroughcounty.org/parks.

10 EDWARD MEDARD PARK AND RESERVOIR

Scenic rating: 9

east of Brandon

Once a phosphate mine, this 1,284-acre tract near the Alafia River includes a 700-acre reservoir with a white-sand swimming beach. The emphasis is on fishing. Bream, speckled perch, and catfish are plentiful, but officials are trying hard to increase the population of the coveted largemouth bass. Paradoxically, to encourage bigger, better bass, anglers are urged to harvest those under 14 inches; that's so the older fish can mature and grow. And to really get the frenzy going, two fish feeders have been placed in the lake near the Burnt Stump dock and a footbridge. You're invited to bring commercial fish food, dry dog food, oatmeal, and even bread to use as chum. Boaters are instructed to anchor away from four fish attractors in deeper water and to cast toward them. The state's regulations on largemouth bass don't apply here, where it's a whole different ball game. For more angling tips, get a copy of the park's fishing brochure.

The heavily wooded campsites are arranged in two loops near the lake, and horseback-riding trails wind through the park. Allow four hours for a round-trip ride on the bridle paths. (You can rent horses by the hour at the stable just north of the park.) Because no reservations are accepted and the park receives about 500,000 visitors a year, try to time your visit for the middle of the week and on nonholiday weekends.

Phosphate, used to manufacture agricultural fertilizer, is dug from enormous earth-scarring pits, and it's interesting to see how land used for such a purpose can be reclaimed for public recreation. The soil around the so-called Sacred Hills play and picnic area was dug from the mine.

RV sites, facilities: This Hillsborough County park has 40 sites with water, electricity, picnic tables, and grills. Restrooms, showers, a dump station, a boat ramp, a fishing pier, a playground, nature trails, horseshoe pits, and horseback-riding trails are available. Groceries, restaurants, and laundry facilities are within 0.8 mile. Children and pets are welcome.

Reservations, fees: Reservations are not accepted. Sites are $16 per night. Credit cards are not accepted. Campers must register one-half hour before sunset. If the sign says the campground is full, drive through and check, then go back and tell the ranger about any empty spots. The maximum stay is 14 days.

Directions: From I-75, take Exit 257 and drive east on State Road 60 through Brandon. Continue six miles farther. At Turkey Creek Road, turn and drive one mile south to the park.

Contact: Edward Medard Park and Reservoir, 5276 Panther Loop, Plant City, FL 33567, 813/757-3802, fax 813/757-3939. Hillsborough County Parks and Recreation Administrative Office: 1101 East River Cove Street, Tampa, FL 33604, 813/975-2160, www.hillsborough-county.org/parks.

course. There's also a 2.5-mile nature trail. Planned activities are held November–April, and about half the park is occupied year-round. Favorite things to do are lounging by the pool, biking, walking, and working out in the exercise room.

RV sites, facilities: All 350 RV sites have full hookups, 30-amp electrical service, and concrete patios. There are 150 sites with 50-amp service. Ten sites are drive-through. Lot sizes are variable, but RVs up to 40 feet long and slide-outs can be accommodated. An Internet connection is available in the clubhouse. On the premises are picnic tables, restrooms, showers, laundry facilities, a dump station, a pool, a boat ramp, boat docks, a playground, a nature trail, a small golf course, horseshoe pits, a volleyball area, a game room, rental trailers, a camp circle, and a one-acre lake. The common areas are wheelchair accessible. Adults are preferred, but children are welcome for short stays. Pets are permitted. Annual residents are especially welcome.

Reservations, fees: Reservations are recommended. Sites are $30 per night for two people, plus $2 for each additional person. Credit cards are not accepted. Long-term rates are available.

Directions: From I-75, take Exit 250 and drive east on Gibsonton Drive/Boyette Road for 2.5 miles. At McMullen Loop Road, turn north and drive 0.8 mile to the park.

Contact: Hidden River Travel Resort, 12500 McMullen Loop Road, Riverview, FL 33569, 813/677-1515, www.hiddenriverrv.com.

11 HIDDEN RIVER TRAVEL RESORT

Scenic rating: 7

in Riverview

BEST (

The quiet, peaceful Alafia River runs the length of the resort. Fish from the docks on the river, swim in the heated pool, relax by the one-acre lake, or drive a few golf balls on the three-hole

12 ALAFIA RIVER RV RESORT

Scenic rating: 7

in Riverview

Swim in the heated pool or launch your fishing boat from the boat ramp on the Alafia River. Shade trees and river views give the park a natural atmosphere, even though it's conveniently close to the interstate.

RV sites, facilities: All 203 RV sites (four pull-through) have full hookups and 30-amp electricity; cable TV and telephone service are available for long-term visitors. A wireless Internet network is available in the park. Restrooms, showers, laundry facilities, a dump station, a pool, a clubhouse, horseshoe pits, shuffleboard courts, and a boat ramp are provided. The restrooms and clubhouse are wheelchair accessible. Children are welcome. Leashed pets under 25 pounds are permitted.

Reservations, fees: Reservations are recommended. Sites are $32–36 per night for two people, plus $2.50 for each extra person. Credit cards are accepted. Long-term rates are available.

Directions: From I-75, take Exit 250 east and drive 0.25 mile to the park.

Contact: Alafia River RV Resort, 9812 Gibsonton Drive, Riverview, FL 33569, 813/677-1997 or 800/555-4384, www.alafiariverrvresort.com.

13 RICE CREEK RV RESORT

Scenic rating: 7

in Riverview

The park attracts snowbirds with its paved, lighted streets, a mix of sunny and shady sites with concrete patios, and a tree canopy of massive oaks. All sorts of recreational facilities are available, including craft and pool rooms and a lounge. Entertainers are booked into the 15,000-square-foot clubhouse. Groceries, restaurants, and golf courses are nearby.

RV sites, facilities: The RV resort has 573 full-hookup sites. Cable TV, telephone service, restrooms, showers, laundry facilities, a heated pool, a whirlpool tub, a clubhouse, an exercise room, a library, horseshoe pits, and shuffleboard courts are available. Campers over age 55 are preferred; children are allowed for short visits. Leashed pets are permitted.

Reservations, fees: Reservations are required in winter and recommended the rest of the year.

Sites are $26 per night for two people, plus $2.50 for each additional person. Credit cards are accepted. Long-term rates are available.

Directions: From I-75, take Exit 250 and drive east on Gibsonton Drive/Boyette Road for one mile to U.S. 301. Turn south and drive 0.25 mile to the park, which is on the left.

Contact: Rice Creek RV Resort, 10714 U.S. 301 South, Riverview, FL 33569, 813/677-6640, fax 813/677-1373, www.rvresorts.com.

14 ALAFIA RIVER STATE PARK

Scenic rating: 10

east of Riverview

BEST (

These 6,879 acres were once a phosphate mine. Today, this land is becoming famed as the site of some of the best mountain-bike trails in Florida. But the news for everyone else is that campers, equestrians, and canoeists will find a home here, too. The park was originally opened for day use only in 1998, but in 2003 a campground was completed. There is a ranger station on-site and a picnic area. The park has 14 miles of off-road biking for users of varying skills (in the parlance of one biker, the red markers for advanced users really do mean "advanced"). Horseback riders can meander around on 16 miles of trails, and there are 4 miles of hiking paths. The park fronts onto 12 miles of the Alafia River's south prong, and the canoeing is considered quite good.

RV sites, facilities: Thirty campsites with water and 30/50-amp electricity also have grills, fire rings, and picnic tables. RVs up to 55 feet long and slide-outs can be accommodated. Fifteen sites are drive-through. Facilities include restrooms, showers, and paved roads. The bathhouse and office are wheelchair accessible. Groceries and restaurants are within eight miles. Children are welcome. Leashed pets are permitted.

Reservations, fees: Reservations are recommended; contact ReserveAmerica at 800/336-3521 or reserveamerica.com. Sites are $18 per night for up to eight people. Credit cards are accepted. The maximum length of stay is 14 days.

Directions: From southbound I-75, take Exit 246 east on Big Bend Road for one mile. At U.S. 301, turn south for 1.5 miles. Turn east onto County Road 672 and drive 12 miles. Turn north onto County Road 39 and proceed 1.5 miles to the park on the right side. If traveling north, take I-75 Exit 240 and drive east on State Road 674 for 15 miles. At County Road 39, turn north and drive five miles to the park. From the east, take I-45 westbound to Exit 22. Turn left onto Park Road and proceed 2.5 miles. Bear right onto 39B. Turn left onto State Road 39 (also known as James Redman Parkway) and drive 15 miles to the park on the left side.

Contact: Alafia River State Park, 14502 South County Road 39, Lithia, FL 33547, 813/672-5132, www.floridastateparks.org.

15 E. G. SIMMONS PARK
🏊 🎣 🚤 🏕 🐎 🚐 ⛺

Scenic rating: 8

west of Ruskin

Views of sparkling-blue Tampa Bay are marvelous from several places in this 469-acre park, but the camping areas are set in mangroves and overlook a bayou. There's a swimming beach about one mile away from the campsites. Fish from the piers or launch your boat at the ramp. Like many Florida parks so close to urban areas, the spot gets a lot of use on weekends and holidays. You can camp in two separate loops. Shade and privacy are minimal.

RV sites, facilities: All 88 sites in this Hillsborough County park have water; 70 have electricity. Picnic tables, grills, fire rings, restrooms, showers, a dump station, a boat ramp, and a playground are provided. Children are welcome. Leashed pets are permitted.

Reservations, fees: Reservations are not accepted. Sites are $16 per night. Credit cards are not accepted. The maximum stay is 14 days.

Directions: From I-75, take Exit 240 and drive west on State Road 674 for three miles. At U.S. 41, turn north and go one mile. Head west on 19th Avenue Northeast about two miles to the park.

Contact: E. G. Simmons Park, 2401 19th Avenue Northwest, Ruskin, FL 33570, 813/671-7655. Hillsborough County Parks and Recreation Administrative Office: 1101 East River Cove Street, Tampa, FL 33604, 813/975-2160, www.hillsboroughcounty.org/parks.

16 HAWAIIAN ISLES
🏊 🎣 🐎 ♿ 🚐

Scenic rating: 7

outside of Ruskin on Bay Road

The Hawaiian mystique sells, even in tropical Florida. The lighted, paved roads in this RV park boast names like Aloha Boulevard, Waikiki Way, and Leilani Lane, but don't look too closely for hula girls except on the park brochure. The Wilder Resort Parks chain understands its market—snowbirds who want a resort experience combined with cruise-ship style luxuries. Hawaiian Isles scores with an Olympic-sized swimming pool (heated, of course), a two-story "sky lounge" cabana overlooking the pool, a whopping 33-unit laundry room, two huge recreation halls with card and billiard rooms, a one-mile nature trail, 16 championship shuffleboard courts, and many waterfront campsites. The park overlooks Cockroach Bay and canals. Golf courses and tennis courts are a short distance away. Reserve early because campers tend to reserve for next winter before they leave at season's end.

RV sites, facilities: This mobile-home/RV park has 1,000 full-hookup sites with 30/50-amp electrical service. Cable TV, telephone service, restrooms, showers, two enormous recreation halls, a pool, a whirlpool, horseshoe pits, shuffleboard courts, and laundry facilities are available. Adult campers are preferred; children are allowed for short visits. Pets under 25 pounds are permitted.

Reservations, fees: Reservations are recommended. Sites are $26 per night for two people, plus $2.50 for each additional person. Credit cards are accepted. Long-term stays are okay.
Directions: From I-75, take Exit 240 and drive west on State Road 674 for three miles. Turn south on U.S. 41 and drive two miles to the park.
Contact: Hawaiian Isles, 4120 Cockroach Bay Road, Ruskin, FL 33570, 813/645-1098, www .rvresorts.com.

17 HIDE-A-WAY RV RESORT

Scenic rating: 7

in Ruskin

BEST (

Set on the Little Manatee River, the park is laid out lengthwise to take maximum advantage of the waterfront. At the heart of the park is a pool, a recreation room, a fishing pier, and a campfire circle. About 25 percent of the park is occupied year-round. There's room for 34 boats to tie up at the docks, and the river offers access to Tampa Bay and the Gulf of Mexico. Golfing, flea markets, and Sun City Center are nearby.

RV sites, facilities: All 307 RV sites have full hookups; 257 have 30-amp electrical service, and 50 have 50-amp. Sites vary in size. They can accommodate rigs up to 40 feet long and slide-outs. A wireless Internet connection is available in the library. On the premises are picnic tables, restrooms, showers, a dump station, recreation hall, a boat ramp, docks, a pool, a whirlpool tub, horseshoe pits, shuffleboard courts, a fishing pier, and laundry facilities (most areas are wheelchair accessible). Streets are paved. Groceries and restaurants are seven miles away. Children are welcome. A maximum of two pets are permitted, provided they stand no taller than 18 inches at the shoulder.

Reservations, fees: Reservations are required. Sites are $28 per night for two people, plus $2 for each additional person and $2 if you use

air-conditioning. Credit cards are accepted. Long-term rates are available.
Directions: From I-75, take Exit 240 and drive west on State Road 674 for three miles. Turn south on U.S. 41 and drive 2.5 miles to Chaney Road, then go east on Chaney to the park.
Contact: Hide-A-Way RV Resort, 2206 Chaney Road, Ruskin, FL 33570, 813/645-6037 or 800/607-2532, www.hideawayrvresort.com.

18 LITTLE MANATEE RIVER STATE PARK

Scenic rating: 10

south of Wimauma

Opened in 1987, this little-known state park has modern facilities on the Little Manatee River, a narrow, tannin-stained tributary that widens as it flows southwest to the Gulf of Mexico. Rent canoes from Canoe Outpost just north of the park on U.S. 301, or bring your own. The campsites are nestled in a sand pine scrub forest, with lush screening from your neighbors. There's plenty to do here: In addition to canoeing, check out the 6.5-mile hiking trail (part of the Florida National Trail), which skirts the park's northern wilderness area, or explore on horseback. Ten miles of horseback trails wind through the rest of the park. You might see bobcats roaming remote areas in the 2,416-acre park.

RV sites, facilities: This park has 34 sites with water, electricity, picnic tables, grills, and fire rings. Ten sites have 50-amp electrical service; the rest have 30-amp. Sites average 24–50 feet wide, and some can accommodate RVs up to 50 feet long and slide-outs. None of the sites are drive-through. Restrooms, showers, a dump station, a canoe ramp, canoe rentals, a playground, a nature trail, and horse stalls are available. The campground, picnic area, and restrooms are wheelchair accessible. Groceries are within five miles. Children are welcome. Pets are permitted with proof of vaccination.

A primitive backpacking site is also available; hikers must obtain a permit at the ranger station. In addition, four campsites are set aside for equestrians.

Reservations, fees: Reservations are recommended; contact ReserveAmerica at 800/336-3521 or reserveamerica.com. Sites are $18 per night for up to eight people. Credit cards are accepted. The maximum stay is 14 days.

Directions: From I-75, take Exit 240 and drive east on State Road 674 for six miles. In Wimauma, turn south on U.S. 301 and drive five miles. At Lightfoot Road, turn west and go 0.2 mile to the park.

Contact: Little Manatee River State Park, 215 Lightfoot Road, Wimauma, FL 33598, 813/671-5005, fax 813/671-5009, www.floridastateparks.org.

SARASOTA/ BRADENTON

BEST RV PARKS AND CAMPGROUNDS

◖ Families
Arcadia's Peace River Campground, page 380

◖ Privately Owned Beachfront RV Parks
Gulf Beach Campground, page 382

The barrier island beauty of St. Petersburg

and Clearwater continues in Sarasota, yet the region retains its own unique flavor. Visitors can enter the area at the southern end of the Sunshine Skyway Bridge (I-275), a spectacular, almost dizzying drive that takes motorists 150 feet above the waters of Tampa Bay. The RV parks in this region are generally divided among family-oriented beach destinations and wintertime homes for older visitors who come every year to get out of the cold. A handful of superb parks in natural settings add a third element here.

In 1539, Spanish explorer Hernando de Soto landed with 600 soldiers near what is now Bradenton with a mandate to colonize Florida for Spain. The effort was the first large-scale European mission into North America, and the National Park Service commemorates this spot at the De Soto National Memorial in Bradenton. Visitors should include a trip to the Gamble Plantation State Historic Site, the last surviving antebellum mansion in the southern half of the state. Today, the house is furnished in the manner of the mid-19th century and depicts the lifestyle of the times.

Sarasota is the state's cultural center, and its downtown contains an opera house, theaters, and art galleries. The John and Mable Ringling Museum of Art is here as well, and displays contemporary pieces and baroque works. Ringling, of circus fame, lived in Sarasota and was also an avid art collector.

Sarasota-area attractions include the Mote Marine Science Aquarium and the Pelican Man Bird Sanctuary, both within 20 miles. The aquarium includes a shark tank among its exhibits; the sanctuary rehabilitates injured birds. Also nearby are the Lionel Train Museum, the Sarasota Classic Car Museum, Jungle Gardens, a dog-racing track, Sunken Gardens, and Busch Gardens.

For a beach experience, check out Gulf Beach Campground on Siesta Key at the Gulf of Mexico. The much-lauded beaches are renowned for their white and powdery sand. RVers can watch from the campground as pelicans skim above the water's surface, or they can head down to the beach to tan, build sand castles, or play in the surf. The gentle waves are perfect for kids.

Escape the busy traffic of U.S. 41 at Oscar Scherer State Park in the nearby town of Osprey, exchanging the strip shopping centers, auto dealerships, and commercial chaos for 1,384 acres of woods and tranquillity. The park, which has a freshwater swimming lake and a tidal creek for canoeing, is also home to many endangered animals.

Farther inland, the Myakka River and Peace River run eastward into agricultural lands and undeveloped areas, as well as some outstanding places to canoe, kayak, or relax in the woods. The Myakka River, one of only two designated Wild and Scenic rivers in Florida, runs through one of Florida's largest state parks. Myakka River State Park is 28,875 acres and is noted for its wide variety and number of birds, especially turkeys and hawks, as well as wildlife. Wildlife tours are offered by tram and boat; guests may see alligators, deer, bobcats, and cottontail rabbits.

Traveling southward to Punta Gorda, RVers will find tranquil destinations along the Gulf of Mexico, such as Anna Maria Island and Longboat Key. Golf courses are within easy driving distance, and groceries and restaurants are close.

At the eastern border of the region, the privately owned Arcadia's Peace River Campground gives you the conveniences of full-service RV camping and access to vast acres of wild beauty of the Peace River, considered one of the best canoeing routes in the state.

St Petersburg
page 340

see
Tampa
page 354

ST PETERSBURG

Hillsborough
Bay

Gibsonton

Brandon

Mulberry

Barte

Tampa Bay

Ruskin

Fort Mea

Mullet
Key

Parrish

Bowling Green

Palmetto

Manatee River

Bradenton

Lake
Manatee

Wauchula

Longboat
Key

Zolfo Springs

Sarasota

Lido Key

Siesta Key

Myakka City

Osprey

Lake
Myakka

Myakka River
State Park

Lower
Lake
Myakka

Casey Key

Arcadia

Nokomis
Venice

Nocatee

North Port

Fort Ogden

Mexico

Gulf of

Port Charlotte

Englewood

El Jobean

Charlotte
Harbor
Punta Gorda

see
Lake Okeechobe
page 396

Boca Grande

Charlotte
Harbor

see
Fort Myers/
Naples
page 438

Bokeelia

Pine
Island

Pineland

North Fort
Myers

**SARASOTA/
BRADENTON**

AL GA

Gulf

of

Mexico

© AVALON TRAVEL PUBLISHING,

1 FROG CREEK CAMPGROUND AND RV PARK

Scenic rating: 6

in Palmetto

Steady improvements have been made to this all-ages park since 2000, including a heated pool and a 100- by 100- foot, fenced dog-play area A fishing stream runs through the park, which is a short drive from the beaches, deep-sea fishing, museums, and other attractions. The managers maintain a blog on the Internet so visitors can keep in touch with the latest news. About one-third of the sites are occupied year-round. The location is near the Sunshine Skyway Bridge (I-275), a spectacular, almost dizzying drive that takes motorists 150 feet above the waters of Tampa Bay. Also nearby is the site where explorer Hernando de Soto and 600 soldiers landed in 1539 with a mandate to colonize Florida for Spain. The National Park Service, which says that the effort was the first large-scale European mission into North America, commemorates this spot at the De Soto National Memorial in Bradenton (941/792-0458).

RV sites, facilities: RVers can choose from 173 grassy or gravel lots with 30-amp or 50-amp electrical service, concrete pads, and picnic tables. A wireless Internet network is available in the clubhouse and at most of the campsites. RVs up to 45 feet long and slide-outs can be accommodated. Sixteen sites are pull-through. On the premises are restrooms, showers, laundry facilities, a dump station, shuffleboard courts, horseshoe pits, a dog field, and a recreation hall. All areas are wheelchair accessible. Groceries, restaurants, and malls are within five miles. A boat ramp is within one mile. Children under 16 are welcome, but they must be supervised by an adult in public areas. Leashed pets are permitted.

Reservations, fees: Reservations are recommended. Sites are $30 per night for two people, plus $3 for each additional person, $3 for electricity, and $1 for pets. Credit cards are accepted. Long-term stays are okay.

Directions: From I-75, take Exit 228 and drive one mile west on I-275. Exit northbound on U.S. 41 and continue 0.5 mile to Bayshore Road. Turn west and drive 0.6 mile.

Contact: Frog Creek Campground and RV Park, 8515 Bayshore Road, Palmetto, FL 34221, 941/722-6154 or 800/771-3764, www.frogcreekrv.com.

2 FIESTA GROVE RV RESORT

Scenic rating: 6

in Palmetto

This park, once a citrus grove, is dotted with orange trees, and guests are welcome to pick and eat the fruit. Activities in the recreation hall include aerobics, line dancing, card games, bingo, ice-cream socials, bowling, bicycle rides, bus trips, and coffees.

RV sites, facilities: Most of the 220 lots are taken by park models, but about one-third are RV sites. The RVers have full hookups and cable TV, except in 15 sites that have water and electricity only. Restrooms, showers, laundry facilities, a heated pool, shuffleboard, boccie ball (lawn bowling), a wheelchair-accessible recreation hall, and a dump station are available. Children under 17 must be supervised in public areas. Pets are permitted.

Reservations, fees: Reservations are recommended. Sites are $24 per night for two people, plus $1.50 for each additional person and $1 for cable TV. Credit cards are not accepted. Long-term stays are okay.

Directions: From I-75, take Exit 228 and drive one mile west on I-275. Exit northbound on U.S. 41 and continue 0.5 mile to Bayshore Road. Turn west and drive 0.5 mile.

Contact: Fiesta Grove RV Resort, 8615 Bayshore Road, Palmetto, FL 34221, 941/722-7661.

3 TERRA CEIA VILLAGE RV RESORT

Scenic rating: 4

in Palmetto

Oak trees and lush landscaping enhance the park grounds, which also contain a stocked pond for fishing. It's an adult-oriented, 15-acre resort that is 12 miles from the beach and is close to golf courses, Indian Mound Park, and the Sunshine Skyway Bridge. Planned activities are held November–mid-April. About two-thirds of the sites are occupied year-round.

RV sites, facilities: Sixty of the 203 RV lots are available to travelers and offer full hookups, including 30-amp and 50-amp electrical service, cable TV, and telephone access. Six sites are pull-through. RVs up to 45 feet long and slide-outs can be accommodated. On the premises are restrooms, showers, laundry facilities, a dump station, a heated pool, a stocked pond, horseshoes, shuffleboard, boccie ball (lawn bowling), and a clubhouse. The bathhouse, clubhouse, and pool area are wheelchair accessible. Streets are paved. A convenience store is at the corner. The nearest restaurant is about two miles away; a supermarket is about five miles away. Children are welcome for short-term visits. Leashed pets are permitted.

Reservations, fees: Reservations are required. Sites are $32 per night for two people, plus $5 for each additional person. Credit cards are accepted. Year-round stays are okay.

Directions: From I-75, take Exit 228 and go west to U.S. 41 (Exit 1). Go north on U.S. 41 for 0.75 mile to the park, at left.

Contact: Terra Ceia Village RV Resort, 9303 Bayshore Road, Palmetto, FL 34221, 941/729-4422, www.rvonthego.com.

4 WINTERSET PARK

Scenic rating: 4

in Palmetto

Frog Creek, a fishing stream, borders the property. Several golf courses and driving ranges are within a few minutes' drive of this over-age-55 manufactured-home and RV community, where park models are for sale. About 15 percent of the sites are occupied year-round. Most visitors come from Canada, Ohio, Michigan, Iowa, Maine, Massachusetts, Kentucky, Tennessee, and New York. Planned activities during the winter season include bingo, potluck dinners, crafts, wood carving, golf, day trips, cards, Bible study, church services, and games. Nearby is the Gamble Plantation State Historic Site (941/723-4536), the last surviving antebellum mansion in the southern half of the state. It was originally the home of Major Robert Gamble, an early settler who built a 3,500-acre sugar plantation on the banks of the Manatee River. The home is also notable for providing refuge to the Confederate secretary of state, Judah P. Benjamin, after the fall of the Confederacy. Today, the house is furnished in the manner of the mid-19th century and depicts the lifestyle of the times.

RV sites, facilities: Out of a total of 213 sites, 6 are available for overnighters. They overlook the tennis courts and horseshoes area. Campsites have full hookups, concrete patios, and picnic tables. Lot size is 30 by 40 feet, and RVs up to 40 feet long and slide-outs can be accommodated. Facilities include restrooms, showers, laundry facilities, shuffleboard courts, two pools, a wheelchair-accessible recreation room, tennis courts, and a dog-walk area. A wireless Internet connection is available in the clubhouse and a few other places in the park. All areas are wheelchair accessible. Grocery stores and restaurants are within five miles. This is an adults-only park. Pets under 25 pounds are allowed.

Reservations, fees: Reservations are recommended. Sites are $28 per night for two people, plus $1.75 per additional person. Credit cards are not accepted. Long-term rates are available.

Directions: From I-75, take Exit 228 and drive one mile west on I-275. Exit northbound on U.S. 41 and continue 0.5 mile to the park.

Contact: Winterset Park, 8515 U.S. 41 North, Palmetto, FL 34221, 941/722-4884, fax 941/722-5820, www.wintersetrvresort.com.

5 FISHERMAN'S COVE RESORT

Scenic rating: 4

near Palmetto

Don't forget to pack your racquet because this is one of the few RV parks in Florida to have tennis courts right on the property. If that's not your game, then launch your boat from the campground boat ramp and you'll be right on Terra Ceia Bay, which has access to Tampa Bay and the Gulf of Mexico. St. Petersburg is a quick ride away over the spectacular Sunshine Skyway Bridge, which soars 150 feet above the water. Golf courses are within easy driving distance, and groceries and restaurants are within two miles. Social programs are held in the recreation hall year-round. Campsites are grassy with concrete pads and are large enough to accommodate even bigger rigs; however, there are no pull-through sites. About two-thirds of the park is occupied by year-round residents. Most visitors come from New England, Michigan, and Florida.

RV sites, facilities: All 80 RV lots have full hookups with 30/50-amp electrical service, cable TV, and telephone access. RVs up to 38 feet long and slide-outs can be accommodated. An Internet connection is available in the clubhouse. On the premises are restrooms, showers, a dump station, laundry facilities, a heated pool with a whirlpool tub, a boat ramp, tennis courts, a clubhouse, exercise and game rooms, and a tiki hut for camp gatherings. A full social calendar in the winter season includes arts and crafts and other activities; in the summertime, organized events are more limited. All areas are wheelchair accessible. Streets are paved. Children may visit for short periods. Pets are permitted.

Reservations, fees: Reservations are recommended. Sites are $40 per night for two people, plus $2 for each additional person. Credit cards are accepted. Long-term rates are available.

Directions: Southbound on the Sunshine Skyway Bridge (I-275/U.S. 19), continue two miles south from the toll plaza to the park, set on the east side of U.S. 19 after you cross Terra Ceia Bay. Northbound on I-275, turn south at U.S. 41 and drive 2.3 miles. At U.S. 19, drive north one mile. The park is just before the Sunshine Skyway Bridge toll plaza.

Contact: Fisherman's Cove Resort, 100 Palmview Road, Palmetto, FL 34221, 941/729-3685, fax 941/721-0614, www.myfishermanscove.com.

6 TROPIC ISLES MOBILE HOME PARK

Scenic rating: 4

in Palmetto

As a visitor at Tropic Isles Mobile Home Park, you automatically earn the privilege of using the permanent boating facilities and marina, just as long-term residents do. Boaters will appreciate the location: access to the Gulf of Mexico and its fishing grounds is first-rate. The open and sunny park overlooks Terra Ceia Bay, and many sites are waterfront. During the winter, the clubhouse buzzes with activity, with weekly social hours (coffee and doughnuts are served), potluck suppers, game nights, bingo, and card parties. There's even an auditorium with a stage for large functions. The park has a bus that takes residents out for weekly shopping trips; group outings to local attractions are also available. Note that bicycles have the right-of-way on the park's paved roads. About 30 percent of the park is occupied year-round. Most visitors hail from Ohio, Michigan, Wisconsin, and

Canada. Lots and mobile homes are for sale; many permanent residents run their own businesses from their homes.

RV sites, facilities: All lots in this adults-only, 362-unit mobile-home park have full hookups and concrete patios. Twenty-four sites are for RVs up to 40 feet long and slide-outs; seven are drive-through. RVs must be self-contained; there are no showers or restrooms. On the premises are a heated pool, 12 championship shuffleboard courts, horseshoe pits, a clubhouse, a wheelchair-accessible auditorium and yacht club, a boat ramp, docks, a marina, a grocery store, laundry facilities, and a beauty parlor. For cable TV and telephone service, you must call the proper utility. Only people age 55 and older are welcome as campers, but children may visit for short periods. Small, leashed pets are permitted but must not be tied outside units.

Reservations, fees: Reservations are recommended. Sites are $40 per night for two people, plus $5 per extra person. Credit cards are not accepted. Stays up to six months are allowed.

Directions: From I-75, take Exit 224 westbound on U.S. 301 and drive 10.5 miles to the park, at right.

Contact: Tropic Isles Mobile Home Park, 3100 10th Street West, Palmetto, FL 34221, 941/721-8888, fax 941/729-0687, www.tropicisles.org.

▇ ELLENTON GARDENS TRAVEL RESORT

Scenic rating: 3

in Ellenton

For people who like to shop, this 16-acre park is a find. Factory outlets, malls, and all manner of other stores are nearby. Even doctors' offices, a hospital, and a library are within one mile. A small fishing lake lies at the center of the park, which is home to a lot of semipermanent trailers and manufactured homes. Activities held in the recreation hall include exercise and arts-and-crafts classes, line dancing, and bingo. Campsites have concrete pads fronting paved roads.

RV sites, facilities: All 196 sites have full hookups with 30-amp electrical service, optional telephone service, and cable TV. About 70 sites are available for overnight or short visits. RVs must be self-contained. Restrooms, showers, laundry facilities, a heated pool, shuffleboard courts, a lake, a dump station, and a recreation hall are on-site. Grocery stores are within 0.75 mile. All areas are wheelchair accessible. Children are welcome for short-term visits only. Small dogs and cats are permitted.

Reservations, fees: Reservations are recommended. Sites are $32 per night for two people, plus $2 for each additional person. Credit cards are not accepted. Long-term rates are available.

Directions: From I-75, take Exit 224 and head northeast on U.S. 301 for 1.4 miles to the park entrance on the left side of the road.

Contact: Ellenton Gardens Travel Resort, 7310 U.S. 301 North, Ellenton, FL 34222, 941/722-0341, fax 941/723-6121.

▇ PALM BAY RV PARK

Scenic rating: 3

north of Bradenton

A private walk provides pedestrian access from this adult-oriented park to a large shopping center. Churches and the Manatee Memorial Hospital are within one mile. This park is geared toward senior citizens who are staying 3–4 months at a time.

RV sites, facilities: These 78 full-hookup RV spots are set inside a 164-unit, adult-oriented mobile-home park. Sites have 30-amp electrical service and vary in size. Some lots can accommodate RVs up to 40 feet long. Facilities include restrooms, showers, a laundry room, a pool, a billiard and card room, shuffleboard courts, and a clubhouse. Children may stay a maximum of two weeks. Pets aren't allowed, not even with visitors.

Reservations, fees: Reservations are recommended. Sites are $25 per night for two people, plus $2 for each additional person. Credit cards are not accepted. Long-term stays are okay.

Directions: From I-75, take Exit 224 and drive west on U.S. 301 for 3.1 miles. The park is 0.25 mile west of U.S. 41.

Contact: Palm Bay RV Park, 751 10th Street East, Palmetto, FL 34221, 941/722-7048.

⁹ WINTER QUARTERS MANATEE RV RESORT

Scenic rating: 9

near Bradenton

Spotless sites with concrete pads and patios are arranged in a circle around 17-acre Lake Mohoina, which is stocked with fish. Four spots are pull-through, and unlike many private RV parks in Florida, this 70-acre alternative has picnic tables at each site. An activities director keeps campers busy during the winter with games and other recreation in the two-story clubhouse. Among the more unusual planned activities are stained-glass classes. A small boat ramp puts you on the Manatee River, which accesses the Gulf of Mexico. Restaurants, shops, and a golf course are within one or two miles. Most visitors come from Canada, Michigan, Ohio, New York, Indiana, and West Virginia.

RV sites, facilities: All 200 RV sites have picnic tables and full hookups, with 50-amp electrical service, cable TV, and telephone availability. RVs up to 45 feet long can be accommodated, as well as slide-outs. Some sites are waterfront. Lot size averages 25 by 60 feet. A wireless Internet connection is available in the clubhouse and in parts of the park. On the premises are two heated pools, a spa, a clubhouse, picnic area, restrooms, showers, a small boat ramp, an exercise and game room, horseshoes, billiards, limited supplies, a lake, a dump station,

and golf nets. All areas are wheelchair accessible. Children are permitted. Leashed pets are permitted.

Reservations, fees: Reservations are recommended. Sites are $26–60 per night. Credit cards are accepted. Long-term rates are available.

Directions: From I-75, take Exit 220 westbound 0.5 mile on State Road 64 to Kay Road. Turn northeast and drive 0.9 mile to the park entrance on the left.

Contact: Winter Quarters Manatee RV Resort, 800 Kay Road Northeast, Bradenton, FL 34212, 239/745-2600 or 800/678-2131, fax 239/748-8964, www.rvonthego.com.

¹⁰ LAKE MANATEE STATE PARK

Scenic rating: 10

on the south shore of Lake Manatee

The thickly landscaped camping area is within walking distance of Lake Manatee's swimming area and a playground. Although the shrubs are not tall enough to provide shade, they form a dense screen between each site, so you'll feel secluded from your neighbor. There are 30 sites on each of two campground loops, further promoting a sense of privacy. Groceries and laundry facilities are nine miles away. The 2,400-acre lake, which is part of the reservoir that supplies drinking water to Manatee and Sarasota Counties, is ideal for canoeing and fishing. Note that boat motors are limited to 20 horsepower. A grassy beach slopes gently down to the water in the swimming area. Watch out for alligators, the park rangers warn. The gators are monitored but not fenced. If you see one near the beach, report it to the office, and, of course, don't harass it. A one-mile-long nature trail offers a chance to learn more about the park's biological communities: flat woods and sand-pine scrub. Among the animals regularly seen in the park are cottontail and marsh rabbits, cotton rats, and gray squirrels.

Occasionally, you may see bobcats, gray foxes, and deer.

RV sites, facilities: There are 60 sites with water and 30-amp electricity. RVs up to 40 feet long and slide-outs can be accommodated. Restrooms, showers, picnic tables, fire rings, grills, a playground, a boat ramp, a dock, a nature trail, and a dump station are provided. Boats are available for rent. One campsite, the bathhouse, docks, and office are wheelchair accessible. Groceries and restaurants are five miles away. Children are welcome. Pets are permitted with proof of vaccination.

Reservations, fees: Reservations are recommended; contact ReserveAmerica at 800/336-3521 or reserveamerica.com. Sites are $18 per night for four people. Credit cards are accepted. Stays are limited to two weeks.

Directions: From I-75, take Exit 220 eastbound nine miles on State Road 64 to the park on the left.

Contact: Lake Manatee State Park, 20007 State Road 64, Bradenton, FL 34212, 941/741-3028 (3 P.M.–5 P.M.), fax 941/741-3486, www.floridastateparks.org.

11 SARASOTA BAY TRAVEL TRAILER PARK

Scenic rating: 4

in Bradenton

The park's Friendship Hall offers pool tables, table tennis, and a full schedule of social activities, including a computer club with classes for new users. Campers can build things in the woodworking shop, tinker with their boats, or work out in the exercise room, which is stocked with Nautilus equipment. A public beach is one mile away, and managers are considering plans to build a pool in the coming years. The park overlooks Sarasota Bay, where pelicans and seagulls wheel and turn in the breeze. Follow the bay by boat, and it leads to the ocean. Most guests leave their

rigs here year-round, and many have added carports, porches, and screened rooms to their trailers. Located in a suburban neighborhood on a main road leading to the beach, the neatly kept park is near shops and restaurants. Its roads are paved, and Norfolk pines and queen palms provide a little greenery. If you hail from Michigan or Canada, and come to escape the frigid winters, you'll find plenty of fellow campers from your neck of the woods. This park is part of a mobile-home community called Paradise Bay.

RV sites, facilities: There are 241 spots in this park, with about 60 full hookup sites available for overnighters and seasonal visitors. Most folks stay for winter and leave their rigs on-site during the summer; around 25 people live in the park year-round. All sites have 50-amp electrical service. RVs up to 45 feet long and slide-outs can be accommodated. An Internet connection is available in the clubhouse. Restrooms, showers, laundry facilities, a recreation hall, shuffleboard courts, horseshoe pits, boat ramps, a boat repair area, docks, an exercise room, and a woodworking shop are available. The bathhouse, clubhouse, and office are wheelchair accessible. Streets are paved. Restaurants and groceries are within two miles. Children may visit for up to two weeks for $2 per person per night. Pets are prohibited.

Reservations, fees: Reservations are recommended. Sites are $40 per night for two people, plus $2 for each additional person. Credit cards are not accepted. Long-term rates are available. The maximum length of stay is six months.

Directions: From I-75, take Exit 217 and drive west on State Road 70 for about 11 miles to State Road 684/Cortez Road. Turn left. Drive two miles west to the park entrance, at left.

Contact: Sarasota Bay Travel Trailer Park, 10777 Cortez Road West, Bradenton, FL 34210, 941/794-1200 or 800/247-8361, fax 941/761-0629, www.paradisebay-sarasota bayrvpark.com.

12 HOLIDAY COVE RV RESORT

Scenic rating: 5

in Cortez

Set in a stand of Australian pines and palm trees, this resort has water access to Sarasota Bay and the Intracoastal Waterway. Boat slips are available, and you can fish from the docks in the park. The long white-sand beaches of Anna Maria Island and Longboat Key are nearby, and you can walk to restaurants, shops, and the beachfront less than a mile away. Many visitors come for the season and park models are for rent, but this park is decidedly RV-oriented, with only 1 percent of its sites occupied by year-round residents. Most visitors from all over the nation, as well as the United Kingdom, Germany, and the Netherlands.

RV sites, facilities: All 112 sites have full hookups with electricity and cable TV. Lots vary in size, but rigs up to 42 feet and slide-outs can be accommodated. There's a wireless Internet connection in the clubhouse and at the sites. Restrooms, showers, picnic tables, a heated pool, shuffleboard courts, horseshoe pits, laundry facilities, a recreation hall, and a boat ramp are provided. A small camp store sells ice, camping supplies, and souvenirs. All areas are wheelchair accessible. Groceries and a restaurant are across the street. Children are welcome. Pets are permitted.

Reservations, fees: Reservations are recommended. Sites are $36–39 per night for two people, plus $5 for each additional person. Credit cards are accepted. Long-term rates are available. The maximum length of stay is six months.

Directions: From I-75, take Exit 217 and drive west on State Road 70 for 13 miles to Cortez Road. Turn left and drive five miles. The park entrance is on the north side.

Contact: Holiday Cove RV Resort, 11900 Cortez Road West/P.O. Box 713, Cortez, FL 34215, 941/792-1111 or 800/346-9224, fax 941-761-4662, www.holidaycoverv.com.

13 PLEASANT LAKE RV RESORT

Scenic rating: 4

in Bradenton

In the center of this sunny, manicured park is a rectangular man-made lake, which is stocked for bass fishing and has grassy slopes where campers pull ashore their johnboats. You'll have to confine your swimming to the pool, however. Like most bodies of freshwater in Florida, there's always a possibility that an alligator may be lurking nearby. Suitable for big RVs, the park has large sites with concrete pads and few trees to get in the way. A guardhouse and golf-cart patrols provide a feeling of security. Park models are for sale, and about 20 percent of the park is occupied year-round. Visitors hail from New York, Ohio, Michigan, New Hampshire, and Maine. Down the street is a large shopping plaza with a grocery store, restaurants, banks, and a gas station. Tourist attractions in the area include gulf beaches, the Ringling Museum of Art, the Gamble Plantation Historic Site, the Lionel Train Museum, Jungle Gardens, a dog-racing track, Sunken Gardens, and Busch Gardens.

RV sites, facilities: All 120 sites have full hookups with 30/50-amp electrical outlets. Telephone and cable TV service are available. A wireless Internet connection is available in the clubhouse. Lots are 40 by 50 feet, accommodating RVs up to 42 feet long and slide-outs. On the premises are restrooms, showers, laundry facilities, a pool, shuffleboard courts, horseshoe pits, boccie ball (lawn bowling) courts, a fishing lake, and a recreation room. The restrooms, laundry, and recreation room are wheelchair accessible. This is an over-age-55 park, but families with children may stay for up to two weeks. Leashed pets are permitted.

Reservations, fees: Reservations are recommended. Sites are $45 per night for two people, plus $2 for each additional person. Credit cards are accepted. Long-term rates are available.

Directions: From I-75, take Exit 217 and drive

west on State Road 70 for 0.3 mile to the park, which is on the north side of the road.
Contact: Pleasant Lake RV Resort, 6633 State Road 70 East, Bradenton, FL 34203, 941/756-5076 or 800/283-5076, www.pleasant lakervresort.com.

14 TROPICAL GARDENS RV PARK

Scenic rating: 2

in Bradenton

Although many of the units in this suburban park are permanent, overnighters are welcome at the 48 available spaces. Sites are small with concrete pads. During the winter, planned social activities in the clubhouse keep residents entertained, and church services are held on Sundays. The security gate is locked at night. About 60 percent of the park is occupied year-round. The location is convenient for exploring nearby tourist attractions, such as the Gamble Plantation Historic Site. Within a couple hours' drive are Sea World, Disney World, and Silver Springs.

RV sites, facilities: This park's 136 grassy, sunny, full-hookup sites have 30/50-amp electrical service and concrete patios. Telephone and cable TV access are available by arrangement with the local utilities. Lot sizes vary, but RVs up to 40 feet long and slide-outs can be accommodated. Twenty-five sites are drive-through. On the premises are restrooms, showers, a screened pool, shuffleboard, a dump station, laundry facilities, and a recreation hall. All areas are wheelchair accessible. Within two blocks are a supermarket, a drugstore, a medical center, and a restaurant. Adults are preferred, but children are allowed to visit. Leashed pets under 25 pounds are permitted.

Reservations, fees: Reservations are recommended. Sites are $30 per night for two people, plus $3 for each additional person. Credit cards are not accepted. Long-term rates are available.

Directions: From I-75, take Exit 217 (if you're southbound) or 217B (northbound) and drive west on State Road 70 for about six miles to the park, which is on the south side of the road, just past 15th Street East/Old 301 Boulevard.
Contact: Tropical Gardens RV Park, 1120 53rd Avenue East, Bradenton, FL 34203, 941/756-1135, www.tropicalgardensrv.com.

15 HORSESHOE COVE RESORT

Scenic rating: 7

in Bradenton

At the heart of this all-ages park is a lovely 12-acre island with a nature trail, picnic areas with barbecue grills, lighted fishing docks, boating facilities, and a gazebo. During the winter, there's plenty to do in the 2,000-square-foot recreation hall, including square dancing, quilting, wood carving, billiards, bingo, and social activities. In summer, kids can catch fish off the docks, swim in the pool, or ride bikes on the paved road. Some sites overlook the Braden River. Unlike many parks with security gates, this park's gate is secured 24 hours a day, not just at night. About 75 percent of the park is occupied by year-round residents.

RV sites, facilities: This all-ages park has 476 full-hookup sites, where 125 are available for RVs (no tents are permitted). Each has 50-amp electrical service, concrete patios, and picnic tables. A wireless Internet connection is available in the clubhouse and other parts of the park. For cable TV and telephone service, call the appropriate utility company. RVs up to 40 feet long and slide-outs can be accommodated. Restrooms, showers, laundry facilities, a recreation hall, a game room, a pool, a spa, shuffleboard, horseshoes, two fishing docks, boat docks, a picnic shelter and separate picnic area, and a nature trail are on the property. The bathhouse, clubhouse, office, pool area, and docks are wheelchair accessible. Streets are paved. Groceries are within two miles. Children are welcome for up to 30 days per year. Leashed pets are allowed if you get an RV spot in the pet section.

Reservations, fees: Reservations are recommended in winter. Sites are $27–42 per night for two people, plus $3 for each additional person. Credit cards are accepted. Long-term rates are available.

Directions: From I-75, take Exit 217 westbound on State Road 70 for 1.1 miles to the first traffic light at Caruso Road/60th Street East. Turn north and proceed to the park on the west side of the road.

Contact: Horseshoe Cove Resort, 5100 60th Street East, Bradenton, FL 34203, 941/758-5335 or 800/291-3446, www.horseshoecove .zzn.com.

16 LINGER LODGE RV RESORT

Scenic rating: 5

near Bradenton

Linger Lodge borders the Braden River, a peaceful stream where you'll see blue herons wading on the banks and other birds roosting in low overhanging branches. Anglers regularly hook bass, bluegill, crappie, and catfish. A few campsites are near the river, but travelers passing through tend to sleep at upland sites and have standard views of other trailers and park models. Fried "local farm-raised" alligator is the big seller at the unusual restaurant, which also offers seafood, sandwiches, and indoor and screened outdoor seating overlooking the river; it draws crowds on weekends, and you'll hear cars coming and going from 11 A.M. until closing time at 9 P.M. (8 P.M. on Sundays; the restaurant is closed on Mondays). The 10-acre park also contains a small aviary, which is home to peacocks and other exotic birds. The showers, restrooms, and laundry facilities are toward the back of the building that houses the restaurant. Also on display is a stuffed "short-horned deer," which has a story behind it: In 1992, a

hurricane picked up a Florida deer and swept it off to Texas, where it bred with a long-horned steer. A Texas tornado then allegedly blew the rare offspring back to Linger Lodge. About 75 percent of the park is occupied year-round.

RV sites, facilities: One-hundred sites have full hookups with 30-amp electrical service, concrete pads, and picnic tables. Five sites have 50-amp electricity. The number of sites available for overnighters varies. Rigs up to 40 feet can be accommodated. Restrooms, showers, laundry facilities, a dump station, a boat ramp, boat docks, a restaurant, and a store that sells ice, propane, and souvenirs are on the premises. The bathhouse and docks are wheelchair accessible. Groceries are within two miles. This is an adults-only park, but children are allowed to stay 15 days up to twice per year. Small, leashed pets are permitted in one section.

Reservations, fees: Reservations are recommended. Sites are $23 per night for two people, plus $2 for each extra person. Credit cards are accepted. Long-term rates are available.

Directions: From I-75, take Exit 217 and drive west on State Road 70 for 0.2 mile to Tara Boulevard. Turn south and drive four miles. Note that the road changes names to Linger Lodge Road, then turns sharply east and crosses I-75. At the stop sign at Oak Hammock Road, turn south and drive 0.3 mile into the park.

Contact: Linger Lodge RV Resort, 7205 Linger Lodge Road, Bradenton, FL 34202, 941/755-2757, fax 941/758-0718.

17 ARBOR TERRACE RV RESORT

Scenic rating: 4

in Bradenton

Located between Bradenton and Sarasota, this park has easy access to local attractions. Groceries and restaurants are within 0.5 mile. Road warriors can relax: Lots of spaces are pull-through. You'll also find some well-shaded spots. Mobile homes and park models are for sale.

RV sites, facilities: Set on 40 acres, the 402-unit resort has 189 available RV sites with full hookups; telephone service is available at most spots. On the premises are restrooms, showers, a dump station, horseshoe pits, shuffleboard courts, a pool, two recreation rooms, and laundry facilities. Campers of all ages are welcome. Pets are accepted.

Reservations, fees: Reservations are recommended. The fee for two people is $39 per night. Add $4 for each additional person. Credit cards are accepted. Long-term rates are available.

Directions: From I-75, take Exit 217 and drive west on State Road 70 for 10 miles. Turn south on U.S. 41 and continue one mile. At 57th Avenue West, turn left by the Red Lobster and drive east for about 0.25 mile.

Contact: Arbor Terrace RV Resort, 405 57th Avenue West, Bradenton, FL 34207, 941/755-6494 or 800/828-6992, fax 941/755-8177, www.suncommunities.com.

18 SUN-N-FUN RV RESORT

Scenic rating: 7

in Sarasota

As the name implies, the emphasis here is on fun. A full-time activities director coordinates dozens of programs each day for guests, most of whom are snowbirds and retired people from all over the United States, Canada, and England. They have plenty to choose from, including swimming in a heated Olympic-sized pool with two whirlpool tubs, exercising in the fitness center, fishing in the private lake, playing at the nine-hole miniature golf course, or lobbing tennis balls on the three lighted courts. Also offered are crafts classes, theme parties and dances, variety shows, and boccie (lawn bowling). The park has a total of 1,600 sites, many of them shaded by oaks, and is close to some RV service centers. Beaches are eight miles to the west, and shopping and outlet malls are within a 15-minute drive.

RV sites, facilities: The 1,600-unit resort park with park models and rental units has about 500 RV sunny sites with full hookups, concrete patios, and picnic tables. A wireless Internet network is available throughout the park. Restrooms, showers, laundry facilities, a dump station, several recreation rooms, rental units, a lake, two whirlpool tubs, a pool, an exercise room, horseshoe pits, rental trailers, The Sandbar Grill restaurant (open during the season), and courts for shuffleboard, volleyball, boccie ball (lawn bowling), and tennis, are on-site. Snacks, souvenirs, and propane are for sale. The clubhouse, office, and pool area are wheelchair accessible. Streets are paved. Groceries and restaurants are within two miles. All ages are welcome. Pets are allowed.

Reservations, fees: Reservations are recommended. Sites are $25–65 per night. Credit cards are accepted. The maximum stay is nine months. Long-term rates are available.

Directions: From I-75, take Exit 210 eastbound on Fruitville Road and drive one mile. The park is on the north side.

Contact: Sun-n-Fun RV Resort, 7125 Fruitville Road, Sarasota, FL 34240, 941/377-8250 or 800/843-2421, fax 941/378-4810, www.sun-nfunfl.com.

19 WINDWARD ISLE RV PARK

Scenic rating: 2

in Sarasota

The open and sunny park is convenient to the interstate for overnighters, but note that there is no bathhouse or dump station. Next door is a Waffle House, plus three fast-food joints. A golf course is across the street. A supermarket is about 0.25 mile away.

RV sites, facilities: This mobile-home park has 99 grassy, full-hookup sites with 50-amp electrical service for self-contained RVs. Just 30 are available for overnighters; the rest of the sites are taken by people who stay year-round or choose to leave their rigs during the hot summer months. There are no showers or restroom facilities. A pool, horseshoe pits, shuffleboard courts, laundry facilities, picnic tables, putting green, social programs, and a recreation room are available. Children may stay a maximum of 15 days, twice a year. Pets are prohibited.

Reservations, fees: Reservations are recommended. Sites are $30–40 per night for two people, plus $2 for each additional person. Credit cards are not accepted. Long-term stays are okay.

Directions: From I-75, take Exit 205 westbound on State Road 72. Drive 0.1 mile to the park on the north side of the road.

Contact: Windward Isle RV Park, 1 Catamaran Drive, Sarasota, FL 34233, 941/922-3090.

20 MYAKKA RIVER STATE PARK

🏃 🚲 🎣 🚐 👪 ♿ 🚍 ⛰

Scenic rating: 10

outside of Sarasota on the Myakka River

One of only two rivers in Florida designated as Wild and Scenic, the Myakka River is the centerpiece of this 28,875-acre state park, one of Florida's largest. Bird-watchers, canoeists, anglers, hikers, backpackers, horseback riders, and tourists flock here year-round to experience nature close at hand. The park is especially noted for its wide variety and large number of birds, especially turkeys and hawks, although many other forms of wildlife abound, including alligators, deer, bobcats, and cottontail rabbits. In fact, one-fourth of the park is a wilderness preserve open to a limited number of users.

Because it's so popular, the two main campgrounds seem to squeeze everyone together, but the park does provide fast, easy access to canoeing, mountain-biking and hiking trails, the boat basin, tram tours of the hammocks and river floodplain, and airboat tours. An elevated, 125-foot walkway allows a good view of the forest tree canopy. The river flows 34 miles through the park and widens into two large lakes. Don't think about taking a dip, though, because no swimming is permitted anywhere. You'll understand why when you realize that the "log" right next to your canoe is actually a huge alligator.

Anglers routinely catch bass, bream, and catfish. There's a boat ramp on Upper Myakka Lake, but the water is shallow and your keel should not have draw. A fishing pier is wheelchair-accessible. It's best to pick up supplies before you arrive; a snack bar operates within the park, but groceries and restaurants are 10–15 miles away. Wildlife tours are offered by tram and boat.

RV sites, facilities: The two campgrounds have a total of 76 sites for RVs. Sites have 30-amp electricity and water; they vary in size, but RVs up to 35 feet long can be accommodated. The Old Prairie Campground, the smallest of the two with 25 sites, also has five cabins for rent. The other campground, Big Flats, is about three miles from the main gate. Each campsite has a picnic table and a grill or fire ring/grill combination. Restrooms, showers, laundry facilities, a dump station, a playground, boat rentals, a boat ramp, and rental cabins are available. There are too many trees at most sites for a camper to use a satellite dish. The visitors center, restrooms, fishing pier, nature trail, picnic areas, and concession building are wheelchair accessible. A camp store sells ice, camping supplies, snacks, and souvenirs. Groceries are 15 miles away; restaurants are within 9 miles. Children are welcome, but pets are prohibited.

Reservations, fees: Reservations are recommended; contact ReserveAmerica at 800/336-3521 or reserveamerica.com. Sites are $22 for up to eight people. Electricity costs $2 per night. Credit cards are accepted. The maximum stay is 14 days.

Directions: From I-75, take Exit 205 eastbound on State Road 72 and drive nine miles to the park.

Contact: Myakka River State Park, 13207 State Road 72, Sarasota, FL 34241, 941/361-6511, fax 941/361-6501, www.floridastateparks.org.

21 ARCADIA'S PEACE RIVER CAMPGROUND

Scenic rating: 10

in Arcadia

BEST (

Ready for something amazing? You get the best of both worlds at this 151-acre private campground: the conveniences of full-service RV camping vast and vast acres of wild beauty of the Peace River. In addition to the RV section, which has a selection of shady and sunny sites, a whopping two-thirds of the park is left wild. At the center of the park are the mysterious-looking ruins of a chautauqua, an open-air stadium that burned down in the 1930s. The park also is laced with nature trails and dirt roads for walking and biking, and there's a dock on the river that offers a scenic overlook. Other recreational amenities include fishing, paddleboat rentals, and an 18-hole miniature golf course. An unusual feature is that you can go fossil hunting in the wilderness. Planned activities include the usual bingo and potlucks, but also dog parades and kids' games.

For the adventurous, canoe outfitters provide shuttle transportation and equipment for exploring and camping expeditions along the Peace River Canoe Trail, a popular 67-mile waterway that once marked the boundary between Indian territory on the east and pioneer settlements on the west. The river trail has swift-flowing narrows and occasional rapids, and is bordered by dense forests teeming with wildlife: wild hogs, armadillos, egrets, and the like. For more information and reservations, call Canoe Outpost at 863/494-1215 or Canoe Safari at 863/494-7865.

RV sites, facilities: The campground has 182 RV sites with full hookups, 30-amp electrical service, and picnic tables. Six sites have 50-amp service, and some sites have concrete patios. RVs up to 45 feet long and slide-outs can be accommodated in the park. On the premises are restrooms, showers, laundry facilities, a dump station, a convenience store, a pool, a play-ground, a fishing pond, a miniature golf course, a recreation room, horseshoe pits, shuffleboard courts, and two paintball fields. There are also a large number of wilderness sites without water, electricity, or other facilities (RVs are not allowed on these sites). The office, store, recreation hall, and restrooms are wheelchair accessible; in addition, you can rent golf carts to drive anywhere in the 150 acres. Children are welcome. Leashed pets are permitted.

Reservations, fees: Reservations are recommended. Sites are $39 per night for two people, plus $5 for each additional person over age 12, and $3 for using air conditioners or electric heaters. Credit cards are accepted. Long-term stays are okay.

Directions: From southbound I-75, take Exit 217 onto State Road 70 and drive 38 miles east to the park, at the junction of State Road 72. From northbound I-75, take Exit 164 onto U.S. 17 and drive north for 24 miles to State Road 70 in Arcadia. Turn west and drive two miles to the park at the State Road 72 junction.

Contact: Arcadia's Peace River Campground, 2998 Northwest Highway 70, Arcadia, FL 33821, 863/494-9693 or 800/559-4011, fax 863/494-9110, www.peacerivercampground.com.

22 BIG TREE RV RESORT

Scenic rating: 4

east of Arcadia

Big Tree attracts active senior citizens by offering a busy schedule of social activities and crafts sessions. Aside from a pool and a huge spa, the largely open and sunny park has pool tables. There's a bowling alley one mile down the street and a Wal-Mart shopping center practically next door; it's connected to the park by a paved bicycle path. Down the road is historic Arcadia with its bounty of antiques shops and restaurants. About 10 percent of the park is occupied year-round.

RV sites, facilities: All 409 full-hookup RV

sites are for people age 55 and older. Sites are 40 by 55 feet, accommodating RVs up to 40 feet long and slide-outs. None are drive-through. On the premises are restrooms, showers, laundry facilities, a recreation hall, a heated pool and spa, a billiards hall, shuffleboard courts, and horseshoes. Children may visit for a few days but not camp. Dogs are not allowed; cats are permitted, but they must be confined.

Reservations, fees: Reservations are recommended. Sites are $35 per night for two people, plus $5 per extra person. Credit cards are not accepted. Long-term rates are available.

Directions: From southbound I-75, take Exit 217 onto State Road 70 and drive 42 miles east to the intersection of U.S. 17 in Arcadia. Continue 1.8 miles on State Road 70 to the park. From northbound I-75, take Exit 164 onto U.S. 17 and drive north for 24 miles to State Road 70. Turn right and drive 1.8 miles east to the park, at left.

Contact: Big Tree RV Park, 2626 Northeast Highway 70, Arcadia, FL 34266, 863/494-7247 or 800/741-7875.

23 TOBY'S RV RESORT

Scenic rating: 6

on the east side of Arcadia

Targeted to retirees seeking a "home away from home," the park is within bicycling distance to Wal-Mart and a grocery store. Much of the infrastructure was built in the early part of the decade, so everything feels new and well maintained. In the clubhouse, campers can socialize and take part in all kinds of planned activities, including computer classes, arts and crafts, bingo, and line dancing. "We have any activity under the sun," say the managers. Campers can use the park's computer to get online. Sites are large enough to fit any size RV, and they're nice and sunny, the better to thaw out snowbirds weary from the cold up North.

RV sites, facilities: Of 379 total RV sites at this age-50-and-older park, 60 are available for overnighters and 319 for seasonal guests. Sites have full hookups and 50-amp service; all have concrete pads, picnic tables, and phone service availability. On the premises are restrooms, showers, a dump station, laundry facilities, a heated pool and spa, a driving range, miniature golf, a nature trail, a lake with a dock, propane gas sales, a dog-walk area, and courts for *pétanque* (French-style bowling), boccie (lawn bowling), shuffleboard, and horseshoes. All areas are wheelchair accessible. Children are not welcome. Leashed pets under 35 pounds are permitted.

Reservations, fees: Reservations are recommended. Sites are $28 per night for two people, plus $1 per extra person. Credit cards are not accepted. Long-term stays are permitted.

Directions: From I-75, take Exit 217 eastbound on State Road 70 for 45 miles through Arcadia. The park is one mile east of the Wal-Mart on the north side of the road.

Contact: Toby's RV Resort, 3550 Northeast Highway 70, Arcadia, FL 34266, 800/307-0768 (reservations only) or 863/494-1744, fax 863/494-2944, www.rvonthego.com.

24 LITTLE WILLIE'S RV RESORT

Scenic rating: 3

north of Arcadia

This adults-only park overlooks wide-open farm country and is convenient for passersby on U.S. 17. Most sites are on an open field. There's not a whole lot to do beyond swimming in the heated pool, but canoeing, boating, and golf are nearby.

RV sites, facilities: All 331 RV sites have full hookups and concrete patios. Facilities include restrooms, showers, laundry facilities, a clubhouse, a heated pool, horseshoes, and shuffleboard. A convenience store is across the street. Children are not welcome as campers but may visit short-term. Leashed pets are allowed; no aggressive breeds.

Reservations, fees: Reservations are recommended. Sites are $30 per night for two people, plus $3 for electricity. Credit cards are not accepted. The park traditionally is closed May 15–September 15.

Directions: From southbound I-75, take Exit 217 onto State Road 70 and drive 42 miles east to the intersection of U.S. 17 in Arcadia. Turn north and drive five miles to the park. From northbound I-75, take Exit 164 onto U.S. 17 and drive north for 24 miles into Arcadia at State Road 70. Continue north on U.S. 17 for five miles to the park.

Contact: Little Willie's RV Resort, 5905 Northeast Cubitis Avenue, Arcadia, FL 34266, 863/494-2717.

25 CRAIG'S RV PARK

Scenic rating: 4

north of Arcadia

The 65-acre park caters to snowbirds and bluegrass lovers, offering bus tours of the area, daily exercise programs, weekend socials, church services, bingo, golf putting greens, and a driving range. It's near the Peace River, which is a good spot for fishing and boating. Close by is the historic village of Arcadia, whose downtown is dotted with restored turn-of-the-20th-century buildings and antiques stores. This is also cowboy country: Rodeos are a highlight in March and July. The park is host to several bluegrass festivals.

RV sites, facilities: The park has 328 RV sites with full hookups. Most have 50-amp electrical service and concrete patios. RVs up to 40 feet long can be accommodated. A wireless Internet network is available in the office and in other areas of the park. On the premises are restrooms, showers, laundry facilities, a dump station, a pool, a recreation hall, a golf driving range, horseshoe pits, and shuffleboard courts. All areas are wheelchair accessible. Streets are paved. Children are allowed to visit during the winter. Pets are not allowed.

Reservations, fees: Reservations are required in winter. Sites are $25 per night for two people, plus $1 for each additional person. Credit cards are accepted. Long-term stays are okay.

Directions: From southbound I-75, take Exit 205 onto State Road 72 and drive 40 miles east to Arcadia, then travel 7 miles north on U.S. 17 to the park. From northbound I-75, take Exit 164 onto U.S. 17 and drive north. The park is seven miles north of Arcadia.

Contact: Craig's RV Park, 7895 Northeast Cubitis Avenue, Arcadia, FL 34266, 863/494-1820 or 877/750-5129, fax 863/494-1079, www .craigsrv.com.

26 GULF BEACH CAMPGROUND

Scenic rating: 10

on Siesta Key

BEST (

At these prices you should expect something special, and Gulf Beach Campground delivers. This park is on the much-lauded beaches of Siesta Key on the Gulf of Mexico. Siesta Key's sand is considered among the whitest and most powdery stuff in the world. From a bench at the edge of the campground, you can watch the pelicans skim inches above the surface of the water. Or, down on the beach, you can play in the surf, build a sand castle, or work on your tan. The campground is next to a county park, so on one side, at least, you're not hemmed in by buildings. Waves are gentle most of the time, perfect for little kids, but don't bring your surfboard. Australian pines provide relief from the sun. Sites are a bit close together and are laid out in two long rows stretching perpendicular from the street to the beach, with a driveway in the middle. Nearby is a bike path; you'll find restaurants, stores, and beach supplies two miles north in Siesta Village.

RV sites, facilities: RVs can be accommodated on 48 campsites with full hookups, 30/50-amp electrical service, cable TV, and picnic tables. Sites vary in length; if you have a big rig, you should call first to see if a large site is available. All sites are back-in. A dial-up Internet connection is available in the laundry. Restrooms, showers, and laundry facilities are available. Children are welcome. Call for current pet policy; it varies by season and by location in the park.

Reservations, fees: Reservations are recommended. The fee for two people varies seasonally from $28 nightly in summer to a high of $61 nightly in winter. Rates vary according to how close you are to the beach. Add $2 for each additional person. There are also $2 surcharges each for use of cable TV, air conditioners, and electric heaters. Credit cards are accepted. Seasonal rates are available.

Directions: From I-75, take Exit 205 west for about seven miles to the dead end at Midnight Pass Road. Turn left (south) and travel 2.3 miles to the park, on the right.

Contact: Gulf Beach Campground, 8862 Midnight Pass Road, Sarasota, FL 34242, 941/349-3839.

27 OSCAR SCHERER STATE PARK

Scenic rating: 10

in Osprey midway between Sarasota and Venice

The seclusion and natural beauty of this park will surprise you. After battling traffic on busy U.S. 41, which is lined with strip shopping centers, auto dealerships, and commercial chaos, you'll enter 1,384 acres of woods and tranquillity. Home to many endangered animals, notably the Florida scrub jay, the park has a freshwater swimming lake and a tidal creek for canoeing. Canoes are available for rent at the ranger station ($5 per hour or $25 per day); you are not permitted to pull boats or canoes on the creek bank because they cause erosion. Here's a paradox: You may catch bass, bream, or catfish above the dam on South Creek if you have a freshwater fishing license; however, if you fish

below the dam for snook, redfish, or snapper, then a saltwater license is a must. Two nature trails run along the creek. Got a hankering for beaches on the Gulf of Mexico? They're three miles west of the park. You'll just have to face that traffic again.

RV sites, facilities: There are 104 campsites with water, 30-amp electricity, picnic tables, grills, and fire rings; among these, 6 have 50-amp service. Six sites are drive-through; RVs up to 35 feet long and slide-outs can be accommodated. Restrooms, showers, a dump station, a playground, a lake, and canoe and kayak rentals are available. Wheelchair-accessible areas include some sites, the docks, the office, the bathhouse, and the picnic areas. Children are welcome. Pets are permitted with proof of vaccination.

Reservations, fees: Reservations are recommended; contact ReserveAmerica at 800/336-3521 or reserveamerica.com. Sites are $24 per night for up to eight people. Credit cards are accepted. The maximum stay is 14 days.

Directions: From I-75 traveling north, take Exit 195 westbound on Laurel Road for two miles. At U.S. 41, turn north and drive two miles. The park is on the east side. If you're traveling south, use Exit 200.

Contact: Oscar Scherer State Park, 1843 South Tamiami Trail, Osprey, FL 34229, 941/483-5956.

28 ROYAL COACHMAN RV RESORT

Scenic rating: 9

east of Nokomis

This deluxe park on Dona Bay is a huge hit with retired snowbirds who spend the cooler months in Florida, but it has plenty of things to keep people of all ages occupied: golf, two pro sand volleyball courts, four tennis courts, and basketball, for example. The heated, 120,000-gallon pool is big enough for laps and water aerobics.

But it's not all about sports; opportunities to socialize run the gamut from theme parties (Germanfest, lobster feasts, country-and-western dinner shows) to bingo, card games, arts and crafts, and auctions. Professional shows and concerts are held in an outdoor amphitheater. There's even a business center with fax, copier, Internet access, and computers. "We're kind of like a small town all to ourselves," say the managers.

RV sites, facilities: There are 167 sites for RVs. Full hookups, 30/50-amp electrical service, cable TV, telephone service, and picnic tables are available. Also on-site are restrooms, showers, laundry facilities, a dump station, a pool, a recreation hall, an outdoor amphitheater, a model train room, a nature walk, a clubhouse, a game arcade, four tennis courts, a golf practice complex, a miniature golf course, a volleyball area, a fitness center, a kid's pirate ship play fort, a library with children's room, a basketball court, horseshoe pits, shuffleboard courts, a tool and craft shop, boat storage, and a boccie ball (lawn bowling) park. Most areas are wheelchair accessible. Children are welcome. Leashed pets are permitted.

Reservations, fees: Reservations are recommended. Sites are $48 per night for two people, plus $2 for each additional person. Credit cards are accepted. Long-term rates are available.

Directions: From I-75, take Exit 195 westbound on Laurel Road for one mile. Look for the park to your left.

Contact: Royal Coachman RV Resort, 1070 Laurel Road East, Nokomis, FL 34275, 941/488-9674 or 800/548-8678, fax 941/485-5678, www.rvonthego.com.

29 COUNTRY CLUB ESTATES

Scenic rating: 2

in Venice

The Intracoastal Waterway borders the community on the east, and Gulf of Mexico beaches are less than one mile to the west. Shopping centers, restaurants, banks, doctors' offices, and a hospital are all within two blocks. There's even a golf course nearby, which is fitting because the park itself is a former golf course, as hinted by street names such as Bogie and Turf. Dock your boat for an additional fee; a lagoon in the park provides access to the Intracoastal Waterway. RVers have access to the common areas of the mobile-home park, including a heated pool and a recreation hall with an auditorium, a stage, a card room, and a ceramics room. The place also has a bowling league, tennis groups, and golf leagues for men and women.

RV sites, facilities: A 509-unit mobile-home community for adults only, Country Club Estates has 10 RV sites for travelers with full hookups and cable TV. Restrooms, showers, a pool with a spa, boat docks, shuffleboard courts, boccie (lawn bowling) courts, and a recreation hall are available. You must be 55 or older to camp. Pets are prohibited in the RV section.

Reservations, fees: Reservations are recommended. Sites are $35–45 per night. Credit cards are not accepted. Six-month stays are permitted.

Directions: From the intersection of U.S. 41 and Business Route 41 on the north side of Venice, drive south on the business route for 1.5 miles and turn into the park, which is behind the Publix supermarket. The park entrance is located directly off the main highway.

Contact: Country Club Estates, 700 Waterway, Venice, FL 34285, 941/488-2111, fax 941/483-4958.

30 FLORIDA PINES MOBILE HOME COURT

Scenic rating: 2

in Venice

Social programs are held for residents between October 15 and April 15 in this clean, well-landscaped mobile-home and RV community for retirement living near the Gulf of Mexico. Shopping, restaurants, and supplies are available 0.25 mile away.

RV sites, facilities: There are 30 paved RV sites with cement patios in this mobile-home community for retirees. Full hookups, cable TV, restrooms, showers, laundry facilities, a dump station, horseshoe pits, shuffleboard courts, and a wheelchair-accessible recreation room are available. Big rigs can be accommodated. You must be 55 or older to stay here. Pets are prohibited.

Reservations, fees: Reservations are recommended. Sites are $32 per night for two people, plus $1.50 for each additional person and for air-conditioning use, and $2.50 for using electrical heaters. Credit cards are not accepted.

Directions: From I-75, take Exit 193 southwest for 6.5 miles. At State Road 776, turn right and drive two blocks.

Contact: Florida Pines Mobile Home Court, 150 Satulah Circle, Venice, FL 34293, 941/493-0019.

31 VENICE CAMPGROUND

Scenic rating: 8

east of Venice

Want to get out of the sun? Set on the scenic Myakka River, Venice Campground is tucked into an old-growth oak hammock that casts shady relief. Some RV sites overlook an inlet off the river. Three miles of nature trails offer views of the river, which is popular with canoeists and anglers. A restaurant is next door, but there's not much else in the way of development; the park has a secluded, back-to-nature ambience. A security gate keeps out the curious. The campground sells some groceries—ice, soda, and even a few RV supplies—but you'll have to drive into Venice three miles west for most items. Venice, like its Italian namesake, is laced with canals and waterways, but it's best known for an unusual beachcombing sport: Instead

of shells, people look for fossilized shark teeth. North of Venice is a popular surfing spot at North Jetty Park.

RV sites, facilities: This 25-acre campground has 104 RV sites with full hookups and 30-amp electrical service. Picnic tables, restrooms, showers, laundry facilities, a dump station, a pool, a boat ramp, boat and canoe rentals, cabin rentals, a playground, a game room, horseshoe pits, shuffleboard courts, a volleyball field, and a limited store are available. A supermarket is about 3.5 miles away. Children are welcome. Leashed pets are permitted at RV sites only.

Reservations, fees: Reservations are recommended. RV sites are $45. Prices are for four people; add $2.75 for each additional person over age six. Credit cards are accepted. The maximum stay is nine months.

Directions: From I-75, take Exit 191 southbound on River Road and drive one mile. Turn left on Venice Avenue (a gravel road) and continue 0.5 mile east to the campground.

Contact: Venice Campground, 4085 East Venice Avenue, Venice, FL 34292, 941/488-0850, fax 941/485-1666, www.campvenice.com.

32 RAMBLERS REST RESORT CAMPGROUND

Scenic rating: 6

east of Venice

Towering slash pines welcome campers to this 100-acre park on the Myakka River in an area little touched by development. Many of the sites are occupied by retirees in park models. Bingo, arts and crafts, choir singing, wood carving, and square dancing are among the activities held in the recreation hall. Fish from the riverfront dock or launch your boat and head south for the Gulf of Mexico. The swimming pool is heated. Within 20 miles are Sarasota-area attractions such as the John and Mable Ringling Museum of Art (941/359-5700), which displays contemporary pieces and baroque works from the Old Masters.

Although the name of John Ringling, who lived in Sarasota, is synonymous with the circus, he was also an avid art collector; his Italianate mansion and formal gardens are open to the public. Sarasota considers itself the state's center of all things cultural, with an opera house, theaters, and art galleries concentrated downtown. Other attractions in Sarasota are the Mote Marine Science Aquarium (941/388-1385), which has a shark tank among other exhibits, and the Pelican Man Bird Sanctuary (941/388-4444), a rehabilitation center for injured birds.

RV sites, facilities: There are 589 RV sites, 563 of which have full hookups and 30-amp or 50-amp electricity. Some nonsewer sites are also available. On the premises are picnic tables, restrooms, showers, a dump station, a clubroom, a pool with a whirlpool tub, a boat ramp, a dock, a playground, an exercise room, horseshoe pits, shuffleboard courts, a convenience store, and laundry facilities. Most areas are wheelchair accessible. Children are welcome. Pets under 20 pounds are allowed; they may be walked in remote areas only.

Reservations, fees: Reservations are recommended. Sites are $33–38 per night for two people, plus $2 for each additional person. Credit cards are not accepted. Long-term rates are available for seasonal visitors.

Directions: From I-75, take Exit 191 southbound on River Road and drive three miles. The campground is on the east side.

Contact: Ramblers Rest Resort Campground, 1300 North River Road, Venice, FL 34293, 941/493-4354, fax 941/496-9520, www.rvinthesun.com.

if you can get a site on the south side of the 40-acre park. The sites are big enough for 40-foot rigs; two sites even accommodate 48-footers. About two-thirds of the park is taken up by park models. Nearby is North Port, which has seen less development than many of the fast-growing cities on Florida's west coast. The town is home to Warm Mineral Springs (941/426-1692), a health spa that calls itself a "fountain of youth." The water stays at 87°F year-round. You can swim there for $16 a day.

RV sites, facilities: You'll find 33 grassy RV sites with full hookups, 30-amp and 50-amp electrical service, picnic tables, and concrete patios, as well as 56 park-model sites. Sites vary in size. A wireless Internet network is available in the clubhouse and in the office. Restrooms, showers, laundry facilities, shuffleboard, a pool, rental units, picnic tables, a patio with a barbecue, a clubhouse, and a canoe launch are available. The bathhouse and clubhouse are wheelchair accessible. Streets are paved. A public boat ramp for bigger vessels is three miles away. Two supermarkets are within two miles. Children are welcome. Leashed pets are permitted.

Reservations, fees: Reservations are recommended. Sites are $29–43 per night, plus $1 for electricity. Credit cards are accepted. Long-term rates are available.

Directions: From I-75, take Exit 191 southbound on River Road and drive six miles to U.S. 41. Turn left and drive 0.5 mile. The park is on the right side of the road, just beyond the bridge.

Contact: Myakka River RV Park, 10400 Tamiami Trail, Venice, FL 34287, 941/426-5040, fax 941/426-5712, www.myakkariverrv.com.

33 MYAKKA RIVER RV PARK

Scenic rating: 3

west of North Port

This park is located at the delta of the Myakka River, in an area overlooking the river floodplain. The location is good for bird-watching

34 RIVERSIDE RV RESORT AND CAMPGROUND

Scenic rating: 10

south of Arcadia

More than 70 acres in size, this park is convenient to I-75 travelers. It caters to young families—some weekend activities are specifically for children—but it also offers river canoeing, kayaking, and fishing, which appeal to teenagers and adults. There's a video arcade, and the proximity of the playground to the swimming pools—one designed for water volleyball—was established with parental supervision in mind. These oak-shaded and sunny sites are large, buffered by a wildlife area and the Peace River, near its mouth on the Gulf of Mexico. It's a true RV park; the only sites occupied year-round are those of the park employees. The park attracts families April 20–December 15, and older snowbirds from the Midwest during the winter season, roughly December 15–April 20.

RV sites, facilities: This park offers 356 full-hookup sites with picnic tables, fire rings, and concrete patios. Thirty-amp electrical service is available at 120 sites; 236 have 50-amp. A wireless Internet network is available in the clubhouse. Some sites are waterfront. RVs as long as 40 feet or more and slide-outs can be accommodated. Lots vary in size, with the largest "premium" sites measuring 40 by 70 feet. There are restrooms, showers, laundry facilities, a dump station, a canoe launch, a boat ramp, and rentals, a recreation hall, a playground, horseshoes, shuffleboard, a volleyball field, two pools (one heated), a spa, a limited store with propane, ice, snacks, souvenirs, fishing tackle, and RV supplies, and a boat dock on the Peace River. All areas are said to be wheelchair accessible. Groceries and restaurants are within 4.5 miles. Children are welcome. Leashed cats and dogs are permitted; a pet-walking area is provided.

Reservations, fees: Reservations are recommended. Fee for two people is $34–47. Add $2.50 for each extra person. Credit cards are accepted. Long-term rates are available.

Directions: From I-75, take Exit 170 onto Kings Highway/County Road 769 and drive five miles east to the park.

Contact: Riverside RV Resort and Campground, 9770 Southwest County Road 769, Arcadia, FL 34266, 863/993-2111 or 800/795-9733, fax 863/993-2021, www.riversidervresort.com.

35 LETTUCE LAKE TRAVEL RESORT

Scenic rating: 5

near Fort Ogden

Greeted by Canadian flags, campers at this manicured park tend to stay for winter or even longer in their RVs or park models. The big attraction is a county boat ramp that gives anglers and boaters access to Lettuce Lake, a wide spot on the Peace River as it flows into the Gulf of Mexico. The campground has a dock on the "lake" and a pretty wooded area on the banks where you can sit at picnic tables with a drink in hand and while away the hours. It's a rural spot; it's out there with the orange groves and cattle, and it has shell-rock roads, as well as oaks, palms, and hibiscus. That rural flavor is part of its appeal.

RV sites, facilities: There are 247 sites with full hookups, 30-amp electrical service, and picnic tables; about half of the sites have concrete pads. RVs up to 40 feet long can be accommodated. Restrooms, showers, laundry facilities, a pool, a recreation center, a lakefront dock, horseshoes, and shuffleboard courts are available. A public boat ramp is next door. A supermarket is 7.5 miles away. Children are permitted if they are well supervised. Leashed, supervised pets under 20 pounds are allowed.

Reservations, fees: Reservations are recommended. Sites are $28 per night for two people, plus $2.50 for each additional person. Credit cards are not accepted. Long-term stays are okay.

Directions: From southbound I-75, take Exit 170 onto Kings Highway/County Road 769 and drive northeast for six miles to County Road 761. Turn southeast, go two miles, then take Lettuce Lake Avenue to the park. From northbound I-75, take Exit 164 onto U.S. 17 and drive north 10 miles to County Road 761. Turn west, go two miles, then take Lettuce Lake Avenue to the park, which is right next to Oak Haven Park.

Contact: Lettuce Lake Travel Resort, 8644 Southwest Reese Street, Arcadia, FL 34269, 863/494-6057, fax 863/494-4254, www.lettucelake.com.

36 OAK HAVEN PARK

Scenic rating: 4

near Fort Ogden

Oak Haven Park is adjacent to Lettuce Lake Park, which has a public boat ramp. A small golf course is down the block. The park is on the same street as Lettuce Lake Travel Resort (see previous campground). Says the management: "We are country. You come here to rest."

RV sites, facilities: All 119 RV sites have full hookups with 30-amp and 50-amp electrical service; about 22 are available for overnighters and new seasonal visitors. On the premises are restrooms, showers, laundry facilities, a pool and spa, shuffleboard, horseshoes, and a small library for guests. A supermarket and restaurants are eight miles away. The park is senior-oriented, but children may visit. Leashed pets under 45 pounds are permitted in a separate section.

Reservations, fees: Reservations are recommended. Sites are $25 per night for two people, plus $3 per extra person. Credit cards are not accepted. Long-term stays are the norm.

Directions: From southbound I-75, take Exit 170 onto County Road 769 and drive northeast for six miles to County Road 761. Turn southeast, go two miles, then take Lettuce Lake Avenue to the park. From northbound I-75, take Exit 164 onto U.S. 17 and drive north for 10 miles to County Road 761. Turn west, go two miles, then take Lettuce Lake Avenue to the park.

Contact: Oak Haven Park, 10307 Southwest Lettuce Lake Avenue, Arcadia, FL 34269, 863/494-4578.

37 LIVE OAK RV RESORT

Scenic rating: 6

south of Arcadia, off I-75

This 80-acre park with a security gate is nestled in an area of horse ranches, farms, and fruit groves along the Peace River near historic Punta Gorda. The park caters to upscale retirees, with an executive golf course on the property and plenty of recreational activities. During the winter season, the park hosts dances, dinners, other social events, choir singing, and religious services.

RV sites, facilities: The resort has 399 RV sites, most with full hookups, 30/50-amp electrical service, and concrete pads. Pop-up trailers, pickup-truck campers, and tenters will be turned away; RVs must be at least 23 feet long. On the premises are showers, restrooms, laundry facilities, a pool and a whirlpool tub, two recreation halls, an exercise room, a game room, a golf putting and chipping green, horseshoe pits, shuffleboard courts, and boccie ball (lawn bowling) courts. A supermarket and restaurants are eight miles away. Children may visit but not camp. Leashed pets are permitted.

Reservations, fees: Reservations are taken. Sites are $28 per night. Credit cards are accepted. Long-term stays are okay.

Directions: From I-75, take Exit 164 onto U.S. 17 and drive 10 miles north to the entrance.

Contact: Live Oak RV Resort, 12865 Southwest Highway 17, Arcadia, FL 34266, 863/993-4014 or 800/833-4236, fax 863/993-0940.

38 HARBOR LAKES RV RESORT

Scenic rating: 8

in the community of El Jobean near the Myakka River

About half of the 528 concrete-pad sites in this well-manicured mobile-home community are available for RVs, although none are pull-through. Lots are roomy, measuring 30 by 80 feet. You won't find much shade in the camping area, but there is a view of pine trees near the lakes. A path winding through the complex has mile markers so joggers and bicyclists can keep track of their exercise progress. The park is minutes from the Texas Rangers' winter training camp, the Charlotte Towne Center mall, Englewood Beach, Gasparilla Island State Park, the Thomas Edison Home, and the Ringling Brothers and Barnum and Bailey Circus and Museum.

RV sites, facilities: The adults-only resort has 268 RV sites with full hookups and telephone access. The property contains four spring-fed lakes, shuffleboard courts, a pool, horseshoe pits, laundry, and a recreation hall used for dances, exercise classes, and other activities. Leashed pets are allowed.

Reservations, fees: Reservations are recommended. Sites are $32–37 per night for two people, plus $3 for each additional person. Credit cards are accepted. Long-term stays are permitted.

Directions: From I-75, take Exit 179 onto Toledo Blade Boulevard heading southwest. Go 6.5 miles to State Road 776/El Jobean Road and turn south. The park is 3.3 miles ahead on the right.

Contact: Harbor Lakes RV Resort, 3737 El Jobean Road, Port Charlotte, FL 33953, 941/624-4511 or 800/468-5022, fax 941/624-5238, www.rvonthego.com.

39 PALMS AND PINES RIVERSIDE RESORT

Scenic rating: 2

on the south side of the Peace River east of Punta Gorda

Palms and Pines Riverside Resort, primarily a residential trailer park, faces the scenic Peace River. Some lots have boat docks; however, swimming is not permitted because of the presence of alligators. Close by are boat ramps,

fishing piers, a golf course, and shopping. Life in Charlotte County revolves around boating, so you'll find plenty of marinas and boating supply stores nearby. In the wintertime, manatees are commonly seen along the Peace River and in the harbor.

RV sites, facilities: Overlooking the Peace River, this 114-unit mobile-home park offers overnighters 40 concrete-pad RV sites with full hookups, 50-amp electrical service, picnic tables, cable TV, and telephone access. RVs up to 39 feet can be accommodated. On the premises are a boat ramp, fishing paddleboats, a wheelchair-accessible recreation room, horseshoe pits, and shuffleboard courts. There are no restrooms, so rigs must be self-contained. Children are allowed. Pets are welcome.

Reservations, fees: Reservations are recommended in winter. Sites are $26 per night for two people, plus $5 for each additional person. Rates are subject to change. Credit cards are not accepted. Long-term stays are encouraged.

Directions: From I-75, take Exit 164 and drive 1.8 miles north on U.S. 17 to Cleveland Avenue. Turn west and drive 0.3 mile to Riverside Drive, then head north for one-half block.

Contact: Palms and Pines Riverside Resort, 5400 Riverside Drive, Punta Gorda, FL 33982, 941/639-5461, www.palmsandpinesinc.com.

40 SHELL CREEK RESORT

Scenic rating: 6

east of Punta Gorda

Set far from urban sights, this open and sunny park overlooks scenic Shell Creek, a tributary of the Peace River. Also nearby is the Fred C. Babcock/Cecil M. Webb Wildlife Management Area, a 65,000-acre hunting park famous for its doves, quail, deer, and wild hogs and for freshwater fishing and frog gigging. But frankly, this adult-oriented park welcomes visitors for more civilized fun. During the winter months, visitors can keep in shape with an aquacise program in the heated pool, and anglers will delight in the great fishing. Bands entertain at holiday dances held five times a year.

RV sites, facilities: RVers over age 55 are welcome at the 185 full-hookup RV spots and 30-amp electrical service. Cable TV access, wheelchair-accessible restrooms, showers, laundry facilities, a pool and spa, a billiards room, tournament shuffleboard courts, a boat ramp, a marina, and a store are on the grounds. A supermarket and pizza parlor are within seven miles. Children can visit for up to 30 days. Leashed pets are permitted and must use the designated dog-walk area.

Reservations, fees: Reservations are recommended. Sites are $35 per night for two people, plus $4 per extra person. Credit cards are accepted. Long-term stays are okay.

Directions: From I-75, take Exit 164 northbound on U.S. 17 and go four miles. At County Road 764, turn east and drive 4.5 miles to the park.

Contact: Shell Creek Resort, 35711 Washington Loop Road, Punta Gorda, FL 33982, 941/639-4234, fax 941/639-2801.

41 PUNTA GORDA RV RESORT

Scenic rating: 6

off U.S. 41 in Punta Gorda

This palm-dotted 30-acre park and mobile-home community is set on a canal offering direct access to Alligator Creek and the Gulf of Mexico for fishing; even sailboats can cruise right out to the open water without encountering bridges. A bait and tackle store is next door. A par-three golf course is across the street, and a restaurant is within walking distance. A monthly activity calendar and newsletter keep campers apprised of the on-site social programs. About 80 percent of the park is occupied year-round.

RV sites, facilities: The adult-oriented RV park has 223 sites with full hookups, cable

TV, and telephone access. Most spots are waterfront. An Internet connection is available in the office. Restrooms, showers, picnic tables, a clubhouse, two spas, a boat ramp, an exercise room, horseshoes, shuffleboard, a convenience store, a beauty salon/barbershop, laundry facilities, and both city water and well water are available. There's also a pool with a tiki hut. The recreation hall, bathhouse, and pool area are accessible to wheelchairs. Streets are paved. Groceries are within 0.5 mile. Children are not welcome as campers, but grandkids can visit for short stays. Small, leashed pets (one per site) are permitted.

Reservations, fees: Reservations are recommended in summer and required in the winter season. Sites are $29 per night for two people, plus $4.50 for each additional person. Credit cards are not accepted. Long-term rates are available.

Directions: From I-75, take Exit 164 and drive 2.3 miles west on U.S. 17 to U.S. 41. Go south for two miles, turn west onto Rio Villa Drive, and take the second left at the sign.

Contact: Punta Gorda RV Resort, 3701 Baynard Drive, Punta Gorda, FL 33950, 941/639-2010, fax 941/637-4931, www.pgrvresort.com.

42 ALLIGATOR MOBILE HOME AND RV PARK

Scenic rating: 3

south of Punta Gorda

In the cool of the evening you'll see a few tenants gather outside their trailers to exchange news, but the center of activity is a large two-story recreation hall in the middle of the grounds. Catering to retirees who are staying for the season, this ownership and site-share park is on a quiet side road five miles south of downtown Punta Gorda with good access to local attractions. A golf course, restaurants, and groceries are within two miles. Although the park is age-restricted (one person must be at least 55, the spouse at least 45).

RV sites, facilities: This mobile-home park has 166 sites available for RVs, offering full hookups, 30-amp and 50-amp electrical service, cable TV, and telephone access. On the premises are restrooms, showers, a dump station, a wheelchair-accessible clubhouse, a pool, shuffleboard courts, a pool table, and laundry facilities. Families with children are not allowed, but grandchildren may visit. Leashed pets are permitted.

Reservations, fees: Reservations are recommended. Sites are $26 per night for two people, plus $3 for each additional person. Credit cards are accepted. Long-term rates are available.

Directions: From I-75 take Exit 161 onto Jones Loop Road and drive 0.5 mile west. Turn south onto County Road 765A/Taylor Road and drive one mile to the park.

Contact: Alligator Mobile Home and RV Park, 6400 Taylor Road, Lot 112, Punta Gorda, FL 33950, 941/639-7000 or 941/639-7916, www .alligatorpark.com.

station, laundry facilities, a pool with a spa, a playground, horseshoes, a volleyball field, a small camp store, and paddleboat rentals are available. All areas are wheelchair accessible. This is an over-55 park. Leashed pets are permitted.

Reservations, fees: Reservations are recommended. RV sites are $32.50–40.50 per night for two people, plus $4 for each additional adult. Credit cards are accepted. Maximum stay is six months.

Directions: From I-75, take Exit 161 onto Jones Loop Road and drive east for 500 feet. Turn north onto Piper Road and drive 2.7 miles. Piper Road becomes Golf Course Boulevard; the campground is just 0.5 mile past the four-way stop sign at Airport Road.

Contact: Water's Edge RV Resort, 6800 Golf Course Boulevard, Punta Gorda, FL 33982, 941/637-4677 or 941/637-1188 or 800/637-9224, fax 941/637-9543, www.watersedgerv resort.com.

43 WATER'S EDGE RV RESORT

Scenic rating: 5

east of Punta Gorda

A 1,500-square-foot recreation room adjacent to the pool is the hub of activity, hosting pancake breakfasts, potlucks, wine-and-cheese parties, ice-cream socials, and crafts classes. The campsites, which are big enough to accommodate RVs up to 45 feet long, form a half circle around a 20-acre fishing lake. Canoes and paddleboats are available for rent. A few pine trees provide a touch of greenery, but there isn't much shade.

RV sites, facilities: This resort has 98 roomy sites for RVs up to 45 feet long, slide-outs, trailers, and campers. The sunny sites are 45 by 70 feet; some have concrete patios and picnic tables. Thirty spots are drive-through. An Internet connection is available in the clubhouse. Restrooms, showers, picnic tables, a dump

44 GULFVIEW RV RESORT

Scenic rating: 8

south of Punta Gorda

Brown pelicans rest atop dock posts here, taking a break after their latest round of fishing. Campers, too, can fish at this well-kept, boating-oriented resort with a stream running past. That is, if they're not busy with the golf outings, movies, dancing, potlucks, and weekly bingo games offered in winter. The campground is screened from the road by lots of greenery, and the sites are a cut above those at most RV parks.

RV sites, facilities: All 182 RV sites have full hookups and 30/50-amp electrical service. RVs up to 40 feet long can be accommodated. Restrooms, showers, picnic tables, laundry facilities, a boat ramp, a heated pool with a spa, a game room, shuffleboard courts, horseshoes, and propane are available. For cable and telephone service, call the appropriate utility company. Children may stay a few days or visit; the typical camper at this retiree-oriented park is around age 70, a staffer says. Leashed pets are permitted.

Reservations, fees: Reservations are recommended. Sites are $29 and up per night for two people. Credit cards are accepted. Long-term stays are okay.

Directions: From I-75, take Exit 161 onto Jones Loop Road and drive west for 0.75 mile to U.S. 41. Cross U.S. 41 and continue 0.5 mile to the park, at right.

Contact: Gulfview RV Resort, 10205 Burnt Store Road, Punta Gorda, FL 33950, 941/639-3978 or 877/237-2757, fax 941/639-8073, www.rvonthego.com.

45 SUN-N-SHADE CAMPGROUND

Scenic rating: 6

south of Punta Gorda

Mostly sunny, this campground is favored by retirees and snowbirds seeking to get out of the cold from the long winter up north. A few trees provide shade and landscaping. Planned activities keep folks busy in the recreation hall.

RV sites, facilities: Of the total 191 full-hookup RV sites, 25 are available for overnighters. All sites have concrete pads and phone service availability. Restrooms, showers, a dump station, and two laundry facilities round out the basic facilities. Amenities are a pool, a recreation hall, shuffleboard courts, two dog-walk areas, and a nature trail. In season, planned activities include bingo, games, cards, parties, dinners, and breakfasts. The clubhouse, pool area, and restrooms are wheelchair accessible. Children are not allowed. Leashed pets are permitted, but not aggressive breeds.

Reservations, fees: Reservations are recommended. Sites are $33 per night for two people, plus $3.50 per extra person. Credit cards are accepted. Long-term or seasonal stays are preferred.

Directions: From I-75, take Exit 158 and drive one mile west on Tucker's Grade/State Road 762. At U.S. 41, turn south and go 3.5 miles.

Contact: Sun-n-Shade Campground, 14880 Tamiami Trail, Punta Gorda, FL 33955, 941/639-5388, fax 941/639-0368, www.sunnshade.com.

LAKE OKEECHOBEE

© PETER TRITLEY

BEST RV PARKS AND CAMPGROUNDS

€ **Fishing**
North Lake Estates RV Resort, page 405
The Marina RV Resort, page 413

€ **Most Unusual**
Pioneer Park of Hardee County, page 397

The area in and around Lake Okeechobee is one of the most underappreciated areas of Florida. Forgotten on the theme-park trail, ignored by many but the most hard-core anglers and boaters, the Lake O area has the taste of "Old Florida" that is lost by the glitzy tourist developments, beachside resorts, and hip urbanism that swamps most of the state south of Orlando. The lake area has escaped the developer's bulldozer, for the most part, and retains a rural charm.

Driving around Lake Okeechobee is a favorite route for motorcyclists and curious drivers. The harder way is to circumnavigate the lake 148 miles on a mountain bike or in hiking boots atop a mostly gravel, sunbaked levee, camping along the way. Fortunately, RVers don't have to do all that work to enjoy bird sightings, wildlife surprises, and the relaxing lifestyle that is easily found in this primarily agricultural area.

First, a word about Lake O (Okeechobee means "big water" in the Seminole Indian language). It is the second-largest inland lake in the United States, and the largest in Florida – 730 square miles. With an average depth of 10 feet, the lake and the Kissimmee River on the north shore were once the headwaters to the Everglades, allowing water to seep southward through the "river of grass." After devastating hurricanes flooded waterside communities in the 1930s, the U.S. Army Corps of Engineers reined in the lake with a towering 34-foot dike and a series of drainage canals. These controlled flooding and allowed development of the cities on the Atlantic Coast.

The lake provides amazing blue, oceanlike views on the northeast and south side; on the west side, the shore is thick marshland. The waters teem with bass and many other kinds of fish. In the hunting season, camo-clad adventurers line up at boat ramps to head out in small open-water skiffs. Snowbirds and retirees flock here in the winter months, many staying the entire season and returning to the same RV park year after year. Asked what there is to do at one RV park, the manager summed it up easily: "Fish, fish, fish."

For the boater, Lake Okeechobee is a watery path that cuts 152 miles across the state from the Atlantic Ocean on the east to the Gulf of Mexico on the west, passing through several locks that equalize the water level. For landlubbers, the paradox is that you can't see the water unless you get above the levee, which is also part of the Lake Okeechobee Scenic Trail and the Great Florida Birding Trail. About 60 miles of the old gravel levee road were paved in 2004 and 2005 (from the town of Okeechobee past Port Mayaca). This development was an instant hit with pedestrians out for their evening stroll and with bicyclists. The end result is that the levee experience is more accessible to less-hardy types.

All around the lake is farm country, with cattle ranches dominating in the north. In the south area, you'll find sugarcane fields and nurseries that produce turf grass and greenery grown for Midwestern malls and fancy housing developments around the state. Although sugarcane is no longer harvested by migrant workers (it's now done by machinery), other vegetable crops are grown here, and you'll see Mexican, Caribbean, and Central American conclaves with their wonderful cookery and groceries, as well as "remittance" centers where workers send their hard-earned dollars home. The foreign flavor adds spice to the "Old South" feel of towns like Clewiston, where you'll find down-home barbecue joints and the antebellum-style Clewiston Inn.

Lake Okeechobee has the variety, the thrills, the adventure, and the relaxation that warms the heart of many snowbirds and active visitors. If you have the time and interest, this area is worth including on your to-do list.

❶ PIONEER PARK OF HARDEE COUNTY

🐟 🛶 🐕 👫 🚐 ⛰️

Scenic rating: 7

on the Peace River in Zolfo Springs

BEST (

You won't soon forget this focal point of Hardee County, if only for its wildlife refuge near the campground in Pioneer Park and museum celebrating the early settlers of this agricultural region. In the refuge, animals move freely in a natural habitat while visitors watch from an elevated boardwalk. The animals include cougars and two black bears. All the denizens of this refuge cannot be returned to the wild for one reason or another, and they had been previously kept in a caged, zoolike environment here. One of the bears is a retired professional wrestler (declawed). The cougar was given up by its owners when the pet—once fist-sized—grew too big. Each has its own personality, and of course, a name. The refuge is open daily 10 A.M.–4 P.M., except Wednesdays, Thanksgiving, and Christmas Day. Admission of $1–2 per person helps contribute to support the animals and their habitat.

The campground offers grassy sites in this 115-acre county-owned park, which is favored by retirees, snowbirds, and family campers. A dike and a handful of short walking trails are by the Peace River, where anglers try for panfish. This sleepy region also attracts weekend canoeists who launch here and paddle past cattle farms and woods on the slow-moving river, ending the overnight journey 23 miles downstream in Arcadia, or closer to home for half-day trips. Among the area canoe outfitters is Canoe Outpost (2816 Northwest County Road 661 in Arcadia, 863/494-1215). If your dog will be joining you, try Canoe Safari (3020 Northwest County Road 661 in Arcadia, 800/262-1119). Other outfitters typically nix pets.

The big event here is Pioneer Park Days, a five-day festival usually held around the first weekend in March (call 863/773-2161 for exact dates). The festival gets off to a rousing start with an old-fashioned parade through downtown Wauchula, and continues with displays of antique farm equipment, entertainers, and a 500-booth flea market in the park. Year-round, visitors can tour the Pioneer Park Museum, which has an 1879 cabin and blacksmith display, demonstrations of how cane syrup is made, and an exhibit depicting mastodon bones found in the area by Boy Scouts several years ago. The original bones were sent to the Smithsonian for study. The museum is open Monday–Saturday 9 A.M.–5:30 P.M.

This area was hard-hit by the 2004 hurricane season. Aside from the economic and infrastructure damage, many trees were lost. It will take years for the tree canopy to recover fully, but the community has rallied to create a Peace River Heritage trail and promote tourism and business revitalization.

RV sites, facilities: There are 62 campsites for RVs. Most sites have water and electricity, but not sewer hookups. Showers, restrooms, a small museum, a playground, nature trails, fishing ponds, an entertainment pavilion, a picnic area, and a dump station are available. A restaurant, a convenience store, a bank, and bait are within 0.25 mile. Children and leashed pets are permitted. Pets must be kept under control at all times; pet "disturbances" will not be tolerated "at any time." Alcohol is forbidden.

Reservations, fees: Reservations are not accepted. Sites are $7 per night for two people, plus $2 per extra person and $4 for electricity. Credit cards are not accepted. Stays are limited to 150 days per year.

Directions: The park is at the intersection of U.S. 17 and State Road 64 in Zolfo Springs.

Contact: Pioneer Park of Hardee County, c/o Hardee County Public Works Department, 205 Hanchey Road, Wauchula, FL 33873, 863/735-0330. Contact the wildlife refuge and museum at 650 Animal Way, Zolfo Springs, FL 33890, 863/735-0119.

◢ BUTTONWOOD BAY

Scenic rating: 9

on Lake Josephine south of Sebring

"A great place to live" and "your fun-filled winter home" are two of the ways this deluxe 130-acre resort describes itself. Geared to the retired set (but you can stay if you are 19 or older), the park is set in the middle of orange groves on 1,300-acre Lake Josephine. A small stream runs through the property, as well.

Paved, lighted streets lead to two pools and two recreation centers, where bingo, cards, and dancing entertain snowbirds from more than half of the United States. Golf aficionados can warm up at an on-site driving range before heading to any of the 15 golf courses within 15 miles. If the 1.5-mile-long nature trail gets to be old hat, try the trails at Highlands Hammock State Park.

RV sites, facilities: This adults-only park has 150 full-hookup RV sites, and 850 manufactured homes with year-round residents. The sites are quite large at 40 by 50 feet, and many have paved patios. Two recreation centers, two heated pools, an exercise room, a nature trail, miniature golf, a driving range, horseshoes, lighted tennis courts, a boccie ball (lawn bowling) court, snacks (in winter), a woodworking shop, pool tables, shuffleboard, and organized activities entertain campers. On the premises are restrooms, showers, a dump station, laundry facilities, a boat ramp, and a dock. Management says the buildings and common areas are wheelchair accessible. Hook up to the Internet in the clubhouse. You can store your RV or boat on-site. Groceries are 5–10 minutes away. Restaurants are about two miles away. Children may visit only for short stays. Pets are welcome.

Reservations, fees: Reservations are recommended. Sites are $23–32 per night for two people, plus $4 for each additional person. Credit cards are accepted. Long-term stays are okay.

Directions: From Sebring, take U.S. 27 five miles south and look for the RV resort on the right.

Contact: Buttonwood Bay, 10001 U.S. 27 South, Sebring, FL 33870, 866/655-5565 or 863/655-1122, www.buttonwoodbay.com.

◢ CYPRESS ISLE RV PARK AND MARINA

Scenic rating: 3

on Lake Istokpoga in Lake Placid

Fishing is the name of the vacation game at Cypress Isle. Wild shiners and lake access are the amenities the proprietors mention first when asked about their park. Eleven-mile-long Lake Istokpoga is well known for its bass, bream, and crappie fishing. Boating is a popular pursuit, and each campsite has a covered boat slip. A fair number of cypress trees shade the grassy sites.

RV sites, facilities: All 30 grassy, shaded sites have full hookups and 30-amp electrical service. Some of the campsites have the lake at their back doors. RVs up to 35 feet long can be accommodated; none of the sites are drive-through. On the premises are restrooms, showers, a dump station, laundry facilities, a recreation room, rental cabins, trailer rentals, a boat ramp, boat rentals, charter fishing services, covered boat slips, a convenience store, and bait and tackle. Groceries and stores are about seven miles away. RV storage is available. Children and leashed pets are permitted.

Reservations, fees: Reservations are recommended but drive-ins are usually available. Sites are $15–30 per night for two people, plus $7 for each additional person. Credit cards are not accepted. Maximum stay is six months.

Directions: From U.S. 27 in Lake Placid, take East County Road 621 for 7.5 miles east to Cypress Isle Road. Turn left. Go to the end of the road and turn right.

Contact: Cypress Isle RV Park and Marina, East County Road 621, Lake Placid, FL 33852, 863/465-5241, www.geocities.com/cypressislesrv.

4 MOSSY COVE FISH CAMP AND RV RESORT

Scenic rating: 5

east of Lake Istokpoga

These seven acres are on the quiet, scenic, little-used eastern side of cypress-ringed Lake Istokpoga. You may spot wildlife along the shore, although most visitors turn their attention toward the fish in the 43-square-mile lake, going after crappies, bass, and bluegill. Several bass fishing tournaments are organized here. You can also charter an airboat ride.

RV sites, facilities: New owners have cleaned up and enlarged this fish camp to 48 full-hookup RV spots, plus 11 cabins. Sites have crushed-shell surfaces, and all have 30-amp electrical service. About 80 percent of the occupants live here year-round. On the premises are restrooms, showers, a dump station, laundry facilities, rental cottages, a boat ramp, a wheelchair-accessible dock, a convenience store, and bait and tackle. Activities include the usual holiday dinners and recreation center, with the added twist of "clogging" (sort of like Irish step-dancing) and airboat tours. The open-air clubhouse has been enclosed and is now known as the "Tree House," because it is surrounded by woods. RV storage is available. Children and pets are welcome.

Reservations, fees: Reservations are recommended. Sites are $28 per night for two people, plus $3 for each additional person. Lakeside lots are more expensive, varying by season and availability. Credit cards are not accepted. Long-term stays are okay.

Directions: From Lorida, drive about three miles east on U.S. 98. Turn right (south) on County Road 621. In about five miles, turn right (west) on Godwin Road and proceed to the fish camp.

Contact: Mossy Cove Fish Camp and RV Resort, 3 Mossy Cove Drive, Lorida, FL 33857, 863/655-0119 or 800/833-2683, www.mossy-cove.us.

5 FISHEATING CREEK CAMPGROUND

Scenic rating: 10

on Fisheating Creek in Palmdale

Fisheating Creek is one of Florida's prettiest natural areas and has attracted generations of picnickers, swimmers, and canoeists. Bring or rent a canoe at the campground, and you can paddle through marshes and past raised banks where you'll sometimes see rope swings that kids once used to jump into the water (be on the lookout for alligators). Enjoy a picnic on riverbanks fringed by moss-draped oaks and cypress trees. Wildlife abounds along the creek, particularly wading birds, alligators, otters, and turtles. Back in the woods, you'll sometimes see deer, wild hogs, and armadillos. The swimming beach is a delight, located on a normally breezy, oak-shaded, five-acre, spring-fed lake. Astronomy buffs come here because it is one of the few places where city lights won't blot out the stars. The park is part of 18,000 acres of wilderness.

RV sites, facilities: About 60 primitive sites with fire rings and picnic tables are available along the creek and near the swimming lake. Another 50 full-hookup RV sites have 30/50-amp electrical service. Restrooms, showers, laundry facilities, a boat ramp, canoe and kayak rentals, and a campground store are available. A supermarket is located within 15 miles. Swim in the lake, but it's against the rules to swim in the creek. If you plan an overnight canoe trip, call the park first to determine if the water is high enough. Transportation is available to your starting point, and you can leave your car at the campground. Primitive sites are available along the river for trips as long as two days. Children are permitted. Leashed pets are allowed, but must be kept under control at all times.

Reservations, fees: Reservations are recommended. RV sites with full hookups are $25. Credit cards are accepted. Long-term rates are available.

Directions: From Moore Haven, go north on U.S. 27 for 16 miles to the entrance. The wildlife management area is one mile north of State Road 29 at Fisheating Creek.

Contact: Fisheating Creek Campground, 7555 North U.S. 27, Palmdale, FL 33944, 863/675-5999, www.fisheatingcreek.com. Or contact the Florida Fish and Wildlife Conservation Commission, 3900 Drane Field Road, Lakeland, FL 33811-1299, 863/648-3203.

6 SUNSHINE RV RESORT

Scenic rating: 6

south of Lake Placid

Formerly known as Sunburst RV Resort, this home of wintertime dances, crafts, bingo, potlucks, gospel music, a "kitchen" band, western/country music jams, and special events is geared toward retirees who spend months or years at these RV sites and mobile homes. An activities director runs these activities in season, and lots of RV rally clubs gather here for fun. Campers who want to go it alone can bicycle past surrounding orange groves. Of the 27 area lakes, perhaps 2 are most famous for fishing and waterskiing—Lake Placid, about three miles northwest, and 43-square-mile Lake Istokpoga, farther northeast.

RV sites, facilities: At this 300-site mobile-home/RV park, about 125 sites are available for RVs; the rest are occupied by year-round residents. The majority have 30-amp electrical service; 50-amp service is available at 10 sites. Between 15 and 20 sites are considered drive-through. A recreation hall, a heated pool, boccie ball (lawn bowling) courts, billiards, horseshoes, shuffleboard, tennis, and winter social programs entertain campers. Restrooms, showers, a dump station, laundry facilities, park-model rentals, cable TV hookups, and telephone service are available. Groceries are within walking distance. One bathhouse, the laundry, clubhouse, and recreation hall are

wheelchair accessible. Restaurants and shopping are about three miles away. RV storage is available. Children are permitted and leashed pets under 40 pounds are accepted.

Reservations, fees: Reservations are recommended. Sites are $25–28 per night for two people, plus $5 per extra person and $2 for cable TV. Credit cards are accepted. Long-term stays are okay.

Directions: From Lake Placid, drive south on U.S. 27 for 6.5 miles to State Road 70. Turn left. The park is 0.5 mile ahead, on the right.

Contact: Sunshine RV Resort, 303 State Road 70 East, Lake Placid, FL 33852, 863/465-4815 or 877/317-2757, fax 863/465-1077, www.sunshinervresorts.com.

7 CAMP FLORIDA RESORT

Scenic rating: 8

south of Lake Placid

This resort employs an unusual circular layout—a nice change from the rectangular sameness of other RV parks. Set on Lake Grassy, everything is spotless—from the landscaping to the infrastructure. Lots are sort of pie-shaped, giving you breathing space from your neighbors, and each circle is separated from the next one by a road. Nearby are 27 lakes for fishing and boating, 12 golf courses, and historical attractions, but there's more than enough to do in the park, including tennis, a nature trail, a marina, and docks. Park models are for rent.

RV sites, facilities: There are 180 full-hookup RV sites, all available for overnighters and seasonal visitors. Most sites have concrete pads and picnic tables. Restrooms, showers, laundry facilities, and telephone service are available. On the premises are a pool, a boat ramp, a clubhouse, shuffleboard courts, a dog-walk area, and miniature golf. A grocery store and many restaurants are within 0.5 mile. Children are welcome, though retirees are more frequent than families. Leashed pets under 20 pounds are permitted.

Reservations, fees: Reservations are recommended. Sites are $28 per night. Credit cards are accepted. Long-term rates are available.

Directions: From Lake Placid, drive south on U.S. 27 about five miles to the park. From the intersection of U.S. 27 and State Road 70, drive north on U.S. 27 about six miles.

Contact: Camp Florida Resort, 100 Shoreline Drive, Lake Placid, FL 33852, 863/699-1991 or 800/226-5188, fax 863/699-1995, www.campfla.com.

⑧ NINE MILE GRADE CAMPGROUND

Scenic rating: 8

east of Lorida on the Kissimmee River

In exchange for the longer trips you'll have to make for such conveniences as groceries, you'll get a secluded, quiet campground alongside the Kissimmee River. It's the kind of place where you can roast marshmallows at campfire rings for a relaxing, old-style camping experience. Many visitors rave about it (though they'd understandably like to keep its location secret). You can fish along 1,500 feet of riverfront shoreline to catch bass, bluegill, peacock bass, and oscars.

The campground is set in one of the old oak hammocks that mark the edge of the historic floodplain of the Kissimmee River, where fishing, boating, and canoeing are popular. The once-meandering stream has been straitjacketed by federal engineers into a big, angular ditch. But the U.S. Army Corps of Engineers and the South Florida Water Management District are working to restore the river to its natural state, in which it overflows and drenches the marshy areas along its banks, providing a home for waterfowl and other creatures. However, the restoration project will not cause changes at Nine Mile Grade since it does not reach this far past the Lake Okeechobee locks, which control water flow.

Canoeists in particular might enjoy exploring some of the river's old oxbows, which are set to be reinvigorated during the restoration. Bring your own watercraft or make plans to rent a boat in the area. Near the campground are eight miles of hiking and biking trails. You also can cross the river north of here to hike along the Florida National Scenic Trail.

RV sites, facilities: This campground offers eight RV sites with water and electricity (two are drive-through), and eight primitive sites. Each site, which measures 20 by 30 feet, has a picnic table, a fire ring, and a grill. On the premises are restrooms, showers, a dump station, a boat ramp, a playground, basketball courts, and baseball and soccer fields. All areas are wheelchair accessible. Groceries and restaurants are six miles away. The nearest laundry facilities are eight miles away. Children and pets are permitted.

Reservations, fees: Reservations are not accepted. Sites are $10 per night for six people. Credit cards are not accepted. Long-term stays are okay.

Directions: From Okeechobee, take State Road 70 west 16 miles to County Road 721 north. Turn right and go 4.5 miles to Butlers Bluff Road (on the right). Turn left. Proceed to the end of the road.

Contact: Nine Mile Grade Campground, 992 Butlers Bluff Road, Lorida, FL 33857, 863/763-3113.

⑨ WHISPER CREEK RV RESORT

Scenic rating: 4

near the Caloosahatchee River in La Belle

Besides a little lake and the surrounding woods, this 57-acre park has the advantage of being just one mile north of the Caloosahatchee River, which is a plus for some anglers. If that won't do, head one-half hour east to the bass haven of Lake Okeechobee. Don't worry if fishing is not your only interest: The owners say this is a "destination" park where 75 percent of guests are snowbirds here for winter, and there are plenty of scheduled activities for landlubbers. Sunny sites will warm your bones in winter.

RV sites, facilities: All 396 sites in this wheel-chair-accessible, adults-only park have full hookups, including telephone and cable TV, plus 30-amp and 50-amp electrical service. Lots are 40 by 50 feet, with 10- by 30-foot concrete patios. None are drive-through, but they can accommodate rigs up to 40 feet long. About 80 percent of the sites are occupied by year-round residents. Popup campers are discouraged. Facilities include a solar-heated pool, horseshoes, shuffleboard, and a 5,000-square-foot clubhouse, which has a large auditorium with an elevated stage, a community kitchen, a game room with pool tables, and a library. Socialize with fellow age-55-plus campers at Saturday-night dances, bingo, exercise classes, potluck suppers, arts and crafts, shuffleboard tournaments, Bible study, and nondenominational church services on Sunday mornings. Showers, restrooms, a dump station, laundry facilities, and propane delivery also are available. Internet access is available in the office. Grocery stores, a restaurant, bait, and tackle are located one mile away. All the public areas, including the pool, laundry, recreation hall, and restrooms, are readily accessible to the physically challenged—an amenity in which the owners take pride. Children are permitted for short visits. Two leashed pets per household are permitted.

Reservations, fees: Reservations are recommended. Sites are $30 per night. Credit cards are not accepted. Long-term stays are encouraged.

Directions: From State Road 80 in the town of La Belle, turn north onto State Road 29. Continue for about one mile to the park entrance.

Contact: Whisper Creek RV Resort, 1980 Hickory Drive/State Road 29 North, La Belle, FL 33975, 863/675-6888, fax 863/675-2323, www.whispercreek.com.

10 GRANDMA'S GROVE RV PARK

Scenic rating: 4

near the Caloosahatchee River in La Belle

Guests can pluck free fruit off orange trees in the surrounding 40-acre grove during the citrus season, where fragrant orange blossoms peak in March and April. A walking trail passes by the fragrant grove and circles much of the 18-acre, adults-only RV park. This campground has been in business more than 25 years under the same ownership; most of the visitors are repeat customers and people who hear about the park by word of mouth. Anglers tend to strike out for the nearby Caloosahatchee River or farther east for Lake Okeechobee, about one-half hour away. Potluck dinners and street names like Grandma's Boulevard and Feather Bed Lane lend a folksy air. Groceries and restaurants are within two miles. Like other grandmothers, this Grandma lays down some strict rules: No converted school buses are permitted, clotheslines must be hung at the rear of units, and quiet hours begin at 10 P.M.

RV sites, facilities: All 208 RV sites at this wheelchair-accessible, age-55-plus park offer full hookups with 30-amp electrical service. Each site has a picnic table and a concrete patio with gravel driveway. Most sites are roomy at 50 by 75 feet, and elbow room between neighbors is easily 20 feet. About 25 percent of the occupants are year-round residents. A pool, dances, arts and crafts, exercises, shuffleboard, horseshoe pits, a social club, fitness classes, bingo, potluck dinners, dances, and a walking trail entertain guests. Showers, restrooms, a campfire ring, a barbecue grill, laundry facilities, propane delivery, and on-site cable TV and telephone service (for long-term campers) are available. The restrooms and recreation hall are wheelchair accessible. This is an adults-only park. Pets should use the designated dog walk near an orange grove.

Reservations, fees: Reservations are recommended. Sites are $25 per night for two people.

Credit cards are not accepted. Long-term rates are available.

Directions: From Fort Myers, drive 22 miles east on State Road 80 to the campground on the left.

Contact: Grandma's Grove RV Park, 2250 State Road 80 West, La Belle, FL 33935, 863/675-2567.

11 ORTONA SOUTH CAMPGROUND

Scenic rating: 9

on the Caloosahatchee River east of La Belle

Visitors tend to fall into one of two groups: The first set adores this remote and peaceful 25-acre recreation area with a view of cow pastures and the off chance of hearing a distant rooster crow. The other likes the quick access to boating and fishing from this U.S. Army Corps of Engineers campground on the Caloosahatchee River. Ortona's faithful fans (many of them retirees) normally keep the 51 sites filled through winter. Don't count on finding an open spot in time to hear bluegrass music at the one-day Ortona Cane Grinding Festival, held each February. The sun-washed campsites are lined up in rows, creating sort of a parking-lot feel; however all areas are wheelchair accessible to federal standards. A pair of bald eagles nests nearby, to the delight of birders. Don't miss the drama of walking across the narrow, steel-grate footbridge directly over the rushing waters of the Caloosahatchee River lock and dam. An ongoing project is the planting of magnolia, red maple, cypress, and cocoplum trees to replace nonnative plants; this work is being carried out by Scout troops and the local Civil Air Patrol.

RV sites, facilities: All 51 sites have water and 30/50-amp electrical hookups, picnic tables, grills, fire rings, and concrete pads surrounded by gravel. None of the sites are drive-through. Besides two fishing piers and a boat ramp, the campground offers showers, restrooms, a dump

station, and laundry facilities. Three wheelchair-accessible campsites are near restrooms; other accessible areas are the laundry room and one fishing pier. Groceries are available nine miles away in La Belle; convenience stores are within five miles. Children are allowed. Leashed pets are permitted.

Reservations, fees: Reservations are accepted by calling 877/444-6777 or online at www.reserve usa.com/nrrs/fl/orto. The fee is $16 per night during the season and $12 May 1–September 30. Credit cards are accepted. Stays are limited to 14 days in a 30-day period.

Directions: From La Belle, go east on State Road 80 for 10 miles to Dalton Lane. Turn north and follow the signs to the campground. From Clewiston, drive nine miles north on U.S. 27. At State Road 80, turn west and drive 14 miles to Dalton Lane.

Contact: Ortona South Campground, 4330 Dalton Lane SW, Moore Haven, FL 33471, 863/675-8400, www.saj.usace.army.mil/recreation/ortonas/orindex.htm. For more information, contact the U.S. Army Corps of Engineers, South Florida Operations Office, 525 Ridgelawn Road, Clewiston, FL 33440-5399, 863/983-8101.

12 MEADOWLARK CAMPGROUND

Scenic rating: 4

on the Caloosahatchee River in Moore Haven

Regulars escape the snowy Midwest, Canada, and the Northeast to winter at this neatly laid-out park, one of the few set on the Caloosahatchee River. The laid-back place allows boats to be parked on the oversized lots. In the summertime, locals and families play here. Under new owner Dan Short, 32 boat docks and two boat ramps were improved in 2005, and Internet connectivity was added.

RV sites, facilities: This adults-only park has 160 full-hookup sites (2 pull-through) for RVs up to 42 feet long; about two-thirds are available for overnighters and seasonal visitors. All sites have 30-amp electrical service. Half have cement pads. A game room, horseshoes, shuffleboard, quilting classes, and wintertime activities entertain campers. Showers, restrooms, picnic tables, cable TV, a dump station, a pool, propane gas sales, and laundry facilities are available. Most of the facilities are wheelchair accessible. RV storage is available. Groceries can be purchased 12 miles away. Children are permitted to visit. Leashed pets are permitted but may not be tied up outside.

Reservations, fees: Reservations are recommended. Sites are $28 per night for two people, plus $3 for each additional person. Credit cards are not accepted. Long-term rates are available, and you can stay as long as you like

Directions: From La Belle, take State Road 29 north. Turn right (east) at State Road 78. Turn right at Ortona Road. The campground is two miles ahead (stay straight at the fork in the road).

Contact: Meadowlark Campground, 12525 Williams Road Southwest, Moore Haven, FL 33471, 863/675-2243 or 800/889-5636, www.meadowlarkcampground.com.

13 LAKEPORT RV RESORT

Scenic rating: 5

near Lake Okeechobee in Lakeport

This over-55 park has sunny spots overlooking the Rim Canal; some lots are on the waterfront. The park's claim to fame: "Really big (70- by 40-foot) sites." Visitors (mostly retirees) escape blustery winters in Michigan, New York, Ohio, and other snowy parts of the country here, and about 90 percent of the sites are occupied or reserved year-round. Bass anglers can head out of the canal to get to Florida's largest lake—Okeechobee. Hike or cycle on the dike above the lake, but the managers strongly suggest: "Fish! Fish!" Groceries and restaurants are

within one mile. The famous Gatorama tourist attraction is about eight miles away (see details in the listing for *Clewiston/Lake Okeechobee KOA* in this chapter).

RV sites, facilities: There are about 89 sunny full-hookup RV sites, of which a few are available for season-long stays. Six sites are available for overnighters. Most spots have cement pads, and the 12-acre park has paved roads. Facilities include showers, restrooms, a laundry, a boat ramp, a dock, and a recreation building where bingo, cards, a quilting club, and organized dinners are on tap. The restrooms and recreation hall are wheelchair accessible. Children may stay no longer than one month. Leashed pets with good dispositions are permitted. Bring proof of up-to-date rabies shots.

Reservations, fees: Reservations are recommended. Sites are $25–30 per night. Credit cards are not accepted. Long-term rates are available.

Directions: From Moore Haven, drive about nine miles north on State Road 78 to Lakeport. Turn left at State Road 74. In 0.5 mile, turn left by the water tower onto Ted Beck Road, which curves into Milum Drive. The campground is the first RV park on Milum Drive.

Contact: Lakeport RV Resort, 2800 Milum Drive, Moore Haven, FL 33471, 863/946-1415, email: lakeportrvresort@direcway.com.

14 ARUBA RV RESORT

Scenic rating: 4

near Lake Okeechobee in Lakeport

Fishing is popular here. A boat launch and moorings, plus two fish-cleaning areas, make this obvious. Anglers hoping for bass and speckled perch use the campground boat ramp for access to 467,000-acre Lake Okeechobee, but you can also fish from a bank. You must spend at least two months at the 14-acre RV park to get a waterfront site in winter. Like most RV parks circling Lake

Okeechobee, this place is mostly flat and sunny with a relatively sparse sprinkling of palms, oaks, and towering Australian pines. A nearby trailhead leads hikers and bicyclists to the top of the Herbert Hoover Dike encircling the fabled lake. The views in the Big O region are often rewarding: Boaters are said to have spotted as many as 32 types of birds during an outing on the lake. If you tire of roughing it, drive about 15 minutes to use the video games and poker tables at Brighton Seminole Bingo (863/467-9998) located at the Indian tribe's reservation off Highway 721, west of Lake Okeechobee.

RV sites, facilities: All 136 RV sites have full hookups and picnic tables; cable TV is available, though most visitors use satellite dishes for their TV fix. Internet services is available at the sites, which are exceptionally large at 40 by 52 feet. Some are grassy and have shade; most have concrete slabs. None of the sites are occupied by year-round residents. A heated pool and exercise room, fishing guide services, bank fishing, pontoon-boat fishing or sightseeing, a dance floor, shuffleboard, a clubhouse, horseshoes, and a community fire ring entertain campers. Moorings are available for most boats. Showers, restrooms, a boat ramp, on-water fuel pumps, tackle, bait, a dump station, and laundry facilities are on the premises. A small grocery store is across the street. Children are permitted. Dogs should use the pet walk next to the dump station.

Reservations, fees: Reservations are recommended. Sites are $20 per night for two people, plus $5 for each additional adult and $3 per child. Credit cards are accepted. Long-term stays are okay.

Directions: From Okeechobee, take Highway 78 west about 25 miles to County Road 74 in Lakeport, then turn right. The park is ahead at left.

Contact: Aruba RV Resort, 1825 Old Lakeport Road, Lakeport, FL 33471, 863/946-1324, fax 863/946-1270, www.okeedirect.com/arubarv.htm.

15 NORTH LAKE ESTATES RV RESORT

Scenic rating: 6

near Lake Okeechobee in Lakeport

BEST(

The paved, lighted streets at this 36-acre RV community have names like Mallard Drive and Perch Lane—a reflection of its visitors' interest in fishing and duck hunting on nearby Lake Okeechobee. Boaters launch from North Lake Marina adjacent to the park. Don't expect to rough it. This may be the neatest, cleanest, most manicured RV park on this side of the lake. With trash pickup, a $325,000 clubhouse, resident managers, and concrete pads that extend to the streets, the RV park feels like a residential community. Many people stay at least two months. Nearly all campers are retirees. For a view of the park's ornamental lake, request a waterfront site on Bass Drive or Widgeon Lane. Alternatively, most Pintail Lane sites back onto a canal. Campers on Mallard Drive and Widgeon Lane have the shortest walk to the pool.

RV sites, facilities: This 300-unit, adult-oriented park accepts RVs at all 100 full-hookup sites, each with a 700-square-foot concrete pad. All sites have 30/50-amp electrical service. RVs up to 40 feet long can be accommodated. A boat ramp, clubhouse (with a deck and pool), horseshoes, shuffleboard, a game room, an exercise room, a crafts room, and wintertime activities entertain guests. Showers, restrooms, picnic tables, on-site park-model sales, and laundry facilities are available. Management says buildings are wheelchair accessible. Convenience stores, restaurants, groceries, and a public boat ramp are within two miles. This is an over-age-55 park; children tend to visit long-term campers for a week or so, then leave. Leashed pets are permitted.

Reservations, fees: Reservations are recommended. Sites are $30 per night for two people, plus $3 per extra person. Credit cards are not accepted. Long-term rates are available.

Directions: From Moore Haven, go north for nine miles on State Road 78 to the campground, at right.
Contact: North Lake Estates RV Resort, 765 East State Road 78, Moore Haven, FL 33471, 863/946-0700.

16 GATOR'S RV

Scenic rating: 2

near Lake Okeechobee in Lakeport

Devoted to this casual spot, retirees and snowbirds come to snag easy-to-catch speckled perch at Lake Okeechobee and fry up dinners of the flaky white meat. Boaters launch from Harney Pond Canal one block from the campground to fish or hunt ducks at the nation's second-largest natural lake. About two-thirds of the park is occupied by year-round residents. Visitors tend to come from Ohio, Illinois, and Kentucky.

RV sites, facilities: Thirteen full-hookup sites (three pull-through) are for RVs as long as 26 feet. Thirty-amp electrical service, showers, restrooms, a dump station, cable TV access, and limited laundry facilities are available. Most campers use a laundry business one block away. Boat launches, a convenience store, restaurants, and bait are also one block away. There's a supermarket within five miles. Children are permitted, although there is little for them to do; management says kids usually visit long-term campers for a week or so, then leave. Leashed pets are permitted.

Reservations, fees: Reservations are recommended in winter but are not necessary in summer. Sites are $20 per night. Credit cards are not accepted. Long-term rates are available.
Directions: From Okeechobee, go south on U.S. 441. Turn right at State Road 78 and continue about 27 miles to the entrance. The campground is one block west of Harney Pond Canal.
Contact: Gator's RV, 900 East State Road 78, Lakeport, FL 33471, 863/983-9155. Mailing address: P.O. Box 974, Moore Haven, FL 33471.

17 BUCKHEAD RIDGE MARINA

Scenic rating: 4

at Lake Okeechobee in Buckhead Ridge

Some down-home anglers cotton to Buckhead Ridge, a small, backwoods town that hasn't been ruined yet by overdevelopment. At sunny Buckhead Ridge Marina, "everyone fishes." The flat campground has a smattering of palms and other native trees. About 90 sites overlook a canal and have water views. A few sites are occupied by year-round residents; annual leases and mobile-home spots are available.

Folks tend to be here for one thing: to go out onto the lake, found beyond a set of locks farther down the canal rimming the campground. Veteran bass guide Captain Mac Russell can tell you whether you should use a June Bug Worm for bass or if bluegills are biting at the mouth of the campground-area canal; call 863/467-4516. Pontoon boats, johnboats, and canoes are available for rent.

RV sites, facilities: All 120 full-hookup campsites are paved; most have 30-amp electrical service. Each site has a picnic table. Recreational offerings include a pool, fishing guide services, a recreation hall, and boat rentals. You'll also find a restaurant, a snack bar, a boat ramp, boat storage, waterfront mobile-home rentals, a dump station, and laundry facilities. Most areas are wheelchair accessible. Children are welcome. Pets are permitted.

Reservations, fees: Reservations are recommended. Sites are $15–25 per night. Credit cards are accepted. Long-term stays are okay.
Directions: From Okeechobee, turn right onto State Road 78 and continue about 10 miles. Turn left on State Road 78B and drive 1.5 miles to the marina/campground on the left. The campground is one mile past the Kissimmee River.
Contact: Buckhead Ridge Marina, 670 State Road 78B, Okeechobee, FL 34974, 863/763-2826 or 800/367-1358, www.buckheadridgerv.com.

18 OKEE-TANTIE CAMPGROUND AND MARINA

Scenic rating: 5

at Lake Okeechobee and the Kissimmee River, 4.5 miles west of Highway 441

This county-owned, peninsular park is a local landmark on the north shore of Lake Okeechobee at the mouth of the Kissimmee River, with boat ramps providing direct access to both bodies of water. It could be a good base camp for fishing, as well as a chance to enjoy the outdoors and view wildlife, but it's been down-rated due to complaints following the 2004 hurricanes. Hikers and bicyclists can get a rare view of Lake Okeechobee from atop the 34-foot-high, 107-mile-long Herbert Hoover Dike, which is also part of the Lake Okeechobee Scenic Trail and the Great Florida Birding Trail. Campsites are very sunny, and a hat and sunscreen are always recommended. Paved roads lead to the gravel/grassy sites. The park has a restaurant and serves as tournament headquarters for various bass fishing contests.

RV sites, facilities: There are 280 large RV sites (164 full hookup, with 20 pull-through, and 107 with water and electricity). More than half the sites have 50-amp electrical service, the rest have 30-amp. Six sites are accessible by wheelchair, as are the docks, boat ramp, and store. All sites have a picnic table and a grill. You'll find showers, restrooms, laundry facilities, a day-use picnic area and playground, public boat ramps and fish-cleaning stations, boat rentals, a marina and fuel dock, bait and tackle, limited groceries and firewood, and a seafood restaurant. Propane can be delivered to your site once a week. The nearest full grocery store is about four miles away. Children are welcome. Leashed pets are permitted.

Reservations, fees: Reservations are recommended. From May 1 through October 31, sites are $16 per night for two people (base rate), plus $5 for each additional adult and $3 per child (under age six is free). The base rate November 1–

April 30 is $31. Credit cards are accepted. Long-term rates are available.

Directions: From State Road 70 and U.S. 441/Parrott Avenue in the town of Okeechobee, go south on U.S. 441/Parrott Avenue. Turn right on State Road 78 West and continue about 4.5 miles to the campground entrance on the left, just before the Kissimmee River bridge.

Contact: Okee-Tantie Campground and Marina, 10430 Highway 78 West, Okeechobee, FL 34974, 863/763-2622, fax 863/763-8136, email: okeetantie@yahoo.com.

19 BIG LAKE LODGE AND RV PARK

Scenic rating: 7

southwest of Okeechobee

Want to keep your boat close by? This well-maintained, all-ages fish camp has a boat dock at almost every campsite, making it easy to carry out those cleaning, loading, and maintenance chores. You'll overlook the wide blue waters of the rim canal leading to Lake Okeechobee and catch glimpses of the fantastic variety of birds that make this area their home. The park attracts anglers and birdwatchers, and brags that it's only 40 miles east of the Atlantic Ocean, making it convenient for snowbirds visiting the Fort Pierce or West Palm Beach area. Owner Betty Arrington describes the fish camp as "down to earth, in a country atmosphere... We don't compete with Holiday Inn or the Joneses." Stores are nine miles away. Only about 10 percent of the park is occupied by year-round residents.

RV sites, facilities: There are 37 roomy RV sites for rigs up to 45 feet long; eight sites are pull-through. Each has concrete pads, full hookups with 50-amp electrical service, grills, and cable TV, and 32 are waterfront with boat docks. Internet service is available at the sites. Restrooms, showers, laundry facilities, and telephone service are available. On the premises are a boat ramp, a fish-cleaning station, rental units, and planned activities, such as fish fries, barbecues, and potluck suppers. Children are welcome. Leashed pets under 20 pounds are permitted, but they are not encouraged and should stay in the RV most of the time.

Reservations, fees: Reservations are recommended. Sites are $25 per night. Credit cards are not accepted. Long-term rates are available, and you can stay as long as you like.

Directions: From the town of Okeechobee, drive south on U.S. 441 to the park at the intersection with County Road 15A.

Contact: Big Lake Lodge and RV Park, 8680 Highway 441 Southeast, Okeechobee, FL 34974, 863/763-4638 or 866/256-5566.

20 LAKEVIEW MANOR RV PARK (FORMERLY WINDSOR)

Scenic rating: 2

southwest of Okeechobee

Open October 15–May 1, this sunny park attracts boaters and anglers who sign yearlong or seasonal leases. They leave their rigs on the premises year-round to avoid the hassle of hauling them back home at the end of the season. A boat ramp leading to Lake Okeechobee is across from the park entrance, and plenty of boat trailer storage is available.

RV sites, facilities: There are 42 sites for RVs, 2 of them pull-through. All have full hookups, 50-amp electrical service, grills, picnic tables, and concrete patios. Restrooms, showers, a dump station, laundry facilities, and telephone service are available. On the premises are a fish-cleaning station, a recreation hall, horseshoe pits, shuffleboard courts, a gazebo, and planned social activities. Campers must be 55 years and older. Pets are not welcome.

Reservations, fees: Reservations are recommended. Sites are $20 per night for two people. Only two people per site are permitted. Credit cards are not accepted. Long-term rates are available.

Directions: From Okeechobee, head south on Highway 78 West for six miles to the park.

Contact: Lakeview Manor RV Park, 10000 Highway 78 West, Okeechobee, FL 34974, 863/467-1833, fax 863/384-1241.

21 LAKE OKEECHOBEE RESORT KOA

Scenic rating: 9

in Okeechobee

Beyond the security gate sits the continent's largest KOA, covering 117 acres. Here you won't find a simple recreation hall but a 20,000-square-foot "convention center and RV rally site" where dances, bingo, meetings, and the clatter of table-tennis balls bring the place alive. And there's not just a pool. Instead, one heated pool serves families, and a separate adults-only pool has a tiki-style bar set in a fountain-filled pond. A third pool is for kids.

The horseshoe-shaped park is built around the putting greens and fairways of a nine-hole golf course. From the big windows of the park's fitness center (formerly a restaurant), you can overlook the golf course from behind the first tee. Wintertime campers have been known to show up from every state east of the Mississippi River to camp at the grassy, paved sites. Some coastal urbanites use the place as a weekend fishing or boating getaway. One-quarter mile south is Lake Okeechobee, where several large-mouth bass tournaments are held each year. Disney World is less than two hours north.

RV sites, facilities: About half of the 748 full-hookup sites are for RVs up to 45 feet long; the rest are for permanent residents. Recreational facilities include three pools (one for families, one for adults, and one for children), a hot tub, a nine-hole golf course, a game room, a playground, horseshoes, tennis courts, volleyball, shuffleboard, pool tables, a recreation hall, and wintertime social programs. Showers, restrooms, a fitness center, cable TV, telephone hookups, limited groceries, park-model sites, and laundry facilities are available. Wireless Internet access is available at most sites. Management says bathhouses, pools, the recreation center, and laundry facilities are wheelchair accessible. RV storage is available. Children are welcome. Leashed pets are permitted. Stay as long as you like.

Reservations, fees: Reservations are recommended. Sites are $37–70 per night for two people, plus $4–6 per extra person. Cable TV costs $3 per day. Credit cards are accepted.

Directions: If you're traveling south on Florida's Turnpike, exit at Yeehaw Junction. Follow U.S. 441 south for 33 miles to the park. If you're traveling north on Florida's Turnpike, exit at PGA Boulevard. Go west to the Beeline Highway/State Road 710. Turn right and follow this road to the town of Okeechobee. Turn left (west) onto State Road 70, then turn left (south) on U.S. 441. The park is ahead, near the junction with State Road 78.

Contact: Lake Okeechobee Resort KOA, 4276 U.S. 441 South, Okeechobee, FL 34974, 863/763-0231 or 800/562-7748, fax 863/763-0531, www.koa.com.

22 LAKESIDE RV PARK

Scenic rating: 3

southwest of Okeechobee

Year after year, seasonal visitors return to this small park south of Okeechobee for "great fishing and even better fishing stories." The town of Okeechobee has dozens of these semi-permanent RV parks, set jowl to jowl on U.S. 441. This park, for example, also competes with a Veterans of Foreign Wars (VFW) clubhouse nearby that allows its members to stay for free. But those folks won't have the chance to fish from Lakeside RV Park's shoreline. "Bigger fish are caught right around the fish-cleaning station than were ever caught in a boat," says manager Gary Rupert. Five miles from the

park is downtown Okeechobee with shopping and supplies. A Labor Day rodeo is held there, and the Brighton Seminole Indian reservation casino is nearby.

RV sites, facilities: Anglers and outdoors lovers occupy these 72 grassy sites with concrete pads and 30-amp electrical service. Sites vary in size, but rigs up to 40 feet in length can be accommodated at some. All have full hookups. Restrooms, showers, laundry facilities, and telephone service are available. Nearly half the park is occupied by year-round residents. The park is partially shaded and restaurants, boating supply stores, and other conveniences are within two miles. Planned activities are held in winter, such as dinners and chili cook-offs on Super Bowl Sunday. Children are okay, though there is no playground nor other facilities for them. Leashed pets are permitted.

Reservations, fees: Reservations are recommended. Sites are $15 per night for two people, plus $2 per extra person. Credit cards are not accepted. Long-term rates are available.

Directions: From the intersection of State Road 70 and U.S. 441, head south to the park.

Contact: Lakeside RV Park, 4074 U.S. Highway 441 Southeast, Okeechobee, FL 34974, 863/467-1530.

23 ZACHARY TAYLOR CAMPING RESORT

Scenic rating: 6

south of Okeechobee

This green place offers more shade than many Lake Okeechobee–area campgrounds, which may explain why it can't guarantee a site preference at reservation time. In fact, the park is now encouraging yearlong lot leases, rather than overnight stays or short-term vacations.

Cypress trees and native palms shade these 20 acres set along 1,500 feet of lazy Taylor Creek, and some campers end up becoming equity owners. Although a heated pool and planned activities at the waterfront recreation hall are provided, fishing remains the god of all activities here in the shadow of the nation's second-largest inland freshwater lake. An on-site concrete boat ramp leads to the Big O.

RV sites, facilities: There are 250 full-hookup sites with 30-amp and 50-amp electrical service. For recreation, there's a pool, a recreation hall, horseshoes, shuffleboard, and planned activities. Showers, a boat ramp, a dock, rental units, picnic tables, bait, and laundry facilities are available. Trips with fishing guides can be arranged. Cable TV and phone service are available if you stay at least one month. The recreation hall and restrooms are wheelchair accessible. Children are permitted for short stays. Leashed pets are accepted for $2 daily.

Reservations, fees: Reservations are preferred. Sites are $35 per night for two people, plus $3 per extra person, $2 for electricity, and $1 or pets. Credit cards are not accepted. Long-term stays are preferred.

Directions: From State Road 70 and U.S. 441/Parrott Avenue in the town of Okeechobee, go south on U.S. 441/Parrott Avenue to Lake Okeechobee. Turn left to continue east on U.S. 441. Turn left at Southeast 30th Terrace. The campground is ahead.

Contact: Zachary Taylor Camping Resort, 2995 U.S. 441 Southeast, Okeechobee, FL 34974, 863/763-3377 or 888/282-6523, fax 863/763-6301.

24 TAYLOR CREEK RESORT RV PARK

Scenic rating: 6

south of Okeechobee

The driving ambition of visitors here is catching speckled perch, bass, bluegill, and catfish at Taylor Creek and nearby 467,000-acre Lake Okeechobee. Its location is ideal: just a few feet from the Taylor Creek lock, the only one on the lake that has no restrictions on boat height.

Other angler-oriented amenities are covered boat slips (remodeled in 2005), a fish-cleaning station, bait, tackle, and a nearby fishing guide service. Those who want to go it alone can rent a boat for $80 daily or $45 for a half day. Some sites have water views, but most are inland. Many water-view sites are reserved for residents of the park's 48 mobile homes, which are squeezed together. Under new ownership since 2005, the campsites and docks were renovated in 2006.

RV sites, facilities: All 96 sites have sewer, water, and 30-amp electricity; two sites have 50-amp service. Restrooms, showers, cabins, boat rentals, boat slips, snacks, and bait and tackle are available. The bathhouse, office, and docks are wheelchair accessible. Streets are paved. Children are welcome except for permanent stays. Small pets are permitted, but must be approved by the management.

Reservations, fees: Reservations are advised. Sites are $30–40 per night for two people, plus $5 for each additional person and $2 for electric service. Credit cards are not accepted.

Directions: From State Road 70 and U.S. 441/Parrott Avenue in the town of Okeechobee, go south on U.S. 441/Parrott Avenue to Lake Okeechobee. Turn left to continue east on U.S. 441 and proceed about four miles to the campground.

Contact: Taylor Creek Resort RV Park, 2730 U.S. 441 Southeast, Okeechobee, FL 34974, 863/763-4417, fax 863/763-8517, www.taylorcreekresort.com. Mailing address: P.O. Box 1796, Okeechobee, FL 34973-1796.

25 PRIMROSE RV PARK

Scenic rating: 4

south of Okeechobee

One of a dozen or so adults-preferred RV parks on the northern side of Lake Okeechobee, Primrose RV Park is easily accessible from both the west and east coast of Florida. It overlooks the deep-blue water of the rim canal leading to the lake, and tends to attract anglers and snowbirds staying for the mild Florida winter. Waterfront sites are available; others are set under tall oak trees. New owners arrived in 2003, and they upgraded the electrical service and added a seawall to the 1,180-foot waterfront. Additional work is to be carried out through the next few years. Most of the visitors are into fishing (on the canal, lake, or creek), and many are repeat customers from Missouri, Illinois and Virginia. About half the sites are occupied year-round.

RV sites, facilities: Of the 59 sites in this community, about half are available for overnighters and seasonal visitors in rigs up to 40 feet and slide-out units. Two sites are pull-through, and all but 13 have concrete pads. All RV sites have full hookups and picnic tables. Restrooms, showers, a dump station, laundry facilities, propane service, cable TV, and telephone service are available. On the premises are a boat ramp, 38 boat docks, a fish cleaning station, and a wheelchair-accessible clubhouse, where planned activities include potluck suppers, "ladies' day out," craft days, charter fishing, boat trips, and bingo. RV storage is available for a monthly fee. Children are welcome, but this is primarily an adults-oriented park where about half the occupants live year-round. Small leashed pets are permitted.

Reservations, fees: Reservations are recommended. Sites are $20 a night. Credit cards are not accepted. Long-term stays are the norm.

Directions: From the intersection of U.S. 98 and U.S. 441 with State Road 78 in Okeechobee, drive 4.3 miles south to the park.

Contact: Primrose RV Park, 6070 Highway 441 Southeast, Okeechobee, FL 34974, 863/763-8711, www.primroserv.com.

26 FIJIAN RV PARK

🚴 🛶 🛻 🐕 🚐

Scenic rating: 4

south of Okeechobee

Under new ownership since July 2005, this "fisherman's park" is now open year-round.

Sitting on the northern end of 740-square-mile Lake Okeechobee, this 3.5-acre park has an understandable focus—the lake. Campers (mostly retirees) launch boats from a park ramp to follow a canal to the watery home of bass and specks. Some campers fish from the bank; the open and sunny park has 850 feet of waterfront. With no swimming pool, playground, or shuffleboard, these grassy sites with concrete patios are best left to grown-up anglers and boaters. In the wintertime, live entertainment in the 5,000-square-foot recreation building provides another way to pass time. Activities include bingo, potluck dinners, dancing, holiday parties, and bus trips to historical sites, amusement parks, and dining. Shopping and supplies are within eight miles.

RV sites, facilities: Campers age 55 and older are welcome at the 40 full-hookup grassy RV sites in this 77-unit park; half the park is occupied by year-round residents. Sites are about 20 feet wide by 35 feet deep. Winter social programs, a game room, a recreation room, showers, restrooms, a dump station, a boat ramp, a dock, cable TV, telephone hookups, and laundry facilities are available. RV storage is available in the summer season. Children are permitted for short-term stays or to visit long-term campers. Small, leashed pets are accepted; use the designated dog walk.

Reservations, fees: Reservations are recommended. Sites are $30 per night for two people, plus $5 per extra person. Credit cards are not accepted. Long-term rates are available.

Directions: From State Road 70 and U.S. 441/Parrott Avenue in the town of Okeechobee, go south on U.S. 441/Parrott Avenue to Lake Okeechobee. Turn left to continue east on U.S. 441. Proceed about five miles, past Nubbin Slough, to the park entrance at right.

Contact: Fijian RV Park, 6500 U.S. 441 Southeast, Okeechobee, FL 34974, 863/763-6200.

27 BOB'S BIG BASS RV PARK

Scenic rating: 4

southeast of Okeechobee

The name is a hint that bass fishing at nearby 740-square-mile Lake Okeechobee is popular among the snowbirds and retirees who come here. Be sure to bring along fishing rods and a motorboat to traverse the two miles from the park's rim canal to locks leading to the Big O. Now there's another reason to choose this park: For bicyclists, the attraction is the bike trail atop the levee. This section of the trail that encircles the lake has been paved, and it's become a huge hit with strollers out for their evening exercise, and even road riders putting in their speedy miles unhindered by stoplights or car traffic. The pavement runs from Port Myakka to the Kissimmee River, and will eventually extend down to the south side of the lake. Manager Howard Lamb is so excited about the paved trail that he insists that it is "underadvertised." It's the perfect place for someone who loves nature because you can see for miles. Birds are abundant, and the lake view from this side is spectacular.

RV sites, facilities: This adults-preferred park has 43 full-hookup RV sites (4 are pull-through). Each site has a picnic table. Sites are irregular in size, but all have patios and are level and fairly shaded with oaks and palm trees. A few sites are on the water overlooking the rim canal. About 10 percent of the occupants live here year-round. A recreation room, showers, restrooms, a boat ramp, a camp circle for campfires, firewood, cable TV, and laundry facilities are available. Groceries, bait, and restaurants are 12 miles away. Hook up to the Internet at the clubhouse. RV storage is available for an extra fee. Adults are preferred, but children are allowed for short-term stays. Leashed pets are permitted.

Reservations, fees: Reservations are recommended. The camping fee is $20 per night for two people, plus $5 per extra person.

Credit cards are not accepted. Long-term rates are available.

Directions: From State Road 70 and U.S. 441/Parrott Avenue in the town of Okeechobee, go south on U.S. 441/Parrott Avenue to Lake Okeechobee. Turn left to continue east on U.S. 441 and proceed about eight miles to the entrance.

Contact: Bob's Big Bass RV Park, 12766 U.S. 441 Southeast, Okeechobee, FL 34974, 863/763-2638, www.bobsbigbassrvpark.com.

28 UNCLE JOE'S FISH CAMP

Scenic rating: 3

south of Moore Haven

If you love fishing for bass or hunting for ducks at Lake Okeechobee, then you'll like these grassy or concrete-pad campsites. (You can also use this as an access point for bicycling and hiking on the dike.) This family-owned fish camp is just what the name implies—a place to sleep so you can rise early the next day to catch finned critters. Forget swimming pools or shuffleboard; you won't find such amenities here, though that's not really the point. During the season, planned activities include weekly fish fries, and a pub serves up beer and jukebox music. Boaters will be glad that the boat ramp has direct access to Lake Okeechobee, meaning they won't face the hassle of waiting to get past a lock. I happened to stop by on the first day of duck-hunting season, and the boat ramp was a beehive of activity. Hunters clad in green camouflage waited in line to launch their watercraft, some of which were edged with frilly dried plant matter—the better to fool the ducks.

Some folks stay at this five-acre camp for months, earning a free, reserved boat dock after a four-month stay. Says manager Ed Massey: "This is the best place in the world to live from November through May. From June to September, it's one of the worst—because of the high humidity and heat." Nonetheless, he says he's happy to be home "in a little country town along the lake." Maybe that's why about 75 percent of the occupants live here year-round.

Motorboats rent for $60 daily. If someone in your party is dying for a hot meal in front of a TV after so much solitude on the lake, then the cabins with kitchenettes (renting for $42 and up) will provide a little extra comfort. The real Uncle Joe arrived in the early 1940s and built a few cabins, and the park still has that "Old Florida" feel. Joe has passed away, but his legacy continues.

RV sites, facilities: All 18 full-hookup sites are for RVs up to 38 feet long. Fishing guides and boat rentals are available. Showers, restrooms, a dump station, cabin rentals, a boat ramp, limited groceries, snacks, sandwiches, firewood, bait, boat gas, dock space, and laundry facilities are on the premises. Most areas are wheelchair accessible. Restaurants and a supermarket are 10 minutes away. Families with small children and pets are welcome.

Reservations, fees: Reservations are not necessary. Sites are $20 per night, plus $5 if your party has more than two people. Credit cards are not accepted. Stay as long as you like.

Directions: From Clewiston, take U.S. 27 west to State Road 720 and turn right. Continue four miles, then turn right at the Uncle Joe's sign.

Contact: Uncle Joe's Fish Camp, 2005 Griffin Road Southeast, Moore Haven, FL 33471, 863/983-9421, email: unclejoefishcamp@ aol.com.

29 THE MARINA RV RESORT

Scenic rating: 7

southwest of Okeechobee

BEST

This renovated park is on federal lands adjacent to the Moore Haven Lock that connects eastern Lake Okeechobee to the Caloosahatchee River leading to Fort Myers and the Gulf Coast; management leases the land from the U.S. Army Corps of Engineers. The campground is popular with boaters, anglers, hunters, and locals, but also offers access to the dike for bicycling and hiking. Renovations include a swimming pool, recreation buildings, and wireless Internet access. There is a gated security entrance and plenty of parking for boat trailers. Managers live on-site. Most sites have views of the water—not the lake, but the wooded canals that lead to the lake. Palms dot the park, but shade is not significant on these 40 acres. About 20 percent of the park is occupied by year-round residents.

RV sites, facilities: Among 151 paved or gravel sites, 59 have full hookups and the rest have water and electric (30-amp and 50-amp services). For the best sites along the water, ask for lots 82–98 on Fisherman's Lane. Restrooms, showers, a dump station, laundry facilities, and rental units are available. On the premises are a swimming pool, a boat ramp, a fish-cleaning station, a clubhouse, a gazebo, horseshoe pits, shuffleboard courts, a bait house with fishing supplies, and gas pumps. A large kitchen area is available, where community breakfasts and dinners are prepared (bring your own utensils unless you don't mind using plastic forks and paper plates). Other activities include dancing, gospel music, and jam sessions, plus the usual bingo and crafts. The laundry, bathhouse, and clubhouse are wheelchair accessible. You can store your RV in the off-season summer months. Children are welcome. Leashed pets are permitted.

Reservations, fees: Reservations are recommended. Sites are $18 per night. Credit cards are accepted. Long-term rates are available.

Directions: From the intersection of U.S. 27 and State Road 78, go north on 78 for about a mile. Turn right on Canal Road and drive through a residential area until the road ends at the park.

Contact: The Marina RV Resort, 900 County Road 720, Moore Haven, FL 33471, 863/946-2255 or 904/824-7063 (reservations).

30 CLEWISTON/LAKE OKEECHOBEE KOA

Scenic rating: 5

west of Clewiston

Formerly known as Holiday Trav-L-Park, this campground has been completely renovated and is under new professional KOA management. It's more than a convenient place to sleep if you want to walk or cycle along the lake's 107-mile-long dike or take your boat out to fish for largemouth bass. Within three miles of the campground are a golf course, tennis and racquetball facilities, a Lake Okeechobee boat launch, shopping, and a hospital in the quaint town of Clewiston.

The RV park boasts a smattering of exotic fruit trees, such as loquats, and offers large (35 foot by 55 foot) grassy, level sites. Although half the park is occupied by year-round residents, the managers emphasize this is a campground, not a trailer park, welcoming snowbirds and family campers. It's become a favorite of Scout troops and church groups.

Just 15 miles north on U.S. 27 is Gatorama (863/675-0623, www.gatorama.com), a fascinating tourist attraction and working alligator farm. One of Florida's earliest alligator parks, it typifies the classic roadside attraction of the mid-1950s. These days, it has been modernized and is a commercial success, as well as a tourist destination that will stay in your mind forever after seeing the reptiles up close. It houses 2,000 gators and crocodiles by age and size in open-air pens, as well as a variety of other animals. The really big gators swim freely in the adjacent ponds. Walk on the shaded boardwalk all the way to the end, or you'll miss seeing Goliath. He's known as the "serial killer" American crocodile, who had to be segregated in his own pen because he killed so many of his neighbors in territorial battles. Gatorama's breeding operation also harvests 1,000 alligators a year for meat and hide.

RV sites, facilities: There are 124 RV sites, of which 100 have full hookups. Almost all the sites are pull-through, and RVs up to 40 feet long can be accommodated. Both 35-amp and 50-amp electrical service are offered, and 12 sites are set aside for pop-up campers who need just water and electricity. Propane gas can be delivered to your site. Connect to the Internet via wireless connection right from your RV. Although cable TV hookups are not available, broadcast reception is good, with approximately 15 TV channels. Facilities include restrooms, showers, a dump station, a store, cabin rentals, and laundry facilities. There's also a hot tub, a pool, a horseshoe pit, a game room, a playground, a shuffleboard court, and an adult activity room. Fishing tournaments, movies, bingo, potluck suppers, card games, and crafts also keep guests entertained. All areas are wheelchair accessible. Children are permitted; parents are responsible for the safety of their kids at the pool. Leashed dogs must use a pet walk at the back of the park. You can store your RV here during the off-season.

Reservations, fees: Reservations are required December–March. Sites are $32 per night for two people, plus $5 for each additional person. Credit cards are accepted. Six-month stays are permitted for new visitors.

Directions: From Clewiston, travel about two miles west on U.S. 27 and then turn right at County Road 720. The campground entrance is located about 700 feet ahead on the right.

Contact: Clewiston/Lake Okeechobee KOA, 194 County Road 720, Clewiston, FL 33440, 863/983-7078 or 800/562-2174, www.clokoa.com.

31 ROBIN'S NEST RV RESORT

Scenic rating: 3

north of Moore Haven

This family-owned park opened in 2002 and the trees have not matured, so if you like sun and lots of visual elbow room between your neighbors, you'll like this community. It targets seasonal visitors who are looking for a convenient base for Lake Okeechobee's charms that is also near citylike amenities (Wal-Mart, restaurants, and other shopping). Open year-round now, the park lies neatly under the sun along U.S. 27, accommodating even the biggest rigs. This park has affiliations with The Marina RV Resort on Lake Okeechobee (see listing in this chapter) and membership privileges with several private RV time-share clubs, though nonmembers are very welcome. About 5 percent of the park is occupied by year-round residents, a number that is showing signs of increase. The big selling point here is a musical note: You'll find everything from karaoke and square dancing to jam sessions and live gospel singing. A pastor lives on the premises and holds nondenominational Sunday services.

RV sites, facilities: There are 248 large RV sites (30 by 50 feet) with full hookups, concrete pads, and picnic tables on 87 acres, of which 25 acres are not developed. Restrooms, showers, laundry facilities, cable TV, telephone service, a dump station, and propane gas are available. Wireless Internet access is planned for the future. All sites have 50-amp service, and asphalt roads lead to the paved RV sites. On the premises are a heated pool, two clubhouses, a four-hole golf course, shuffleboard courts, and a snack bar. Live music is scheduled every weekend from December through the end of March. Planned activities include music, games, group meals, and church services. Restaurants and grocery shops are located seven miles away in Moore Haven and 18 miles away in Clewiston. Management says the bath, laundry, and clubhouse have wheelchair access. RV storage is available. Children are welcome for short stays only at this age-50-plus preferred park. Leashed pets are permitted. Stay here and get full-day use of the owners' boat and recreational facilities at The Marina RV Resort on Lake Okeechobee.

Reservations, fees: Reservations are recommended. Sites are $18 per night. Credit cards are accepted. Long-term rates are available.

Directions: From Moore Haven, drive nine miles north on U.S. 27 to the park, which is on the west side.

Contact: Robin's Nest RV Resort, 2365 North U.S. 27, Moore Haven, Fl 33471, 863/946-3782, fax 863/946-3883.

32 OKEECHOBEE LANDINGS

Scenic rating: 3

in Clewiston

Purchasers of park models, trailer lots, and seasonal visitors in big RVs people this 27-acre community, which attracts anglers and retirees from Canada and the Midwestern states. Big grassy sites are the park's crowning glory, promising "peace and quiet" for campers, according to management. Speckled perch, bluegill, largemouth bass, and catfish tempt them from nearby Lake Okeechobee. This park is a member of several private time-share RV clubs. You won't be able to see the "Big O" from here or, for that matter, from most places around the lake, because the levee is so high. If you'd like a water view, request a campsite near the park's seven-acre lake.

RV sites, facilities: All 270 large RV sites are set on paved streets with lots 30 by 50 feet in size, accommodating rigs up to 44 feet long. They have full hookups, including cable TV; 249 sites have 30-amp electrical service and 26 have 50-amp. A pool, a whirlpool tub, shuffleboard, horseshoes, a tennis court, a game room, bingo, and special events entertain guests. Showers, restrooms, picnic tables, a dump station, and laundry facilities are available. Internet access is available from the park office. Propane is delivered to your site once a week during the winter season. Campers can store a boat, car, or RV for $60 a month. Groceries can be purchased 1 mile away; a restaurant and bait shop are within 0.5 mile. Management says the office, bathhouse, and clubhouse are wheelchair accessible. Children are welcome. Leashed pets are permitted if they weigh less than 40 pounds, and aggressive breeds are verboten.

Reservations, fees: Reservations are recommended. Sites are $30 per night for four people and $2 per extra person. Campers who stay for six months or more must pay additional charges for electricity. Credit cards are accepted. Long-term stays are okay.

Directions: From downtown Clewiston, go east on U.S. 27 to the park entrance. Signs on the highway mark the turnoff to the park, which is at the eastern end of town.

Contact: Okeechobee Landings, 420 Holiday Boulevard, Clewiston, FL 33440, 863/983-4144, email: info@okeechobeelandings.com.

33 CROOKED HOOK RV RESORT

Scenic rating: 6

east of Clewiston

One of the cleanest private parks around Lake Okeechobee, anglers seek Crooked Hook out for its proximity to the bass haven. But seasonal visitors fill up the park fast in the wintertime for line dancing, bowling outings, or other daily activities, and it is close to shopping and restaurants in Clewiston. In a region where sunbaked RV sites tend to be the norm, this 30-acre, retiree-oriented place offers something different: It has shaded campsites and greenery that make it feel tropical and relaxing. Because it was developed long ago, the sites are irregular in size (ranging from 25- by 25-foot to 30- by 40-foot). The cookie-cutter feel of parks plotted out on cleared land is a nice absence. More than 200 fruit trees are on the property, of which many are edible, including mango. The levee is across the highway, hiding the big blue waters of the lake—not that it makes any difference to the folks who come here year after year.

Owners Dan and Laurel Darlington indicate the park has more of a neighborhood feel, with so many planned activities that the "chief complaint is there are too many things to do." Visitors have to be selective with their time, whether it's focused on golf, fishing, poker tournaments, casino nights, poker, card games, or crafts room. In season (meaning the winter months), cookouts are held every weekend. "There is something to do every day," they say. An unusual activity we've rarely heard of is the park's "holey board" field, where eight competitors toss items called "washers" at boards with holes in them for points. The Darlingtons have upgraded many sites to 50 amps to accommodate visitors. About 35 percent of the park is occupied by year-round residents because housing choices in this area are scarce. Park models are available for sale.

RV sites, facilities: Three of the 200 full-hookup RV sites are pull-through. A heated pool, a recreation room, a playground, an exercise room, horseshoes, shuffleboard, *pétanque* (French-style bowling), and wintertime daily activities entertain campers. Showers, restrooms, picnic tables, and laundry facilities are available. Three miles away are restaurants, groceries, an 18-hole golf course, and bait. Wal-Mart (called by park visitors "Wally Mart") is the biggest store for miles around, and it's just six miles north. Some visitors leave their RVs or boats on-site during the hot summer months; the park will store them for six months for $30 per month. Children are welcome, although the park mainly attracts retirees. Small, leashed pets are permitted.

Reservations, fees: Reservations are required. Sites are $30 per night for two people, plus $3 per extra person. Credit cards are accepted. Long-term stays are the norm, though a few sites are available for overnighters in winter. Stay as long as you wish.

Directions: From Clewiston, go three miles east on U.S. 27 to the campground entrance.

Contact: Crooked Hook RV Resort, 51700 U.S. Highway 27, Clewiston, FL 33440, 863/983-7112, www.crookedhookrv.biz.

34 SOUTH BAY RV CAMPGROUND

Scenic rating: 10

in South Bay

This is one of the cleanest, best-managed campgrounds on the lakeshore, with particular appeal to RVers. It's just on the edge of the town of South Bay, and across the levee from fishing, hiking, cycling, and bird-watching on the lake. If you have a boat, you'll appreciate the city boat ramp/day-use picnic area across from the park; please note that the approach to the ramp is up and over a steep one-way drive over the 34-foot levee. A 24-hour on-site manager lives within footsteps of the county-run campground's office. The large paved campsites are sunny and are set along two elongated loops named Shellcracker Circle and Bluegill Circle. Plenty of elbow room exists between the sites, and the landscaping is well maintained. Most of the sites have views overlooking a mowed field and Shiner Lake, which has a short walking trail on the shoreline. There's also a screened-in picnic area with large grills for gatherings, and an air-conditioned recreational hall with a pool table, card tables, and a color TV. A campfire ring offers socializing opportunities. Swimming is not allowed, and other rules are enforced (no loud music or disruptive behavior, no barking dogs, for example). A security gate is kept closed 9 P.M.–7 A.M.

One visitor tells the story of a favorite jacket left outside during a storm. Imagine her surprise when the campground manager returned it to her by courier a week after she got home. Someone had found it hanging in a tree on the other side of the park.

RV sites, facilities: The 72 campsites have water, electricity, and cable TV. Both 30-amp and 50-amp electrical service is available. Showers, restrooms, a playground, a game room, a dump station, laundry facilities, horseshoes, and pool tables are in the park. A boat ramp is nearby. Nearly 20 campsites are wheelchair accessible. Children are welcome. Leashed, attended pets (no pit bulls) are permitted; no more than two pets per site.

Reservations, fees: Reservations can be made up to 90 days in advance, unless reserving by phone, which requires 14 days' notice. Sites are $17–18 per night for five people, plus $2 for each additional person. Credit cards are accepted. Monthly rates are available; however, stays are limited to 100 days within a 12-month period.

Directions: From U.S. 27 and State Road 80 in South Bay, follow U.S. 27 northwest about 2.5 miles. Turn right at Levee Road, then turn right into the campground.

Contact: South Bay RV Campground, 100 Levee Road, South Bay, FL 33493, 561/992-9045 or 877/992-9915. Additional information: Palm Beach County Parks and Recreation Department, 561/966-6600, www.pbcgov.com/parks.

35 BELLE GLADE MARINA CAMPGROUND

Scenic rating: 4

on Lake Okeechobee's Torry Island

If you're coming from eastern Palm Beach County, this is probably the closest place to hook up a rig at Lake Okeechobee, particularly if you want a golf course practically on the premises. The nicely kept Belle Glade Country Club is across from the campground, which is popular with bass anglers and boaters who seek to experience the nation's second-largest inland freshwater lake. Many sites have personal docking facilities with lake access. It's not the most fancy-looking park with so many long-term visitors settling in with all their gear, but having your boat that close is definitely a plus. Belle Glade is a farming community and the largest city on Lake Okeechobee.

RV sites, facilities: There are 350 concrete-pad campsites with picnic tables. Most have electricity, water, and sewer hookups. None of the sites are drive-through, and many sites are arranged on waterfront loops that overlook reedy, pond-like waters. For recreation, there's horseshoes, shuffleboard, organized activities, and fishing guides. Some sites have boat docks or overlook lagoons dotted with lily pads on the rim canal that leads to the lake. Near the entrance to the campground are pavilions for rent to the public, and you might spy a birthday party or baby shower going on. Eight public boat ramps, plus showers, restrooms, barbecue/picnic areas, and laundry facilities are available. Within walking distance are a golf course, boat rentals, a restaurant, bait, and tackle. Internet access is available in the office for a $5 fee. Children and pets are permitted.

Reservations, fees: Camping is first-come, first-served. Sites are $21 per night for two people, plus $2 for each additional person. Credit cards are accepted. Long-term stays are allowed.

Directions: From U.S. 27 and State Road 80 in South Bay, go east nearly two miles on State Road 80. Turn left at State Road 715 and proceed about 2.25 miles. Turn left at West Canal Street North/State Road 717. Continue about two miles west to the campground entrance on Torry Island. (On Torry Island, State Road 717 is known as Chosen–Torry Island Road.)

Contact: Belle Glade Marina Campground, 110 Southwest Avenue E, Belle Glade, FL 33430, 561/996-6322. Or contact the City of Belle Glade Office of Parks and Recreation, Municipal Complex, Belle Glade, FL 33430, 561/996-0100.

36 EVERGLADES ADVENTURES RV AND SAILING RESORT

Scenic rating: 8

at Lake Okeechobee

Formerly known as Pahokee Marina and Campground, this park has a unique setting. It boasts the only developed lakefront campsites on the eastern shore of Lake Okeechobee. The grassy campsites are directly on the banks of the lake, providing unrivaled water views. From this point, the lake shimmers blue like an ocean, and you can gaze into the unobstructed horizon to see sailboats and other vessels under way. The shoreline is rocky (not a beach). The steep berm that surrounds the lake is behind the park, so you'll actually drive up and over the dike and then down to the park. It's also convenient to groceries and the small shops of Pahokee, a farming community. Although the park has some trees, expect plenty of sunshine. Fishing and boating are the main attraction, but access to the hiking and bicycling options on the dike is excellent. All ages are welcome. Part of the park has cabins for rent or sale.

RV sites, facilities: There are 100 level, grassy sites with full hookups. None of the sites are drive-through, but the access road is paved. The sites vary in size from 20 to 24 feet wide and 60 to 75 feet long. About 10 percent of the sites are used by year-round residents, but most visitors here are anglers. Shuffleboard, horseshoes, a playground, restrooms, showers, cabin rentals, a dump station, a honey wagon, a boat ramp, bait, tackle, and limited groceries are available. The park has 86 deep-water slips in its marina, two fishing piers, three boat ramps, and trailer storage. If you didn't bring your boat, you can rent pontoon boats and Boston whalers fully equipped for fishing. Bicycle, canoe, and kayak rentals are on-site. Groceries are available within one mile. All areas are wheelchair accessible. Children and pets are permitted.

Reservations, fees: Reservations are recommended. Sites are $37 per night for eight people January 1–April 30, and $29 per night for the rest of the year. Credit cards are accepted. Stay as long as you like.

Directions: The park is on Lake Okeechobee in the heart of Pahokee. Head west over the levee from the intersection of U.S. 441 and State Road 715.

Contact: Everglades Adventures RV and Sailing Resort, 190 North Lake Avenue, Pahokee,

FL 33476, 561/924-7832 or 800/335-6560, fax 561/924-7271, www.evergladesadventures-resort.com.

37 BIG CYPRESS RV RESORT

Scenic rating: 7

in the Everglades on the Big Cypress Seminole
Indian Reservation

Back when Native American tribes were forced to follow the Trail of Tears to reservations out West, the resistant Seminoles had the distinction of never surrendering to federal troops. Eventually, three wars with United States soldiers forced the Seminoles southward through the length of Florida to vanish into the mysterious Everglades. There they lived for decades until they struck peace, but did not sign a treaty, with the federal government. The Seminoles today say they remain "unconquered." To underline the point, the Big Cypress Seminole Indian Reservation welcomes tourists with many more attractions than a casino. The 54-acre RV park is a citified choice in what was once wilderness. The well-tended lawn encircling the basketball and shuffleboard courts could be mistaken for suburban parkland if it weren't for the park's native thatched-roof shelters (called "chickees"), which shade some of the picnic tables.

Oaks and cabbage palms dot the landscape and help separate RV campsites, although trees don't totally block views of neighbors. Free buses will take you to one of the tribe's gambling casinos, and there are ice-cream socials, potluck dinners, and other planned activities in the recreation room. A new casino is planned across the street from the RV resort. A motocross track, popular with families, is being expanded to 85 acres, making it the largest lighted course in the United States. Open since late 2003, the track hosts races and practice sessions throughout the year.

Within one mile, the tribe's Kissimmee Billie Swamp Safari Wildlife Park offers airboat rides and swamp-buggy ecotours. Frog legs and alligator-tail nuggets are served at the safari's Swamp Water Cafe. Hunters can track such animals as trophy boars and red stag deer year-round at the tribe's 3,000-acre Big Cypress Hunting Adventures hunting preserve; call 800/689-2378 for reservations. Also nearby is the Ah-Tah-Thi-Ki Museum, which tells the story of the tribe's history and culture. The museum (863/902-1113) is worth the trip: It has perhaps the prettiest and longest nature boardwalks in Florida, winding more than a mile through bald cypress and native trees. Incredible carpentry went into the construction of the boardwalk, which is also completely wheelchair accessible.

Special note: The speed limit of 25 mph inside the reservation is strictly enforced by police.

RV sites, facilities: There are 60 roomy RV campsites, of which 9 are pull-through. Streets are paved, making access easy for even the largest RVs. Some sites are shady. RV sites have concrete pads and full hookups. Facilities include a clubhouse, a pool, a hot tub for adults only, miniature golf, basketball courts, shuffleboard, horseshoes, a playground, and a weight room. Showers, restrooms, cabins, and laundry facilities are available. Telephone service and Internet access are available at each site, but not cable TV. A small store offers ice and snacks. All areas are wheelchair accessible. Children are welcome. Leashed pets are permitted. You can leave your RV in storage for a monthly fee.

Reservations, fees: Reservations are suggested. Sites are $25 per night for two adults and two children, plus $5 for each extra person. Credit cards are accepted. Maximum length of stay is six months.

Directions: From Fort Lauderdale, take I-75 west to Exit 49, then head north for about 19 miles to the campground. From Naples, take I-75 east for 52 miles to Exit 49, then go north to the campground.

Contact: Big Cypress RV Resort, HC 61, P.O. Box 54-A, Clewiston, FL 33440, 863/983-1330 or 800/437-4102, www.bigcypress-rvresort.com.

TREASURE COAST

BEST RV PARKS AND CAMPGROUNDS

◖ **Most Unusual**
Sunnier Palms Nudist Campground, page 428

Blessed with outdoor attributes, the Treasure Coast offers beaches, the ocean, and woods, as well as top-notch golfing, boating, and relaxation. The Atlantic Ocean defines the region on the east, and towns such as Vero Beach, Fort Pierce, and Stuart hug the coast. They are quieter and more relaxed than their southern big-city cousins, and they pride themselves on controlling development and playing up their natural features.

At the same time, the area beckons visitors for more touristy pursuits. The Los Angeles Dodgers have played spring-training baseball games since 1953 in Vero Beach, and fans can watch them practice at "Dodgertown." In Port St. Lucie, the PGA Village is home to 72 holes of championship golf and a learning center for duffers who want to perfect their game. Public beachfront parks are plentiful.

Although RV parks are few in this area, many provide interesting places to park your rig. The St. Lucie Lock Recreation Area offers a view of how engineers use their skills to control nature. The St. Lucie Canal, built by the U.S. Army Corps of Engineers as part of South Florida's massive drainage system, is the east-west waterway from Lake Okeechobee to the ocean. Visitors can stand above the massive lock system and watch boats travel beneath their feet. At this restful, sunny spot, daytime picnickers and campers alike stop to watch the action.

Head farther south to the always-popular Jonathan Dickinson State Park for something that will please almost everyone in your party. Campers can choose from easy, level hiking trails well suited for a day trip, horseback riding, mountain biking, fishing, nature study, and side trips to nearby beaches. The Loxahatchee, the only federally designated Wild and Scenic River in this part of the state, is worth exploring by canoe or kayak. Paddling seaward, you'll pass through dark, brooding cypress forests to where the freshwater turns salty and mangroves appear on the banks. You're virtually certain to see alligators (maybe a manatee, if you're lucky) and bald eagles are also sighted along with the hawklike osprey. The park is populated throughout by deer, Florida sandhill cranes, wading birds, alligators, raccoons, and other wild animals.

Fishing is good, both in the Loxahatchee River and the nearby Indian River. Redfish, trout, and snook are among the favored game fish. Some anglers prefer surfcasting in the nearby Atlantic Ocean for whiting, pompano, and jack. For a side trip, visit the Jupiter Lighthouse and Museum, where Confederate soldiers captured the light and doused it, and Blowing Rocks Preserve, where water jets up through blow-holes in an intriguing rock formation.

TREASURE COAST

see Space Coast page 326

441

60

Lokosee

Yeehaw Junction

Blue Cypres Lake

4

512

1

95

Micco

Indian River

Roseland

Sebastian

2
3

A1A

60

Vero Beach

AL
GA

Gulf of Mexico

441

70

see Lake Okeechobee page 396

Sunland Gardens

St Lucie

5

6

8

7

Fort Pierce

ATLANTIC

OCEAN

95

Port St Lucie

Lake

Okeechobee

A1A

9

10

Jensen Beach

Palm City

Port Salerno

St Lucie 76 Canal

Indiantown

726

12-13

11

1

Hobe Sound

Bryant

710

441

28

706

95

Tequesta

0   5 mi

0   5 km

see Gold Coast page 464

© AVALON TRAVEL PUBLISHING,

1 SUNSHINE TRAVEL-ENCORE RESORT VERO BEACH

Scenic rating: 7

off I-95 north of Vero Beach

This 35-acre RV resort is so civilized that garbage is picked up at your campsite, by the concrete-paved road, at 10 A.M. daily, and loud radios are forbidden. It's owned by a chain of manufactured-home communities, so expect professional landscaping and services. The park is designed for RVers looking to spend one month or longer in a resort community, but overnight travelers also show up at the large sites and plunge into the 22- by 36-foot, kidney-shaped heated pool.

King Palm Drive is the closest to nearby I-95. On the other side of the park is a pine forest. The Los Angeles Dodgers have played spring-training baseball games since 1953, eight miles to the south at 4001 26th Street, Vero Beach; for tickets, call 772/569-6858.

RV sites, facilities: All 300 sites have full hookups, 30-amp and 50-amp electrical service, and cable TV. Some sites are pull-through. For recreation, there's a heated pool, a game room, horseshoes, miniature golf, a playground, shuffleboard, boccie ball (lawn bowling), croquet, table tennis, a lending library, two recreation halls (one with a kitchen), and scheduled winter activities. Showers, restrooms, a general store, picnic tables, rental park models, and laundry facilities are available. Restaurants and grocery stores are within three miles. Children are welcome. Leashed pets are permitted.

Reservations, fees: Reservations are advised. Sites are $22–43 per night for two people, plus $2 per extra person. Credit cards are accepted. Long-term rates are available.

Directions: From I-95 at Exit 156, drive east for one block on County Road 512/Fellsmere Road to the park entrance on your right at 108th Avenue. The park is behind McDonald's.

Contact: Sunshine Travel-Encore Resort Vero Beach, 9455 108th Avenue, Vero Beach, FL 32967, 772/589-7828 or 877/362-6736, fax 772/628-7081.

2 WHISPERING PALMS RV PARK

Scenic rating: 5

on U.S. 1 in Wabasso

Retirees escaping frosty Northern winters are targeted by this sprawling 35-acre home of not one, but two, heated pools and two recreation rooms, located four miles west of Atlantic Ocean beaches. The sunny, concrete-pad RV sites are outnumbered by the 328 mobile homes. The nicely kept park is set in a sleepy area and is bordered by U.S. 1 and FEC Railroad tracks. Most visitors here are from Canada. Anglers often travel a few miles northeast to the Indian River/Brevard County line to crowd the jetty at the 500-acre Sebastian Inlet State Park.

RV sites, facilities: This adult-oriented park has 257 full-hookup RV sites with 30-amp and 50-amp electrical service. Two pools, horseshoes, shuffleboard, winter social programs, two recreation rooms, and two tennis courts entertain campers. Showers, restrooms, a dump station, and laundry facilities are available. The pull-through sites are wheelchair accessible. Groceries, snacks, and restaurants are one mile away. Children are allowed for short-term visits only. Leashed pets under 25 pounds are permitted.

Reservations, fees: Reservations are recommended. Sites are $25–35 per night for two people, plus $3 for each additional person. Credit cards are accepted. Long-term stays are okay.

Directions: From I-95 at Exit 156, drive east for six miles on County State Road 512 to U.S. 1. Turn right and continue 2.1 miles south to the campground.

Contact: Whispering Palms RV Park, 10305 U.S. 1, Sebastian, FL 32958, 772/589-3481.

3 VERO BEACH KAMP

Scenic rating: 6

on U.S. 1 north of Vero Beach

A hair salon, a ceramics shop, and other businesses set a commercial tone for the road that fronts this 14-acre campground—U.S. 1. Still, the region focuses on its pretty outdoor attributes, with Atlantic Ocean beaches 2 miles east, a boat ramp on the Indian River 0.5 mile from the campground, deep-sea fishing at offshore reefs, and shelling and clamming nearby. Visitors come from all over the United States, plus Canada and Germany. Favorite things to do are fishing and going to the beach.

RV sites, facilities: Five rows of grassy RV slots line up campers side by side, about 20 sites per row for a total of 120 sites. Seventy sites have 30-amp electrical service, and 30 have 50-amp. All sites have concrete patios, grills, and picnic tables. For recreation, there's a pool, a playground, shuffleboard, winter social programs, and a recreation room. Showers, grills, fire rings, a dump station, cabins, a convenience store, a deli, a gift shop, cable TV, and laundry facilities are available. Restrooms, the office, and the activity building are wheelchair accessible. Groceries and restaurants are within two miles. Children are welcome. Leashed, attended pets are permitted.

Reservations, fees: Reservations are required in winter and recommended at other times. Sites are $40 per night for two people, plus $3 for each additional person. Credit cards are accepted. Long-term rates are available.

Directions: From I-95 at Exit 156, drive east for two miles on County Road 512 to County Road 510 and turn right. Continue six miles, following the curve to the left, to U.S. 1. Turn left. The campground is 0.25 mile ahead, on the right.

Contact: Vero Beach Kamp, 8850 U.S. 1, Sebastian, FL 32958, 772/589-5665 or 877/589-5643, fax 561/388-5722.

4 MIDDLETON'S FISH CAMP

Scenic rating: 4

at Blue Cypress Lake west of Vero Beach

Even though serious anglers try for speckled perch and bass at 6,500-acre Blue Cypress Lake, this wild region holds promise for bird-watchers, wildlife admirers, duck hunters, and anyone who doesn't mind giving up niceties like electric hookups for a night. Some Midwesterners return to this rustic campground year after year, lured by 80°F-plus winter temperatures and the call of the outdoors. The primitive camp is surrounded by huge, government-owned lands set aside for wildlife.

At dusk, deer cross the five-mile dirt road that leads to cypress-lined Blue Cypress Lake, which is named for the trees' blue appearance at sunrise. Alert campers may see otters, eagles, hawks, alligators, and osprey. Yet, as the name suggests, fishing is the highlight at the only camp on the lake, which is the headwaters to the St. Johns River. Motorboats start at $55 for four hours. You can also rent pontoon boats and kayaks.

RV sites, facilities: This primitive, county-owned camping area offers approximately a dozen or so RV sites. There are no hookups, but showers, restrooms, a boat ramp, boat and canoe rentals, fishing guides, cabins, and rental trailers are available. Most areas are said to be wheelchair accessible. Children and leashed pets are permitted.

Reservations, fees: Sites are first-come, first-served, and there is no fee. There is a $10 deposit for pets. Credit cards are accepted for cabin and boat rentals. The maximum stay is one week.

Directions: From I-95 at Exit 147, drive west for 18 miles on State Road 60, veering around a bend known as 20 Mile Bend and passing a waterway called Padgett Branch. Signs will instruct you to turn right at Blue Cypress Lake Road. If you pass a microwave tower on State Road 60, then you've missed the turn to the lake. Follow Blue Cypress Lake Road for five miles to its end to reach the fish camp.

Contact: Middleton's Fish Camp, 21704 73rd Manor, Vero Beach, FL 32966, 772/778-0150, www.middletonsfishcamp.com.

5 PORT ST. LUCIE RV RESORT

Scenic rating: 8

in Port St. Lucie

Port St. Lucie RV Resort fills a void for campers with large motorhomes and trailers who want to explore the Treasure Coast. Just five miles from the ocean, the well-manicured park opened in 2000 with all new facilities. Within one block are several shopping centers, two groceries, and many restaurants; visitors can access a Wal-Mart behind the park through a side gate.

RV sites, facilities: The park has 117 sites with full hookups, 30/50-amp electrical service, picnic tables, and concrete pads. Four sites are pull-through, and there are no size restrictions. Each site has telephone hookups for modem use or telephone calls. About half the sites have cable TV. Restrooms, showers, laundry facilities, a pool, and a recreation hall are available. All areas are wheelchair accessible. Children are welcome, but adults are preferred. Leashed pets are permitted.

Reservations, fees: Reservations are recommended. Sites are $36–44 nightly for two people, plus $2 per extra person and $1.63 for cable TV sites. A onetime fee of $2 is charged for pets. Credit cards are accepted. Seasonal stays are permitted.

Directions: From I-95 southbound, take Exit 121 east to U.S. 1 and follow directions below. From I-95 northbound, use Exit 118 and go east to U.S. 1. From the Florida Turnpike, use Exit 142 and go east to U.S. 1. From the intersection of Port St. Lucie Boulevard and U.S. 1, drive north about 0.5 mile. Turn right on Jennings Road; the park will on your right about 2,000 feet ahead.

Contact: Port St. Lucie RV Resort, 3703 Jennings Road, Port St. Lucie, FL 34952, 772/337-3340 or 877/405-2333, fax 772/337-7347, http://portstlucievresort.com.

6 ROAD RUNNER TRAVEL RESORT

Scenic rating: 6

west of Fort Pierce

This 38-acre blend of citified amenities in a wooded, rural setting lures some people to live here and others to visit. Besides the campground's heated pool and unusual offerings such as a *pétanque* (French-style bowling) court, a par-three golf course, and three recreation halls, owners Jim and Marilyn Minix's park rules aim to satisfy urban sensibilities: Keep your campsite neat. Overnighters should place garbage bags at the paved road in front of their campsite before checking out. Long-term campers should rake lawn debris into a pile in front of their lots to be picked up. Still, the park won't soon be mistaken for a suburban subdivision, if only for its pines and sabal palms. Roads are paved. And how many suburbs boast a fishing pond by a general store? About 40 percent of the park is occupied year-round.

For fun, boaters and anglers can drive 5–6 miles to Atlantic Ocean beaches, the Indian River, or the St. Lucie Inlet. Back at the campground, the packed winter activities schedule keeps visitors busy. A sample day: 7 A.M. walk, 8 A.M. flea market trip, 9 A.M. exercises, 2 P.M. water exercises, 7 P.M. cards. To sleep beside the park's lake, ask about the sunny, nearly treeless campsites on Lincoln Circle. For a canopy of shade trees, ask about campsites on Madison and Eisenhower Drives (although several other streets have at least some shade). The park is near the small St. Lucie County Airport.

RV sites, facilities: These 452 full-hookup campsites have mostly 50-amp electrical service; 75 have 30-amp. RVs up to 45 feet in length and slide-outs can be accommodated. Twelve sites are drive-through. A pool, a tennis court, a *pétanque* court, shuffleboard, horseshoes, winter activities, and three recreation halls keep campers entertained. Showers, restrooms, a restaurant, groceries, a dump station, rental park models, rental villas, the on-site convenience store, and laundry facilities are available. Most areas are wheelchair accessible. Streets are paved. Children under 12 must be adult-supervised at the pool and other public areas. Leashed pets are permitted.

Reservations, fees: Reservations are advised. Sites are $32 per night for two people, plus $3 for each additional person. Credit cards are accepted. Long-term rates are available.

Directions: From I-95 at Exit 131B, go west on Orange Avenue/State Road 68 a short distance to the first light. Turn right at Kings Highway/State Road 713. Turn right in 2.5 miles at St. Lucie Boulevard. The campground is one mile ahead on your left.

Contact: Road Runner Travel Resort, 5500 St. Lucie Boulevard, Fort Pierce, FL 34946, 772/464-0969 or 800/833-7108, www.road-runnertravelresort.com.

⑦ SUNNIER PALMS NUDIST CAMPGROUND

Scenic rating: 5

off I-95 west of Fort Pierce

BEST (

Everyone at this 24-acre park is expected to participate in the nudist lifestyle and must be nude in the pool or hot tub. But there is a definite nature orientation, and even activism: The park helped save a rare plant and a butterfly species that lost their habitat to development by allowing the colonies to be moved to the park land. Foot trails lead through a sun-dappled forest of pines and spiky palmettos interspersed with shady oaks. Some campers at this private, flat, fenced park hike or take blankets out to lie naked in the 12 acres or so of woods. You'll get a taste of both worlds here:

The reasonably close highway and fast-food joints are reminders of city life. Favorite things to do are sightseeing and fishing, and there's a potluck dinner every Sunday. Most visitors are from the Northeast and from Canada.

RV sites, facilities: This nudist resort has 13 full-hookup RV sites with 50-amp electricity and picnic tables. Rigs up to 40 feet long and slide-outs can be accommodated. A pool, a hot tub, organic gardening, nature trails, a playground, and a butterfly exhibit entertain campers. A certain amount of decorum is expected: "Your behavior is your passport." Part of the park is a 12-acre nature sanctuary. Showers, restrooms, a dump station, a grocery store, rental villas, and laundry facilities are available. The bathhouse is wheelchair accessible. Groceries and restaurants are within three miles. Children are welcome. Pets are prohibited.

Reservations, fees: Reservations are necessary in winter. Sites are $45 per night, plus $1 for electricity. Credit cards are accepted. Long-term rates are available. The maximum length of stay is six months.

Directions: From I-95 at Exit 129, drive west on Okeechobee Road/State Road 70 for about 1.5 miles to the campground. The park is one mile west of Florida's Turnpike (Exit 152).

Contact: Sunnier Palms Nudist Campground, 8800 Okeechobee Road, Fort Pierce, FL 34945, 772/468-8512, www.sunnier.com.

⑧ OUTDOOR RESORTS AT ST. LUCIE WEST

Scenic rating: 10

west of Port St. Lucie between I-95 and Florida's Turnpike

This resort is for Class A motor homes 25 feet or longer—which gives you an expectation of the kinds of amenities to expect: several swimming pools, lighted tennis courts, a golf course, and deluxe paved sites on which to park that expensive rig. It's three miles from the famous PGA Golf Club, but already has nine holes of its own on-site. When fully built out, the resort will have 510 sites (many for ownership), five swimming pools, four tennis courts, 18 holes of golf, a fitness center, an owner's lounge, and more. About 5 percent of the park is occupied by year-round residents.

RV sites, facilities: There are 249 campsites, each with 30/50-amp electrical service, cement pads, picnic tables, full hookups, telephone, wireless Internet access, and cable TV. Motor coaches 25–45 feet long can be accommodated. On the premises are three pools, two lighted tennis courts, a nine-hole golf course, and a large clubhouse. Security and on-site staff are available 24 hours. Restrooms, showers, a dump station, three dog-walk areas, and laundry facilities are also provided. Most areas are wheelchair accessible. Freestanding satellite dishes are not allowed. Children are welcome. Leashed pets are permitted.

Reservations, fees: Reservations are recommended. Sites are $45–65 per night for four people, plus $5 per extra person. No more than six people are allowed per site. Credit cards are accepted. Long-term rates are available.

Directions: From I-95, take Exit 121 onto St. Lucie West Boulevard in an eastbound direction. Drive 0.3 mile, and turn left on Northwest Peacock Boulevard. Continue 1.3 miles to the park entrance on the left. From Florida's Turnpike, take Exit 152 at Fort Pierce. Follow the signs to I-95 and proceed with the directions above.

Contact: Outdoor Resorts at St. Lucie West, 800 Northwest Peacock Boulevard, Port St. Lucie, FL 34986, 772/336-1136 or 866/456-2303, fax 772/336-1193, www.outdoor-resorts-slw.com.

9 THE SAVANNAS RECREATIONAL AREA

Scenic rating: 5

east of U.S. 1 in southeastern Fort Pierce

Some people rave about the rustic Savannas, a 550-acre county park/camping getaway where

boaters snag bass and visitors lazily paddle rental canoes. Inside the gate, in day-use area No. 2, you can eat a picnic lunch, then walk along the Everglades-like marsh on a hiking trail shaded by shaggy Australian pines. The trail leads to a sort of makeshift observation tower, where you can peer out over the saw grass and cattails. You'll hear frogs croaking—after all, this is a wild retreat. Rent a canoe for $4 hourly for an up-close view of the marsh.

Although the park is large, it feels fairly small if you don't head out into the marsh. The limited dry land is hemmed in by the watery prairie. Expect to see your neighbors from your no-frills, grassy campsite. To help minimize that, spring for a water-view site.

County promoters say the Savannas is Florida's last freshwater lagoon system. The preserve actually extends outside this campground to take in about eight square miles of marsh and uplands between White City Road/State Road 172 and Jensen Beach Boulevard/State Road 707A. From the campground, Atlantic Ocean beaches are nine miles east, for those who want to swim or sunbathe.

RV sites, facilities: There are 33 campsites for RVs with water and electricity; some also have sewer hookups. Canoe rentals, nature trails, a playground, a dump station, showers, restrooms, a boat ramp, a picnic shelter, and laundry facilities are available. Groceries can be purchased within two miles. A restaurant is within 10 miles. Children are welcome. Leashed dogs are permitted.

Reservations, fees: Reservations are accepted. Sites are $13–20 per night for four people, plus $1–2 for each extra person. There is an additional admission fee of $1 per car. Credit cards are accepted. RVers can stay as long as two months.

Directions: From I-95 at Exit 131A, drive east for about four miles on Orange Avenue/State Road 68. Turn right (south) at South 4th Street/U.S. 1. Continue almost five miles to Midway Road/County Road 712. Turn left and proceed east to the park entrance, about 1.5 miles ahead.

Contact: The Savannas Recreational Area, 1400 East Midway Road, Fort Pierce, FL 34982, 772/464-7855 or 800/789-5776, fax 772/464-1765, www.stlucieco.gov/leisure/savanna.htm.

10 THE VILLAGE AT NETTLES ISLAND

Scenic rating: 7

on the Atlantic Ocean on Hutchinson Island

This 130-acre, ocean-to-river island resort feels like a residential community. Before you pull into the concrete driveway beside your RV site and personal patio, you'll follow paved roads that pass park models with attached Florida rooms, lots with docks on the Intracoastal Waterway, and maybe even a retirement-ready, double-wide mobile home with a front porch and garden. It seems like every square inch of this sun-washed barrier island is covered with villas, RVs, and park models, although roads and green ribbons of lawn separate sleeping spots. At the resort's center is its hub of activity—a clubhouse, a pool, and sports courts. From the marina (bring your own boat), you can embark on a day of boating or fishing in the Intracoastal Waterway, the Atlantic Ocean, or the Indian River Lagoon.

The Intracoastal Waterway stretches one mile from the wee backyards of western waterfront lots. RV sites are scattered throughout this barrier island off Florida's Treasure Coast. Although the island technically has 1,578 sites, only 50–125 at any given time may be open to campers who bring their own rigs. The other sites here at this condominium-concept park largely are devoted to vacation rentals. February is the busiest time of the year, so call early if that's when you'll be coming.

RV sites, facilities: All 1,578 sites have full hookups, but only 50 or so are available for self-contained RVs staying overnight or for the season. Pop-ups and other small trailers without facilities are not allowed. For recreation, there's

a pool, miniature golf, a clubhouse, horseshoes, a playground, tennis, shuffleboard, and volleyball. Showers, restrooms, a cafe, a dump station, a grocery store, cable TV, park models, a marina, and laundry facilities are available. Children are permitted. Leashed pets are allowed on park streets and in a dog walk in front.

Reservations, fees: Reservations are advised. Sites are $37–64 per night, plus $3 for electricity. Credit cards are accepted. Long-term stays are okay.

Directions: From Stuart, drive north on Highway A1A/Ocean Drive to Hutchinson Island past the county line. Nettles Island is located just ahead, on the left side of the road.

Contact: VNI Realty, 9803 South Ocean Drive, Jensen Beach, FL 34957, 772/229-1300, www.vnirealty.com.

11 PHIPPS PARK

Scenic rating: 4

on the St. Lucie Canal west of Stuart

This 57-acre, grassy, county-operated park on the St. Lucie Canal has huge spaces and lots of room for big rigs on its grassy camping spots. Boats under 20 feet can launch from Phipps Park, whereas campers with bigger boats should opt for the nearby St. Lucie Lock and Dam. Feel free to keep your boat at your site. Locals and out-of-towners alike camp at the park, which is on the saltwater side of the St. Lucie Lock and Dam. Anglers take boats out to try for snook and bass. The park restrooms are not real modern, but there's lots of room for everyone in the park and you won't feel crowded, even in the high winter season. A locked gate nightly and on-site manager provides a feel of security.

RV sites, facilities: The 54 officially numbered campsites and open field of about 17 overflow sites are for RVs, but no hookups are offered. Each site has a picnic table, a grill, and a fire ring. A playground, a nearby boat launch, showers, a dump station, and wheelchair-accessible restrooms are available. Restaurants, laundry facilities, a bank, and a supermarket are five or six miles away. Children are welcome. Pets are forbidden.

Reservations, fees: Reservations are not accepted. Sites are $6 per night. Credit cards are not accepted. You may stay up to 15 days per year.

Directions: From I-95, take Exit 101 and go west on State Road 76. Pass Florida's Turnpike. Turn right at Locks Road. Proceed one mile to the park entrance at right.

Contact: Phipps Park, 2175 Southwest Locks Road, Stuart, FL 34997, 772/287-6565.

12 ST. LUCIE LOCK RECREATION AREA

Scenic rating: 8

on the St. Lucie Canal west of Stuart

This 154-acre area run by the U.S. Army Corps of Engineers combines the opportunity to commune with nature and marvel at the ingenuity of the human mind. The drama of standing above the massive lock system and watching boats travel beneath your feet is one attraction of this restful, sunny spot on the St. Lucie Canal. Daytime picnickers and campers alike stop to watch the action. As boats spend 15–20 minutes passing through the lock, the curious look downward to read the home ports on the boat transoms to get an idea of just how far the vessels have traveled. It's an awesome sight to behold. A one-mile nature trail is available for hikers on the north side of the lock/dam with an observation area overlooking Hog Creek. You may spot alligators and gopher tortoises near the trail and on Killingbeck Island. To the east of the campground is a 2,500-square-foot visitors center with a free lending library, a movie, and exhibits on the Okeechobee Waterway.

Tall Australian pines provide some shade for the concrete-pad RV sites. Meanwhile, boaters can motor up to this camping area and sleep aboard their vessels at the eight boat campsites. Anglers can launch from the camping area to go up the canal for bass. Others catch mullet and catfish from the lock's pier. Tip: Cross the lock if you want to try for snook. This campground is another example of the U.S. Army Corps of Engineers' taste for precision, from its immaculate sites to its attention to detail.

RV sites, facilities: Eight RV sites with 30-amp electricity and water hookups are offered. Each site has a picnic table, a grill, and a fire ring. A playground, a boat ramp, showers, a dump station, and wheelchair-accessible restrooms are available. A convenience store and a deli are two miles away; a laundry and a supermarket are six miles away. Children are welcome. Leashed pets are permitted.

Reservations, fees: Reservations are accepted. RVers pay $16 nightly. Credit cards are accepted. You may stay 14 days in a 30-day period. If you're lucky and plan ahead, you can get a free campsite in exchange for 24–30 hours of weekly volunteer service; these opportunities are naturally limited during the popular winter months.

Directions: From I-95, take Exit 101 and go west on State Road 76 for about two miles, passing Florida's Turnpike. Turn right at Locks Road. Continue 1.5 miles to the end of the road, then turn left at Canal Street and proceed to the campground.

Contact: St. Lucie Lock Recreation Area, 2170 Southwest Canal Street, Stuart, FL 34997, 772/219-4575. For reservations, call 877/444-6777 or see www.reserveusa.com/nrrs/fl/stlu/stlu.htm.

13 JONATHAN DICKINSON STATE PARK

Scenic rating: 10

near the Atlantic Ocean in Hobe Sound

This place is excellent for a family outing because something will please almost everyone in your party. You can hike to the top of piney hills and, if you stand and look toward the Indian River in the distance, you can imagine how these were once huge sand dunes at the edge of Florida, aeons ago when the oceans were much deeper. Much of the hiking here is easy, level, and suited to a day excursion with the kids. Horseback riding is popular, as is canoeing in the Loxahatchee River, fishing, nature study, and side trips to nearby beaches. Mountain-biking trails complete the picture; ask about "Camp Murphy," which served as an Army base for 6,000 troops during World War II. You're likely to see deer, Florida sandhill cranes, wading birds, and other wild animals throughout the park.

The park is named for a Quaker merchant who shipwrecked nearby in 1696. But probably the most colorful of the historic figures is a 20th-century addition to the local lore known as Trapper Nelson. Taking a canoe or narrated riverboat tour up to the site of Trapper Nelson's old camp on the Loxahatchee River is highly recommend. Nelson was a hermit who came to live on the banks of the beautiful Loxahatchee during the Great Depression, eking out an existence by trapping animals for their fur. Before dying under mysterious circumstances more than three decades later, he built a small zoo at his place and added to his income by charging tourists who were passing by on the river a fee to see the menagerie. After his death the site was preserved, complete with the animal pens, his cabin, a "chickee" shelter (Seminole-style thatched-roof dwelling), and exotic trees, including wild almond, bamboo, sausage tree, guava, and java plum.

If you're handy with a canoe or kayak, try an all-day paddle down the Loxahatchee, which is designated by the federal government as the only Wild and Scenic River in this part of the state. From the spot where Indiantown Road crosses the Loxahatchee, you'll paddle seaward, past dark, brooding cypress forests to where the freshwater turns salty and mangroves appear on the banks. Some parts of the trip are achingly beautiful and serene, although you will pass underneath I-95 and Florida's Turnpike at one point. You're virtually certain to see alligators (in fact, one of the few documented cases of an alligator attacking a human occurred here a few years ago when an old, sick gator attacked and killed a young boy). If you're lucky, you might even see a manatee, that lumbering but lovable endangered mammal also known as the sea cow. Bald eagles, once endangered but now on the upswing, also are sighted sometimes, along with the hawklike osprey. The park rents canoes, but the area's mostpopular canoe livery is Canoe Outfitters of Florida, which charges $50 for three people in a canoe and $40 for a kayak, with shuttle service; call 772/746-7053.

Fishing is good, both in the Loxahatchee River and the nearby Indian River. Redfish, trout, and snook are among the favored game fish. Some anglers prefer surfcasting in the nearby Atlantic Ocean for whiting, pompano, and jack, while other members of the family sunbathe.

Also consider two other side trips: At the Jupiter Lighthouse and Museum, a short drive away, you can learn how Confederate soldiers captured the light and doused it—without firing a shot—to aid ships running the Yankee blockade. Also, don't miss a trip to Blowing Rocks Preserve, within a 30-minute drive, where water jets up through blowholes in an intriguing rock formation in what's known as Anastasia limestone. The wave action has worn the relatively soft stone into fascinating and beautiful shapes. At high tide, watch water spout through the blowholes. At low tide, explore the caves and tidal pools. Guided nature walks are offered Thursday at 2 P.M. and Sunday at 11 A.M. Call 772/747-3113.

RV sites, facilities: All 135 back-in sites have water and 30-amp electrical hookups; of these, 16 have 50-amp service. Each site has a grill, a fire ring, and a picnic table. None of the sites are pull-through. Boat tours, canoe rentals, a playground, horseback-riding trails, four nature trails, and a bicycling trail entertain campers. Showers, a boat ramp, limited groceries, and rental cabins are available. About two miles away are restaurants, bait, and laundry facilities. Some areas of the park are wheelchair accessible. Children are welcome. One pet is permitted in the campground with proof of vaccination.

Reservations, fees: Reservations are recommended; contact ReserveAmerica at 800/336-3521 or reserveamerica.com. Sites are $22 per night for up to eight people. Credit cards are accepted. The maximum stay is 14 nights.

Directions: From I-95, take Exit 87A and go east on State Road 706. Turn left at U.S. 1. Look for the park entrance on the left.

Contact: Jonathan Dickinson State Park, 16450 Southeast Federal Highway, Hobe Sound, FL 33455, 772/546-2771, www.florida stateparks.org.

FORT MYERS/ NAPLES

COURTESY OF VISIT FLORIDA

BEST RV PARKS AND CAMPGROUNDS

《 Privately Owned Beachfront RV Parks
Red Coconut RV Resort, page 446

《 Most Luxurious
RiverBend Motorcoach Resort, page 442
Silver Lakes RV Resort and Golf Club, page 458

The Fort Myers and Naples area is a popular

vacation spot for many reasons: broad, sugar-white beaches, abundant fishing in saltwater and on rivers, undeveloped barrier islands where nature still reigns, and wildlife ranging from the endangered manatee to all manner of wading birds. However, the coastline is under heavy development pressure. Construction booms year-round, as vacation and retirement homes are built for affluent buyers from the Northern states, mostly retirees. As one of the nation's fastest-growing and most affluent areas, it is constantly changing.

Fort Myers attractions include the Edison Winter Home and Laboratory, where inventor Thomas A. Edison, who gave us the lightbulb and the phonograph among hundreds of other things, spent his winters. Next door is the home of auto magnate Henry Ford, where you can see some perfectly preserved Model Ts. A few RV parks are near Fort Myers Beach, which overlooks the Gulf of Mexico. When you tire of beachside fun, you can charter a fishing excursion or head for the Times Square restaurant area clustered around the bridge to the mainland.

Sanibel Island, Captiva Island, and Marco Island offer public beaches known for good shelling. However, it's illegal to collect live shells. When you find an empty one, try soaking it in a bucket of water with bleach to make it look nearly as perfect as those for sale at the Shell Factory. The huge Fort Myers store claims to have the largest collection of seashells and coral in the world (for sale, of course). All three islands have expensive vacation homes, fancy resort hotels, and quaint boutiques selling pastel-colored vacation clothing and knickknacks made of shells. Among the three, only Sanibel has a campground. Many people park their RVs or cars just off the causeway to Sanibel, and then go fishing, swimming, or windsurfing.

Nature sanctuaries in this area include the J. N. "Ding" Darling National Wildlife Refuge, Six-Mile Cypress Slough Preserve, and the National Audubon Society's Corkscrew Swamp Sanctuary, a unique forest of towering 500-year-old bald cypress bisected by a two-mile boardwalk. The refuge teems with nearly 200 species of birds, including nesting wood storks, plus alligators, deer, and bobcat.

Some part-time residents choose to stay in the area's many RV parks, and traffic is noticeably heavier when tourists are in town. (The "high season" runs roughly November 15–April 15, peaking January–Easter.) A typical adult park might find repeat visitors from the Midwest and Canada. In older parks, many have added carports, porches, and screened rooms to their trailers. Residents spend the winter months socializing, shopping, and taking part in organized activities in the RV park recreation hall, such as square dancing, quilting, wood carving, billiards, bingo, arts-and-crafts classes, card games, ice-cream socials, and potluck dinners. Tennis, horseshoe, and shuffleboard tournaments are also popular.

Some newer parks cater to upscale RVs, specifically allowing only Class A motor homes or fifth wheels. Older travel trailers are not welcome. One park has RV sites with space for two cars, 50-foot concrete pads, and a patio; its 12,000-square-foot recreation hall has a $30,000 sound system. Often, these deluxe parks will also sell lots or park models, which the owners can rent out part-time as a source of income.

1 TAMIAMI RV PARK

Scenic rating: 3

north of Fort Myers

With its fitness classes on land and in the pool, this park perhaps is the epitome of the "active" retirement lifestyle people seek in Florida. The idea is to experience first the RV park, then decide to stay longer. More seriously speaking, the community has established a veteran's memorial garden to commemorate those who served the United States in wartimes. Across the street from this sun-drenched park is the Shell Factory, a 70,000-square-foot store that claims to have the largest collection of seashells and coral in the world (for sale, of course). Next door is an enormous mobile-home community (a sister park, Tamiami Village, with 700 sites) and a barbershop. Speaking of shells, it's illegal to collect live shells from the beach; those are the ones with the little critters still inside them. When you find an empty one, try soaking it in a bucket of water with bleach to remove algae and make it look nearly as perfect as those for sale at the Shell Factory. Another method for cleaning shells is to leave them outside in the Florida rain and sun for a few days.

RV sites, facilities: This park has a total of 243 full-hookup RV sites with cable TV and telephone service available. About half are taken by visitors who stay six months and then store their trailers, and one-third are permanent residents. The rest are available for shorter-term visitors. Big rigs up to 45 feet long and slide-outs can be accommodated. Forty sites have 50-amp electrical service; the rest have 30-amp. A wireless Internet network is available in the park. Restrooms, showers, laundry facilities, three shuffleboard courts, three recreation halls, three swimming pools, horseshoe pits, and two pool tables are on-site. The restrooms, laundry room, and recreation hall are wheelchair accessible. Groceries and restaurants are within two miles; malls and hospitals are eight miles away. Streets are paved. Children are welcome for short visits. Two pets under 25 pounds are allowed.

Reservations, fees: Reservations are recommended. Sites are $23–27 per night for two people, plus $3 for each additional person. Credit cards are accepted. Long-term rates are available.

Directions: From I-75, take Exit 158 westbound eight miles to new U.S. 41. Turn north at Cleveland Avenue. Don't be fooled into turning north on Business Route 41, one mile before you reach U.S. 41.

Contact: Tamiami RV Park, 16555-A North Cleveland Avenue, North Fort Myers, FL 33903, 239/995-7747, 239/997-2697, or 888/609-9697, www.tamiamirvpark.com.

2 SWAN LAKE VILLAGE AND RV RESORT

Scenic rating: 5

in North Fort Myers

Snowbirds who patronize this park are so devoted that one woman even wrote a poem about the place. What sets Swan Lake apart is that, unlike many campgrounds married to a mobile-home park, here the RV area is removed from highway noise and separate from the manufactured homes. It even has its own clubhouse with an adjacent pool. Slash pines and palm trees shade the 60-acre park, which has two fishing lakes and a citrus grove. Shopping, the Shell Factory, and Fort Myers attractions are close by. Fort Myers is a popular vacation spot for many reasons: broad, sugar-white beaches, abundant fishing in both saltwater and on rivers, undeveloped barrier islands where nature still reigns, and wildlife ranging from the endangered manatee to all manner of wading birds.

RV sites, facilities: This 156-unit mobile-home community has an attached RV park with 104 full-hookup sites that accommodate RVs up to 40 feet long. Each site has a picnic table and 30-amp electrical service. Restrooms, showers, laundry facilities, a pool, a clubhouse with wireless Internet access, two lakes, a recreation room, horseshoes, shuffleboard, daily wintertime activities, and an open field (where some campers hit golf balls) are available. For cable TV and telephone service, you must call the proper utility. A supermarket is one mile away. Adults over 50 are preferred; children are not permitted. Leashed pets that weigh under 20 pounds are permitted, and you can walk your dog in a special pooches area.

Reservations, fees: Reservations are recommended. Sites are $28 per night for two people, plus $3 per extra person. Credit cards are not accepted. Long-term stays are okay.

Directions: Take I-75 to Exit 143 and go west on State Road 78 for 5.2 miles to Business Route 41. Turn north (right) and drive a little over one mile to the park, on the right.

Contact: Swan Lake Village and RV Resort, 2400 North Tamiami Trail, North Fort Myers, FL 33903, 239/995-3397, fax 239/995-7879, www.swanlakevillage.com.

🄳 PIONEER VILLAGE

Scenic rating: 7

in North Fort Myers

RVers may not want to leave if they stay overnight in this 80-acre deluxe snowbird resort, where more than half the sites go to visitors who stay for the season. It's plenty close to the local attractions, but so many sports facilities and other activities are available on-site that you may want to stay a month or more. Under the direction of an activities director during the high season (November 15–April 15), residents can compete in tennis, horseshoe, and shuffleboard tournaments, and the recreation hall is Action Central for arts-and-crafts classes, bingo, card games, square dancing, quilting, ice-cream socials, and potluck dinners. A few mature oaks shade some sites, but many spots are sunny. Not too far away is the Edison Win-

ter Home and Laboratory (239/334-3614), where inventor Thomas A. Edison, who gave us, among other things, the lightbulb and the phonograph, spent his winters. Next door is the home of auto magnate Henry Ford, which is also open to the public and reached at the same phone number. Six-Mile Cypress Slough Preserve (239/432-2004) is a 2,000-acre wetland northeast of Fort Myers. It features a self-guided nature boardwalk and an opportunity to see alligators in the wild.

RV sites, facilities: This community has 470 RV sites (no size restrictions, and most are pull-through) with full hookups and 30/50-amp electrical service; 200 are available for over-nighters. A heated, oversized swimming pool with whirlpool and cabana, an 8,700-square-foot clubhouse, and a putting-and-chipping green are available. Volleyball, billiards, tennis, shuffleboard, basketball, horseshoes, a library, laundry facilities, showers, and restrooms also are on the premises. The park is oriented to active retirees, but families with children are permitted for short-term stays. Leashed animals are permitted, and there's a dog-walk area.

Reservations, fees: Reservations are recommended. Sites are $30 and up per night for two people, plus $2.50 for each extra person. Credit cards are accepted. Long-term stays are the norm.

Directions: From I-75, take Exit 143 westbound on Bayshore Road for one mile. At Samville Road, turn south and go 0.2 mile.

Contact: Pioneer Village, 7974 Samville Road, North Fort Myers, FL 33917, 239/543-3303 or 877/897-2757, fax 239/543-3498, www.rvonthego.com.

🄴 SEMINOLE CAMPGROUND

Scenic rating: 1

near North Fort Myers

Set on 20 acres, this rustic campground is convenient for overnighters. You may request an adults-only or family-only area. Take a look around before you decide; the clientele varies.

RV sites, facilities: The park has 129 sites with full hookups, 30-amp electrical service, cable TV, restrooms, showers, picnic tables, a dump station, a pool, a playground, a game room, laundry facilities, and rental trailers are on-site. Children are welcome, but not pets.

Reservations, fees: Reservations are not necessary. Sites are $11–15 per night for two people, plus $1 to $2 for each additional person. Credit cards are not accepted. Long-term stays are okay.

Directions: From I-75, take Exit 143 eastbound on State Road 78/Bayshore Road for 0.25 mile. Turn north on Wells Road and go 0.25 mile. At Triplett Road, turn west and proceed to the park.

Contact: Seminole Campground, 8991 Triplett Road, North Fort Myers, FL 33917, 239/543-2919, fax 239/731-2598.

5 UPRIVER CAMPGROUND RV RESORT

Scenic rating: 8

in North Fort Myers on the Caloosahatchee River

Some sites overlook a short inlet leading to the Caloosahatchee River, so you can feed pelicans from your own private dock or look for a manatee trying to stay warm in the river during the cooler months. A full-time activities director makes sure campers are entertained in winter. This self-described "luxury" campground is exceptional in that it is set back from the road with a huge open golf chipping range in front; it also has lots of trees. The surrounding area is somewhat rural. Still, there's plenty to do (fishing and boating on the river, swimming in the pool), and the park is a popular destination for snowbirds and retirees. Park models are for sale.

RV sites, facilities: Catering to RVers 55 and older, the park has 350 sites with full hookups,

30/50-amp electrical service, large concrete patios, cable TV, and telephone availability. Fifty sites are pull-through. A high-speed Internet connection is available in the clubhouse. Restrooms, showers, picnic tables, a boat ramp, an exercise-and-game room, a golf chipping course, three laundry facilities, a pool, and tennis courts are provided. The restrooms, laundry room, and recreation hall are wheelchair accessible. Children are welcome for short periods in summer. One small pet is allowed per site.

Reservations, fees: Reservations are recommended. Sites are $28–51 per night for two people, plus $2 for each additional person. Credit cards are accepted. Long-term rates are available.

Directions: From I-75, take Exit 143 eastbound on State Road 78 for 1.5 miles. The campground is on the south side.

Contact: Upriver Campground RV Resort, 17021 Upriver Drive, North Fort Myers, FL 33917, 239/543-3330 or 800/848-1652, fax 239/543-6663, www.upriver.com.

6 W. P. FRANKLIN LOCK AND DAM CAMPGROUND

Scenic rating: 8

east of Fort Myers

This is the westernmost campground run by the U.S. Army Corps of Engineers on the 152-mile Okeechobee Waterway, which crosses Lake Okeechobee and ends on the east coast of Florida near Stuart. This section on the Caloosahatchee River is the most scenic because it still has the old river oxbows outside of the main boating channel. You can ski in the channel, but at that speed you'll likely miss seeing wildlife such as alligators, river otters, bobcats, eagles, ospreys, hawks, and black vultures. The endangered West Indian manatee swims upstream to warmer waters in winter; sometimes, manatees get penned in with boats going through the locks and hitch a ride farther upstream. Campsites are paved and shade is minimal, although all sites overlook the river and a small inlet where boat campers can tie up their craft.

RV sites, facilities: There are 30 sites for RVs with water and 30-amp electrical service. Showers, restrooms, laundry facilities, a dump station, and a boat ramp are provided. A supermarket is 12 miles away. Children and leashed pets are welcome.

Reservations, fees: Reservations are recommended; contact ReserveAmerica at 800/336-3521 or reserveamerica.com. Sites are $20 per night. Credit cards are accepted. Maximum stay is 14 days in a 30-day period.

Directions: From I-75, take Exit 141 eastbound on State Road 80 for 10 miles. While driving, you will come to a stop sign after five miles; turn north and continue on State Road 78 as it winds around south again and west. The campground is on the south side of the road.

Contact: W. P. Franklin Lock and Dam Campground, 17850 North Franklin Lock Road, Alva, FL 33920, 239/694-8770; visitor center: 239/694-2582. Or, call the U.S. Army Corps of Engineers headquarters at 863/983-8101 (weekdays).

⑦ RIVERBEND MOTORCOACH RESORT

Scenic rating: 9

north of Fort Myers on the Caloosahatchee River

BEST (

This luxury resort, which opened in 2003, welcomes Class A motor coaches only. About 50 of the sites are available for rent; the rest are condominium lots. Ten percent of the park is occupied by year-round residents, and visitors come from as far away as Canada, Australia, and Germany. The park has 1,000 feet of frontage on the Caloosahatchee River's northern shore, and 25 acres are preserved as nature areas. Favorite things to do include enjoying group campfires, talent nights, karaoke, happy

hours, breakfasts, swimming, massages, and planned activities. East of here in the town of Alva is the Eden Harbor Winery, where you can observe the wine-making process and taste the homegrown product, which is reminiscent of sweet German wines.

RV sites, facilities: All 315 sites have full hookups with 50-amp electrical service, wireless Internet connection, concrete patios, and phone service available. Lots are landscaped, and the developers have kept some natural preserve areas on the site, including an oak grove along the river. About half the sites are drive-through. Restrooms, showers, laundry facilities, a pool, a boat ramp, a dock, pontoon boat rentals, three clubhouses, horseshoe pits, shuffleboard courts, a snack bar, a store, and nature trails are available. All areas are wheelchair accessible. The store sells ice, food, camping supplies, snacks, and souvenirs. Groceries and restaurants are within five miles. Malls are 20 miles away, and hospitals are 12 miles. Children are welcome, but no more than four people are allowed per coach. Leashed pets are permitted.

Reservations, fees: Reservations are recommended. Sites are $55–85 per night for two people. Credit cards are accepted. Stay as long as you like.

Directions: From I-75, take Exit 141 and go east on State Road 80 for 17 miles. The park will be on your left.

Contact: RiverBend Motorcoach Resort, 5800 West State Road 80, Alva, FL, 33920, 866/568-7368 or 863/674-0085, fax 863/674-0089, www.riverbendflorida.com.

⑧ ORANGE HARBOR MOBILE HOME AND RV PARK

Scenic rating: 4

in Fort Myers

As you cross the soaring bridge over the Caloosahatchee River, you can see this sprawling mobile-home and RV park on the south bank. It's near a manatee haven and bird sanctuary on the

Caloosahatchee and Orange Rivers. The open and sunny RV area is separate from the 364-unit mobile-home community, where there seems to be a golf cart parked in every driveway; campers may use the pool and common areas there. Near this park is Manatee World (239/694-4042), where you can book a river cruise through one of the state's most populated manatee sanctuaries. The endangered manatees (or sea cow, as this gentle animal is sometimes called) are often injured or killed by speeding boats; many bear the scars of past encounters with propellers because they stay close to the surface to breathe. On this cruise, the captain shuts off the engines so you can float quietly among the creatures. Reservations are recommended.

RV sites, facilities: Overnighters are not allowed. Long-term visiting senior citizens are the preferred campers at this park, which offers 130 full-hookup sites for RVs. Restrooms, showers, a pool, laundry facilities, a boat ramp, boat docks, and a recreation room are provided. A supermarket is 0.5 mile away. Children are not accepted, except to visit campers. Pets are forbidden.

Reservations, fees: Reservations are recommended. Sites are $1,100 for two months or $1,585 for three months, plus the cost of electricity. Add $50 per month for 50-amp service. Big rigs may be charged an additional fee. Credit cards are not accepted. Minimum stay is two months.

Directions: From I-75, take Exit 141 eastbound on State Road 80/Palm Beach Boulevard for 0.5 mile, then turn north into the park.

Contact: Orange Harbor Mobile Home and RV Park, 5749 Palm Beach Boulevard, Fort Myers, FL 33905, 239/694-3707, www.orangeharbor.com.

⑨ CYPRESS WOODS RV RESORT

Scenic rating: 8

east of Fort Myers

This park was among the first of the new breed of Florida luxury resorts targeted to

motor coaches, fifth wheels, and travel trailers—"one of the most beautiful and private outdoor resorts ever created," according to the color brochure. Sites have space for two cars and 50-foot concrete pads and a patio. The 12,000-square-foot recreation hall has a $30,000 sound system. The property is architecturally planned to incorporate nature preserves and open spaces. Besides RV spots, lots are being sold for homes.

RV sites, facilities: This luxury campground has 290 RV sites large enough to accommodate the biggest of rigs. Each site has concrete pads, full hookups, and cable TV; telephone service is available. Restrooms, showers, and laundry facilities are available. On the premises are a heated pool and spa, a lake, a recreation hall, and a dog-walk area. All areas are wheelchair accessible. Children are allowed for stays up to 30 days. Leashed pets are permitted; limit of two per site.

Reservations, fees: Reservations are recommended, and require a 25 percent deposit. No refunds are allowed if you cancel within 30 days of your arrival date, nor are they permitted for early checkouts. Sites are $36 per night May 1–September 30. From October 1 to April 30, the fee is $60 per night for two people, plus $5 for each additional person. Rates are subject to change. Credit cards are accepted. Long-term stays are okay.

Directions: From I-75, take Exit 139 eastbound about 0.5 mile to the resort entrance on the left.

Contact: Cypress Woods RV Resort, 5551 Luckett Road, Fort Myers, FL 33905, 239/694-2191, fax 239/694-4969, www.cypresswoodsrv.com.

⑩ FORT MYERS/ PINE ISLAND KOA

Scenic rating: 7

on the southern end of Pine Island

Lapped by the warm waters of the Gulf of Mexico, Pine Island's climate is so tropical that fruit is grown here commercially. The island has seen little development until recently. Nearby is the Matlacha fishing village, site of the "fishing-est bridge" in the United States. Of course, the fishing is great in all the waters nearby. The two-wheeled set can take their bikes for a spin around the quiet town of St. James City.

If you don't have a boat, then call one of the many local marinas to rent one so you can see all the interesting islands around Bokeelia. Among them, Cabbage Key is home to a little restaurant and inn where patrons over the decades have made wallpaper out of dollar bills. Supposedly, this is where Jimmy Buffett was inspired to write "Cheeseburger in Paradise," although his former neighbors in Key West would surely dispute that claim. Or cruise by Useppa Island, where wealthy people from all over the world have constructed the kind of fabulous getaways we all would build (in even better taste, of course) if we ever won the lottery.

RV sites, facilities: This 370-unit KOA offers RV sites with full hookups, 50-amp electrical service, cable TV, and telephone service. Restrooms, showers, picnic tables, a playground, shuffleboard courts, a pool, a spa, tennis courts, three fishing lakes, horseshoe pits, a pool table, a clubhouse with a kitchen and a stage, saunas, laundry facilities, a store, and a gift shop are available. Children and leashed pets are welcome.

Reservations, fees: Reservations are recommended. Sites are $28–60 per night for two adults. Kids camp free; the charge for extra adults is $5. Major credit cards are accepted.

Directions: From I-75, take Exit 143 westbound on State Road 78 for 20 miles to Pine Island. When you reach the dead end at Pine Island Center, turn south on Stringfellow Road/State Road 767 and drive 10 miles to the park.

Contact: Fort Myers/Pine Island KOA, 5120 Stringfellow Road, St. James City, FL 33956, 239/283-2415 or 800/562-8505, www.koa.com.

11 THE GROVES RV RESORT

Scenic rating: 7

in Fort Myers

This park boasts it is the closest RV park to Sanibel Island, which is saying something since the fabled isle houses only one campground and hundreds of luxury condos and homes. Social activities are planned during winter. The Sanibel Factory Shops outlet mall is nearby. To get to Sanibel Island beaches, located just across the causeway, you'll have to pay a toll of $3. Many people park their RVs or cars just off the causeway and then go fishing, swimming, or windsurfing; they don't beat the toll, but these wide spots in the road have Australian pines, a modicum of privacy, and vistas of water, water everywhere.

RV sites, facilities: All 306 grassy RV sites have full hookups, picnic tables, cable TV, and telephone availability. Lots are for sale. Restrooms, showers, picnic tables, concrete patios, laundry facilities, a pool, a library, a game room, shuffleboard, horseshoes, boccie ball (lawn bowling), an exercise room, wintertime social programs, and a dump station are available. Management says the clubhouse is wheelchair accessible. An 18-hole golf course is nearby; a supermarket is about five miles away. Children are welcome. Leashed pets under 35 pounds are permitted.

Reservations, fees: Reservations are recommended. Sites are $42 per night for two people, plus $4 for each additional person. Credit cards are accepted. Long-term rates are available.

Directions: From I-75, take Exit 131 west on Daniels Parkway for 5.5 miles to State Road 869/Summerlin Road. Turn southwest on State Road 869 and drive 6.6 miles to John Morris Boulevard. Turn north and go 0.8 mile to the park.

Contact: The Groves RV Resort, 16175 John Morris Road, Fort Myers, FL 33908, 239/466-5909, 239/466-4300, or 800/828-6992, fax 239/466-6310, www.suncommunities.com.

12 SIESTA BAY RV RESORT

Scenic rating: 5

east of Sanibel Island on the mainland

Favored by busy, busy wintering retirees who like lots of activity, this sparkling-clean park is three miles from the beach on Sanibel Island. There are more double-wide mobile homes here than RVs, and a sense of permanence and community holds forth, at least in the wintertime when everyone is here. Sabal palms and two lakes give a touch of greenery. Don't feed the swans on the lake, although you are welcome to watch them float lazily on the water. The broad, smooth concrete roadways are perfect for bicycling; plenty of residents have adult tricycles parked in front of their units.

RV sites, facilities: The sprawling mobile-home/RV park has 162 RV sites with full hookups and concrete pads available for over-nighters and seasonal visitors. Lots are for sale. Restrooms, showers, two pools, a whirlpool tub, horseshoe pits, shuffleboard and three lighted tennis courts, volleyball, a putting green and driving range, laundry facilities, fishing lakes, two recreation halls, a library, a card room, and a fitness center are available. Tours, field trips, theme parties, dances, clubs, classes, music groups, and competitive sports keep visitors more than occupied. Management says all buildings are wheelchair accessible. Golf is two miles away. Children are permitted for short visits only. Pets are forbidden.

Reservations, fees: Reservations are required. Sites are $46 per night for two people, plus $4 for each additional person. Credit cards are accepted. Long-term rates are available.

Directions: From I-75, take Exit 131 west on Daniels Parkway for 5.5 miles to State Road 869/Summerlin Road. Turn southwest on State Road 869 and drive 6.5 miles to the park.

Contact: Siesta Bay RV Resort, 19333 Summerlin Road, Fort Myers, FL 33908, 239/466-8988 or 800/828-6992, www.sun-communities.com.

13 PERIWINKLE PARK

Scenic rating: 8

on Sanibel Island

Periwinkle Park is the only campground on Sanibel Island, which is famed around the world for its wonderful shelling beaches. If you camp here instead of on the mainland, you'll at least avoid paying the $3 toll each time you cross the causeway to experience Sanibel. The island has expensive vacation homes, fancy resort hotels, and quaint boutiques selling pastel-colored vacation clothing and knickknacks made of shells, but it retains much of its jungle-like lushness and small-town atmosphere. A two-lane road winds north to the J. N. "Ding" Darling National Wildlife Refuge, where camping is not permitted. Hike the nature trails in this 5,030-acre sanctuary (closed on Fridays) or paddle your canoe; less-adventurous types or those in a hurry can see much of the refuge on the five-mile road that winds through it.

Also on Sanibel is a historic village and museum, a lighthouse built in 1884, and several shell and marine-life attractions. More great beaches are farther north on Captiva Island, so named because the pirate Jose Gasparilla had a camp there and kept captives on it. The campground stays in island character with shady trees and roads built of crushed shells and gravel. It's 0.5 mile from the beach; from the back of the campground, you can ride a fat-tired bike on an unpaved access road or walk to the Gulf of Mexico. Some sites overlook a little pond next to an aviary filled with exotic birds.

RV sites, facilities: Eighty RVs can be accommodated on tropical wooded sites with full hookups in this 326-unit park; 50 sites have telephone access. Seven sites are pull-through. Restrooms, showers, a dump station, laundry facilities, and a recreation room are on the premises. Children are allowed. Dogs are forbidden.

Reservations, fees: Reservations are recommended January–March and on holiday weekends. Sites are $32–39 per night for two people, plus $2 for each additional person. Credit cards are not accepted. Long-term rates are available.

Directions: From I-75, take Exit 131 west on Daniels Parkway for 5.5 miles to State Road 869/Summerlin Road. Turn left on State Road 869 and drive 9.5 miles to the Sanibel Island Causeway. Continue over the causeway to the four-way intersection, then turn north on Periwinkle Way and go 0.25 mile. The park is on the left.

Contact: Periwinkle Park, 1119 Periwinkle Way, Sanibel, FL 33957, 239/472-1433, www.sanibelcamping.com.

14 RED COCONUT RV RESORT

Scenic rating: 9

on Estero Island at Fort Myers Beach

BEST (

How close do you want to be to the beach? This is the only Fort Myers campground that is directly on the Gulf of Mexico. The best (and most expensive) sites are on the beach side and enjoy shade from tall Australian pines. Less-pricey sites are across the street; they're also less crowded, are shaded by Norfolk pines and coconut trees, and put you within walking distance of the beach. Nine-hole golf courses and boat/canoe rentals are close by. When you tire of beachside fun, ride your bike north to the Times Square area clustered around the bridge to the mainland. It's great for people-watching, even if you're not interested in the honky-tonk T-shirt shops, pizzerias, and ice-cream parlors.

RV sites, facilities: All 176 full-hookup sites have electricity, cable TV, and wireless Internet access. Restrooms, showers, picnic tables, a dump station, horseshoe pits, shuffleboard courts, laundry facilities, and a recreation room featuring a six-foot TV screen and movies are on the premises. Rental trailers are available. Children are welcome. Leashed pets are permitted.

Reservations, fees: Reservations are recommended. Sites are $31–60 per night for two people, depending on location of the site and time of year, plus $6 for each additional person in your party. Credit cards are accepted. The minimum stay is three nights, and long-term rates are available. The pet fee is $3; you must provide proof of inoculation and a photograph of the animal.

Directions: From I-75, take Exit 131 west on Daniels Parkway for 5.5 miles to State Road 869/Summerlin Road. Turn southwest on State Road 869 and drive 5.5 miles to San Carlos Boulevard. Turn south (left) on that road and go one mile until it ends on Estero Island. Turn left on Estero Boulevard and drive 1.5 miles.

Contact: Red Coconut RV Resort, 3001 Estero Boulevard, Fort Myers Beach, FL 33931, 239/463-7200, ext. 200, or 888/262-6226, fax 239/463-2609, www.redcoconut.com.

15 GULF WATERS RV RESORT

Scenic rating: 9

in Fort Myers Beach

Just minutes from the beach, this park is so manicured it looks more like a hotel property. It's usually booked solid November–April. A security gate keeps the park secluded, though it is close to bicycle paths and shopping is within one mile. Lots are for sale, but management says no one lives here year-round. Tennis courts and shuttle service to the beach are a complement to the busy planned activities schedule. If you drive a fancy, newer RV, you will feel at home: All motor homes, fifth wheels, and travel trailers must be 26 feet or longer, and any unit 10 years and older needs to be approved.

RV sites, facilities: There are 319 full-hookup RV sites, all with 50-amp electrical service, picnic tables, cable TV, and telephone service availability. Rigs up to 45 feet long and slide-outs can be accommodated on huge lots measuring 30 by 100 feet. Restrooms, showers, laundry facilities, a computer room with wireless Internet network, a heated pool, a spa, a poolside tiki bar, a 5,000-square-foot clubhouse with wireless Internet access, horseshoe pits, shuffleboard courts, basketball, and a dog-walk area are available. All areas are wheelchair accessible. Streets are paved. Children are welcome. Leashed pets are permitted.

Reservations, fees: Reservations are recommended during winter. Sites are $60 per night, and rates are subject to change. Credit cards are accepted. Long-term rates are available.

Directions: From I-75, take Exit 131 west on Daniels Parkway for 5.5 miles to State Road 869/Summerlin Road. Turn southwest on Summerlin Road and drive 5.5 miles to Pine Ridge Road. Turn left, and then make an immediate right on Summerlin Square Drive. The park will be on your left.

Contact: Gulf Waters RV Resort, 11301 Summerlin Square Drive, Fort Myers Beach, FL 33931, 239/437-5888, fax 239/437-5922, www .gulfwatersrv.com.

16 FORT MYERS BEACH RV RESORT

Scenic rating: 5

in Fort Myers Beach

This 15-acre park is centrally located near gulf beaches, the Thomas Edison and Henry Ford homes, Sanibel Island, and Fort Myers Beach. Paved interior roads lead to grassy sites with concrete patios.

RV sites, facilities: RVs up to 40 feet in length are accommodated at the 305 full-hookup sites with cable TV and telephone access. Sites have 30/50-amp electrical service. Restrooms, showers, picnic tables, a dump station, a pool, a whirlpool tub, an exercise room, wireless Internet access, shuffleboard courts, laundry facilities, rental trailers, and winter entertainment are available. Families with children are welcome. Leashed pets are permitted.

Reservations, fees: Reservations are required. Sites are $45 per night for two people, plus $5 for each additional person. Credit cards are accepted. Campers can stay as long as seven months.

Directions: From I-75, take Exit 131 west on Daniels Parkway for 5.5 miles to State Road 869/Summerlin Road. Turn southwest on State Road 869 and drive 5.5 miles to San Carlos Boulevard. Turn north (right) on that road and go 0.7 mile to the park on the right.

Contact: Fort Myers Beach RV Resort, 16299 San Carlos Boulevard, Fort Myers, FL 33908, 239/466-7171 or 800/553-7484, fax 239/466-6544.

17 GULF AIR RV PARK

Scenic rating: 7

in Fort Myers Beach

A nest for snowbirds, this mobile-home/RV park dotted with queen palms hosts coffee hours for its campers along with many other social activities, including bingo, potluck dinners, dances, and arts and crafts. The park is central to the Minnesota Twins spring training camp, golf courses, dog racing, shelling, a bird sanctuary, marinas, deep-sea fishing charters, and miles of white-sand beaches. A shopping center is located next door.

RV sites, facilities: The adult-oriented park has 55 full-hookup sites with 50-amp electrical service. Restrooms, showers, picnic tables, laundry facilities, wireless Internet network, shuffleboard courts, a recreation hall, a pool, a dump station, and horseshoe pits are available. Activity programs run November 15–April 15. Children are welcome for short-term stays only. Leashed pets are allowed.

Reservations, fees: Reservations are recommended. Sites are $29 per night for two people. Credit cards are accepted. Long-term stays are okay.

Directions: From I-75, take Exit 131 west on

Daniels Parkway for 5.5 miles to State Road 869/Summerlin Road. Turn southwest on State Road 869 and drive 5.5 miles to San Carlos Boulevard. Turn south and go 0.5 mile to the park on the left.

Contact: Gulf Air RV Park-Fort Myers Beach, 17279 San Carlos Boulevard Southwest, Fort Myers Beach, FL 33931, 239/466-8100 or 877/937-2757, fax 239/466-4044, www .rvonthego.com.

18 SAN CARLOS RV PARK AND ISLANDS

Scenic rating: 5

near Fort Myers Beach

Fish from some of the campsites at this seven-acre boating-oriented campground, which extends off a causeway onto a peninsula surrounded by mangroves. You may see porpoises, manatees, mullets, and numerous tropical birds. If you're into deep-sea fishing, this is a great location: Charter boats are within walking distance, and you can tie up your own boat at the docks. There's a one-mile bicycling and walking path to the beach; restaurants are close by. The campground, which is shaded by Australian pines, lies at the base of the busy Matanzas Pass Bridge, the only access road to the Gulf of Mexico and Estero Island. Sometimes traffic backs up at this spot in front of the park.

RV sites, facilities: RVs up to 40 feet long can stay at the 122 full-hookup sites, which have 30/50-amp electrical service and concrete pads. Restrooms, showers, picnic tables, a dump station, a pool, a whirlpool tub, a boat ramp, kayak rentals, shuffleboard and horseshoe areas, laundry facilities, and a recreation room are on-site. Management also rents out 19 mobile homes to vacationers. The office and recreation hall are wheelchair accessible. Children and leashed pets are welcome.

Reservations, fees: Reservations are recommended. Sites are $43 per night for two

people, plus $2 for each additional person and $2 for using air-conditioning. Credit cards are accepted.

Directions: From I-75, take Exit 131 west on Daniels Parkway for 5.5 miles to State Road 869/Summerlin Road. Turn southwest on State Road 869 and drive 5.5 miles to San Carlos Boulevard. Turn south and go two miles.

Contact: San Carlos RV Park and Islands, 18701 San Carlos Boulevard, Fort Myers Beach, FL 33931, 239/466-3133 or 800/525-7275, www.gocampingamerica.com/sancarlos.

19 INDIAN CREEK PARK

Scenic rating: 6

in Fort Myers Beach

In winter, people from Michigan, Ohio, New York, Massachusetts, and Quebec flock to this sprawling but immaculate park, which is one of the largest in Florida if you count the number of sites. Many visitors leave their rigs here year-round; they've built Florida rooms (typically with windows on all sides) onto their trailers and added utility sheds. Park models are for sale. On the scale of a small city's recreation department, the park offers three swimming pools, 16 shuffleboard courts, three tennis courts, a year-round recreation director, and a tournament-sized pool hall. Nineteen small lakes dot the park, which is two miles from the beach and next door to a miniature golf course. Social activities, needless to say, are ubiquitous.

RV sites, facilities: Set on 200 acres, this senior-oriented park has a whopping 1,140 RV sites (plus another 300 mobile-home sites) with full hookups, 30/50-amp electrical service, cable TV, wireless Internet access, telephone service, concrete patios, and picnic tables. Lots are 30 feet wide by 55 feet deep. Rigs as long as 40 feet and slide-outs can be accommodated. On the premises are restrooms, showers, a dump station, three pools, whirlpool tubs, 19 lakes, three clubhouses with Internet access, horseshoe pits, shuffleboard, three tennis courts, and laundry facilities. An 18-hole golf course is two miles away. The clubhouses and bathhouses are wheelchair accessible. Streets are paved. Groceries and restaurants are within 0.5 mile; malls and hospitals are within 3 miles. Children are welcome for stays no longer than 30 days. Small pets are permitted at certain sites only.

Reservations, fees: Reservations are required. Sites are $42 per night for two people, plus $4 for each additional person. Credit cards are accepted. Long-term rates are available.

Directions: From I-75, take Exit 131 west on Daniels Parkway for 5.5 miles to State Road 869/Summerlin Road. Turn southwest (left) on State Road 869 and drive 5.5 miles to San Carlos Boulevard. Turn left onto San Carlos Boulevard. The park is 0.2 mile ahead.

Contact: Indian Creek Park, 17340 San Carlos Boulevard, Fort Myers Beach, FL 33931, 239/466-6060 or 800/828-6992, fax 239/466-7475, www.sunrvresorts.com.

20 FORT MYERS RV RESORT

Scenic rating: 6

in Fort Myers

"We pamper the camper," insist the owners of neatly kept Fort Myers RV Resort, and they've certainly included nearly every amenity seen in an RV park, from an 18-hole miniature golf course to a post office and beer sales. What you won't find is a beach, so drive about eight miles to Sanibel Island or Fort Myers Beach if you pine for sand. Although part of the park fronts on busy U.S. 41, the place is so large that campers toward the back won't be conscious of much noise. Some spots are on a creek where you can fish. Greenery includes slash pine, queen palms, and Australian pines. Shopping centers are close by.

RV sites, facilities: All 345 grassy RV sites offer full hookups with a mix of 30-amp and 50-amp

electrical service. Restrooms, showers, some picnic tables, a dump station, a playground, a pool, wireless Internet network, a boat ramp, a dock, horseshoes, shuffleboard, a miniature golf course, a recreation hall, a pool table, a volleyball field, a store, and laundry facilities are on-site. Children and pets are welcome.

Reservations, fees: Reservations are required from October to April. Sites are $32 per night for two people, plus $2.50 for each additional person. Credit cards are accepted. Long-term stays are okay.

Directions: From I-75, take Exit 128 westbound on Alico Road for three miles. Turn north (right) on U.S. 41. Drive 0.6 mile to the park on the west side of the highway.

Contact: Fort Myers RV Resort, 16800 South Tamiami Trail, Fort Myers, FL 33908, 239/267-2141 or 239/267-2211.

21 WOODSMOKE CAMPING RESORT

Scenic rating: 7

south of Fort Myers

Slash pines, melaleucas, and lakeside cypress trees cast shade throughout the park. Resist the temptation to feed the ducks, but feel free to watch their antics. Hike on a short boardwalk nature trail. Two miles away is the Koreshan State Historic Site (see listing in this chapter). Woodsmoke is within easy driving distance of beaches, deep-sea fishing charters, Sanibel Island and nature preserves, the Henry Ford and Thomas Edison homes, the Shell Factory, and the Corkscrew Swamp Sanctuary. Most visitors here are staying for the season.

RV sites, facilities: You'll find 300 sites, all with full hookups and 30/50-amp electrical service. Seventy-five are pull-through. For cable TV and telephone, you must call the appropriate utility company. Restrooms, showers, a heated pool, a spa, a recreation hall, three lakes, a large pavilion, shuffleboard, horseshoes, dial-up modem, and laundry facilities are available. Children are welcome. Leashed pets are permitted, except for Doberman pinschers, pit bulls, German shepherds, and rottweilers.

Reservations, fees: Reservations are recommended, particularly in winter. Sites are $30–50 per night for two people, plus $3.50 for each additional adult. Credit cards are accepted. Long-term stays are okay.

Directions: From I-75, take Exit 123 westbound on Corkscrew Road for two miles. Turn north on U.S. 41 and drive two miles. The park is between Hickory Street and Sanibel Boulevard.

Contact: Woodsmoke Camping Resort, 19551 U.S. 41 South, Fort Myers, FL 33908, 239/267-3456 or 800/231-5053, fax 239/267-6719, http://woodsmokecampingresort.com/index.html.

22 SHADY ACRES RV PARK

Scenic rating: 7

south of Fort Myers

On cool nights, folks gather around the community campfire for socializing in this well-shaded, lushly landscaped park. Orange-colored flame vine and purple bougainvillea add color. Watch squirrels scramble up the sabal palms. In winter, a restaurant and snack bar are open on the grounds, and social activities, such as crafts, bingo, dances, pool parties with live entertainment, exercise classes, and singing, are available. A golf course is within two miles. Some sites overlook a pond and a creek. Although U.S. 41 is a congested highway, this park is nicely secluded from the road. Shopping centers and tourist attractions are nearby. About 30 percent of the sites are occupied year-round.

RV sites, facilities: The retiree-oriented park has 356 full-hookup RV sites with 30-amp and 50-amp electrical service, wireless Internet access, concrete patios, and picnic tables. Three sites are pull-through. RVs up to 50 feet long and slide-outs can be accom-

modated. Restrooms, showers, picnic tables, a dump station, a pool, laundry facilities, cable TV, a playground, horseshoe pits (tournaments during winter), shuffleboard courts, propane sales, and a recreation room with pool tables and table tennis are provided. Grocery stores are within two miles. Streets are paved, and most areas are wheelchair accessible. Children may camp for two weeks only. Leashed pets are permitted, except for rottweilers, pit bulls, German shepherds, and Doberman pinschers.

Reservations, fees: Reservations are recommended. Sites are $34 per night for two people, plus $3 for each additional person. Credit cards are accepted. Long-term rates are available.

Directions: From I-75, take Exit 128 westbound for three miles on Alico Road. Turn south on U.S. 41 and go three miles. At the campground sign, turn west and drive 0.25 mile to the park.

Contact: Shady Acres RV Park, 19370 South Tamiami Trail, Fort Myers, FL 33908, 239/267-8448, fax 239/267-7026, www.shady-acresfl.com.

23 KORESHAN STATE HISTORIC SITE

Scenic rating: 10

in Estero

Adjoining the Estero River, the campground is part of a state historic site that memorializes a Utopian communal religious settlement founded in 1870 by a New York doctor who planned to construct a "New Jerusalem" here to follow the religion of "Koreshanity." Cyrus Teed was inspired by the Bible to take the name Koresh, a Hebrew transliteration of Cyrus, which was the name of the Persian king who allowed the Jews held captive in Babylon to return to Israel.

Tours of the Koreshan communal settlement are held regularly, including views of the founder's house, the bakery, outbuildings, and the "planetary court." Followers believed that Earth was a hollow sphere with the planets inside. The governing council consisted of seven women who ran the day-to-day operations of the settlement; leaders of the religion were celibate. Many of the followers came from Chicago with all their furnishings, much of which still can be seen. Teed thought he was immortal, but he died in 1908. Even his tomb has not lasted; it was destroyed in a hurricane in the 1920s. When the settlement dwindled to four members, they donated this land in 1961 to the state; however, the Koreshan Unity Foundation still runs a library and museum near the state park. Don't miss touring the historic site while you're camped here, and imagine what it would be like if Teed's plans for settling 8–10 million people had come to fruition. The campground is shady and cool—a real treat in itself. Swimming is not permitted in the Estero River; canoeing, cycling, boating, and fishing are the things to do. Canoes are for rent on the river, which is part of a state-designated canoe trail.

RV sites, facilities: The 156-acre state park has 48 sites with water and 30-amp electricity. Restrooms, showers, picnic tables, grills, a dump station, laundry facilities, a playground, rental canoes, a camp circle, and a boat ramp are available. Some camp sites, the tour areas, and the restrooms are wheelchair accessible, and the shell roads are wide and level. Most areas and four campsites are wheelchair accessible. Children are welcome. Pets are allowed with proof of vaccination.

Reservations, fees: Reservations are recommended; contact ReserveAmerica at 800/336-3521 or reserveamerica.com. Sites vary seasonally from $22 per night. Credit cards are accepted. The maximum stay is 14 days.

Directions: From I-75, take Exit 123 westbound on Corkscrew Road for two miles. Cross U.S. 41 and continue 0.25 mile west to the park.

Contact: Koreshan State Historic Site, P.O. Box 7, Estero, FL 33928, 239/992-0311, fax 239/992-1607, www.floridastateparks.org and http://koreshan.mwweb.org.

24 BONITA BEACH TRAILER PARK

Scenic rating: 4

in Bonita Springs

Tall slash pines, scarlet bougainvillea blossoms, and perfectly formed Norfolk pines give visitors a sense of being sheltered from the busy road that leads to the beach nearby. You'll find pool tables and—in winter—dances, bingo, and card games in the recreation hall. About 80 percent of the park is occupied year-round. A miniature-golf course is across the street. Ride your bicycle to Barefoot Beach Preserve two miles west or take a free trolley. The Gulf of Mexico is 1.25 miles away, and Lover's Key State Park (239/463-4588) is 7 miles distant.

RV sites, facilities: The 12.5-acre park has 20 RV sites with full hookups, 30-amp electrical service, and cable TV. Four sites can accept rigs up to 40 feet long. There is an Internet connection in the clubhouse. Restrooms, showers, picnic tables, a dump station, a clubhouse, shuffleboard, a pool, winter activities, and telephone service are available. A supermarket is two blocks away. Children are allowed. Only one leashed pet under 20 pounds is permitted per site.

Reservations, fees: Reservations are recommended. Sites are $37 per night for two people, plus $3 for each additional person. Credit cards are not accepted. Long-term rates are available.

Directions: From I-75, take Exit 116 westbound on Bonita Beach Road for five miles. The park is two blocks west of U.S. 41. Turn north on Meadowlark Lane, and go one block to the park entrance.

Contact: Bonita Beach Trailer Park, 27800 Meadowlark Lane, Bonita Springs, FL 34134, 239/498-1605 or 800/654-9907, email: bbtp-coop@aol.com.

25 IMPERIAL BONITA ESTATES

Scenic rating: 4

in Bonita Springs

Located on the Imperial River, this resident-owned manufactured-home community and RV park has social activities year-round, although winter is the more active season. Grocery stores and restaurants are within three miles, and beaches are close by. Many of the barrier island beaches at this end of the county are government-owned and protected from development. Lover's Key State Park (239/463-4588), a 434-acre collection of islands, canals, tidal lagoons, and mangroves, is accessible by road or by water for fishing, boating, canoeing, and swimming. You can't swim in the canals, but why would you want to when there are sugar-white beaches on Lover's Key? A footbridge connects some of these little islands, so you'll have more of an opportunity to spot wildlife, including several species of woodpeckers and shorebirds. Look for roseate spoonbills and egrets as they hunt for food. You may also see porpoises and manatees near shore.

RV sites, facilities: There are 145 RV sites with full hookups and 30/50/100-amp electrical service available for transient travelers. The RV section includes 347 lots, of which about half have units that are tied down permanently. The rest of the park is a 247-unit manufactured-home community, which is wheelchair accessible. Restrooms, showers, picnic tables, a dump station, two laundry facilities, a large heated pool, horseshoe pits, shuffleboard courts, a recreation room, and a computer room with both dial-up and high-speed Internet access are on-site. Visitors should be age 55 or older, but children may visit, and those under 10 must be accompanied outside the RV. House pets are permitted; be sure to clean up after them and keep them leashed.

Reservations, fees: Reservations are recommended. Sites are $40–50 per night January–March, and $35–40 April–December. Credit cards are accepted. Long-term visits are okay.

Directions: From I-75, take Exit 116 westbound on Bonita Beach Road for 1.1 miles. Turn north on Imperial Street and drive 0.3 mile. At Dean Street, turn east and go two blocks. The park is on the left.

Contact: Imperial Bonita Estates, 27700 Bourbonniere Drive, Bonita Springs, FL 34135, 239/992-0511 or 800/690-6619, fax 239/992-6126, www.imperialbonitaestates.com.

26 CITRUS PARK

Scenic rating: 5

in Bonita Springs

This RV resort and manufactured-home community offers 968 sites for vacationers, seasonal visitors, and full-timers. Its claim to fame: more activities than you can shake a stick at. The motto seems to be, "Be active!" The roster of things to do fills four pages of the park's monthly newsletter. For example: a theater troupe, softball, a driving range, tennis, exercise classes, film screenings, choral groups, square dancing, and the usual trips, potlucks, bingo, cards, and so forth. About 20 percent of the occupants live here year-round; others leave their rigs on-site after their vacations are over.

RV sites, facilities: All 968 sites have full hookups, 50-amp electrical service, and cable TV. Picnic tables are available upon request. Twenty-five sites are pull-through. A wireless Internet network is available. Restrooms, showers, laundry facilities, and telephone service are available. On the premises are two pools, a recreation hall, several lakes, horseshoe pits, shuffleboard courts, a driving range, two softball fields, a dog-walk area, and *pétanque* and boccie (lawn bowling)courts. All areas are wheelchair accessible. This is an age-55-plus park; children are allowed for short visits only. Leashed pets are permitted.

Reservations, fees: Reservations are recom-

mended. Sites are $25 per night for two people, plus $5 per extra person. Credit cards are not accepted. Long-term rates are available.

Directions: From I-75, take Exit 116 eastbound on Bonita Beach Road 0.5 mile. Turn north on Bonita Grande Road and proceed one mile to East Terry Drive. Turn left on East Terry Drive and drive 0.5 mile to Trost Boulevard. Turn north on Trost Boulevard and drive one mile to the park.

Contact: Citrus Park, 25501 Trost Boulevard, Bonita Springs, FL 34135, 239/992-3030, fax 239/992-4130, www.citrusparkrvmobile.com.

27 GULF COAST CAMPING RESORT

Scenic rating: 3

in Bonita Springs

At Christmastime, at least one camping couple has been known to set out baskets of grapefruit for their neighbors to take—a sign of both friendliness and the abundance of winter citrus yields among the slowly dwindling fruit trees. Set in a neighborhood of small, warehouse-based businesses, this park has a little pond and an undeveloped jungly area behind. It tends to attract boaters and snowbirds. As more people buy lots here, the number of spots for overnighters shrinks, but most sites still cater to people passing through or looking to spend a few winter months in a warm retreat. About one-third of the park is occupied by mobile homes.

RV sites, facilities: Catering to people age 55 and older, this 270-unit park offers about 196 full-hookup grassy sites for RVs up to 37 feet long. Sites have 30-amp and 50-amp electrical service. For cable TV and telephone service, call the appropriate utility company. Restrooms, showers, a pool, a recreation hall, shuffleboard courts, horseshoe pits, and wintertime social programs are available. Children may visit campers. Small, leashed dogs are allowed.

Reservations, fees: Reservations are recom-

mended in winter or any time for stays of three months or longer. Sites are $29 per night for two people, plus $3 for each additional person. Credit cards are not accepted. Long-term rates are available.

Directions: From the intersection of Old U.S. 41 and U.S. 41 in North Bonita Springs, drive 0.25 mile north on U.S. 41. Turn east at the sign and go two blocks.

Contact: Gulf Coast Camping Resort, 24020 Production Circle, Bonita Springs, FL 34135, 239/992-3808.

28 BONITA LAKE RV RESORT

Scenic rating: 5

in Bonita Springs

Most campers here are retired folks spending winter in the sunshine, and there's plenty of that. A few fruit trees offer greenery; the pool is heated in winter, and the whirlpool is open year-round for soothing weary muscles. A fishing lake might yield hours of relaxation. Some people eat lunch at what is considered a small picnic island. Everglades Wonder Gardens, an old-time tourist attraction with birds, alligators, otters, snakes, and other wildlife, is nearby.

RV sites, facilities: The 167 grassy sites at this 10-acre park have full hookups with 30-amp and 50-amp electrical service and are for RVs up to 40 feet long. All sites have picnic tables. Telephone service and a wireless Internet network are available. Restrooms, showers, a dump station, a pool, a whirlpool tub, horseshoe pits, shuffleboard courts, laundry facilities, a recreation hall, and wintertime social programs are available. An 18-hole golf course is five miles away. Children are allowed. Small, leashed pets are permitted.

Reservations, fees: Reservations are recommended. Sites are $39 per night for two people, plus $3 for each additional person. Credit cards are accepted. Long-term stays are permitted.

Directions: From I-75, take Exit 116 westbound

on County Road 865/Bonita Beach Boulevard for two miles. At County Road 887/Old U.S. 41, turn north and drive 1.7 miles to the park.
Contact: Bonita Lake RV Resort, 26325 Old U.S. 41, Bonita Springs, FL 34135, 239/992-2481 or 800/828-6992, fax 239/992-2357.

29 LAKE SAN MARINO RV PARK

Scenic rating: 6

north of Naples

Visitors to this over-age-55 park keep a keen edge: Shuffleboard is so competitive that the courts are surrounded by bleachers for spectator seating. The pastime seems to be taken as seriously as a Wimbledon tennis match. Campsites are grassy with adjoining concrete patios. Lake San Marino RV Park is strategically poised for enjoying Greater Naples, close to shopping and restaurants, and several golf courses, and two miles from the spectacular beachfront Delnor-Wiggins Pass State Park (239/597-6196). The state park, south from here on U.S. 41, then east on County Road 846, is open for day use only. There's gulf-front swimming and shelling, fishing, a boat ramp, and an observation tower. West on County Road 846 is the National Audubon Society's Corkscrew Swamp Sanctuary, a unique forest of towering 500-year-old bald cypress bisected by a two-mile boardwalk. The refuge teems with nearly 200 species of birds, including nesting wood storks, plus alligators, deer, and bobcat. For details, call 239/657-3771.

RV sites, facilities: The 35-acre park has 415 sites with full hookups, 30/50-amp electrical service, wireless Internet network, and picnic tables. About half are available for new seasonal visitors; the rest are taken by folks who leave their units on-site in summer. Restrooms, showers, laundry facilities, a pool, horseshoe pits, shuffleboard courts, a clubhouse, telephone service, wintertime social programs, a camp circle for gatherings, and a small fishing lake with a pier are available. Management says the pool area and bathhouse are wheelchair accessible. Two miles away are groceries, a restaurant, bait, and LP gas. Children are permitted, but in winter the park is predominantly retiree oriented. One leashed pet under 35 pounds is permitted per site.

Reservations, fees: Reservations are required. Sites are $29–42 per night for two people, plus $4 for each additional person. Credit cards are accepted. Long-term stays are okay.

Directions: From I-75 Exit 111, go west to U.S. 41, then north (right) to Wiggins Pass Road. Turn right onto Wiggins Pass. The park is 0.25 mile ahead at right. Alternatively, from U.S. 41 in Bonita Springs, drive two miles south to Wiggins Pass Road. Turn east and go 0.25 mile.

Contact: Lake San Marino RV Park, 1000 Wiggins Pass Road, Naples, FL 34110, 239/597-4202 or 800/828-6992, fax 239/592-0790, www.suncommunities.com.

30 PALM RIVER MOBILE HOME PARK

Scenic rating: 2

north of Naples

Set on the Cocohatchee River, this senior-oriented park hosts potluck dinners, pancake breakfasts, cards, bingo, and crafts during the winter season. Campers can fish from the docks, which accommodate boats up to 20 feet long for an extra charge. Paved, lighted roads lead to concrete sites at this open and sunny park. Shopping, medical facilities, churches, and restaurants are nearby. At least one camper in your party must be over the age of 55.

RV sites, facilities: This 68-unit condominium mobile-home park is targeted to people over age 55. There are 10 RV sites with full hookups, a clubhouse, and boat docks. Groceries are 0.5 mile away. Children and pets are not allowed.

Reservations, fees: Reservations are recommended. Sites are $25 per night. Credit cards are not accepted. Long-term stays are okay.

Directions: From U.S. 41 in Bonita Springs, drive three miles south to Walker Bilt Road, which intersects with the highway on the south side of the Cocohatchee River. Turn west on Walker Bilt Road and drive a short distance to the park.

Contact: Palm River Mobile Home Park, 793 Walker Bilt Road, Naples, FL 34110, 239/597-3639.

31 LAKE TRAFFORD MARINA AND CAMPGROUND

Scenic rating: 3

in Immokalee

Immokalee—meaning "my home" in the Seminole Indian tongue—is home to sprawling cattle ranches, citrus and vegetable farms, and anglers, which makes it an offbeat destination for campers. This fishing camp is nestled on the shores of Lake Trafford, a 1,600-acre basin described as "infested" with largemouth bass, as well as crappie, bluegill, and shellcracker. Children are welcome, although parents should be sure to keep an eye on them: "Too many alligators!" warns the camp's management. The park also offers boat tours, fishing guides, and airboat rides. Fishing is the main draw, but there are other attractions: a Cinco de Mayo festival in May celebrating the culture of Mexican migrant farmworkers who flock here September–June; the Immokalee Harvest Festival in April; and the Immokalee Horse Trails equestrian competition in February.

RV sites, facilities: There are 63 sites with full hookups and 30-amp electrical service. Internet connection is available. On the premises are restrooms, showers, a dump station, a boat ramp, a lakeside pier, and a marina with a bait and tackle store, boat rentals, and fishing guides. The office is wheelchair accessible. Groceries and restaurants are within three miles. Children and pets are welcome.

Reservations, fees: Reservations are taken.

Sites are $24 per night for two people, plus $2 for each additional person. Credit cards are accepted. Long-term rates are available. The maximum length of stay is six months.

Directions: From I-75, take Exit 111 east onto County Road 846 and drive 30 miles to Immokalee. Turn west on State Road 29 and drive about two miles to County Road 890/Lake Trafford Road. Continue three miles west to the campground.

Contact: Lake Trafford Marina and Campground, 6001 Lake Trafford Road, Immokalee, FL 34142, 239/657-2214, fax 239/658-2401, email: laketraffordmarina@earthlink.net.

32 ROCK CREEK RV RESORT AND CAMPGROUND

Scenic rating: 6

in Naples

Overnight visitors need luck to get into this suburban park, but it's worth a try to sleep so close to Naples attractions. Despite being in the heart of the city, the place is shady and jungly with sabal palms, bougainvillea, oaks, and flowering hibiscus. The 17-acre park sits on the banks of pretty Rock Creek, which flows into the Gulf of Mexico. Seasonal guests don't seem to mind the noise of traffic from the small airport next door. A short 2.5-mile drive away are downtown Naples' quaint but pricey marketplaces, such as Tin City, a trendy enclave of restaurants and shops on the city's old fishing wharves. From there, charter boats are waiting to embark on gulf fishing excursions. Tour boats are available, as well. Also near the park are the Collier County Museum, a big regional mall, and Caribbean Gardens, formerly known as Jungle Larry's, a tourist zoo famous for its boat tours of islands inhabited by monkeys and apes. For more information, call 239/262-5409.

RV sites, facilities: The 225-unit park has lots with picnic tables, full hookups, 30-amp electrical service, and cable TV. Park models are for sale, and many older units are being removed and replaced. Restrooms, showers, laundry facilities, a dump station, a large heated pool, two recreation halls, a boat ramp, horseshoe pits, shuffleboard courts, wintertime planned activities, and a chickee hut (Seminole-style thatched-roof dwelling) for gatherings are available. Children and overnighters are welcome only in summer for short periods; in the winter months, this is an adults-only park. Call for current pet policy.

Reservations, fees: Reservations are required for the few campsites available in the winter season; they are not necessary in summer. Sites are $45–56 per night for two people, plus $3 for each additional person. Credit cards are not accepted. Long-term stays are okay.

Directions: From I-75, take Exit 107 and turn right onto Pine Ridge Road. Drive two miles, then turn left onto Airport Pulling Road. Continue south for 4.5 miles, then turn right onto North Road. The park entrance sign is 100 yards ahead. The park is just south of Naples Municipal Airport.

Contact: Rock Creek RV Resort and Campground, 3100 North Road, Naples, FL 34104, 239/643-3100, fax 239/643-3101, www.rockcreekrv.com.

33 CLUB NAPLES RV RESORT

Scenic rating: 5

southeast of Naples

To eastbound travelers on I-75, Exit 101 is the last opportunity for easy-on, easy-off camping before reaching Greater Fort Lauderdale, which typically takes two hours. Popular with campers age 55 and up, this well-kept campground has paved roads and grassy sites set on 20 acres. The first of several campgrounds near the interstate along Collier Boulevard (County Road 951), it is also convenient to fast-food restaurants, gas stations, and Naples-area tourist attractions. South on Collier Boulevard, about a 20-minute drive, is Marco Island, a resort town with plenty of golfing, fishing, boating, fine dining, and shopping options, plus Tigertail Beach on the Gulf of Mexico, which is open to the public. This is also the way to reach U.S. 41/Tamiami Trail, the eastbound route to Big Cypress National Preserve and Everglades National Park.

RV sites, facilities: There are 307 sites with full hookups, cable TV, and picnic tables. About 65 percent of the lots have 30-amp electrical service; the rest have 50-amp. RVs up to 40 feet long can be accommodated. On the premises are restrooms, showers, laundry facilities, a dump station, propane supply, a small general store, a swimming pool and whirlpool, a playground, activity rooms, rental park models, a miniature golf course, volleyball, *pétanque,* basketball, horseshoe pits, shuffleboard courts, and modem hookup for computers. The restrooms, clubhouse, pool area, store, and office are wheelchair accessible. Children are welcome. Leashed pets are permitted.

Reservations, fees: Reservations are recommended. Sites are $45 per night for two people, plus $2.50 for each extra person. Credit cards are accepted. Long-term stays are okay.

Directions: From I-75, take Exit 101 south on Collier Boulevard (County Road 951). Turn east on Beck Boulevard and drive one mile to the resort.

Contact: Club Naples RV Resort, 3180 Beck Boulevard, Naples, FL 34114, 239/455-7275 or 888/795-2780, fax 239/455-7271, www.clubnaplesrv.com.

34 KOUNTREE KAMPINN RV RESORT

Scenic rating: 6

south of Naples

Shade, glorious shade. A tropical forest canopy of pines and palms envelops this campground near Everglades National Park, Marco Island, the Ten Thousand Islands, and Naples. A gun range and golf courses are nearby. Pick up supplies three miles away at shopping centers on the corner of County Road 951/Collier Boulevard and U.S. 41/Tamiami Trail. About 10 percent of the park is occupied by year-round residents. Within a short hike from the park, you'll find a flea market and a rustic county-owned sports complex that has a go-cart track and spectator bleachers for swamp-buggy races.

RV sites, facilities: All 161 RV sites have full hookups (most with 30-amp electrical service; 36 with 50-amp), concrete patios, picnic tables, cable TV, and telephone availability. Lots are 25 by 50 feet, on average. RVs up to 45 feet long and slide-outs can be accommodated. You can access a wireless Internet network in the office and the clubhouse, as well as a few other areas of the park. Restrooms, showers, picnic tables, laundry facilities, a pool, horseshoe pits, a recreation room, boccie (lawn bowling), shuffleboard courts, and wintertime social programs are available. A camp store sells ice, snacks, propane, and camping supplies. All areas are wheelchair accessible. Children are welcome. Leashed pets under 30 pounds are permitted.

Reservations, fees: Reservations are recommended. Sites are $45 per night for two people, plus $3 per extra person. Children under 12 are free. Cable TV is free, but a $2 fee applies if you need to hook up to 50-amp electrical service. Credit cards are accepted. Long-term rates are available.

Directions: From I-75, take Exit 101 and head south on County Road 951/Collier Boulevard for five miles to the park. To enter the park, you must pass the campground and make a U-turn 0.25 mile past Edison College. From U.S. 41/Tamiami Trail, turn north on County Road 951 and drive three miles.

Contact: Kountree Kampinn RV Resort, 8230 Collier Boulevard, Naples, FL 34114, 239/775-4340, fax 239/775-2269, www.kountreekampinn.com.

35 MARCO-NAPLES HITCHING POST TRAVEL TRAILER RESORT

Scenic rating: 4

south of Naples

These sun-drenched pull-through sites measure a roomy 30 by 60 feet with 8- by 20-foot concrete patios. The park is within seven miles of two beaches and close to "U-pick" vegetable and fruit farms, shopping centers, bowling alleys, golf courses, grocery stores, and restaurants. But the park's recreation hall activities may keep campers close to home, with an action-packed schedule that includes blood-pressure checks every other week, Jazzercise, water aerobics in the pool, a library, square dances, cookouts, and outings such as cruises. There's even a ladies' horseshoe-throwing group.

RV sites, facilities: This wheelchair-accessible park has 300 sites with full hookups, 30-amp electrical service, and picnic tables. About 236 are available for seasonal visitors, and 50 for vacationers. Sites are about 30 feet wide by 50 feet deep, accommodating RVs up to 40 feet long and slide-outs. A wireless Internet network is available. Restrooms, showers, laundry facilities, a dump station, a recreation building, a pool, shuffleboard and handball courts, and horseshoe pits are available. All areas are wheelchair accessible. Children are permitted for short stays only. Leashed pets are allowed.

Reservations, fees: Reservations are recommended. Sites are $30 per night for two people, plus $2.50 for each additional person. Credit cards are not accepted. The maximum stay is seven months. The park is open October 1–April 30.

Directions: From I-75, take Exit 101 and head south on County Road 951 for 6.8 miles. Turn north at U.S. 41/Tamiami Trail and drive 1.3 miles to Barefoot Williams Road. Turn south and continue to the park entrance.

Contact: Marco-Naples Hitching Post Travel Trailer Resort, 100 Barefoot Williams Road,

Naples, FL 34113, 239/774-1259 or 800/362-8968, fax 239/774-9552, www.hitchingpostrv.com.

36 NAPLES/MARCO ISLAND KOA KAMPGROUND

Scenic rating: 6

south of Naples

This KOA and the Silver Lakes RV Resort (see listing in this chapter) are best situated for campers who want all the amenities of a developed park plus convenient access to Marco Island. For those with pop-tops, this is the only close option because Silver Lakes won't open its gate to these campers. The sites are fairly crowded but designed for easy parking, and planned activities entertain folks during the season. The boat ramp provides access to the Gulf of Mexico and for canoeing in Henderson Creek and the Audubon Society's Rookery Bay Wildlife Sanctuary, which is a short paddle downstream. The mangroves offer good saltwater fishing grounds for snapper, sheepshead, redfish, and—albeit rarely—snook. A license is required, and you must be sure to follow the rules and season restrictions, as well as boating speed limits, because Florida Marine Patrol enforcement is strict.

RV sites, facilities: There are 172 sites with full hookups, 30-amp and 50-amp electrical service, cable TV, and picnic tables. RVs can pull through half the sites. On the premises are restrooms, showers, laundry facilities, a dump station, a pool and hot tub, a playground, wireless Internet network, a game room, shuffleboard and boccie ball (lawn bowling) courts, canoe and banana bike rentals, a boat ramp, cabin rentals, and two pet walks. The restrooms, recreation hall, and some campsites are wheelchair accessible. Children are welcome. Leashed pets are permitted.

Reservations, fees: Reservations are recommended. Sites are $62–72 per night for two people, plus $4 for each additional child and

$6 per extra adult. Credit cards are accepted. Long-term stays are okay.

Directions: From I-75, take Exit 101 and drive eight miles south on County Road 951. At the intersection with U.S. 41/Tamiami Trail, continue south on County Road 951 for 0.5 mile. Turn west on Tower Road, then drive one more mile to the park entrance.

Contact: Naples/Marco Island KOA Kampground, 1700 Barefoot Williams Road, Naples, FL 33962, 239/774-5455.

37 SILVER LAKES RV RESORT AND GOLF CLUB

Scenic rating: 10

north of Marco Island

BEST (

Their slogan: "An Invitation to the Good Life!" The emphasis is on "the good life" because this park is marketed to older adults who've made significant investments in their RVs and are willing to spend $60 a night—among the higher prices I've seen. Of course, you get what you pay for: The gated park has spent awesome bucks on amenities, from a pristinely maintained nine-hole executive golf course to two swimming pools. Lots (measuring 45 by 90 feet, with 24- by 40-foot concrete pads) are for sale for those who want to return each winter, but owners are permitted to rent them to overnighters. Worried about the lawn in your absence? Automatic sprinklers make sure the grass stays green. The park, which is close to Marco Island, is two miles from a public boat ramp with direct access to the Gulf of Mexico and the Ten Thousand Islands. A factory outlet shopping mall is next door, and department and grocery stores are within five minutes' drive. About two miles south on County Road 951 at Shell Island Road is the Stephen F. Briggs Memorial Nature Center at Rookery Bay, a nature exhibit and interpretive boardwalk through a mangrove estuary ecosystem. Here's where you can see how Southwest Florida looked before development: low-lying foliage that's home to an array of birds, lizards, snakes, and the almost-extinct Florida panther. For information, call 239/775-8569.

RV sites, facilities: This ultradeluxe, adult-oriented condominium RV resort has 520 full-hookup lots with 30-amp and 50-amp electrical service, telephone service, cable TV, restrooms, showers, and laundry facilities available. Three stocked freshwater fishing lakes, a nine-hole golf course, two heated swimming pools, two spas, three tennis courts, six shuffleboard courts, six regulation horseshoe pits, a fitness center, two clubhouses with dial-up Internet access, pool tables, and a pro shop are on-site. The "Diamond Club House" has banquet facilities, a dance floor, a library, and a TV room. RV and boat storage is available so you can leave your stuff in spring. All areas are wheelchair accessible. Converted trailers, pop-up campers, and truck campers are prohibited. Children are welcome for short stays. Two pets are permitted per site.

Reservations, fees: Reservations are recommended. Sites are $35 per night, except for January, February, and March, when the rate is $75 per night. Credit cards are accepted. Long-term stays are okay.

Directions: From I-75, take Exit 101 southbound on County Road 951 for seven miles to the intersection with U.S. 41/Tamiami Trail. Continue on County Road 951 for 1.5 miles to the park entrance on the south side.

Contact: Silver Lakes RV Resort and Golf Club, 1001 Silver Lakes Boulevard, Naples, FL 33114, 239/775-2575 or 800/843-2836, fax 239/775-9989.

38 GREYSTONE PARK

Scenic rating: 3

north of Marco Island

On the highway between Naples and Everglades City, Greystone Park also is midway between the primitive wonders of Big Cypress Swamp and the luxurious, manicured ambience of Marco Island. The sun-swept park borders on Henderson Creek, which at high tide allows small boats (18 feet long or smaller) access to the Gulf of Mexico.

RV sites, facilities: The 200-unit mobile-home park has 65 concrete-pad RV sites with full hookups for overnighters and seasonal visitors; cable TV is available. Restrooms, showers, picnic tables, laundry facilities, a store, a recreation hall, shuffleboard courts, pool tables, horseshoes, wintertime social programs, and a pool are provided. Supermarkets and Kmart are 0.25 mile away. The pool area, recreation hall, and laundry are wheelchair accessible. This is an age-55-plus park; children may visit residents only. Small, leashed pets under 30 pounds are allowed, and a dog-walk area accommodates their needs.

Reservations, fees: Reservations are accepted. Sites are $42 per night for two people, plus $2 for each additional person. Credit cards are accepted. Long-term stays are encouraged.

Directions: From I-75 Exit 101, go south on County Road 951 for nine miles to U.S. 41/Tamiami Trail. Turn left. The park is 0.25 mile ahead at right.

Contact: Greystone Park, 13300 East Tamiami Trail, Naples, FL 34114, 239/774-4044, fax 239/774-0105, www.greystonervpark.com.

39 PARADISE POINTE RV RESORT

Scenic rating: 8

north of Marco Island

Paradise Pointe is the younger sister of Greystone Park (see previous listing) and was developed by the same investors. The newer facility, however, targets the upscale RV crowd: RVs must be at least 24 feet long, and pop-up campers and camping vans are not welcome. The sites have huge concrete pads for easy parking. The relatively young landscaping is growing in, adding an increasing lushness to the grounds. The park, built around five lakes, has a luxurious air-conditioned clubhouse with pool tables, a TV room, and a large gathering hall for parties. The other amenities are resort-class: tennis courts, a large swimming pool and whirlpool tub, and a fully equipped health spa.

RV sites, facilities: The 56-acre park offers 383 full-hookup sites with 30-amp and 50-amp electrical service, cable TV, wireless Internet network, and telephone access. Restrooms, showers, a pool, a spa, tennis and shuffleboard courts, horseshoe pits, a clubhouse with a kitchen, a TV room, a game room, laundry facilities, a small putting green, and a health spa with a massage therapist and weights are on the premises. RVs must be at least 24 feet long; pop-up campers and vans are not welcome. A supermarket and restaurants are two miles away. Children are allowed for two weeks. Pets are permitted.

Reservations, fees: Reservations are recommended. Sites are $45 per night. Credit cards are accepted. Long-term stays are allowed.

Directions: From the intersection of U.S. 41/ Tamiami Trail and County Road 951, drive east on U.S. 41 for 2.5 miles.

Contact: Paradise Pointe RV Resort, 14500 East Tamiami Trail, Naples, FL 34114, 239/793-6886 or 877/4-NAPLES (877/462-7537).

GOLD COAST

BEST RV PARKS AND CAMPGROUNDS

❮ Best for Biking
Markham Park, page 477

❮ Families
Lion Country Safari KOA, page 468

❮ Most Unusual
Sunsport Gardens, page 467
Lion Country Safari KOA, page 468
Seminole Health Club, page 477

As one of the best-known destinations on the planet, the Gold Coast lures visitors from all over the globe with its beaches, cosmopolitan lifestyle, and fast-paced — sometimes exotic — tempo. Stretching from Palm Beach in the north, to Fort Lauderdale in the middle, and finally, Miami in the south, the eastern half of what is also called South Florida is knitted together by office towers and condominiums that bump up against the Atlantic Ocean. On the west side, sprawling bedroom suburbs end abruptly at the levees that define the edge of the Everglades, the legendary "river of grass."

Palm Beach County is home to 1,100 tennis courts and 160 golf courses — including the famous PGA National Resort and Spa. Fishing charters are available along the Atlantic coast, and the waters off of Palm Beach County offer first-rate scuba diving. In the tiny posh town of Palm Beach, the main attractions are the luxury retailers of Worth Avenue and the waterfront mansions of socialites and captains of industry, both historic and modern. Palm Beach is among several Florida east coast resorts put on the map by pioneer developer Henry Flagler, who planned them in the 1920s as refuges for well-heeled travelers in search of tropical climates. Palm Beach's larger cousin is the city of West Palm Beach, across the Intracoastal Waterway, which once housed servants for its fancier neighbor and is now representative of the typical South Florida downtown skyline. Nearby are quaint Jupiter, which boasts a historic lighthouse, and Lake Okeechobee, the second-largest freshwater lake in the United States.

Fort Lauderdale is often referred to as the "Venice of America" because of its network of artificial canals that wind through neighborhoods and past boatyards. The water theme doesn't end there: Sailboats and pleasure craft are parked along nearly every foot of waterfront and the beaches are stars of many a family vacation. The New River leads to the fishing grounds of the Gulf Stream; other waterways access backcountry fishing spots.

I-75 is the easiest Everglades access point from Fort Lauderdale. While there is no camping allowed on the high-speed thoroughfare that stretches from Fort Lauderdale to Naples, recreation areas and rest stops have boat ramps and covered picnic tables. Several camping parks are nestled along the urban/Everglades boundary.

Miami-Dade County is probably the most famous spot on the Gold Coast, known as the gateway to Latin America and the Caribbean, the cruise ship capital of the world, and as the Manhattan of the South for attracting the ultra-hip from all over the globe. The heart of the area is downtown Miami, which boasts a breath-taking skyline of modern architecture. To the west, north, and south is urban sprawl, punctuated by Coral Gables, Aventura, Bal Harbour, Key Biscayne, and neighborhoods that reflect Miami's ethnic diversity. To the east lies the city of Miami Beach, which is what most visitors think of when they hear "Miami." The beaches are almost beside the point. There is so much else to do: late-night clubs, pedestrian-friendly Lincoln Road, and a burgeoning arts and music scene.

South of Miami are the main entrances to two national parks: Everglades and Biscayne, both located near the farmlands and horticultural fields of Homestead. Biscayne National Park has no camping – in fact, you'll need a boat to experience most of it. The main entrance to Everglades National Park is on the west side of Homestead.

Unfortunately the traffic, continuous construction projects, and parking problems make the eastern part of the Gold Coast unfriendly to RVs. Many campers use it as a jumping-off point to the Florida Keys and Central Florida, both of which are easy drives. For other RV campers, the Gold Coast can combine the excitement of city entertainment and access to the sawgrass wilds of the Everglades.

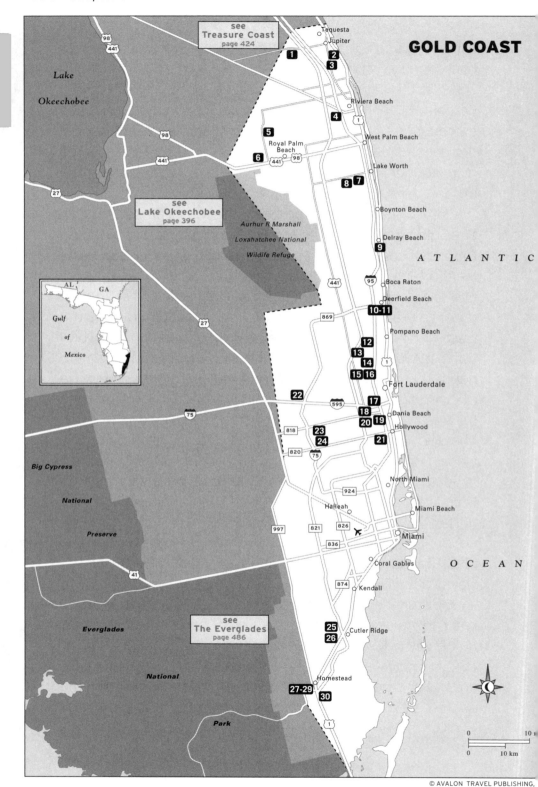

GOLD COAST

see
Treasure Coast
page 424

see
Lake Okeechobee
page 396

see
The Everglades
page 486

Lake
Okeechobee

Aurhur R Marshall
Loxahatchee National
Wildife Refuge

AL   GA

Gulf
of
Mexico

Big Cypress

National

Preserve

Everglades

National

Park

Tequesta
Jupiter

Riviera Beach

West Palm Beach

Royal Palm
Beach

Lake Worth

Boynton Beach

Delray Beach

A T L A N T I C

Boca Raton

Deerfield Beach

Pompano Beach

Fort Lauderdale

Dania Beach

Hollywood

North Miami

Hialeah

Miami Beach

Miami

O C E A N

Coral Gables

Kendall

Cutler Ridge

Homestead

0   10 mi

0   10 km

◼ WEST JUPITER CAMPING RESORT

Scenic rating: 10

west of Jupiter

Fan-shaped palm fronds and the long needles of Florida slash pine trees shade portions of this improved 10-acre campground, but odds are that the paved roads will lead you to a sunny RV campsite. Some campers pluck their own breakfasts of grapefruits and oranges from the park's fruit trees in winter. Video games are found in a large tiki hut, and monthly entertainment may bring a band, a magician, or a disc jockey to the campground. Favorite thing to do? "Have fun!" say the owners. The beach is about a 10-minute drive east, and the St. Louis Cardinals play spring-training games one highway exit south at Roger Dean Stadium (4751 Main Street, Jupiter); for baseball tickets, call 561/775-1818. Within a 30-minute drive are Lion Country Safari and fishing charters at Lake Okeechobee. In Jupiter, the oldest lighthouse in Palm Beach County is open for tours Sunday–Wednesday and has a small museum at its base; call 561/747-6639.

RV sites, facilities: The 74 full-hookup RV sites in this resort have 30-amp (22 sites) and 50-amp (52 sites) electrical hookups; a few sites are pull-through (available in summer only). Lots are 25 by 45 feet and can accommodate RVs up to 45 feet long and slide-outs. A pool, a playground, tennis, volleyball, horseshoes, shuffleboard, monthly entertainment, a basketball court, a catch-and-release fishing pond, and a game room with video games and pool tables entertain campers. Showers, restrooms, picnic tables, concrete pads and patios, a convenience store, deli foods, cable TV, telephone hookups, rental RVs, LP gas, and laundry facilities are available. Nearby are canoe rentals, a golf course, and a theater. Most areas are wheelchair accessible. Streets are paved. Groceries are within three miles. Children are permitted. Pets are allowed, but small dogs are preferred.

Reservations, fees: Reservations are recommended. Fees for two people are $25–35 per night for RVs. Add $3 per additional adult and $4 for cable TV. Credit cards are accepted. Long-term stays are okay, but the maximum stay is six months and one day.

Directions: From I-95, take Exit 87B and go west about five miles on State Road 706/Indiantown Road. Turn left (south) at 130th Avenue North and proceed to the campground entrance at the first right.

Contact: West Jupiter Camping Resort, 17801 130th Avenue North, Jupiter, FL 33478, 561/746-6073 or 888/746-6073, fax 561/743-3738, www.westjupitercampingresort.com.

◼ JUNO BEACH RV PARK

Scenic rating: 6

off U.S. 1 in Juno Beach

The lapping waves of the Atlantic Ocean are within walking distance of this sunny 25-acre park, where paved streets (maximum speed of 10 mph) pass two rectangular fishing lakes, a playground, and a heated pool with a hot tub. If the place feels like a residential community, the park's condominium concept explains why: A monthly maintenance fee for the condo owners includes niceties such as lawn upkeep and underground sprinklers, and some campers opt to buy their concrete-pad RV sites at about half the cost of monthly rental rates. (The fee does not apply for overnighters or seasonal visitors.)

RV sites, facilities: Among the 264 sites in this condominium resort, 100 full-hookup spots are for transient RVs up to 45 feet long and have a picnic table and a fire ring. A pool with a sundeck and a hot tub, a recreation room, a playground, horseshoes, shuffleboard, two fishing lakes, and social programs keep campers busy. Restrooms, a dump station, rental trailers, and two laundry facilities are available. Groceries and restaurants are within 1.1 miles. Management says most areas are wheelchair accessible.

Young children must be adult-supervised, and everyone under 18 is subject to a 10 P.M. curfew. Leashed pets (a maximum of two are allowed per site) must walk in designated areas.

Reservations, fees: Reservations are recommended. If you arrive after office hours, the park posts available sites on the office door. Sites are $28–40 per night for two people, plus $3 for each additional person or pet. Add $3 for electrical service; cable TV is included in the base rate. Credit cards are accepted. Long-term stays are okay.

Directions: From I-95, take Exit 87A and go east a little over four miles on Indiantown Road to U.S. 1. Turn right (south). In about three miles, you'll see a shopping center called The Bluffs on the left side. Turn right at the corner of SunTrust Bank. The RV park is one block ahead to your right.

Contact: Juno Beach RV Park, 900 Juno Ocean Walk, Juno Beach, FL 33408, 561/622-7500, fax 561/627-6595.

❸ PALM BEACH GARDENS RV PARK

Scenic rating: 4

in Palm Beach Gardens

Plunging into the heated pool, tossing horseshoes, or playing a wintertime game of bingo at the recreation room are the main activities for folks at these grassy and gravel RV sites, but they may wish to venture out of the 10-acre park for more action. Within 2.5 miles are the PGA National Resort and Spa and the full-service yacht harbor of Soverel Harbour. More down to earth, the big rolling dunes and fairly wide stretch of sand at Juno Beach are about three miles east of this former KOA. In spring, the St. Louis Cardinals play practice games at nearby Roger Dean Stadium, 4751 Main Street in Jupiter; for tickets, call 561/775-1818. Farther west, drag racers and racing-school students attend more than 150 events per year

at the 200-acre Moroso Motorsports Park; call 561/622-1400. Most visitors to this park stay for a month or two or the entire winter.

RV sites, facilities: All 106 full-hookup RV sites (most of them pull-through) have picnic tables with 30-amp electricity. A pool, a recreation room, horseshoes, propane gas sales, showers, restrooms, limited RV parts, and a dump station are available. A supermarket, restaurants, and Palm Beach Gardens Mall are about one mile away. Children are allowed for short-term stays, and leashed pets are permitted.

Reservations, fees: Reservations are not necessary. Sites are $36 per night for two people, plus $5 for each additional adult and $2 per child. Credit cards are not accepted. Long-term stays are allowed.

Directions: From I-95, take Exit 83 and go east about 1.5 miles on Donald Ross Road to Military Trail. Turn right. Proceed less than 1.5 miles to Hood Road. Turn left (east). The park is about 0.25 mile ahead.

Contact: Palm Beach Gardens RV Park, 4063 Hood Road, Palm Beach Gardens, FL 33410, 561/622-8212.

❹ VACATION INN RESORT

Scenic rating: 6

west of West Palm Beach

Major William Lauderdale and his Tennessee Volunteers cut their way through a jungly subtropical forest during the Second Seminole War of the mid-1800s to create the now-busy thoroughfare that fronts this campground. Continue farther south to Fort Lauderdale, and you'll see how Major Lauderdale's trail has been transformed into an asphalt street crammed with neon lights and strip shopping centers with too-small parking lots. But I digress.

Beyond the security gate sits a manicured campground tailored to the resort crowd vacationing in what sometimes is called the state's wealthiest (per capita) county—Palm

Beach. Ask for a brochure and you'll be able to choose from four campsite designs, all with lighted patios, automatic lawn sprinklers, paved sites, and cable TV. Some people buy their lots, so the number of spaces available to campers varies.

To reach the ocean, drive about five miles east on Blue Heron Boulevard, passing through some dingy neighborhoods, and cross a bridge to Singer Island, the one-time winter playground of the late industrialist John D. MacArthur. You can use one of three municipal beaches in the small town of Palm Beach Shores. For a more woodsy oceanfront experience, head north a few miles on Highway A1A to swim in the ocean or wade in the Intracoastal Waterway at the state park named for MacArthur. Fishing is also popular there.

RV sites, facilities: All 400 full-hookup sites are for self-contained RVs. Facilities include restrooms, showers, picnic tables, cable TV, and laundry. Two pools, a TV lounge, racquetball, tennis, a clubhouse, billiards, an exercise room, horseshoes, and two hot tubs entertain campers. Children and leashed pets are permitted.

Reservations, fees: Reservations are advised. Sites are $50 per night for two people, plus $3 for each additional person. Credit cards are accepted for daily rates. Long-term rates are available.

Directions: Exit I-95 at Blue Heron Boulevard (Exit 76). Head west a few blocks to Military Trail. Turn left and look for the park about 0.5 mile ahead on the east side of the road.

Contact: Vacation Inn Resort, 6500 North Military Trail, West Palm Beach, FL 33407, 561/848-6166 or 800/262-9681.

◢ SUNSPORT GARDENS

Scenic rating: 7

in Loxahatchee west of West Palm Beach

BEST (

At this family-targeted nudist retreat located in rural Loxahatchee, everyone is expected to be in the altogether while swimming in the pool or the hot tub, although exceptions are made in other areas of the 42-acre resort. For afternoon shade, duck into the screened pavilion for a game of darts or cards. The restaurant serves breakfast, lunch, and dinner, and every February this park is the home of the Midwinter Naturist Festival. Lion Country Safari, golf courses, and shopping are nearby. Prince Charles has climbed onto polo ponies at the nearby 125-acre Palm Beach Polo and Country Club, where matches are held in winter; call 561/798-7000.

RV sites, facilities: This 42-acre family nudist retreat has 100 RV sites, 50 sites with 30-amp service, and 20 with 50-amp electricity. Sewer hookup sites are available. A heated pool, a hot tub, a sauna, a playground, a Kidz Club, a game room, two lighted tennis courts, regulation volleyball courts, two *pétanque* (French-style bowling) courts, paddleboats, horseshoe pits, a game room with table-tennis and pool tables, a sundeck, and a 0.25-mile nature trail keep campers busy. Dances are held Saturday nights in the pavilion. Showers, restrooms, two dump stations, rental trailers and cabins, firewood, laundry facilities, snacks, and a restaurant are on the premises. All areas are wheelchair accessible. Groceries are six miles away. Children are welcome. Leashed pets are okay.

Reservations, fees: Reservations are required. Sites are $18–35 per night. Additionally, you will be charged a $25 daily grounds fee for each person in your party. Credit cards are accepted. Long-term rates are available.

Directions: From I-95, take Exit 70B and go west on Okeechobee Boulevard about 14 miles, passing through Royal Palm Beach. At D Road, turn right. Continue 2.5 miles until it dead-ends into North Road. Turn right, then take the first left to enter the campground.

Contact: Sunsport Gardens, 14125 North Road, Loxahatchee, FL 33470, 561/793-0423 or 800/551-7217, fax 561/793-6370, www .sunsportgarden.com.

6 LION COUNTRY SAFARI KOA

Scenic rating: 7

in Loxahatchee west of West Palm Beach

BEST(

Wake to the roar of lions. No kidding. The kings of the jungle tend to express their opinions around their 6:30 A.M. feeding time next door at the 500-acre Lion Country Safari wildlife park, where tourists drive within inches of the freely roaming cats, 2.5-ton white rhinos, and more than 1,000 other creatures. In the afternoon, monkeys get into the verbal act. You'll hear them from your partially shaded or sunny shell-rock campsite.

Although a heated pool and social activities can keep campers busy, sleeping next to the nation's first drive-through cageless zoo (opened in 1967) is the prime reason to stay at the remote 20-acre campground. There is precious little else to do in this fairly rural region, where roadside vegetable stands sometimes can be found along State Road 80. So campers understandably head next door to the safari's amusement park rides and drive-through zoo, where they stop to let elephants cross in front of their cars.

Elsewhere, hikers who travel about four miles west of the KOA can see the northern Everglades by visiting one of the largest water-pumping stations in the world—the S5-A, which is bigger than most houses. Walk down the little-explored levee separating sugarcane fields from the Everglades. To your left, you'll probably see alligators, wading birds, and waterfowl such as ducks and coots. Within the first mile, you'll see an experimental project aimed at cleaning dirty sugarcane water before it reaches the Everglades, and maybe get a glimpse of more wildlife. To get to the S5-A pump station, turn right from the KOA onto State Road 80/Southern Boulevard. Head west about four miles to where the road bends (called 20 Mile Bend). Instead of taking the main road to the right, make a left across the metal bridge crossing the canal, then immediately turn left.

Take that road east to the dead end by a picnic area and then park. Look to the southwest and you'll see a gate preventing vehicular access to the levee. Just walk around the gate and hike as far south as you'd like.

RV sites, facilities: There are 211 full-hookup RV sites (158 pull-through) with 30-amp and 50-amp electricity. For recreation, there's a pool, a playground, a game room, volleyball, basketball, shuffleboard, horseshoes, miniature golf, winter and summer social programs, rental cabins, and a recreation room. Showers, restrooms, a dump station, picnic tables, limited groceries, LP gas sales, and laundry facilities are on the premises. Management says wheelchairs have access to the store, showers, restrooms, pool, and laundry room. Children are welcome. Leashed pets are okay.

Reservations, fees: Reservations are recommended. Sites are $36–44 per night for two people, plus $7 for each additional person over age two, and $1.50–2.50 for electricity. Credit cards are accepted. The maximum stay is three months.

Directions: From I-95, take Exit 68 and go west on U.S. 98/Southern Boulevard for 15 miles to the campground at right.

Contact: Lion Country Safari KOA, P.O. Box 16066, 2000 Lion Country Safari Road, Loxahatchee FL 33470, 561/793-9797 or 800/562-9115, fax 561/763-9603, www.lioncountrysafari.com.

7 JOHN PRINCE PARK CAMPGROUND

Scenic rating: 6

on Lake Osborne west of Lake Worth

The placid waters of Lake Osborne provide a pleasant backdrop for joggers and bicyclists following the five-mile exercise path that winds through 726-acre John Prince Park, a county-run recreation complex big enough to merit three entrances. The 48-acre campground is set in the southern portion of the sunny park. Golfers can take their pick of a driving range, an 18-hole miniature golf, or a par-3 golf course. At the park's focal point—Lake Osborne—you can boat, water-ski, or fish for bass (just bring the gear). Tennis courts and volleyball areas are also in the park.

Don't expect much shade; hurricanes have damaged the tree canopy. Inquire about water-view sites on Explorer Lane or Allegro Road if you don't plan to camp for more than two weeks (the limit at those sites). For the best lake-view spots on a loop drive with a central community campfire circle, try sites 38–41. Fifty-three sites are paved; the rest have a shell-rock surface. Rules clearly state that alligators and snakes are considered residents that should be respected and left alone. You needn't worry, though, because alligators and snakes pose little threat if you don't bother them. Just don't feed the gators. A security gate is closed 24 hours a day.

RV sites, facilities: All 265 campsites have water, 30-amp electricity, and picnic tables. RVs up to 45 feet long and slide-outs can be accommodated. Six sites are drive-through. Restrooms, fire rings, a boat ramp, a dump station, and four playgrounds are on-site. At the park beyond the entrance gate are a fitness trail, a golf course, a driving range, tennis courts, a nature area, and picnic areas. The bathhouse, office, and docks are wheelchair accessible. Streets are paved. Children are welcome. Leashed, attended pets (no pit bulls) are permitted.

Reservations, fees: Reservations are recommended. Sites are $20 per night for five people, plus $2 for each additional person. Credit cards are accepted. Long-term rates are available, but camping is limited to 100 days per year. The maximum stay at waterfront sites with the best views is 14 days.

Directions: From I-95, take Exit 63 and go west on Sixth Avenue South to Congress Avenue. Turn left. The campground entrance is about 0.5 mile ahead on the left. From the Florida

Turnpike, take the Lake Worth Road exit and turn left. Drive 5.2 miles to Congress Avenue and turn right. Drive 0.9 mile to the park.

Contact: John Prince Park Campground, 4759 South Congress Avenue, Lake Worth, Florida 33461. Or contact the Palm Beach County Parks and Recreation Department, 2700 Sixth Avenue South, Lake Worth, FL 33461, 561/582-7992 or 877/992-9925, fax 561/588-5469, www.pbcgov.com/parks.

8 PALM BEACH TRAVELER PARK

Scenic rating: 1

in Lantana

This 7.5-acre suburban home of wintertime bingo games and potluck dinners attracts a 50-50 mix of permanent residents and travelers. The paved park roads, which have a 10-mph speed limit, form a rough figure eight through the grounds, passing staggered, instead of rigidly side-by-side, sleeping spots. Atlantic Ocean beaches are four miles east. A few minutes away is Lake Worth, which is ignored by many tourists. Still, head that way for some bright spots: a 1,000-foot ocean fishing pier, a beach where early birds get the best parking spots, and free concerts at the Bryant Park band shell on the Intracoastal Waterway.

RV sites, facilities: This adult-oriented park has 100 full-hookup sites for RVs, some with 20/30-amp service and some with 50-amp. A pool, shuffleboard, a clubhouse, horseshoes, rental trailers, laundry facilities, and volunteer wintertime social programs are available. The pool and clubhouse are wheelchair accessible. Children may visit a registered camper for no more than two weeks per year. Pets are forbidden.

Reservations, fees: Reservations are recommended. Sites are $50 per night for two people, plus $5 per additional person. Credit cards are accepted. Long-term stays are okay.

Directions: From I-95, take Exit 61 and go west

a little more than two miles on Lantana Road/ County Road 812. Turn left at Lawrence Road. The park is 0.5 mile ahead on the right.

Contact: Palm Beach Traveler Park, 6159 Lawrence Road, Lantana, FL 33462, 561/967-3139, email: jerryrv@msn.com.

❾ DEL-RATON TRAVEL TRAILER PARK

Scenic rating: 4

on U.S. 1 in Delray Beach

If you want to sleep in your RV near the beach in southern Palm Beach County, this is pretty much your only choice. Tourists sometimes are astounded by the seemingly endless stream of condominiums and shopping centers spanning almost the length of U.S. 1 in South Florida, and this neck of the woods is no exception. Car dealerships, shops, eateries, and more hubs of commerce line the street on the approach to the five-acre park. Once you pass the security gate, the straight, paved roads (with 5-mph speed limits) pass tree-dotted yet largely sunny concrete-pad campsites separated from each other by grassy lawns. The park is the closest to the tony shops at Mizner Park in Boca Raton. The Atlantic Ocean is a short drive east. Only a handful call this park home, and it is oriented to visitors in motor homes and travel trailers who stop in for the night or stay for the winter season.

RV sites, facilities: All 60 full-hookup sites (25 pull-through) are for RVs up to 36 feet long, with 30-amp and 50-amp service. Showers, restrooms, a dump station, a recreation room, LP gas sales, and laundry facilities are available. Groceries and a restaurant are across the street. Children are welcome short-term but not as monthly residents. Pets are forbidden.

Reservations, fees: Reservations are recommended, except in summer. Sites are $32–36 per night for two people, plus $1 per extra person. Credit cards are not accepted. Long-term stays are permitted for adults.

Directions: From I-95, take Exit 51 and go east one mile on Linton Boulevard to U.S. 1/South Federal Highway. Turn right. Proceed one mile to the trailer park.

Contact: Del-Raton Travel Trailer Park, 2998 South Federal Highway, Delray Beach, FL 33483, 561/278-4633, email: delraton@aol.com.

🔟 BREEZY HILL RV RESORT

Scenic rating: 3

in Pompano Beach

Security gates and a concrete-block wall guards the entry to this neatly kept RV park and mobile-home community dotted by palm trees and Norfolk pines. It's preferred by French Canadians, many of whom leave their rigs here year-round. During the winter, campers keep busy by taking English classes, reading a newsletter in French, bowling, playing boccie ball (lawn bowling), *pétanque* (French-style bowling), or shuffleboard, and participating in other activities. All sites have concrete pads and accommodate RVs up to 40 feet long. This is one of three well-established snowbird refuges within two blocks of each other.

RV sites, facilities: Among the 749 full-hookup sites, seven are designated for overnighters and the rest are available for seasonal RVs or prefabricated homes. About 33 percent of the park is occupied by permanent residents. Telephone and cable TV are available for long-term visitors. Restrooms, showers, laundry facilities, a billiard hall, horseshoes, and shuffleboard are available. There are two pools (one heated) and two recreation halls. Most facilities are wheelchair accessible. A convenience store is one block away. A supermarket and the ocean are three miles away. Propane can be delivered to your site during the winter months. You must be 55 or older to stay here, and pop-up campers are not allowed. Children and pets are prohibited.

Reservations, fees: Reservations are recom-

mended. Sites are $37 per night for two people, plus $3 per additional person. Major credit cards are accepted. Long-term stays are permitted.

Directions: From I-95, take Exit 39 east on Sample Road and drive 0.25 mile. At Northeast 3rd Avenue, turn north and go 1.5 miles to Northeast 48th Street. Turn east and use the second park entrance.

Contact: Breezy Hill RV Resort, 800 Northeast 48th Street, Pompano Beach, FL 33064, 954/942-8688, www.mhchomes.com.

11 HIGHLAND WOODS RV RESORT

Scenic rating: 2

in Pompano Beach

If you have business in the area or are visiting relatives, then this place might do, though it is transitioning to manufacturing homes. The quiet park is "age qualified," meaning it is geared to people over 55. Paved interior roads lead to the concrete sites, each offering a grassy area in back and to the side. This park is selling homesites, reducing the number of RV spots available to 68, with 30-amp and 50-amp electrical service. Fort Lauderdale's famous sandy beaches are four miles away.

RV sites, facilities: This 147-site adult-oriented mobile-home park offers full hookups, restrooms, showers, a swimming pool, a recreation room, *pétanque* (French-style bowling), horseshoes, shuffleboard, pool tables, two laundry rooms, and wintertime activities such as bingo and darts. Groceries, restaurants, movies, and a flea market require about a five-minute drive. Children are allowed to visit. Pets are permitted in a designated area.

Reservations, fees: Reservations are recommended. Sites are $27 per night for two people, plus $3 per extra person. Credit cards are accepted. Long-term stays are okay.

Directions: From I-95, take Exit 39 east on Sample Road and drive 0.25 mile. At Northeast

3rd Avenue, turn north and go 1.5 miles to Northeast 48th Street. Turn east; the park is on the south side of the road.

Contact: Highland Woods RV Resort, 900 Northeast 48th Street, Pompano Beach, FL 33064, 954/942-6254, www.mhchomes.com.

12 GOLF VIEW ESTATES

Scenic rating: 3

in Pompano Beach

An immaculate walled manufactured-home community wedged between a busy highway and a warehouse area, this resort has the feel of a permanent upscale neighborhood. Many big RVs are parked here year-round, and their owners have built on Florida rooms (screened porches). An adult tricycle is parked in almost every well-tended driveway. Nightly security patrols, a heated swimming pool with a whirlpool tub, saunas for men and women, and a sundeck complete the picture. About 90 percent of the visitors and residents are from Canada.

RV sites, facilities: Open to campers 55 and older, this RV park/mobile-home community offers 127 RV sites with full hookups. About half have 30-amp service; the other have 50-amp. Paved lots vary from 32 to 45 feet in length; they are 12 feet wide. One-third of the community is occupied by full-timers. Shuffleboard courts, a heated pool, a whirlpool tub, saunas, a dump station, and two wheelchair-accessible clubhouses are provided. Favorite things to do are cards, parties, exercise classes, and cruises. Groceries and shopping are within 0.5 mile. RV storage is available in the off-season. Children and pets are prohibited.

Reservations, fees: Reservations are recommended. Sites are $30–55 per night for two people. Credit cards are accepted. Long-term rates are available.

Directions: From I-95, take Exit 36 and drive 2.5 miles west on Atlantic Boulevard to Northwest 31st Avenue. Turn north; the entrance to the park is on the west side. From Florida's Turnpike, take Exit 67 and go 0.5 mile south on Northwest 31st Avenue.

Contact: Golf View Estates, 901 Northwest 31st Avenue, Pompano Beach, FL 33069, 954/972-4140, fax 954/972-3041, www.golf viewestates.com.

13 KOZY KAMPERS RV PARK

Scenic rating: 2

in Fort Lauderdale

Despite its urban locale, this pine-needle–blanketed park is notable for its forest of 100-foot-tall Australian pines. You can park even the biggest rig under towering trees that shelter many of the concrete-pad or grassy sites. Shopping centers and restaurants are nearby, and the location offers good access to local attractions, such as the *Jungle Queen* riverboat cruise, the Sawgrass Mills outlet mall, Pompano Harness Racing, and Dania Jai Alai. Although kids are permitted, parents are warned that they must assume financial responsibility for any damage or injury caused by their children "regardless of age." About half the park is occupied by year-round residents.

RV sites, facilities: All 104 sites have full hookups with 30-amp and 50-amp service, cable TV, and telephone availability. Thirteen are pull-through. During busy times, an overflow area with water and electricity only is opened for additional campers. Sites vary in size from 30 by 40 feet to 25 by 50 feet. Dial-up Internet service is available in the clubhouse. Restrooms, showers, a laundry room, a dump station, a small store, and a recreation hall are provided. All areas are said to be wheelchair accessible. RV and boat storage is available for a monthly fee. Shopping centers and restaurants are within 0.2 mile. Children are welcome but must be supervised by an adult in all areas of the park. Leashed dogs are permitted; a small dog-walk area has been set aside.

Reservations, fees: Reservations are recommended. Sites are $28–38 per night for two people, plus $3 for each additional person over the age of 12. Major credit cards are accepted. Long-term stays are okay.

Directions: From I-95, take Exit 32 on Commercial Boulevard and drive west three miles to the park, which is on the north side. From Florida's Turnpike, take Exit 62 and go east on Commercial Boulevard 0.5 mile.

Contact: Kozy Kampers RV Park, 3631 West Commercial Boulevard, Fort Lauderdale, FL 33309, 954/731-8570, fax 954/731-3140, www. kozykampers.com.

14 JOHN D. EASTERLIN PARK

Scenic rating: 7

in Oakland Park

Until mid-2007, this park is being used as a shelter for people displaced by Hurricane Wilma and it is unknown if camping will resume. Call to see if the RV park is open to the public.

It's hard to believe you're still in urban Fort Lauderdale. Some cypress trees are more than 200 years old and stand 100 feet tall. A magnificent canopy of cypress, cabbage palms, and oaks shades the grassy sites. Don't miss the winding nature trail, where you'll see ferns, wild-coffee bushes, red maple trees, and cabbage palms in a 0.75-mile walk. This Designated Urban Wilderness Area was acquired by the county in 1944 by foreclosure and originally named Cypress Park; it was renamed after a county commissioner in 1965. You can fish in the lake, but you're encouraged to release your catch; swimming is not allowed. The winding paved road is good for leisurely cycling. During the winter season, you'll find visitors from Europe and Canada, as well as Floridians year-round.

RV sites, facilities: The 46-acre county park has 46 shady, paved RV sites, and seven tent sites with electricity, water, restrooms, showers, picnic tables, and grills. The biggest RVs on the road can be accommodated. All sites have 20/30/50-amp service and full hookups. Also in the park are a dump station, a lake, a one-mile nature trail, two playgrounds, horseshoe pits, shuffleboard courts, and a volleyball field. Limited Internet access is available by dial-up in the office. Five campsites and the bathhouse are wheelchair accessible. Groceries and shopping are within two miles. No alcohol or firearms are permitted. Children are welcome. Pets are permitted with proof of vaccination.

Reservations, fees: Reservations are recommended. Sites are $19–23 per night for four people, plus $2–2.50 for each additional person. Credit cards are accepted. The maximum stay is 14 days; if you pay by the month, you can stay up to six months.

Directions: From I-95 southbound, take Exit 32 and head west on Commercial Boulevard for 0.1 mile. Turn south at Powerline Road and go 0.9 mile. Turn west at Northwest 38th Street; you'll see the park entrance on the south side of the road. From I-95 northbound, take Exit 31 and go east to Powerline Road. Go north on Powerline Road to Northwest 38th Street. Turn west and drive under the interstate and across the railroad tracks. The entrance is just past the tracks.

Contact: John D. Easterlin Park, 1000 Northwest 38th Street, Oakland Park, FL 33309, 954/938-0610, fax 954/938-0625, www.broward.org/parks.

15 SUNSHINE HOLIDAY RV RESORT

Scenic rating: 2

in Fort Lauderdale

Only self-contained RVs are allowed in this family-friendly park, where about a third of the tenants stay year-round. It has a security gate that requires you to punch in an entrance code. Some sites on the east side are shaded by mature oaks, but much of the park is sunny. A shopping center is across the street. A majority of the visitors and mobile-home residents are from Quebec; you'll hear plenty of French spoken here.

RV sites, facilities: There are 100 full-hookup RV sites set apart from the 300-unit mobile-home park for families. The campsites are 22 by 60 feet, including a paved patio area 11 feet long, and they have 30-amp and 50-amp electrical service. There is no bathhouse, but you'll find a pool, laundry facilities, a 33-acre lake, a clubhouse with dial-up Internet access, and shuffleboard courts. A social committee comprised of campers organize activities in winter. Children are welcome. Pets are permitted.

Reservations, fees: Reservations are recommended. Sites are $28–37 per night. Major credit cards are accepted. Long-term stays are permitted.

Directions: From I-95, take Exit 31B and drive 1.5 miles west on Oakland Park Boulevard. The park entrance is on the south side.

Contact: Sunshine Holiday RV Resort, 2802 West Oakland Park Boulevard, Fort Lauderdale, FL 33311, 954/731-1722 or 877/327-2757, fax 954/731-0451, www.rvonthego.com.

16 PARADISE ISLAND RV RESORT

Scenic rating: 4

in Fort Lauderdale

This is a homey kind of place where campers grow potted geraniums in their front yards and hang little wooden signs with their names on their rigs. A high ficus hedge surrounds the clean, manicured RV resort, cutting it off from city sights. Mature oaks and palm trees shade some campsites. A security gate offers peace of mind. About half the folks here are permanent residents. Most visitors are snowbirds, and the managers say that there's not a lot for kids to do except swim in the pool.

RV sites, facilities: There are 150 RV sites with full hookups and 50-amp electrical service in this 232-unit park with 18 drive-through spots. RVs up to 45 feet long can be accommodated. The park has paved streets and some oaks and palm trees. Sites are grassy or paved, varying in size up to 45 feet long and 25 feet wide. Many have concrete pads. Wireless Internet connection is available at each campsite, but not cable TV. Restrooms, showers, laundry facilities, a pool, a recreation hall, two adults-only lounges, a barbecue pavilion, and shuffleboard, boccie ball (lawn bowling), and *pétanque* (French-style bowling) courts are available. In winter, dinner dances, breakfasts, and card games also entertain. A small store offers RV supplies but not food. Grocery stores are about three miles away. Children under 16 must be accompanied by an adult in the clubhouse, pool, bathrooms, and laundry. Two leashed pets per site are permitted.

Reservations, fees: Reservations are recommended. Sites are $31–38 per night for two people, plus $3 for each additional person. Major credit cards are accepted. Long-term stays are okay.

Directions: From I-95, take Exit 31B and drive 0.25 mile west on Oakland Park Boulevard. Turn south onto Northwest 21st Avenue; the park entrance is on the west side of the street.

Contact: Paradise Island RV Resort, 2121 Northwest 29th Court, Fort Lauderdale, FL 33311, 954/485-1150 or 800/487-7395, fax 954/485-5701, www.paradiserv.com.

17 YACHT HAVEN PARK MARINA

Scenic rating: 7

in Fort Lauderdale

For a taste of the "Venice of America," as Fort Lauderdale is often called, this high-end RV resort and marina has much to offer. About half the sites are on the New River; you might find a CEO's yacht or an oceangoing sailboat parked at the dock near your site. Try to get a spot on Perry Street or Magellan Drive, which overlook the river and the trees of the Secret Woods Nature Center, a county park. Other sites offer postcard-quality vistas of expensive waterfront homes. There's a security gate, and most sites have a raised concrete patio next to the RV pad. The pool is heated in winter. The New River leads to the fishing grounds of the Gulf Stream, meaning that boats have access to the ocean.

RV sites, facilities: All 250 sites have full hookups and 30/50-amp electrical service. About 30 percent of the park is occupied by year-round residents. RVs up to 45 feet long can be accommodated. Restrooms, showers, laundry facilities, a dump station, a pool, a spa, a recreation hall with planned activities during the winter, shuffleboard courts, boat docks, and a boat ramp are available. Two sites are wheelchair accessible. Groceries and restaurants are within one mile. Children are welcome. Leashed pets are permitted.

Reservations, fees: Reservations are recommended. Sites are $29–50 per night for two people, plus $5 for each additional person. You can moor your boat for an extra charge. Credit cards are accepted. Long-term stays are okay.

Directions: From I-95, take Exit 25 toward Marina Mile Road for 0.4 mile. At the intersection with State Road 84 go west to the entrance 0.1 mile. Look for the entrance on the north side of the highway.

Contact: Yacht Haven Park Marina, 2323 State Road 84, Fort Lauderdale, FL 33312, 954/583-2322 or 800/581-2322, www.yachthavenpark.com.

18 TWIN LAKES TRAVEL PARK

Scenic rating: 3

in Fort Lauderdale

Tucked into an industrial neighborhood in a web of major highways, Twin Lakes is a peaceful, sunny campground dotted with tabebuia and mature shade trees. A sign at the entrance announces *"Il est imposible de parquer ici"* ("It is impossible to park here"), evidence of the French-Canadian clientele. About 95 percent of the visitors here are from Canada; 10 percent live here year-round. Besides being a good base from which to explore the Everglades, it's convenient to Sawgrass Mills, the world's largest outlet mall; Blockbuster Golf and Games entertainment park; and the Old West–theme town of Davie, where even the McDonald's has hitching posts.

RV sites, facilities: All 374 sites have full hookups; almost all drive-through and 70 feet long, "like having your own little yard." Rigs as long as 45 feet can be accommodated. Cable TV is available, and you can access the Internet in the laundry room by the pool. Restrooms, showers, a pool, wading pool for tots, laundry facilities, *pétanque* (French-style bowling) and shuffleboard courts, horseshoe pits, a recreation hall, a dump station, and propane delivery are on-site. A small store sells beer and soda; groceries are within one mile. All buildings have wheelchair ramps. Children are welcome. Small leashed pets are permitted.

Reservations, fees: Reservations are recommended. Sites are $35–45 per night for two people, plus $5 per additional person. Major credit cards are accepted. Long-term stays are allowed.

Directions: From I-595, or Florida's Turnpike, exit onto U.S. 441 and go 0.4 mile south. Turn west (right) on Southwest 36th Court/Oakes Road and drive two blocks, then turn north on Burris Road. Continue 0.5 mile to the park.

Contact: Twin Lakes Travel Park, 3055 Burris Road, Fort Lauderdale, FL 33314, 954/587-0101 or 800/327-8182, fax 954/587-9512.

19 SEMINOLE PARK

Scenic rating: 3

in Hollywood

This private campground on land leased from the Seminole Indian tribe welcomes older travelers, 95 percent of whom return year after year from Canada and the North. You'll have to reserve as much as a year in advance to get a spot here in the winter season. Bingo, potluck dinners, and dances keep people busy, but the real attraction is the Seminole Hard Rock Hotel and Casino (866-502-7529) within 0.5 mile. Some sites are paved, but others are grassy. Stores are within walking distance, but be careful because the highway carries heavy traffic.

RV sites, facilities: All 102 RV sites have full hookups, plus cable TV and telephone access for long-term visitors. Amenities include restrooms, showers, a pool, two recreation halls, and *pétanque* (French-style bowling) and shuffleboard courts. Most of the sites have 30-amp electrical service; a few have 50-amp. A volunteer group of park guests organize planned activities such as cards, dances, and bicycle outings. The office, recreation halls, laundry, bathhouses, and pool are wheelchair accessible. RV storage is available. Adult campers are preferred, but children are allowed for short visits. Only pets under 10 pounds are permitted.

Reservations, fees: Reservations are recommended. Sites are $32 per night for two people, plus $2 per extra person. Credit cards are not accepted. Long-term rates are available.

Directions: From I-95, take Exit 25 westbound for 2.8 miles on Stirling Road. Turn south at U.S. 441/State Road 7 and drive 0.2 mile to the park, on the east side of the road.

Contact: Seminole Park, 3301 North State Road 7, Hollywood, FL 33021, 954/987-6961.

20 T. Y. PARK

Scenic rating: 5

in Hollywood

This campground was closed for renovations in April 2006; call to see if it has reopened.

Bring a fishing pole to try your luck in the well-stocked lake that is the centerpiece of this

150-acre oak-shaded park in the middle of the metropolitan area. (You'll also need a Florida fishing license.) A two-mile path around the lake is a favorite with joggers and bicyclists. On weekends, the park is jammed with local kids and families picnicking on the grounds and swimming in the lake. In winter, many Canadians use this campground as their vacation base. Art fairs and community festivals are sometimes held here, too, adding to the crowds. What does T. Y. stand for? "Topee-keegee Yugnee" is what the Seminoles called "the gathering place."

RV sites, facilities: There are 48 campsites, including 40 that are drive-through in this county park. While six-month stays are allowed if sites are available, no visitors live here year-round, and the normal limit is 14 days. Water, electricity, grills, picnic tables, and patios are provided at RV sites. Restrooms, showers, laundry facilities, a dump station, a trading post, bicycle and boat rentals, a swimming lagoon with a waterslide, and basketball and volleyball courts are available. One campsite, the bathhouse, and laundry are wheelchair accessible. Children are welcome. Leashed pets are permitted at campsites and in the park but may not be taken on the beach; they must be preregistered at the park office. Twenty-four-hour security is provided.

Reservations, fees: Reservations are recommended. Sites are $18–25 per night for four people, plus $2 for each additional person. Credit cards are accepted. The maximum stay is six months if paid each month in advance. Long-term rates are available.

Directions: From I-95 in Hollywood, take Exit 21 west on Sheridan Street for 0.7 mile. Turn north at Park Road and drive 0.2 mile to the entrance.

Contact: T. Y. Park, 3300 North Park Road, Hollywood, FL 33021, 954/985-1980, fax 954/961-5950, www.broward.org/parks.

21 LAKE TRINITY ESTATES

Scenic rating: 4

in Pembroke Park

This 61-acre park is ingeniously slipped underneath a Christian TV station's towering antenna and studios, which broadcasts live religious programming and screens movies in a state-of-the-art surround-sound theater. On the south side of the property is a lake with a golf driving range on the shore. Putt-putt golf is available if you want to try your hand. The sites are well landscaped. Each winter, campers, many of them French Canadians, compete in *pétanque* (French-style bowling) and shuffleboard contests. About 80 percent of the inhabitants live here year-round, and park models are for sale. The beach is about six miles east, and the Miami Dolphins play pro football about a 10-minute drive west; for tickets, call 305/620-2578.

RV sites, facilities: This 284-unit community hosts 117 RV-only sites with 30-amp electrical service and full hookups. Most sites fit rigs up to 40 feet and have concrete patios and 10 feet of space of elbow room. Restrooms, showers, laundry facilities, a swimming pool, a dump station, a gift shop, shuffleboard, and *pétanque* (French-style bowling) are available. Some areas are wheelchair accessible. Groceries, shopping, and tourist attractions are within two miles. Children are welcome. Dogs are not permitted, but cats and birds are allowed. The park requires sites to be kept neat, clean and quiet; profanity, fighting, and drunkenness can result in eviction.

Reservations, fees: Reservations are recommended in winter. Sites are $27–29 per night for two people, plus $1 for each additional person. Major credit cards are accepted. Long-term stays are okay.

Directions: From I-95, take Exit 19 westbound on Pembroke Road for 0.5 mile to the park, which is on the south side.

Contact: Lake Trinity Estates, 3300 Pembroke Road, 1 Lake Trinity Estates, Pembroke Park, FL 33021, 954/962-7400, email: laketrinityestates@tbn.org.

22 MARKHAM PARK

Scenic rating: 10

near the Everglades

BEST (

This campground was closed in early 2006 for hurricane renovations. Call to see if it has reopened.

You'd have to spend weeks at this 665-acre county park before you could sample everything there is to do here. For one, there's a mountain-biking trail with sharp turns and what passes for altitude in flat South Florida. (The other two popular mountain-biking parks are Oleta State Park in North Miami and Amelia Earhart Park in Hialeah, both in Miami-Dade County south of here. Markham Park is said to be the most technical, requiring more skill than the others.) You can also bicycle on paved roads that wind through the park and in the campground clusters. If your tastes run to the cosmic, there's stargazing in the observatory every Saturday. Gun enthusiasts come from all over to take aim on the 50-yard and 100-meter target ranges, which are said to be Florida's best. There are two dog parks, one for pets under 25 pounds, and one for heavier canines, where you can let your friend off leash. Water scooters are allowed to buzz around in a lake on weekends.

From the concrete boat ramps, you can launch your craft into the L-35A Canal, which stretches along the eastern edge of the Everglades, or the New River Canal, which runs east to west. Hike through the Australian pine forest to the levee that separates the vast watery prairie of the Everglades from civilization; from atop the levee, you can see for miles. When you get hot, cool down in the oversized pool (swimming is not allowed in the lake or the canals). The pool is open from spring break to Labor Day. On weekends, the campground fills up fast, so be sure to make reservations. During the week, you can relax at your large, wooded RV site in peace and quiet.

RV sites, facilities: Split among 12 campground clusters are 88 spots with water and electricity. Each cluster has a paved site for wheelchair access. Eight drive-through sites have full hookups. An additional 10 tent sites have no water or electricity. Pods A, B, C, D, and E are shady; pod F is less shaded. If you like to sunbathe, choose pods G–L. All have picnic tables, grills, and fire rings. Restrooms, showers, and a dump station are available. For fun, take your pick from the pool, the lake, two boat ramps, boat rentals, racquetball and tennis courts, mountain-biking trails, playgrounds, gun ranges, horseshoe pits, volleyball courts, an observatory, a personal-watercraft lake, a biking/jogging path, a 0.5-mile nature trail, a 1-mile-long equestrian trail, and a model airplane field. With two miles are grocery stores, restaurants, and upscale shopping. Most areas are wheelchair accessible, including some paved campsites. Children and leashed dogs are welcome.

Reservations, fees: Reservations are recommended, especially on weekends, and are accepted up to one year in advance. Sites are $19–23 per night for four people, plus $2 for each additional person. Major credit cards are accepted. Most overnighters stay 14 days. Maximum length of stay is six months if paid in advance month to month.

Directions: From Fort Lauderdale, take I-595 west eight miles to Exit 1A at State Road 84. Continue on State Road 84 west to the second traffic light (Weston Road), then turn north into the park entrance.

Contact: Markham Park, 16001 State Road 84, Sunrise, FL 33326, 954/389-2000, www .broward.org/parks.

23 SEMINOLE HEALTH CLUB

Scenic rating: 3

in Davie

BEST (

Coconut palms, orchids, and banana and mango trees give this wooded 11-acre naturist park a tropical feel, even though it's rapidly being surrounded by housing subdivisions. Horses and a goat or pig (or two) on the premises will make you think of the farm. In the center of the park's pond is Monkee Island where real primates run loose—a treat for children. As at most nudist campgrounds, the managers are careful to screen out curiosity seekers and to protect the privacy of their guests. If you pass muster, you'll get the ultimate tan. A plus for those who travel with their pets: There's also a free-roaming area for dogs.

RV sites, facilities: This nudist resort offers 50 RV slots and five tent sites with water and 30-amp electricity hookups. Restrooms, showers, two laundry rooms, a dump station, an outdoor gym, a game room, a dance floor, a restaurant, motel rooms with color TVs but no bathrooms, a large swimming pool, and courts for tennis, shuffleboard, horseback-riding lessons, and *pétanque* (French-style bowling) are available. Internet access is available in the office. Most areas are wheelchair accessible. Visitors are asked to spend the day here before camping to make sure everyone is comfortable with each other. Families with children are welcome. Leashed pets are permitted.

Reservations, fees: Reservations are required. Sites are $40 per night for two people or a family. Beyond that, add $10 per extra person. Credit cards are not accepted. Long-term stays are okay.

Directions: From Fort Lauderdale, take I-595 west for seven miles to Southwest 136th Avenue. Drive three miles south to Southwest 26th Street. Turn west and continue 1.6 miles to Southwest 142nd Avenue, then turn left. At 37th Court, turn left, then immediately turn right onto a paved road that leads to the park entrance. From I-75, take the Griffin Road exit eastbound about three miles to the first traffic light that allows you to cross the canal to Orange Drive, which parallels Griffin Road. On Orange Drive, turn west and drive to Southwest 142nd Avenue. Go north past the mountainlike county park (it used to be a dump), and the RV place will be on your right.

Contact: Seminole Health Club, 3800 Southwest 142nd Avenue, Davie, FL 33330, 954/473-0231, fax 954/476-7042, email: sonshiners@aol.com.

24 C. B. SMITH PARK

Scenic rating: 7

in Pembroke Pines

The park was being used after the 2005 hurricanes to shelter people whose homes had been damaged in storms; it is expected to reopen by 2007. Call ahead to see if the park is open to camping.

Kids flop down a waterslide on inner tubes at this 320-acre county park, but you won't be able to hear their gleeful shouts from the sunny, palm-dotted campground on the park's other side. The lake is the focus of attention. For fun, try the waterslide, sunbathe at the beach, tool around in a paddleboat, play racquetball, tennis, or volleyball, visit the playground, or toss a few horseshoes at the horseshoe pits.

RV sites, facilities: Sixty full-hookup RV sites (30 pull-through) and 12 tent sites overlook an 80-acre lake. Restrooms, showers, picnic tables, grills, and laundry facilities are available. Children are welcome. Leashed pets are permitted.

Reservations, fees: Reservations are recommended. Sites are $19 per night for four people, plus $2 for each additional person. Major credit cards are accepted. Unlike most public parks, this one permits long-term stays of up to six months.

Directions: From I-75, take Exit 9A east on Pines Boulevard for one mile to Flamingo Road. Turn north and go to the park at 900 North Flamingo Road.

Contact: C. B. Smith Park, 900 North Flamingo Road, Pembroke Pines, FL 33028, 954/437-2650, www.broward.org/parks.

25 LARRY AND PENNY THOMPSON MEMORIAL PARK AND CAMPGROUND

Scenic rating: 10

west of Perrine near Metrozoo

This is likely the best base camp for exploring the Miami area. It's a bit far from Miami Beach, but it's close to tourist attractions like Coral Castle, Monkey Jungle, Miami Metrozoo, and Biscayne Bay. With 240 RV sites and 30 tent spots, you might expect this urban campground to have a more crowded feel, but the sites are thoughtfully laid out in spoke-and-wheel groups of 15–20 spots each. Trees are plentiful in the campground, with mango and avocado orchards nearby (no picking allowed).

The secret is out, too. While traveling in Canada a couple of years ago, I met Canadians who have come to this county park to catch some winter sunshine and the ambience of 275 acres of woodlands. They couldn't always remember then name of the park, but they recalled the details of their good times here. The fishing lake and swimming beach get crowded on weekends with day-trippers and locals using the picnic shelters for birthday parties and other festivities. When Miami's only county-run waterslides reopen for summer here (Memorial Day–Halloween), platoons of kids each weekend climb up a wooden platform to reach the top of a rocky palm-dotted hill, then plunge down three slides into the 72–75°F clear waters of a well-fed lake. Wednesday is the slowest day at the slides. The Florida Keys are one hour away.

RV sites, facilities: All 240 sites have full hookups and 30/50-amp electrical service. Twenty sites are pull-through. Restrooms, showers, picnic tables, laundry facilities, a dump station, and ice are available. Within the county park are a lake, a swimming beach, three waterslides, a fishing pier, a concession stand, bridle trails, and picnic pavilions. A supermarket is one mile away. The laundry, restrooms, and playground are wheelchair accessible. Rules requiring neatness and quiet hours are enforced. Internet access is available in the office. Children are welcome. Leashed pets may camp but are forbidden in the rest of the county park. All pets must be properly licensed and are welcome if kept under control and quiet. Pets may not be tied to trees or left unattended.

Reservations, fees: Reservations are taken, but you cannot reserve specific sites. Sites are $22 per night for four people, plus $2–5 for each extra person over age four. Credit cards are accepted. Stays are limited to three months, but an extension is available for another three months, and weekly and monthly rates are available.

Directions: From Florida's Turnpike, exit west on Eureka Drive/Southwest 184th Street. Continue one mile to the park entrance at 12451 Southwest 184th Street on the north side of the road.

Contact: Larry and Penny Thompson Memorial Park and Campground, 12451 Southwest 184th Street, Miami, FL 33177, 305/232-1049, fax 305/293-4529, www.metrodade.com.

26 MIAMI EVERGLADES CAMPGROUND

Scenic rating: 7

in southern Dade County on Southwest 162nd Avenue between Quail Roost Drive and Hainlin Mill Road

Pick free avocados and mangoes right off the trees at this farm country campground, which is convenient to such attractions as Monkey Jungle, Metrozoo, Parrot Jungle, the Everglades, and the Florida Keys. Nearby is the Redland, Dade County's agricultural area, where much of the nation's limes are grown, as well as tropical crops, including yucca and malanga. These tubers are often cooked like potatoes and served with "mojo," a mixture of vinegar, spices, and olive oil. Staples of the Cuban-American diet, yucca and malanga have become trendy with chefs of the "New World" cooking school. In these parts, think tree farm and what you get are acres and acres of palm trees, soon to be planted outdoors in Florida subdivisions and inside Midwestern shopping malls. The real plus of this park is its rural feel, yet it is close to restaurants and shopping.

RV sites, facilities: This former KOA has 330 RV sites (140 are pull-through) and 20 tent spots. About 15 percent of the sites are occupied by year-round residents. The park offers full hookups; 50-amp service at one-third of the sites and 30-amp service at the remaining sites. Facilities include picnic tables, restrooms, showers, laundry facilities, a circular pool with hot tub, horseshoe pits, paved biking trail, restaurant, shuffleboard, volleyball, and basketball courts, an adult lounge, rental cabins, a dump station, propane, and a convenience store. The bathhouses, store, and recreation hall are wheelchair accessible. Wireless Internet service is available in some of the common areas; there are phone jacks and two computers in the lounge. Slide-out RVs and rigs up to 45 feet can be accommodated. Grocery shops and restaurants are within one mile. Children under 14 must be accompanied by a responsible adult at all times. Leashed pets are welcome.

Reservations, fees: Reservations are recommended; however, a $30 deposit is required, and the park requires seven days' notice for cancellations. Sites are $34–65 per night for two people, plus $3 for each additional person. Rates are higher during special events. Holiday weekends require a three-night stay. Credit cards are accepted. Long-term stays are permitted.

Directions: From Florida's Turnpike, exit west on Quail Roost Drive and proceed five miles to Southwest 162nd Avenue, then turn south. The park entrance is 0.5 mile ahead on the east side of the road. From U.S. 1, drive 4.5 miles west on Southwest 216th Street to Southwest 162nd Avenue, then turn north and continue to the park.

Contact: Miami Everglades Campground, 20675 Southwest 162nd Avenue, Homestead, FL 33187, 305/233-5300 or 800/917-4923, www.miamicamp.com.

27 THE BOARDWALK

Scenic rating: 5

in Homestead

This mobile-home and RV park is a gated community close to city amenities, Everglades National Park, the Florida Keys, and Biscayne Bay. About three-fourths of the land is dedicated to manufactured homes, but you'll also find RV spaces available for overnighters and seasonal visitors in a their own section. Everything is neat and spotlessly maintained—from the swimming pool and suburban-style landscaping to the fitness center, clubhouse, and social areas. A concrete wall surrounds the park, and a security gate keeps out curiosity seekers. A speed limit of 15 mph is enforced.

RV sites, facilities: There are 108 RV sites with concrete pads and full hookups. The entire park is laid out in checkerboard fashion, with the RV section confined to one corner; some RV spots are up against the property line. The rest of the park is occupied by mobile homes. About 25 percent of the RV sites have 50-amp electrical service; the rest are 30 amp. Most sites have concrete patios, and rigs up to 44 feet can be accommodated. Restrooms, showers, and laundry facilities are available. On the premises are a heated pool, a clubhouse with billiards and card room, a fitness center, planned activities in winter, lighted shuffleboard courts, horseshoe pits, propane, and a barbecue area. The office has an Internet connection. Children are welcome. Leashed pets of small and medium size are permitted. Visitors must register in the office and should be off-premises by 10 P.M.

Reservations, fees: Reservations are recommended; however, a $150 deposit is required. Sites are $35–65 per night for two people, plus $6 per extra person. Credit cards are accepted. Long-term rates are available.

Directions: From the Florida Turnpike, take Exit 2 west on Campbell Drive and proceed to U.S. 1. Turn left on U.S. 1 and drive 0.3 mile to Northeast 6th Avenue.

Contact: The Boardwalk, 100 Northeast 6th Avenue, Homestead, FL 33030, 305/248-2487 or 888/233-9255, fax 305/248-2075, www .boardwalkcommunity.com.

28 GOLDCOASTER MOBILE HOME AND RV PARK

Scenic rating: 3

in Homestead

Part of the Sun Communities mobile-home and RV park chain that owns dozens of parks across the nation, Goldcoaster Mobile Home and RV Park is a squeaky-clean, professionally landscaped and managed destination for snowbirds, retirees, and local workers, about half of whom live here year-round. A concrete wall encircles the park, and there's a security gate. Four miles of paved roads are ideal for bicycling and strolling. Big rigs are welcome, and a full-time recreation director is in charge of the social program. It's convenient to the Florida Keys and Biscayne Bay, and 15 minutes from the main entrance to Everglades National Park. Nearby is a large outlet mall, as well as the Homestead motor-sports racing complex. Surrounding this area is the South Dade farming area, where vegetables—including tomatoes, green beans, and more—flourish in the winter sun. For a fun and different experience, drive to one of the "you-pick" strawberry fields and gather your own harvest of sweet berries.

RV sites, facilities: This 548-site manufactured-home community offers around 150 full-hookup sites for travelers, who can use the restrooms, showers, craft and card room, laundry facilities, deluxe shuffleboard courts, heated pool, and whirlpool tub. Most sites have 30/50-amp electrical service; 20 have 50-amp service. The pool, clubhouse, bathhouse,

and laundry are wheelchair accessible. In the wintertime, bingo, dances, pancake breakfasts, crafting classes, water aerobics, and bicycle trips are held to entertain visitors. Children and leashed pets are welcome.

Reservations, fees: Reservations are taken. Sites are $30–43 per night for two people, plus $3 for each additional person. Credit cards are accepted.

Directions: From U.S. 1 in Florida City, turn west at Palm Drive/Southwest 344th Street and proceed 1.5 miles to Southwest 187th Avenue/Redland Road, then turn south. The park entrance is on the west side.

Contact: Goldcoaster Mobile Home and RV Park, 34850 Southwest 187th Avenue, Homestead, FL 33034, 305/248-5462 or 800/828-6992, fax 305/248-5467, www.suncommunities.com.

29 CITY OF FLORIDA CITY CAMP SITE AND RV PARK

Scenic rating: 2

in Florida City

Parts of this park are little more than an open, grassy field, but some shady old oaks can be found on the west side. The rest of the park is laid out in gridlike fashion. Converted school buses are not allowed, and all RVs must have up-to-date inspections, tags, and insurance. A manager lives on the property, and about 40 percent of the sites are occupied by year-round residents, mostly construction and power-plant employees. Because this is a city-owned park, it is patrolled by the Florida City Police Department. Many rules are in place, including no open fires, quiet times, and limits on operation of generators. RVs staying longer than 180 days must use PVC pipes for hooking up to the sewers.

RV sites, facilities: This city-owned urban campground has 300 grassy campsites, 30 of which are for tents. None are drive-through.

Full hookups, restrooms, showers, picnic tables, laundry facilities, and shuffleboard courts are available. Electrical service includes 20-amp, 30-amp, and 50-amp hookups; the majority are 30-amp sites. An Internet connection is available in the office. RVs up to 40 feet can be accommodated. Shopping and restaurants are within 0.5 mile. The restrooms are wheelchair accessible. Children are welcome. Leashed pets are permitted, except for dogs weighing more than 40 pounds.

Reservations, fees: Reservations are not necessary. Sites are $22 per night for two people, plus $2 for each additional person. Credit cards are accepted. Long-term stays are okay.

Directions: From Florida's Turnpike, take Exit 1 and drive straight two blocks to Northwest 2nd Avenue. The park entrance is 500 feet on the right.

Contact: City of Florida City Camp Site and RV Park, 601 Northwest 3rd Avenue, Florida City, FL 33034, 305/248-7889, fax 305/248-1738.

30 SOUTHERN COMFORT RV RESORT

Scenic rating: 7

in Florida City

With its swaying royal palms, fruit trees, and a rainbow of hibiscus flowers, the park displays a Caribbean mood. It's convenient to the Florida Keys, national parks, and other attractions; a discount shopping mall, the Florida Keys Factory Shops, is across the street. If you're driving to the Florida Keys, this is the last resort-style overnight campground near U.S. 1—something to note if there's an accident on the highway between Florida City and Key Largo. Often, the road is completely shut down in both directions and you're stuck for hours. Traffic may be rerouted on Card Sound Road, but that can be slow going in a crowd.

RV sites, facilities: There are 338 full-hookup RV sites (50 pull-through) and 10 tent-only sites with water and electricity. Picnic tables, restrooms, showers, laundry facilities, a pool, a recreation room, shuffleboard, and a tiki bar are on the premises. Organized activities are offered, including aerobic exercises, bingo, and dances in winter. Rigs up to 40 feet long can be accommodated. You can connect to the Internet in the recreation hall. Children are welcome. Leashed pets, except rottweilers and pit bulls, are permitted.

Reservations, fees: Reservations are recommended. Sites are $30–38 per night for two people, plus $5 for each additional person. Rates may be higher during special events. Credit cards are accepted. Long-term stays up to six months are okay.

Directions: From U.S. 1 in Florida City, turn east at Palm Drive and proceed one block to the park entrance on the south side.

Contact: Southern Comfort RV Resort, 345 East Palm Drive, Florida City, FL 33034, 305/248-6909, fax 305/245-1345, www.gzinc.com/comfortrv.

THE EVERGLADES

BEST RV PARKS AND CAMPGROUNDS

◖ **Biking**
Long Pine Key Campground, page 495

More than any other natural feature, the

Everglades define south Florida. They are, in the true sense of the word, unique. Author Marjory Stoneman Douglas recognized this in her 1947 classic, *The Everglades: River of Grass,* when she penned these famous words: "There are no other Everglades in the world."

The river of grass she referred to was the 50-mile-wide band of wispy saw grass that looks from afar like a dry prairie, until your boots sink knee-deep into the watery bottom. The broad expanse is punctuated by small rises covered with trees (known as tree islands or "hammocks") and stretches from Lake Okeechobee to Florida Bay, and from the area east of Naples to the western suburbs of Fort Lauderdale and Miami. Water levels in the river fluctuate naturally, from ankle- to chest-deep. Modern drainage efforts have thrown that hydrologic equilibrium out of whack, but much of the Everglades' original appeal still can be enjoyed by modern-day visitors. Meanwhile, the state and federal governments are working overtime to restore what remains of the original wilderness. It's a good thing, too; more than 1.5 million people per year visit the Everglades.

Each winter, thousands of winged visitors head to the vicinity of the Everglades, one of the largest migrations in the nation. Winter is the best time to visit the southern tip of undeveloped Florida because you'll have less trouble with the 40-odd types of resident mosquitoes. (Still, bring repellent of your choice. Some people prefer those containing DEET). From muggy May to November, temperatures reach the high 80s°F to high 90s°F, and lightning storms and torrential local downpours are common. From January to mid-March, temperatures are usually moderate and skies tend to be clear.

Almost anywhere in this area, you're certain to see an alligator sunning itself on a canal bank, even as you drive by, or laying across a hiking or biking trail on a levee. A note of caution about alligators: Do not feed them. Also, don't throw your fish-cleaning remains into the water. First of all, it's against the law. Second, alligators that become acclimated to human company expect food from us, and may eventually chomp off someone's hand or foot. If an alligator approaches you, assume that it has been improperly fed and try to get away. Most alligators I've encountered in the wild will run from you as soon as it perceives your presence; you'll hear a big splash. Others that are more tame will lollygag around in the sun. I've seen one or two approach people, and these are gators wisely avoided.

The place that most tourists visit is Everglades National Park, considered by the United Nations to be as significant as the Egyptian pyramids and Australia's Great Barrier Reef. It is twice the size of Rhode Island and offers 2,356 square miles to explore. The Big Cypress Preserve adjoins Everglades National Park on the northwestern side. The trees are indeed bald cypress, but most of the big ones were felled for lumber decades ago. This is a different view of the prairie and prettier in many ways. Fishing is excellent throughout Everglades National Park and the Big Cypress Preserve. Be aware that even though you're on national land, you'll need a Florida fishing license.

Two main east–west roads cross the Everglades and Big Cypress: I-75, which connects Naples and Fort Lauderdale, and U.S. 41, also called Tamiami Trail. U.S. 41 is a pretty drive; however, keep in mind that it is a two-lane highway. You should drive with your headlights on at all times. Gasoline is limited on both roads. For the best views of wildlife, choose Tamiami Trail and take a detour on Loop Road. This 26-mile stretch is only partially paved. It may take more than an hour to drive this part-gravel road, but it's a terrific experience with plenty of places to stop and gaze into the woods.

THE EVERGLADES

see
Gold Coast
page 464

see
Lake Okeechobee
page 396

see
Florida Keys
page 500

see
Fort Myers/Naples
page 438

ATLANTIC

OCEAN

Gulf

of

Mexico

❶ COLLIER SEMINOLE STATE PARK

🧍🏊🚴🐎⛵♿🚐⛺

Scenic rating: 10

south of Naples

A gateway to the Ten Thousand Islands and the western side of the Everglades and Big Cypress National Parks, this popular state park is a showcase for South Florida's unique landscape of mangrove and cypress swamps, salt marshes, and pine flat woods. Common to the park are royal palms, tropical hammock trees typical of the West Indies; and wildlife ranging from pelicans, wood storks, and bald eagles to the American crocodile and black bear. Mosquitoes tend to be less bothersome in the cooler months.

Think of what it must have been like here before the advent of mosquito repellent. When the Tamiami Trail (the road linking Tampa and Miami, hence the name) was built in the 1920s, crews labored in chest-deep water under nearly impossible conditions. An enormous piece of their equipment, known as a "walking dredge," is on display in the state park, which was named for Barron Collier (the developer of much of Naples) and for the Seminole Indians who lived on these lands.

Adventurers can get a taste of those difficult days (as well as a sense of the abundant birds and other wildlife that were present then, including the wood stork, brown pelican, osprey, and roseate spoonbill) by canoeing the 13.6-mile tidal creek into the park's 4,760-acre wilderness preserve.

Pick up supplies in Naples or on Marco Island. From here, you can explore Everglades City, Corkscrew Swamp Sanctuary, and the Fakahatchee Strand State Preserve.

RV sites, facilities: Part of a 6,243-acre state park and wilderness preserve, the campground offers 118 sites for RVs; all have 30-amp electricity and water; 45 sites have 50-amp service. Sites tend to be 20 by 40 feet in size, and some are shady. One unique feature: The park has a screen room with an Internet connection available during the winter. Restrooms, showers, fire rings with grills, picnic tables, a dump station, laundry facilities, two playgrounds, a boat ramp, and hiking trails are within the park, which is mostly wheelchair accessible. Call ahead to see if canoes are available for rent. Children are welcome. Pets are allowed with proof of vaccination.

Reservations, fees: Reservations are recommended; contact ReserveAmerica at 800/336-3521 or reserveamerica.com. Sites are $18 per night for eight people. Credit cards are accepted. The maximum stay is 14 days.

Directions: From Naples, travel 14 miles east on U.S. 41/Tamiami Trail. The campground entrance is just east of the junction with County Road 92.

Contact: Collier Seminole State Park, 20200 East Tamiami Trail, Naples, FL 34114, 239/394-3397, fax 239/394- 5113, www.floridastateparks.org.

❷ PORT OF THE ISLANDS RV RESORT

Scenic rating: 7

on the Tamiami Trail

This is a tight-knit community for RVers who come year after year to relax in the sun. About 80 percent are repeat visitors; many store their rigs here in the off-season. They even keep in touch via a volunteer-edited newsletter. Nearby is the Port of the Islands resort hotel. Campers are free to stop by the hotel restaurant and lounge if they get hungry; otherwise, there's nothing much commercial near here. The campground, which is on the north side of the road, is surrounded by a million acres of federal preserves. From the hotel, pontoon tour boats are available for a two-hour cruise through the Everglades and the Ten Thousand Islands, or you can launch a canoe and explore the area on your own. There's also a full-service gun club, shuffleboard, dinner parties, pig roasts, and other social activities. About 60 percent of the sites are occupied year-round. The management keeps mosquitoes at bay with regular ground spraying.

RV sites, facilities: All 99 RV sites have full hookups with 30-amp electrical service. Fourteen sites are drive-through. RVs as large as 40 feet or with as many as three slide-outs can be accommodated. Sites are grassy with plenty of elbow room. On the premises are restrooms, showers, laundry facilities, a clubhouse, two boat ramps, two dump stations, bike paths, hiking trails, and a fish- cleaning station. Most areas are wheelchair accessible. This is primarily an adult park; children are welcome for short stays only. Pets must be leashed.

Reservations, fees: Reservations are recommended. Sites are $33–38 per night for two people, plus $3 per extra person and $1 for electricity. Credit cards are accepted. Long-term stays are okay.

Directions: From Miami, take U.S. 41/Tamiami Trail west for 80 miles. The campground is on the north side of the highway when you reach Port of the Islands. From Naples, travel 25 miles east on U.S. 41.

Contact: Port of the Islands RV Resort, 12425 Union Road, Naples, FL 34114, 239/642-5343 or 800/319-4447, www.portoftheislands.com.

3 GLADES HAVEN

Scenic rating: 7

in Everglades City

Nestled between Everglades City and Chokoloskee Island, this campground is an ideal base camp for exploring the Wilderness Waterway, a backwater route flush with fish and feathered wildlife, that meanders along the edge of Everglades National Park. From the causeway bridge, it takes 2–5 hours, depending on the tide and wind, to reach Comer Key, once home to hermit/mangrove philoso-

pher Robert Osmer. He holed up here a half century ago with his favorite books and a coffeepot ready for strangers and friends who were welcome to drop by for a cup and some conversation. For information, call Kitty Hawk Kayaks (800/948-0759). Everglades National Park Boat Tours rents canoes and conducts nearly two-hour scenic boat rides for the less adventuresome. Boats leave the center every 30 minutes. For information, call 239/695-2591.

RV sites, facilities: All 51 sites have full hookups and picnic tables. On the premises are restrooms, showers, laundry facilities, a dump station, a boat ramp, a full- service marina, boat and canoe rentals, a restaurant, a delicatessen, cabins, a chickee (thatched-roof) bar, and a general store. Children are welcome. Leashed pets are permitted.

Reservations, fees: Reservations are recommended October–April. Sites are $20–30 per night for two people, plus $5 for each additional person. Credit cards are accepted. Long-term stays are okay.

Directions: From Naples, take U.S. 41/Tamiami Trail east to State Road 29. Turn south and drive about three miles to Everglades City. The park is on the south side of town, across from the Everglades National Park Gulf Coast Visitor Center.

Contact: Glades Haven, P.O. Box 580 (or 800 Copeland Avenue), Everglades City, FL 34139, 239/695-2746, fax 239/695-2091, www.gladeshaven.com.

4 CHOKOLOSKEE ISLAND PARK

Scenic rating: 4

on Chokoloskee Island south of Everglades City

Fishing is the name of the game at this waterfront mobile-home and RV park. It has the rustic charm of an old seaside motor court, although it's a bit cluttered with boat trailers and the like. The setting is right on the water, with boat and canoe rentals available, as well as charter fishing services. There's a busy social schedule during the winter, including potluck dinners, bingo, and crafts. You'll find a full-service marina selling cold drinks, bait, ice, oil, and gas, as well as sheltered docks with 67 boat slips. Park rules say that quiet times are enforced and that drunkenness, profanity, and offensive conduct will not be tolerated.

One interesting place in Chokoloskee is Smallwood's store museum. This is the site where turn-of-the-20th- century murder suspect Ed Watson was shot to death in 1910. A hulking, bearded man, Watson supposedly moved to the Everglades to flee pursuers who believed he had killed, among others, the famous female outlaw Belle Star. Soon, Watson's hired hands began to disappear—funny, right around payday. Nervous neighbors suspected the boss had killed them. After the body of Hannah Smith was seen floating nearby in 1910, frightened townsfolk took matters into their own hands and killed him. To add dimension to your stay, bring along Peter Matthiessen's book *Killing Mr. Watson,* a fictionalized yet largely historical account of the secretive man's exploits.

RV sites, facilities: The 87-unit park has 20 grassy sites with 30-amp electrical service available for RVs; the rest are occupied by year-round residents. Full hookups, wheelchair-accessible restrooms, showers, picnic tables, a dump station, a boat ramp, horseshoe pits, shuffleboard courts, and laundry facilities are available. RVs up to 27 feet long can be accommodated. Sites vary in size up to 20 by 45 feet, and the park has palms and other landscaping. A few sites are drive-through. Internet access is available in the office. Children are welcome. Leashed pets are permitted.

Reservations, fees: Reservations are recommended. Sites are $38 per night for two people, plus $2 for each additional person and $1.50 for electricity during summer months. Cable TV is included in the camping fee. Credit cards are accepted. Long-term stays are okay.

Directions: From Naples, take U.S. 41/Tamiami Trail east to State Road 29. Turn south and drive about three miles to Everglades City, then continue about three miles to Chokoloskee Island. Turn west (right) at the post office and follow the signs to the park at 1175 Hamilton Lane.
Contact: Chokoloskee Island Park, P.O. Box 430, Chokoloskee, FL 34138, 239/695-2414, http://chokoloskee.com/cip.html.

⑤ OUTDOOR RESORTS OF CHOKOLOSKEE ISLAND

Scenic rating: 9

on Chokoloskee Island south of Everglades City

Tiny, secluded Chokoloskee Island, linked to the mainland by a causeway, is the snook-fishing capital of the world. It's within one hour's drive of most Naples and Everglades attractions, but the focus is on canoeing, boating, and fishing—and with good reason. These waters are great for teaching little ones to fish; just about any persistent kid or novice can pick up enough skills in a few hours to hook a small snapper or sheepshead right from the dock. Bigger anglers in search of game fish such as snook should venture into the mangroves or to the fishing holes a short distance offshore. There's nothing like heading toward a spot where you see the gulls circling. Pop your line into the middle of a school of blue runner or amberjack; they're fun to catch, practically jumping into the boat, although not great to eat. Nearby is Everglades City, famous for its stone crab and seafood festival, held the first full weekend in February. Boat and canoe rentals are available in the park, and many fishing guides and charter boats can be hired close by. More than 160 campsites have docks available; 86 are on canals or gulf-side. Shade is minimal, but, hey, you're on the water, which is presumably what you came for. Spring for a waterfront site if your budget allows. It's strictly a vacation spot; no full-timers are allowed.

RV sites, facilities: This condominium park has 283 full-hookup RV sites with cable TV and 30/50-amp outlets. All sites are back-in, but rigs as long as 45 feet can be accommodated. Restrooms, showers, laundry facilities, and groceries are on the premises. In addition, the park has three recreation centers, three pools, three hot tubs, a health club, shuffleboard courts, lighted tennis courts, a marina, boat docks, motel rooms, bait, tackle, canoe and kayak rentals, and wintertime activities. The restrooms and laundry are wheelchair-accessible. Internet access is available in the marina office. Children are welcome. Two leashed pets are permitted per site, as long as they do not annoy other guests. You must provide proof of rabies vaccination. Pop-up campers, vans, and are prohibited.

Reservations, fees: Reservations are recommended. Sites are $79–99 per night for two people; these rates are subject to change. The maximum number of people per site is four. Some lots are available for resale, but overnighters can rent sites from the park. Credit cards are accepted.

Directions: From Naples, take U.S. 41/Tamiami Trail east to State Road 29. Turn south and drive about three miles to Everglades City, then continue about three miles to Chokoloskee Island. Look for the park at left.

Contact: Outdoor Resorts of Chokoloskee Island, P.O. Box 39, Chokoloskee Island, FL 34138, 239/695-3788, fax 239/695-3338, www.outdoor-resorts.com.

6 BIG CYPRESS TRAIL LAKES CAMPGROUND

Scenic rating: 5

on the Tamiami Trail in Big Cypress National Preserve

Keep an eye out for the giant concrete panther sitting out front, along with a sign that says: "Alligators, snakes, ice cream." For Big Cypress campers in search of full hookups, this is one of only two fully developed campgrounds around. The sunny campsites surround two ponds, and

the place is a bit rustic. The world's smallest post office—a tiny little building about the size of a parking lot attendant's booth—is just down the road in Ochopee and draws the occasional tour bus. Owner David Shealy says the campground land has been in the family since the 1800s, which is practically an epoch in Florida historical terms. An animal exhibit sits in front of the campground office, which also serves as a gift shop. Most visitors are hunters, anglers, and international travelers. Occasionally, concerts are held here. A stage accommodates music bands or other events.

RV sites, facilities: There are 100 gravel RV sites with full hookups, 30-amp electrical service, and picnic tables. About 30 percent of the occupants live here year-round. On the premises are restrooms, showers, a dump station, laundry facilities, and a store for groceries and souvenirs. An activities house and the restrooms are wheelchair accessible. Children are welcome. Leashed pets are permitted.

Reservations, fees: Reservations are recommended. Sites are $14–16 per night for two people, plus $5 for each additional person. Children under 10 are not charged extra. Credit cards are accepted. Long-term stays are okay.

Directions: From Naples, drive east on U.S. 41/Tamiami Trail to the intersection of State Road 29. Continue on U.S. 41 for six miles to the campground, on the south side of the highway. From Florida's Turnpike in Miami, exit at U.S. 41 and drive west for 53 miles.

Contact: Big Cypress Trail Lakes Campground, U.S. 41, Ochopee, FL 33943, 239/695-2275 or 239/695-3063, email: traillakes@netscape.net.

7 BURNS LAKE CAMPGROUND

Scenic rating: 3

on the Tamiami Trail in Big Cypress National Preserve

This free campground is open only during hunting season, basically September 1–January 2. Aside from hunters, it's a base for exploring

728,000-acre Big Cypress National Preserve, and you will find hardy snowbirds here soaking up the sunshine. Sunny, rustic campsites surround a small lake, which is off-limits to swimmers. No sites are marked; just stake out a spot in the clearing. Bring everything, including drinking water. The only camper comforts are a couple of portable toilets. Camping is no-frills. The reward is getting away from it all: The croaks of frogs, the chirps of cicadas, and panther-crossing signs are reminders that you're far from the city.

RV sites, facilities: At this clearing set around a lake, there is room for about 55 RVs. There are no hookups. Rigs as large as 45 feet can find a home here. The campground has two chemical toilets, but the nearest source of drinking water is Dona Drive, four miles west on U.S. 41. Bring mosquito repellent, food, water, and any supplies you'll need. Children are welcome. Pets must be on a six- foot leash and restrained at all times.

Reservations, fees: Reservations are not accepted, and there is no fee. Stays are limited to 14 days.

Directions: From Naples, drive east on U.S. 41/Tamiami Trail to the intersection of State Road 29. Continue on U.S. 41 for seven miles, then turn north on Burns Road. Drive one mile on gravel to the campground. From Florida's Turnpike in Miami, exit at U.S. 41 and drive west for 52 miles. Turn north on Burns Road.

Contact: Big Cypress National Preserve, HCR 61, P.O. Box 110, Ochopee, FL 34141, 239/695-1201 or 239/695-2000, www.nps.gov/bicy. For hunting information, call 239/695- 2040.

8 MONUMENT LAKE CAMPGROUND

Scenic rating: 6

on the Tamiami Trail in Big Cypress National Preserve

The preserve's managers have upgraded this site to offer niceties you won't find at most public camping spots within 728,000-acre Big Cypress National Preserve. Here, you'll find actual restrooms with running water and an outdoor shower (but not electricity). Monument Lake otherwise is a rustic, bare-bones place where sunny sites surround a lake. Swimming is prohibited, lest you encounter an alligator. Winter is the best time to camp: Mosquitoes are bearable, the weather is cool, and the ground is unlikely to be sodden by summer-style rains. One of my favorite things about Big Cypress is listening to the building crescendo of sounds at night—the croaking frogs, the maracas music of cicadas. It feels a world away from urban Miami, yet it's within easy reach for a quick weekend getaway. The campground is used primarily by retirees, anglers, and Scout groups.

Near the campground is Monroe Station, a roadhouse dating back to the building of U.S. 41, or the Tamiami Trail. The Herculean effort was launched in 1917 and took 11 years to finish, with progress stymied by labor shortages during World War I and the difficulties encountered when dynamiting limestone for the roadbed. Cranes on giant barges dredged up the rock, creating the canal as they built up the roadbed.

Behind Monroe Station is the Loop Road Scenic Drive, a 26-mile single lane leading deep into the preserve's southern reaches. Watch out for potholes and flooding. Along the road is the Tree Snail Hammock Nature Trail, with signs explaining the preserve's plants and animals. The loop leads to two more campgrounds, Pinecrest and Mitchell's Landing (see campgrounds in this chapter), before connecting with U.S. 41 at Forty Mile Bend.

RV sites, facilities: At this clearing set around a lake, there is room for about 30 RVs. There are no electrical or water hookups. Wheelchair-accessible restrooms with running water and sinks, plus an outdoor shower that can be used if you wear a bathing suit are provided. Rigs as long as 45 feet can be accommodated. Some sites have fire rings or grills. Registered campers can use the dump station at Dona Drive for free. The Oasis Visitor Center is five miles east on U.S. 41/Tamiami Trail. Bring water, food, mosquito repellent, and any supplies you'll need. Children are welcome. Pets must be on a six-foot leash and restrained at all times.

Reservations, fees: Reservations are not accepted. Fee is $16 a site per night December 15–April 15. There is no charge during the rest of the year. The campground often is filled on weekends in January and February. Stays are limited to 14 days.

Directions: From Florida's Turnpike in Miami, exit on U.S. 41/Tamiami Trail and drive 46 miles west to the campground on the north side of the highway. From Naples, drive east on U.S. 41 to the intersection of State Road 29, then continue east on the same road for 13 miles.

Contact: Big Cypress National Preserve, HCR 61, P.O. Box 110, Ochopee, FL 34141, 239/695-1201 or 239/695-2000, www.nps.gov/bicy. For hunting information, call 239/695- 2040.

9 MIDWAY CAMPGROUND

Scenic rating: 5

on the Tamiami Trail in Big Cypress National Preserve

Finally, you'll find an Everglades campground with electricity, which was added in December 2005. Other improvements at Midway are flush toilets, cement pads, picnic tables, fire rings, and grills—welcome additions for RVers accustomed to more primitive setups at other campgrounds in the Big Cypress preserve. Midway is closest to the Oasis Visitor Center. From here, hikers can pick up the Florida National Scenic Trail and walk deep into the preserve. The sometimes-flooded path meanders for 31 miles. Oasis is a nerve center for activities in the preserve: ranger-led bicycling, hiking, and canoe trips; group campfires; and nature talks. Inside the center are films and exhibits detailing the preserve's rich environment. For program information,

call 239/695-1201. Lots of alligators tend to hang out near the visitors center.

RV sites, facilities: At this clearing around a lake, 26 campsites with water hookups are available for RVs. Electrical service is 20/30/50-amp. There is a wheelchair- accessible restroom with flush toilets. Children are welcome. Pets must be on a six-foot leash and restrained at all times.

Reservations, fees: Reservations are not accepted. The fee is $19 per night per campsite. The campground often is filled on weekends in January and February. Stays are limited to 14 days.

Directions: From Florida's Turnpike in Miami, exit on U.S. 41/Tamiami Trail and drive 41 miles west to the park on the north side of the highway. From Naples, drive east on U.S. 41 to the intersection of State Road 29. Proceed east on U.S. 41 for about 22 miles, then turn north into the campground.

Contact: Big Cypress National Preserve, HCR 61, P.O. Box 110, Ochopee, FL 34141, 239/695-1201 or 239/695-2000, www.nps.gov/bicy. For hunting information, call 239/695- 2040.

10 MITCHELL'S LANDING

Scenic rating: 5

off Loop Road in Big Cypress National Preserve

Airboats launch from this part of 1,138-square-mile Big Cypress National Preserve, so you may hear the rumble of their engines as the craft roar off into the distance. The road leading to this remote clearing is not paved. For some tastes, campers sometimes may seem rougher than normal, and no park volunteer is stationed here to keep an eye on things. On weekdays, you may have the place to yourself; on weekends, you may share it with Boy Scout troops or groups of frog hunters. Winter is the best time to camp anywhere in otherwise-buggy Big Cypress, which offers many miles of hiking trails, seasonal hunting, and fishing in scattered areas. Bring a mountain bike to follow trails in the northern part of the preserve. You're virtually certain to see an alligator during your visit to the preserve.

RV sites, facilities: At this clearing outfitted with two portable toilets, about 20 sites are available. A few have improvised fire rings. There are no hookups or picnic tables. A paved boat ramp is provided, but there are no other facilities. Bring water, food, mosquito repellent, a hat, and everything else you'll need. Children are welcome. Pets must be on a six-foot leash and restrained at all times.

Reservations, fees: Reservations are not accepted, and there is no fee.

Directions: From Florida's Turnpike in Miami, exit on U.S. 41/Tamiami Trail and drive about 28 miles west, passing the Shark Valley entrance to Everglades National Park and the Miccosukee tribe cultural center. Don't veer right when the road jogs north. Instead, bear a tad left onto a little road called Loop Road; it's marked by a sign that reads "Hunters Must Check In." Follow Loop Road a little more than 10 miles to the Mitchell's Landing primitive camping area on the south side of the road. You'll see a brown tent sign instead of the posted name of the site; drive onto a rough-grade road to reach the camping area.

Contact: Big Cypress National Preserve, HCR 61, P.O. Box 110, Ochopee, FL 34141, 239/695-1201 or 239/695-2000, www.nps.gov/bicy. For hunting information, call 239/695- 2040.

11 PINECREST CAMPGROUND

Scenic rating: 7

off Loop Road in Big Cypress National Preserve

Peace. Quiet. Remoteness. That's what you get at this open and sunny clearing in 1,138-square-mile Big Cypress National Preserve. Daytime visitors to the preserve travel slowly down Loop Road by car, motorcycle, or bicycle, in hopes of catching glimpses at deer, alligators, birds, and the occasional bobcat or bear. Very rarely, you may catch sight of an endangered Florida panther hurrying across Loop Road. Many miles of hiking trails can be accessed from right here. Trails suitable for mountain bikes are found in the northern part of Big Cypress; get a map from a ranger. Fishing is possible in the canals along Tamiami Trail, Turner River Road, and other spots. This campground is more favored by RV campers than Mitchell's Landing (see campground in this chapter). You might bring a canoe if you want to paddle the Turner River and Halfway Creek south to Chokoloskee Bay. The Turner River is just west of H. P. Williams Roadside Park, which is at U.S. 41 and Highway 839. Halfway Creek is about five miles west, just beyond the intersection of U.S. 41 and Highway 841.

RV sites, facilities: At this clearing outfitted with portable toilets, about 20 RVs can be accommodated. There are no hookups. Bring water, food, mosquito repellent, a hat, and everything else you'll need. Children are welcome. Pets must be on a six-foot leash and restrained at all times.

Reservations, fees: Reservations are not accepted, and there is no fee.

Directions: From Florida's Turnpike in Miami, exit on U.S. 41/Tamiami Trail and drive about 28 miles west, passing the Shark Valley entrance to Everglades National Park and the Miccosukee tribe cultural center. Don't veer right when the road jogs north. Instead, bear a tad left onto a little road called Loop Road; it's marked by a sign that reads "Hunters Must Check In." Follow Loop Road about five to six miles to the Pinecrest primitive camping area on the north side of the road. You'll see a brown tent sign instead of the posted name of the site; drive into that driveway and follow it to a clearing that serves as the camping area.

Contact: Big Cypress National Preserve, HCR 61, P.O. Box 110, Ochopee, FL 34141, 239/695-1201 or 239/695-2000, www.nps.gov/bicy. For hunting information, call 239/695- 2040.

GATOR PARK

Scenic rating: 4

on the Tamiami Trail west of Coopertown

Gator-headed mannequins welcome visitors from the front porch, an eye-catching gimmick designed to lure motorists off the Tamiami Trail. Gator Park is a tourist stop with a campground out back, offering airboat tours of the Everglades, and a gator pen. This is a popular spot for tour buses that come from Miami loaded with international travelers. About 25–40 percent of the park is occupied year-round. The last chance for groceries and gas is six miles east at Dade Corners, the intersection of U.S. 41 and State Road 997, also known as Krome Avenue. Also at this intersection is the popular Miccosukee Indian casino and hotel. Drive very carefully; I've seen a lot of car accidents at this intersection.

RV sites, facilities: Self-contained rigs are accepted at these 21 sites with water and 30-amp electric hookups. Usually, about eight sites are available for traveling RVs. On the premises are a dump station, cooking grills, chickee (thatched-roof) huts, an airboat concession, a souvenir shop, and a restaurant. The park has palms, black olive trees, and a small pond. Children are welcome. Leashed pets are permitted.

Reservations, fees: Reservations are not necessary. Sites are $30 per night; dry camping is allowed for $10 per night. Credit cards are accepted. Long-term stays are okay.

Directions: From Florida's Turnpike in Miami, exit on U.S. 41/Tamiami Trail and drive west for 12 miles. The park is on the south side of the road, behind a tourist shop.

Contact: Gator Park, 24050 Southwest 8th Street, Miami, FL 33187, 305/559-2255 or 800/559-2205, www.gatorpark.com.

EVERGLADES HOLIDAY PARK

Scenic rating: 6

west of Fort Lauderdale in the Everglades

Favored by locals for weekend getaways, this rustic bass-fishing haven and gateway to the Everglades is known by tourists for its narrated one-hour-long airboat rides. International visitors arrive by the busload for the airboats. It's also popular with motorcycle riders, who make a pit stop here to relax on the covered deck with a refreshment or two. But fishing is a big thing here—you can be out on the water at daybreak if you use this 30-acre park as your base camp. You can rent fishing rods and boats, or hike or cycle atop the levee for miles. You're sure to see an alligator or two and some long-legged wading birds hunting for their dinner. The mosquitoes aren't as plentiful in the cooler winter months, but they'll eat you alive in summer if you're not prepared. Pick up groceries and other items in Fort Lauderdale because there's nothing much around here. Some supplies are sold 24 hours a day at the general store, souvenir shop, and bait shop. There's also a restaurant that serves take-out hamburgers and sandwiches.

RV sites, facilities: There are 90 RV sites with 30-amp electrical service and sewer hookups. RVs up to 40 feet long can be accommodated. Most of the sites have concrete slabs and are shaded by palms, oaks, and palmettos. Twenty sites are drive-through. About 75 percent of the park is occupied by year-round residents. Restrooms, showers, and picnic tables are provided. Airboat tours, fishing charters, a two-acre lake, a tackle shop, and boat rentals are available. You can also rent a rod and reel. The bathhouses and laundry are wheelchair accessible. All ages are welcome. Pets must be on handheld leashes, which is wise because alligators live in the nearby saw grass and canals.

Reservations, fees: Reservations are recommended for November–May (reserve no later than August). Sites are $22 per night for two people, plus $5 per extra person. Credit cards are accepted. Long-term stays are okay.

Directions: From I-95 in Fort Lauderdale, drive west on I-595 for eight miles until the road becomes I-75. Continue six miles following the signs for northbound traffic on I-75. At the exit for U.S. 27, turn south and drive 6.5 miles. Turn west on Griffin Road and drive 0.5 mile to the park.

Contact: Everglades Holiday Park, 21940 Griffin Road, Fort Lauderdale, FL 33332, 954/434-8111 or 800/226- 2244, www.evergladesholidaypark.com.

14 LONG PINE KEY CAMPGROUND

Scenic rating: 10

in Everglades National Park

BEST (

The pine-dotted campground is the closest to the most popular walking trails and the main park entrance. It's ideal for self-contained RVs. You can view plentiful birds along the nearby Anhinga Trail boardwalk in winter, and you will still see, a few pine trunks snapped in two by 1992's Hurricane Andrew along the Long Pine Key Trail leading west from the campground. Rangers speak at the amphitheater in winter and answer questions year-round at the visitors center to the east. There's a great six-mile, one-way bike trail just across the road from the campground, leading fat- tire bikes through a double-track dirt road in a winding pine forest and more. You can make it a 12-mile loop by exiting the trail onto the main highway, turning north, and heading back on the road to the campground. Another little-used biking trail is the Old Ingraham Highway, built in the 1920s; it's a 21-mile trip out and back on an old rutted road where alligators will flee your approach and you'll spook blue herons and other birds from their hiding places.

For a woodsy walk, drive west along the sole road to reach the thicker canopy of Mahogany Hammock (bring mosquito repellent). Its parking area is at the first turnoff after Pa-hay-okee

Overlook, one of several stops along the 38-mile park road leading to Flamingo. Although the beauty of Pa- hay-okee's sea of saw grass typically is described as subtle, even a first-time visitor might notice the huge white clouds—sometimes described as "Florida's mountains"— building over the pancake-flat prairie.

RV sites, facilities: The 108 campsites have no water or electricity, but the roads are paved. You will find restrooms (but no showers), picnic tables, grills, a pay phone, a dump station, an amphitheater for winter programs, several nearby hiking trails, and a fishing pond. Children and leashed pets are permitted.

Reservations, fees: Reservations are accepted up to five months in advance at 301/722-1257 or 800/365-CAMP (800/365-2267). Sites are $14 per night for up to eight people. Group sites are $28 for up to 15 people. Campers also must pay a $10 entrance fee, which is good for one week. Credit cards are accepted. The maximum stay is 14 days between November 1 and April 30, or 30 days per year.

Directions: From Miami, take Florida's Turnpike to its southern terminus at U.S. 1. In about one block, turn right at Palm Drive. Cross the railroad tracks and pass the Circle K. At the traffic light at 192nd Avenue/State Road 9336, turn left by the Robert Is Here fruit stand. Proceed south about two miles. When State Road 9336 veers right, follow it to the right instead of going straight toward the alligator farm. The park entrance is four miles ahead. The campground is on the left about four miles beyond the entrance.

Contact: Everglades National Park, 40001 State Road 9336, Homestead, FL 33034, 305/242-7700, www.nps.gov/ever.

15 FLAMINGO CAMPGROUND

Scenic rating: 10

on Florida Bay in Everglades National Park

If you want to see a manatee, the goose-sized limpkin bird, and other Everglades animals all in one day, one place to try is Flamingo Marina, east of this campground in Everglades National Park. You're sure to spot some sort of wildlife there—maybe alligators, wading birds, or the occasional American crocodile. Flamingo is at the end of the 38-mile main park road and is one of the prettiest spots reachable by car. You'll find visitors here from all over the world. Hurricanes have destroyed some of the shade, the adjacent hotel and other buildings, and no fuel, food, or services are available as of May 2006. Dredging of the harbor was due to be completed by mid-summer 2006.

The campground overlooks the smooth, blue-green waters of Florida Bay and far-off mangrove islands. Campers drag canoes to their campsites or tie them near the water in anticipation of a morning launch to sightsee or fish for snook, snapper, jacks, trout, redfish, and sheepshead. Motorboaters launch to the east at the marina to fish for big-game tarpon or cross the bay to the Florida Keys.

Canoes, single-person kayaks, motorized skiffs, and bicycles are available for rent at the marina. Tickets to a tram tour and the worthwhile Bald Eagle and Pelican sightseeing boats also are sold there. A 12-hour advance reservation is required for the Cape Sable beach and birding cruise; call 239/695-3101.

RV sites, facilities: This is the biggest campground in Everglades National Park. It offers 234 drive-up campsites for tents, trailers, or RVs and 64 walk-up tent sites. There are no electrical hookups or showers, but you will find restrooms, picnic tables, grills, a pay phone, two dump stations, an amphitheater for winter programs, and two hiking trails. RVs up to 45 feet can be accommodated. The restrooms are wheelchair accessible. Several mountain biking trails can be started from here; ask the park office for maps. Children and leashed pets are permitted.

Reservations, fees: Reservations are accepted up to five months in advance at 301/722-1257 or 800/365-CAMP (800/365-2267). Sites are $14 per night for up to eight people. Group sites are $28 nightly for up to 15 people. Campers also pay a $10 park entrance fee, which is good for seven days. Credit cards are accepted. The maximum stay is 14 days between November 1 and April 30, or 30 days per year.

Directions: From Miami, take Florida's Turnpike to its southern terminus at U.S. 1. In about one block, turn west at Palm Drive. Cross the railroad tracks and pass the Circle K. At the traffic light at Southwest 192nd Avenue/State Road 9336, turn left by the Robert Is Here fruit stand. Proceed south about two miles. When State Road 9336 veers right, follow it to the right instead of going straight toward the alligator farm. The park entrance is four miles ahead. Follow the main park road about 38 miles to the campground on the left, beyond the marina.

Contact: Everglades National Park, 40001 State Road 9336, Homestead, FL 33034, 305/242-7700. For questions about Flamingo, contact the Flamingo Visitor Center at 239/695- 2945 or www.nps.gov/ever.

FLORIDA KEYS

BEST RV PARKS AND CAMPGROUNDS

◖ Most Luxurious
Bluewater Key RV Park, page 508

◖ Publicly Managed Beachfront Campgrounds
Long Key State Park, page 503
Bahia Honda State Park, page 505

If you're looking for the feel of the Caribbean,

head south to the Florida Keys. Beginning at Key Largo and ending at Key West, the Keys are actually a string of small islands connected by one highway, with sparkling crystalline blue waters on either side. Not only is the water incredibly clear, it reflects so many shades of blue and green you'll be glad to have polarized sunglasses.

Just an hour from fast-paced Miami, the Keys have a reputation for being laid-back and casual. Favorite activities are snorkeling, scuba diving, boating, and fishing. You can rent equipment for just about any water sport; there are plenty of dive boats, fishing guides, and paddling tours; and if you don't want to get wet, a glass-bottom boat tour will take you to the beautiful reefs offshore. What you will not find is many beaches; most of the shoreline that is accessible to the public is rocky.

As you approach the Keys, note the mile marker posts along U.S. 1, also known as the Overseas Highway, that continues south for 113 miles and across 43 bridges. The numbers start at 0 in Key West, and all addresses along U.S. 1 coincide with the mile marker posts. For instance, a campground at 106003 Overseas Highway is near mile marker 106. Addresses often are further described as "ocean side" (on the Atlantic Ocean side of the road) or "bay side" (on the north side of U.S. 1, generally on Florida Bay).

At the end of the journey is Key West, a city celebrated by songwriters (Jimmy Buffett's "Margaritaville"), authors (Ernest Hemingway, Tennessee Williams), artists (John James Audubon), and even presidents (Harry S. Truman, who started the Hawaiian-shirt craze here). Today, Key West is so far from the mainland that it's hard to believe this was once a major Florida trading port, bustling with early settlers from the Bahamas, pirates, treasure salvors, and rumrunners. Many of the ginger-bread houses that were home to these early residents have been restored. Modern-day "Conchs" (pronounced "konks"), as Keys natives call themselves, now make their living from art galleries, boutiques, souvenir and T-shirt shops, or by giving circus-style performances on Mallory Square.

The real-estate boom of the mid-2000s is profoundly changing the face of the Keys. Many RV parks and campgrounds were closed to allow building of condominiums and hotel resorts. However, some stand-out parks remain. John Pennekamp State Park in Key Largo is the first underwater state park in the United States. It's a marvelous place to learn to snorkel, even for small children. At Long Key State Park, you can snag a campsite on a sandy beach with a gentle shoreline. Bahia Honda State Park also has a lovely beach. The Keys also boast the southernmost KOA in the nation. The closest campgrounds to famous Key West are now on Stock Island, about five miles outside the town.

Wherever you plan to stay, reservations are a must. Camping in parking lots is not an option, and RVs are prohibited from parking along U.S. 1 after 11 P.M. That said, you'll enjoy having your RV with you if you stop along the way and take in the water views.

Getting to the Keys is simple. From Florida City just south of Homestead, U.S. 1 is the main route. U.S. 1 was built on the roadbed of railroad tracks that Henry Flagler created to link Key West to the mainland. An alternate route between Florida City and Key Largo is Card Sound Road. The two roads converge in Key Largo. If there's a car accident on the upper stretch of U.S. 1, many times traffic is rerouted onto Card Sound Road. Elsewhere, you'll just have to wait for the wreck to be cleared.

Anywhere in the Keys, drive carefully. Since U.S. 1 is the only major artery to which all side streets lead, traffic can be a problem, especially on the weekends when Miamians come south to play, or when visitors pile in during the winter tourist season. Speed limits are strictly enforced, as are laws against drunken driving. Plan on four hours of driving to cover the 163 miles from Miami to Key West.

Ultimately, the Keys, part luxury resort, part natural paradise, are worth the drive, no matter how far you venture.

FLORIDA KEYS

EAST SIDE

WEST SIDE

1 JOHN PENNEKAMP CORAL REEF STATE PARK

Scenic rating: 10

in Key Largo on U.S. 1/Overseas Highway

This, the first underwater state park in the United States, is also one of the finest parks in Florida, with a sandy beach and boat service to diving or snorkeling reefs three to six miles offshore. Please note that the coral reefs are accessible only by boat; however, you can practice snorkeling or diving skills at the beach, where you'll see colorful fish and sunken cannons. It's a rare setting of tropical hardwood hammocks, mangroves, and crystal-clear water bordering the Key Largo Coral Reef National Marine Sanctuary, which covers 178 nautical square miles. Paddle a canoe or visit the interpretive center. The park gets a lot of traffic from international and United States tourists and locals alike, and the gates often close by midday when crowds reach capacity. It has been called the world's most-traveled-to dive destination, and the cars of daytime visitors may stretch for 200 yards waiting to get into this home of brain coral and barracuda. Don't forget mosquito repellent in the hot months.

This is the perfect place for novice snorkelers, and especially children. The gently sloping swimming beach near the visitors center lets them try out their skills without worries. Once proficient, they can swim farther out. Just 130 feet from the water's edge lies a reconstruction of an early Spanish shipwreck. You'll see 14 cannons, an anchor, and ballast stones recovered from a ship lost in a 1715 hurricane.

RV sites, facilities: This state park has 47 mostly shaded sites with water, 30-amp and 50-amp electricity, picnic tables, and grills. None are drive-through; a few are large enough to accommodate rigs larger than 35 feet. Palm trees and native landscaping provide buffer between sites. Restrooms, showers, and laundry facilities are provided. Three sites are wheelchair accessible, as are the bathhouses and the laundry. In the main part of the park are two beaches, two nature trails, a playground, a visitors center with a 30,000-gallon saltwater aquarium, a marina, a dive shop, boat and canoe rentals, and a snack shop. Scuba instruction, snorkeling, and glass-bottom boat tours are available. Restaurants and grocery stores are with two miles. Children are welcome. Pets are not allowed in the campground or on the beach.

Reservations, fees: Reservations are recommended; contact ReserveAmerica at 800/336-3521 or reserveamerica.com. Sites are $32 per night for up to eight people. Major credit cards are accepted. The maximum stay is 14 days. Reservations are advised for snorkeling trips, which cost $25–30 per person, plus $5 to rent a snorkel and mask; reserve at 305/451-1621.

Directions: Follow U.S. 1/Overseas Highway to mile marker 102.5 in Key Largo. The park is on the ocean side.

Contact: John Pennekamp Coral Reef State Park, P.O. Box 487, Key Largo, FL 33037, 305/451-1202, www.floridastateparks.org.

2 KEY LARGO KAMPGROUND AND MARINA

Scenic rating: 9

in Key Largo south of U.S. 1/Overseas Highway

One of the nicest campgrounds in the Florida Keys, this resort reflects thoughtful planning designed to please nearly everyone. RVs are accommodated under shade trees or on water-view sites with private docks. The sites have been sold as condominium spaces but are often rented to tourists, usually divers or visitors from Europe. In the winter, understandably, owners tend to be in town, so transient spaces are scarcer then. Spring for a site with your own private dock overlooking the long boat channel. Isolated from the beaten track, the waters don't get as stirred up as they do at other places. You'll see stingrays, tarpon, and snapper when you're snorkeling over the grassy sea bottom off the two beaches. The surrounding woods and uninhabited mangrove islands give this deluxe campground a secluded feeling, even though it's close to shopping and Key Largo attractions.

RV sites, facilities: There are 171 full-hookup slots with 50-amp electrical service for RVs up to 40 feet long. About one-third are drive-through sites. Facilities include cable TV, restrooms, showers, a dump station, a pool, a boat ramp, two recreation halls, small camp store, chickee huts (Seminole Indian thatched-roof dwellings), horseshoe pits, two sandy beaches, and volleyball, basketball, and shuffleboard courts are available. Some sites have gravel surfaces, while others have concrete pads. The pool and laundry area are wheelchair accessible. Groceries are within one mile. A gate provides security. Limited RV storage is available. Children are welcome. Leashed pets are permitted.

Reservations, fees: Reservations are recommended. Sites are $46–63 per night for two adults and two children under 12, plus $3 for each additional person. No more than six people are allowed per site. Major credit cards are accepted. Long-term stays are okay.

Directions: From U.S. 1/Overseas Highway at mile marker 101.5 in Key Largo, turn south at Samson Road, which dead-ends at the park entrance, on the ocean side.

Contact: Key Largo Kampground and Marina, 101551 Overseas Highway, Key Largo, FL 33037-4596, 305/451-1431 or 800/526-7688, fax 305/451-8083, www.keylargokampground.com.

3 KING'S KAMP RV PARK MARINA AND MOTEL

Scenic rating: 1

in Key Largo on U.S. 1/Overseas Highway

A boat ramp and a small swimming beach provide good access to Blackwater Sound and Florida Bay; the pull-up RV sites are said to accommodate rigs as long as 40 feet. Most people

are here to stay, rooted nearly as strong as the lush royal poinciana and gumbo-limbo trees that shade the park. But the location is worth the effort to see if a site is available. Sunsets are magnificent. Motel rooms and rental units are also available, and you can dock your boat in the marina for an additional fee of $10 per day. The park is near restaurants and shopping.

RV sites, facilities: The park has 60 sites, of which only 7 are available for RVs. Water, electricity, restrooms, showers, picnic tables, and fire grills are available. There is a boat ramp, a dock, and a jetty. Grocery shops and restaurants are within one mile. Children and leashed pets are permitted.

Reservations, fees: Reservations are highly recommended since space is at a premium. Sites are $40–50 per night for two people, plus $5 for each additional person. Major credit cards are accepted. Long-term stays are permitted.

Directions: Follow U.S. 1/Overseas Highway to mile marker 103.5 in Key Largo. The park is on the bay side.

Contact: King's Kamp RV Park Marina and Motel, 103620 Overseas Highway, Key Largo, FL 33037, 305/451-0010, www.kingskamp.com.

4 THE RIPTIDE RV PARK AND MOTEL

Scenic rating: 5

in Key Largo on U.S. 1/Overseas Highway

This well-kept trailer park has great views of Florida Bay and pretty coconut palms. It's a quiet place that mixes seasonal residents with travelers. Sites line a hairpin drive that leads to Florida Bay, a dock, and picnic tables by the water.

RV sites, facilities: Of the 36 trailer sites, 5 are set aside for RV travelers in rigs up to 30 feet long (none of the sites are pull-through). Full hookups, 30-amp electrical service, cable TV, picnic tables, restrooms, showers, a dock, and rental units are available; two waterfront sites have water and electricity only (no sewer hookups). The campground caters primarily to retirees, but children are allowed to visit. Pets are not permitted.

Reservations, fees: Reservations are recommended. Sites are $55 per night for two people, plus $10 for each additional person. Major credit cards are accepted. Long-term stays are okay. The park is open October 1–May 1.

Directions: Follow U.S. 1/Overseas Highway to Key Largo. The park is at mile marker 97.6 on the bay side.

Contact: The Riptide RV Park and Motel, 97680 Overseas Highway, Lot 1, Key Largo, FL 33037, 305/852-8481.

5 LONG KEY STATE PARK

Scenic rating: 10

on Long Key south of Layton

BEST (

With so few sites, the campground in this 980-acre state park is often filled, but don't let that deter you from trying. The camping area has a gently curving natural shoreline and all sites are at beachfront. Get up in the morning and walk a few feet right into the water. There's almost always a breeze (sometimes too much of one!). The Australian pines and several of the trees of Caribbean origin that shaded most spots were blown down during a series of hurricanes, so campsites are now sunny. Expect little in the way of natural vegetative buffers; without the pines, many campsites and even the pedestrians on the park's beloved walking path are now visible to cars passing by on U.S. 1. A few campsites are big enough, however, to give the illusion of being far from neighbors. And vegetation in Florida grows back quickly, so by the time you read this, some of the landscaping may be back.

At low tide, kids can look for fiddler crabs and minnows in rocky tidal pools at the east end of the campground. The sea level was 20–30 feet higher 100,000 years ago, but today

the water is so shallow that you can wade a half mile out to sea and only get waist deep. That makes it a great place to learn to snorkel, although you won't see dramatic coral formations and big fish unless you go far offshore in a boat. However a world-record bonefish was caught on the grassy flats at Long Key, according to park rangers. The Long Key Lakes Canoe Trail winds through mangrove flats and a shallow lagoon. Nearby is the Golden Orb Trail, a 40-minute nature walk. On the bay side (across U.S. 1 and east of the campground) is the Layton Trail, a meandering path through a dark, almost impenetrable tropical hardwood hammock.

RV sites, facilities: This state park has 50 sites for RVs. Water and 30-amp electricity are available at all. Picnic tables, grills, restrooms, and showers are provided. There's a canoe trail, a 1.25-mile nature trail, and an interpretive program. A convenience store is within 0.5 mile; a grocery store is 15 miles away. Children are welcome. Pets are prohibited.

Reservations, fees: Reservations are recommended; contact ReserveAmerica at 800/336-3521 or reserveamerica.com. Sites are $32 per night for up to eight people. Major credit cards are accepted. The maximum stay is 14 days.

Directions: From the town of Layton on Long Key, drive south on U.S. 1/Overseas Highway to mile marker 67. Turn south at the park sign.

Contact: Long Key State Park, P.O. Box 776, Long Key, FL 33001, 305/664-4815, www.floridastateparks.org.

6 PELICAN MOTEL AND TRAILER PARK

Scenic rating: 6

on Grassy Key near Marathon

In wintertime, you'll find senior citizens enjoying boating, fishing, water sports, and activities in the recreation room, and relaxing in the sheltered picnic area next to the water. This trailer-park/motel complex on the gulf side is next door to a full-service marina and near a dolphin research center.

RV sites, facilities: A varying number of RV sites (usually around 10) are available for over-nighters and short-term visitors in this 85-unit trailer park, where 25 percent of the occupants live year-round. All sites have full hookups, 30-amp electrical service, picnic tables, cable TV, and optional telephone service. Restrooms, showers, a dump station, and laundry facilities are available. On the premises are a pool, a boat ramp, a dock, a clubhouse with planned activities during the winter, shuffleboard courts, a dog-walk area, and a picnic area. RV storage is available. Children are welcome, but adults and senior citizens are preferred. Small, leashed pets are permitted.

Reservations, fees: Reservations are recommended. Sites are $25–38 per night for two people, plus $3 per extra person. Major credit cards are accepted. Long-term (up to six months) stays are allowed.

Directions: From Follow Overseas Highway to mile marker 59; the park is on the gulf side.

Contact: Pelican Motel and Trailer Park, 59151 Overseas Highway, Marathon, FL 33050, 305/289-0011.

◼ KEY RV PARK

Scenic rating: 3

in Marathon

This well-kept park caters to boaters who want ocean access near their campsite and visitors who stay for the season. Shade is minimal. A small lighthouse and park benches overlook the water. Sites line a paved road around a narrow boat channel; about half are on the canal. The park is within two blocks of restaurants and shopping, and convenient to an 18-hole, par-3 golf course, public tennis courts, groceries, and miniature golf.

RV sites, facilities: There are 200 RV-only sites, most with full hookups and some with 50-amp electrical service. About 30 percent of the park is occupied by year-round residents, who also moor their boats at the docks. This makes dockage for transient visitors rather scarce. Sites are gravel and many have concrete slabs. Restrooms, showers, a boat ramp, a boat dock ($4-a-day charge), picnic tables, three laundry rooms, and a recreation hall are available. Social programs are directed by an activities committee during the winter months. Internet access is available in the clubhouse. Children are allowed. Small friendly pets are accepted.

Reservations, fees: Reservations are recommended. Sites are $45–75 per night for up to four people, plus $4 for each additional person. Major credit cards are accepted. Long-term rates are available.

Directions: The park is in Marathon, on U.S. 1/Overseas Highway between mile markers 50 and 51, on the ocean side.

Contact: Key RV Park, 6099 Overseas Highway, Marathon, FL 33050, 305/743-5164 or 800/288-5164.

◼ SUNSHINE KEY RV RESORT

Scenic rating: 8

on Ohio Key

At 75 acres, this is one of the largest campgrounds in the Keys. Surrounded by crystal-clear seas, the park bills itself as a water-sports wonderland, with a 172-slip marina for anglers and a narrow swimming beach. From the marina, scuba divers, snorkelers, sailors, canoeists, and ocean kayakers have access to both bay and ocean waters. But there are plenty of activities on land, too—even a game arcade for teens who feel they're too grown-up to hang out with their parents. Coconut palms give the campground that tropical island feel. There are walking trails on 35 acres. RVs up to 12 feet wide can be accommodated, and a remarkable 325 sites are pull-through. Although seasonal stays are allowed and RV storage is available, no one lives here year-round.

RV sites, facilities: All 400 grassy or gravel sites are for RVs up to 48 feet long; all sites have full hookups and 30-amp/50-amp service. The sites are a mix of shady and sunny spots, varying in size from 25 to 30 feet wide and 40 to 50 feet long. Pull your rig through at 325 sites. Picnic tables, restrooms, showers, a pool, a boat ramp, two recreation halls, a horseshoe pit, shuffleboard and basketball courts, tennis, wintertime planned activities, cable TV, propane, a dump station, honeywagon service (a truck pumps out the sewer bilges from your RV), a dive shop, a boat ramp, boat rentals, a fishing pier, and diving and snorkeling trips are on the premises. Planned activities include bingo, dancing, dinners, and fishing tournaments. Also on-site are groceries, a snack bar, bait and tackle, laundry facilities, and rental cottages. Internet service is available in the office. Children are welcome. Leashed pets are permitted; a dog kennel is provided.

Reservations, fees: Reservations are recommended. Sites are $60–105 per night. Major credit cards are accepted. Six-month stays are allowed.

Directions: The park is on Ohio Key, on U.S. 1/Overseas Highway at mile marker 39 on the bay side.

Contact: Sunshine Key RV Resort, 38801 Overseas Highway, Big Pine Key, FL 33043, 305/872-2217 or 800/852-0348, fax 305/872-3801, rvonthego.com. Reserve campsites or dive and snorkel trips at 800/852-0348.

9 BAHIA HONDA STATE PARK

Scenic rating: 10

on Bahia Honda Key

BEST (

This beautiful state park's two swimming beaches, routinely named among the top 10 in the nation, are spectacular. One overlooks the Bahia Honda bridge, and the other is on the ocean. You can spend hours lazing on a raft and imagine yourself floating across the Atlantic, or toss a beach ball around on the shore. Hike up to the old roadbed that once served as Henry Flagler's original rail line to Key West; on the top deck is the old highway. It juts eerily into space because the state removed the central span when the new road was built.

RV sites, facilities: The two camping areas have a total of 80 sites with piped water, electricity, picnic tables, and nearby restrooms and showers. On the south side of the park, smaller sites are tucked into a lush hardwood hammock. On the north side, campers stay on a sun-drenched gravel promontory suitable for RVs. Some sites and the restrooms are wheelchair accessible. A snack bar, a gift shop, snorkeling tours, ocean-kayak and beach-bike rentals, and diving equipment are provided by a concessionaire. In addition, 19 boat slips (where you can also stay overnight) are available (reservations are recommended). Children are welcome, but pets are not permitted.

Reservations, fees: Reservations are recommended; contact ReserveAmerica at 800/336-3521 or reserveamerica.com. Sites are $24 per night for four people, plus $2 for each additional person and $2 for electricity. Boat slips cost $1 per linear foot (minimum charge is $22) and include water, electricity, and use of the park facilities. Major credit cards are accepted. The maximum stay is 14 days.

Directions: The park is on Bahia Honda Key, at mile marker 37 on U.S. 1/Overseas Highway, on the ocean side.

Contact: Bahia Honda State Park, 36850 Overseas Highway, Big Pine Key, FL 33043, 305/872-2353.

10 BIG PINE KEY FISHING LODGE

Scenic rating: 8

on Big Pine Key

A sprawling motel/campground resort on 10 acres, Big Pine Key Fishing Lodge is paradise for anglers. The complex has a spectacular location, bordering on Looe Key National Underwater Marine Sanctuary and the ocean. An unusually well-developed canopy of tropical trees (frangipani, gumbo-limbo, and buttonwood, among others) creates a natural ambience even in the interior of the campground. Swimmers can bask in lawn chairs near the coral rock shoreline (not a beach) or at the pool. Kids will find lots of things to keep them busy, and boaters have all the amenities they could need on hand, from fishing guides to a full-service marina. The boat ramp has an immediate drop-off from the seawall edge, however, and you're advised to launch with caution. When you come home with your catch, you must use the fish-cleaning tables near the boat basin. During most of the year (except for September and October), planned activities include dances, parties, card games, "banana split" nights, and trips to golf clubs and theaters in Key West.

RV sites, facilities: There are 94 RV sites with full hookups (accommodating rigs up to 34 feet long) and 58 primitive tent-only sites with community water spigots and grills. Ten of the RV sites have 50-amp electrical service; the rest have 30 amps. Picnic tables, restrooms, showers, laundry facilities, a dump station, honeywagon service, docks, a boat ramp, boat rentals, charter fishing and diving services, a pool, a beach, horseshoe pits, shuffleboard courts, a playground, a recreation room, and a game room are available. A convenience store, a bait and tackle shop, and rental units are on the premises. Most areas are wheelchair accessible. Internet service is available in the office. Groceries are 2 miles away; Key West is 28 miles south. Children are welcome. Dogs are prohibited because they are likely to scare the endangered key deer; other pets are welcome.

Reservations, fees: Reservations are required during holidays and recommended at other times. Sites are $41–45 per night for two people, plus $7 for each person over age seven. Children under seven are free. Major credit cards are accepted. Long-term stays are not permitted.

Directions: From U.S. 1/Overseas Highway at mile marker 33 on Big Pine Key, turn south at the park entrance on the ocean side.

Contact: Big Pine Key Fishing Lodge, 33000 Overseas Highway, P.O. Box 430513, Big Pine Key, FL 33043, 305/872-2351, fax 305/872-3868.

11 BREEZY PINES RV ESTATES

Scenic rating: 4

on Big Pine Key

Trees, tropical flowers, and shrubs dot this 4.5-acre inland park. Boating, fishing, charter services, scuba diving, and snorkeling are available nearby. Also nearby is the National Key Deer Refuge, home of the elusive, endangered miniature deer, and a bicycle path along U.S. 1.

RV sites, facilities: The 90 paved RV sites have full hookups and cable TV, and a few have 50-amp service. About 70 percent of the park is occupied by year-round residents. Rigs up to 34 feet long can be accommodated; none of the sites are pull-through. Sites are 18–20 feet wide and 35–40 feet long. Heavy traffic makes it difficult to turn in and out of the park onto U.S. 1. Restrooms, showers, a pool, shuffleboard, a recreation room, wintertime planned activities, a small laundry facility, and a rental unit are available. A supermarket, restaurants, and a flea market are within 0.5 mile. Internet access is available in the recreation room. RVs can be stored during the off-season. Children are welcome, but the park does not cater to their needs. Leashed pets under 30 pounds are permitted.

Reservations, fees: Reservations are required in winter. Sites are $33 per night for two people, plus $3 for each additional person. Credit cards are not accepted. Long-term stays are okay.

Directions: From U.S. 1/Overseas Highway near mile marker 30 on Big Pine Key, turn north into the park entrance.

Contact: Breezy Pines RV Estates, 29859 Overseas Highway, Big Pine Key, FL 33043, 305/872-9041.

12 SUGARLOAF KEY RESORT KOA KAMPGROUND

Scenic rating: 8

on Sugarloaf Key

The southernmost KOA in North America has much to offer families who want a resort-style vacation along with the waterfront necessities that define the Florida Keys experience. Ficus, sea grape, palm trees, and ocean vistas enhance the campsites. Fifteen sites are at waterfront; the tent area is in a large, shady, grassy clearing. There are plenty of amenities, including a private sandy beach with tiki huts for sunning and playing, plus the Crews Nest social pavilion, and planned activities. RVs and cabins are available for rent. Boaters and anglers can use the campground's full-service marina, which has 25 boat slips. An inlet leads from the marina to the Atlantic Ocean. Canoes and other boats are available for rent. Like everywhere on the waterfront in the Keys, the waters are crystal clear for snorkeling. Located just 14 miles from Key West, this is a good base camp for touring the city and its attractions.

RV sites, facilities: There are 200 gravel sites with full hookups, plus 30/50-amp electrical services and picnic tables. Slide-outs and RVs up to 40 feet long can be accommodated. None of the sites are drive-through. Facilities include restrooms, showers, dump station, honeywagon service, propane, a sandy beach, a heated pool with a hot tub, a restaurant, café, a marina, a boat ramp, a convenience store, a game room, miniature golf, laundry facilities, trailer rentals, basketball, volleyball, horseshoe pits, a bar with wintertime live entertainment, and rentals of bicycles, boats, and canoes are available. Planned activities are held during the winter season, and the park sponsors a dolphin-fishing tournament in June. Internet hookup is available in the office; a wireless connection can be found near the cafe. The bathrooms and laundry are wheelchair accessible. Children are welcome. Leashed pets are permitted.

Reservations, fees: Reservations are recommended. Sites are $67–112 per night for two people, plus $9 per extra person. Major credit cards are accepted. Stays are limited to 30 days.

Directions: From U.S. 1/Overseas Highway at mile marker 20 on Sugarloaf Key, turn south and drive 0.2 mile to the park entrance.

Contact: Sugarloaf Key Resort KOA Kampground, 251 County Road 939, Sugarloaf Key, FL 33042, 305/745-3549 or 800/562-7731, fax 305/745-9889, www.koa.com.

13 LAZY LAKES CAMPGROUND

Scenic rating: 6

on Sugarloaf Key

The six-acre artificial lake, an almost perfect rectangle nearly split in two by a promenade that ends in a swim ladder, is the focus of this campground. Snorkeling, swimming, windsurfing, and fishing are popular camper activities. If you get a waterfront site, be careful with children; the lake is 20 feet deep (even at the shoreline in some places). In fact, children under 14 must be accompanied by an adult when near the lake, the pool, or the bathhouse. Always use a flashlight when walking at night. Scuba divers are welcome, but they're not allowed to use spears or guns in the lake. Motorboats are forbidden. Coconut palms and Australian pines are counterpoints to the rather barren terrain, but many sites have no shade and little vegetation. Cool off in the pool, or work off some calories while line dancing. In the recreation hall, where planned activities take place in the wintertime, you can curl up with a good book or relax in front of the TV.

RV sites, facilities: Full hookups, cable TV, and telephone access are available at 80 RV sites, which accommodate rigs up to 40 feet long. Both 50-amp and 30-amp electrical service is available. Picnic tables, restrooms, showers, a dump station, a pool, a lake, boat docks, rental units, laundry facilities, a basketball court, and a recreation hall are available. Most areas are wheelchair accessible. Children are welcome. Two leashed pets are permitted per site.

Reservations, fees: Reservations are recommended. Sites are $28–51 per night for two people, plus $5 for each additional person and $2 for cable TV. Major credit cards are accepted. Long-term stays are okay.

Directions: From U.S. 1/Overseas Highway at mile marker 19.8 on Sugarloaf Key, turn south on Johnson Road. Drive 0.25 mile to the park.

Contact: Lazy Lakes Campground, 311 Johnson Road, Sugarloaf Key, FL 33042, 305/745-4129 or 800/354-5524, fax 305/745-1680, www .rvonthego.com.

14 BLUEWATER KEY RV PARK

Scenic rating: 10

on Sugarloaf Key

BEST (

You can park your big rig at poolside, on a canal lot, or on the bay front in this deluxe park, which has a three-story clubhouse and a resort-style pool. The park is set in a quiet, residential neighborhood. Key West is only 10 miles away. Waterfront sites have their own docks and tiki huts.

RV sites, facilities: Rigs up to 47 feet can be accommodated at this 81-site ownership park. Your RV must use full hookups and be at least 26 feet long; tents are not permitted. Electrical service at each site is both 30 amps and 50 amps. Picnic tables, restrooms, showers, and laundry facilities are provided. Waterfront sites have swimming, docks, tiki huts, and coconut palms. There's also a boat ramp, a pool, a clubhouse, and a security gate. The clubroom, laundry, and showers are wheelchair accessible. Propane delivery service can be scheduled once a week. Internet hookup is available in the clubhouse. Children are welcome. Two leashed pets are permitted per site.

Reservations, fees: Reservations are required.

Sites are $110 per night for two people, plus $10 per additional person. Cable TV is included. Telephone service is available at $2 per night. Rates are higher during Fantasy Fest (usually held mid-to-late October) and holidays. Major credit cards are accepted. Long-term stays are welcome; however, only a few occupants live here year-round.

Directions: On Sugarloaf Key, from U.S. 1/ Overseas Highway at mile marker 14.5, turn on Bluewater Drive toward the ocean side and proceed to the park entrance.

Contact: Bluewater Key RV Park, 2950 U.S. Highway 1, Key West, FL 33040, 305/745-2494 or 800/237-2266, fax 305/745-2433, www.bluewaterkey.com.

15 GEIGER KEY MARINA AND RV PARK

Scenic rating: 3

on Geiger Key

Waterfront lots "on the back side of paradise" are the draw here. This secluded, sunny campground overlooks Saddlehill and Bird Keys, both uninhabited, and it has good access to the water, especially for canoes and kayaks. Some campers fish from the seawall or explore the area in kayaks or snorkel fins (bring your own gear). Campsites are gravel, so bring a sleeping pad if you're tenting. You'll probably see jets from the nearby Key West Naval Air Station streak across the sky in formation. About 15 percent of the park is occupied by year-round residents.

RV sites, facilities: There are 35 RV sites with full hookups and 30-amp electrical service, and a small area for about four tents. None of the sites are drive-through; however, they are mostly gravel, sunny, and have reasonable elbow room between each other. Rigs up to 40 feet can be accommodated. Restrooms, showers, a dump station, a recreation room, a restaurant, a tiki bar, bait, tackle, laundry facilities, and weekend live entertainment are available. Boat slips are for rent. The restaurant is wheelchair accessible. Limited Web access is available in the office. Key West attractions and shopping are six miles away; a beach is within one mile. Children are welcome "if they're quiet and considerate." Leashed pets are permitted.

Reservations, fees: Reservations are required. Sites are $60–85 per night for two people, plus $5 for each additional person. Major credit cards are accepted. Long-term stays are okay.

Directions: From U.S. 1/Overseas Highway at mile marker 10.5 on Geiger Key, turn south at the Circle K onto Boca Chica Road. Go 1.5 miles, then turn east onto Geiger Road. Drive two blocks to the park entrance.

Contact: Geiger Key Marina and RV Park, 5 Geiger Road, Key West, FL 33040, 305/296-3553, fax 305/293-9319, www.geigerkeymarina.com.

16 LEO'S CAMPGROUND

Scenic rating: 2

on Stock Island

Set on two wooded acres, this quiet, shady campground is convenient to Key West's historic area, beaches, dive shops, and fishing charters. From here, you could ride your bicycle into town or catch a bus. Parking in Key West is notoriously difficult, and a lot of visitors rent moped scooters to get around. Some sights you shouldn't miss: the buoy marking the southernmost point in the United States, only 90 miles from Cuba; sunset at Mallory Square; the Audubon House and Tropical Gardens; the Hemingway Home and Museum; and the Mel Fisher Maritime Heritage Society Museum. Fisher is a modern-day treasure salvor who discovered the wreck of a gold-laden Spanish galleon and brought his booty ashore.

RV sites, facilities: The 34 grassy, shaded campsites come with picnic tables; 7 have 50-amp electrical service and 27 have 30-amp. RVs up to 40 feet long can be accommodated; however,

be advised that none are drive-through. There is no dump station. Most sites are 24 feet wide. A separate tent section offers 12 sites overlooking a small lake. About 10 percent of the occupants live here year-round. Restrooms, showers, and a laundry facility are available. Internet service is available in the office. A bus stop is on the corner and serves Key West–bound passengers. Restaurants, parasailing, and kayak and water scooter rentals are within two blocks; grocery stores are one mile away. Children are welcome. Leashed pets under 30 pounds are permitted in RVs only.

Reservations, fees: Reservations are not necessary. Sites are $49 per night for two people, plus $8 for each extra person and $1 per pet. Rates are higher during Fantasy Fest (in October), Christmas, and New Year's. Major credit cards are accepted. Long-term stays are okay.

Directions: On Stock Island, from U.S. 1/Overseas Highway at mile marker 4.5, turn south at Cross Street and drive one block to the campground on Suncrest Road.

Contact: Leo's Campground, 5236 Suncrest Road, Key West, FL 33040, 305/296-5260.

17 BOYD'S KEY WEST CAMPGROUND

Scenic rating: 5

on Stock Island

Although set in a busy urban area just outside the Key West city limits, this 12-acre campground manages to sustain a tropical ambience, with a swimming beach, water views, and coconut palms. Like Key West, it attracts all kinds of people. Here, you might see a tent cooled by a room air conditioner on concrete blocks, as well as luxury-loving campers parked in $150,000 RVs. The proprietors say most visitors here are "very active" snowbirds in their fifties or sixties, as well as families. This is the largest park close to Key West, a city celebrated by songwriters (Jimmy Buffett's "Margaritaville"), authors

(Ernest Hemingway, Tennessee Williams), artists (John James Audubon), and even presidents (Harry S. Truman, who started the Hawaiian-shirt craze here).

Today, Key West is so far from the mainland that it's hard to believe this was once a major Florida trading port, bustling with early settlers from the Bahamas, pirates, treasure salvors, and rumrunners. Many of the gingerbread houses that were home to these early residents have been restored. Modern-day "Conchs" (pronounced "konks"), as Keys natives call themselves, now make their living from art galleries, boutiques, souvenir and T-shirt shops, or by giving circus-style performances on Mallory Square.

RV sites, facilities: There are 150 full-hookup RV sites and 53 spots set apart for tents. Ninety sites have 50-amp electrical service; 60 have 30-amp. You'll find concrete patios at some sites, and some with scrub bushes to provide a modicum of privacy. Restrooms, showers, picnic tables, laundry facilities, a dump station, a heated pool, a beach, a game room, a boat ramp, telephone service, cable TV, a camp store with limited supplies, and a dock are available. Planned activities including cards, crafting classes, snorkeling, and parties. All areas are wheelchair accessible. Children are welcome. Pets are permitted on leashes; however Dobermans, pit bulls, rottweilers, chows, wolf hybrids, German shepherds, and nondomesticated animals are prohibited. RV storage is available only in the summer months.

Reservations, fees: Reservations are recommended. Sites are $45–110 per night for two people, plus $10 for each additional person over the age of 12. Major credit cards are accepted. Long-term stays are okay.

Directions: From U.S. 1/Overseas Highway, turn south at mile marker 5 onto 3rd Street. Drive one block and turn east onto Maloney Avenue/State Road 941. The park is at 6401 Maloney Avenue.

Contact: Boyd's Key West Campground, 6401 Maloney Avenue, Key West, FL 33040, 305/294-1465, fax 305/293-9301, www.boyd-scampground.com.

18 EL MAR RV RESORT

Scenic rating: 6

on Stock Island

Modeling itself as "upscale," El Mar RV Resort has sunny waterfront sites for self-contained RVs that are 26 feet or longer. No tents, truck campers, or pop-ups are allowed. Indeed, expensive motor coaches and fifth-wheelers are the norm at this sparsely landscaped park that offers eastward views of the beautiful Keys waters. Adults are the preferred visitors.

RV sites, facilities: There are five waterfront sites and five inland sites. All have full hookups with 30/50-amp service and are available for overnighters or snowbirds. Picnic tables, cable TV, and phone availability are at each site, which measure 30 by 75 feet with concrete patios. Interior roads are paved. RVs must be self-contained; no restrooms or showers are provided. Children are discouraged. Leashed pets under 25 pounds are permitted.

Reservations, fees: Reservations are recommended. Sites are $65–95 per night for two people, plus $10 per extra person. Major credit cards are accepted. Long-term rates are available.

Directions: From U.S. 1/Overseas Highway, turn south at mile marker 5 onto 3rd Street. Drive one block and turn east onto Maloney Avenue/State Road 941. The park is 0.5 mile away at 6700 Maloney Avenue.

Contact: El Mar RV Resort, 6700 Maloney Avenue, Key West, FL 33040, 305/294-0857 or 315/524-8687, fax 603/880-8187, www.elmarrvresort.com.

RESOURCES

Resources

U.S. NATIONAL FORESTS
For further information about National Forests in Florida, write, call, or visit the the following forest services:

Apalachicola National Forest
www.r8web.com/florida/forests/
apalachicola.htm
Divided into two ranger districts:
Wakulla Ranger District
P.O. Box 579
Bristol, FL 32321
850/643-2282

Wakulla Ranger District
57 Taft Drive
Crawfordville, FL 32327
850/926-3561

Florida Forest Supervisor's Office
325 John Knox Road, Suite F-100
Tallahassee, FL 32303
850/532-8500
TDD: 850/942-9351

Ocala National Forest
www.r8web.com/florida/forests/ocala.htm
Divided into two ranger districts:
Seminole Ranger District
40929 State Road 19
Umatilla, FL 32784
352/669-3153

Lake George Ranger District
17147 East Highway 40
Silver Springs, FL 34488
352/625-2520

Osceola National Forest
P.O. Box 70
Olustee, FL 32072
386/752-2577
www.r8web.com/florida/forests/osceola.htm

USDA Forest Service
Southern Region
1720 Peachtree Road Northwest
Atlanta, GA 30367
404/347-4177
www.r8web.com

U.S. NATIONAL PARKS
For further information about National Park units in Florida, write, call, or visit the websites of the following:

Big Cypress National Preserve
HCR61, P.O. Box 110
Ochopee, FL 34141
239/695-1201
www.nps.gov/bicy

Biscayne National Park
9700 Southwest 328th Street
Homestead, FL 33033-5634
305/230-1144 or 305/230-7275
email: bisc_information@nps.gov
www.nps.gov/bisc

Canaveral National Seashore Park Headquarters
308 Julia Street
Titusville, FL 32796
407/267-1110
email: cana_superintendent@nps.gov
www.nps.gov/cana

Castillo de San Marcos National Monument
One South Castillo Drive
St. Augustine, FL 32084
904/829-6506
email: casa_ranger_activities@nps.gov
www.nps.gov/casa

De Soto National Memorial
P.O. Box 15390
Bradenton, FL 34280
941/792-0458
fax 941/792-5094
email: eso_superintendent@nps.gov
www.nps.gov/deso

Everglades National Park
40001 State Road 9336
Homestead, FL 33034-6733
305/242-7700
email: ever_information@nps.gov
www.nps.gov/ever

Fort Caroline National Memorial/
Timucuan Preserve
12713 Fort Caroline Road
Jacksonville, FL 32225
904/641-7155
email: timu_interpretation@nps.gov
www.nps.gov/foca

Fort Matanzas National Monument
8635 Highway A1A South
St. Augustine, FL 32080
904/471-0116
email: FOMA_Site_Supervisor@nps.gov
www.nps.gov/foma

Gulf Islands National Seashore
Florida District
1801 Gulf Breeze Parkway
Gulf Breeze, FL 32561
850/934-2600
email: terry_colby@nps.gov
www.nps.gov/guis

Reservations service
800/365-CAMP (800/365-2267)
http://reservations.nps.gov

Southeast Region
National Park Service
100 Alabama Street Southwest, 1924
Building
Atlanta, GA 30303
404/562-3100
www.nps.gov

Timucuan Ecological and Historic Preserve
13165 Mount Pleasant Road
Jacksonville, FL 32225

or write to
12713 Fort Caroline Road
Jacksonville, FL 32225
904/221-5568
email: timu_interpretation@nps.gov
www.nps.gov/timu

U.S. FISH AND WILDLIFE SERVICE

For further information about U.S. Fish and Wildlife Service units, including National Wildlife Refuges in Florida, visit the websites of the following:

National Wildlife Refuges directory
http://refuges.fws.gov

Southeast Regional Office
http://southeast.fws.gov

U.S. ARMY CORPS OF ENGINEERS

The U.S. Army Corps of Engineers regulates, among other things, recreational activities at several sites in Florida. For more information, contact:

Jacksonville District
P.O. Box 4970
Jacksonville, FL 32232-0019
Public Affairs Office:
904/232-2568
fax 904/232-2237
www.saj.usace.army.mil/recreation/
index.html
Governs Lake Okeechobee and most of Florida.

Lake Seminole Resource Management Office:
P.O. Box 96
Chattahoochee, FL 32324
229/662-2001

Mobile District
P.O. Box 2288
Mobile, AL 36628-0001
334/471-5966
www.sam.usace.army.mil/op/rec/seminole
Governs Lake Seminole on the Florida-Georgia
state border.

South Florida Operations Office:
525 Ridgelawn Road
Clewiston, FL 33440-5399
863/983-8101

FLORIDA STATE PARKS

Almost 150 parks are part of the award-winning
Florida State Parks system. The *Florida State
Parks Guide* is available from:

**Florida Department of
Environmental Protection**
Parks Information
Mail Station #535
3900 Commonwealth Boulevard
Tallahassee, FL 32399-3000
850/245-2157
www.floridastateparks.org
Order the guide online or download park information and park maps at www.dep.state.
fl.us/parks/communications/guide.html. You
can search for individual Florida State Parks at
www.dep.state.fl.us/parks/parksby.htm.

FLORIDA DIVISION
OF FORESTRY

For a trailwalker's guide to exploring Florida's state
forests, visit www.trailwalker.fl-ag.com, which
lists individual trails throughout the state.
For information about Florida's 30 state
forests, contact the following:

Florida Division of Forestry
3125 Conner Boulevard
Tallahassee, FL 32399-1650
850/488-4274
fax 850/488-0863
www.fl-dof.com

Download state forest maps in Adobe Acrobat
format at www.fl-dof.com/Pubs/index.html.

Florida Division of Forestry
Field Unit/District Offices

Blackwater Forestry Center
11650 Munson Highway
Milton, FL 32570
850/957-6140
fax 850/957-6143

Bunnell District Office
5001 U.S. Highway 1
North Bunnell, FL 32110
904/446-6785
fax 904/446-6789

Caloosahatchee District Office
10941 State Road 80
Fort Myers, FL 33905
239/690-3500
fax 239/690-3504

Everglades District
3315 Southwest College Avenue
Davie, FL 33314
954/475-4120
fax 954/475-4126

Jacksonville District
7247 Big Oaks Road
Bryceville, FL 32009
904/266-5001
fax 904/266-5018

Lakeland District Office
5745 South Florida Avenue
Lakeland, FL 33813
863/648-3163
fax 863/648-3169

Myakka District Office
4723 53rd Avenue East
Bradenton, FL 34203
941/751-7627
fax 941/751-7631

Orlando Office
8431 South Orange Blossom Trail
Orlando, FL 32809
407/856-6512
fax 407/856-6514

Perry District Office
618 Plantation Road
Perry, FL 32348
850/838-2299
fax 850/838-2284

Suwannee District Office
Route 7, P.O. Box 369
Lake City, FL 32055
386/758-5700
fax 386/758-5725

Tallahassee District
865 Geddie Road
Tallahassee, FL 32304
850/488-1871
fax 850/922-2107

Waccasassa Forestry Center
1600 Northeast 23rd Avenue
Gainesville, FL 32609
352/955-2005
fax 352/955-2125

Withlacoochee Forestry Center
15019 Broad Street
Brooksville, FL 34601-4201
352/754-6777
fax 352/754-6751

SELECTED INDIVIDUAL STATE FORESTS

Big Shoals State Forest
7620 133rd Road
Live Oak, FL 32055
904/208-1460

Blackwater River State Forest
11650 Munson Highway
Milton, FL 32570
850/957-6140
fax 850/957-6143

Cary State Forest
Route 2, P.O. Box 60
Bryceville, FL 32009
904/266-5021 or 904/266-5022

Etoniah Creek State Forest
390 Holloway Road
Florahome, FL 32140
386/329-2552
fax: 386/329-2554

Goethe State Forest
8250 Southeast County Road 336
Dunnellon, FL 34431
352/447-2202
fax 352/447-1358

Jennings State Forest
1337 Longhorn Road
Middleburg, FL 32068
904/291-5530
fax 904/291-5537

Lake George State Forest
5460 North Highway 17
DeLeon Springs, FL 32120
386/985-7820

Lake Talquin State Forest
865 Geddie Road
Tallahassee, FL 32304
850/488-1871
fax 850/922-2107

Lake Wales Ridge State Forest
452 School Bus Road
Frostproof, FL 33843
941/635-7801
fax 941/635-7837

Little Big Econ State Forest
1350 Snow Hill Road
Geneva, FL 32732
407/971-3500

Myakka State Forest
4723 53rd Avenue East
Bradenton, FL 34203
941/255-7653

Picayune Strand State Forest
2121 52nd Avenue Southeast
Naples, FL 34117
239/348-7557
fax 239/348-7559

Pine Log State Forest
715 West 15th Street
Panama City, FL 32401
850/747-5639
fax 850/872-4879

Point Washington State Forest
715 West 15th Street
Panama City, FL 32401
850/747-5639
fax 850/872-4879

Ralph E. Simmons State Forest
Route 3, P.O. Box 299
Hillard, FL 32046
904/845-3597

Seminole State Forest
Leesburg Forestry Station, 9610 CR 44
Leesburg, FL 34788
352/360-6675 or 352/360-667

Tate's Hell State Forest
1621 Highway 98 East
Carrabelle, FL 32322
850/697-3734
fax 850/697-2892

Tiger Bay State Forest
4316 West International Speedway Boulevard
Daytona Beach, FL 32124
386/226-0250
fax 386/226-0251

Twin Rivers State Forest
7620 133rd Road
Live Oak, FL 32060
386/208-1460
fax 386/208-1465

Welaka State Forest
P.O. Box 174
Welaka, FL 32193-0174
386/467-2388
fax 386/467-2740

Withlacoochee State Forest
15003 Broad Street
Brooksville, FL 34601
352/754-6896

FLORIDA FISH AND WILDLIFE CONSERVATION COMMISSION

The Florida Fish and Wildlife Conservation Commission supervises hunting and fishing activities, as well as wildlife conservation. For more information, contact:

Florida Fish and Wildlife Conservation Commission
620 South Meridian Street
Tallahassee, FL 32399-1600
850/488-4676

For recreation use permits, hunting season information, freshwater and saltwater fishing licenses, and information about wildlife management area regulations, see www.florida conservation.org.

Florida Fish and Wildlife Conservation Commission District Offices

North Central Region
Route 7, P.O. Box 440
Lake City, FL 32055-8713
386/758-0525

Northeast Region
1239 Southwest 10th Street
Ocala, FL 34474-2797
352/732-1225

Northwest Region
3911 Highway 2321
Panama City, FL 32409-1658
850/265-3676

South Region
8535 Northlake Boulevard
West Palm Beach, FL 33412
561/625-5122

Southwest Region
3900 Drane Field Road
Lakeland, FL 33811-1299
863/648-3203

FLORIDA WATER MANAGEMENT DISTRICTS

In addition to managing the quality and quantity of water throughout Florida, five water management districts provide recreational opportunities on lands they control. Contact the following:

Northwest Florida Water Management District
81 Water Management Drive
Havana, FL 32333
850/539-5999
fax 850/539-4380
http://sun6.dms.state.fl.us/nwfwmd

South Florida Water Management District
3301 Gun Club Road
West Palm Beach, FL 33406
561/686-8800
www.sfwmd.gov

Southwest Florida Water Management District
2379 Broad Street
Brooksville, FL 34609-6899
352/796-7211
www.swfwmd.state.fl.us

St. Johns River Water Management District
P.O. Box 1429
Palatka, FL 32178-1429
386/329-4500 or 800/451-7106
http://sjr.state.fl.us

Suwannee River Water Management District
9225 County Road 49
Live Oak, FL 32060
386/362-1001
www.srwmd.state.fl.us

Florida has a rapidly growing program for the development of new trails. For more information, contact:

Cross Florida Greenway Field Office
8282 Southeast Highway 314
Ocala, FL 34470
352/236-7143

Office of Greenways and Trails
Florida Department of
Environmental Protection
3900 Commonwealth Boulevard, MS 795
Tallahassee, FL 32399-3000
850/245-2052 or 877/822-5208
www.dep.state.fl.us/gwt/index.htm

ACTIVE VOLUNTEERING

All outdoors-oriented agencies or civic groups need money, but some also want your energy. The following want volunteer help or hands-on support.

Florida State Parks

If you are interested in volunteering at a particular state park or in becoming a campground host, contact the park directly. Each park screens its own volunteers. An application can be downloaded online or contact:

Coordinator of Volunteer Services
Bureau of Operational Services
Division of Recreation and Parks
3900 Commonwealth Boulevard, MS 535
Tallahassee, FL 32399
http://floridastateparks.org/volunteers

Florida Trail Association
5415 Southwest 13th Street
Gainesville, FL 32608
352/378-8823
email: fta@florida-trail.org
www.florida-trail.org

Friends of Florida State Forests
3125 Conner Boulevard, Suite C-21
Tallahassee, FL 32399-1650
850/414-9974
email: ffsf@doacs.state.fl.us

Volunteer Florida

www.volunteerflorida.org/volcenters/centerslisting.cfm
This statewide organization coordinates volunteer efforts for a variety of good causes. Local opportunities are listed online.

Index

Page numbers in **bold** indicate maps.

Acknowledgments

Susan Windrem, Joanne S. Moore, and Sally Deneen provided valuable assistance in the preparation of this book.

Notes

Notes

www.moon.com

For helpful advice on planning a trip, visit www.moon.com for the **TRAVEL PLANNER** and get access to useful travel strategies and valuable information about great places to visit. When you travel with Moon, expect an experience that is uncommon and truly unique.

OUTDOORS

"A smart new look provides just one more reason to travel with Moon Outdoors. Well-written, thoroughly researched, and packed full of useful information and advice, these guides really do get you into the outdoors."

—GORP.COM

ALSO AVAILABLE AS FOGHORN OUTDOORS ACTIVITY GUIDES:

101 Great Hikes of the
 San Francisco Bay Area
250 Great Hikes in
 California's National Parks
Baja Camping
Bay Area Biking
California Beaches
California Camping
California Fishing
California Golf
California Hiking
California Recreational
 Lakes & Rivers
California Waterfalls
California Wildlife
Camper's Companion
Easy Biking in Northern
 California

Easy Hiking in Northern
 California
Easy Hiking in Southern
 California
Florida Beaches
Florida Camping
Georgia & Alabama Camping
Great Lakes Camping
Maine Hiking
Massachusetts Hiking
Montana, Wyoming & Idaho
 Camping
New England Biking
New England Cabins
 & Cottages
New England Camping
New England Hiking
New Hampshire Hiking

Northern California Biking
Oregon Hiking
Pacific Northwest Hiking
Southern California
 Cabins & Cottages
Tom Stienstra's Bay Area
 Recreation
Utah Camping
Utah Hiking
Vermont Hiking
Washington Boating
 & Water Sports
Washington Fishing
Washington Hiking
West Coast RV Camping

MOON FLORIDA RV CAMPING

Avalon Travel Publishing
an Imprint of
Avalon Publishing Group, Inc.

AVALON
publishing group incorporated

1400 65th Street, Suite 250
Emeryville, CA 94608, USA
www.moon.com

Editors: Sabrina Young, Shari Husain
Series Manager: Sabrina Young
Acquisitions Manager: Rebecca K. Browning
Copy Editor: Gerardyne Madigan
Graphics Coordinator: Stefano Boni
Production Coordinator: Darren Alessi
Cover Designer: Gerilyn Attebery
Interior Designer: Darren Alessi
Map Editor: Kevin Anglin
Cartographer: Suzanne Service
Cartography Director: Mike Morgenfeld
Indexer: Greg Jewett

ISBN-10: 1-56691-988-6
ISBN-13: 978-1-56691-988-3
ISSN: 1930-8752

Printing History
1st Edition – November 2006
5 4 3 2 1

Text © 2006 by Marilyn A. Moore.
Maps © 2006 by Avalon Travel Publishing, Inc.
All rights reserved.

Some photos and illustrations are used by permission and
are the property of the original copyright owners.

Front cover photo: Photo by Andy Newman/
   Courtesy of Florida Keys News Bureau
Title page photo: Courtesy of Florida Keys Tourist
   Development Council
Back cover photo: © Digital Vision / Getty Images

Printed in the United States by Malloy Inc.

KEEPING CURRENT

We are committed to making this book the most accurate and enjoyable RV camping guide to
Florida. You can rest assured that every campground in this book has been carefully reviewed
in an effort to keep this book as up-to-date as possible. However, by the time you read this
book, some of the fees listed herein may have changed and campgrounds may have closed
unexpectedly.

   If you have a favorite gem you'd like to see included in the next edition, or see anything that
needs updating, clarification, or correction, please drop us a line. Send your comments via email
to feedback@moon.com, or use the address above.